PROFESSIONAL RESPONSIBILITY FOR BUSINESS LAWYERS

EDITORIAL ADVISORS

Rachel E. Barkow
Vice Dean and Charles Seligson Professor of Law
Segal Family Professor of Regulatory Law and Policy
Faculty Director, Center on the Administration of Criminal Law
New York University School of Law

Erwin Chemerinsky
Dean and Jesse H. Choper Distinguished Professor of Law
University of California, Berkeley School of Law

Richard A. Epstein
Laurence A. Tisch Professor of Law
New York University School of Law
Peter and Kirsten Bedford Senior Fellow
The Hoover Institution
Senior Lecturer in Law
The University of Chicago

Ronald J. Gilson
Charles J. Meyers Professor of Law and Business
Stanford University
Marc and Eva Stern Professor of Law and Business
Columbia Law School

James E. Krier
Earl Warren DeLano Professor of Law Emeritus
The University of Michigan Law School

Tracey L. Meares
Walton Hale Hamilton Professor of Law
Director, The Justice Collaboratory
Yale Law School

Richard K. Neumann, Jr.
Alexander Bickel Professor of Law
Maurice A. Deane School of Law at Hofstra University

Robert H. Sitkoff
Austin Wakeman Scott Professor of Law
John L. Gray Professor of Law
Harvard Law School

David Alan Sklansky
Stanley Morrison Professor of Law
Faculty Co-Director, Stanford Criminal Justice Center
Stanford Law School

ASPEN CASEBOOK SERIES

PROFESSIONAL RESPONSIBILITY FOR BUSINESS LAWYERS

NANCY J. MOORE
Professor of Law
Nancy E. Barton Scholar
Boston University School of Law

Wolters Kluwer

Copyright © 2022 CCH Incorporated. All Rights Reserved.

Published by Wolters Kluwer in New York.

Wolters Kluwer Legal & Regulatory U.S. serves customers worldwide with CCH, Aspen Publishers, and Kluwer Law International products. (www.WKLegaledu.com)

No part of this publication may be reproduced or transmitted in any form or by any means, electronic or mechanical, including photocopy, recording, or utilized by any information storage or retrieval system, without written permission from the publisher. For information about permissions or to request permissions online, visit us at www.WKLegaledu.com, or a written request may be faxed to our permissions department at 212-771-0803.

To contact Customer Service, e-mail customer.service@wolterskluwer.com, call 1-800-234-1660, fax 1-800-901-9075, or mail correspondence to:

> Wolters Kluwer
> Attn: Order Department
> PO Box 990
> Frederick, MD 21705

Printed in the United States of America.

1 2 3 4 5 6 7 8 9 0

ISBN 978-1-5438-2596-1

Library of Congress Cataloging-in-Publication Data

Library of Congress Cataloging-in-Publication Data application is in process.

About Wolters Kluwer Legal & Regulatory U.S.

Wolters Kluwer Legal & Regulatory U.S. delivers expert content and solutions in the areas of law, corporate compliance, health compliance, reimbursement, and legal education. Its practical solutions help customers successfully navigate the demands of a changing environment to drive their daily activities, enhance decision quality, and inspire confident outcomes.

Serving customers worldwide, its legal and regulatory portfolio includes products under the Aspen Publishers, CCH Incorporated, Kluwer Law International, ftwilliam.com, and MediRegs names. They are regarded as exceptional and trusted resources for general legal and practice-specific knowledge, compliance and risk management, dynamic workflow solutions, and expert commentary.

To my loving and supportive family—
my husband, Steve Kanes,
our two daughters, Sarah Kanes and Emily Kanes Snyder, and
our four grandchildren, Bea and Zac Snyder and Thomas and Annabel Johnston

SUMMARY OF CONTENTS

Contents	xi
Preface	xix
Acknowledgments	xxi

CHAPTER 1
Why a Course in Professional Responsibility?   1

PART I
CORE CONCEPTS   15

CHAPTER 2
Formation, Scope, and Termination of the Attorney-Client Relationship   17

CHAPTER 3
Competence and Diligence; Control and Communication; Fees   41

CHAPTER 4
Privilege and Confidentiality   67

CHAPTER 5
Conflicts of Interest: Current Clients   101

CHAPTER 6
Conflicts of Interest: Former Clients, Prospective Clients, and Government Lawyers   151

CHAPTER 7
Limits of Zealous Representation I: Litigation   181

CHAPTER 8
Limits of Zealous Representation II: Transactions   217

PART II
REPRESENTING ENTITIES   255

CHAPTER 9
Who's My Client?   257

CHAPTER 10
Privilege and Confidentiality Revisited   281

CHAPTER 11
Conflicts of Interest in Entity Representation   321

CHAPTER 12
Corporate Wrongdoing   353

CHAPTER 13
In-House Counsel   391

PART III
REGULATING THE PROFESSION   421

CHAPTER 14
Admission and Discipline   423

CHAPTER 15
Unauthorized Practice of Law and Multijurisdictional Practice   445

CHAPTER 16
**Nonlawyer Ownership, Multidisciplinary Practice, and
Alternative Legal Service Providers**   471

CHAPTER 17
Marketing Legal Services   499

Table of Cases   523
Index   527

CONTENTS

Preface	xix
Acknowledgments	xxi

CHAPTER 1
Why a Course in Professional Responsibility? | 1

A. Introduction to the Subject Matter	2
Richard B. Schmitt: Lawyers Pressed to Report Fraud	
Under New Law	3
B. The Law of Lawyering	5
1. The ABA Model Codes	6
2. The Restatement of the Law Governing Lawyers and "Other Law"	7
3. Researching the Law of Lawyering	8
4. The Underdeveloped State of the Law of Lawyering	9
C. The Ethics of Lawyering	10
D. Why Professional Responsibility for Business Lawyers?	13

PART I
CORE CONCEPTS | 15

CHAPTER 2
Formation, Scope, and Termination of the Attorney-Client Relationship | 17

A. Forming the Attorney-Client Relationship	17
Sin Ho Nam v. Quichocho	18
B. Scope of the Representation	23
Model Rules 1.2, 1.4, 1.5	23
Genesis Merchant Partners, L.P. v. Gilbride, Tusa, Last &	
Spellane, LLC	23
SCB Diversified Municipal Portfolio v. Crews & Associates	26
C. Terminating the Attorney-Client Relationship	31
Model Rule 1.16	31
Manoir-ElectroAlloys Corp. v. Amalloy Corp	31
D. Should I Represent This Client?	35
Model Rules 1.2, 1.16	35
Review Problems	38

CHAPTER 3
Competence and Diligence; Control and Communication; Fees 41

A. Competence	41
Model Rule 1.1	41
State v. Orr	42
B. Diligence	46
Model Rule 1.3	46
C. Control	47
Model Rules 1.2, 1.4, 1.16	47
Olfe v. Gordon	48
D. Communication	53
Model Rule 1.4	53
E. Legal Fees	54
Model Rules 1.5, 1.15, 6.1	54
1. The Reasonableness Standard Generally	54
2. Different Types of Fee Arrangements	56
3. Modifying the Fee Agreement	60
4. Pro Bono Public Service	60
Review Problems	63

CHAPTER 4
Privilege and Confidentiality 67

Model Rules 1.6, 1.8(b), 1.9(c), 1.18(b)	67
A. Distinguishing Between Attorney-Client Privilege and the Rule of Confidentiality	67
Purcell v. District Attorney for the Suffolk District	68
B. Prima Facie Protection of Client Information	70
1. Attorney-Client Privilege	70
a. Communications	71
b. Between Privileged Persons	71
c. In Confidence	72
d. For the Purpose of Obtaining or Providing Legal Assistance	73
2. Professional Duty of Confidentiality	74
C. Applicable Exceptions	75
1. Attorney-Client Privilege	75
a. Crime-Fraud Exception	75
Purcell v. District Attorney for the Suffolk District	75
b. Joint Clients in Action Between Them	80
c. Consent and Waiver	81
2. Professional Duty of Confidentiality	82
a. Informed Consent	82
b. Implied Authority	83

c. Rule 1.6(b) Exceptions	83
(1) Preventing Physical Harm	84
(2) Preventing Economic Harm	84
The Saga of Singer Hutner and O.P.M.	85
(3) Past Crimes or Frauds	89
(4) Lawyer Securing Legal Advice	89
(5) Self-Defense and Asserting Claims Against the Client	90
Meyerhofer v. Empire Fire and Marine Insurance Co.	91
(6) Complying with Other Law	96
(7) Detecting Conflicts of Interest	97
D. Acting Competently to Protect Confidentiality	98
E. Work Product Immunity	98
Review Problems	99

CHAPTER 5
Conflicts of Interest: Current Clients
101

Model Rules 1.7, 1.8, 1.10	101
A. Conflicts Among Current Clients	103
1. Material Limitation Conflicts	103
a. Material Limitation Conflicts in Transactions	103
Simpson v. James	104
b. Material Limitation Conflicts in Litigation	112
Kramer v. Ciba-Geigy Corp.	113
2. Directly Adverse Conflicts	120
a. Directly Adverse Conflicts in Litigation	120
Sheppard, Mullin, Richter & Hampton, LLP v. J-M	
Manufacturing Co	123
b. Directly Adverse Conflicts in Transactions	133
3. Imputation of Conflicts Among Associated Lawyers	135
B. Conflicts Between Lawyer and Client	136
1. Personal Interest Conflicts	136
2. Business and Other Financial Transactions with a Client	137
Passante v. McWilliam	138
3. Other Specific Conflicts Rules	142
C. Conflicts in Criminal Cases: The Constitutional Standards	143
Cuyler v. Sullivan	143
Review Problems	148

CHAPTER 6
Conflicts of Interest: Former Clients, Prospective Clients, and Government Lawyers
151

Model Rules 1.9, 1.10, 1.11, 1.18	151
A. Former Client Conflicts	152
1. The Individual Private Lawyer in a Stable Firm	152

Analytica, Inc. v. NPD Research, Inc.	152
2. The Individual Private Lawyer Who Migrates to Another Firm	161
Silver Chrysler Plymouth, Inc. v. Chrysler Motors Corp.	161
3. The New Law Firm of the Individual Migratory Lawyer: Rebuttable or Irrebuttable Presumption?	166
Schiessle v. Stephens	166
B. Prospective Client Conflicts	172
Eileen Libby: www.warning.law: Websites May Trigger Unforeseen Ethics Obligations to Prospective Clients	173
C. Former Government Lawyers	176
Review Problems	178

CHAPTER 7

Limits of Zealous Representation I: Litigation $\hphantom{}$ 181

Model Rules 3.1, 3.3, 3.4	181
A. The Anglo-American Adversary System of Justice	182
Edward F. Barrett: The Adversary System and the Ethics of Advocacy	182
Marvin E. Frankel: Partisan Justice	183
B. Limits on Adversary Zeal	188
1. Pleadings in Civil and Criminal Cases	188
2. Lawyer Misrepresentation to a Court or Other Tribunal	191
3. Failure to Disclose Adverse Law or Facts	194
Tyler v. State	194
4. Client and Other Witness Perjury	201
Nix v. Whiteside	202
5. Fairness to Opposing Party and Counsel	214
Review Problems	215

CHAPTER 8

Limits of Zealous Representation II: Transactions $\hphantom{}$ 217

Model Rules 1.2(d), 1.6, 4.1, 4.2, 4.3	217
A. Lawyer Discipline: Knowingly Counseling or Assisting a Client's Crime or Fraud	218
1. Active Counseling or Assisting	218
2. Failure to Disclose	221
3. Knowingly Counseling or Assisting Other Wrongful Client Acts	223
B. Lawyer Discipline: Lawyer Interactions with Persons Other Than Clients	224
1. Truthfulness in Statements to Others	224
The Florida Bar v. Joy	224
2. Communication with Person Represented by Counsel	229
Neil J. Wertlieb & Nancy T. Avedissian: *Ex Parte* Communications in a Transactional Practice	230

3. Communication with an Unrepresented Person	236

C. Lawyers' Liability for Aiding and Abetting a Client's Crime or Fraud or Other Tortious Conduct ... 238
  Chem-Age Industries, Inc. v. Glover ... 239
D. Lawyers' Liability to Nonclients for Negligence ... 245
  Greycas, Inc. v. Proud ... 246
  Review Problems ... 251

PART II
REPRESENTING ENTITIES ... 255

CHAPTER 9
Who's My Client? ... 257

Model Rule 1.13 ... 257
A. Client Identification ... 258
  1. Large, Publicly Held Corporations ... 258
    E.F. Hutton & Company v. Brown ... 259
  2. Closely Held Corporations ... 264
    Bobbitt v. Victorian House, Inc. ... 264
    Rosman v. Shapiro ... 267
  3. General and Limited Partnerships, Limited Liability Companies ... 272
  4. Other Formal and Informal Associations ... 273
B. Control ... 274
    Legal Ethics Committee of the D.C. Bar: Representation of Closely Held Corporation in Action Against Corporate Shareholder ... 274
C. Communication ... 277
D. Contacting a Represented Entity ... 279
  Review Problems ... 279

CHAPTER 10
Privilege and Confidentiality Revisited ... 281

Model Rules 1.6, 3.4(f), 4.2, cmt [7], 4.3, 4.4(a) ... 281
A. Attorney-Client Privilege ... 281
  1. Basic Doctrinal Approaches ... 281
    Consol. Coal Co. v. Bucyrus-Erie Co. ... 282
    Upjohn Co. v. United States ... 285
  2. Application of Privilege to Third-Party Agents and Consultants ... 292
    Pearlstein v. Blackberry Ltd. ... 293
    In Re Copper Market Antitrust Litigation ... 294
  3. Application of Privilege After Changes in Entity Control ... 300
    Tekni-Plex, Inc. v. Meyner and Landis ... 300
    Great Hill Equity Partners IV, LP v. SIG Growth Equity Fund I, LLLP ... 307
B. Professional Rule of Confidentiality ... 312

C. Contacting a Represented Entity	313
Professional Ethics Committee of the State Bar of Wisconsin: Contact With Current and Former Constituents of a Represented Organization	313
Review Problems	319

CHAPTER 11
Conflicts of Interest in Entity Representation — 321

Model Rules 1.7, 1.9, Rule 1.13(g)	321
A. Current Clients: Simultaneously Representing an Entity and a Constituent	321
United States v. Nicholas	322
Musheno v. Gensemer	330
B. Current Clients: Corporate Family Conflicts	337
GSI Commerce Solutions, Inc. v. BabyCenter, L.L.C.	338
C. Former Clients: The Accommodation Client	346
Douglas R. Richmond: Accommodation Clients	346
Review Problems	352

CHAPTER 12
Corporate Wrongdoing — 353

Model Rules 1.2(d), 1.6, 4.1, 1.13, 5.2	353
A. Reporting Up	353
Complaint: SEC v. Isselmann	354
Outline of SEC's "Reporting Up" Regulations	358
B. Reporting Out	361
Outline of SEC's "Reporting Out" Regulations	362
C. Lawyer Liability	366
1. Liability to the Client Entity	366
Peterson v. Winston & Strawn LLP	367
Peterson v. Katten Muchin Rosenman LLP	369
2. Liability to Others for Violating Securities Laws	374
Pacific Inv. Management Co. LLC v. Mayer Brown LLP	374
Lorenzo v. SEC	384
Review Problems	390

CHAPTER 13
In-House Counsel — 391

Model Rules 1.6, 1.7, 1.8, 1.13, 1.16, 1.18, 2.1	391
A. The Evolving Role of In-House Counsel	391
1. The Emergence of the Modern In-House Counsel	391
Mary C. Daly: The Cultural, Ethical, and Legal Challenges in Lawyering for a Global Organization: The Role of General Counsel	391

2. Questioning the "Independence" of Modern In-House Counsel	396
Pam Jenoff: Going Native: Incentive, Identity, and the Inherent Ethical Problem of In-House Counsel	396
B. Difficulties in Establishing the Attorney-Client Privilege	402
Leazure v. Apria Healthcare Inc.	402
C. Lawyers as Compliance Officers	405
Jennifer M. Pacella: The Regulation of Lawyers in Compliance	406
D. Wrongful Discharge	411
Crews v. Buckman Laboratories International, Inc.	412
Review Problems	419

PART III
REGULATING THE PROFESSION
421

CHAPTER 14
Admission and Discipline
423

Model Rules 8.1, 8.3, 8.4	423
A. Admission to Practice	423
1. Educational Requirements	424
2. Bar Examinations	424
3. Character and Fitness	425
In Re Application of Burch	426
B. Discipline	432
1. Common Grounds for Discipline	433
a. Mishandling Client Funds	433
b. Other Forms of Dishonesty	433
c. Criminal Conduct	434
2. Failure to Report Another Lawyer's Serious Misconduct	435
3. Bias, Prejudice, Harassment, and Discrimination	436
The Florida Bar v. Martocci	437
Review Problems	443

CHAPTER 15
Unauthorized Practice of Law and Multijurisdictional Practice
445

Model Rules 5.5, 8.5	445
A. UPL by Nonlawyers	445
B. UPL by Lawyers	447
1. The MJP Problem	447
Birbrower, Montalbano, Condon & Frank, P.C. v. Superior Court	448
2. The ABA's "Safe Harbors" Solution	456
a. Safe Harbors for Temporary Practice	457
In Re Charges of Unprofessional Conduct in Panel File No. 39302	457
b. Safe Harbors for Systematic Presence	466

xviii Contents

3. Regulating Out-of-State Lawyers	467
a. Authority to Discipline	467
b. Choice of Law	468
Review Problems	469

CHAPTER 16
Nonlawyer Ownership, Multidisciplinary Practice, and Alternative Legal Service Providers
469... 471

Model Rule 5.4	471
A. UPL, Model Rule 5.4, and the Current Structure of Law Practice	472
B. Prohibiting Nonlawyer Ownership of Law Firms	473
1. Nonlawyers Actively Assisting in Client Representation	473
2. Passive Investment in Law firms	475
Jacoby & Meyers, LLP v. Presiding Justices	475
C. Prohibiting Multidisciplinary Practices	478
1. Interdisciplinary Service Providers	479
State Bar of Wisconsin: Lawyer Practicing in Interdisciplinary Organization	479
2. Retail and Other Commercial Businesses Offering Legal Services	483
D. Developments Outside the United States: Permitting Alternative Business Structures	484
Judith McMorrow, UK Alternative Business Structures for Legal Practice: Emerging Models and Lessons for the US	485
E. Recent Developments in the United States	491
Andrew M. Perlman: Reflections on the Future of Legal Services	494
Review Problems	497

CHAPTER 17
Marketing Legal Services
499

Model Rules 7.1, 7.2, 7.3, 8.4(c)	499
A. Restrictions on Lawyer Advertising	501
Alexander v. Cahill	502
B. Restrictions on Lawyer Solicitation	511
Ohralik v. Ohio State Bar Ass'n	512
C. Paying for Referrals	519
Review Problems	522

Table of Cases	523
Index	527

PREFACE

This casebook is designed to introduce law students to the law and ethics of lawyering. Unlike traditional Professional Responsibility casebooks, this one focuses more on business and other transactional lawyers than on litigators. Nevertheless, there are plenty of cases involving litigation lawyers, and the casebook is designed to provide a basic introduction to the subject matter for all law students, regardless of the type of practice they will enter.

The casebook is structured around text, edited cases, notes and questions, and review problems. The text introduces the concepts and provides explanations of many of the rules discussed, allowing the instructor to focus on the more difficult aspects of each subject area. The notes and questions following the cases are designed to highlight what is most important in the case, and to explore whether and how the result might be different if the facts are varied. We anticipate that the instructor will discuss some but not all of the notes and questions in class, but will be receptive to student questions based on any of the assigned material not specifically mentioned in class. Review problems are provided at the end of each chapter and are intended to be used at the discretion of the instructor. Some instructors may use particular problems during the initial discussion of the material; others will use them at the end of the chapter for purposes of review; still others will not assign them at all, but students may want to use them for purposes of review on an ongoing basis or for the final examination in the course.

Chapter 1 describes the various sources of the law of lawyering, including rules of professional conduct, which are typically adopted by a state's highest court. The casebook focuses largely on the American Bar Association's Model Rules of Professional Conduct; however, some cases rely on state court versions that may differ from the Model Rules, and both the text and the footnotes frequently indicate common state variations. The casebook is deliberately designed to emphasize the extent to which state rules differ from the Model Rules and the importance of lawyers knowing what their own state rules provide. Indeed, the Teacher's Manual to this casebook suggests that the instructor ask students to choose one or more state court versions to monitor throughout the semester and to determine for each chapter how their state's rules differ from the Model Rules. Ideally, students will choose the state where they are most likely to practice.

All of the main cases are edited to clarify the court's discussion of the ethical issues relevant to the material being discussed in the chapter in which the case appears. We use ellipses or brackets to indicate omissions from the court's opinion; however, omitted citations and footnotes are generally not identified. We sometimes add a footnote to an opinion, labeled "Ed. Note," to provide an explanation helpful to students reading the opinion. We include some footnotes that are original to the opinion, clearly identified as such, including providing the original footnote number.

Citations to cases and other authorities generally follow the most recent version of The Bluebook: A Uniform System of Citation, but with some omissions designed to make the citations more succinct. For example, we typically cite to regional reporters only and often omit the subsequent history of a case. Also, we provide Internet citations only when we believe that the material will otherwise be difficult for students to find.

When discussing the American Bar Association's Model Rules of Professional Conduct in text, we typically refer to the "Model Rules," and when citing the Model Rules, we use the abbreviation "MR." In referring to a particular rule in text, we use either "Model Rule [x]" or "Rule [x]." When citing either a current Model Rule or the current state court rule, we do not provide the year; therefore, students should assume that the citation is to the most recent edition of those rules at the time the casebook was written. If we provide a year, it is because we are referring to an earlier version of the rule, which has since been changed.

In addition to the Model Rules, this casebook frequently discusses and cites the American Law Institute's Restatement (Third) of the Law of Lawyering (2000). We refer to this restatement in text as "the Restatement" and we cite it as "RLGL." When we occasionally reference other restatements of the American Law Institute, such as the Restatement (Third) of Agency (2006), we use the full name and provide full citation information.

ACKNOWLEDGMENTS

I owe the deepest debt of gratitude to Rick Mixter, who was Senior Acquisitions Editor at Wolters Kluwer when I first broached the idea of publishing a casebook on Professional Responsibility for Business Lawyers. I had known Rick from an earlier project that, due to no fault of Rick's, was never completed. I contacted Rick at an early stage, hoping merely for some indication whether he thought this was a worthwhile project. To my surprise and delight, he expressed immediate enthusiasm about my idea, discussed it with me at length on the telephone, and urged me to submit a detailed book proposal. I had initially envisioned a small paperback to be used in an advanced course or seminar, like the one I was then teaching on Professional Responsibility for Business Lawyers. Rick, however, firmly believed that the project should be expanded to include all the necessary materials for a typical introductory course on Professional Responsibility (as well as an advanced offering in the area of ethics for business lawyers), for use by instructors who may or may not have a particular interest in business and other transactional lawyering. And indeed, as I developed the individual chapters, I began using them in my own Professional Responsibility course and was pleased to learn that my students enjoyed and appreciated the materials, regardless of the type of practice they envisioned. Rick left Wolters Kluwer before my casebook was concluded, but he has remained interested in the project and we have stayed in touch. I look forward to sending him a complimentary copy as soon as the book is in print.

I am also indebted to the rest of "the team" at Wolters Kluwer, which provided detailed suggestions and guidance at every stage of the project, including submitting my initial book proposal and a couple of sample chapters to anonymous external reviewers, as well as submitting all of my completed draft chapters to the same or different reviewers. These reviewers provided me with incredibly helpful suggestions and constructive criticism at various stages of the project. Special thanks: to Anton Yakovlev, who took the lead role from Rick when Rick left; to Kathy Langone at The Froebe Group, who provided substantial assistance with my style questions as the book progressed and shepherded the production process; and to Michelle Humphrey, also at The Froebe Group, who helped me with copyright permissions.

Two of my anonymous external reviewers have identified themselves to me. While I am thankful to all my reviewers, I am especially thankful to Peter Kostant, who graciously met with me in several Zoom sessions and corresponded with me by email, and to Paul Tremblay, who provided me with both overall comments and detailed edits of each of the chapters he reviewed.

I was blessed with outstanding research assistance from Kate Cochrane, a Legal Information Librarian at BU Law School, who has been my library liaison for teaching and research for many years, and from the following student research assistants: Kimberly Crowley, Eduardo Gonzalez, Daniel Fradin, and Rebecca Reeve. Joe Graham, my capable Administrative Assistant, helped me enormously with all sorts of practical problems I encountered in producing the chapters for the casebook.

Countless of my Professional Responsibility students, including students in my Professional Responsibility for Business Lawyers seminar, contributed to the improvement of the casebook by commenting on the draft chapters I assigned them. I am continually amazed by the ability of my students to raise questions I have never previously considered despite the number of years I have taught this material. Thanks for remaining engaged, even during our Zoom sessions in the midst of the COVID-19 pandemic!

I appreciate the support given me by Boston University, in the form of summer research grants, student research assistance funding, and a sabbatical that came at a critical time in my drafting of the initial chapters of the casebook. I am also incredibly grateful to the Nancy E. Barton Foundation for funding me as a Nancy E. Barton Scholar for many years, including all of the years in which I wrote this casebook.

PROFESSIONAL RESPONSIBILITY FOR BUSINESS LAWYERS

CHAPTER 1

WHY A COURSE IN PROFESSIONAL RESPONSIBILITY?

Many, perhaps most, of you enrolled in this course because your law school requires that you take a minimum number of credits in the subject area of professional responsibility. You may wonder why this is a requirement. One quick answer is that to obtain accreditation by the American Bar Association ("ABA"), law schools must require students to complete "one course of at least two hours in professional responsibility."[1] This requirement, in turn, stems from the ABA's broader view that a rigorous program of legal education is one that "prepares its students, upon graduation, for admission to the bar and for effective, ethical, and responsible participation as members of the legal profession."[2]

According to the Preamble to the ABA's Model Rules of Professional Conduct, "[a] lawyer, as a member of the legal profession, is a representative of clients, an officer of the legal system and a public citizen having special responsibility for the quality of justice." In these various roles, lawyers are in a position to significantly affect the well-being of their clients and others, as well as the integrity and reputation of the legal system. With such power comes responsibility, including the obligation to act within the various laws that govern lawyer conduct and to exercise discretion, where available, in a thoughtful manner, with due regard for the impact of a lawyer's conduct on both individuals and the legal system.

Most of you will not specialize in practicing "professional responsibility" law. As a result, when you are in practice, you may not recognize when your conduct

---

1. ABA Standards and Rules of Procedure for Approval of Law Schools 2020-2021, Standard 303(a)(1). The significance of ABA-accreditation is discussed in Chapter 14: Admission and Discipline.
2. *Id.* at Standard 301(a).

(or the conduct of others) raises professional responsibility issues. One of the most important goals of the professional responsibility course is to prepare you to navigate the ethical realities of law practice, including: (1) recognizing when ethical issues arise; (2) knowing what resources are available to assist you in analyzing these issues; and (3) understanding the values implicated by the different choices available to you, so that you can make more responsible decisions.

The purpose of this brief introductory chapter is to acquaint you with the nature of the subject matter of a professional responsibility course, as well as the various sources of professional responsibility law and some of the resources available to find that law. It also introduces you to the concept of "legal ethics," which includes not only the policies underlying the law of lawyering, but also the values that you can draw on in exercising the considerable discretion that the law allows. An ethical practice is one that views the legal requirements as a floor, not a ceiling; however, individual lawyers differ in the ideals they seek to embody in their legal careers. Finally, the chapter explains why I have chosen to publish a casebook focusing on the professional responsibilities of "business lawyers," a phrase that is meant to refer to lawyers who do primarily advising or transactional work rather than litigation.

A. INTRODUCTION TO THE SUBJECT MATTER

Courses in professional responsibility typically cover both the law and ethics of lawyering, with an emphasis on the former. The law of lawyering consists of the legal regulations that govern the conduct of lawyers, including rules of professional conduct (sometimes confusingly described as "legal ethics codes")[3] and "other law,"[4] such as the common law of contracts, agency, and torts, as well as state and federal statutes and agency regulations.

The ethics component of a professional responsibility course is far more amorphous. At its most theoretical, it draws on the work of moral philosophers who seek to understand and critique the legal and moral obligations of lawyers.[5] This material is fascinating and definitely worthy of study,[6] but our focus will be on the

---

3. E.g., Fred C. Zacharias, Steroids and Legal Ethics Codes: Are Lawyers Rational Actors?, 85 Notre Dame L. Rev. 671 (2010).

4. Restatement (Third) of the Law Governing Lawyers §1, cmt. b (2000) (hereinafter "RLGL").

5. For some prominent examples, *see, e.g.*, David Luban, ed., The Good Lawyer (1984); Alan Goldman, The Moral Foundations of Professional Ethics (1980); Thomas Shaffer, Legal Ethics and the Good Client, 36 Cath. U. L. Rev. 319 (1987); Richard Wassertrom, Lawyers as Professionals: Some Moral Issues, 5 ABA Human Rights 1 (1975); William H. Simon, Ethical Discretion in Lawyering, 101 Harv. L. Rev. 1083 (1988).

6. A common question is whether a good lawyer can be a good person, i.e., whether the lawyer's role justifies actions that would be condemned by the lawyer's personal morality. *See, e.g.*, Luban, *supra* n. 5, at 1 (essays in book address the following question: "Does the professional role of lawyers impose duties that are different from, or even in conflict with ordinary morality?"). For a criticism of the philosophical approach to legal ethics, *see* Monroe H. Freedman, A Critique of Philosophizing about Legal Ethics, 25 Geo. J. Legal Ethics 91 (2012).

more day-to-day questions confronting lawyers and the legal profession. For our purposes, the ethics of lawyering will consist primarily of the more familiar public policy debates that underlie ongoing efforts at legal reform, including identifying the values that underlie the different sides of a debate. In addition, you will be asked to consider how you might exercise discretion when the law permits you to do so and whether it is ever morally appropriate, perhaps even morally imperative, to refuse to comply with a particular legal rule.[7] You are encouraged to bring your own ethical and moral standards to the discussions and to begin to picture what your own personal vision of "ethical lawyering" looks like.

In introducing law students to the law and ethics of lawyering, I like to use a real-life story to illustrate how lawyers are currently regulated by law and how that regulation might be changing as a result of developments affecting the legal profession. One example I have used is particularly compelling for future business lawyers. It concerns the adoption by the federal Securities and Exchange Commission ("SEC") of Standards of Conduct for Attorneys pursuant to congressional passage of the Sarbanes-Oxley Act ("SOX") in 2002.[8] The relevant provisions of the SEC standards require company lawyers to report violations of securities laws to the client company's chief legal officer or chief executive officer, and if the reporting lawyer does not receive an appropriate response, the lawyer must continue "up the ladder" and report to the company's board of directors. Both the federal statute and the SEC regulations were enacted over the vigorous objection of the ABA, following public outrage over corporate accounting scandals such as Enron and WorldCom, which bankrupted some of the country's biggest companies.[9] Consider the following article that was written as Congress was adopting the historic legislation.

Richard B. Schmitt

Lawyers Pressed to Report Fraud Under New Law
Wall Street Journal, Eastern ed.; New York, N.Y., July 25, 2002: B.1

A little-noticed feature in the sweeping corporate reform bill approved by key members of Congress yesterday steps up pressure on lawyers to report evidence of fraud and other misconduct by corporate managers—even their bosses. Under the provision, lawyers will for the first time be obligated to alert senior officers, such as the chief legal counsel or chief executive officer,

---

7. *See, e.g.,* Louis Fisher, Civil Disobedience as Legal Ethics: The Tension between Morality and "Lawyering Law," 51 Harv. CR-CL L. Rev. 481 (2016).

8. For a more detailed discussion of the statute and the attorney-conduct regulations, *see infra* Chapter 12: Corporate Wrongdoing.

9. For a detailed discussion of the professional responsibility issues raised by the Enron scandal, *see* Roger C. Cramton, Enron and the Corporate Lawyer: A Primer on the Legal and Ethical Issues, 58 Bus. Law. 143 (2002).

of evidence of corporate misconduct in the companies they represent. If those officials fail to address problems, the lawyers are then required to report the misconduct to the board.

This thorny legal issue has long been a subject of debate among lawyers and legal ethics specialists. Most state laws, modeled after American Bar Association recommendations, give lawyers discretion on how to handle evidence of fraud so long as they are acting in the companies' best interests. But critics say lawyers have been hesitant to expose paying clients, and that shareholders have suffered. . . .

The lawyer-as-stool-pigeon provision is part of a potentially sweeping new regulatory system for corporate attorneys. The rules, which will be administered by the Securities and Exchange Commission, require the SEC to establish "minimum standards of professional conduct" for the thousands of lawyers who practice before the commission. . . .

The legislation's progress — with the provis[ion] intact — could be a defeat for the 400,000 member ABA, which has been opposing federal regulation of lawyers for decades and which lobbied against the measure.

"This is a grant of licensing authority, and it is pernicious," says Edward Fleischman, a former SEC commissioner, and now a lawyer at Linklaters law firm in New York. "That radically changes the relationship between the lawyer and the regulator."

Lawyers are concerned that SEC rules will conflict with state laws, and cause confusion about lawyers' ethical duties and obligations, . . .

Yesterday, in an apparent last-ditch effort to head off the bill's passage, the ABA proposed changes in some of its own rules through a report from its "Task Force on Corporate Responsibility," created in March to examine possible changes in the corporate governance laws amid the swirl of accounting scandals. . . .

As this article notes, the grounds on which the ABA lobbied against the proposed federal action were both *procedural* and *substantive*. Procedurally, the ABA argued that historically it has been the states — not the federal government — that regulate the conduct of lawyers, most prominently through state-adopted rules of professional conduct. The ABA has consistently opposed efforts by the federal government, including Congress and various federal agencies, to regulate the conduct of lawyers. Substantively, the ABA argued that the proposed federal regulation interfered with the attorney-client relationship by discouraging candid communication between client and attorney.

In an effort to avoid or limit the scope of the proposed federal law, the ABA adopted changes to its Model Rules of Professional Conduct that were designed to move the rules further in the direction of (but not as far as) the federal government's proposals. These changes strengthened corporate lawyers' up-the-ladder reporting obligation and granted them permission to disclose client crimes or fraud to prevent or rectify economic harm to others. This gambit did not work, the federal regulation was implemented,[10] and the ABA was left with newly adopted rules that some factions within the ABA had been resisting for years.

The SOX story has much to tell us about the law of lawyering, including the differing roles of the states, the ABA, and the federal government. It also tells us something about the ethics of lawyering.

B. THE LAW OF LAWYERING

The ABA was correct that, historically, the states have been the primary regulators of lawyer conduct. Lawyers are typically licensed to practice pursuant to state court rules establishing standards for admission to the bar.[11] In addition, each state has adopted rules of professional conduct,[12] typically by action of the state's highest court.[13] Rules of professional conduct are designed to serve as a basis for lawyer discipline (using a disciplinary process also governed by state court regulation), but the rules are often referenced in other legal contexts, such as lawyer disqualification and legal malpractice. For example, the court-appointed examiner in the Enron bankruptcy proceeding concluded that Enron's lawyers were potentially liable to Enron for malpractice based on a Texas professional conduct rule, as well as for aiding and abetting breaches of fiduciary duty by Enron officers, and for malpractice based on common law negligence.[14]

When professional conduct rules are used in contexts other than lawyer discipline, courts are free to use their common law authority to modify the

---

10. The ABA was successful, however, in getting the SEC to back off an initial proposal that would have required lawyers who do not receive an appropriate response from the board to withdraw from the representation and inform the SEC of the withdrawal, disaffirming any reports filed with the SEC that the lawyer knows were inaccurate. *See infra* Chapter 12: Corporate Wrongdoing. The ABA's adoption of a more expansive permission to disclose client crimes or frauds likely explains the SEC's decision not to adopt the mandatory "reporting out" obligation.

11. For more detail on admission standards and the disciplinary process, *see infra* Chapter 14: Admission and Discipline.

12. Court rules outside a state's rules of professional conduct sometimes contain provisions similar to those found elsewhere in rules of professional conduct. For example, New York's provision requiring that most fee agreements be written is found in a court rule separate from the New York Rules of Professional Conduct. *See* 22 N.Y.C.R.R. §1215.1.

13. Exceptions include New York, where the rules of professional conduct are adopted jointly by the four appellate divisions of the New York Supreme Court (and not the New York Court of Appeals, which is the state's highest appellate court) and California, where the state legislature and the California Supreme Court share responsibility for regulating the conduct of lawyers.

14. *See, e.g.*, Final Report of Neal Batson, App. C at 48-49 (2003), In re Enron, No. 1:01-bk-16034 (Bankr. S.D.N.Y. 2003), ECF No. 14455 (reporting conclusions concerning potential liability of Vinson & Elkins, one of several outside counsel to Enron). *See also* RLGL, §1, cmt b.

specific legal standard, and they often do so, particularly when a litigant seeks to disqualify an opponent's lawyer because of an ethical violation.[15]

State rules of professional conduct are commonly based on ABA model codes, but there are many important state variations; for example, state rules on client confidentiality and lawyer advertising differ substantially from state to state.[16] Federal courts and agencies (such as the SEC) commonly adopt their own conduct rules for lawyers appearing before them; however, with the exception of rules like the SOX regulations, the federal rules are usually based on either an ABA model code or on state professional conduct rules (as is typically the case with federal district courts).[17] Although Congress likely has the authority to preempt state rules and adopt uniform licensing and conduct rules for all lawyers,[18] so far it has not had the appetite to do so; rather, it regulates selectively, as in the case of SOX.[19] Commentators have noted the extent to which the federal government has been expanding its selective regulation of lawyers in recent decades,[20] a development of great concern to both the ABA and some state courts.

1. The ABA Model Codes

The ABA itself has no authority to regulate lawyers; therefore, the ABA model codes bind no one, not even lawyers who are ABA members. However, as the leading national association of lawyers, the ABA plays an important role in proposing comprehensive lawyer codes for the states to adopt. Although all state codes are now based on the current ABA Model Rules of Professional Conduct,[21] you will commonly see references in cases and ethics committee opinions to prior ABA codes (or even an earlier version of a particular ABA code). As a result, lawyers need to be aware of the historical evolution of these codes.

---

15. *See infra* Chapter 5: Conflicts of Interest: Current Clients.

16. The ABA Center for Professional Responsibility provides charts illustrating how state rules differ from the ABA Model Rules, including the rules on confidentiality and advertising. *See* https://www.americanbar.org/groups/professional_responsibility/policy/rule_charts.html.

17. *See, e.g.,* Daniel R. Coquilette & Judith A. McMorrow, Zacharias's Prophecy: The Federalization of Legal Ethics Through Legislative, Court, and Agency Regulation, 48 San Diego L. Rev. 123 (2011). For a comprehensive look at regulation by federal and state agencies, *see* George M. Cohen, The Laws of Agency Lawyering, 84 Fordham L. Rev. 1963 (2016).

18. *See, e.g.,* Fred C. Zacharias, Federalizing Legal Ethics, 73 Tex. L. Rev. 335, 337 & n. 4 (1994).

19. *See generally* Coquillette & McMorrow, *supra* n. 17.

20. *See id.*

21. California was the last holdout. Until recently, California refused to base its lawyer code on any version of the ABA model codes, but rather relied on its own formulation, which used a completely different organization and numbering system, thereby making it difficult for lawyers to compare the California rules with the rules in other jurisdictions. Effective November 2018, the newly adopted California Rules of Professional Conduct largely follow the format and numbering system of the ABA Model Rules, although as with other state rules, there is considerable variation from the ABA rules. The California Supreme Court continues to share regulatory jurisdiction over lawyers with the California legislature.

The first ABA code was enacted in 1908 when the ABA promulgated its Canons of Professional Ethics. The Canons, often criticized for their brevity and lack of specificity, were replaced in 1969 by the Model Code of Professional Responsibility. The Model Code consisted of nine general Canons, each of which contained both aspirational Ethical Considerations and mandatory Disciplinary Rules. The format was confusing, and in 1983 the ABA adopted the Model Rules of Professional Conduct, using a format based on the black-letter text and explanatory comments of the American Law Institute ("ALI") Restatements. The Model Rules have been amended from time to time, including extensive changes in 2002. The ABA continually reviews the Model Rules and from time to time considers specific proposals for reform, as when it adopted a controversial new antidiscrimination rule in 2017.[22] As a result, when researching either the Model Rules, or a state or federal rule, be sure that you are focusing on the version in force during the relevant time period.

2. The Restatement of the Law Governing Lawyers and "Other Law"

When I first began teaching Professional Responsibility in the 1970s, the casebooks were quite thin and focused almost exclusively on codes of professional conduct, with an occasional U.S. Supreme Court case invalidating a state court rule on the ground that it violated a federal statute[23] or the U.S. Constitution.[24] Since then, however, lawyers and law professors have become increasingly aware that there is a considerable body of "other law" that governs the conduct of lawyers. One reason for this growing awareness was the ALI's decision in 1986 to undertake an entirely new Restatement of the Law Governing Lawyers ("Restatement" or "RLGL"), which was adopted in 2000. This Restatement included references to rules of professional conduct, but focused primarily on "other law," including the common law of agency, fiduciary duties, contracts, and torts, as well as state and federal statutes and agency regulations.[25] In addition, the Restatement emphasized the different remedies available for violations of the law governing lawyers, including not only disciplinary proceedings that can result in a reprimand, suspension, or

---

22. As of June 2020, Model Rule 8.4(g) had been adopted with only minor changes by two states (New Mexico and Vermont), adopted in part by another state (Maine), and rejected by a number of states (including Louisiana, Nevada, and South Carolina). Many other states have antidiscrimination and harassment rules that are more limited than the ABA version. *See infra* Chapter 14: Admission and Discipline.

23. *E.g.,* Goldfarb v. Virginia State Bar, 421 U.S. 773 (1975) (minimum fee schedules published by county bar constituted price-fixing in violation of Sherman Act).

24. *E.g.,* Bates v. State Bar of Ariz., 433 U.S. 350 (1977) (state ban on virtually all forms of lawyer advertising held to violate First Amendment).

25. *See* RLGL, Foreword.

disbarment, but also remedies such as fee forfeiture, civil damage actions, disqualification, court sanctions, injunctions, or even, in extreme cases, criminal prosecution.[26] Modern professional responsibility casebooks are filled with examples of this extremely important "other law."

3. Researching the Law of Lawyering

For guidance in interpreting and applying the ABA Model Rules, you should first determine if any of the terms of the rule are defined. Many important and recurring terms, such as "fraud," "knowingly," "informed consent," and "writing," are defined in Model Rule 1.0. Next, you should always read the detailed comments following each black-letter rule. These comments were expanded as part of the ABA's extensive 2002 revisions, for the express purpose of providing additional guidance to lawyers. In addition, the ABA's Standing Committee on Ethics and Professional Responsibility issues advisory opinions from time to time on questions of concern to lawyers.

Most state courts also have adopted comments to their rules of professional conduct, typically based on the ABA comments, although some have not done so.[27] These comments, like the rules themselves, may vary significantly from the ABA comments. State courts that have not adopted the comments will often refer to the ABA comments in interpreting similar state rules.[28] State and local bar association committees also issue ethics committee opinions, which, like the ABA ethics opinions, are usually merely advisory. All ABA opinions and some state and local bar opinions are available on Westlaw and Lexis Advance; they also can be found on Bloomberg Law's ABA/Bloomberg Law Lawyers' Manual on Professional Conduct. For additional guidance in identifying relevant state and local ethics opinions, consult your law school librarians. Many law school law libraries have compiled research guides for professional responsibility issues.

Additional resources for interpreting both the ABA and state rules of professional conduct include the ABA's Annotated Model Rules of Professional Conduct, Bloomberg Law's ABA/Bloomberg Law Lawyers' Manual on Professional Conduct,[29] treatises on the law of lawyering[30] and legal malpractice,[31] as well as numerous articles in law reviews and bar journals. Lawyers can

---

26. *See id.*

27. *See, e.g.,* N.J. Rules of Prof'l Conduct. The New York courts adopted only the black-letter text of each of its Rules of Professional Conduct. The comments, however, are adopted and published by the New York State Bar Association for the guidance of lawyers.

28. *See, e.g.,* Matter of Op. 668 of Advisory Comm. On Prof'l Ethics, 134 N.J. 294 (1993).

29. The ABA/Bloomberg Law Lawyer's Manual on Professional Conduct has an excellent series of Practice Guides, which address particular topics and include state variations of the Model Rules, case law, and secondary sources.

30. *See, e.g.,* Geoffrey C. Hazard, Jr. et al., The Law of Lawyering (two-volume treatise updated annually). *See also* Gregory C. Sisk et al., Legal Ethics, Professional Responsibility, and the Legal Profession (2018) (single-volume treatise).

31. *See, e.g.,* Ronald E. Mallen, Legal Malpractice (six-volume treatise with annual editions).

request advisory opinions from bar association ethics committees, some of which also offer ethics "hotlines" to call for advice.

As for researching "other law," the Restatement itself is an excellent resource, including the Reporter's Notes, which identify illustrative rules, court decisions, and secondary sources that were relied upon by the Reporters in drafting each section. Services such as Westlaw and Lexis Advance will allow you to find court decisions that have either adopted or discussed a particular Restatement provision. In addition to the Restatement, Bloomberg Law's ABA/Bloomberg Law Lawyer's Manual of Professional Conduct includes a discussion of "other law," where applicable, as do the above-mentioned treatises. Law review articles and bar publications are also excellent resources. Finally, for issues involving "other law," don't forget to check other ALI Restatements, such as the Restatement (Third) of Agency, the Restatement (Second) of Contracts, and the Restatements (Second) and (Third) of Torts.[32] In addition, don't forget treatises such as those on Evidence and the Federal Rules of Civil Procedure.

4. The Underdeveloped State of the Law of Lawyering

As you research various questions involving the law of lawyering, you will often be frustrated to learn how often you cannot find a clear answer to the question you are asking. This happens with other subjects, but some aspects of the law of lawyering are considerably less developed than other areas of the law. The primary reason for this is the lack of opportunities for courts to address certain fundamental issues. Most lawyer discipline cases do not result in published opinions, and because disciplinary authorities typically pursue only the most egregious cases, many of the perplexing issues that arise in the daily practice of law are never addressed by anyone. Bar association ethics committees try to address some of these issues in ethics opinions, but these opinions are not binding, and there are only so many questions they can address.

The problem is particularly frustrating for business and other transactional lawyers. The ethical conduct of litigators is frequently raised by their clients' adversaries during the course of a lawsuit, thereby requiring the court to rule on a motion to disqualify or for court sanctions and, in doing so, to explain whether and why the lawyer's conduct was improper. Although it is possible for a transactional client to seek a court injunction to prevent lawyer misconduct,[33] clients rarely do so. Moreover, although a transactional lawyer's

---

32. The ALI is still in the process of restating the law of torts, and there is no single current Restatement for all of torts. Parts of the Restatement (Second) of Torts are still in force, whereas some aspects of tort law have been more recently updated in the Restatement (Third) of Torts: Apportionment of Liability (2000), Restatement (Third) of Torts: Physical and Emotional Harm (2010), and the Restatement (Third) of Torts: Liability for Economic Harm (2020). Ongoing projects include the Restatement (Third) of Torts: Intentional Torts to Persons.

33. *See, e.g.,* Maritrans GP Inc. v. Pepper, Hamilton & Scheetz, 602 A.2d 1277 (Pa. 1992).

misconduct can often be litigated in a malpractice or breach of fiduciary duty lawsuit, the complainant typically must prove that the lawyer's misconduct caused legally cognizable damages, a daunting prospect that deters many such lawsuits.

A final reason for the underdeveloped state of the law governing lawyers is that most lawyers do not practice "professional responsibility" law; as a result, they are less likely to spot issues and raise them in a context in which these issues might get litigated. Fortunately, this state of affairs is gradually changing, as more lawyers begin to specialize in this field.[34] Many states require legal ethics to be covered in mandatory continuing education, and law firms are increasingly asking lawyers to perform various ethics-related functions, including serving on conflicts of interest committees or becoming law firm "general counsel," whose responsibility includes educating firm lawyers as to their professional responsibilities and adopting proactive policies and procedures to avoid lawyer discipline, legal malpractice, and other civil liability.

C. THE ETHICS OF LAWYERING

The SOX story directly addresses the ethics of lawyering only in the sense that it identifies different policy concerns underlying debates over when corporate lawyers should be required to report possible constituent misconduct "up-the-ladder," and whether lawyers should be permitted, perhaps even required, to report client crimes or frauds when necessary to prevent or rectify substantial economic harm to others.[35] These debates are similar to the kinds of policy debates you encounter in other courses, but there is one way in which they are unique in the professional responsibility context. In other courses, we debate laws that govern the conduct of other people, including those who will be our clients. Professional responsibility debates are more personal because they are directed toward our own behavior. And while others may feel free to advocate their own interests in lobbying for or against the adoption of particular laws, lawyers are arguably under a special, ethical obligation to consider how the regulation of lawyer conduct affects the broader public interest. The source of this obligation is the concept of *professionalism*.

Professionalism involves many aspects, including a set of ideals to which lawyers aspire.[36] What I am referring to here is the concept that professions

---

34. There is even a specialized organization, the Association of Professional Responsibility Lawyers (APRL), which includes not only bar counsel and lawyers who represent respondents in disciplinary cases, but also lawyers who provide advice to lawyers on legal ethics issues, defend lawyers in civil liability cases, and perform ethics-related functions in law firms. *See* https://aprl.net/about-aprl/.

35. *See* Schmitt, *supra*. *See also infra* Chapter 4: Privilege and Confidentiality.

36. *See generally* Nancy J. Moore, Professionalism: Rekindled, Reconsidered or Reformulated, 19 Cap. U. L. Rev. 1121 (1990).

differ from other occupations in that they are more self-regulating.[37] Professional codes are then explained and justified as the result of an implied contract between society and the profession, in which the profession agrees to regulate itself in the public interest in return for the benefits and privileges of a legal monopoly.[38] Of course, no profession is free from external regulation, and the legal profession is no exception. However, lawyers are *more* self-regulating than other professions because lawyer regulation comes to a large extent from courts, and courts are comprised of judges, who are themselves lawyers.[39] Moreover, state court regulation is often either initiated or largely influenced by bar association proposals, although many courts have become more active in recent decades.

Critics of professionalism argue that professional codes (and other aspects of professionalism) are part of the ideology that an occupation uses to achieve or maintain its special rights and privileges.[40] But while it is true that these codes might contain much false rhetoric (thereby deceiving not only the public, but also the professionals themselves),[41] they also serve to establish standards by which the profession can be held to public account. And if society perceives that the public interest is not well-served by lawyer self-regulation, then society can and should take over that regulation, by-passing lawyers' proposals in favor of its own.[42] This is apparently what happened in the SOX saga, in which Congress stepped in because it was concerned that state court regulation, dominated by lawyers, was insufficient to protect the public interest in preventing corporate crimes or frauds.

The ethics of lawyering also concerns an individual lawyer's exercise of the discretion permitted by much of the law of lawyering.[43] For example, under both the current Model Rules and the SOX regulations, lawyers have a choice whether or not to disclose confidential information to third persons

---

37. *See* ABA Comm'n on Professionalism, ". . . In the Spirit of Public Service:" A Blueprint for the Rekindling of Lawyer Professionalism at 10 (1986).

38. *See* Nancy J. Moore, The Usefulness of Ethical Codes, 1989 Ann. Survey of Amer. Law 7, 12-13 (1989).

39. *Id.* at 14-15.

40. *See* Moore, *supra* n. 36, at 1124-25.

41. For example, the comment to Model Rule 5.4 explains that the rule against lawyers sharing legal fees with nonlawyers, which, inter alia, prevents law firms from making nonlawyers partners and prevents lawyers from practicing law in a company owned even partly by nonlawyers, is designed "to protect the lawyer's professional independence of judgment." MR 5.4, cmt [1]. Critics contend that the prohibition is in fact designed to maintain lawyers' monopoly over the provision of legal services, which makes access to justice more difficult for many middle and low-income clients. *See infra* Chapter 16: Nonlawyer Ownership, Multidisciplinary Practice, and Alternative Legal Service Providers. This is an example of what I mean by "false rhetoric."

42. *See* Moore, *supra* n. 36 at 1128.

43. William Simon has developed a theoretical approach to lawyers' exercise of discretion, which he intended to be applied to both "ethical analysis relevant to a regulatory body promulgating rules of professional conduct and analysis relevant to an individual lawyer operating within the limited of promulgated rules." William H. Simon, Ethical Discretion in Lawyering, 101 Harv. L. Rev. 1083, 1084 (1988).

in order to prevent or rectify a client crime or fraud.[44] When would you (or should you) be willing to do so? Why do so few lawyers blow the whistle on their clients?[45] Another example concerns the ethics of client counseling. Rules of professional conduct provide that clients have the right to be informed and make decisions about the objectives of the representation, such as whether or not to accept an offer made during a contract negotiation.[46] If your client, say an inexperienced entrepreneur, is inclined to accept an onerous provision that you, an experienced business lawyer, are convinced is not in the client's best interest, should you attempt to persuade the client to reject that provision, even if it means that there will be no deal? If so, how far should you go in using your powers of persuasion to overcome the client's inclination?[47]

Finally, the ethics of lawyering includes the question whether there are some circumstances in which it is morally appropriate, perhaps even morally imperative, for a lawyer to refuse to comply with a clear rule of law.[48] For example, unlike the Model Rules, the newly adopted California Rules of Professional Conduct permit the disclosure of confidential information to prevent death or serious bodily harm only when the lawyer can do so by preventing a crime that is likely to produce such a result.[49] What if your client has already committed the crime, for example, by knowingly selling adulterated food, or what if your client's threatened conduct is not criminal?[50] Are lawyers uniquely bound by the rule of law, or are they, like other persons, morally (if not legally) free to resist the application of law in circumstances in which

---

44. *See* MR 1.6(b)(2), (3); 17 C.F.R. § 205.3(d)(2)(i), (iii). Some state rules *require* disclosure when necessary to prevent a client crime or fraud. *See infra* Chapter 4: Privilege and Confidentiality.

45. The federal government is increasingly relying on financial rewards to encourage whistleblowers, including lawyers, to ferret out fraud. For a discussion of a myriad of issues confronting lawyers who might seek these whistleblower rewards, *see generally* Kathleen Clark & Nancy J. Moore, Financial Rewards for Whistleblowing Lawyers, 56 B.C. L. Rev. 1697 (2015).

46. *See* MR 1.2(a), 1.4. *See also infra* Chapter 3: Competence and Diligence; Control and Communication; Fees.

47. *See, e.g.*, David Luban, Paternalism and the Legal Profession, 1981 Wis. L. Rev. 454 (1981).

48. Most scholars who have written on this topic invoke examples from either criminal or civil litigation. *See, e.g.*, David Luban, The Adversary System Excuse, in The Good Lawyer 83, 118 (D. Luban ed. 1983); Fisher, *supra* note 7.

49. *Compare* MR 1.6(b)(1) (disclosure permissible "to prevent reasonably certain death or substantial bodily harm" *with* Cal. Rules of Prof'l Conduct, R. 1.6(b) (disclosure permissible "to prevent a criminal act that the lawyer reasonably believes is likely to result in the death of, or substantial bodily harm to, an individual"). *See also infra* Chapter 4: Privilege and Confidentiality.

50. A lawyer who learned that his client had AIDS requested an opinion from the Delaware Bar Association Professional Ethics Committee whether he had either a duty or permission to disclose the information to the woman with whom his client lived, as he suspected that the client had not told her. The Committee concluded that the lawyer was neither obligated nor allowed to disclose under the Delaware Rules, but that "[i]f [his] moral code is such that he cannot abide by this duty, he may be pressed to the point of civil disobedience because obeying the letter of the law may require him to sacrifice more than he can bear of his own moral code." Del. Bar. Assoc. Prof. Ethics Comm., Op. 1988-2.

application of the rule would be unjust? Of course, lawyers who do so will have to accept the legal consequences of their actions, but might disciplinary authorities exercise their own discretion not to prosecute under at least some circumstances?[51]

D. WHY PROFESSIONAL RESPONSIBILITY FOR BUSINESS LAWYERS?

Professional responsibility is notoriously one of the most difficult subjects to teach to law students because it is often the only required upper-level course, which means that many students are there against their will. As a result, faculty often report their students' resistance or passivity to the subject, as well as their need to be convinced of the utility of the materials and analysis.

Having taught the course in various formats and contexts for over 30 years, I know that my students are most engaged when the issues raised in class are ones that they see themselves encountering in their own future law practices. As a result, many law schools offer contextual courses that focus on ethical issues in a single practice area. These courses have tended to focus on litigation practice, such as criminal prosecution, criminal defense, or civil litigation. A few law schools, including my own, now offer a course in professional responsibility for the business or transactional lawyer.

Not all, or even most, students know exactly what they want to do after law school, but increasingly students are taking advantage of new opportunities to explore the transactional practice of law, typically in a business setting. These offerings include simulated courses in contract drafting and deals, externships in corporate counsel offices and transactional legal clinics where students assist budding entrepreneurs, community groups, small businesses, and other for-profit or nonprofit organizations.

Although students in these different types of courses are undoubtedly exposed to at least some of the professional responsibility issues that arise in a business law practice, I believe these students will nevertheless benefit from a more substantial immersion in the broader framework and in-depth analysis provided in a semester-long course in professional responsibility. Given that they are required to take some professional responsibility course, why not make it easier for such students to satisfy the professional responsibility requirement through a course or seminar that covers the fundamental components of the traditional professional responsibility course, but with a focus on how these issues arise in a transactional business law practice?

---

51. *See id.* (Committee advised that the lawyer "should inform his client of the decision to disclose and should be prepared to accept discipline if he cannot convince a disciplinary authority to read in a 'moral compulsion' exception to the letter of Rule 1.6.")

Although the goal of this casebook is to provide the basis of a contextual professional responsibility course in the area of business transactions, do not despair if you are not planning a career in business law. As noted above, the casebook covers the fundamental components of a traditional professional responsibility course, including the litigator's unique duties of candor to the court and to a litigation adversary. In addition, although the casebook provides more cases and other materials involving lawyers in a transactional setting than do most other casebooks, it also contains plenty of material involving litigators. One reason for this, as mentioned earlier, is that ethical issues involving litigators are more likely to be resolved by a court than ethical issues involving transactional lawyers.

Finally, a note on the structure of this casebook. Part I addresses core professional responsibility concepts in the context of either an individual client or a company where the organizational status of the client is not relevant. Part II then examines some unique difficulties that arise when applying these core concepts to a client that is an organization, such as a partnership or corporation. Some faculty will prefer to assign one or more of the chapters in Part II with the corresponding chapter in Part I—for example, discussing confidentiality and attorney-client privilege for the individual client, followed immediately by the application of this material when the client is an organization. The casebook is structured to permit this variation in the order of chapters.

Both Parts I and II address ethical issues that arise in the day-to-day practice of law. Part III, on the other hand, addresses broader issues in the regulation of lawyers as a profession, including admission, discipline, and the changing nature of both the delivery of legal services and the regulation of those who provide these services. These later chapters offer a glimpse into the world of the future, for which many have predicted radical changes in the nature of the practice of law.

PART I

CORE CONCEPTS

CHAPTER 2

FORMATION, SCOPE, AND TERMINATION OF THE ATTORNEY-CLIENT RELATIONSHIP

Lawyers owe some duties to nonclients, including prospective clients, but once an attorney-client relationship is formed, the lawyer owes a full panoply of duties to that client—competence, diligence, communication, confidentiality, and loyalty. As a result, it becomes important to know when and how such relationships are formed and when they end. In most instances, the lawyer and client expressly agree that the lawyer will represent the client in a particular matter. Representation typically begins at the time of the agreement and ends when the matter is concluded. But all too often, there is no express agreement, and the scope of the representation is either general or ill-defined; as a result, it may be unclear whether and when the relationship ended. And if the scope of the representation is either general or ill-defined, it also may be difficult to determine the scope of the lawyer's duty to protect the client. These are some of the complexities this chapter addresses.

A. FORMING THE ATTORNEY-CLIENT RELATIONSHIP

In most jurisdictions, lawyers may orally agree to represent a client, although they are constantly urged to use written retention agreements whenever possible.[1] Even when there is no express agreement, either oral or written, the

---

1. *See, e.g.*, MR 1.5(b) ("[t]he scope of the representation and the basis or rate of the fee and expenses for which the client will be responsible shall be communicated to the client, *preferably in writing*, before or within a reasonable time after commencing the representation") (emphasis added). Some jurisdictions require that the scope of the representation and the basis or rate of the fee and expenses be communicated *in writing* to the client except in some circumstances, as when the lawyer reasonably expects that the fee will be under $500. *See, e.g.*, Mass. Rules of Prof'l Conduct, R. 1.5(b). *See also* N.Y.C.R.R. §1215.1 (similar requirement set forth in court rule separate from rules of professional conduct). Virtually all jurisdictions follow the Model Rules in requiring lawyers to use a written fee agreement, signed by the client, before charging a contingent fee. *See* ABA Model Rule 1.5(c).

attorney-client relationship may be implied from the parties' conduct. For example, if an individual meets with a lawyer, asks the lawyer to represent him or her in the sale of her business, and the lawyer begins providing legal services in that matter, a court will readily imply an attorney-client relationship. But not all instances of implied representation are that straightforward.

Consider the following case involving a foreign businessman who signed a lease agreement with a lawyer–property owner who drafted the lease and explained its terms to the businessman, through a translator. The events took place in Saipan, which is the largest island in the Commonwealth of the Northern Mariana Islands, a territory of the United States located in the western Pacific Ocean, and the litigation was brought in federal district court there. Lawyers in the Northern Mariana Islands, like lawyers in the territory of Puerto Rico, are governed by standards similar to those governing lawyers in the 50 states and the District of Columbia.

Nam was a Korean businessman who had signed a 55-year ground lease with Quichocho,[2] a Saipan lawyer licensed to practice law in the Northern Mariana Islands, and another co-owner. The lessors attempted to terminate Nam's lease after only two years, and Nam filed a lawsuit asserting a claim of breach of fiduciary duty against Quichocho, as well as claims of breach of contract and restitution against both lessors. Each of the parties moved for summary judgment on each claim.

Sin Ho Nam v. Quichocho
841 F. Supp.2d 1152 (D.N. Mar. I. 2011)

Mark W. Bennett, District Judge

[Nam first met Quichocho when Nam and his translator, Mr. Ha, came to Quichocho's law office to execute the lease. Mr. Ha had negotiated the ground lease with the co-owner. The parties agreed that Quichocho had prepared the ground lease, in English, for Nam's signature. Quichocho explained the terms of the lease to Nam, through Mr. Ha, the translator. Nam and Ha left Quichocho's office with the lease and returned later that day to execute it. Two days later, Nam paid Quichocho $1,500 for drafting and filing Articles of Incorporation and By-Laws of Sin Ho Nam Corporation. Quichocho admitted the existence of an attorney-client relationship at that point, but argued that the relationship began *after* the ground lease was executed. The breach of fiduciary duty claim was based on Quichocho's alleged failure to satisfy the requirements of Rule 1.8(a) of the Model Rules of Professional Conduct, which provides that a lawyer may not enter into a business transaction with an existing client except after complying with certain conditions. The following portion of the district judge's opinion with respect to the parties' motions for summary judgment is limited to the breach of fiduciary duty claim.]

---

2. The correct American pronunciation is probably "kwee-*cho*-cho."

[A]n attorney-client relationship is an essential element of a claim for malpractice based on breach of fiduciary duty. Circumstances in which such a relationship arises are the following:

(1) a person manifests to a lawyer the person's intent that the lawyer provide legal services for the person; and either
(a) the lawyer manifests to the person consent to do so; or
(b) the lawyer fails to manifest lack of consent to do so, and the lawyer knows or reasonably should know that the person reasonably relies on the lawyer to provide the services; or
(2) a tribunal with power to do so appoints the lawyer to provide the services.

Restatement (Third) of the Law Governing Lawyers § 14. Contrary to the defendants' contentions, I believe that a reasonable juror could find from the evidence adduced by Nam that he did have an attorney-client relationship with Quichocho with regard to the Ground Lease, although I do not believe that Nam has shown this beyond dispute. . . . Nam at least arguably manifested to Quichocho that he was requesting that Quichocho provide legal services for him by asking him to draft the Ground Lease, and just as importantly, Quichocho did not manifest a lack of consent to do so. Indeed, a reasonable jury could find that, at least under circumstances involving a foreign national who did not speak English, was not familiar with Commonwealth law, and who sought or at least received an explanation of the terms of the Ground Lease drafted by the attorney, that the attorney reasonably should have known that the person was relying on him to provide services. Contrary to the defendants' contentions, while ¶ 29 of the Ground Lease might make clear to reasonably sophisticated English speakers that the attorney did not represent the Lessee, it does not necessarily make Nam's reliance on Quichocho as his attorney unreasonable.[3] Neither party is entitled to summary judgment on this element of the claim.

NOTES AND QUESTIONS

1. Having previously learned that the ABA Model Rules are not binding on anyone, you may wonder why one of those rules formed the basis for Quichocho's alleged breach of fiduciary duty to Nam. The reason is that the Supreme Court for the Northern Mariana Islands has adopted as its rules of attorney conduct the most recent version of the ABA Model Rules.[4]

---

3. [Paragraph 29 of the lease provided in part: "This Lease has been prepared for the Lessor and may be submitted by the Lessee to Lessee's attorney for approval. No representation or recommendation is made by the Lessor as to the legal sufficiency, legal effect, or tax consequences of this Lease or the transaction relating thereto; the parties shall rely solely upon the advice of their own legal counsel as to the legal and tax consequences of this Lease." —Ed.]

4. *See* Northern Mariana Islands Rules of Attorney Discipline and Procedure, https://www.cnilaw.org/pdf/courtrules/R07.pdf. The conflicts of interest arising from a lawyer's financial transactions with clients are discussed in Chapter 5: Conflicts of Interest: Current Clients.

2. Although the district judge cited the Model Rules as evidence of a lawyer's fiduciary duty when entering into a business transaction with a client, the judge did not cite them on the issue involving forming an attorney-client relationship. This is because the Model Rules do not address that question. Rather, as provided in the Scope section, "for purposes of determining the lawyer's authority and responsibility, principles of substantive law external to the Rules determine whether a client-lawyer relationship exists."[5] Section 14(b)(1)(b) of the Restatement adopts a "reasonable expectations of the client" test to forming an attorney-client relationship. That test is based on judicial decisions in a wide variety of common law cases, including promissory estoppel.[6]

3. As a result of the court's denial of the parties' motions for summary judgment, a jury was required to determine whether an attorney-client relationship was formed. Formulate the arguments you would make to a jury on behalf of both Nam and Quichocho. In doing so, consider what the relevance was, if any, of the fact that two days after Nam executed the lease, he expressly retained Quichocho to represent him in forming a business entity, paying him $1,500 to do so. It is commonly said that payment of a fee is not a necessary aspect of an attorney-client relationship, but is it nevertheless relevant that Nam did not pay Quichocho a fee to prepare the lease? As the lawyer for either party, are there additional facts you would want to know for the purpose of presenting additional evidence or making arguments to the jury?

4. In Johnson v. Schultz, 691 S.E. 2d 701 (N.C. 2010), the closing attorney in a sale of real estate[7] embezzled financing funds provided by the lender, leaving the sellers with a check from the closing attorney's trust account that could not be cashed due to insufficient funds. The court held that the buyers, who had hired the lawyer to be the closing attorney, were responsible for the loss. Following common practice in North Carolina, the closing attorney prepared the deed for the seller. The court remanded the case for determination whether an attorney-client relationship also existed between *the sellers* and the attorney, in which case the sellers would share the risk of loss. The evidence cited by the court as raising a question whether the attorney represented the sellers,

---

5. MR, Scope [17].

6. Promissory estoppel is the legal principle that a promise is enforceable by law, even if made without formal consideration, when a promisor has made a promise to a promisee who then relies on that promise to the promisee's subsequent detriment. The "reasonable expectations" test has elements of both contract and tort law. *See* Togstad v. Vesely, Otto, Miller & Keefe, 291 N.W.2d 686, 693, n.4 (Minn. 1980) (explaining that contract analysis requires rendering of legal advice pursuant to another's request, whereas under a negligence approach, the relationship can exist when a person reasonably relies on legal advice, not necessarily at the person's request).

7. A closing attorney is responsible for organizing, carrying out, and finalizing real estate closings.

as well as the buyers, was that the sellers paid the attorney $125 to prepare the deed and that the sellers had a prior professional relationship with the attorney. The court provided the following guidance to the trial court:

> To determine whether an attorney-client relationship in fact existed between sellers and [the attorney], the trial court should consider the guidance offered in the [North Carolina State Bar] Ethics Opinion[8] as to how a closing attorney "may prepare the deed as an accommodation to the needs of her client, the buyer, without becoming the lawyer for the Seller." To avoid establishment of an attorney-client relationship, the Ethics Opinion instructs lawyers to make certain clarifications and disclosures about their role in the transaction as well as to abstain from giving the seller legal advice. On remand, we instruct the trial court to consider these factors and determine whether [the attorney] exceeded the ethical safe harbor in the Ethics Opinion and established an attorney-client relationship with sellers.

As the lawyer for either party, what other facts would you want to know for the purpose of presenting additional evidence or making arguments to the trial court in determining whether the closing attorney represented both the sellers and the buyers? Keep in mind that the seller wants to argue that no attorney-client relationship existed, and it's the buyer who wants to argue that there was in fact an attorney-client relationship with the seller. If the sellers wanted to sue the closing attorney for malpractice, then it would be the sellers arguing in favor of the existence of an attorney-client relationship.

5. There are many circumstances in which contacts with an attorney in a non-office setting may give rise to an attorney-client relationship. A California ethics opinion analyzed three hypotheticals involving: (1) a stranger approaching a lawyer in a courthouse hallway; (2) a guest approaching the lawyer at a party after learning from the host that the lawyer is an attorney; and (3) a lawyer who receives a phone call requesting advice from a cousin. *See* State Bar of California Formal Op. 2003-161. The opinion advised that a number of factors may be considered in determining whether an "implied-in-fact attorney-client relationship exists," including the following: whether the lawyer "volunteered his or her services to a prospective client," whether the lawyer "agreed to investigate a case and provide legal advice to a prospective client about the possible merits of the case," whether "the lawyer previously represented the individual, particularly where the representation occurred over a lengthy period of time or in several matters," whether "the individual sought legal advice from the attorney in the matter in question and whether the attorney provided advice," whether

---

8. [The ethics opinion cited by the court was N.C. St. B. Formal Ethics Op. 10 (July 14, 2004).—Ed.]

"the individual paid fees or other consideration to the attorney," whether "the individual consulted the attorney in confidence," and whether "the individual reasonably believes that he or she is consulting a lawyer in a professional capacity." Have your friends or family consulted you on legal matters? When they do so after you are admitted to the bar, should you answer their questions? Assist them in preparing legal documents, such as a simple contract or an apartment lease?

6. The California ethics opinion discusses not only whether and when an attorney-client relationship is established, but also whether the lawyer might owe a duty of confidentiality to the speaker as a *prospective client*. For more on the duty of confidentiality owed to prospective clients, including determining when a person is a prospective client, *see infra* Chapter 4: Privilege and Confidentiality.

7. Although the risk of unintended or "accidental" clients has always existed, that risk has recently escalated as a result of lawyers' increasing use of digital technology, including social networking websites, for marketing purposes. Many law firm websites encourage visitors to contact firm lawyers, sometimes including a link for them to do so, and some lawyers actively participate in online discussions of legal issues. A lawyer who elicits specific information about a person's particular legal problem, and then responds by providing specific legal advice, may inadvertently form an attorney-client relationship with that person. Lawyers can sometimes avoid doing so by using disclaimers that proclaim that no attorney-client relationship is being formed. These disclaimers must be clearly worded and prominently displayed, and they will not protect lawyers who nevertheless provide specific legal advice in response to detailed questions about specific legal matters.[9] In addition, the disclaimer should explain whether the lawyer will maintain the confidentiality of any communications.

8. A recent ABA ethics opinion identified a type of client called "an episodic client, meaning a client who engages the lawyer whenever the client requires legal representation, but whose legal needs are not constant or continuous." ABA Formal Ethics Op. 18-481 (2018). If the client reasonably expects that the professional relationship continues during intervals between matters, then the client is a current (and not a former) client, as to whom various duties are owed, including the duty to inform the client of a lawyer's material error. *Id.* (citing authorities describing factors to determine the reasonableness of a client's expectation of ongoing representation). For a discussion of the significance of clarifying the status of an episodic client, *see infra* Section C on terminating the attorney-client relationship.

---

9. *See, e.g.,* S.C. Ethics Op. 12-03 (2012).

B. SCOPE OF THE REPRESENTATION

Model Rules 1.2, 1.4, 1.5

Model Rule 1.5(b) provides that except when the lawyer will represent a regularly represented client on the same basis or rate, "[t]he scope of the representation and the basis or rate of the fee and the expenses for which the client will be responsible shall be communicated to the client, preferably in writing, before or within a reasonable time after commencing the representation."[10] The importance of advising the client up front of the basis of legal fees is obvious: once the lawyer begins the work, it becomes difficult for the client to switch lawyers if the client objects to the proposed fee arrangement. But why is it so important that clients understand the scope of the representation? One reason is that knowing what services are included may affect the client's willingness to pay the proposed fee. For example, if the lawyer is charging a fixed legal fee, the client needs to know whether any additional services might be needed, as when the representation will be limited to forming an entity and will not include drafting any necessary licensing or employment agreements. Even under an hourly fee agreement, knowing which tasks are included and which are not will assist the client in estimating the total amount of legal or other fees the client will end up paying to accomplish the client's goal.

Apart from legal fees, both the client and the lawyer need to know the types of services the lawyer is obligated to provide: the lawyer to avoid malpractice, and the client to make alternative arrangements for any tasks not covered by the representation. Consider the following two cases in which a client claimed that a lawyer committed malpractice when the lawyer failed to provide a necessary service.

The first case involved a legal malpractice action based on the failure of the lawyers in the defendant law firm to perfect security interests in life insurance policies. The plaintiff-lenders (collectively "Genesis") agreed to make four secured loans totaling $4.425 million to a nonparty ("Progressive") to finance Progressive's purchase of several portfolios of life insurance policies. The agreement provided that the loans would be secured by the insurance policies themselves.

Genesis Merchant Partners, L.P. v. Gilbride, Tusa, Last & Spellane, LLC
69 N.Y.S.3d 30 (N.Y. App. Div. 2018)

Order, Supreme Court, New York County (Nancy M. BANNON, J.). . . .

[Genesis retained the defendant law firm ("Gilbride") to draft the loan documents and file UCC financing statements for all four loans. When Progressive subsequently defaulted on three of the loans, Genesis contacted the

---

10. The rule also provides that "[a]ny changes in the basis or rate of the fee or expenses shall also be communicated to the client."

underwriting insurers to collect on the life insurance policies. The underwriters refused to provide any information on the policies because they had no record of the collateral assignments of the policies to Genesis. These collateral assignments were required by state law to perfect Genesis's security interest in the insurance policy proceeds.[11] Genesis then sued Gilbride, alleging that the firm committed legal malpractice by failing to perfect Genesis's security interests in the life insurance policies, resulting in the loss of millions of dollars.]

The crux of the factual dispute is whether Gilbride had a duty to perfect Genesis's security interests in the collateral. Genesis alleges that Gilbride was retained to advise it on the loans, including drafting the loan documents and ensuring that Genesis's security interests in the collateral were secured and perfected under applicable law. Gilbride maintains that it was retained only to draft the loan documents and that this limited representation was at the express instruction of Genesis. . . .

THE SCOPE OF GILBRIDE'S REPRESENTATION

On this record, the parties' competing affidavits, the Collateral Assignment of Contracts, and the emails raise issues of fact as to whether Gilbride's role was limited to drafting the loan documents and preparing the closing binders at the specific instructions of Genesis.

There is no engagement letter that defines the scope of Gilbride's representation. Steven Sands, Senior Portfolio Manager of Genesis, states in an affidavit that "[Genesis] initially retained [Gilbride] to draft loan documents for a loan to [Progressive] that required collateral assignments of life insurance policies and other assets as collateral for the loan. This engagement included perfecting the collateral."

Jonathan Wells, an attorney at Gilbride who represented Genesis, disputes that the law firm had a duty to perfect the security interests. He states that "Genesis specifically restricted Gilbride from undertaking" the tasks of the actual filing of the collateral assignment forms.

In order for Gilbride to limit the scope of its representation, it had a duty to ensure that Genesis understood the limits of its representation [citing authorities including New York Rule of Professional Conduct 1.2(c): "A lawyer may limit the scope of the representation if the limitation is reasonable under the circumstances, the client gives informed consent and where necessary notice is provided to the tribunal and/or opposing counsel"]. An attorney may not be held liable for failing to act outside the scope of the retainer.

Here, the Collateral Assignment of Contracts raises a question as to the scope of the representation. Section 11(c) of the contract provides, in relevant part, that

---

11. Perfecting a security interest in an asset means registering it with the appropriate statutory authority, thereby ensuring its enforceability.

"[a]dditionally, [Progressive] shall deliver to [Genesis] evidence of a perfection of [Genesis's] security interest in, and evidence of the acceptance of filing of Assignments of Policy as Collateral Security Agreements, or their equivalent, in favor of [Genesis], from the respective insurance carriers with regard to the Contracts within twenty one (21) days of the date hereof."

The provision unambiguously requires Progressive to deliver to Genesis documents evidencing perfection of Genesis's security interest in, and the acceptance of, the collateral assignment agreements from the insurance carriers.

Gilbride asserts that the final provision was added at Genesis's insistence and that it included the mechanism and direction for perfecting the security interests. Wells maintains that the structuring and negotiation of the loans were between Genesis and Progressive as evidenced by the draft term sheets.

In addition, the provision suggests that Progressive and Genesis, not Gilbride, were tasked with the responsibility of taking the mechanical steps necessary to perfect the security interest. Furthermore, the provision arguably supports Gilbride's position that despite the filing of the UCC-1 financing statements, the parties understood that the security interests in the insurance policies could only be perfected by Genesis obtaining a collateral assignment of the policies. . . .

Accordingly, there are issues of fact as to the scope of Gilbride's representation, and if limited, whether Gilbride ensured that Genesis understood that Gilbride was not responsible for perfecting the security interests in the life insurance policies.

Note that the court did not discuss Gilbride's obligations under the New York equivalent of Rule 1.5(b). Rather, the court discussed New York Rule 1.2(c), which like Model Rule 1.2(c), permits a lawyer to limit the scope of the representation only when the limitation is "reasonable under the circumstances [and] the client gives informed consent."[12] The court decided that whether the representation was limited and, if so, whether Genesis had given its informed consent, were questions of fact to be determined at trial.

In the next case, a Louisiana federal trial court granted summary judgment for the law firm defendant on the ground that the law firm had no duty to perform environmental due diligence for a real estate developer, although there was no evidence that the firm obtained the developer's informed consent to exclude environmental due diligence from the scope of the representation. As you read this case, consider whether it is reconcilable with *Genesis*.

---

12. The New York rule differs from the Model Rule by also requiring that the lawyer provide any necessary notice "to the tribunal and/or opposing counsel."

SCB Diversified Municipal Portfolio v. Crews & Associates
2012 WL 13708 (E.D. La. 2012)

Kurt D. Engelhardt, District Judge

[A partnership purchased 324 acres of real property for the purpose of building a planned residential community. To fund a portion of the development, the partnership formed a community development district ("District") under Louisiana law to issue bonds.[13] The District retained the defendant law firm McGlinchey Stafford PLLC ("McGlinchey") to organize the District and to act as bond counsel in connection with the issuance of the bonds,[14] and the parties executed an engagement agreement. As part of the bond transaction, McGlinchey issued three opinions addressing various aspects of the bond issuance. Defendant Crews and Associates underwrote and purchased the bonds from the District and thereafter offered them for repurchase to other plaintiffs including SCB Diversified Municipal Portfolio. Subsequently, after the development of the project, it came to light that the U.S. Army Corps of Engineers had used portions of the development property to provide gunnery, rocket, and bombing practice for pilots. When the local engineer announced that no further building permits or approvals would be issued until there was no risk of contamination, the project development stopped. The District defaulted on the bonds and sought to recover damages against McGlinchey. The complaint alleged various legal theories, including "legal malpractice for failure to conduct environmental due diligence [and] failure to obtain informed consent for the limited scope of representation it outlined in its engagement letter."]

In order to prevail on a legal malpractice claim, a plaintiff must demonstrate 1) "the existence of an attorney-client relationship, 2) negligent representation by an attorney, and 3) loss caused by that negligence." The existence and scope of an attorney client relationship is defined by the mutual intent of the parties to the agreement. . . . An attorney does not create an attorney-client relationship with respect to all legal or business affairs of a client when he agrees to represent the client in a specific legal matter. . . .

In order to prove negligent representation by an attorney, some plaintiffs must retain an expert witness to testify regarding the standard of care an attorney must meet in the relevant locality. However, in many cases, the trial court may evaluate the adequacy of an attorney's representation based on its knowledge of the standards of practice in the community without the need for expert testimony. In some cases, the failure of the attorney to comply with the community standard of care may be so obvious as to render expert testimony unnecessary.

---

13. [A bond is a fixed income instrument that represents a loan made by an investor to a borrower, typically a corporation or a governmental entity. Bonds are used to finance projects and operations. Bond owners are creditors of the issuer.—Ed.]

14. [Bond counsel is customarily retained by the issuer of the bonds to give an opinion that the bonds are validly issued and, in the case of governmental bonds, that the bonds are tax-exempt.—Ed.]

Here, Plaintiff and McGlinchey established an attorney-client relationship when they executed an engagement letter dated June 28, 2006. Under the terms of the engagement letter, McGlinchey undertook to represent Plaintiff "as special counsel to [Plaintiff] in connection with its organization and establishment and also as bond counsel to [Plaintiff] in connection with the proposed issuance, sale and delivery of the Bonds." The engagement letter outlines the scope of the engagement and the duties McGlinchey would perform as special counsel and bond counsel, including: preparing documents required to create Plaintiff; rendering legal opinions regarding the validity of the Bonds, the source of payment and security for the Bonds and the excludability of interest on the Bonds from gross income for tax purposes; preparing and reviewing documents in connection with the authorization, issuance and delivery of the Bonds, coordinating the authorization and execution of such documents and reviewing enabling legislation; assisting Plaintiff in seeking from other governmental authorities such approvals, permission and exemptions as McGlinchey determined were necessary or appropriate in connection with authorization, issuance and delivery of the Bonds; reviewing legal issues relating to the structure of the transaction; reviewing those sections of the [offering memorandum] involving the Plaintiff, the Bonds and the security therefore, together with such matters as are consistent with the role of bond counsel; and preparing the continuing disclosure undertaking of Plaintiff, if such undertaking is required. In the engagement letter, McGlinchey stated, "During the course of our engagement, we will rely on [Plaintiff] to provide us with complete and timely information on all developments pertaining to the Bonds, including but not limited to the project and facilities to be constructed or provided with bond proceeds, timetable and cost of construction, and matters relating to security for the Bonds."

The engagement letter clearly defines the scope of the representation contemplated between Plaintiff and McGlinchey. McGlinchey's role in the venture consisted of assisting Plaintiff in its formation under Louisiana law and in issuing bonds. As expressly stated, McGlinchey's review of the [offering memorandum] did *not* include the section regarding the development, which is where the mention of a Phase I Environmental Site Assessment is located. . . .

Plaintiff argues that McGlinchey violated the rules of professional conduct for attorneys by drafting an engagement letter limiting its representation of Plaintiff without obtaining informed consent to such limited representation. Plaintiff cites several rules of conduct from various sources which state that a lawyer must consult with client when narrowing his representation from what his traditional role as counsel would be. In order to demonstrate a violation of these rules, Plaintiff must show that McGlinchey failed to perform some duty which is traditionally included in the role of bond counsel.

In an attempt to establish the scope of McGlinchey's duties, Plaintiff submits the expert report of Sean Rafferty, a title attorney based in New Orleans, Louisiana. In his report, Mr. Rafferty opines that "an attorney representing a client intending to conduct a Louisiana commercial real estate development project has a professional duty to advise his client of the acute need to obtain appropriate environmental review of the project property." However, Mr. Rafferty does not address McGlinchey's duties to Plaintiff specifically or the role of bond counsel generally. Rather, Mr. Rafferty asserts that *any* attorney representing, in *any* capacity, a client who is engaged in developing real estate must advise a client about the need for environmental reviews. Based on the Court's familiarity with the standard of practice in this community, this broad contention cannot be sustained. For instance, a tax attorney who works only on tax issues surrounding a real estate development would certainly have no obligation to advise the client of the need for environmental studies of the property. Mr. Rafferty states that he has experience representing clients in real property acquisitions and that he works as a title attorney. In these roles, such an attorney would most likely have a duty to advise a client regarding environmental issues, but this duty does not extend to every attorney who comes into contact with a client developing real estate. . . . On the other hand, McGlinchey submits the expert report of M[s]. Jane Dickey, an attorney with experience in municipal finance who served as President of the National Association of Bond Lawyers, stating that environmental issues are outside the scope of bond counsel's traditional role in municipal finance transactions such as the one at issue herein. Based on Ms. Dickey's testimony and the Court's knowledge of standards of practice observed in this community, the Court finds that Plaintiff has failed to show that environmental issues were within the scope of McGlinchey's duty as bond counsel. Because environmental due diligence was not in the scope of McGlinchey's particular duty to Plaintiff, McGlinchey did not commit legal malpractice by reviewing the [offering memorandum] and failing to notice the mention of a Phase I Environmental Site Assessment.

NOTES AND QUESTIONS

1. In *SCB Diversified*, the court found that the engagement letter clearly limited McGlinchey's duties to those specified and thereby excluded any obligation to conduct an environmental assessment. This alone distinguishes the case from *Genesis*. But why wasn't McGlinchey obligated by Rule 1.2(c) to obtain the District's "informed consent" to a limited representation? Model Rule 1.0(e) defines "[i]nformed consent" to denote "the agreement by a person to a proposed course of conduct after the lawyer has communicated adequate information and explanation about the material risks of and reasonably available alternatives to the proposed course of conduct." Wouldn't this require McGlinchey to inform the District of the risk of failing to conduct an environmental assessment and the need to engage another firm to do so? It may help to know that in a footnote in the opinion, the court noted that the Restatement provides that the client must consent if the lawyer wants "to limit a duty that a lawyer would *otherwise* owe to a client" and that

a report by the National Association of Bond Lawyers Committee on Professional Responsibility states that under Model Rule 1.2(c) "a bond lawyer may . . . limit the scope of representation more narrowly than the *traditional bond counsel function* provided the client consents after consultation with the attorney." 2012 WL 13708 at n. 2 (emphasis in original). Does this footnote help you to understand why Rule 1.2(c) may have applied in *Genesis* but not in *SCB Diversified*? And why the *SCB Diversified* court appeared to agree that lawyers representing clients in real property acquisitions (such as the plaintiff's expert) most likely have a duty to advise a client regarding environmental issues? If the representation in *Genesis* was limited as Gilbride contended, and Rule 1.2(c) applied, what information should Gilbride have given Genesis in order to obtain its "informed consent" to the limited representation?

2. In Nichols v. Keller, 19 Cal. Rptr. 2d 601 (Cal. Ct. App. 1993), an injured employee retained two lawyers to pursue a workers' compensation claim against the employer. The lawyers failed to inform the employee that he might also have civil tort claims against third parties, and the employee did not learn of that possibility until the statute of limitations had run. The court of appeals reversed summary judgment for the lawyers in a malpractice action, stating that "a workers' compensation attorney should be able to limit the retention to the compensation claim if the client is cautioned (1) there may be other remedies which the attorney will not investigate and (2) other counsel should be consulted on such matters." No such caution had been given. Is *Nichols* distinguishable from *SCB Diversified*? Isn't it clear that a lawyer engaged to file a workers' compensation claim is not "otherwise" obligated to pursue a civil lawsuit against possibly liable third parties? Should it matter whether the lawyers advertised themselves as workers' compensation lawyers and whether the employee understood that the lawyers were being retained to pursue a workers' compensation claim? Does the sophistication of the client matter? For example, would the employee in *Nichols* have understood that another source of compensation might be available?

3. The court in *Nichols* went on to hold that "even when a retention is expressly limited, the attorney may still have a duty to alert the client to legal problems which are reasonably apparent, even though they fall outside the scope of the representation." Is this communication mandated by Rule 1.2(c) or might it be required under the lawyer's general duty to communicate information relevant to the representation under Rule 1.4?[15] If the communication was mandated by Rule 1.4 and not

---

15. Model Rule 1.4, entitled "Communication" applies to all representations, not just those that are limited in scope. For a more detailed discussion of that rule, *see infra* Chapter 3: Competence and Diligence, Control and Communication; Fees.

Rule 1.2(c), did McGlinchey have a similar obligation in *SCB Diversified* even if Rule 1.2(c) did not apply?

4. None of these cases—*Genesis*, *SCB Diversified*, or *Nichols*—discussed the additional requirement of Rule 1.2(c) that any limited representation be "reasonable under the circumstances." Is that because it was obvious that the limited scope representations in these cases were reasonable? Why or why not? When would a limitation be *unreasonable*, even with the client's informed consent? Comment [2] to MR 1.2 does not provide a general standard, but rather gives an example of a client who wants to secure "general information about the law the client needs in order to handle a common and typically uncomplicated legal problem." The comment concludes that such a limitation "would not be reasonable if the time allotted was not sufficient to yield advice upon which the client could rely." A Michigan ethics opinion relies on Rule 1.1, which provides that "[a] lawyer shall provide competent representation to a client." As a result, it concludes that "a lawyer wishing to limit the scope of the representation . . . must determine objectively whether the client would be competently represented in light of the proposed limitations."[16] Is this any more helpful? Does it matter whether it is the lawyer or the client who proposes, indeed insists upon, the limitation?

5. Limited scope representations are common in real estate and bankruptcy matters. *See, e.g.,* S.C. Ethics Advisory Opinion 5-18 (2005) (lawyer asked to perform real estate closing without participating in pre- or post-closing activities); *compare, e.g.,* In re Collmar, 417 B.R. 920 (Bankr. N.D. Ind. 2009) (unreasonable for Chapter 7 debtor's lawyer to exclude participation in reaffirmation agreements)[17] *with* Mich. Inf. Ethics Op. RI -348 (2010) (bankruptcy lawyer may ethically exclude representation on reaffirmation agreements). Typically, the limitation is one negotiated between the client and the lawyer. Sometimes, however, there is a third party involved. For example, a nonlawyer, such as a real estate broker, may request a lawyer to perform a single task, such as preparing closing documents, leaving the nonlawyer to perform all of the other necessary tasks. In such a case, the lawyer must be careful not only to comply with Rule 1.2(c), but also to avoid aiding the nonlawyer in the unauthorized practice of law. *See* Ill. State Bar Assoc. Advisory Opinion 94-01 (1994).[18]

---

16. Mich. Inf. Ethics Op. RI-348 (2010) (limiting representation of individual debtors in bankruptcy proceedings).

17. A reaffirmation agreement between a creditor and a debtor in bankruptcy waives discharge of a debt that would otherwise be discharged. Such an agreement may be necessary if the creditor has a security interest in property, such as a car or an appliance, and the debtor wants to keep the property. It is also used when a third person, such as a family member, has guaranteed the debt, and the debtor does not want that person to be responsible for paying the debt.

18. Unauthorized practice of law by nonlawyers is discussed in Chapter 15: Unauthorized Practice of Law and Multijurisdictional Practice.

6. "Unbundled" or discrete-task representation is most commonly discussed in the context of lawyers assisting pro se litigants in civil litigation and has been embraced by many as critical in the effort to secure access to justice for low- and middle-income clients. Increasingly, unbundled legal services are being used in a wide variety of settings, including corporate and intellectual property law. This practice has been embraced not only by solo lawyers competing with online document preparation services such as LegalZoom,[19] but also by law firms seeking to attract startups and entrepreneurs, some of whom will eventually become regular clients of the firm. The ABA maintains a helpful compilation of articles, cases, and ethics opinions in its online Unbundling Resource Center.[20]

C. TERMINATING THE ATTORNEY-CLIENT RELATIONSHIP

Model Rule 1.16

Lawyers owe some duties to former clients, including duties of confidentiality and loyalty, but these duties are less stringent than their duties to current clients.[21] For example, the ABA Standing Committee on Ethics and Professional Responsibility has opined that a lawyer must inform a current client, but not a former client, if the lawyer believes that the lawyer committed a material error during the representation.[22] In the following case, the issue concerned the applicability of a more stringent conflicts rule for current clients than for former clients. We will address the conflicts issues in subsequent chapters.[23] For now, focus on the court's analysis as to whether the Hannoch law firm was representing third-party defendant Iacono when it filed a lawsuit against him, in an unrelated matter, on behalf of the Borin Group, the third-party plaintiff.

Manoir-ElectroAlloys Corp. v. Amalloy Corp.
711 F. Supp. 188 (D.N.J. 1989)

BARRY, District Judge.

[The Borin Group entered into a written agreement to sell the assets of a foundry to a French conglomerate in which Manoir-ElectroAlloys was a participant. The sale was finalized in early October 1988. Almost immediately

---

19. For a discussion of the legal issues involved in the provision of online document preparation services, including a lawyer providing legal services through an entity with nonlawyer ownership, *see infra* Chapter 16: Nonlawyer Ownership, Multidisciplinary Practice, and Alternative Legal Service Providers.

20. *See* https://www.americanbar.org/groups/delivery_legal_services/resources/.

21. *See infra* Chapter 4: Privilege and Confidentiality; Chapter 6: Conflicts of Interest: Former Clients, Prospective Clients, and Government Lawyers.

22. *See* ABA Formal Opinion Ethics Op. 18-491 (2018).

23. *See infra* Chapter 5: Conflicts of Interest: Current Clients; Chapter 6: Conflicts of Interest: Former Clients, Prospective Clients, and Government Lawyers.

thereafter, the French conglomerate learned that the Borin Group had apparently misrepresented the foundry's annual earnings, inflating the purchase price of the assets and defrauding the purchasers. In late October the plaintiffs, including Manoir-ElectroAlloys, sued the Borin Group for fraud. One month later, the Borin Group filed an answer, a counterclaim, and a third-party complaint against third-party defendants, including Carmelo Iacono, president of one of the plaintiff companies. Iacono moved to disqualify the law firm of Hannoch Weisman ("Hannoch") from representing the Borin Group on the ground that Iacono was a current client of Hannoch. The Borin Group and Hannoch resisted the motion to disqualify on the ground that Iacono was a *former* client, not a *current* client, and the conflict of interest rules for former clients did not require the law firm's disqualification.

During the negotiations for the sale of the foundry, the Borin Group had been represented by Hannoch. Iacono, president of the companies purchasing the foundry, was present at some of the negotiating sessions, including one on July 22, 1988, at Hannoch's offices. At that meeting, Iacono told one of the Hannoch lawyers that he had a relationship with the Hannoch firm, stating that the firm "are my lawyers."]

Hannoch's representation of Iacono had, in fact, begun in approximately 1976 when Iacono was referred to the firm. . . . Since that time, Hannoch has handled several matters for Iacono and his wife Josephine. Hannoch prepared the wills of both Mr. and Mrs. Iacono, retaining the wills at its Roseland office, and established a trust for their children. Additionally, it assisted Iacono with tax planning and provided him with income, estate and gift tax advice.

In 1983, [Hannoch trusts and estates lawyer] D'Avella wrote to Iacono, informing him of recent changes in the tax laws and suggesting that Iacono contact the firm to update his will. According to D'Avella, Iacono never responded to that letter. Also, in 1983, however, Iacono was re-negotiating his employment contract with Pompey Steel and wrote to D'Avella requesting advice as to certain provisions of the new contract. Apparently D'Avella turned the matter over to [Hannoch lawyer] Marcus who provided the requested advice to Iacono and enlisted the aid of a New York attorney, Joseph Sierchio, to interpret the contract with regard to New York law. In a letter to Sierchio, Marcus referred to Iacono as "our client" no less than five times. [Iacono was billed for these services.] This was the last matter for which Hannoch billed Iacono.

Iacono contends that following the July 22, 1988 negotiating session, and while at the Hannoch offices, he visited D'Avella and discussed the possibility of updating his will. D'Avella agrees that this meeting took place, and states, referring to Iacono, "I commented to him that he had never responded to my letters suggesting that he consider updating his will to take into consideration changes in the tax laws.". . . D'Avella claims that the discussion ended without either party making a commitment to get back to the other.

[On October 28, 1988, after learning of the apparent fraud, the plaintiffs sued the Borin Group. Hannoch announced that it was representing the Borin

Group in the lawsuit. Iacono received a copy of this announcement as president of one of the plaintiff companies. On November 23, 1988, the Borin Group filed its answer and counterclaim, as well as the third-party complaint against third-party defendants, including Iacono, charging them with fraud.]

The third-party complaint was served on Iacono on December 2, 1988. Also on December 2, Hannoch sent a letter to Iacono and his wife, urging them to call Hannoch to arrange a meeting to discuss changes in the tax laws and their impact on Iacono's retirement benefits. The letter began "Dear Mel and Josephine," and was signed by D'Avella. It discussed the changes in the law and concluded:

> This subject must be dealt with before year end. Thus, you should accumulate the appropriate information as soon as possible, so we have sufficient time to properly deal with this important matter.

[Iacono] phoned D'Avella on December 8, 1988 to reiterate his desire to update his will. Several days later, after consulting with the firm's attorneys representing the Borin Group, D'Avella told Iacono that Hannoch could not provide further services to Iacono.

[Iacono sought to disqualify Hannoch from representing the Borin Group for taking a position adverse to Iacono, a current client of that firm. Under the applicable rules of professional conduct, representation adverse to a *current* client without that client's consent, even in an unrelated matter, warranted disqualification. Hannoch, however, argued that at the time the third-party complaint was filed, Iacono was a *former* client, in which case the less-stringent conflicts rule applicable to former clients required disqualification only if the adverse matter was "substantially related" to the subject of the former representation.]

The threshold issue is whether Iacono was a present or a former client of the Hannoch firm in November of 1988. Hannoch argues that the last time the firm performed legal services for Iacono was in 1983-1984, when it undertook the "limited" task of issuing a legal opinion in connection with the renegotiation of Iacono's employment contract. It claims that no inference may be drawn from Hannoch's retention of the Iaconos' wills as this is standard firm practice. Moreover, it continues, it sent what it describes as "standard law firm follow-up letters" to Iacono in 1983 and in December of 1988, letters it also describes as "form letters." Thus, according to Hannoch, when suit was instituted against Iacono by the Borin Group, he had not been a client of the law firm for over four years, and the 1988 letter was, therefore, a letter to a former client. . . . In support of its argument, Hannoch cites *Heathcoat v. Santa Fe International Corp.*, which it claims is directly on point. In *Heathcoat*, the plaintiff attempted to disqualify defendants' attorneys, who had prepared plaintiff's will in 1966. No further legal services had been sought by plaintiff after that time. In September of 1981, the firm sent a follow-up letter to plaintiff, addressed "Dear Friend" and signed only with the firm name, advising of recent tax law changes and suggesting that plaintiff update her will.

Plaintiff forwarded the letter to her attorney in the pending action and the disqualification motion was filed. [The *Heathcoat* court denied the motion for disqualification.]

I do not agree with Hannoch that the *Heathcoat* case is "strikingly similar" to the matter before me. The preparation of Iacono's will was not the sole matter undertaken for him by the Hannoch firm. Rather, Iacono was referred to Hannoch . . . in or about 1976 and over the years, [Hannoch] provided legal services for Iacono whenever required and assisted him, in his individual capacity, with a number of matters. Iacono contacted D'Avella when a legal matter arose, and Hannoch provided the necessary services. . . .

Iacono's relationship with Hannoch, up to and including December of 1988 was sufficiently continuous, and the mere fortuity that he did not require more extensive or frequent services than he did cannot be the escape hatch Hannoch would have it be.

Moreover, Hannoch itself seems to have believed that a continuous relationship existed, and, in fact, encouraged that relationship. In his 1984 letter to Siercho, Marcus repeatedly referred to Iacono as "our client." D'Avella admits that when Iacono visited his office in July of 1988, he chastised Iacono for not having responded to the follow-up letters suggesting changes in Iacono's will, and they discussed updating Iacono's will. Not five months later, on the very day that the third-party complaint was served upon Iacono, Iacono received a letter, signed personally by D'Avella, urging "Mel and Josephine" to prepare materials and get in touch with D'Avella so that "we," quite clearly meaning the Iaconos and D'Avella, could deal with the "important matter." Certainly it was reasonable for Iacono to construe Hannoch's actions as the actions of attorneys vis-à-vis their present client. And just as Hannoch treated Iacono as if he was the firm's client, he talked to at least one member of the firm as if he was talking to his attorney. . . .

Although the issue is not free from doubt, it is my considered opinion that on November 23, 1988, when Hannoch filed the third-party action against Iacono on behalf of its client, the Borin Group, Iacono was also a present client of the firm and, thus, there has been a breach of the well-established rule that an attorney may not represent one client in a lawsuit against another.

[The court concluded that Iacono had not consented to the adverse representation and granted the motion for disqualification.]

NOTES AND QUESTIONS

1. *Manoir-ElectroAlloys* represents what the ABA Standing Committee on Ethics and Professional Responsibility has called an "episodic client.[24] What were the critical facts supporting the court's conclusion that

---

24. *See* ABA Formal Ethics Op. 18-481 (2018).

Iacono was a *current* and not a *former* client of Hannoch at the time Hannoch filed a lawsuit against Iacono on behalf of the Borin Group? Would the result have been different if Hannoch had not represented Iacono with respect to his renegotiation of his employment contract in 1983? Do you understand why it mattered whether he was a current or a former client?

2. Even if there was no continuous attorney-client relationship spanning the years between 1976 and 1988, might Iacono have believed that a prior attorney-client relationship was reestablished as a result of the 1988 communications concerning the redrafting of the Iaconos' wills? Would the *Heathcoat* case then be determinative, or was it still at least arguably distinguishable?

3. Unless there is an ongoing attorney-client relationship, as the court found in *Manoir-ElectroAlloys*, representation typically ends when the work is completed. Sometimes, however, either the client or the lawyer becomes dissatisfied with the relationship and wants to terminate it midstream. Ordinarily, a client may discharge a lawyer for any reason. A lawyer, on the other hand, must have good cause to withdraw, except when withdrawal will not result in any material adverse effect on the client. *See* Model Rule 1.16 (providing examples of circumstances requiring or permitting a lawyer to withdraw); RLGL §31 (termination of a lawyer's actual and apparent authority to act for a client). In any event, once the representation ends, the lawyer must act reasonably to protect the client's interests. Model Rule 1.16(d). To see how midstream termination impacts a lawyer's ability to collect a legal fee, *see infra* Chapter 3: Competence and Diligence; Control and Communication; Fees. The ability of in-house counsel to sue for wrongful termination is discussed in Chapter 13: In-House Counsel.

D. SHOULD I REPRESENT THIS CLIENT?

Model Rules 1.2, 1.16

Practical considerations aside, such as the need to earn a living, U.S. lawyers almost always have discretion in deciding whether to represent a client.[25] Even when a lawyer has accepted representation, the lawyer is permitted to

---

25. For an unusual exception to this rule, *see* Nathanson v. Mass. Comm'n Against Discrimination, 2003 WL 22480688 (Mass Super. Ct. 2003) (lawyer who only represented women in her divorce practice violated state statute prohibiting gender discrimination in a place of public accommodation). A newly adopted Model Rule prohibiting gender and other forms of discrimination by lawyers does not appear to apply when a lawyer declines representation on the basis of gender or other protected status, although a comment suggests that a lawyer who violates an antidiscrimination statute may be disciplined under this rule. *See* Model Rule 8.4(g) & cmt [3]. For a more detailed discussion of this rule, *see infra* Chapter 14: Admission and Discipline.

withdraw when "the client insists upon taking action that the lawyer considers repugnant or with which the lawyer has a fundamental disagreement." MR 1.16(b)(4). *Should* a lawyer refuse to represent a prospective client, or withdraw from representing a current client, when the lawyer finds either the client or the client's cause to be morally repugnant? Model Rule 1.2(b) encourages lawyers to represent clients "whose cause is controversial or the subject of popular disapproval" by pronouncing that a lawyer's agreement to represent a particular client "does not constitute an endorsement of the client's political, economic, social or moral views or activities." *See* MR 1.2(c) & cmt [5].

The late Monroe Freedman, a former law professor at Hofstra Law School and a well-known advocate of zealously representing criminal defendants, took a contrary view. In a 1992 essay entitled "Must You Be the Devil's Advocate?," Freedman argued that lawyers who have the ability to choose their clients are "morally accountable" for their choices, "in the sense of being under a burden of public justification" of their representation of any particular client. He was responding to New York law firm Sullivan & Cromwell's refusal to represent the man charged with involvement in the car-bombing of the World Trade Center "because the bombing was 'such a heinous crime' and because the defendant is 'so personally objectionable.'"[26] Freedman acknowledged that he had previously taken a contrary position, but explained that what changed his mind was a debate concerning the picketing of D.C. law firm Wilmer, Cutler & Pickering by Ralph Nader and a group of law students protesting the law firm's representation of General Motors in an air pollution case. Although Freedman had publicly defended the law firm at the time, he declared in his later essay that his then debate opponent (Michael Tigar) "won the debate" by arguing "that it was entirely proper for demonstrators to challenge lawyers at the firm to ask themselves: 'Is this really the kind of client to which I want to dedicate my training, my knowledge, and my skills as a lawyer? Did I go to law school to help a client that harms other human beings by polluting the atmosphere with poisonous gases?'" Is Freedman correct that moral nonaccountability is inconsistent with the freedom of lawyers to "pick and choose their clients as they please"?[27] Do junior lawyers in large corporate law firms have the ability to choose what matters they work on? What about their decision to join a firm that represents some morally repugnant clients or causes?

---

26. Monroe Freedman, Must You Be the Devil's Advocate?, Legal Times, D.C. Aug. 23, 1993, at 19. Freedman notes, however, that "the firm was also concerned about adverse reactions from some of its current clients." *Id.*

27. *See* Tchia (Tia) Schacar, The Ethics of Client Selection: A Moral Justification for Representing Unpopular Clients, 6 DePaul J. Soc. Just. 1, 11 (2012). Schacar suggests that in answering the question whether representing an unpopular client is a moral good, lawyers should view "lawyering as representation of rights and liberties, rather than of people." *Id.* at 21.

Lonnie Brown disagrees that lawyers, particularly criminal defense lawyers, ought to feel compelled to publicly justify their decision to represent a particular client, because "[a] lukewarm explanation such as 'everyone is entitled to a defense' connotes procedural obligation rather than uncompromising loyalty and zeal," which can undermine the effectiveness of the representation.[28] Public justification aside, should lawyers feel a need to even privately justify their decision to represent a morally reprehensible client or cause? Does it matter whether the client is a wealthy corporation, which can easily find legal representation elsewhere, or an indigent or low-income individual who is unlikely to find alternative legal representation?

Stephen Pepper rejected the argument that economic inequality undermines the value of "the lawyer's amoral role." For him the distribution of access to lawyers is a different question than the content of what is being distributed.[29] He also rejected the argument that the lawyer's amoral role is justified primarily in the adversary system of litigation, in which the existence of a lawyer on the other side and a neutral judge and jury tempers the lawyer's efforts to assist the client. Rather, Pepper addressed primarily the situation of an office lawyer implementing a wide range of available legal devices, such as a trust or a corporation.[30] Pepper's argument in support of the lawyer's amoral role — reflected in Rule 1.2(b) — was as follows: law is a public good that increases autonomy; increasing individual autonomy is morally good; in a highly legalized society, autonomy is frequently dependent upon access to law, and access to law is realistically available only with the help of a lawyer. He further argued that "[f]or the lawyer to have a moral obligation to refuse to facilitate that which the lawyer believes to be immoral, is to substitute lawyers' beliefs for individual autonomy and diversity."[31] David Luban disagreed, arguing that Pepper placed too much value on the moral worth of assisting clients' autonomy when what they are doing is morally wrong. Luban had no problem with lawyers acting as informal moral filters, analogizing them to a client's "associates or partners or friends or family or financial backers or employees" whose refusal to help may discourage the client's immoral behavior.[32] Which of these views do you find more persuasive?

Although generally a critic of the profession's standard nonaccountability principle, Luban vigorously defended the standard conception of the lawyer's zealous adversary role in representing criminal defendants. Here he

---

28. Lonnie T. Brown, Jr., In Defense of the Devil's Advocate, 44 Hofstra L. Rev. 1037, 1038 (2016).

29. Stephen L. Pepper, The Lawyer's Amoral Ethical Role: A Defense, a Problem, and Some Possibilities, 1986 Am. B Found. Res. J. 613, 619-20 (1986).

30. *Id.* at 621-22.

31. *Id.* at 617.

32. David Luban, The Lysistratian Prerogative: A Response to Stephen Pepper, 1986 Am. B. Found. Res. J. 637, 642 (1986).

argued that given the power of the state over the individual, criminal defense lawyers are often entitled to engage in conduct that conflicts with ordinary morality.[33] What is your view of Sullivan & Cromwell's refusal to represent the man charged with involvement in the car-bombing of the World Trade Center? Large law firms often accept pro bono representation, including representation of criminal defendants.

In England, barristers—lawyers who are authorized to represent clients in all courts—are subject to the so-called "cab rank" rule, under which they must take cases within their knowledge and expertise provided they are free to do so. In 2013, there was an effort to remove this rule on the ground that it was no longer relevant; however, in the face of an independent report commissioned by the regulatory authority, that effort was unsuccessful. The report concluded that the rule protects barristers from any social stigma arising from representing an unpopular client, and therefore its removal would threaten access to justice.[34] Would you support the adoption of a cab rank rule for U.S. lawyers? Is there any justification for limiting such a rule to court lawyers?[35]

Review Problems

2-1 A lawyer contacted his former professional responsibility teacher and asked to meet with her concerning a confidential matter. The professor, who was admitted to practice in the jurisdiction, agreed to do so. They met at the professor's office, and the lawyer explained that he had inadvertently given a client legal advice that he now understood was incorrect, but that he didn't want to tell the client or anyone in his firm for fear that he would be fired, as this was not his first mistake. The professor explained that it was the lawyer's legal responsibility to communicate his mistake both to the client and to the law firm, but the lawyer indicated that he would not do so. The professor is good friends with a partner in the lawyer's firm and, concerned that the lawyer was breaching his fiduciary duties to both the client and the law firm, the professor called the partner and relayed what she had learned. The lawyer was immediately fired and filed a lawsuit against the professor for breaching her duty of confidentiality to him. The professor responded that no attorney-client relationship was formed, but rather that she gave the lawyer—a former student—informal advice in her capacity as his former law

---

33. *See* David Luban, Lawyers and Justice 145-47 (1988).

34. The cab rank rule applies only to barristers taking cases referred by another lawyer and not to so-called "public access" cases where clients may contact barristers directly. The Bar Standards Board has declined to extend the rule to "public access" cases on the ground that it would make barristers less likely to make accept these cases—and thereby reduce access to justice. *See* Max Walters, Bar confirms no cab rank rule extension (Oct. 27, 2017), available at https://www.lawgazette.co.uk/law/bar-confirms-no-cab-rank-rule-extension/5063449.article.

35. English solicitors are now authorized to represent clients in some court proceedings, but their work consists primarily of providing legal advice, assisting in negotiations between parties, and drafting legal instruments. Barristers and solicitors are regulated separately.

professor. Although she has a consulting business in which she represents an occasional client for a modest fee, she meets with her law clients in her home, not at the law school, and she never charged the former law student a fee. Did the professor form an attorney-client relationship with the lawyer? Should the professor have handled the meeting differently?

2-2 After a husband learned that his wife had been having an affair, he sued for divorce. The couple agreed to mediation and as a result, a written Property Settlement Agreement (PSA) emerged. The mediator suggested that each spouse retain a lawyer to review the PSA before they signed it. The wife retained a well-known matrimonial lawyer. She told him that she was satisfied with the terms of the agreement, which included a lump sum settlement for the wife of $500,000 and 15 percent of the stock the two had acquired during the marriage. The lawyer told her that without reviewing documentation concerning their respective incomes, assets, liabilities, and other financial information, he could not advise her whether the PSA represented a fair and reasonable compromise of the issues concerning equitable distribution. She said that was fine, and that all she wanted was for him to review the PSA for clarification and make sure she understood its terms. He did so, and the couple signed the PSA, which became incorporated in the divorce decree. Several years later, the stock they owned tripled in value, and the wife was upset that the husband was receiving much more of that value than she was. As a result, she filed a lawsuit against the lawyer for malpractice. The lawsuit alleges that because the wife had felt guilty about her affair, she was passive in the mediation and reluctant to delve into the fairness of the PSA. It further alleges that the lawyer, knowing of her affair, should have obtained the underlying financial information before recommending that she sign the PSA. The lawyer filed a motion for summary judgment on the ground that the representation was limited in scope and that he had no duty to obtain further factual information or assess the fairness of the PSA. Is the lawyer likely to prevail on the motion for summary judgment? Does it matter whether the limitation on the scope of the representation was oral or in writing? What, if anything, should the lawyer have done differently?

2-3 A real estate consultant is suing a commercial real estate developer for money owed for services rendered pursuant to a consulting services agreement. The developer filed a motion to disqualify the consultant's law firm, alleging that the law firm was currently representing the developer in an unrelated matter. The developer had retained the law firm five years ago to represent it in connection with various financing efforts, including meeting with prospective investors and financial partners. The engagement letter signed that year confirmed that the firm had been retained "to provide legal services in connection with certain potential financing alternatives." The law firm recorded hundreds of hours over the course of two years, billing on a monthly basis. At the end of two years, the developer paused in its efforts to obtain financial investors, and there were no further hours recorded or billings. During the last year, the developer recommenced its efforts to obtain financing. The developer's CEO contacted the senior partner at the law firm who had been lead lawyer on the representation and asked her to introduce the CEO to a potential investor who was an acquaintance of the partner.

The partner arranged a meeting between the CEO and the potential investor and, at the CEO's request, passed along a folder containing financial information of the developer. Although the partner concedes that the law firm never sent the developer a termination letter, she is adamant that the attorney-client relationship ended three years ago. The partner claims that she was a social friend of the CEO and agreed to set up the meeting merely as a favor to a friend. She did not open the package containing the developer's financial information, she recorded no hours, and she did not bill the developer. The subject matter of the current lawsuit is unrelated to the legal work the law firm did for the developer pursuant to the engagement agreement, so the success of the lawsuit depends on the developer establishing that it is a current client of the law firm. Is the motion for disqualification likely to succeed?

CHAPTER 3

COMPETENCE AND DILIGENCE; CONTROL AND COMMUNICATION; FEES

Once an attorney-client relationship is formed, and the lawyer and client both understand the scope of the engagement, the lawyer will begin the legal work. In performing this work, the lawyer needs to keep in mind several core duties owed by lawyer-fiduciaries to their client-beneficiaries. These duties include competently carrying out the representation, acting diligently on the client's behalf, properly allocating control of decision-making between lawyer and client, and reasonably communicating with the client at all stages of the representation. In addition to addressing these basic duties, this chapter briefly addresses some recurring issues concerning legal fees, including modification of the fee agreement during the course of the representation and the (unenforced) professional obligation to render pro bono legal services.

A. COMPETENCE

Model Rule 1.1

Model Rule 1.1 requires that a lawyer "provide competent representation to a client." Competence is defined as "the legal knowledge, skill, thoroughness and preparation reasonably necessary for the representation." Incompetence is rarely the subject of discipline unless there is also neglect, a pattern of incompetent representation, or gross incompetence. If, however, the client suffers harm as a result of the lawyer's negligence, even a single incompetent representation by a lawyer with an otherwise unblemished record may result in civil liability for malpractice.

Particularly worrisome for lawyers is accepting representation in an unfamiliar subject area. As much as law firms would like to hire "practice ready" graduates, no newly admitted lawyer is ready to provide competent representation in more than a few subject areas, at least without adequate supervision. And the same is true of more experienced lawyers venturing into a new field.

42   Chapter 3 Competence and Diligence; Control and Communication; Fees

Comment [2] to Rule 1.1 provides that "[a] lawyer need not necessarily have special training or prior experience to handle legal problems of a type with which the lawyer is unfamiliar." However, the comment then warns that adequate representation "in a wholly novel field" will likely require "necessary study" or "the association of a lawyer of established competence in the field in question."

Consider the following case as a cautionary tale about an experienced lawyer, with no prior complaints or penalties, who was disciplined for gross incompetence in an isolated occurrence involving a single client.

State v. Orr
759 N.W.2d 702 (Neb. 2009)

PER CURIAM. . . .

The underlying conduct in this case involves Orr's representation of Steve Sickler and Cathy Mettenbrink in connection with the franchising of a coffee shop business. Sickler and Mettenbrink had opened their first coffee shop together, Barista's Daily Grind (Barista's), in Kearney, Nebraska, in December 2001. In September 2002, Sickler met with Orr and asked whether Orr could help Sickler and Mettenbrink franchise their business.

Orr was engaged in private practice in Kearney and his experience with franchising was limited. Orr testified that he had read franchise agreements on behalf of clients who either were or were interested in becoming franchisees, but had never represented a franchisor. Orr's role in those cases had been to generally advise clients as to the rights of a franchisor and duties of a franchisee under the agreement. Orr's experience had required him to review franchise agreements and disclosure statements, but he had not reviewed state or federal law governing franchising. . . .

Although he had never before drafted a franchise agreement, Orr believed it was simply "a matter of contract drafting," which he believed he was competent to do. Orr contacted an attorney in Washington, D.C., for assistance with the trademark and copyright portions of franchising, and that attorney warned Orr that franchising was a specialized field.

In December 2002, Orr drafted a disclosure statement. Orr used the disclosure statement he had recently reviewed on behalf of the previously mentioned franchisee, as well as "FTC documents," to finish the statement in January 2003. Orr's understanding was that a disclosure statement was required by the Federal Trade Commission (FTC) in order to inform the franchisee of the more important terms and conditions of the franchise agreement.

From 2003 to 2006, Barista's sold 21 franchises. In July 2004, Sickler was contacted by a banker in Colorado, inquiring on behalf of a prospective franchisee. The banker requested the "UFOC" of Barista's, and, unaware of what a UFOC was,[1] Sickler referred the banker to Orr. Orr determined that the then-current disclosure statement of Barista's was "compliant and valid" and could be used anywhere. Sickler testified that Orr told him that the UFOC was a requirement of federal law which Barista's was "probably going to have to get" if it was "going to be selling franchises out of state."

In August 2004, Orr revised the franchise agreement and disclosure statement at Sickler's request due to problems Barista's was having with a franchisee in Iowa. The Iowa franchisee had been provided with copies of the initial franchise agreement and disclosure statement. However, in February 2004, the Iowa franchisee's attorney sent a letter to Sickler suggesting that Barista's had not complied with federal disclosure requirements.

. . . [D]espite being aware that Barista's was working with prospective franchisees in Iowa and Colorado, Orr did not advise Sickler to seek input from local counsel in those states. And Sickler testified that the revised franchise agreement and disclosure statement were also provided to prospective franchisees in Kansas.

In October 2004, due to an unrelated dispute, Sickler and Mettenbrink sued the Colorado franchisees to terminate the franchises. A counterclaim was filed alleging deceptive and unfair trade practices, violation of FTC rules, and violation of Nebraska's Seller-Assisted Marketing Plan Act. . . .

Disagreements were also ongoing with the Iowa franchisees, who eventually demanded rescission of the franchise agreement based on Barista's failure to comply with federal and Iowa disclosure laws. . . .

Orr stated that before the third revision of the disclosure statement, he had been under the impression that FTC requirements overrode state law. . . .

The Iowa franchisee filed suit in Iowa and, according to Sickler, obtained personal judgments against Sickler and Mettenbrink. Barista's sold seven more franchises using the third disclosure statement, but was notified by the FTC in November 2005 that Barista's was under investigation. [Orr's associate] contacted an attorney specializing in franchise law regarding the FTC investigation. The specializing attorney reviewed the franchise documents of Barista's and concluded that these documents—including the third disclosure statement—did not comply with the FTC rules. The attorney characterized the deficiencies as "major."

[Orr's firm withdrew. The franchise specialist continued to represent Sickler and Mettenbrink, and an FTC civil penalty was suspended indefinitely so long as the disclosures of Barista's were truthful. But the franchising of Barista's had "virtually been shut down." Orr's firm paid for the specialist's work, including necessary revisions to the franchise documents. A court-appointed referee found that Orr had violated Rule 1.1, as well as the analogous former Code provision on competence. Orr accepted the referee's report, and the

---

1. ["UFOC" stands for Uniform Franchising Offering Circular. It is a regulatory document describing a franchising opportunity. It has since been renamed as a Franchise Disclosure Document ("FDD"). — ED.]

only remaining issue was the sanction to be imposed. Based on the referee's finding of numerous mitigating factors, including that Orr had practiced law for 40 years with no prior complaints or penalties, that only one client was involved, and that his misconduct appeared to be "an isolated occurrence rather than part of a recurring pattern," the court agreed with the referee's recommendation for a public reprimand.]

That is not to say we are unconcerned about Orr's conduct. We have said that "[i]t is inexcusable for an attorney to attempt any legal procedure without ascertaining the law governing that procedure." As a lawyer who has been practicing law for over 40 years, Orr should have been aware that he was not competent to represent franchisors, and he was warned by another attorney that franchise law was a specialized area. At the very least, Orr should have done the research necessary to become competent in the area of franchise law. The fact that Orr did little or no research into state or federal franchising law until long after he first received notice that there was a problem with the franchising documents is inexcusable.

We take this opportunity to caution general practitioners against taking on cases in areas of law with which they have no experience, unless they are prepared to do the necessary research to become competent in such areas or associate with an attorney who is competent in such areas. General practitioners must be particularly careful when practicing in specialty areas. "If a general practitioner plunges into a field in which he or she is not competent, and as a consequence makes mistakes that demonstrate incompetence, the [professional conduct rule] demands that discipline be imposed. . . ."

NOTES AND QUESTIONS

1. Was Orr precluded from accepting the representation of Sickler and Mettenbrink? If not, what should he have done once he agreed to represent them? Although lawyers may not misrepresent their experience, they are not generally obliged to disclose their lack of experience in a particular subject area. Should they be required to do so?

2. The court's opinion did not indicate whether the business owners sued Orr for malpractice. If they did, the question might arise what standard of care Orr was required to follow. Lawyers are required to "exercise the skill and knowledge ordinarily possessed by attorneys under similar circumstances."[2] Lawyers who hold themselves out as specialists are held to the standards of other specialists, not a general practitioner. What about a general practitioner like Orr who is consulted in a matter involving a specialty field? Courts have held that such a practitioner should either refer the client to a specialist or seek the assistance of a

---

2. Ronald E. Mallen, 2 Legal Malpractice §20:2 at p. 1321 (2017).

specialist. And if the general practitioner fails to do so, and is subsequently sued for malpractice, the practitioner will be held to the specialists' standard.[3]

3. Another area of potential concern involves ongoing developments in the practice of law. In 2009, the ABA appointed the Commission on Ethics 20/20 to study the ethical and regulatory challenges posed by the manner in which both technology and globalization have transformed legal practice.[4] Among other changes, the Commission recommended, and the ABA concurred, that the comment to MR 1.1 be amended to include the following statement: "To maintain the requisite knowledge and skill, a lawyer should keep abreast of changes in the law and its practice, including the benefits and risks associated with relevant technology. . . ."[5] The risks associated with new technologies include the inadvertent or unauthorized disclosure of digitally stored client information, which will be addressed in Chapter 4: Privilege and Confidentiality. The potential benefits of technology include not only the ability to access documents from remote locations, but also the use of new tools, such as social media, to obtain relevant information about adversaries or prospective business partners. Lawyers need not keep up with all of the latest gadgets, but they do need to be aware of significant risks and benefits as these developing technologies become part of the toolkit of the ordinary practitioner. As a result of the work of the Commission, the ABA has established a Legal Technology Resource Center, which provides legal technology resources to ABA members, including a technology blog, publications, webinars, and an extensive website.[6] Some state and local bar associations provide similar resources for lawyers in different types of practices.[7]

4. According to Jan Jacobowitz, another consequence of the global environment created by technology is that lawyers increasingly recognize "the value of cultural competence for the legal profession."[8] Lawyers who do not understand the differing cultures of their clients and others,

---

3. *See id.* at §20:4.

4. *See generally* ABA Commission on Ethics 20/20 Introduction and Overview (August 2012) (summarizing the work of the Commission and introducing a series of Resolutions and Reports recommending ABA action, including limited changes to the Model Rules of Professional Conduct).

5. MR 1.1, cmt. [8].

6. *See* ABA Legal Technology Resource Center, at https://www.americanbar.org/groups /departments_offices/legal_technology_resources/.

7. For example, the New York State Bar Association recently established a Committee on Technology and the Legal Profession to make recommendations on providing CLE and other tools to assist members in achieving reasonable technological competence in their practices. *See* https://www.nysba.org/techcommittee/.

8. Jan L. Jacobowitz, Lawyers Beware: You Are What You Post — The Case for Integrating Cultural Competence, Legal Ethics, and Social Media, 17 SMU Science and Tech. L. Rev. 541, 553 (2014).

including business partners or employees, may make costly mistakes. She gives the following example of contrasting communication styles in eastern and western cultures: "An American businessman travels to China to negotiate a business deal. He enters the conference room, offers a firm handshake while making direct eye contact, and launches almost immediately into his business presentation, which is a miserable failure. The American businessman has offended his Chinese counterpart with his direct eye contact, aggressive handshake, and failure to engage in personal conversation before discussing the business deal."[9] Assume it was the businessman's U.S. lawyer who traveled to China to negotiate the deal. What should the lawyer have done to avoid the problem that the businessman encountered? Can you think of similar examples that do not involve foreign travel? Should the lawyer expect that U.S. citizens of eastern ancestry share their ancestors' culture? Isn't that itself an example of cultural or implicit bias?

B. DILIGENCE

Model Rule 1.3

Model Rule 1.3 provides that "[a] lawyer shall act with reasonable diligence and promptness in representing a client." The rule requires not only that lawyers perform the work in a *timely manner*, but also that they "act with *commitment and dedication* to the interests of the client and with zeal in advocacy upon the client's behalf."[10] This, in turn, means that lawyers should "take whatever lawful and ethical measures are required to vindicate a client's cause or endeavor."[11]

When Jeffrey Orr failed to engage in the necessary research or to associate with an already-competent franchising lawyer, he violated both MR 1.1 and MR 1.3.[12] Indeed, a comment to Rule 1.3 acknowledges the overlap between the two rules when it specifies that "[a] lawyer's work must be controlled so that each matter can be handled competently."[13]

Recognizing that lawyers have obligations to other clients, as well as personal interests and commitments, MR 1.3 requires only that the lawyer act

---

9. *Id.* at 546.
10. MR 1.3, cmt [1] (emphasis added).
11. *Id.*
12. Orr was charged under both the Nebraska version of the Model Code and its more recently adopted version of the Model Rules. He was found to have violated Code provisions DR 6-101(1) and (2), which include both incompetence and "handl[ing] a legal matter without preparation adequate in the circumstance," which is now addressed in Model Rule 1.3. Although he was not charged with violating Rule 1.3, it appears that he did indeed violate that provision, as well as Rule 1.1.
13. MR 1.3, cmt [2].

with *reasonable* diligence and promptness. The pressing needs of one client will take priority over the less-pressing needs of another client, and a lawyer is both entitled and expected to maintain a healthy work-life balance,[14] whether by attending a child's soccer game or taking a family vacation. So long as each client's matter is performed in a timely manner, the lawyer will have complied with this rule.

Similarly, lawyers are not required to act with *unqualified* "commitment and dedication" to a client or a client's cause. As the comment states, "[a] lawyer is not bound, however, to press for every advantage that might be realized for a client."[15] Lawyers have some discretion in choosing the means for achieving the client's objectives; in particular,"[t]he lawyer's duty to act with reasonable diligence does not require the use of offensive tactics or preclude the treating of all persons involved in the legal process with courtesy and respect."[16] Bar associations and courts have expressed concern for excessive zeal that results in unnecessarily harsh language and malicious tactics, particularly in litigation.[17] As one commentator noted, "A lawyer's duty of faithful representation does not justify his or her departure from ordinary social norms of civility and fair dealing."[18]

C. CONTROL

Model Rules 1.2, 1.4, 1.16

Model Rule 1.2(a) addresses the allocation of decision-making authority between lawyer and client. It states that generally "a lawyer shall abide by a client's decisions concerning the objectives of the representation, and, as required by Rule 1.4, shall consult with the client as to the means by which they are to be pursued." Without reading further, a lawyer might interpret this statement as providing that "objectives" are for the client to decide, whereas the "means" of achieving these objectives are for the lawyer, subject only to an obligation to "consult" the client as required under Rule 1.4. The rule, however, is not that simple. For example, it expressly provides that certain

---

14. Recent bar association studies on lawyer well-being have concluded that many lawyers struggle with physical and mental health issues as a result of the pace of today's law practice. A Massachusetts Supreme Judicial Court commission has recommended numerous ways in which courts and the bar can support a healthy work-life balance, including revising the e-filing deadline for all Massachusetts courts, then set at 11:59, thereby creating an expectation that lawyers routinely work into the middle of the night.

15. MR 1.3, cmt [1].

16. *Id.*

17. *See, e.g.*, Comm. on Professionalism and Lawyer Competence, Conference of Chief Justices, A National Action Plan on Lawyer Conduct and Professionalism (1999).

18. Albert W. Alschuler, How to Win the Trial of the Century: The Ethics of Lord Brougham and the O.J. Simpson Defense Team, 29 McGeorge L. Rev. 291, 319 (1998).

decisions are for the client to make, regardless of whether they are characterized as "objectives" or "means": whether to settle a matter, and, in a criminal case, what plea to be entered, whether to waive a jury trial, and whether the client will testify. Moreover, the rule also states that "[a] lawyer may take such action on behalf of the client as is impliedly authorized to carry out the representation," although neither the rule nor the comment explains when a lawyer has such implied authority over the means of the representation.[19]

Finally, the rule does not explain what happens when a lawyer who has no implied authority consults with the client, but the lawyer and client cannot agree on the best way to proceed. Does the lawyer have the right to decide, subject to the risk of being discharged by the client?[20] Or is the lawyer obligated to follow the client's instructions, subject to the lawyer's ability to withdraw over a "fundamental disagreement" with the client?[21]

Many of these ambiguities can be explored by examining the following opinion, in which the Wisconsin Supreme Court held that a lawyer could be held liable in malpractice for failing to follow a client's instructions with respect to taking a mortgage on the sale of her home.

Olfe v. Gordon
286 N.W.2d 573 (Wis. 1980)

CALLOW, Justice

[Olfe was a 62-year-old widow who was approached by a man who proposed buying her house and the land it was on to construct an office building. After Olfe and the man orally agreed on a purchase price, Olfe retained Gordon, an attorney, and told him that she wanted a first mortgage.[22] Subsequently, Gordon and his real estate partner presented Olfe with a document to sign. Before signing, Olfe asked, "This isn't a second mortgage is it?" Gordon did not

---

19. For an argument that "impliedly authorized" means that the circumstances are such that the lawyer reasonably believes that the action is one that the client would want the lawyer to take, including whether the client would want to be consulted before the lawyer acts, *see* Nancy J. Moore, Why Is There No Clear Doctrine of Informed Consent for Lawyers?, 47 U. of Tol. L. Rev. 133, 152-53 (2015) (contrasting this position with a Restatement comment that lawyers are impliedly authorized "to take any lawful measure 'reasonably calculated to advance a client's objectives'"). The term "impliedly authorized" in Rule 1.2(a) mirrors the use of the same term in the rule governing confidentiality. *See infra* Chapter 4: Privilege and Confidentiality.

20. *See* MR 1.16(a)(3) (lawyer must withdraw when lawyer is discharged).

21. *See* MR 1.16(b)(4) (except when court approval is required, lawyer may withdraw when "the client insists upon taking action that the lawyer considers repugnant or with which the lawyer has a fundamental disagreement").

22. Having a mortgage gives a lender (in this case the seller herself, although it's typically a bank), the right to sell the property to satisfy an unpaid debt. A first mortgage gives the lender the first right to any sale proceeds, up to the amount of the unpaid debt. A second mortgage would require the lender to wait to see if there are any sale proceeds left after the first mortgage has been satisfied. As a result, a second mortgage is clearly riskier than a first mortgage.

respond, and his partner replied: "It is second only to the cost of construction." Understanding this to mean that the second mortgage was only on the new building, and that she had a first mortgage on the land and the home on it, Olfe signed the agreement. When the buyer subsequently defaulted and the holder of the first mortgage foreclosed on the entire property, Olfe was forced to sell her second mortgage at a substantially discounted rate. She then sued Gordon for negligence. The trial court dismissed the case on the ground of insufficient evidence, including the lack of expert testimony related to the standard of care required of attorneys in a legal malpractice case. The Wisconsin Supreme Court reversed, holding that Olfe was entitled to present her case to the jury.]

Since Olfe did not present expert testimony to establish the standard of care and a departure from that standard, we must determine whether Gordon's actions fall within the exception to the rule requiring expert testimony. Olfe's first two allegations, that Gordon failed to provide in the offer to purchase that Olfe's security interest would be a first mortgage and that he failed to draft or cause to be drafted a mortgage that would be senior to any other [the buyer] would obtain on the premises of sale, are contentions that Gordon is liable for damages caused by his negligent disregard of Olfe's instructions. The legal theory on which these allegations are premised is well established:

> It has generally been recognized that an attorney may be liable for all losses caused by his failure to follow with reasonable promptness and care the explicit instructions of his client. Moreover, an attorney's honest belief that the instructions were not in the best interests of his client, provides no defense to a suit for malpractice.

The attorney-client relationship in such contexts is one of agent to principal, and as an agent the attorney "must act in conformity with his authority and instructions and is responsible to his principal if he violates this duty." While actions for disregard of instructions can be based upon fiduciary and contractual principles, the principal's cause of action for an agent's breach of duty may also lie in tort. "[I]f a paid agent does something wrongful, either knowing it to be wrong, or acting negligently, the principal may have either an action of tort, or an action of contract."... Expert testimony is not required to show that the agent (attorney) has violated his duty.

NOTES AND QUESTIONS

1. Was securing a first mortgage an "objective" of the representation, or was it merely a "means" to provide security for payment of the remaining purchase price to Olfe? What if Olfe told Gordon that her primary objective was to get the highest possible purchase price, and Gordon then determined that in order to get that price, Olfe would have to accept a second mortgage?

2. In the actual case, it appears that Gordon and his partner were not candid with Olfe as to whether she was accepting a first or second

mortgage. Assume that Gordon was completely candid and that he reasonably believed that taking a second mortgage would not present a substantial financial risk in the circumstances. Finally, assume that in order to get a first mortgage, Olfe would have had to accept a purchase price well below what Gordon reasonably believed the property was worth. If Olfe insisted on taking a first mortgage, was Gordon obligated to follow Olfe's instructions? The Wisconsin Supreme Court seems to say that he was because a lawyer "may be liable for all losses caused by his failure to follow . . . the explicit instructions of his client," and the opinion does not differentiate between the "objectives" and the "means" of the representation. This position is supported by Section 21(2) of the Restatement, which provides that, subject to certain limitations,[23] "[a] client may instruct a lawyer during the representation."

3. Contrary to *Olfe*[24] and Restatement Section 21(2), Model Rule 1.2(a) does not subject a lawyer to discipline for failing to follow a client's instructions as to the means of the representation. Comment [2] provides the following explanation for the ABA's deliberate refusal to allocate decision-making authority to either the lawyer or the client in these circumstances:

> On occasion, however, a lawyer and a client may disagree about the means to be used to accomplish the client's objectives. Clients normally defer to the special knowledge and skill of their lawyer with respect to the means to be used to accomplish their objectives, particularly with respect to technical, legal and tactical matters. Conversely, lawyers usually defer to the client regarding such questions as the expense to be incurred and concern for third persons who might be adversely affected. Because of the varied nature of the matters about which a lawyer and client might disagree and because the actions in question may implicate the interests of a tribunal or other persons, *this Rule does not prescribe how such disagreements are to be resolved*. Other law, however, may be applicable and should be consulted by the lawyer. The lawyer should also consult with the client and seek a mutually acceptable resolution of the disagreement. If such efforts are unavailing and the lawyer has a fundamental disagreement with the client, the lawyer may withdraw from the representation. See Rule 1.16(b)(4). Conversely, the client may resolve the disagreement by discharging the lawyer. See Rule 1.16(a)(3). [Emphasis added.]

In Wisconsin, "other law" includes decisions such as *Olfe*, in which case a lawyer who disregards a client's instructions as to the means of the representation would not be subject to discipline, but might be subject to civil liability for malpractice.

---

23. The limitations include the rules of professional conduct and other law, as well as a prior agreement between lawyer and client as to "which of them will make specified decisions." RLGL §§21-23.

24. The statement in *Olfe* that a lawyer must follow explicit instructions of a client may be dictum because it is likely that for Olfe herself, obtaining a first mortgage was an objective of the representation.

4. Comment [2] may rest on the assumption that clients know better than lawyers how much they can or are willing to spend, as well as the importance to them of respecting the interests of third persons. Clients also know their own tolerance for risk. Lawyers, on the other hand, are more knowledgeable on questions of legal and tactical matters, which is why clients normally defer to them. Of course, not all decisions fit neatly into this dichotomy. Consider a client who wants to save money by limiting the lawyer's research or due diligence, whereas the lawyer believes that doing more work will significantly enhance the likelihood that the client will achieve her desired result. Who knows better whether achieving a greater likelihood of prevailing is worth the extra cost—the client or the lawyer? At some point, following client instructions may cause the lawyer to perform the work incompetently, in violation of Rule 1.1, in which case the lawyer must withdraw.[25]

5. Client autonomy is one of the concerns underlying Comment [2], and it is this value that most clearly justifies the strongly client-centered position taken in both *Olfe* and Restatement Section 21(2). A recent law review article asked whether this client-centered position isn't "clearly correct, as a matter of ethics and morality, in concluding that clients *should* have the right to make decisions in [all] matters that affect them because lawyers who disregard lawful client instructions are failing to respect the client's dignity and autonomy?"[26] Having posed the question, the article attempted a brief response:

> If only it was so simple. But as many courts and commentators have recognized, there are interests at stake other than those of the client: the interests of courts and adversaries in efficient trial management; the interests of lawyers in professional autonomy, professional identity, and "a craft interest in not being forced to do substandard work;" and the public's interest in preventing lawyers from "approach[ing] the limits of ethical behavior because of their perceptions of the clients' wishes." And even with respect to the client's own interests, there are those who firmly believe that a client's long-term interests are frequently best served by permitting lawyers to make certain tactical and strategic decisions, even when client values may be implicated.[27]

Is a lawyer's interest in professional autonomy, professional identity, and "a craft interest in not being forced to do substandard work" a legitimate interest when it conflicts with client autonomy? Imagine having a client insisting on rewriting every sentence in a brief or a contract or otherwise micromanaging the representation. How should lawyers balance client and lawyer autonomy? Do courts and third parties have legitimate interests in permitting lawyers to make some decisions over

---

25. *See* MR 1.16(a)(1) (lawyer must withdraw when representation will result in violating a rule of professional conduct).

26. Moore, *supra* n. 19, at 157.

27. *Id.* at 157-58.

the objections of their clients? Be sure to consider the interests of third parties outside the litigation context, such as an unsophisticated tenant who is unlikely to know that a particular lease provision the landlord insists on including is unenforceable. Is the landlord's lawyer justified in refusing to draft such a provision on the ground that it is unfair to the tenant?[28]

6. Given the client's right to discharge a recalcitrant attorney, as well as the attorney's right to withdraw over a "fundamental disagreement" with the client, the questions raised here may seem merely theoretical. But consider that Olfe might have been materially prejudiced in her ability to sell her home quickly if Gordon withdrew rather than follow her instruction to pursue either a cash deal or a first mortgage for an extremely low purchase price. Model Rule 1.16 might permit Gordon to withdraw, but would it have been morally right for him to do so if Olfe might have difficulty replacing him? And what happens in litigation, when court approval is required but the court refuses the lawyer permission to withdraw?[29]

7. As an agent of the client-principal, a lawyer's acts are binding on the client when the lawyer has actual or apparent authority. *Actual authority* exists when the client has expressly or impliedly authorized the act or when the client subsequently ratifies the act.[30] *Apparent authority* exists when a third person reasonably assumes that the lawyer is authorized to act based on the client's having manifested such authorization.[31] Merely by retaining a lawyer, the client manifests consent to conduct that appears reasonably appropriate to carry out the representation, but not to decisions that are reserved to the client, unless the client has objectively manifested consent that the lawyer may act on the client's behalf. For example, a court held that a buyer's lawyer had the apparent authority to extend a closing date by one day to avoid closing on a holiday, even if the buyer suffered harm as a result of the extension; as a result, the buyer lost his deposit when he attempted to revoke the contract after the seller did not appear on the original closing date.[32] Would the client be bound if the lawyer had agreed to reduce the purchase price? To extend the closing date by more than one day?

---

28. For a discussion whether drafting a clearly unenforceable contract provision is ethically permissible, *see infra* Chapter 8: Limits of Zealous Representation II: Transactions. For purposes of answering this question, assume that drafting such a provision would not subject the lawyer to discipline.

29. *See* MR 1.16(c) (lawyer must comply with law requiring notice to or permission of a tribunal before withdrawing).

30. *See* RLGL §26 (also including decisions reserved to the lawyer, which cannot be overridden by the client, such as acts that are required by law).

31. *See id.* at §27.

32. *See* Tesini v. Zawistowski, 479 So.2d 775 (Fla. App. 1985).

If the client is harmed as a result of the lawyer having agreed to extend the closing date by one day, without actual authority to do so, how is it fair to bind the client to the impermissible acts of the lawyer? Can you square this consequence with the lawyer's role as a fiduciary on whom the client-beneficiary necessarily depends? Does the client have a remedy against the lawyer?

D. COMMUNICATION

Model Rule 1.4

Model Rule 1.4 addresses the lawyer's duty to communicate with the client. Lawyers are rarely disciplined for a violation of Rule 1.4 in the absence of harm to the client or other rule violations, and yet the failure to communicate is one of the two most common sources of client complaints to disciplinary agencies.[33] Imagine the "heartache and frustration and pain" lawyers cause by failing to respond to a client's need to know what is happening in a matter,[34] as when five weeks after taking custody of a baby, a prospective adoptive mother could not find out from her lawyer when the natural mother would sign the required relinquishment papers necessary to finalize the adoption.[35]

Rule 1.4(a) instructs lawyers *when* they must communicate, identifying five events that trigger the lawyer's duty to provide information to a client: (1) to inform the client about decisions as to which the client's informed consent is required;[36] (2) to reasonably consult about the means of achieving the client's objectives; (3) to "keep the client reasonably informed about the status of a matter"; (4) to "promptly comply with reasonable requests for information"; and (5) to inform the client about limits on the lawyer's conduct "when the client expects assistance not permitted by the Rules of Professional Conduct or other law." How can a lawyer "promptly comply" with requests for information when the lawyer is occupied day and night with a deal about to close or a lengthy trial?

---

33. *See* Martin Cole, The Hardiest Perennials, 64 Bench & B. Minn. 12 (2007) (other most common complaint is neglect).

34. Robert S. Caine, A Lawyer's View of Being a Litigant, letter, N.Y.L.J., May 16, 1994, at 2.

35. *See* Discipline Corner, 20 Utah Bar Journal 52 (Jan-Feb 2007). The lawyer's failure to communicate in that case was likely an effort to cover up her neglect. Frustrated by the lawyer's unresponsiveness, the client made her own arrangements for the natural mother to appear before the judge to sign the relinquishment papers. The natural mother refused to sign and demanded return of the baby, which the court then ordered. The lawyer was disciplined for violating numerous rules, including the rules requiring competence, diligence, communication, and fees.

36. The only example provided of when a client's informed consent is required is Rule 1.2(a), although that rule does not expressly require the client's informed consent. *See* MR 1.4, cmt [2]. Rules expressly requiring a client's informed consent are those concerning limited representations (MR 1.2(c)), waivers of confidentiality (MR 1.6), waivers of conflicts of interest (e.g., MR 1.7; 1.8(a), (f), (g); MR 1.9), and evaluations likely to materially and adversely affect the client's interests (MR 2.3).

When Rule 1.4(a) triggers the lawyer's duty to communicate, Rule 1.4(b) addresses the *type of explanation* to be provided. This rule requires the lawyer to "explain a matter to the extent reasonably necessary to permit the client to make informed decisions regarding the representation." If the matter is one for which another rule requires the client's "informed consent," Rule 1.0(e) provides that the lawyer must communicate "adequate information and explanation about the material risks of and reasonably available alternatives to the proposed course of conduct."

E. LEGAL FEES

Model Rules 1.5, 1.15, 6.1

Model Rule 1.5 addresses many aspects of legal fees, including requiring that fees and expenses be reasonable and that the basis or rate of the fee and expenses be communicated to the client, "preferably in writing, before or within a reasonable time after commencing the representation." The rule permits contingent fees, except in criminal cases and in certain domestic relations matters, but requires that agreements for contingent fees be in a writing signed by the client and that they make certain detailed disclosures. Finally, the rule addresses the limited circumstances in which lawyers not in the same firm may divide legal fees.

1. The Reasonableness Standard Generally

Determining the reasonableness of legal fees is not an easy matter, partly because lawyers use a variety of billing methods, including hourly fees, contingent fees, and fixed fees, as well as an expanding number of "alternative fee arrangements." Rule 1.5(a) provides a non-exclusive list of factors to consider in determining the reasonableness of a fee:

> (1) the time and labor required, the novelty and difficulty of the questions involved, and the skill requisite to perform the legal service properly;
> (2) the likelihood, if apparent to the client, that the acceptance of the particular employment will preclude other employment by the lawyer;
> (3) the fee customarily charged in the locality for similar legal services;
> (4) the amount involved and the results obtained; the time limitations imposed by the client or by the circumstances;
> (5) the nature and length of the professional relationship with the client;
> (6) the experience, reputation, and ability of the lawyer or lawyers performing the services; and
> (7) whether the fee is fixed or contingent.

Concerned that this rule was drafted with litigation rather than transactional services in mind, an ABA Committee on Lawyer Business Ethics proposed that two additional factors be added to Rule 1.5(a):

> (1) the size and complexity of the transaction or matter for which the lawyer is retained; and
>
> (2) the client's sophistication and extent of experience in business matters.[37]

The Committee also urged that "reasonableness should be presumed 'if the client and the lawyer reach an agreement with respect to a billing arrangement after disclosure and understanding and fees are charged in accordance with that agreement.'"[38] The ABA did not adopt these recommendations; however, the recommendation may continue to serve as a useful guideline for business lawyers.

"Reasonableness" is not the standard for determining the validity of contracts generally, but Rule 1.5 provides no explanation for departing from the contract standard of "unconscionability."[39] If a fee contract is entered into *after* an attorney-client relationship is formed, then the attorney is a fiduciary, and fiduciary principles justify a more client-protective approach. But what about contracts entered into *before* the attorney-client relationship is formed, when the client might be expected to bargain over price? Here is the explanation given by the Restatement:

> Courts are concerned to protect clients, particularly those who are unsophisticated in matters of lawyers' compensation, when a lawyer has overreached. Information about fees for legal services is often difficult for prospective clients to obtain. Many clients do not bargain effectively because of their need and inexperience. The services required are often unclear beforehand and difficult to monitor as a lawyer provides them. Lawyers usually encourage their clients to trust them. Lawyers, therefore, owe their clients greater duties than are owed under the general law of contracts.[40]

Is this explanation sufficient to distinguish legal fees from other consumer expenses, such as hiring a plumber to install a new bathroom? Is the stricter standard also explained by the status of law as a profession, in which its members agree to police each other for the benefit of the public generally?[41] The ABA Committee on Lawyer Business Ethics' presumed-reasonableness standard may be friendlier to lawyers than MR 1.5(a); however, it is noteworthy that the proposal would have required lawyers "to assure that the client fully understands and agrees to the basis for billing for legal services rendered."[42] Should such a requirement be added to Rule 1.5(a)?

---

37. Committee on Lawyer Business Ethics, Business and Ethics Implications of Alternative Billing Practices: Report on Alternative Billing Arrangements, 54 Bus. Law. 175, 204 (1998).

38. *Id.* (quoting Task Force on Lawyer Business Ethics, Statements of Principles, 51 Bus. Law. 1303, 1311 (1996)).

39. *See* Restatement (Second) of Contracts §208 (1981) (unconscionable contracts).

40. RLGL §34, cmt b.

41. *See supra* Chapter 1: Why a Course in Professional Responsibility?

42. Task Force on Lawyer Business Ethics, Statements of Principles, 51 Bus. Law.1303, 1311 (1996).

2. Different Types of Fee Arrangements

The most common forms of fee arrangements are hourly fees, fixed fees, and contingent fees. Here are some common problems that arise with each, followed by a brief description of some recently adopted "alternative billing arrangements."

Hourly Fees. The reasonableness of hourly fees is typically measured by what fees are commonly charged by similarly experienced lawyers in similar matters in the locality, with an understanding that there is often a wide range of customary billing rates. The problem with hourly fees, which have been harshly criticized in recent years, is that they are subject to a variety of abuses, ranging from outright fraud,[43] to bill padding (through such devices as minimum billing increments[44] and overstaffing), to the absence of an incentive for efficiency. Absent dishonesty, it is rare for a lawyer to be disciplined for charging excessive hourly fees. One such lawyer was Laurence Fordham, who although not a criminal lawyer, agreed to represent a man in a drunk driving case. The man's father had been quoted fixed fees between $3,000 and $10,000 by experienced criminal lawyers, but agreed to pay Fordham's regular hourly rate instead. Fordham and his associate billed 227 hours for a total of $50,022.25. Although the son was acquitted, due largely to a creative approach resulting in the suppression of breathalyzer tests, Fordham was disciplined for spending too much time learning the basics of criminal representation in a drunk driving case. The court concluded:

> Fordham's inexperience in criminal defense work and [DUI] cases in particular cannot justify the extraordinarily high fee. It cannot be that an inexperienced lawyer is entitled to charge three or four times as much as an experienced lawyer for the same service. A client "should not be expected to pay for the education of a lawyer when he spends excessive amounts of time on tasks which, with reasonable experience, become matters of routine."[45]

But if Fordham's approach was "creative," and the son was acquitted as a result, didn't Fordham earn his fee? Unfortunately for Fordham, the client agreed to pay an hourly fee, not a success fee,[46] and in any event, success fees in criminal cases are prohibited. The lesson from *Fordham* is that lawyers venturing into entirely new territory must be extremely careful in determining precisely how much of the time they spend learning the new subject is properly billed to the client.

---

43. *See, e.g.,* Lisa G. Lerman, Lying to Clients, 138 U. Penn. L. Rev. 659 (1990).

44. *See, e.g.,* Republican Party of Minn. v. White, 456 F.3d 912, 920 (8th Cir. 2006) (criticizing law firm's practice of billing in quarter-hour increments, as opposed to tenth-hour increments).

45. In re Laurence S. Fordham, 668 N.E.2d 816, 823 (Mass. 1996).

46. Success fees are a form of contingent fee and are increasingly being used as a form of alternative billing arrangement in transactional cases, as discussed later in this section.

Fixed Fees. A set fee is most common for routine matters where the legal time required is relatively predictable. Remember the experienced criminal lawyers in *Fordham* who quoted fixed fees ranging from $3,000 to $10,000 for a drunk driving case. Similarly, business lawyers may charge fixed fees for such discrete tasks such as forming a company, issuing stock, and preparing shareholder agreements.[47] The representation may take more or less time than anticipated; however, both lawyers and clients benefit from knowing in advance how much the representation will cost. There is an added benefit for lawyers, who may be permitted to place the entire fee in their operating account—as opposed to a client trust account[48]—as earned on receipt.[49] And there is an added benefit for clients, who can more readily compare the total cost of retaining different lawyers. Despite the obvious benefits, however, many legal matters are not routine and are therefore not suitable for fixed fees.

Fixed fees are unlikely to be controversial when the lawyer completes the services for which the lawyer was retained. The trouble comes when lawyers designate flat fees (or even a portion thereof) as "nonrefundable," and the client discharges the lawyer before the contemplated services have been rendered. Many jurisdictions prohibit *nonrefundable legal fees*, except in the rare case of a "general retainer," where the fee is for obtaining the availability of the lawyer when needed, and the client will pay additional fees for legal services if and when performed. But are such fees truly nonrefundable? What if the lawyer becomes seriously ill and is not available during the designated period? Wouldn't the lawyer have to refund a portion of the general retainer fees?

Most nonrefundable legal fees are not general retainers, but are rather fixed fees for specific legal services. In Matter of Cooperman,[50] a New York court held that these types of nonrefundable fees are improper because they limit the right of a client to terminate the lawyer. Some jurisdictions expressly permit nonrefundable fees, with the caveat that lawyers may need to refund a portion of the fee if the representation is terminated before completion.[51] Although such fees are not truly nonrefundable, designating them

---

47. *See, e.g.*, Sarah Boulden, The Business of Startup Law: Alternative Fee Arrangements and Agency Costs in Entrepreneurial Law, 11 J. on Telecomm. & High Tech. L. 279, 296 (2013). *See also id.* at 290 (law firms reporting use of fixed fees for such automated tasks as patent drafting, motions, and some aspects of mergers and acquisitions).

48. Rule 1.15 requires lawyers to safeguard client property, including funds for advanced legal fees and expenses, by keeping such funds in an account separate from the lawyer's own funds. These accounts are known as "client trust accounts."

49. Whether such fees are truly earned on receipt, or might need to be refunded in whole or in part, is controversial, as discussed with respect to "nonrefundable" fees in the next paragraph of this section.

50. 591 N.Y.S.2d 855 (N.Y. App. Div. 1993), order aff'd, 633 N.E.2d 1069 (N.Y. 1964).

51. *See, e.g.*, Ariz. Rules of Prof'l Conduct, ER 1.5(d)(3) (lawyer may not agree to charge "a fee denominated as 'earned upon receipt,' 'nonrefundable' or in similar terms unless the client is simultaneously advised in writing that the client may nevertheless discharge the lawyer at any time and in that event may be entitled to a refund of all or part of the fee based upon the value of the representation").

as such entitles the lawyer to deposit the entire amount in the lawyer's office account, with the understanding that the lawyer may need to return some of the fee under appropriate circumstances.[52] At least one jurisdiction, Vermont, expressly permits nonrefundable fees, earned before legal services are rendered even when the client terminates the representation; however, even here, such fees must be "reasonable under all of the relevant circumstances," and the rule prohibits the lawyer from "making any agreement with a client that prospectively waives the client's right to challenge the reasonableness of a nonrefundable fee."[53] Are nonrefundable fees in Vermont truly nonrefundable? What if the client discharges the lawyer the day after signing the agreement and paying the fee, before any services are rendered; may the client successfully claim that to allow the lawyer to keep the entire payment is unreasonable? If the "nonrefundable" fee is unreasonable under these circumstances, should the lawyer be entitled to keep *any* of the advance payment?

Contingent Fees. Although they are prohibited in many other countries, legal fees that are contingent on the outcome of the representation are expressly permitted in the United States, except in criminal cases and most domestic relations matters.[54] Typically charged by lawyers representing plaintiffs in personal injury and commercial litigation, they are also used by some lawyers on the defense side in the form of "reverse contingency" fees, measured by the savings the lawyer achieves in litigation. Contingent fees are also increasingly common in transactional work, where all or a portion of the legal fees are contingent on achieving an objective, such as closing a deal. Why do you think that contingent fees are prohibited in criminal and most domestic relations matter?

Unlike other fee agreements, which most jurisdictions do not require to be in writing, contingent fee agreements must be "in a writing signed by the client."[55] Model Rule 1.5(c) also requires that the agreement "state the method by which the fee is to be determined, including the percentage or percentages that shall accrue to the lawyer in the event of settlement, trial or appeal," and must describe the "litigation and other expenses to be deducted from the recovery" and "whether such expenses are to be deducted before or after the contingent fee is calculated." Finally, the rule provides that "[t]he agreement must clearly notify the client of any expenses for which the client will be liable whether or not the client is the prevailing party" and requires a written accounting upon the conclusion of the matter.

---

52. *See id* at cmt [7]. If the fee is not earned upon receipt, the lawyer must deposit it as an advanced fee in the lawyer's client trust account. *See* MR 1.15(a).

53. Vt. Rules of Prof'l Conduct, R. 1.5(f).

54. *See* MR 1.5(d) (prohibiting contingent fees for representing a defendant in a criminal case and for fees in a domestic relations matter when the payment or amount "is contingent upon the security of a divorce or upon the amount of alimony or support, or property settlement in lieu thereof").

55. MR 1.5(c).

Courts with jurisdiction over a lawsuit sometimes question the reasonableness of the lawyer's contingent fee, particularly when the court is required to approve a settlement.[56] According to a Restatement comment, courts are most likely to hold that a contingent fee is unreasonable in two types of cases: "those in which there was a high likelihood of substantial recovery by trial or settlement, so that the lawyer bore little risk of nonpayment; and those in which the client's recovery was likely to be so large that the lawyer's fee would clearly exceed the sum appropriate to pay for services performed and risks assumed."[57] Some states have enacted court rules or statutes capping the amount of contingent fees generally or in particular cases, such as medical malpractice lawsuits.

Disputes sometimes arise when a client with a contingent fee matter wants to change lawyers. Because the client has the absolute right to discharge the lawyer, the lawyer may not recover under the contract terms. Rather, courts typically permit the lawyer to recover the lesser of the contractual fee and the fair value of the lawyer's services, measured by a reasonable hourly rate. Regardless of the amount of time expended by the lawyer, the lawyer may not recover unless the client prevails, as provided in the contract.

Alternative Fee Billing. Given both the unpredictability and the potential for abuse in traditional hourly billing, many lawyers have shifted to alternative billing arrangements, primarily as a result of pressure from clients. These clients include not only sophisticated corporate clients with in-house counsel, but also individuals or small business entities that cannot afford to commit an indefinite amount for legal representation. Some of these alternative arrangements are variations on hourly fees, such as fee caps, budgets, and firm estimates, as well as discounted hourly rates and volume rates.[58] Others are variations on the contingent fee, including incentive and value billing, cost-plus arrangements, and result-based billing.[59] More attorneys are using creative fixed fee arrangements, including task-based flat fees and the loaned lawyer (where a client borrows a salaried firm lawyer to work for a period of time with the client, which pays a set fee for these services).[60]

---

56. *See, e.g.,* Goesel v. Boley Int'l (H.K.) Ltd., 806 F.3d 414 (7th Cir. 2015) (state law required judicial approval of contingent fee in settlement of personal injury lawsuit on behalf of a minor).

57. RLGL §35, cmt c. For an excellent discussion of the reasonableness of contingent fees, particularly when they are charged on a routine basis with no consideration of the reasonableness of applying the lawyer's standard fee in a particular case, *see* Geoffrey C. Hazard, Jr. et al., 1 The Law of Lawyering §9.08 (4th ed. 2020) (last updated June 2021) (including a discussion of a controversial ABA opinion defending the use of contingent fees even when liability is clear).

58. *See* Committee on Lawyer Business Ethics, *supra* n. 37, at 182-84 (also discussing unbundled fees, blended rates, partner-based rule structures, and phased billings). For a description of alternative fee arrangements in the representation of start-up companies, including detailed profiles of a range of law firms offering such fees, *see generally* Boulden, *supra* n. 47.

59. *Id.* at 184-86.

60. *Id.*

Ethical issues raised in connection with these alternative fee arrangements include the difficulty of determining the reasonableness of novel fee arrangements in the absence of traditional benchmarks (such as the contingent fee percentages commonly charged in personal injury lawsuits) and issues associated with loaned lawyers, including the inability of outside counsel to select and manage a legal team comprised largely of client employees.[61]

3. Modifying the Fee Agreement

Just as the initial basis or rate of the fee must be communicated to the client at the beginning of the representation, Rule 1.5(b) requires that the lawyer communicate any change in the basis or rate of the fee. It is misleading, however, to suggest that all a lawyer need do is "communicate" a change in the fee basis. Lawyers may not unilaterally impose such a change, and as stated in Section 18 of the Restatement, "if the . . . modification is made beyond a reasonable time after the lawyer has begun to represent the client in the matter, the client may avoid it unless the lawyer shows that the contract and circumstances of its formation were fair and reasonable to the client."[62] The burden will be on the lawyer to establish that the changes were reasonable in light of previously unanticipated circumstances and that the client's agreement was not the result of coercion or duress. Except for routine annual increases in hourly fees, courts view such modifications with suspicion, given that clients may agree to accept them out of concern that refusal may adversely affect the representation and it is difficult to change lawyers in midstream.[63] Renegotiating an existing fee agreement is sometimes deemed a business transaction between lawyer and client, thus triggering additional protections for the client under Model Rule 1.8(a), including that the client be advised in writing of the desirability of consulting independent counsel and that the client's informed consent be in a writing signed by the client.[64]

4. Pro Bono Public Service

Model Rule 6.1 is entitled "Voluntary Pro Bono Publico Service," where "pro bono publico" means for the public good. The rule states that "[e]very lawyer has a professional responsibility to provide legal services to those unable to pay" and then provides that "[a] lawyer should aspire to render at least (50) hours of pro bono public legal services per year." The voluntary nature of the rule is emphasized in the comment, which states that the rule is "not intended to be enforced through disciplinary process."[65] Paragraph (a) of the

---

61. *Id.* at 193-98.
62. RLGL §18(a).
63. *Id.* at cmt e.
64. *See* MR 1.8(a), discussed *infra* Chapter 5: Conflicts of Interest: Current Clients.
65. MR 6.1, cmt [12].

rule provides that a "substantial majority" of the hours should be provided "without fee or expectation of fee" to either "persons of limited means" or nonprofit organizations that "address the needs of persons of limited means." Paragraph (b) provides that the remaining hours may be provided in a variety of alternative ways, including providing legal services at "a substantially reduced fee to persons of limited means" and to individuals or nonprofit organizations in support of various civil rights, civil liberties, religious, and civic goals.

There have been numerous unsuccessful attempts within the ABA and the states to make pro bono service mandatory.[66] Proponents have cited to overwhelming evidence of the unmet need for legal services among persons of limited means, despite the existence of publicly funded legal services for the poor.[67] Opponents such as Ronald Rotunda have responded that lawyers should not be singled out to solve a societal problem. According to Rotunda, "When the government deems the poor in need of food, it provides food stamps; it doesn't order the grocer to give them food as a condition of his business license."[68] Steven Lubet and Cathryn Stewart argued that lawyers are different because government creates law, which is the "product" that lawyers sell, and limits the ability of others to provide that product through unauthorized practice of law statutes.[69]

The debate also centers on whether providing pro bono services is a "charity" or a "duty."[70] Rotunda argued that "*[m]andatory* pro bono, like mandatory charitable donation, is an oxymoron."[71] Just as one gets little pleasure from paying government taxes, lawyers might lose the personal and professional satisfaction they derive from providing pro bono services. Proponents of mandatory pro bono have nevertheless maintained that lawyers, as a profession, commit themselves "to a higher calling"[72] and should therefore "devote professional time and resources and use civic influence to ensure equal access to our system of justice for all those who because of economic or social barriers cannot afford or secure adequate legal counsel."[73]

---

66. *See, e.g.,* Judith L. Maute, Changing Conceptions of Lawyers' Pro Bono Responsibilities: From Chance Noblesse Oblige to Stated Expectations, 77 Tul. L. Rev. 91 (2002).

67. *See, e.g.,* Deborah L. Rhode, Cultures of Commitment: Pro Bono for Lawyers and Law Students, 67 Fordham L. Rev. 2415, 2420-21 (1999). The "access to justice gap" also underlies other efforts to ensure meaningful access to legal services by persons of low and moderate income. These efforts are discussed in Chapter 16: Nonlawyer Ownership, Multidisciplinary Practice, and Alternative Legal Services Providers.

68. Ronald Rotunda, The Wrong Legal "Help" for NY's Poor, N.Y. Post, June 1, 2012, http://nypost.com/2012/06/01/the-wrong-legal-help-for-nys-poor.

69. Steven Lubet & Cathryn Stewart, A Public Assets Theory of Lawyers' Pro Bono Obligations, 145 U.Pa. L. Rev. 1245, 1249-62 (1997).

70. *See, e.g.,* Justin Hansford, Lippman's Law: Debating the Fifty-Hour Pro Bono Requirement for Bar Admission, 41 Fordham Urb. L. J. 1141, 1145-59 (2014).

71. Rotunda, *supra* n. 68 (emphasis in original).

72. Hansford, *supra* n. 70, at 1152-56.

73. MR, Preamble, at [6].

Aside from the theoretical aspects of the debate, there are practical difficulties in implementing any system of mandatory pro bono. Deborah Rhode, herself a proponent of mandatory pro bono, acknowledged the strength of these concerns:

> The stronger arguments against pro bono obligations involve pragmatic rather than moral concerns. Many opponents who support such obligations in principle worry that they would prove ineffective in practice. A threshold problem involves defining the services that would satisfy a pro bono requirement. If the definition is broad, and encompasses any charitable work for a nonprofit organization or needy individual, then experience suggests that poor people will not be the major beneficiaries. . . . A loosely defined requirement is likely to assist predominately middle-class individuals and organizations such as hospitals, museums, and churches. By contrast, limiting a pro bono requirement to low-income clients who have been given preferred status in the ABA's current rule would exclude many crucial public-interest contributions, such as work for environmental, women's rights, or civil rights organizations. Any compromise effort to permit some but not all charitable groups to qualify for pro bono credit would bump up against charges of political bias.
>
> A related objection to mandatory pro bono requirements is that lawyers who lack expertise or motivation to serve under-represented groups will not provide cost-effective assistance. In opponents' view, having corporate lawyers dabble in poverty cases will provide unduly expensive, often incompetent services. . . . Critics also worry that some lawyers' inexperience and insensitivity in dealing with low-income clients will compromise the objectives that pro bono requirements seek to advance.[74]

Another practical question is whether lawyers ought to be able to "buy out of their required service by making a specified financial contribution to a legal-aid program."[75]

Frustrated by the profession's unwillingness to commit to mandatory pro bono for lawyers, Jonathan Lippman, then Chief Justice of the New York Court of Appeals, announced in 2012 that New York would require all applicants to the New York bar to provide evidence of having provided 50 hours of pro bono service as a condition of their admission to the bar.[76] Lippman justified the focus on bar applicants, rather than practicing lawyers, by citing as goals the development of practical skills and the inculcation of a commitment to pro bono as a "core value" of the profession.[77] Effective 2013, the New York law recognizes as "pro bono" a wider variety of activities than is currently recognized in Model Rule 6.1, including participation in law school

---

74. Rhode, *supra* n. 67 at 2423-24.

75. *Id.*

76. *See* Chief Judge Jonathan Lippman's Speech—Law Day 2012, at http://nysbar.com/blogs/EASL/2012/05/chief_judge_jonathan_lippmanip.html.

77. *Id.*

courses, like clinics and externships, for which students already receive credit for graduation, extending even to externships with state and federal judges, which are highly sought by students as a means of career advancement.[78]

Although several state courts have considered implementing a similar requirement,[79] none have done so. In 2016, the California legislature passed a bill that would have required 50 hours of pro bono service as a condition of admission; however, Governor Jerry Brown vetoed the bill, citing the high cost of legal education and the unfairness of burdening students, many of whom "struggle to find employment," with a pro bono requirement.[80]

Do you support mandatory pro bono for either practicing lawyers or bar applicants? Why or why not? A number of law schools have adopted a pro bono requirement as a condition of graduation.[81] Do you support these requirements?

Review Problems

3-1 After a husband learned that his wife had been having an affair, he asked for a divorce. The wife agreed and the couple retained a mediator to help them divide their property, resulting in a written Property Settlement Agreement (PSA). The mediator suggested that each spouse retain a lawyer to review the PSA before they signed it. The lawyer retained by the wife investigated all aspects of the financial situation of both the husband and the wife and is convinced that the PSA represents more than a fair and reasonable compromise of the issues concerning equitable distribution and strongly recommends that the wife sign it. The wife, however, has decided that she was too passive in the mediation and that, given her contributions to the acquisition of the assets in question, she deserves significantly more. She has instructed the lawyer to tell the husband that she will insist on litigating the issues unless he agrees to give her a lump sum settlement of $750,000 and 30 percent of the stock they own. She understands that the husband is unlikely to agree to these terms, but expects that he will agree to significantly enhance what she is currently due under the PSA. On the basis of his extensive experience in negotiating and litigating marital property disputes, the lawyer reasonably believes that this is

---

78. *See* N.Y. Comp. Codes R. & Regs. tit. 22 §520.16; *see also* New York State Bar Admission: Pro Bono Requirement FAQs (2918 rev.1), at http://ww2.nycourts.gov/ATTORNEYS /probono/FAQsBarAdmission.pdf. For a critique of the broad definition of what should count as pro bono under the New York rules, *see* Hansford, *supra* n. 70 , at 1162-65.

79. *See* Hansford, *supra* n. 70, at 1144-45.

80. Debra Cassens Weiss, California governor cites high law school costs in vetoing mandatory pro bono bill, at https://www.abajournal.com/news/article /california_governor_cites_high_law_school_costs_in_vetoing_mandatory_pro_bo.

81. For a description of some of these programs, *see* https://www.americanbar.org/groups /center-pro-bono/resources/directory_of_law_school_public_interest_pro_bono_programs /definitions/pb_structure/.

a poor negotiating tactic that will inevitably backfire, and that the likelihood is that the husband will insist on litigation and that she will end up with less than she would get under the PSA. He has advised her that if she is unhappy with the PSA she should suggest that they go back to mediation in an attempt to resolve the controversy amicably rather than engage in hardball litigation, which is what she wants to do. She is adamant and insists that he convey her terms to the husband. What may or must the lawyer do? Would your views be any different if the wife was insisting on signing an agreement that the lawyer believed was not fair and reasonable, that would likely leave her on the verge of poverty in a few years, and that she was undoubtedly going to regret when she got over her guilt about having an affair?

3-2 A lawyer whose office is in Minnesota is licensed in both Minnesota and North Dakota. She was retained by a businessman to assist him in administrating the estate of his deceased brother, who had resided in North Dakota. The businessman signed an engagement agreement to pay the lawyer $525 per hour for the lawyer's time and services. The lawyer explained to the businessman that her regular hourly rate was $400, but because she was not familiar with North Dakota probate work, and would have to make all new forms for this probate, she would charge more. She estimated that the total fees would likely be between $15,000 and $20,000. She offered to refer him to a North Dakota probate lawyer, who would likely charge less, but the businessman said that he trusted the lawyer and wanted her to represent the estate. The businessman was the primary beneficiary of the estate. When the estate was probated, it was determined that the value of the estate totaled approximately $75,000. The lawyer sought approval from the probate court of approximately $20,000 in legal fees, which will be paid from the estate. By this time the businessman had had a falling out with the lawyer and is objecting to the size of the legal fees, as is a cousin who is also a beneficiary under the will. The businessman has also filed a grievance with the state disciplinary authorities. Is the court likely to approve the legal fees, which will be paid from the estate? Is the lawyer subject to discipline for charging these fees?

3-3 A lawyer has recently left his position as a fifth-year associate and is forming a new law firm with a law school classmate. They are in the process of formulating policies concerning legal fees and expenses. Consider the ethical propriety of the following proposals:

a. When charging hourly fees, the lawyers will bill their time in 15-minute increments. (Most firms in the area charge in 6-minute intervals, but a number of law firms have begun charging in 15-minute increments.)

b. When charging hourly fees, the lawyers will charge their regular hourly rate for travel time, regardless of whether the lawyer is working on the client's matter during that time. If a lawyer chooses to work on a matter for another client during that travel time (e.g., while traveling on a plane), the lawyer will bill that time to both clients.

c. The lawyers will offer fixed fees for such matters as forming an entity, preparing a shareholder agreement, and drafting a routine employment contract. The entire fixed fee must be paid in advance. Half of the fixed fee will represent the administrative costs of setting up the file and ensuring the lawyer's availability, and will therefore be nonrefundable. The remainder of the fixed fee will be subject to refund if the client discharges the lawyer for cause, or the lawyer is unable to complete the representation, but is otherwise nonrefundable.

CHAPTER 4

PRIVILEGE AND CONFIDENTIALITY

Model Rules 1.6, 1.8(b), 1.9(c), 1.18(b)

Lawyers are fiduciaries, that is, persons in whom others have reposed their trust and confidence to act on their behalf, in their best interest. Fiduciaries owe obligations of undivided loyalty and confidentiality, beyond obligations that are created by contract alone. Although the contours of fiduciary obligation vary, and are sometimes in dispute, the two basic fiduciary obligations are *loyalty* and *confidentiality*. We consider the lawyer's loyalty obligations in later chapters on conflicts of interest. In this chapter, we focus on the lawyer's duty of confidentiality, which is embodied in three separate legal doctrines: (1) attorney-client privilege, which is a rule of evidence; (2) work-product immunity, which is a rule of civil procedure; and (3) the professional duty of confidentiality, a common law fiduciary duty now codified in rules of professional conduct. Of these three, the privilege and professional confidentiality doctrines are the most important, particularly for business lawyers.

When a question concerning confidentiality arises, lawyers need to ask themselves the following questions: (1) which of the three doctrines applies; (2) is the information prima facie protected under the applicable doctrine, and, if so, (3) is there an *exception* that removes that protection? The first question is *procedural*: when is each of the three doctrines appropriately invoked in the particular circumstance? The second two questions are *substantive* and determine whether the lawyer is obligated to protect the confidentiality of the information at issue. Given what we will later demonstrate are significant differences in substantive coverage among the three doctrines, the first question becomes critical: which of the three doctrines applies?

A. DISTINGUISHING BETWEEN ATTORNEY-CLIENT PRIVILEGE AND THE RULE OF CONFIDENTIALITY

Putting aside work product immunity, which is of interest primarily to litigators, let's begin with the two most important doctrines for business and other

68   Chapter 4 Privilege and Confidentiality

transactional lawyers: the attorney-client privilege and the professional duty of confidentiality. (We will briefly discuss work product immunity later in the chapter.) The following excerpt from an opinion in a Massachusetts criminal case addresses both of these doctrines. The lawyer became involved when his client was served with an order of eviction, after having been discharged from his job as a maintenance worker in the building where his apartment was located. As you will see, the attorney-client privilege is invoked only with respect to discovery or testimony in an official proceeding. And yet, as numerous commentators have advised, it is critically important for business and other transactional lawyers to be aware of and understand the privilege.[1] As you are reading the opinion, ask yourself why this is so. Consider, for example, that the trial in which the attorney-client privilege was invoked was neither pending nor reasonably anticipated at the time the lawyer learned the information that became the subject of the privilege discussion.

Purcell v. District Attorney for the Suffolk District
676 N.E.2d 436 (Mass. 1997)

WILKINS, Chief Justice.

On June 21, 1994, Joseph Tyree, who had received a court order to vacate his apartment in the Allston section of Boston, consulted the plaintiff, Jeffrey W. Purcell, an attorney employed by Greater Boston Legal Services, which provides representation to low income individuals in civil matters. Tyree had recently been discharged as a maintenance man at the apartment building in which his apartment was located. On the day that Tyree consulted Purcell, Purcell decided, after extensive deliberation, that he should advise appropriate authorities that Tyree might engage in conduct harmful to others. He told a Boston police lieutenant that Tyree had made threats to burn the apartment building.

The next day, constables, accompanied by Boston police officers, went to evict Tyree. At the apartment building, they found incendiary materials, containers of gasoline, and several bottles with wicks attached. Smoke detectors had been disconnected, and gasoline had been poured on a hallway floor. Tyree was arrested and later indicted for attempted arson of a building.

In August, 1995, the district attorney for the Suffolk district subpoenaed Purcell to testify concerning the conversation Purcell had had with Tyree on June 21, 1994. A Superior Court judge granted Purcell's motion to quash the subpoena. The trial ended in a mistrial because the jury was unable to reach a verdict.

---

1. *See, e.g.*, Raymond L. Sweigart, Attorney-Client Privilege: Pitfalls and Pointers for Transactional Attorneys, Bus. Law Today 43 (March/April 2008); Thomas E. Spahn, Business Lawyers: Listen Up, 14 Bus. Law Today 11 (May/June 2005).

The Commonwealth decided to try Tyree again and once more sought Purcell's testimony. Another Superior Court judge concluded that Tyree's statements to Purcell were not protected by the attorney-client privilege, denied Purcell's motion to quash an anticipated subpoena, and ordered Purcell to testify. Purcell then commenced this action. . . .

There is no question before this court, directly or indirectly, concerning the ethical propriety of Purcell's disclosure to the police that Tyree might engage in conduct that would be harmful to others. As bar counsel agreed in a memorandum submitted to the single justice, this court's disciplinary rules regulating the practice of law authorized Purcell to reveal to the police "[t]he intention of his client to commit a crime and the information necessary to prevent the crime." S.J.C. Rule 3:07, Canon 4, DR 4-101(C)(3). . . . The fact that the disciplinary code permitted Purcell to make the disclosure tells us nothing about the admissibility of the information that Purcell disclosed. . . .

NOTES AND QUESTIONS

1. The attorney-client privilege is one of several evidentiary privileges which, by definition, apply only to the production of evidence in proceedings to which the rules of evidence apply. The Federal Rules of Evidence do not codify the applicable privileges, but rather rely on either state law or federal common law, depending on the nature of the federal court's jurisdiction. *See* Fed. R. Evid. 501. The privilege permits clients to resist disclosure of certain confidential communications with their lawyer. Can you see why the court did not refer to the attorney-client privilege in its initial conclusion that Purcell properly disclosed Tyree's threat to the police?

2. The professional duty of confidentiality, however, applies in *all* circumstances, including voluntary disclosures by a lawyer outside of any litigation process.[2] This fiduciary duty arises from agency law but is codified in professional rules of conduct, which are often referenced in breach of fiduciary duty lawsuits brought by clients against their lawyers.[3] In discussing Purcell's contact with the police, the court referred to the then-applicable Massachusetts professional discipline rule, which was based on the ABA Model Code of Professional Responsibility. Massachusetts subsequently adopted a version of the Model Rules.

---

2. The professional rule of confidentiality applies even when a lawyer is subpoenaed to testify at trial, as Purcell was. The rule requires the lawyer to protect the client's confidentiality by asserting the attorney-client privilege, where applicable, but then recognizes an exception permitting the attorney to testify when required by law or court order, as when the court denies the applicability of the attorney-client privilege. *See* MR 1.6, cmt [12].

3. *See, e.g.*, MR, Scope, at [20] ("Violation of a Rule should not itself give rise to a cause of action against a lawyer nor should it create any presumption in such case that a legal duty has been breached. . . . Nevertheless, since the Rules do establish standards of conduct by lawyers, a lawyer's violation of a Rule may be evidence of breach of the applicable standard of conduct.").

3. The professional duty of confidentiality applies outside the litigation process. But what if litigation is already pending when a lawyer learns of a threat to human life in connection with that litigation? Which legal doctrine would apply if, while representing Tyree in his arson trial, Purcell learned that Tyree was planning to kill a prosecution witness, and Purcell wanted to contact law enforcement authorities in order to prevent that harm?[4]

4. If the attorney-client privilege is invoked only in litigation, then why is it important for business lawyers to understand how the privilege works? The answer is that disputes between business parties commonly arise, and these disputes sometimes result in lawsuits: as a result, business lawyers need to be proactive in ensuring that the privilege will apply when sensitive communications are sought in future litigation. As one commentator notes, "[L]itigators go to court to defend their client's privilege or to assault their adversary's privilege claims . . . [b]ut often they are trying to overcome their business partner's mistakes, or take advantage of the other side's business lawyer's ignorance."[5]

To understand what these mistakes might be, we turn now to the substantive requirements of both privilege and confidentiality, first with respect to securing prima facie protection and then to the applicable exceptions. Throughout this material, try to keep in mind the significant differences between the two doctrines.

B. PRIMA FACIE PROTECTION OF CLIENT INFORMATION

1. Attorney-Client Privilege

Section 68 of the Restatement provides a generally accepted formulation of the scope of the prima facie protection of the attorney-client privilege:

> Except as otherwise provided . . . , the attorney-client privilege may be invoked . . . with respect to:
> (1) a communication
> (2) made between privileged persons
> (3) in confidence
> (4) for the purpose of obtaining or providing legal assistance for the client.

---

4. In In re Grand Jury Investigation, 902 N.E.2d 929 (Mass. 2009), a lawyer was representing a father in a care and protection proceeding in juvenile court. After the judge denied the father visitation rights, the lawyer received six voice messages from the father, within a 16-minute period, containing inappropriate comments regarding the juvenile court judge and a social worker, including a message that "some people need to be exterminated with prejudice" and that he knew where the judge lived and that the judge had two children. The lawyer alerted the trial court security department, and the husband was subsequently charged with threatening to commit murder and intimidating a judge.

5. Spahn, *supra* n. 1.

a. Communications

Purcell learned of Tyree's plan based on a conversation he had with Tyree. If Purcell had learned of the plan only because he visited Tyree at his apartment and observed the incendiary materials and other physical evidence, then the attorney-client privilege would not have applied, and he would have been compelled to testify at Tyree's trial. On the other hand, if he had discovered the physical evidence as a direct result of a privileged communication from Tyree, then the evidence would still be subject to prima facie protection.[6] Communications are not limited to words, but also include physical gestures intended to convey information, as well as other nonverbal forms of communication.

b. Between Privileged Persons

Privileged persons include the client (as well a prospective client), the lawyer, agents who facilitate communications between them, and agents of the lawyers who facilitate the representation.[7]

Privileged agents of the lawyer include nonlawyer employees such as receptionists, administrative assistants, and paralegals, as well as independent contractors who facilitate the representation, such as accountants and nontestifying experts. Privileged agents of the client, however, are limited to those agents who facilitate the *communication* itself.[8] This may surprise many business clients, who like to work in teams, including investment bankers and other financial advisors and public relations consultants. The presence of such a non-privileged person in a meeting typically prevents the client's communication from being prima facie protected, and sharing the communication with such a person after the fact often constitutes a waiver of the privilege. For example, in American Legacy Found. v. Lorillard Tobacco Co., 2004 Del. Ch. LEXIS 157 (Del. Ch. 2004), the court held that the client waived the privilege by sharing its law firm's advice with its outside public relations

---

6. *See, e.g.*, People v. Meredith, 631 P.2d 46 (Cal. 1981) (observation by defense counsel or his investigator, which is the product of a privileged communication, may not be admitted unless the defense, by altering or removing physical evidence, has precluded the prosecution from making that same observation).

7. *See* RLGL §70.

8. *See, e.g.*, Pearlstein v. Blackberry Ltd., 2019 WL 2281280 (S.D.N.Y. 2019) (inclusion of company's outside financial advisor in communications with outside counsel did not waive privilege because the advisor was an agent of the client whose role in the communications was limited to explaining the transactions at issue so that the attorneys could provide effective legal advice). Some courts limit this "third party as agent" test to consultants who perform a translator-like function; others more broadly apply the test to third parties who "facilitate" the attorney's ability to render legal advice. *See infra* Chapter 10: Privilege and Confidentiality Revisited.

firm.[9] Lawyers should not permit nonclients to participate in sensitive discussions without first clarifying their role and determining that the benefits of that person's presence outweigh the risk of a subsequent privilege denial.[10]

Would the privilege apply if Purcell overheard Tyree tell his brother that he was going to burn down the building? What if Purcell got a telephone call from Tyree's brother relaying Tyree's threat and requesting Purcell's help in persuading Tyree not to carry out his threat?

c. In Confidence

The presence of a nonprivileged person prevents a client's communication from being protected because the privilege protects only confidential communications. A communication is confidential if the client reasonably believes that it will not be heard or read except by the lawyer or other privileged persons.[11] So if Tyree's brother was present when Tyree communicated his threat to Purcell, the privilege would not have applied.

Lawyers have some control over who is present during in-person discussions, but problems may arise when the client communicates with the lawyer from outside the office, particularly when the communication involves digital technology. In order to preserve the privilege, lawyers should advise their clients to take precautions when making sensitive communications; for example, avoid using an unsecure internet connection or monitored email system.[12]

A client's identity is generally not protected under the attorney-client privilege. However, there are circumstances in which revealing the client's identity will necessarily disclose the content of an otherwise confidential client communication. For example, the Restatement gives the example of a tax lawyer whose client confides that he has not paid back taxes, a fact unknown to the authorities. The lawyer pays the money on the client's behalf, in order to avoid the further accrual of penalties, but does not reveal the client's name. The lawyer cannot be required to testify to the client's identity in that situation because to do so would reveal the client's confidential communication that he owes back taxes.[13]

---

9. The court acknowledged that other courts have held that communications with a client's outside public relations firm may come within the privilege, but only when the outside firm serves as the "functional equivalent" of an in-house public relations department. This controversial doctrine applies primarily to entity clients, where the question arises which constituents act on behalf of the entity in communications to and from its counsel. These are complex questions that we address in a subsequent chapter. *See infra* Chapter 10: Privilege and Confidentiality Revisited.

10. *See* RLGL §70, cmt e.

11. *Id.* at §71.

12. *See, e.g.*, In re Asia Global Crossing, Ltd., 322 B.R. 242, 257 (S.D.N.Y. 2005) (in dispute between employees and their former employer's trustee in bankruptcy, whether privilege protected employees' email communications to their personal attorney, using the employer's email system, depended on whether the employees had a reasonable expectation of privacy, considering: "(1) does the corporation maintain a policy banning personal or other objectionable use, (2) does the company monitor the use of the employee's computer or email, (3) do third parties have a right of access to the computer or emails, and (4) did the corporation notify the employee, or was the employee aware, of the use and monitoring policies.")

13. RLGL, §68, cmt g, Ill. 6.

d. For the Purpose of Obtaining or Providing Legal Assistance

The purpose of the privilege is to encourage clients to confide in their lawyers to enable the lawyer to provide effective legal advice or assistance. So it is not surprising that the privilege is limited to communications made for the purpose of securing legal advice or legal services from a lawyer. Did Tyree tell Purcell that he was planning to burn the apartment building for the purpose of seeking legal advice? As we will see when we read the rest of the *Purcell* opinion, this was an issue raised by the district attorney and resolved by the court in a controversial aspect of the opinion.

The mere fact that the recipient is a lawyer is not sufficient if the communication is for some other purpose. Consider the following illustration from the Restatement:

> Client and Lawyer have had a longstanding relationship. Client sends a letter to Lawyer offering Lawyer an opportunity to participate as an investor in a real-estate project. Lawyer has occasionally given Client legal advice and performed other legal services, and the two have engaged in real-estate transactions on other occasions. In the letter, Client discusses negotiations with the prospective seller, indicating the seller's willingness to sell and the likely price. The letter does not request or refer to any legal assistance. Unless other circumstances compel a contrary inference, a finding is warranted that Client consulted Lawyer for a business purpose.[14]

This example is clear, but real life is often messier. Assume that Client and Lawyer had engaged in many real-estate transactions in which Lawyer had simultaneously acted as business partner and legal representative.[15] Assume also that Client and Lawyer had previously discussed a possible legal problem with the property's title. In communicating with Lawyer, Client may have been seeking *both* legal and business advice. Even when a lawyer is not a participant in the transaction, business clients often rely on their lawyers to provide both legal knowledge and business savvy. When communications have a dual purpose, the privilege will apply only if the "primary" or "predominant" purpose was legal, as opposed to business, in nature.[16]

---

14. *Id.* §72, cmt c, Ill. 1.

15. For a discussion of the conflicts of interest that exist when lawyers engage in business transactions with their clients, *see infra* Chapter 5: Conflicts of Interest: Current Clients.

16. *See, e.g.,* William F. Shea, LLC v. Bonutti Research, Inc., 2013 WL 1499609, *1 (S.D. Ohio 2013) ("When a document contains both legal and other advice (e.g., business or financial advice), the applicability of the privilege turns on whether the 'predominant purpose' of the document was legal advice."); North Shore Gas Co. v. Elgin, Joliet & Eastern Ry. Co., 164 F.R.D. 59, 61 (N.D. Ill. 1995) ("For the privilege to apply, however, the attorney must be involved in a legal, rather than a business capacity, and the confidential communication must be primarily legal in nature."). *But see* RLGL §72 cmt c (dual purpose communication will be protected so long as the client sought "to gain advantage from the lawyer's legal skills and training, . . . even if the client may expect to gain other benefits as well, such as business advice or the comfort of friendship").

Clients sometimes think that copying the lawyer on written communications, or including the lawyer in a meeting with nonlawyers, will result in the communication being privileged. Given that the primary or predominant purpose of the communication must be legal, this tactic is clearly mistaken, and lawyers should take steps to ensure that their clients understand this aspect of the privilege.[17]

2. Professional Duty of Confidentiality

Model Rule 1.6(a) provides that unless there is an applicable exception, "[a] lawyer shall not reveal information relating to the representation of a client."[18] The Model Rules provide similar protection to former and prospective clients.[19] The prima facie coverage of the rule of confidentiality could not be broader. *All* information is prima facie protected if it relates to the representation, no matter how the information was learned or what was its source. No worries about limitations concerning dual purpose communications or the presence of nonprivileged persons. Indeed, the rule protects information that is generally known or even information that is a matter of public record.[20] Unlike the attorney-client privilege, the rule protects the client's identity, which means that, absent client consent, lawyers may not use the names of their clients on their websites or in other forms of advertising.

Rule 1.6(a) is not limited to intentional or knowing disclosures of client information; nevertheless, Rule 1.6(c) expressly provides that "[a] lawyer shall make reasonable efforts to prevent the inadvertent or unauthorized disclosure of, or unauthorized access to, information relating to the representation of a client." We will return to this provision after we examine the applicable exceptions to both privilege and confidentiality.

---

17. Moreover, even when the primary purpose of the communication is legal, the presence of nonprivileged persons will prevent the communication from being privileged, as discussed above.

18. MR 1.8(b) also provides that a lawyer may not "*use* information relating to representation of a client to the disadvantage of a client" (emphasis added), unless there is an applicable exception.

19. The rules governing the disclosure of information relating to a former or prospective client are the same as for current clients. MR 1.9(c)(2); 1.18(b). However, the rules governing the *use* of such information, to the disadvantage of the former or prospective client, are slightly less stringent. *See* MR 1.9(c)(1) (additional exception when the information is "generally known"); 1.18(b) (same rule as for former clients).

20. *See* ABA Formal Ethics Op. 18-480 (2018). In 2013, the Virginia Supreme Court held that the First Amendment protects a lawyer's right to disclose and publicly discuss confidential, even embarrassing, public information about a client without the client's consent, at least in nonpending cases. *See* Hunter v. Virginia State Bar ex rel. Third District Comm., 744 S.E.2d 611 *cert. denied* 570 U.S. 919 (2013). That decision has been criticized by most legal ethicists and appears to be an outlier.

Under the Model Code, prima facie protection was more limited, covering only "confidences," defined as information protected under the attorney-client privilege, and "secrets," defined as "other information gained in the professional relationship that the client has requested be held inviolate or the disclosure of which would be embarrassing or would likely be detrimental to the client." Model Code, DR 4-101. Some jurisdictions have retained versions of Rule 1.6 that are based on the Model Code. *See, e.g.,* N.Y. Rules of Prof'l Conduct, R. 1.6(a).

C. APPLICABLE EXCEPTIONS

1. Attorney-Client Privilege

Generally recognized exceptions to the privilege include communications (1) in furtherance of a crime or fraud; (2) with a deceased client, in a dispute between claimants through that client; (3) relevant to an alleged breach of duty by the lawyer to his client or vice versa; (4) relevant to an issue concerning an attested document, when the lawyer is an attesting witness; and (5) relevant to a matter of common interest between two or more jointly represented clients, in an action between the clients. In addition, a client may expressly consent to disclosure or may impliedly waive protection of the privilege.[21] As we will see, many of these exceptions have analogies to exceptions recognized under the professional rule of confidentiality. The exceptions most relevant to business lawyers are the crime-fraud exception, the joint client exception in an action between the clients, express consent, and implied waiver.

a. Crime-Fraud Exception

Aside from consent or waiver, the *crime-fraud* exception is the most frequently invoked by opponents seeking to avoid application of the privilege. The availability of this exception is addressed in the remainder of the opinion in *Purcell*. The court's discussion is worth analyzing, not only because it highlights distinctions between the crime-fraud exception and an analogous exception under the rule of confidentiality, but also because it raises important distinctions between the crime-fraud exception and the prima facie protection of the privilege. Not everyone agrees with how the *Purcell* court resolved these issues. After reviewing the facts of *Purcell*, consider the following excerpt from the opinion.

Purcell v. District Attorney for the Suffolk District
676 N.E.2d 436 (Mass. 1997)

WILKINS, Chief Justice. . . .

The district attorney announces the issue in his brief to be whether a crime-fraud exception to the testimonial privilege applies in this case. He asserts that, even if Tyree's communication with Purcell was made as part of his consultation concerning the eviction proceeding, Tyree's communication concerning his contemplated criminal conduct is not protected by the privilege. We shall first consider the case on the assumption that Tyree's statements to Purcell are protected by the attorney-client privilege unless the crime-fraud exception applies.

---

21. Strictly speaking, consent and waiver differ from true exceptions because when an exception applies, the privilege never attached.

"It is the purpose of the crime-fraud exception to the attorney-client privilege to assure that the 'seal of secrecy,' . . . between lawyer and client does not extend to communications 'made for the purpose of getting advice for the commission of a fraud' or crime." There is no public interest in the preservation of the secrecy of that kind of communication.

Our cases have not defined a crime-fraud exception to the attorney-client privilege with any precision. . . . The Proposed Massachusetts Rules of Evidence adequately define the crime-fraud exception to the lawyer-client privilege set forth in Rule 502(d)(1) as follows: "If the services of the lawyer were sought or obtained to enable or aid anyone to commit or plan to commit what the client knew or reasonably should have known to be a crime or fraud." We need not at this time consider seemingly minor variations of the exception expressed in various sources. The applicability of the exception, like the existence of the privilege, is a question of fact for the judge.

The district attorney rightly grants that he, as the opponent of the application of the testimonial privilege, has the burden of showing that the exception applies. . . . We conclude that facts supporting the applicability of the crime-fraud exception must be proved by a preponderance of the evidence. However, on a showing of a factual basis adequate to support a reasonable belief that an in camera review of the evidence may establish that the exception applies, the judge has discretion to conduct such an in camera review. Once the judge sees the confidential information, the burden of proof normally will be unimportant.

In this case, in deciding whether to conduct a discretionary in camera review of the substance of the conversation concerning arson between Tyree and Purcell, the judge would have evidence tending to show that Tyree discussed a future crime with Purcell and that thereafter Tyree actively prepared to commit that crime. Without this evidence, the crime of arson would appear to have no connection with Tyree's eviction proceeding and Purcell's representation of Tyree. With this evidence, however, a request that a judge inquire in camera into the circumstances of Tyree's apparent threat to burn the apartment building would not be a call for a "fishing expedition," and a judge might be justified in conducting such an inquiry. The evidence in this case, however, was not sufficient to warrant the judge's finding that Tyree consulted Purcell for the purpose of obtaining advice in furtherance of a crime. Therefore, the order denying the motion to quash because the crime-fraud exception applied cannot be upheld.

There is a consideration in this case that does not appear in other cases that we have seen concerning the attorney-client privilege. The testimony that the prosecution seeks from Purcell is available only because Purcell reflectively made a disclosure, relying on this court's disciplinary rule which permitted him to do so. Purcell was under no ethical duty to disclose Tyree's intention to commit a crime. He did so to protect the lives and property of others, a purpose that underlies a lawyer's discretionary right stated in the disciplinary rules. The limited facts in the record strongly suggest that Purcell's disclosures

C. Applicable Exceptions   77

to the police served the beneficial public purpose on which the disciplinary rule was based.

We must be cautious in permitting the use of client communications that a lawyer has revealed only because of a threat to others. Lawyers will be reluctant to come forward if they know that the information that they may disclose may lead to adverse consequences to their clients. A practice of the use of such disclosures might prompt a lawyer to warn a client in advance that the disclosure of certain information may not be held confidential, thereby chilling free discourse between lawyer and client and reducing the prospect that the lawyer will learn of a serious threat to the well-being of others. To best promote the purposes of the attorney-client privilege, the crime-fraud exception should apply only if the communication seeks assistance in or furtherance of future criminal conduct. When the opponent of the privilege argues that the communication itself may show that the exception applies and seeks its disclosure in camera, the judge, in the exercise of discretion on the question whether to have an in camera proceeding, should consider if the public interest is served by disclosure, even in camera, of a communication whose existence is known only because the lawyer acted against his client's interests under the authority of a disciplinary rule. The facts of each situation must be considered. . . .

[T]he district attorney's brief appears to abandon its earlier concession that all communications between Tyree and Purcell should be treated as protected by the attorney-client privilege unless the crime-fraud exception applies. The question whether the attorney-client privilege is involved at all will be open on remand. We, therefore, discuss the issue.

The attorney-client privilege applies only when the client's communication was for the purpose of facilitating the rendition of legal services. The burden of proving that the attorney-client privilege applies to a communication rests on the party asserting the privilege. The motion judge did not pass on the question whether the attorney-client privilege applied to the communication at all but rather went directly to the issue of the crime-fraud exception, although not using that phrase.

A statement of an intention to commit a crime made in the course of seeking legal advice is protected by the privilege, unless the crime-fraud exception applies. That exception applies only if the client or prospective client seeks advice or assistance in furtherance of criminal conduct. It is agreed that Tyree consulted Purcell concerning his impending eviction. Purcell is a member of the bar, and Tyree either was or sought to become Purcell's client. The serious question concerning the application of the privilege is whether Tyree informed Purcell of the fact of his intention to commit arson for the purpose of receiving legal advice or assistance in furtherance of criminal conduct. Purcell's presentation of the circumstances in which Tyree's statements were made is likely to be the only evidence presented.

This is not a case in which our traditional view that the testimonial privileges should be construed strictly should be applied. A strict construction of the privilege that would leave a gap between the circumstances in which the crime-fraud exception applies and the circumstances in which a communication is protected by the attorney-client privilege would make no sense. The attorney-client privilege "is founded upon the necessity, in the interest and administration of justice, of the aid of persons having knowledge of the law and skilled in its practice, which assistance can only be safely and readily availed of when free from the consequences or apprehension of disclosure." Unless the crime-fraud exception applies, the attorney-client privilege should apply to communications concerning possible future, as well as past, criminal conduct, because an informed lawyer may be able to dissuade the client from improper future conduct and, if not, under the ethical rules may elect in the public interest to make a limited disclosure of the client's threatened conduct.

A judgment should be entered in the county court ordering that the order denying the motion to quash any subpoena issued to Purcell to testify at Tyree's trial is vacated and that the matter is remanded for further proceedings with this opinion. . . .

NOTES AND QUESTIONS

1. The *Purcell* court held that the crime-fraud exception would not apply unless Tyree communicated his threat to burn down the building for the purpose of securing the lawyer's assistance in furthering his criminal intent, which he apparently did not. According to the Restatement, the crime-fraud exception applies when the client "consults a lawyer for the purpose, later accomplished, of obtaining assistance to engage in a crime or fraud or aiding a third person to do so" or when "regardless of the client's purpose at the time of consultation, [the client] uses the lawyer's advice or other services to engage in or assist a crime or fraud." RLGL §82 (2000). It does not matter whether the lawyer was aware of the client's intent or whether the legal services sought were themselves lawful, e.g., drafting the documents necessary to secure and close a business deal. *See id.* at cmt c.

2. If Tyree did not communicate his threat to secure his lawyer's assistance in the intended crime, then why did he reveal his intention to Purcell? Perhaps he made the statement reflexively, in a moment of anger. In any event, if the communication itself was not for the purpose of securing legal advice or assistance, then why was the communication prima facie protected? This is perhaps the most controversial aspect of the *Purcell* opinion. What explanation did the court give? Do you find this explanation satisfactory? Would the court's decision have been more persuasive if the context in which Tyree disclosed his preparations to burn down the building was a discussion in which Purcell was relaying the building owner's offer to find Tyree another apartment and Tyree

was explaining how his anger at the owner for firing and then evicting him prevented him from accepting that offer?

3. As the *Purcell* court noted, the traditional view is that the attorney-client privilege should be "strictly construed," implying that close cases ought to be decided in favor of disclosure. Strict scrutiny is considered appropriate because recognizing the privilege is inconsistent with the general duty to disclose relevant information at trial, and thus the privilege impedes the search for truth.[22] The court nevertheless concluded that this was not a case in which strict scrutiny should be implied. Why not?

4. One concern expressed by the *Purcell* court was that, if the communication did not receive facie protection, then Tyree might not have confided his intent to Purcell; Purcell would not then have been in a position either to attempt to dissuade Tyree or, if that failed, to disclose the threat to prevent the harm from occurring, which he was entitled to do under the disciplinary rule. (To test your understanding of the procedural difference between the privilege and the rule of confidentiality, can you explain how it is that Purcell was permitted to disclose Tyree's threat to law enforcement authorities, but not in testimony at Tyree's trial?) But isn't there a breakdown in logic here? If Tyree knew that the disciplinary rule permitted Purcell to go to the police, wouldn't he also be unlikely to communicate his threat to Purcell? Realistically, shouldn't we assume that Tyree had no understanding of the specific parameters of either the privilege or the rule of confidentiality? If so, then does it matter whether his communication was protected under the privilege?

   The court considered not only Tyree's motivations but also Purcell's. How did the court believe that Purcell's conduct might be affected by the scope of the prima facie protection extended under the evidentiary rule? Do you think Purcell would have acted differently if he thought he might have to testify at Tyree's trial? Would you?

5. Courts outside Massachusetts might find that Tyree's threat was not prima facie protected under the attorney-client privilege.[23] Would they find the threat prima facie protected under Model Rule 1.6(a)? How did the information "relate" to the representation? According to the Restatement, "[i]n the course of representation, a lawyer may learn confidential information about the client that is not necessary for the representation but which is of a personal or proprietary nature or other character such that the client evidently would not wish it disclosed,"

---

22. *See, e.g.,* U.S. v. (Under Seal), 784 F.2d 871, 875 (4th Cir. 1984).

23. *See* U.S. v. Alexander, 289 F.3d 811 (9th Cir. 2002) (lawyer's testimony that client communicated threats to kill others not covered by attorney-client privilege because they were not made for the purpose of seeking legal advice).

and such information is protected by the rule of confidentiality.[24] Do you agree that this type of information should be protected unless an exception applies?

6. One explanation for the stricter rules traditionally applied to the scope of protection under the privilege, as opposed to the duty of confidentiality, is that the purposes of the two doctrines differ. The acknowledged purpose underlying the privilege is strictly consequential—its purpose is to encourage clients to confide in their lawyers in order to receive more effective legal advice. While such encouragement is also an important consideration underlying the broader duty of confidentiality, the fiduciary duty is also viewed as embodying a nonconsequentialist rationale of protecting a client's privacy and autonomy. Think about this in the medical context. Patients confide much harmful or embarrassing information to their physicians, without necessarily understanding whether the information is legally protected, because they trust physicians to be discreet. Even if disclosure were not unlawful, it would be a violation of that trust for a physician to disclose patient information, absent some compelling reason to do so. Professional duties of confidentiality, which were initially designed as aspirational, and not mandatory, express the professions' commitment to maintain that trust.

Clients intending death or serious bodily harm to another may be unlikely to confide in a lawyer for the purpose of seeking assistance in furthering their criminal scheme. And they are unlikely to understand the intricacies of either the privilege or the rule of confidentiality. But clients engaged in economic crimes and frauds frequently need the assistance of a lawyer to further their schemes, and business clients are more likely than others to have at least some understanding of the scope of the lawyer's duty of confidentiality. We will explore these issues further when we get to the analogous "crime-fraud" exceptions to the professional rule of confidentiality. Before doing so, we need to briefly introduce the exception for communications between joint clients and the concepts of *consent* and *waiver*.

b. *Joint Clients in Action Between Them*

When a lawyer jointly represents two or more clients in a matter, the communications of either client to the lawyer related to the subject matter of the joint representation are privileged against third persons, and each client may invoke the privilege regardless of which one of them made the communication. Under an exception to the privilege, however, these communications are not privileged in subsequent litigation between the previously jointly represented clients.[25]

Even when the clients are represented by separate lawyers, the lawyers may enter into a joint defense agreement, in which they agree that the lawyers

---

24. *See* RLGL, §59, cmt d.
25. *See* RLGL §75.

will share confidential communications from their respective clients in order to develop a joint strategy. These agreements are common among separately represented parties in governmental investigations or criminal proceedings. As with previously represented co-clients, however, the joint defense privilege does not apply in subsequent litigation between the clients.[26]

Although the joint defense privilege was developed in matters involving pending or anticipated litigation, it has also been applied to two more clients with a common interest in a nonlitigation matter, such as pre-merger or pre-acquisition discussions concerning matters of common legal interest between the negotiating parties. Widely accepted by federal courts, the extent to which state courts recognize this common interest doctrine outside the litigation context is unclear.[27] Of course, where it is recognized, the privilege cannot be asserted in subsequent litigation between the parties themselves.

c. Consent and Waiver

As we will see, the professional rule of confidentiality recognizes the ability of a client to give "informed consent" to the disclosure of otherwise confidential information. When it comes to the attorney-client privilege, however, "informed" consent is not typically required; either the client, the client's lawyer, or another authorized agent may expressly agree not to assert the privilege, thereby permitting the disclosure of otherwise privileged information, either in discovery or at trial. Sometimes clients want to disclose the information to one adversary, such as a governmental agency investigating alleged misconduct, but to retain the privilege as to other potential adversaries, such as persons who might subsequently sue the client based on the same misconduct. Most authorities do not permit such "selective" or "limited" waivers, on the ground that permitting them is unnecessary to achieve the purpose of encouraging clients to communicate fully with their lawyers.[28] As a result, voluntary agreements to disclose to a single adversary will result in loss of the privilege for all subsequent purposes.

Aside from express consent or agreement, a client or the client's agent may inadvertently *waive* the privilege in a number of ways, for example: (1) failing to raise an objection; (2) mistakenly disclosing the information without taking reasonable precautions to prevent such inadvertent disclosure; and (3) disclosing part of a confidential communication.[29] Lawyers are often the source of an inadvertent waiver; for example, by failing to

---

26. *Id.* at §76.

27. *See, e.g.,* Jared S. Sunshine, The Secrets of Corporate Courtship and Marriage: Evaluating Common Interest Privilege When Companies Combine in Mergers, 60 S.C. L. Rev. 301, 310 (2017).

28. *See, e.g.,* In re Pacific Pictures Corp., 679 F.3d 1121 (9th Cir. 2012).

29. *See generally* RLGL §§78 (agreement, disclaimer, or failure to object); 79 (subsequent disclosure); 80 (putting assistance or communication in issue).

2. Professional Duty of Confidentiality

reasonably guard against disclosing confidential communications to non-privileged persons.[30]

Model Rule 1.6(a) provides that a lawyer may not reveal information related to a client representation "unless the client gives informed consent, the disclosure is impliedly authorized in order to carry out the representation or the disclosure is permitted by paragraph (b)."

a. Informed Consent

"Informed consent" is defined in Rule 1.0(e) as "the agreement by a person to a proposed course of conduct after the lawyer has communicated adequate information and explanation about the material risks of and reasonably available alternatives to the proposed course of conduct." The term is used throughout the Model Rules, including with respect to limited scope representations[31] and conflicts of interest.[32] Because questions concerning the extent of a required consent arise most frequently in conflicts of interest situations, we will defer a detailed discussion of the term until the basic conflicts chapter.[33] For now, the following is a brief description of the lawyer's duty to explain the implications of joint representation for the confidentiality of otherwise protected information.

When a lawyer jointly represents two or more clients in a matter, there is frequently a conflict of interests between them. Most such conflicts are consentable, but in obtaining the informed consent of each client, the lawyer will need to explain the effect of common representation on both the attorney-client privilege and confidentiality. With respect to the latter, the lawyer will usually be required to explain that all information bearing on the matter will be shared among the jointly represented clients and that

---

30. According to one commentator, the leading causes of inadvertent disclosure leading to a privilege waiver are: (1) the sheer volume of recorded communications, including electronic communications, (2) the ease of dissemination (e.g., clicking the opposing attorney's name rather than the client's name, on an email), and (3) lawyers' failure to adequately advise their clients about the need to protect privileged communications. *See* Paula Shaefer, Technology's Triple Threat to the Attorney-Client Privilege, 2013 Prof. Law. 171 (2013).

31. Recall that in Genesis Merchant Partners, LP v. Gilbride, Tusa, Last & Spellane, LLC, discussed in Chapter 2, there were factual questions as to whether the lawyer properly limited the scope of the representation, including whether the law firm "ensured that Genesis understood that [the law firm] was not responsible for perfecting the security interests in the life insurance policies." *See supra* Chapter 2: Formation, Scope, and Termination of the Attorney-Client Relationship. In limited scope representations, New York Rule 1.2(c), like the Model Rule, required that Genesis have given "informed consent" to the limitation.

32. *See infra* Chapter 5: Conflicts of Interest: Current Clients; Chapter 6: Conflicts of Interest: Former Clients, Prospective Clients, and Government Lawyers.

33. *See infra* Chapter 5: Conflicts of Interest: Current Clients.

joint representation is inappropriate if a client wants to keep information from another client.[34]

b. Implied Authority

We previously encountered the term "impliedly authorized" in discussing a lawyer's ability to take action in furtherance of the representation without first consulting the client under Rule 1.2(a).[35] Unfortunately, this term is not defined, and there is no consensus as to its general meaning. One interpretation is that it refers to circumstances where a lawyer reasonably believes that the client would agree to the proposed course of conduct, without prior consultation, as when the benefit of the action is clear and there is no significant risk of harm.[36] Another, potentially broader interpretation is that, in the absence of contrary client instruction, lawyers may take any lawful measure reasonably calculated to advance a client's objectives.[37]

Situations likely to give rise to a finding of implied authority to disclose confidential information include the following: delivering a former client's file to successor counsel to protect the former client's interest;[38] discussing a client's matter with other lawyers in the firm, in the absence of special circumstances;[39] discussing a client's matter with an outside lawyer for the client's benefit, but only when such disclosures will not waive attorney-client privilege or otherwise harm the client;[40] and revealing information relating to a data breach if doing so will advance the client's interests and will not adversely affect the client.[41] Do these authorities indicate a preference for the narrower or broader interpretation of "impliedly authorized"? Which interpretation do you prefer?

c. Rule 1.6(b) Exceptions

Model Rule 1.6(b) provides for seven exceptions. With respect to each, the lawyer is *permitted*, but not required to disclose information relating to the representation. Keep in mind that state rules often differ from the Model Rules, and Rule 1.6 is perhaps the rule most likely to be subject to state variation. One of the ways in which some states vary the exceptions is to *require* disclosure in some circumstances. Because the confidentiality exceptions are subject to considerable state variation, the following discussion will indicate some of the variations you should anticipate finding.

---

34. *See* MR 1.7, cmts [30]-[31].
35. *See supra* Chapter 3: Competence and Diligence; Control and Communication; Fees.
36. *See* Nancy J. Moore, Why Is There No Clear Doctrine of Informed Consent for Lawyers? 47 U. of Tol. L. Rev. 133, 152-53 (2015), discussed *supra* Chapter 3, at n. 19.
37. *See id.* (discussing RLGL §21).
38. *See* N.C. Ethics Op. 2015-5 (2015).
39. *See* MR 1.6, cmt [5].
40. ABA Formal Ethics Op. 98-411 (1998).
41. ABA Formal Ethics Op. 18-483 (2018).

(1) Preventing Physical Harm

Model Rule 1.6(b)(1) provides that a lawyer may disclose client information when reasonably necessary to "prevent reasonably certain death or substantial bodily harm." In finding that the lawyer in *Purcell* properly disclosed Tyree's threat to law enforcement, the court relied on a then-existing Massachusetts disciplinary rule that permitted a lawyer to reveal "[t]he intention of his client to commit a crime and the information necessary to prevent the crime."[42] This was the former Model Code provision, which some states continue to follow.[43] The current Model Rule, which was amended in 2002, is both broader and narrower than the Model Code provision. It is broader because it is not limited to crimes (or even illegal conduct), and it is not limited to conduct by a client. It is narrower because it permits disclosure only when there is a threat of physical harm and that harm will be substantial. Some states continue to use the Model Rule as it was originally adopted in 1983, which permitted disclosure only when necessary "to prevent *the client* from committing a *criminal* act that the lawyer believes is likely to result in *imminent* death or substantial bodily harm."[44]

Some jurisdictions *require* disclosure to prevent death or reasonably certain harm.[45] Why do you think the Model Rule and most states have a rule that is merely permissive? Which rule is preferable? Consider not only the public interest in protecting potential victims, but also the lawyer's own interest in having or avoiding the exercise of discretion in the matter of disclosure.

(2) Preventing Economic Harm

Model Rule 1.6(b)(2) provides that a lawyer may disclose client information when reasonably necessary "to prevent the client from committing a crime or fraud that is reasonably certain to result in substantial injury to the financial interests or property of another and in furtherance of which the client has used or is using the lawyer's services."

States like Michigan retain the former Model Code provision, limiting disclosure to a client's intent to commit a future crime, regardless whether the harm to be prevented is physical or economic.[46] States like Rhode Island retain the original Model Rules provision, which did *not* permit *any* disclosure to prevent merely economic (and not physical) harm, regardless of whether the client's conduct was criminal or fraudulent.[47] Some other states have rules similar to the current Model Rule, but without the requirement

---

42. 676 N.E.2d at 438 (citing DR 4-101(C)(3)).

43. *See, e.g.*, Mich. Rules of Prof'l Conduct, R. 1.6(4).

44. MR. 1.6(b)(1) (emphasis added). For one of a small number of states that continue to use this version of the rule, *see* R.I. Rules of Prof'l Conduct, R. 1.6(b)(1).

45. *See, e.g.*, Iowa Rules of Prof'l Conduct, R. 1.6(c).

46. *See* Mich. Rules of Prof'l Conduct, R. 1.6(4).

47. *See* R.I. Rules of Prof'l Conduct, R. 1.6(b)(1).

that the lawyer's services have been used in furtherance of the crime or fraud.[48] And some states require disclosure of a client's intent to commit a crime or fraud.[49]

Consider a true story involving the Singer, Hutner law firm in New York, which settled lawsuits for around $10 million based on allegations that its lawyers had been accomplices in economic crimes and frauds committed by its client, a company called O.P.M. (which stood for "other people's money"). The following is a summary taken from a detailed and gripping account by journalist Stuart Taylor, which appeared in the *New York Times*.[50] Taylor's article is based on thousands of pages of depositions taken in a bankruptcy investigation of O.P.M. and is definitely worth reading in full.

THE SAGA OF SINGER HUTNER AND O.P.M.

Mordecai Weissman started O.P.M. with his good friend Myron Goodman in 1970. The company borrowed money to purchase computers and other business equipment and then leased the equipment to other companies. By the late 1970s, O.P.M. was one of the country's five largest computer-leasing companies, buying computers from IBM and other well-known companies and leasing them to large corporations such as AT&T and Revlon. Loans were obtained from a variety of reputable banks, insurance companies, and other financial institutions.

> Almost from the start, the company was basically insolvent and survived by means of fraud and bribery. A single computer would be used as collateral for two or three loans with different banks; the value of a given piece of equipment would be inflated to obtain larger loans. (Judge Haight, at the time of sentencing[51] told how "Mr. Goodman would crouch under a glass table with a flashlight and Mr. Weissman would trace the forged signatures.")

During this time, O.P.M.'s legal work was being handled by Andrew Reinhard, of Singer Hutner Levine & Seeman, a New York law firm. The firm's lawyers closed loans and issued the legal opinions relied on by lenders that O.P.M. had title to the computers and that the leases were lawful. The firm later insisted that prior to June 1980, none of them had any idea that O.P.M. was engaged in fraud. Goodman, however, said that Reinhard was a "knowing, although reluctant, participant" in at least one of the frauds.

On June 12, 1980, senior partner Joseph L. Hutner received an unexpected visit from Myron Goodman:

---

48. *See, e.g.,* Mass. Rules of Prof'l Conduct, R. 1.6(b)(2).

49. *See, e.g.,* N.J. Rules of Prof'l Conduct, R. 1.6(b)(1).

50. Stuart Taylor, Jr., Ethics and the Law: A Case History, The New York Times (Jan. 9, 1983), at https://www.nytimes.com/1983/01/09/magazine/ethics-and-the-law-a-case-history.html.

51. [Goodman and Weissman subsequently pleaded guilty to defrauding banks and other lenders of more than $200 million. — ED.]

The O.P.M. executive indicated that he was troubled, that he might have done something wrong in his stewardship of the company — something he could not set right because it involved millions of dollars more than he could raise. But during the meeting, . . . Goodman indicated he had no intention of telling Hutner any details unless he could be sure the attorney would not tell them to anyone else.

Hutner could not promise Goodman confidentiality due to his obligations to the company, which might require him to let Weissman know what Goodman had told him.

What prompted the meeting was that John Clifton, an in-house accountant, had discovered evidence of "the Rockwell lease fraud" and had written a letter to Reinhard, which he was going to deliver and then resign. Reinhard delivered the letter prior to Hutner's meeting with Goodman, but during a break in that meeting, Goodman obtained possession of the letter. Goodman and Singer Hutner later gave conflicting accounts of how that happened.

The lawyers say that Goodman snatched the letter unopened from Reinhard's hand or seized it from the top of the desk. Goodman says this was a "cover story" agreed upon between him and Reinhard – that in fact he found Reinhard reading the letter as he passed his office. By all accounts, Goodman took the Clifton letter with him when he left Singer Hutner that afternoon, still refusing to reveal what he had done wrong but insisting that it was all in the past.

Worried that Clifton might go to the authorities, Goodman promised him money to buy his silence and urged Hutner to speak with Clifton's attorney, William Davis. Davis's description of their meetings was that Hutner "seemed to know more than he let on, but seemed anxious to preserve a 'smoke screen' of deniability." Davis said he "had visions of him clamping his hands over his ears and running out of his office." Hutner denied this account, but a Singer Hutner memorandum from the time stated that Davis told them "that O.P.M. had perpetrated a multimillion-dollar fraud and that the opinion letters Singer Hutner had drawn up to obtain loans for O.P.M. had been based upon false documents." The memorandum also revealed that Davis had told them that, according to Clifton, O.P.M.'s survival depending on continuing the same type of activities.

Singer Hutner sought outside legal advice from a dean of Fordham Law School who later became a federal judge. The dean, who was an expert on attorney-client privilege, but not legal ethics, brought in a legal-ethics expert. Singer Hutner conveyed to them that they would like to continue representing the company unless they were required to withdraw. The Singer Hutner lawyers got the advice they were seeking. They were told that because Goodman had insisted that his wrongdoing was in the past, they were not permitted to disclose his confession of past frauds, except to Weissman. Nor were they required to withdraw the false opinion letters they had unknowingly given to the banks. Finally, they could continue to close new transactions, although the experts recommended that they require O.P.M. "to certify in writing the legitimacy of each new transaction." That was fine with Goodman, who had no scruples against signing false certifications.

The expert's advice was based on their agreement that the Singer Hutner lawyers did not "know" that the fraud was ongoing. But to maintain their lack of "knowledge," the Singer Hutner lawyers had to swallow O.P.M's attempts to explain away such extraordinary events as "bills of sale for computers that O.P.M. apparently did not have the money to buy, a signature on a document that looked [like a forgery; and] the sudden resignation of an outside accounting firm because of its suspicion that Goodman and Weissman had been looting their corporation at a time when it was insolvent."

Singer Hutner continued closing loans for O.P.M., but many of the leases later proved to be fraudulent. When Goodman finally revealed some of the details of his fraud, Singer Hutner decided to withdraw from representing O.P.M., although the lawyers were still being advised that they were not ethically obligated to do so. They withdrew gradually so that they would not prejudice the company while it was locating new counsel. They told no one of their knowledge of at least past frauds, including informing the new law firm Goodman sought to retain that the withdrawal was by mutual agreement. As a result, O.P.M. was able to go on to close more than $15 million in loans secured by fraudulent leases.

NOTES AND QUESTIONS

1. The New York ethics rule at the time was identical to the rule in Massachusetts, permitting a lawyer to disclose only "[t]he intention of his client to commit a crime and the information necessary to prevent the crime." Certainly under this rule, the lawyers were prohibited from revealing entirely past crimes, although it was unclear whether they were required to maintain confidentiality if O.P.M.'s past misconduct was part of an ongoing crime or series of crimes. According to the article, the lawyers (and the ethics expert) defended their silence on the ground that they did not "know" that O.P.M. was continuing to engage in criminal conduct. But did the ethics rule require such knowledge? Does the current Model Rule 1.6(b)(2)? Perhaps the answer to this question did not matter because disclosure was entirely discretionary, and the lawyers never contemplated disclosing what they knew to prevent future criminal activity.[52]

2. In *Purcell*, Tyree had expressly communicated his intent to commit a crime, so Purcell was safe in revealing that threat to the authorities. Under Model Rule 1.6(b)(2), all that is required is that the lawyer

---

52. Their biggest regret was that they deceived their fellow lawyers at Kaye Scholar, the firm that replaced them when they withdrew, thereby preventing those lawyers from avoiding being implicated in any ongoing criminal activity.

"*reasonably believes* [that disclosure is necessary]" to prevent the client from committing the requisite crime or fraud.[53] The "reasonable belief" standard requires that the lawyer subjectively hold that belief and that the belief is objectively reasonable.

3. As noted above, along with the prevention of death or substantial bodily harm, some jurisdictions *require* the lawyer to disclose when the lawyer "reasonably believes" that disclosure is necessary to prevent substantial economic harm.[54] If such a rule had been adopted in New York, could bar counsel have proved that the Singer Hutner lawyers reasonably believed that O.P.M. was continuing to engage in fraudulent transactions?

4. The Singer Hutner lawyers understood that the firm would have to resign if the lawyers "knew" that O.P.M. was continuing to engage in criminal conduct. This is because the professional conduct rules prohibit a lawyer from "knowingly" counseling or assisting a client in criminal or fraudulent conduct.[55] In a later chapter, we will return to the O.P.M. case and ask whether there was any point at which Singer Hutner should have concluded that it had to resign.[56] If the lawyers really believed that they weren't required to do so, why *did* they resign? Does knowing that Singer Hutner was later sued for assisting in O.P.M.'s crimes and frauds, and that the law firm settled those lawsuits for $10 million, help to answer that question? Or at least suggest why other lawyers might withdraw in questionable situations even when they are not required to do so?

5. If a lawyer withdraws because of fear of being implicated in the client's wrongdoing, then choosing to permissively disclose under Rule 1.6(b)(2) may be the best way to avoid being indicted or sued. But what if the lawyer is practicing in a state like Rhode Island, which prohibits disclosure to prevent merely economic harm? In 1983, after the ABA rejected an attempt to provide for permissive disclosure of economic crimes or frauds, the Reporter added a comment to Rule 1.6, which provided for what is now known as a *"noisy withdrawal."*[57] The comment reminded lawyers that they may not knowingly assist clients in crimes or fraud and that they may be required to withdraw in order to avoid doing so, but also stated that nothing in this or any other rule "prevents the

---

53. This is the same standard required for disclosures to prevent physical harm and to prevent, mitigate, or rectify substantial economic harm from a client's past crime or fraud.

54. *See supra* n. 49 & accompanying text.

55. At the time, the New York rule followed the Model Code, which provided that a lawyer shall not "[c]ounsel or assist his client in conduct that the lawyer knows to be illegal or fraudulent." Model Code, DR 7-102(A)(7) (1969). *See also* MR 1.2(d) ("A lawyer shall not counsel a client to engage, or assist a client, in conduct that the lawyer knows is criminal or fraudulent. . . .")

56. *See infra* Chapter 8: Limits of Zealous Representation II: Transactions.

57. For a discussion of the origin and meaning of this term, *see infra* Chapter 8: Limits of Zealous Representation II: Transactions.

lawyer from *giving notice of the fact of withdrawal*, and the lawyer may also *withdraw or disaffirm any opinion, document, affirmation, or the like*."[58] Although subsequently removed from Model Rule 1.6 as no longer necessary, that comment is still in the Rhode Island version of that rule.[59]

6. If the lawsuits against Singer Hutner had gone to trial, instead of being settled, would Goodman's "confession" to Hutner have been protected by the attorney-client privilege?

(3) Past Crimes or Frauds

Model Rule 1.6(b)(3) provides that a lawyer may disclose client information when reasonably necessary "to prevent, mitigate or rectify substantial injury to the financial interest or property of another that is reasonably certain to result or has resulted from the client's commission of a crime or fraud in furtherance of which the client has used the lawyer's services." The ABA adopted this rule in 2002, at the same time that it adopted Rule 1.6(b)(2). If the rule had been in place at the time the Singer Hutner lawyers learned of O.P.M.'s past crimes and frauds, then they could have disclosed that information to the lenders, even if they weren't confident that the wrongdoing was continuing.

Not all states permit the disclosure of past wrongdoing. And those that do typically require, as does the Model Rule, that the lawyer's services have been used in furthering the crime or fraud. That is not the case with the state variations of Rule 1.6(b)(2). What is the justification for distinguishing between past and future wrongdoing, making it easier for lawyers to disclose when the crime or fraud has not yet occurred?

(4) Lawyer Securing Legal Advice

Model Rule 1.6(b)(4) provides that a lawyer may disclose client information when reasonably necessary "to secure legal advice about the lawyer's compliance with these Rules."[60] The reason underlying this exception should be obvious: the rules are not always clear, and if we want to encourage lawyers to comply with their legal obligations, we need to make it possible for them to obtain legal advice. Large law firms typically have in-house ethics experts, but no such option exists for the majority of lawyers, who work either as sole practitioners or in small firms. The risk to clients is minimal because the advice sought must be "legal advice," which means that the consulted lawyer

---

58. MR. 1.6, cmt [15] (1983), in ABA, A Legislative History: The Development of the ABA Model Rules of Professional Conduct, 1982-2013 at 177 (2013) (emphasis added).

59. R.I. Rules of Prof'l Conduct, R. 1.6, cmt [4]. There is also a noisy withdrawal provision in the text of the New York rule. *See* N.Y. Rules of Prof'l Conduct, R. 1.6 (b)(3).

60. Advice concerning a lawyer's obligations under "these Rules" will typically include advice concerning obligations imposed by other law, such as the lawyer's duty to avoid aiding and abetting a client's criminal or fraudulent conduct, which is also set forth in Rule 1.2(d). *See also, e.g.,* MR 8.4(b) (lawyer subject to discipline for "commit[ting] a criminal act that reflects adversely on the lawyer's honest, trustworthiness or fitness as a lawyer in other respects").

in turn has obligations under both the attorney-client privilege and the duty of confidentiality.

This exception did not exist under either the Model Code or the 1983 Model Rules, and it has not been adopted in all states. Were the Singer Hutner lawyers justified in consulting outside lawyers and revealing detailed information concerning their representation of O.P.M.? The Rule 1.6 comment says that "in most situations, disclosing information to secure such advice will be impliedly authorized for the lawyer to carry out the representation."[61] Were the Singer Hutner lawyers impliedly authorized to seek outside legal advice? They wanted to stay in the case and not be forced to withdraw, but they also said that they were prepared to withdraw if that's what was ethically required. Was the advice sought "in order to carry out the representation"? What if they wanted to withdraw and disclose their concern that O.P.M. was continuing to defraud lenders?

Consulting lawyers should be sure that the person they are consulting is authorized to practice law in the jurisdiction because otherwise the advice sought will not be "legal advice," and therefore there is greater risk to the client. Many full-time law faculty are not licensed in the law school jurisdiction, so be careful before you call your former Professional Responsibility teacher for advice![62] Even then, and in states where the exception has not been adopted, you can permissibly seek advice by using a hypothetical situation, "so long as there is no reasonable likelihood that the listener will be able to ascertain the identity of the client or the situation involved."[63]

(5) Self-Defense and Asserting Claims Against the Client

Model Rule 1.6(b)(5) provides that a lawyer may disclose client information when reasonably necessary "to establish a claim or defense on behalf of the lawyer in a controversy between the lawyer and the client, to establish a defense to a criminal charge or civil claim against the lawyer based upon conduct in which the client was involved, or to respond to allegations in any proceeding concerning the lawyer's representation of the client."

The most common situation in which a lawyer asserts a claim against a client (usually a former client) is to collect the lawyer's legal fee. Other situations typically involve an in-house lawyer suing for wrongful termination or perhaps violation of a federal or state antidiscrimination statute. Disclosures limited to those necessary to collect a legal fee are permitted everywhere. However, wrongful termination and other lawsuits by current or former in-house lawyers are definitely controversial and for that reason are

---

61. MR 1.6, cmt [9].

62. For a discussion of the ability of a lawyer licensed in one jurisdiction to provide legal services in another jurisdiction, *see infra* Chapter 15: Unauthorized Practice of Law and Multijurisdictional Practice.

63. MR 1.6, cmt [4].

not recognized in all jurisdictions. We cover this material in a later chapter on special issues facing in-house lawyers.[64]

For now, let's focus on the self-defense exception. Understandably, lawyers are entitled to defend themselves in a "controversy between the lawyer and the client," which includes a client's lawsuit seeking either the recovery of legal fees already paid or damages as a result of either negligence or a breach of fiduciary duty. Similarly, lawyers need to defend themselves against either criminal charges or civil claims brought by someone other than the client but based on a client's conduct; for example, when the Singer Hutner lawyers were ultimately sued by the lenders for allegedly assisting in O.P.M.'s crimes and frauds or if Reinhard had been indicted. What if no charges have actually been brought but the lawyer is afraid that they will be? At what point is the lawyer entitled to disclose client information in order to avoid having charges filed? This question was raised in the following case involving a lawyer who filed an affidavit with the SEC and then gave a copy of that affidavit to counsel for plaintiffs suing the lawyer's former client, as well as the lawyer's former firm and several lawyers in that firm.

The plaintiffs and their counsel appealed from an order disqualifying plaintiffs' counsel and enjoining them and lawyer Stuart Charles Goldberg from disclosing confidential information regarding defendant Empire Fire and Marine Insurance Co. ("Empire"), a former client of Goldberg. Goldberg had previously disclosed confidential information concerning Empire to plaintiffs' counsel in a successful effort to avoid being included as a defendant in the lawsuit.

Meyerhofer v. Empire Fire and Marine Insurance Co.
497 F.2d 1190 (2d Cir. 1974)

MOORE, Circuit Judge:

[In May 1972 Empire made a public offering of 500,000 shares of stock, pursuant to a registration statement filed with the Securities and Exchange Commission ("SEC") in March. Empire was represented by the law firm of Sitomer, Sitomer & Porges ("Sitomer"). Goldberg was a lawyer in the Sitomer firm and had done some work on the registration statement. Plaintiffs purchased shares of Empire stock and subsequently sustained both actual and unrealized losses due to a precipitous fall in the share price, after Empire disclosed that its registration statement had contained material omissions. They retained the firm of Bernson, Hoeniger, Freitag & Abbey ("the Bernson firm") on behalf of themselves and other purchasers alleging violations of the Securities Acts, as well as common law negligence, fraud, and deceit.]

---

64. *See infra* Chapter 13: In-House Counsel.

The lawsuit was apparently inspired by a Form 10-K[65] which Empire filed with the SEC on or about April 12, 1973. This Form revealed that "The Registration Statement under the Securities Act of 1933 with respect to the public offering of the 500,000 shares of Common Stock did not disclose the proposed $200,000 payment to the law firm as well as certain other features of the compensation arrangements between the Company [Empire] and such law firm [defendant Sitomer, Sitomer & Porges]."...

The defendants named were Empire, officers and directors of Empire, the Sitomer firm and its three partners . . . , the managing underwriter, Stuart Charles Goldberg, originally alleged to have been a partner of the Sitomer firm, and certain selling stockholders of Empire shares.

On May 2, 1973, the complaint was served on the Sitomer defendants and [the underwriter]. No service was made on Goldberg who was then no longer associated with the Sitomer firm. However, he was advised by telephone that he had been made a defendant. Goldberg inquired of the Bernson firm as to the nature of the charges against him and was informed generally as to the substance of the complaint and in particular the lack of disclosure of the finder's fee arrangement. Thus informed, Goldberg requested an opportunity to prove his non-involvement in any such arrangement and his lack of knowledge thereof. . . .

Goldberg, after his graduation from Law School in 1968 had rather specialized experience in the securities field and had published various books and treatises on related subjects. He became associated with the Sitomer firm in November 1971. While there Goldberg worked on phases of various registration statements including Empire, although another associate was responsible for the Empire registration statement and prospectus. However, Goldberg expressed concern over what he regarded as excessive fees, the nondisclosure or inadequate disclosure thereof, and the extent to which they might include a "finder's fee," both as to Empire and other issuers.

The Empire registration became effective on May 31, 1972. The excessive fee question had not been put to rest in Goldberg's mind because in middle January 1973 it arose in connection with another registration (referred to as "Glacier"). Goldberg had worked on Glacier. Little purpose will be served by detailing the events during the critical period January 18 to 22, 1973, in which Goldberg and the Sitomer partners were debating the fee disclosure problem. In summary Goldberg insisted on a full and complete disclosure of fees in the Empire and Glacier offerings. The Sitomer partners apparently disagreed and Goldberg resigned from the firm on January 22, 1973.

On January 22, 1973, Goldberg appeared before the SEC and placed before it information subsequently embodied in his affidavit dated January 26, 1973, which becomes crucial to the issues now to be considered.

---

65. [A Form 10-K is an annual filing that publicly traded companies are required to file with the SEC. It contains extensive information about the company and its operations, including disclosure of risks the company faces.—ED.]

Some three months later, upon being informed that he was to be included as a defendant in the impending action, Goldberg asked the Bernson firm for an opportunity to demonstrate that he had been unaware of the finder's fee arrangement which, he said, Empire and the Sitomer firm had concealed from him all along. Goldberg met with members of the Bernson firm on at least two occasions. After consulting his own attorney, as well as William P. Sullivan, Special Counsel with the Securities and Exchange Commission, Division of Enforcement, Goldberg gave plaintiffs' counsel a copy of the January 26th affidavit which he had authored more than three months earlier. He hoped that it would verify his nonparticipation in the finder's fee omission and convince the Bernson firm that he should not be a defendant. After receiving Goldberg's affidavit, the Bernson firm amended plaintiffs' complaint. The amendments added more specific facts but did not change the theory or substance of the original complaint.

By motion dated June 7, 1973, the remaining defendants moved "pursuant to Canons 4 and 9 of the [Model Code][66] and the supervisory power of this Court" for the order of disqualification now on appeal.

By memorandum decision and order, the District Court ordered that the Bernson firm and Goldberg be barred from acting as counsel or participating with counsel for plaintiffs in this or any future action against Empire involving the transactions placed in issue in this lawsuit and from disclosing confidential information to others. . . .

The basis for the Court's decision is the premise that Goldberg had obtained confidential information from his client Empire which, in breach of relevant ethical canons, he revealed to plaintiffs' attorneys in their suit against Empire. . . .

There is no proof — not even a suggestion — that Goldberg had revealed any information, confidential or otherwise, that might have caused the instigation of the suit. To the contrary, it was not until the suit was commenced that Goldberg learned that he was in jeopardy. The District Court recognized that the complaint had been based on Empire's — not Goldberg's disclosures, but concluded because of this that Goldberg was under no further obligation "to reveal the information or to discuss the matter with plaintiffs' counsel."

. . . DR 4-101(C) recognizes that a lawyer may reveal confidences or secrets necessary to defend himself against "an accusation of wrongful conduct." This is exactly what Goldberg had to face when, in their original complaint, plaintiffs named him as a defendant who willfully violated the securities laws.

The charge, of knowing participation in the filing of a false and misleading registration statement, was a serious one. The complaint alleged violation of

---

66. [Canon 4, on preserving confidentiality, included DR 4-101, discussed in *Purcell*, as well as aspirational Ethical Considerations. Canon 9, entitled "Avoiding Even the Appearance of Impropriety" was often invoked in considering a disqualification motion. It has no analogy in the Model Rules, which rejected the appearance of impropriety as a basis for determining lawyer misconduct. — ED.]

criminal statutes and civil liability computable at over four million dollars. The cost in money of simply defending against an action might be very substantial. The damage to his professional reputation which might be occasioned by the mere pendency of such a charge was an even greater cause for concern.

Under these circumstances Goldberg had the right to make an appropriate disclosure with respect to his role in the public offering. Concomitantly, he had the right to support his version of the facts with suitable evidence.

The problem arises from the fact that the method Goldberg used to accomplish this was to deliver to Mr. Abbey, a member of the Bernson firm, the thirty page affidavit, accompanied by sixteen exhibits, which he had submitted to the SEC. This document not only went into extensive detail concerning Goldberg's efforts to cause the Sitomer firm to rectify the nondisclosure with respect to Empire but even more extensive detail concerning how these efforts had been precipitated by counsel for the underwriters having come upon evidence showing that a similar nondisclosure was contemplated with respect to Glacier and their insistence that full corrective measures should be taken. Although Goldberg's description reflected seriously on his employer, the Sitomer firm and, also, in at least some degree, on Glacier, he was clearly in a situation of some urgency. Moreover, before he turned over the affidavit, he consulted both his own attorney and a distinguished practitioner of securities law, and he and Abbey made a joint telephone call to Mr. Sullivan of the SEC. Moreover, it is not clear that, in the context of this case, Canon 4 applies to anything except information gained from Empire. Finally, because of Goldberg's apparent intimacy with the offering, the most effective way for him to substantiate his story was for him to disclose the SEC affidavit. It was the fact that he had written such an affidavit at an earlier date which demonstrated that his story was not simply fabricated in response to plaintiffs' complaint. . . .

To the extent that the District Court's order prohibits Goldberg from *representing* the interests of these or any other plaintiffs in this or similar actions, we affirm that order. We also affirm so much of the District Court's order as enjoins Goldberg from disclosing material information except on discovery or at trial.

NOTES AND QUESTIONS

1. Under DR 4-101(C)(4), the Model Code provision cited by the *Meyerhofer* court, lawyers were permitted to defend themselves against an "accusation" of misconduct. Model Rule 1.6(b)(5), however, arguably limits disclosure to those necessary "to establish a defense to a criminal charge or civil claim against the lawyer" or "to respond to allegations in any proceeding concerning the lawyer's representation of the client." Which of the two Model Rule provisions would have applied to Goldberg? Was disclosure necessary to defend against a civil complaint

that had not yet been served? If not, had an allegation been made in a "proceeding"?

2. How important was it that the complaint naming Goldberg as a defendant had already been publicly filed, although it had not yet been served on him? The comment to Rule 1.6 states: "The lawyer's right to respond arises when an assertion of such complicity has been made. Paragraph (b)(6) does not require the lawyer to await the commencement of an action or proceeding that charges such complicity." What if plaintiffs' counsel had merely threatened to include Goldberg in the complaint or were questioning Goldberg in their initial pre-filing investigation and Goldberg merely suspected (perhaps reasonably) that they were planning to name him as a defendant?

3. Under what circumstances do lawyers find it necessary to defend themselves against "allegations" of misconduct in settings other than criminal charges or civil claims against the lawyer? Settings in which this provision are invoked include disciplinary proceedings, litigation sanctions, and disqualification motions in litigation. What about a lawyer who wants to defend against an allegation of ineffective assistance of counsel by a former client, in a proceeding brought to set aside the client's criminal conviction? ABA Formal Ethics Op. 10-456 (2010) advised that, although lawyers in that situation may invoke the self-defense exception to testify in a judicial proceeding, it is "highly unlikely" that disclosures in informal discussions with a prosecutor will be permitted. How can this be, given that there has been a formal allegation, in a proceeding, and it concerns the lawyer's representation of the client? The opinion conceded that a lawyer subject to such an allegation has a legitimate interest in avoiding a finding in the client's favor, which might "impair the lawyer's reputation or have other adverse, collateral consequences for the lawyer." (What other "adverse, collateral consequences" might the opinion have in mind?) Nevertheless, the opinion concluded that it is unlikely that the lawyer has a "reasonable need" to invoke the self-defense exception outside of the judicial proceeding. Are allegations of ineffective assistance of counsel distinguishable from allegations made in disciplinary proceedings, sanctions, and disqualification motions (or defending against criminal or civil charges), where no one suggests that lawyers may not informally seek to resolve allegations outside of formal judicial proceedings?

4. What about responding to false accusations by a client in informal settings, such as in a negative social media review? There is no "proceeding" here, but isn't it reasonably necessary for the lawyer "to establish a claim or defense . . . in a controversy between the lawyer and the client"? Most ethics opinions have rejected the use of the self-defense exception here, advising that "controversy" should be narrowly confined to circumstances such as judicial or other formal proceedings that

warrant the establishment of either a "claim" or a "defense."[67] Several opinions suggest that the lawyer respond as follows: "A lawyer's duty to keep client confidences has few exceptions and in an abundance of caution I do not feel at liberty to respond in a point-by-point fashion in this forum. Suffice it to say that I do not believe that the post presents a fair and accurate picture of the events."[68]

5. Although the *Meyerhofer* court was certain that "Goldberg had the right to make an appropriate disclosure" to plaintiffs' counsel, and that "he had the right to support his version of the facts with suitable evidence," the court was nevertheless concerned about the amount of information that Goldberg disclosed when he turned over the 30-page affidavit, with its 16 exhibits, that he had filed with the SEC. Arguably, the affidavit contained unnecessary detail and reflected badly not only on the Sitomer firm, but on Glacier, a former client that was not a part of the class action lawsuit. Nevertheless, the court concluded that Goldberg was under a "situation of some urgency," and it rejected the district court's finding that he had violated Canon 4. Do you agree? What might Goldberg have done differently?

6. What did the court mean when it said that "it is not clear that, in the context of this case, Canon 4 applies to anything except information gained from Empire"? What if, as a result of Goldberg's disclosures, a class action lawsuit was filed against Glacier, and Glacier subsequently sued Goldberg for breach of fiduciary duty? Might a court reach a different result?[69] Are there ways that Goldberg could have minimized his risk of subsequently being found to have revealed too much information?

7. The court did not address the propriety of Goldberg's initial filing of the affidavit with the SEC. Was he permitted to do so? On what basis?

(6) Complying with Other Law

Model Rule 1.6(b)(6) provides that a lawyer may disclose client information when reasonably necessary "to comply with other law or a court order."

Your first reaction may be that of course lawyers are obligated to comply with either "other law" or a court order, and of course they should be allowed to disclose client information in order to do so, but why is this exception permissive, and not mandatory? There are a couple of explanations. First, it is not always clear when another law supersedes the lawyer's duty of

---

67. *See, e.g.,* ABA Formal Ethics Op. 21-496 (2021); Pa. Ethic. Op. 2014-200 (2014).

68. *Id. See also* Tex. Ethic. Op. 662 (2016).

69. In a later chapter on conflicts of interest, we will see that courts resolving disqualification motions are not bound to apply the rules of professional conduct in the same manner they would be applied in a disciplinary proceeding. *See infra* Chapter 5: Conflicts of Interest: Current Clients.

confidentiality. For example, a New York appellate court upheld the dismissal of indictments against a criminal defense lawyer for failing to report a death without medical attendance, on the ground that the confidential client communication that led to the lawyer's discovery of several dead bodies was protected by the attorney-client privilege, and the privilege shielded the lawyer from actions that would otherwise violate the Public Health Law.[70] Second, if the issue arises in an official proceeding, the lawyer is obligated to consult the client to determine whether to assert a claim of privilege; moreover, the order or ruling of a lower court or other tribunal may be subject to an appeal. Lawyers need some discretion in order to decide the proper course of action in any given case. Keep in mind, however, that although failure to disclose will not subject the lawyer to discipline under this rule, the lawyer may be subject to a penalty under other law.

(7) Detecting Conflicts of Interest

Model Rule 1.6(b)(7) provides that a lawyer may disclose client information when reasonably necessary "to detect and resolve conflicts of interest arising from the lawyer's change of employment or from changes in the composition or ownership of a firm, but only if the revealed information would not compromise the attorney-client privilege or otherwise prejudice the client."

This exception was adopted in 2012 because of the difficulty experienced by lawyers seeking to move from one law firm to another and by law firms trying to avoid being saddled with conflicts of interest arising from a new hire. As a law student, you may find yourself in a situation in which a prospective employer wants detailed information about your prior legal work. You should read the comment closely. It says, for example, that disclosure is not allowed until "substantive discussions regarding the new relationship have occurred."[71] Moreover, "[a]ny such disclosure should ordinarily include no more than the identity of the persons and entities involved in a matter, a brief summary of the general issues involved, and information about whether the matter has terminated." The importance of this exception will be manifest when we come to the chapters on conflicts of interest, particularly those involving the so-called "transient lawyer."[72]

---

70. *See* People v. Belge, 376 N.Y.S. 2d 771 (N.Y. App. Div. 1951). When the lawyer and his co-counsel finally revealed the existence of the bodies in an attempt to plea bargain on their client's behalf, there was an outcry in the community. The details of this fascinating case are discussed in an article that includes comments by co-counsel Frank Armani. *See* Lisa G. Lerman et al., The Buried Bodies Case: Alive and Well After 30 Years, 2007 Prof. Law. 19 (2007). Armani also participated in a television documentary about the case, in which he poignantly revealed his anguish at not being able to tell a father what had happened to his missing daughter.

71. *See* MR 1.6, cmt [13].

72. *See infra* Chapter 6: Conflicts of Interest: Former Clients, Prospective Clients, and Government Lawyers.

D. ACTING COMPETENTLY TO PROTECT CONFIDENTIALITY

In 2012, the ABA amended the Model Rules to add Rule 1.6(c), which requires lawyers to take reasonable measures to prevent inadvertent or unauthorized disclosures or access to client information. Of course, even without this amendment, Rule 1.1 requires lawyers to act competently, and common law obligates them to use reasonable care to avoid harming their clients. Nevertheless, the 2012 amendment highlights the extent to which recent developments in technology have heightened the risks threatening confidentiality and the need for lawyers to both understand and take reasonable precautions in light of these risks.

The threats to client confidentiality in today's world are almost too numerous to mention. They include problems arising with electronic communications and data storage; portable devices and border searches; metadata in electronic documents; and virtual law offices, social networking websites, blogs, and similar communication modes.[73] There are numerous resources available to lawyers seeking to educate themselves and determine what precautions are reasonably necessary, given their particular type of practice.[74] The ABA, as well as state and local bar associations, provide updated information on various topics involving legal technology and other threats to client confidentiality.[75]

Acting competently to protect confidentiality includes supervising both legal and nonlegal personnel. *See, e.g.* MR 5.1 (responsibilities of partners, managers, and supervisory lawyers); 5.3 (responsibilities regarding nonlawyer assistants). The category of nonlegal personnel is not limited to employees, such as secretaries, administrators, and paralegals, but also includes outside contractors, including third parties retained to perform printing, cloud computing, data storage, and a variety of other services.

E. WORK PRODUCT IMMUNITY

Like the attorney-client privilege, the *work product immunity* doctrine applies only to discovery or other compelled disclosure at trial. Prima facie protection extends primarily to tangible material prepared by a lawyer for pending

---

73. *See, e.g.*, ABA, Annotated Model Rules, Rule 1.6 (9th ed. 2019)(citing cases, ethics opinions, and secondary sources).

74. In addition to the annually updated ABA Annotated Model Rules, *see supra* n. 73, the ABA/Bloomberg Law's Lawyers' Manual on Professional Conduct publishes frequently updated Practice Guides, including one on Electronic Communications. Both sources are available online.

75. For example, the ABA has a Legal Technology Resource Center, including an annual technology report, as well as a technology blog. The New York State Bar Association makes available comprehensive and frequently updated Social Media Ethics Guidelines. These resources, and many more, are typically available online. *See, e.g.*, Legal Technology Resource Center, https://www.americanbar.org/groups/departments_offices/legal_technology_resources/.

litigation or in reasonably anticipated future litigation,[76] such as notes of witness interviews or memoranda concerning trial strategy. *Ordinary* work product may be subject to an exception based on an adversary's substantial need for and inability to obtain the substantial equivalent,[77] whereas *opinion* work product, which consists of the lawyer's opinions or mental impressions,[78] is rarely subject to an exception.[79]

Transactional lawyers who have heard of the work product doctrine may be under the mistaken impression that their work product, such as drafts of documents or memoranda concerning their mental impressions of a transaction, are protected against future disclosure. Because this work is rarely created in anticipation of litigation, it is generally not protected; however, there is at least one jurisdiction, California, which does not require that work product be created in anticipation of litigation.[80]

Review Problems

4-1 A lawyer agreed to represent a businesswoman in a real estate deal. The woman brought her sister, who was her business advisor, to all meetings with the lawyer. The woman's English was poor, and she frequently looked to her sister to help her find the correct words. The woman described the proposed transaction as an all-cash deal involving large amounts of money and requested that the proceeds be deposited in a bank located in a jurisdiction where transactions of this kind are commonly used to conceal terrorist financing or other illegal activities. The lawyer made further inquiries in an effort to dispel the lawyer's concerns, but the woman was evasive and said that the lawyer did not need to know further details of the transaction. The lawyer insisted that the woman answer his questions because if she did not persuade him to the contrary, he would inform the relevant governmental authorities of his belief that she was planning to engage in money laundering, which is a crime under federal law. The woman refused to answer and discharged the lawyer. May the lawyer voluntarily inform the relevant governmental authorities of the woman's proposed transaction? If he does so, and is subsequently subpoenaed to testify for the government in an investigation of the woman's potential money laundering activities, may he testify against her?

---

76. *See* RLGL §87. In federal courts, work product protection is provided for in Rule 26(b)(3) of the Federal Rules of Civil Procedure.

77. RLGL §88.

78. *Id.* at §87(2).

79. *Id.* at §§89, 91-93.

80. *See, e.g.*, City of L.A. v. Superior Court, 98 Cal.Rptr.2d 564, 574 (Cal. Ct. App. 2000) (work product doctrine applies not only to writings created in anticipation of litigation, but also "to writings prepared by an attorney while acting in a nonlitigation capacity").

4-2 May a lawyer disclose information in the following scenarios?

a. A lawyer representing a chemical company just learned that the company inadvertently dumped toxic chemicals into a landfill site near the company's plant. The company is concerned that the toxic chemicals, which can cause cancer if ingested, will reach the town's water supply. The lawyer has urged the company to notify the town's public health authorities, but the company is not yet prepared to do so. It is unclear whether the company has committed any crime. May or must the lawyer notify the town authorities of the situation?

b. A lawyer retained by the personal representative of an estate learned that the representative had misappropriated estate funds. May the lawyer disclose this information to the sole beneficiary?

c. While working on a case, a sole practitioner recognized that she needed further information on the tax consequences of a business transaction. Her brother is a tax lawyer. May she call him and ask him a quick question about the tax consequences of the client's contemplated transaction?

d. A client filed for bankruptcy before paying a lawyer's invoice for legal services. The lawyer has filed a claim with the bankruptcy court for the legal fees that are due. During the representation, the lawyer learned extensive information about the client's assets. May the lawyer disclose that information in the bankruptcy proceeding?

e. A lawyer who formerly represented a business owner was subpoenaed to testify before a grand jury investigating the owner. Reasonably believing that the testimony he was being asked to give was protected by the attorney-client privilege, the lawyer refused to answer the prosecutor's questions, citing the privilege. When the prosecutor raised the issue with the court overseeing the grand jury, the court ruled that the privilege did not apply and ordered the attorney to testify. The attorney continues to reasonably believe that the privilege has been properly asserted. May or must the attorney testify as ordered by the court?

CHAPTER 5

CONFLICTS OF INTEREST: CURRENT CLIENTS

Model Rules 1.7, 1.8, 1.10

As fiduciaries, lawyers owe obligations of both confidentiality and loyalty to their clients. The previous chapter addressed the duty of confidentiality. This chapter, as well as the next three chapters, address the duty of loyalty, as it is embodied in an extensive set of conflict of interest rules. Just the fact that this doctrine is covered in four separate chapters tells you both how important and how complex this doctrine can be.[1] Conflicts affect not only *current* clients, but also *former* and *prospective* clients. In addition, with respect to each of these categories, the conflicts of an individual lawyer are usually *imputed* to other lawyers associated in a practice, thereby requiring elaborate conflicts checking procedures, particularly in increasingly large law firms with thousands of lawyers and branches in multiple cities, states, and countries. Moreover, there are special conflicts rules that apply to current and former *government lawyers* and lawyers who have formerly served as *judges* or *arbitrators*. And if all this isn't sufficiently complex, lawyers also need to consider the specific contexts in which conflicts issues arise, because the standards might be different depending on the particular remedy sought. As we will see, available remedies for impermissible conflicts include not only *discipline*, but also *malpractice* or *breach of fiduciary duty* lawsuits, *disqualification, injunctions, fee forfeiture,* the *voiding of a transaction* between lawyer and client, *reversal of a client's criminal conviction*, and in rare cases, *criminal conviction of the lawyer*.

Conflicts affecting current clients are among the most difficult to analyze. In this chapter, we address three different types of conflicts of interest affecting current clients: (1) conflicts among multiple clients simultaneously represented by a lawyer or a law firm; (2) conflicts between a client and a lawyer;

---

1. To add to the complexity, a later chapter addresses special conflict of interest concerns when the lawyer represents an entity, including conflicts in simultaneously representing an entity and one or more individual constituents. *See infra* Chapter 11: Conflicts of Interest in Entity Representation.

and (3) conflicts between a client and third persons, such as a person or entity that pays the lawyer's fees. Most of these conflicts are governed by Model Rule 1.7, which is the general conflicts of interest rule for current clients, and Model Rule 1.10(a), which imputes most conflicts of an individual lawyer to other lawyers associated in a firm. In addition, Model Rule 1.8 provides more specific rules for a number of common conflicts situations, including business and other financial transactions between lawyer and client. Rule 1.8(k) imputes all but one of these special conflicts to associated lawyers.

Before examining each of these current conflicts categories in detail, it is helpful to have an overview of the type of analysis required under Rule 1.7, which is the rule you will most often be applying. Conflicts analysis under this rule requires the following steps:

(1) clearly identifying the client or clients;

(2) determining whether a conflict of interest exists;

(3) deciding whether the representation may be undertaken despite the existence of a conflict, i.e., whether the conflict is consentable; and

(4) consulting the client or clients and obtaining their informed consent, confirmed in writing.[2]

As for the first step, *client identification*, we have already encountered examples of lawyers who may have failed to identify a conflict because they did not understand who they were representing. For example, in Sin Ho Nam v. Quichocho,[3] the lawyer landlord did not understand that in preparing a lease for a prospective tenant, he may have inadvertently created an attorney-client relationship, thereby triggering the conflict of interest rules. And in Manoir-ElectoAlloys Corp. v. Amalloy Corp.,[4] a case involving imputed conflicts, a law firm lawyer knew that he had once represented a company executive and his wife in drafting their wills, but he mistakenly believed that the firm's representation was no longer current at the time when another lawyer in the firm sought to represent a different client with conflicting interests. In both cases, the courts looked to the reasonable expectations of the client to determine the existence of an attorney-client relationship. Keep in mind that the Model Rules do not attempt to define when an attorney-client relationship exists; rather, this is a matter governed by common law.

The second step of conflicts analysis requires *conflict identification*. Because identifying a conflict does not necessarily mean that the representation is prohibited, it may be helpful to characterize this step as identifying *potentially impermissible conflicts*, that is, conflicts that must be addressed by the lawyer in one way or another. Rule 1.7(a) provides that a current conflict of interest exists if:

---

2. *See* MR 1.7, cmt [2].

3. *See supra* Chapter 2: Formation, Scope, and Termination of the Attorney-Client Relationship.

4. *See id.*

> (1) the representation of one client will be *directly adverse* to another client; or
>
> (2) there is a significant risk that the representation of one or more clients will be *materially limited* by the lawyer's responsibilities to another client, a former client or a third person or by a personal interest of the lawyer.[5]

Directly adverse conflicts apply only in situations involving two or more current clients, whereas material limitation conflicts include conflicts among current clients, conflicts between lawyer and client, and conflicts between a client and a third person. Individual business lawyers are most likely to encounter material limitation conflicts, which commonly arise when a lawyer attempts to represent more than one client in a transaction or in efforts to resolve disputes concerning a transaction.[6] As a result, this chapter will consider these types of conflicts before turning to address directly adverse conflicts, which are more common in litigation. Both concepts will be examined in detail.

The third step requires the lawyer to determine if the identified conflict is *consentable*. Rule 1.7(b) provides for three conditions of consentability. The one most typically in issue is that, notwithstanding the conflict, "the lawyer reasonably believes that the lawyer will be able to provide competent and diligent representation to each affected client." Conflicts present the risk of harm to a client by depriving the client of the lawyer's loyalty and independent judgment,[7] as well as risks to confidentiality and attorney-client privilege. Given the existence of such risks, ask yourself as you read the material in this chapter how a lawyer could reasonably believe that representation burdened with a conflict of interest would be competent and diligent. Are there potential benefits to the representation that might outweigh the risks?

The final step requires the lawyer to consult the client or clients and obtain their *informed consent*. Ask yourself, with respect to each situation discussed, what exactly the lawyer needed to explain to the client in order for the client's consent to be properly informed.

A. CONFLICTS AMONG CURRENT CLIENTS

1. Material Limitation Conflicts

a. Material Limitation Conflicts in Transactions

The following case illustrates a conflict of interest involving multiple clients simultaneously represented by two successive law firm lawyers — Ed Oliver and David James. The context was a malpractice lawsuit brought by the

---

5. MR 1.7(a) (emphasis added).

6. When a lawyer represents multiple clients with adverse interests in a single transaction, there will likely be a directly adverse conflict in addition to the material limitation conflict; however, for purposes of determining both consentability and informed consent, it is important to identify the likely limitations on the lawyer's ability to represent each client under the analysis of a material limitation conflict.

7. MR 1.7, cmt [1].

plaintiffs, including Mrs. Simpson, against both the lawyers and the law firm, with Mrs. Simpson alleging that the defendants failed to protect her interests as the seller of a business previously managed by her late husband. In upholding verdicts in favor of the plaintiffs, the court did not even mention the applicable rules of professional conduct. As you read the case, ask yourself what each lawyer should have done differently under the requirements of Model Rule 1.7.

Simpson v. James
903 F.2d 372 (5th Cir. 1990)

Wisdom, Circuit Judge

This appeal concerns a malpractice suit brought by the sellers of corporate assets against the partners of a law firm that represented both the buyers and the sellers in the transaction. The plaintiffs alleged two incidents of negligence on the part of the attorneys: the handling of the original sale and the subsequent restructuring of the buyers' note in favor of the plaintiffs. After a jury trial, the court rendered judgment in favor of the plaintiffs, awarding the sellers $100,000 for each act of negligence. We affirm.

STATEMENT OF THE CASE

The plaintiffs, Sheila Simpson and Lovie and Morelle Jones, were the sole stockholders in H.P. Enterprises Corporation. The business of H.P. Enterprises was operating and franchising catfish restaurants. Sheila Simpson's late husband, Buck Simpson, handled most of the business affairs of the corporation until his death. Mrs. Simpson then took over operation of the company, but she later decided to sell the corporation to devote more time to her children.

Mrs. Simpson turned to Ed Oliver for help in selling the corporation. Since 1968, Oliver practiced in Texarkana, Texas, with the firm now known as Keeney, Anderson & James. He had represented Mr. Simpson for many years in matters relating to H.P. Enterprises and in personal matters. In November 1983 a group of investors approached Oliver to inquire into purchasing H.P. Enterprises. Oliver formed a corporation for the investors, Tide Creek, and drew up the legal documents to transfer the assets of H.P. Enterprises to Tide Creek. Oliver was the sole source of legal advice for both parties.

The price agreed upon was $500,000, of which $100,000 was paid at the execution of the sale. As security for the sellers, Oliver provided for a lien on the stock of Tide Creek, personal guarantees of the buyers on the corporation's $400,000 note to the sellers, and certain restrictions on operation of the business. The sale took place on November 18, 1983. After the transaction, Mr. Oliver's firm continued to represent Mrs. Simpson in estate and tax matters. During this time, all of her business records were kept at the firm's office.

A. Conflicts Among Current Clients 105

Thereafter, two significant events occurred. In April 1984 a fire destroyed Tide Creek's commissary, which contained its inventory. David James, a partner in Oliver's firm, represented Tide Creek in recovering over $200,000 in insurance proceeds. In October 1984, Oliver left the firm to practice in Houston. The firm was renamed Keeney, Anderson & James. An associate in the firm, Fred Norton, took over tax and estate work for Mrs. Simpson.

Under the original terms of the sale arranged by Oliver, a $200,000 note by Tide Creek in favor of the plaintiffs became due on November 18, 1984. Tide Creek did not meet this obligation. On January 29, 1985, the plaintiffs visited David James at his office. James told them that Tide Creek was having financial difficulties, and that the company could pay them only $50,000 at that time. James restructured the note between the parties. At that meeting, Mrs. Simpson asked James what he would do if her interests and those of Tide Creek diverged. James replied: "We would have to support you."

In the Fall of 1985, Mrs. Simpson became concerned when she heard rumors of Tide Creek's impending bankruptcy. She called Fred Norton, an associate at the firm, and Norton arranged a meeting for her with David James. James advised Mrs. Simpson that her interests were in conflict with those of Tide Creek. He told her that she should find another lawyer to represent her; James was representing Tide Creek.

The plaintiffs received their last payment from Tide Creek on October 1, 1985. Tide Creek then filed for bankruptcy. The plaintiffs filed a claim in bankruptcy court, but received nothing. Their efforts to enforce the personal guarantees proved fruitless; the guarantors filed for personal bankruptcy.

Mrs. Simpson filed suit against the three partners of Keeney, Anderson, and James on January 16, 1987. The suit alleged that acts of negligence by Oliver and James proximately damaged the plaintiffs. The plaintiffs alleged that the defendants had a conflict of interest that prevented them from acting in the plaintiffs' best interests. The jury found that Ed Oliver was negligent in his representation of Mrs. Simpson and the Joneses and awarded them $100,000 damages. It also found David James liable for negligence for his role in restructuring the delinquent note and awarded $100,000 damages to Simpson. The defendants moved for a judgment notwithstanding the verdict, or in the alternative, for a new trial. The court denied both motions.

Discussion . . .

In Texas, an attorney malpractice claim is based on negligence. A plaintiff in a malpractice action must prove four elements to recover: that 1) the defendant owed a duty to the plaintiff; 2) the defendant breached that duty; 3) the breach proximately caused the plaintiff injury; and 4) damages resulted. The defendants challenge the existence of a number of these elements.

A. ATTORNEY-CLIENT RELATIONSHIP: JAMES AND SIMPSON

The defendants argue that no attorney-client relationship existed between David James and Sheila Simpson, and consequently, James owed no duty to her that could form the basis of malpractice liability. . . . [T]he jury found that an attorney-client relationship did exist between the two with respect to the renewal note of January 29, 1985. We review the jury's finding with deference, and will reverse only if no reasonable jury could have so found. . . .

The evidence adduced at trial indicated that Ed Oliver represented the plaintiffs' business interests in H.P. Enterprises before and at the time of the sale of its assets to Tide Creek. After Oliver left, the firm represented Mrs. Simpson in tax and estate matters and continued to maintain all of her business records. Mrs. Simpson testified that on January 29, 1985, at the time the note was restructured, and on a subsequent occasion, James encouraged her about Tide Creek's future economic viability. She added that she relied on those assurances. Significantly, Simpson stated that James advised her that she was entering into a good deal in agreeing to the restructuring. At the same meeting, James assured Simpson that he would stand by her in the event of a conflict of interest between Simpson and Tide Creek. James stated that at no time did Mrs. Simpson specifically ask him to represent her interests against Tide Creek. He testified that he never gave any advice to Mrs. Simpson and never charged her for his time. Nevertheless, the evidence was sufficient for a reasonable jury to conclude that an attorney-client relationship existed, as manifested through the parties' conduct.

B. NEGLIGENCE

Under Texas law, an attorney "is held to the standard of care which would be exercised by a reasonably prudent attorney." This is not a result-oriented analysis; an attorney will not be liable for undesirable effects of a decision that was reasonable at the time it was made.

The plaintiffs alleged negligent acts that arose out of the defendants' conflicts of interest in representing both sides of a transaction. Liability may not be premised solely on the fact that an attorney represented both buyer and seller; after full disclosure by the attorney, it may be proper in some circumstances for an attorney to represent both sides in a real estate transaction.

Both sides in this case presented expert testimony on the propriety of Oliver's representing both the plaintiffs and the investors from Tide Creek. Of course, in the case of conflicting expert testimony, the jury is entitled to make credibility determinations and to believe the witness it considers more trustworthy. Although the defense maintains that Oliver merely reduced a settled agreement to writing, the plaintiffs presented evidence suggesting that Oliver negotiated the sale price for the assets of H.P. Enterprises and determined the "mechanics" of the sale. Moreover, the plaintiffs' expert witness . . . testified that Oliver did not adequately protect Simpson against the possibility that Tide Creek would fail financially. For example, he stated that instead of a lien on Tide Creek stock, Oliver should have provided for a lien on the assets. Oliver also might have named the plaintiffs as beneficiaries of insurance policies. [The expert] added that the interests of the plaintiffs and buyers varied significantly from the beginning. Although the evidence of Oliver's negligence is not overwhelming, we are not persuaded that the jury's conclusion is unreasonable.

David James prepared the instrument whereby Tide Creek's note in favor of Simpson and Jones was restructured. Simpson argues that James did not disclose Tide Creek's desperate financial condition, did not explain other options to her, and did not pursue over $200,000 insurance money for her benefit. The plaintiffs' expert also testified that it was improper for James to represent parties with such divergent interests: a creditor seeking recovery and a debtor in default. We believe that this evidence is sufficient to uphold the jury's finding of negligence.

C. Whether Attorney Negligence Proximately Caused the Plaintiffs' Damages

The plaintiffs have the burden to prove that but for the defendants' negligence, they would have recovered the payments due. The jury found that Oliver and James, by their individual acts of negligence, each caused the plaintiffs $100,000 damages. We review the record to determine whether the plaintiffs proved that amount of damages.

It is apparent that proper conduct on the part of Oliver could have averted the loss of at least $100,000. The plaintiff's expert accountant testified that the sellers of the corporate assets were not adequately protected. Protection could have been provided by a lien on the conveyed assets or by naming the plaintiffs as beneficiaries of property insurance. The evidence is sufficient on this issue.

Whether the plaintiffs proved damages as a result of James's conduct is a closer question. The plaintiffs' expert accountant testified that as of March 1985, Tide Creek had combined equity of over $368,000. His estimate was based on internal corporation figures that were not verified. Had the plaintiffs foreclosed on Tide Creek, however, they would have taken it back with over $477,000 in worthless accounts receivable. Moreover, it is undisputed that as of September 30, 1985, Tide Creek had equity of —$483,427.

However, the plaintiffs presented evidence that James was involved in recovering over $200,000 in insurance proceeds after a fire destroyed the restaurant's commissary. As argued by the plaintiff and admitted by the defendants' expert witness, James could have seized the insurance proceeds to satisfy the delinquent note. Perhaps because of a conflict of interest, James did not mention this possibility to the plaintiffs. We conclude that the plaintiffs proved damages caused by James.

NOTES AND QUESTIONS

1. Once again, an attorney, David James, may have failed to understand that he had an attorney-client relationship, in this case with Mrs. Simpson. When he first met with her, to inform her that Tide Creek could not pay the note in full, he had not personally represented her on any matter. Mrs. Simpson apparently understood that James was representing Tide Creek at that time. What facts led her to reasonably believe that he was also representing her? Would it have made a difference if the jury did not believe her testimony that James told her the firm would support her if her interests and Tide Creek's interests diverged?

2. Consider whether and how Ed Oliver had a conflict of interest in representing both the sellers and the buyers in the sale of H.P. Enterprises to Tide Creek. Commentators have disagreed whether the interests of buyers and sellers are necessarily "directly adverse."[8] Under Rule 1.7(a), it makes no difference because the most likely conflict in these situations involves a "material limitation" on the lawyer's ability to adequately represent both parties. In what sense was there a "significant risk" that Oliver's representation of Mrs. Simpson would be "materially limited" by his responsibilities to his other client, Tide Creek? Comment [8] explains that "[e]ven where there is no direct adverseness, a conflict of interest exists if there is a significant risk that a lawyer's ability to consider, recommend or carry out an appropriate course of action for the client will be materially limited as a result of the lawyer's other responsibilities or interests." Does this help explain how Oliver's loyalty and independent judgment on behalf of Mrs. Simpson could be compromised by his duties to Tide Creek? What about the possible effects on confidentiality and the attorney-client privilege?

3. Oliver argued that he "merely reduced a settled agreement to writing." This is often referred to as the lawyer serving as a "mere scrivener." The court found that there was evidence to the contrary that Oliver negotiated the sale price and "determined the 'mechanics' of the sale." What if the parties had already negotiated the terms of the transaction? Could the lawyer properly serve as a "mere scrivener," perhaps as a form of limited scope representation under Rule 1.2(c)? Does it matter that Mrs. Simpson had no significant business experience of her own? If two sophisticated and experienced businesspersons who have already negotiated the terms of an agreement are permitted to limit the scope of the lawyer's representation to drafting the agreement, thereby satisfying Rule 1.2(c), does that eliminate the existence of a material limitation conflict under Rule 1.7(a)(2)? Remember that acknowledging the existence of a conflict does not necessarily mean that the representation is

---

8. Directly adverse conflicts in transactions are discussed in a later section of this chapter.

impermissible. The conflict might nevertheless be consentable, in which case the lawyer could proceed with the informed consent of both clients.

4. Given Oliver's expanded role as price negotiator and planner of the details of the transaction, there is little question that he had a material limitation conflict. Was that conflict consentable? Rule 1.7(b) provides that conflicts are consentable if:

> (1) the lawyer reasonably believes that the lawyer will be able to provide competent and diligent representation to each affected client;
> (2) the representation is not prohibited by law; [and]
> (3) the representation does not involve the assertion of a claim by one client against another client represented by the lawyer in the same litigation or other proceeding before a tribunal.

Considering these conditions in reverse order, (3) is satisfied because neither client was asserting a claim against the other. We don't necessarily know whether (2) is satisfied. Some types of joint representations are prohibited by federal or state statute (e.g., a state statute prohibiting a governmental agency from consenting to a conflict), and some are prohibited by case law. For example, the New Jersey Supreme Court has adopted a per se rule that "an attorney may not represent both the buyer and the seller in a complex commercial real estate transaction even if both give their informed consent." Baldesarre v. Butler, 132 N.J. 278, 296 (1993). The reason for doing so is that "where large sums of money are at stake, where contracts contain complex contingencies, or where options are numerous . . . [t]he potential for conflict in that type of complex real estate transaction is too great to permit even consensual dual representation of buyer and seller." *Id.* In other words, the New Jersey Supreme Court has made a determination that in these types of cases a lawyer could not satisfy condition (1) that the lawyer could reasonably believe that the representation of each client would be competent and diligent. Why not? What is the significance of the specific factors cited by the court? Were those factors present in *Simpson*?

5. If the conflict confronting Ed Oliver was not per se nonconsentable under paragraph (b)(2), was it nonconsentable under paragraph (b)(1)? How does a lawyer determine whether it is reasonable to believe that, despite the significant risk of material limitation, the representation will be competent and diligent? Comment [15] states that "[c]onsentability is typically determined by considering whether the interests of the clients will be adequately protected if the clients are permitted to give their informed consent." Comment [28] addresses consentability in nonlitigation conflicts generally; comments [29] through [32] raise additional considerations in common representations, that is, representation of multiple clients in the same matter, also referred to as joint representation.

6. According to the Restatement, nonconsentability concerns the potential adverse effect on both the attorney's relationship with the client and the attorney's representation of the client: "[i]n general, if a reasonable and disinterested lawyer would conclude that one or more of the affected clients could not consent to the conflicted representation because the representation would likely fall short in either respect, the conflict is nonconsentable."[9]

7. If there are significant risks to the conflicted representation but the conflict is nevertheless consentable, the reason must be that despite these risks, there are potential benefits to the clients. Were there potential benefits to Mrs. Simpson and Tide Creek of being represented by Oliver, despite the conflict? Consider both the benefit of sharing a common lawyer (either Oliver or someone else), as well as any benefit to each of retaining this particular lawyer. Consider also whether the parties deliberately sought common representation or whether it occurred as a matter of happenstance. Should that matter?

8. In considering whether the potential benefits outweigh the potential risks, we should also consider whether there are factors particular to each situation that enhance the risk. According to the Restatement, "[d]ecisions holding that a conflict is nonconsentable often involve facts suggesting that the client, who is often unsophisticated in retaining lawyers . . . was incapable of adequately appreciating the risks of the conflict."[10] Are there factors that heightened the risk to either Mrs. Simpson or Tide Creek? Consider both the personal characteristics of each client, including the likelihood that the client could adequately weigh the risks and benefits, as well as the lawyer's relationship to each client. Could you have predicted at the outset which client Oliver might be tempted to favor? If there are potential benefits to joint representation, why not permit competent adult clients to consent to any existing conflict, so long as they are fully informed of the risks of doing so?[11]

9. Oliver had also represented the multiple investors who formed Tide Creek. Did that representation present a material limitation conflict of interests? Was it consentable? How was that representation different from the joint representation of Mrs. Simpson and Tide Creek in the sale of Mrs. Simpson's business? Consider the following hypothetical presented by Paul Tremblay:

---

9. RLGL §122, cmt g(iv).

10. *Id.*

11. For a discussion of the possible justification for an admittedly paternalistic rule that does not allow all competent adult clients to decide for themselves whether to proceed with conflicted representation, *see* Nancy J. Moore, Conflicts of Interest in the Simultaneous Representation of Multiple Clients: A Proposed Solution to the Current Confusion and Controversy, 61 Tex. L. Rev. 211, 232-40 (1982).

> Janelle, Arjun, and Netia are all post-docs working at University Hospital in its mental health department. Janelle has been puzzling through an idea for the past year or so for a software program, or perhaps a mobile device app, that could assist social services agencies to track opioid addicts and their outpatient care as well as their interactions with the law enforcement community. Janelle believes that this invention, if it can work, will be valuable to medical professionals around the country. She persuaded Arjun and Netia to work with her to craft the mechanics, the coding, and the possible marketing and business plan for this invention. The trio also has been discussing with Sami, a former roommate of Netia who is an expert coder, the possibility of his assisting on a part-time basis with the technical components of the software program. . . .
>
> The advisors at [a] startup incubator have urged the group to seek some legal assistance earlier rather than later, and so Janelle contacted [a lawyer] in a law firm catering to small business transactional work.[12]

May the lawyer represent Janelle, Arjun, and Netia in forming an entity to monetize their invention?[13] Issues the lawyer would need to raise with the founders include choice of entity, allocation of ownership and control, and the ownership and transfer of any intellectual property to the entity. Tremblay discusses in great detail the ethical issues involved in joint founder representation.[14]

10. Assume that the lawyer concludes that the conflict of interest among Janelle, Arjun, and Netia is consentable, and the lawyer wants to proceed with the joint representation.[15] Rule 1.7(b)(4) requires that "each affected client give[] informed consent, confirmed in writing." Rule 1.0(e) defines "informed consent," a term used throughout the Rules,[16] as "the agreement by a person to a proposed course of conduct after the lawyer has communicated adequate information and explanation about the material risks of and reasonably available alternatives to the proposed course of conduct." Comments [6] and [7] to Rule 1.0 address some aspects of informed consent generally, and Comments [6] and [7] to Rule 1.7 further explain the concept in the context of conflicts of

---

12. Paul R. Tremblay, The Ethics of Representing Founders, 8 William & Mary Bus. L. Rev. 207, 278-79 (2017).

13. In a later chapter, we consider yet another alternative—identifying the client as the prospective entity itself, rather than one or more of the individual founders. *See infra* Chapter 9: Who's My Client?

14. *See* Tremblay, *supra* n. 12.

15. Even when a lawyer determines that a conflict is consentable, the lawyer may decline the representation of more than one client due to prudential concerns. These concerns include the risk that one or more of the clients will be dissatisfied with the outcome of the representation, accuse the lawyer of favoring another client, and sue the lawyer for any resulting harm in a breach of fiduciary duty or malpractice lawsuit. This is exactly what happened in *Simpson*, despite what appears to have been a sincere effort on Oliver's part to provide protection for Mrs. Simpson.

16. *See, e.g., supra* Chapter 2: Formation, Scope, and Termination of the Attorney-Client Relationship (informed consent as a prerequisite to limiting the scope of representation); Chapter 4: Privilege and Confidentiality (informed consent as an exception to the lawyer's duty of confidentiality).

interest. In addition, Comments [29] through [32] to Rule 1.7 provide in great detail the nature of the required disclosures in joint representations. Use these comments to outline the disclosures the lawyer should make to Janelle, Arjun, and Netia. Should the lawyer meet with them individually or together?

11. Rule 1.0(b) defines "confirmed in writing" as "informed consent that is given in writing by the person or a writing that a lawyer promptly transmits to the person confirming an oral informed consent." "Writing" is broadly defined to include "a tangible or electronic record of a communication or representation, including handwriting, typewriting, printing, photostating, photography, audio or videorecording and electronic communications." Keep in mind that some jurisdictions require that the lawyer obtain the clients' informed consent in a writing signed by the client.[17]

12. Analyze the conflict of interest presented when David James simultaneously represented both Tide Creek and Mrs. Simpson. What about causation? What difficulties did Mrs. Simpson confront in establishing that James's conflict caused the sellers harm? Were there similar difficulties in establishing causation as a result of Oliver's conflict?

13. The conflicts of interest in *Simpson* involved representation of multiple clients in the same matter. What if the representation involves different matters? In Bank Brussels Lambert v. Fiddler, Gonzalez & Rodriguez, 305 F.3d 120 (2d Cir. 2002), a law firm represented a consortium of banks, including Bank Brussels, lending money to a company. Other lawyers in the firm were representing the lead bank in the consortium in an unrelated matter in which they received documents indicating that the company receiving the loan had been fraudulently manipulating its financial and accounting reports. When the company subsequently defaulted on the loan, Bank Brussels sued the law firm for breach of fiduciary duty. The law firm argued that there was no conflict of interest because the scope of its representation of Bank Brussels was limited to determining the validity and enforceability of the security interest being acquired by the lending group, and the information it had received from its other client did not relate to that limited question. The Second Circuit disagreed. Was there a conflict of interest? If so, what should the law firm have done? Consider not only the law firm's obligations under Model Rule 1.7, but also its obligations under Model Rule 1.4.

b. *Material Limitation Conflicts in Litigation*

Most litigation conflicts involve either suing a current client on behalf of another client in an unrelated matter (a "directly adverse" conflict) or representation adverse to a former client (which is governed by Rule 1.9). Material

---

17. *See, e.g.,* Cal. Rules of Prof'l Conduct, R. 1.7(a).

A. Conflicts Among Current Clients   **113**

limitation conflicts among current clients in litigation typically involve the representation of co-plaintiffs or co-defendants, as illustrated in the following case, in which a corporate defendant attempted to coerce two co-defendants, former employees of the corporation, into accepting representation by a lawyer whom the co-defendants believed had conflicts of interest.

Kramer v. Ciba-Geigy Corp.
854 A.2d 948 (N.J. Super. Ct. App. Div. 2004)

STERN, P.J.A.D.

[In May 2000, three individuals filed a class action lawsuit asserting common law claims for personal injuries and medical monitoring resulting from "unauthorized disposal of toxic waste over a lengthy period of time at [defendants'] plant in Toms River, New Jersey." The defendants included various Ciba-Geigy Corp. defendants (collectively "CIBA") and four individuals—William P. Bobsein, James A. McPherson, Dr. David Ellis, and Robert Fesen—each of whom had been a CIBA employee at the time of the toxic waste disposal. In 1984, all four individuals had been indicted for their illegal conduct. The indictments were later dismissed, and Dr. Ellis testified under a grant of immunity against Bobsein and McPherson before a second grand jury, which indicted them. Bobsein and McPherson pled guilty to a single fourth degree crime. CIBA also pled guilty and was ordered to pay a large criminal penalty.

[Although Dr. Ellis and Fesen were named in the original class action complaint, an amended complaint voluntarily dismissed them, leaving Bobsein and McPherson, as well as CIBA, as defendants in the case. A second amended complaint asserted an additional claim for concert of action/concerted action against all defendants. By July 2002, the plaintiffs' claims had been settled or dismissed without any financial or other participation by Bobsein and McPherson, who had an indemnification agreement with CIBA. Prior to that time, however, Bobsein and McPherson had filed cross-claims against CIBA seeking payment of the legal fees of their respective lawyers, Henry Furst and Michael Wilbert. The following opinion concerns those cross-claims, in which Bobsein and McPherson alleged conflicts of interest on the part of lawyers that CIBA had offered in satisfaction of their obligation to provide them with "conflict-free counsel." The trial judge had granted summary judgment on Bobsein's and McPherson's cross-complaints and awarded them $212,703.33 and $198,023.66, respectively, in counsel fees and costs. CIBA appealed.]

Bobsein and McPherson are both former employees of CIBA, who during their employment had management positions in the Environmental Technology Department at CIBA's Toms River Plant. When their employment with CIBA ended in the early 1990's, each entered into a consulting agreement with CIBA. . . . Each consulting agreement contained identical indemnification provisions, . . . which read as follows:

11. Except for occurrences of your willful misconduct, CIBA-GEIGY will defend and indemnify you in connection with any claims asserted or litigation commenced after the date hereof and based on your prior employment by CIBA-GEIGY or this consultancy, provided that you give prompt notice to CIBA-GEIGY of such claim or litigation. In such instance, CIBA-GEIGY *shall have the right to assume the defense thereof with counsel of its choice.* You agree to cooperate with CIBA-GEIGY in the defense of any asserted liability and, in any event, shall have the right to participate at your own expense in the defense of the asserted liability. . . .

There is no dispute that the agreement covered claims based on prior conduct, and as already noted, in the criminal proceeding involving their employment at CIBA, both Bobsein and McPherson pled guilty to a fourth degree criminal offense. Both Bobsein and McPherson certified that, in agreeing to plead guilty, they were assured by CIBA that they would be indemnified and provided independent, conflict free counsel in any future litigation arising from their employment with CIBA.

On June 2, 2000, after the first amended complaint was filed in the *Kramer* matter, James Stewart, a partner at the law firm of Lowenstein Sandler, wrote to Bobsein and McPherson separately advising them that his firm was representing CIBA in connection with the litigation and that CIBA had requested that the firm also represent them at CIBA's expense. The letter further provided that such joint representation "is permissible where the facts and circumstances of the case do not indicate the existence of a conflict between the interests of an individual employee co-defendant and CIBA" and "that [b]ased on [Lowenstein's] present knowledge of the underlying facts of the . . . claim, we do not believe any such conflict exists between CIBA and you and do not anticipate that any will arise as this matter progresses." However, Stewart requested that Bobsein and McPherson acknowledge and confirm in writing that "no conflict" existed between the interests of Bobsein and McPherson and those of CIBA "which, if disclosed, could preclude" the joint representation. The letter continued "that in the unlikely event such a conflict should develop during the course of [the joint] representation" or if Lowenstein determined that continued representation was "not appropriate," Lowenstein would "resign . . . representation" of Bobsein and McPherson and "continue to represent CIBA" without their objections. . . .

Bobsein consulted Henry Furst, the attorney who had represented him at CIBA's expense in past matters involving his employment at CIBA, to review the offer of representation contained in the June 2, 2000 letter. By letter dated July 18, 2000, Bobsein informed Stewart of his decision to reject representation by Lowenstein but rather use independent counsel, Furst. Bobsein indicated that having Furst, as "independent counsel of [his] choice, from the start" he "would not have to worry about conflicts" and any resulting effects on the quality of his representation.

McPherson also consulted with the attorney who had previously represented him in the prior litigation involving his employment at CIBA, Michael E. Wilbert. [McPherson] advised Lowenstein that he "would not agree to waive the conflict of interest issue or to allow Lowenstein to drop [him] and continue to represent the corporation in the event of a conflict." Lowenstein "refused that request," and McPherson also declined to be represented by Lowenstein. . . .

On October 13, 2000, Douglas Hefferin, CIBA Vice President for Site Remediation, wrote to Bobsein and McPherson regarding their representation and acknowledged CIBA's obligation to indemnify them. He reiterated that CIBA "remain[ed] willing" to pay their defense costs, "but only with counsel of [CIBA's] choice since it will bear all the expense." However, on November 9, 2000, after discussions with them and their "personal attorneys," Hefferin again wrote to Bobson and McPherson, jointly, and offered to provide a "defense" if they "both" agreed to accept Joseph A. Hayden, Jr. as their counsel. . . .

The letter further explained that if they objected to Hayden, CIBA would "offer [them] another attorney," but CIBA would not retain their "personal attorneys as defense counsel in the pending suits" as CIBA had the "right to choose counsel and to direct the defense as long as it continues to recognize its duty to indemnify." Finally, the letter acknowledged that Bobsein and McPherson could choose "to be represented and defended by [their] personal attorneys," but that in such circumstances, CIBA would "not pay for such a defense."

Both Bobsein and McPherson rejected CIBA's offer to retain Hayden on the basis of a conflict of interest primarily stemming from Hayden's prior representation of Dr. David Ellis, who was an individual co-defendant in the CIBA criminal matter. After the first indictment was dismissed, . . . Hayden negotiated immunity for Ellis, who then testified against Bobsein and McPherson at the second grand jury which returned an indictment against Bobsein and McPherson. In addition, Hayden's firm represented CIBA as trial counsel in related insurance coverage litigation.

[CIBA never offered the services of another attorney.]

After receiving the [mediator's recommendation favoring Bobsein and McPherson] Judge Corodemus reviewed the issues *de novo*, and rendered her October 29, 2002 opinion. She concluded that: . . .

2. "Joint representation of . . . Bobsein and McPherson and CIBA would create a conflict of interest [because the parties'] interests are not coextensive" and "[r]epresentation by Mr. Hayden was laced with inherent conflict[;]"
3. There is a possibility "that Bobsein and McPherson could be held liable for intentional acts for which they would not be] indemnified" in later possible cases, "where the results of this case could likely prejudice them[;]" . . .
5. Neither Bobsein or McPherson "alleged that any conflict existed between themselves thereby eliminating the need for two attorneys . . . [so the] court . . . disallow[ed as duplicative] 50% of the hours expended reviewing correspondence, reviewing privilege logs and conferences with judges [.]" . . .

III.

We affirm the order before us, premised on the conclusion that Bobsein and McPherson were "entitled to . . . conflict-free counsel in accordance with the Rules of Professional Conduct" and ordering CIBA to reimburse Bobsein and McPherson for reasonable counsel fees. . . . There was a reasonable and legitimate basis for both Bobsein and [McPherson] to reject the services of Lowenstein and Hayden, as each had a prior or present conflict of interest. . . . Because of the acknowledged obligation to defend and indemnify, CIBA had the right to select counsel it trusted to represent Bobsein and McPherson, provided the attorney CIBA selected was "conflict free." . . .

IV . . . .

It is undisputed that CIBA offered two different counsel for Bobsein and McPherson and that they never consented to the representation of either or otherwise waived any real or apparent conflicts. The counsel CIBA initially offered, Lowenstein Sandler, has represented CIBA in the past and was CIBA's counsel in the instant litigation. It is also undisputed that the only other counsel offered, Joseph A. Hayden, had represented CIBA in a directly related matter, the insurance coverage litigation involving many of the same underlying claims. In addition, Hayden had previously represented Dr. Ellis, the immunized former employee of CIBA, in the criminal case resulting in the guilty pleas of Bobsein and McPherson. Hayden first negotiated criminal immunity for these matters for Ellis and then represented Ellis when he testified against Bobsein and McPherson, after which Bobsein and McPherson were indicted and ultimately pled guilty. . . .

In this circumstance, a "conflict of interest" exists with respect to both Lowenstein and Hayden because Dr. Ellis and other co-employees could have been called to testify or to point the finger at Bobsein and McPherson, thereby triggering the exception to the duty to indemnify. Under the agreement in question, as Bobsein and McPherson note, no writing "expressly states nor clearly implies that the stated exceptions for 'willful misconduct'" was ever "stricken from the Agreement." Moreover, as Judge Corodemus pointed out, the consulting agreements specifically provided that they can only be amended in writing, and punitive damages were sought in the complaints. These facts are dispositive irrespective of whether New Jersey public policy would prohibit CIBA from ultimately deciding to indemnify Bobsein and McPherson for an award of punitive damages based on a finding of willful misconduct. . . .

Thus, Bobsein and McPherson were entitled to independent counsel because of the potential dispute with CIBA over the scope of indemnification, and the fact that the case has now ended satisfactorily for Bobsein and McPherson does not control whether they were obligated to accept designated counsel while the litigation was ongoing. . . .

In our view, Judge Corodemus properly held that Lowenstein could not adequately represent Bobsein and McPherson and CIBA because its "obligation to CIBA would have required taking a position which would have been adverse to the effective defense of . . . Bobsein and McPherson" because they "blame CIBA for any harm which has come to plaintiffs in the underlying action," whereas plaintiffs asserted "concerted action." The trial judge also properly held that

A. Conflicts Among Current Clients   117

there was a real possibility "that Bobsein and McPherson could later be named as defendants in another suit in which they would not be indemnified for willful conduct, where the results of this case could likely prejudice them."

Judge Corodemus also properly held that Hayden could not properly represent Bobsein and McPherson. Hayden's prior representation of Ellis was adverse to Bobsein and McPherson's interest in the prior litigation, and his representation of Bobsein and McPherson in this matter would be adverse to the interests of Ellis and CIBA, his former clients. Hence, his representation in this case was precluded by *R.P.C. 1.9.* . . .

VI.

On their cross-appeal, Bobsein and McPherson argue that the trial court erred by holding that they should have retained joint counsel because neither alleged that a conflict existed between the two of them, and thus erred by reducing their attorney fee awards by fifty percent. . . .

We do not have enough before us in the record to conclude that the defenses of Bobsein and McPherson could not be adverse, or that the conduct of only one, but not the other, could be deemed "willful." The record demonstrates that they had different roles at different times. For example, their "statement of material uncontroverted facts" states that McPherson, but not Bobsein, conducted seminars that "highlighted disposal practices at the plant that could, or did, cause contamination of the land, air and/or groundwater." . . . Therefore, for the reasons we have previously developed, both were entitled to retain independent counsel with undivided loyalty to represent him. . . .

[The court nevertheless determined that the trial judge properly concluded that the separate attorneys should have made more effort to coordinate the defenses and mitigate costs and therefore remanded for reconsideration of the fee award.]

NOTES AND QUESTIONS

1. Let's begin with Lowenstein's conflict in simultaneously representing CIBA and the two individual co-defendants in the *Kramer* case. The New Jersey conflicts rules are virtually the same as the Model Rules, including Rule 1.7. How was there a significant risk that Lowenstein's duties to its client CIBA would materially limit its duties to Bobsein and McPherson? The court also notes that Lowenstein had previously represented CIBA, although it did not describe the nature of that prior representation. Was the prior representation of CIBA relevant in assessing the existence of a conflict of interest among its current clients in this case? Remember that Rule 1.7 describes material limitations arising not only from a lawyer's duties to another client (or a third person) but from the lawyer's own interests. Did Lowenstein's interests in retaining CIBA as a client have a bearing on the existence of a conflict in simultaneously representing Bobsein and McPherson?

2. In most situations involving simultaneous representation of co-plaintiffs or co-defendants, the parties choose to be represented by the same lawyer, at least initially, and employer and employee co-defendants frequently agree to joint representation.[18] Bobsein and McPherson might have agreed to be represented by Lowenstein, particularly if they believed that CIBA had orally agreed to indemnify them even if they were found to have engaged in willful misconduct. Did Lowenstein nevertheless have at least a potentially impermissible conflict? Why do you think Lowenstein believed that it had no conflict?

3. Although Lowenstein thought it had no conflict in representing Bobsein and McPherson, its letter stated "that in the unlikely event such a conflict should develop during the course of the [joint] representation" or if Lowenstein determined that continued representation was "not appropriate," Lowenstein would resign the representation of Bobsein and McPherson and "continue to represent CIBA." This statement clearly signaled that CIBA was the primary client, and Lowenstein was agreeing to represent Bobsein and McPherson as a so-called "accommodation client." Whether Lowenstein could properly request the former employees to agree to its continued representation of CIBA, in the event of a conflict subsequently arising, is the subject of a later chapter.[19]

4. If Bobsein and McPherson wanted Lowenstein to represent them, would the material limitation conflict be consentable? What are the potential benefits of common representation here? If the conflict is consentable, what disclosures would Lowenstein have to make to the former employees? Does the nature and extent of Lowenstein's interest in retaining CIBA as a client have a bearing on the consentability of the conflict? If so, does that mean that a common lawyer should never represent both an employer company and an individual officer or employee in the same matter? As we will see in a later chapter, this is a common form of joint representation.[20]

5. One of the potential advantages of the joint representation of co-defendants is presenting a united front, including sharing information and coordinating defense strategy. Even when the defendants are separately represented, they may enter into a joint defense agreement. As you may recall, under such an agreement, privileged communications shared among the parties to the agreement remain protected by the attorney-client privilege against disclosure to other parties.[21] Does this affect your view of the consentability of co-defendants using the same lawyer? Even under a joint defense agreement, is there a risk to the

---

18. *See infra* Chapter 11: Conflicts of Interest in Entity Representation.
19. *See id.*
20. *See id.*
21. *See supra* Chapter 4: Privilege and Confidentiality.

parties of sharing privileged information? What happens if one of the co-defendants is offered a favorable settlement (or even dismissal) in return for cooperating with the plaintiffs?[22] Although these agreements are typically made among co-defendants (both criminal and civil), they also apply to co-plaintiffs and even to companies engaged in joint ventures with other businesses. In order for this "common interest" privilege to apply in a transactional context, courts generally hold that the members must be pursuing a common legal interest, not merely a common business interest. *See, e.g.,* United States v. BDO Seidman LLP, 492 F.3d 806, 816 (7th Cir. 2007).[23]

6. Let's turn now to the conflict involving Hayden, the alternative counsel offered by CIBA. Hayden had previously represented Dr. Ellis, the immunized former employee of CIBA, in the criminal case resulting in the guilty pleas of Bobsein and McPherson. In addition, Hayden represented CIBA in related insurance coverage litigation involving many of the same underlying claims, although it was unclear if that representation was pending when CIBA offered to have Hayden represent Bobsein and McPherson. Hayden's relationship with Ellis would certainly be relevant if Hayden continued to represent Ellis, who might be called as a witness to testify against Bobsein and McPherson. Can you see why? But what if Hayden was *not* currently representing Ellis? Rule 1.9 addresses representation adverse to a former client, but the concern under that rule is for the interests of the former client, not the current client. As we will see, lawyers have an obligation not to use or disclose confidential information of a former client for the benefit of a current client.[24] Did Hayden's duty to Ellis as a former client present a significant risk that his representation of Bobsein and McPherson in this case would be materially limited? Similarly, how would Hayden's representation of CIBA in related litigation, either former or current, create a material limitation conflict? Were these conflicts consentable?

7. The court also addressed the right of Bobson and McPherson to collect legal fees from CIBA while being represented by separate lawyers. Remember that the court had previously upheld CIBA's right to condition its agreement to indemnify and pay legal fees on its right to select

---

22. *See id.* (communications otherwise protected under a joint defense agreement are not privileged in subsequent adverse proceeding between the parties, unless the parties have agreed otherwise). In United States v. Krug, 868 F.3d 82 (2d Cir. 2017), the trial court ruled that the privilege applied when the government sought to introduce the testimony of a cooperating co-defendant; however, the order was reversed on the ground that the privilege did not apply to communications between co-defendants themselves, outside the presence of the lawyers, when the communications were not made for the purpose of seeking or relaying advice from one of the lawyers.

23. *See generally* Gregory B. Mauldin, Invoking the Common Interest Privilege in Collaborative Business Ventures, The Federal Lawyer 54 (Nov./Dec. 2009).

24. *See infra* Chapter 6: Conflicts of Interest: Former Clients, Prospective Clients, and Government Lawyers.

counsel, so long as that counsel was "conflict free." Was it clear there was a material limitation conflict for a single lawyer to represent both McPherson and Bobsein?

8. Issues similar to those raised in *Kramer* are presented in cases involving insurance defense litigation, in which the contract of insurance provides that the insurer's obligation of indemnification and defense gives the insurer the right not only to select counsel but to direct the defense. Whether or not the insurer is a co-client varies according to state law. The delegation of authority to a third person to direct the defense is generally unproblematic,[25] and in most instances, the insurer's agreement to defend and indemnify eliminates the significant risk of a material limitation conflict. However, when there is a claim asserted for more than the policy limits, or when there is a question whether a claim against the insured is within the policy coverage, the lawyer may not reveal adverse information of the insured to the insurer without the insured's informed consent. The standardized protection afforded by a regulated industry may permit practices otherwise impermissible for lawyers in noninsurance situations. *See* RLGL §134, cmt f.

2. Directly Adverse Conflicts

a. *Directly Adverse Conflicts in Litigation*

Because directly adverse conflicts arise most frequently in litigation, we begin there. Once we understand how these types of conflicts differ from material limitation conflicts in the litigation setting, we can better understand how courts may determine when they arise in transactions, which is currently an unsettled question.

Rule 1.7(a)(1) provides that a conflict of interest exists whenever "the representation will be directly adverse to another client." Note that unlike material limitation conflicts, this is not a question of a "risk" that the clients' interests will become directly adverse. Rather, there is a conflict under this section only if those interests *are* directly adverse.

When the clients are on opposite sides of a lawsuit, it is rare for a lawyer to undertake to represent both clients in that litigation.[26] It is possible, however, that one lawyer in a firm might agree to represent one side, while another lawyer in the same firm is representing the opposite side. Because of the imputation rule, each lawyer would have to analyze the situation as if a single lawyer

---

25. Under Model Rule 1.2(a), however, the lawyer could not agree to a settlement offer over the insured's objection, although the lawyer would need to inform the insured that rejecting the offer could result in the loss of insurance coverage for the remainder of the defense.

26. This sometimes happens when a lawyer represents both husband and wife in a divorce, and state law requires litigation in order to secure a final decree. It can also happen in multiparty litigation where two parties are aligned directly against each other on one or more issues and are prepared to consent to joint representation as they attempt to negotiate their differences.

represented both clients.[27] The representation of each client would be directly adverse to the other. In addition, there would be a material limitation conflict because the lawyer's duty to each client is materially limited by his or her duties to the other client. When this occurs, it is irrelevant whether the lawyer characterizes the conflict as either "directly adverse" or "materially limited"; the issues of consentability and informed consent are addressed in either case by Rule 1.7(b), and a lawyer may not represent a client in a claim against another client represented by that lawyer (or another firm lawyer) in the same litigation. MR 1.7(b)(3); 1.10(a). The reason these conflicts are nonconsentable is the "institutional interest in vigorous development of each client's position when the clients are aligned directly against each other in the same litigation or other proceeding before a tribunal."[28]

Both directly adverse and material limitation conflicts might also exist when a lawyer represents a client in a matter involving a third party and simultaneously represents another client in related litigation directly adverse to the first client. For example, consider a lawyer who represents Company A in an antitrust suit against a competitor defendant and then agrees to represent yet a third competitor, Company B, in a lawsuit alleging the same basic antitrust violation against Company A. Even if the lawyer will not represent Company A in defending the second lawsuit, there is a directly adverse conflict because the lawyer is representing one client, Company B, in a matter that is directly adverse to another client, Company A. Here, too, there is also a material limitation conflict, if only because the lawyer is likely to learn information about Company A's commercial practices that would be useful to Company B in establishing whether Company A committed an antitrust violation. Here, however, the conflict might be consentable because the lawyer will not represent both parties in the lawsuit between them.

Directly adverse conflicts most often occur when the lawyer represents a client suing a party that the lawyer represents in a different, *unrelated* matter, as in *Manoir-ElectroAlloys Corp.*[29] Here, unlike the previous examples, there may be no material limitation conflict. For example, consider a lawyer who represents a plaintiff in an antitrust lawsuit against a company. At the same time, the lawyer's partners are representing the same company in various unrelated matters. If the facts and circumstances of each matter are entirely unrelated, then there may be no significant risk that the lawyer's representation of the antitrust plaintiff will adversely affect the lawyer or law firm's representation of the company in these other matters. Although there is no material limitation conflict, the company nevertheless may complain that its law firm is representing another client in a directly adverse matter and seek to

---

27. MR 1.10(a). The imputation rule for current clients is discussed in more detail in a later section of this chapter.

28. MR 1.7, cmt [17].

29. *See supra* Chapter 2: Formation, Scope, and Termination of the Attorney-Client Relationship.

disqualify that lawyer in the antitrust litigation. This is exactly what happened in IBM v. Levin, 579 F.2d 271 (3d Cir. 1978), in which the CBM law firm was representing Levin in an antitrust lawsuit against IBM, at the same time that different CBM lawyers were representing IBM on unrelated matters, including labor disputes. Under the Model Code provision in effect at the time, the court upheld the disqualification of CBM from representing Levin, citing the possibly serious effect on the attorney-client relationship when a client (IBM) learns that the client is being sued in a different matter by a person (Levin) represented by the client's (IBM's) own lawyer. Similarly, the comment to Rule 1.7 explains that "[l]oyalty to a current client prohibits undertaking representation directly adverse to that client without that client's informed consent," even when the matters are "wholly unrelated" because "[t]he client as to whom the representation is directly adverse [IBM] is likely to feel betrayed, and the resulting damage to the client-lawyer relationship is likely to impair the lawyer's ability to represent the client effectively." MR 1.7, cmt [6]. When the matters are unrelated, the conflict is almost always consentable.

In these situations, there is also a conflict involving the client on whose behalf the lawsuit is brought, that is, clients in the position of Levin. There is no directly adverse conflict as far as Levin is concerned, because CBM was not representing IBM in any matter that was directly adverse to Levin. But what about the fact that CBM had an attorney-client relationship with IBM? Isn't that a fact that Levin was entitled to know when he decided to retain CBM to sue IBM? This presents what's sometimes called a "punch-pulling" conflict. As the Rule 1.7 Comment explains "the client on whose behalf the adverse representation is undertaken [Levin] reasonably may fear that the lawyer will pursue that client's case less effectively out of deference to the other client, i.e., that the representation may be materially limited by the lawyer's interest in retaining the current client [IBM]." MR 1.7, cmt [6]. As a result, the lawyer will need to determine consentability and obtain informed consent from *both* clients.

Direct adversity arises not only when the second client is an opposing party in a lawsuit, but also when the lawyer will need to cross-examine a witness on behalf of one client, and the witness is simultaneously being represented by the lawyer, typically in an unrelated matter. MR 1.7, cmt [6]. This is because being subjected to an aggressive cross-examination by one's own lawyer is just as likely to result in a feeling of betrayal as being the subject of a lawsuit. Similarly, even if the witness consents, the client on whose behalf the cross-examination is being undertaken may reasonably fear that the lawyer is relaxing his or her style of cross-examination in order to avoid offending the witness.

Directly adverse conflicts cause major headaches for large law firms. Consider a law firm approached by a company to represent it in a small tax matter. On the one hand, the law firm wants to accept the representation and hopes that its excellent work will induce the company to retain it in additional matters. On the other hand, having accepted the company as a client, the result will be that the law firm will need the company's consent to sue it, even in unrelated matters, and even on behalf of long-standing clients of the law firm.[30] Of course, the law firm could decline to represent the company, but what if the company might be willing to waive not only any existing conflicts but those that might arise in the future? Why might it be willing to do so? Perhaps the law firm has unique expertise in a narrow subject area or the company had an existing relationship with a lawyer who recently joined the law firm; in either event, the company's strong desire to retain this particular law firm may outweigh the risk of a directly adverse representation in an unrelated matter.

The validity of these waivers of future conflicts, or advance waivers, has been controversial, as illustrated in the following case. The lawyers were governed by the California Rules of Professional Conduct, but the text of the applicable California rule then in effect did not differ significantly from Model Rule 1.7. Nevertheless, the California court's approach to advance waivers apparently differs from the approach outlined in Comment [22] to the Model Rules, which we discuss in the Notes and Questions to follow.

Sheppard, Mullin, Richter & Hampton, LLP v. J-M Manufacturing Co.
198 Cal. Rptr. 3d 253 (Cal. Ct. App. 2016), *aff'd in part, rev'd in part,*
6 Cal. 5th 59 (Cal. 2018)

COLLINS, J.

INTRODUCTION

Appellant J-M Manufacturing Company, Inc. (J-M) appeals from a judgment in favor of its former attorneys, Sheppard, Mullin, Richter & Hampton, LLP (Sheppard Mullin). Sheppard Mullin sought recovery of attorney fees relating to litigation in which Sheppard Mullin represented J-M. Sheppard Mullin was disqualified from that litigation because, without obtaining informed consent from either client, Sheppard Mullin represented J-M, the defendant in the litigation, while simultaneously representing an adverse party in that case, South Tahoe Public Utility District (South Tahoe) in unrelated matters. J-M argued that its engagement agreement with Sheppard Mullin was unenforceable because it was illegal and it violated the public policy embodied in the California Rules of Professional Conduct Rule 3-310 (Rule 3-310), which bars simultaneous representation of adverse clients. J-M argued that as a result of Sheppard Mullin's violation, J-M did not owe Sheppard Mullin outstanding attorney fees and Sheppard Mullin should return to J-M all attorney fees paid pursuant to the agreement. . . .

---

30. Indeed, the company might be attempting to retain the law firm in a small matter precisely in order to prevent that firm from undertaking representation directly adverse to the company in future matters. A company that spreads its work among many law firms makes it more difficult for its adversaries to find law firms willing to represent them in matters adverse to the company.

Factual and Procedural Background . . .

The Underlying Litigation: The Qui Tam Action[31]

In 2006, a qui tam action was initiated against J-M and [another company] on behalf of approximately 200 real parties in interest, including the United States, seven states, and other state and local government entities. J-M manufactures polyvinyl chloride (PVC) pipe. The Qui Tam Action alleged that J-M falsely represented to its customers that the PVC pipe products it sold conformed to applicable industry standards for water works parts. . . .

Another law firm represented J-M in the initial phases of the Qui Tam Action. By February 2010, the complaint was unsealed, and numerous governmental entities were filing notices of intervention. Camilla Eng, J-M's general counsel, invited Sheppard Mullin attorneys Bryan Daly and Charles Kreindler to meet with her and J-M chief executive officer Walter Wang to discuss replacing J-M's current counsel. They discussed the experience of the Sheppard Mullin attorneys in qui tam actions and their proposed defense strategy. J-M retained Sheppard Mullin shortly thereafter.

Sheppard Mullin represented J-M in the Qui Tam Action for sixteen months, litigating motions, conducting discovery, reviewing documents, and conducting an extensive internal investigation at J-M. It billed J-M nearly $3.8 million for approximately 10,000 hours of work.

A. Conflict Waiver Provision

In March 2010, before J-M retained Sheppard Mullin, Daly and Kreindler ran a conflicts check to determine whether Sheppard Mullin had represented any of the real parties in interest identified in the Qui Tam Action. They discovered that Jeffrey Dinkin, a Sheppard Mullin labor-and-employment partner, had done work for South Tahoe, one of the municipal intervenors in the Qui Tam Action. . . . South Tahoe signed an engagement agreement with Sheppard Mullin in 2002, and it renewed that agreement in 2006. The agreement had a broad advance conflict waiver provision similar to the one in the J-M agreement, discussed below. Dinkin did occasional, as needed labor and employment work for South Tahoe between 2006 and November 2009.

When Sheppard Mullin's conflict check for J-M revealed that South Tahoe was a client, Daly and Kreindler consulted with an assistant general counsel to Sheppard Mullin. That unidentified attorney informed them that South Tahoe had "agreed to an advance conflict waiver and that Sheppard Mullin had done no work for [South Tahoe] for the previous five months (since November 2009)." In addition, Daly and Kreindler discussed the issue with Ronald Ryland, Sheppard Mullin's general counsel, "who analyzed [South

---

31. [In a qui tam action, a private party brings an action on behalf of the government. The action is filed under seal while the government determines whether it wants to intervene. Regardless of whether the government chooses to intervene, if the action is successful, the private party will recover a percentage of the award. — Ed.]

Tahoe's] conflict waiver and informed us that it allowed us to represent J-M in the Qui Tam Action."

Daly met with Eng for two hours on March 4, 2010, to discuss a draft engagement agreement. The draft contained the advance conflict waiver provision that ultimately was included in the final engagement agreement. It stated, "*Conflicts with Other Clients.* [Sheppard, Mullin] has many attorneys and multiple offices. We may *currently or in the future represent one or more other clients (including current, former, and future clients) in matters involving [J-M].* We undertake this engagement on the condition that we may represent another client in a matter in which *we do not represent* [J-M], even if the interests of the other client are adverse to [J-M] (including appearance on behalf of another client adverse to [J-M] in litigation or arbitration) and can also, if necessary, examine or cross-examine [J-M] personnel on behalf of that other client in such proceedings or in other proceedings to which [J-M] is not a party *provided* the other matter is not substantially related to our representation of [J-M] and in the course of representing [J-M] we have not obtained confidential information of [J-M] material to representation of the other client. *By consenting to this arrangement, [J-M] is waiving our obligation of loyalty to it so long as we maintain confidentiality and adhere to the foregoing limitations.* We seek this consent to allow our Firm to meet the needs of existing and future clients, to remain available to those other clients and to render legal services with vigor and competence. Also, if an attorney does not continue an engagement or must withdraw therefrom, the client may incur delay, prejudice or additional cost such as acquainting new counsel with the matter." . . .

According to Daly, Eng carefully reviewed the entire draft agreement with him, and she "did not ask me any questions or express any concern about the advance conflict waiver." Eng declared that Sheppard Mullin attorneys never discussed the conflict waiver provision with her, nor did they explain it. Eng also said that the Sheppard Mullin attorneys assured her there were no conflicts in representing J-M in the Qui Tam Action. J-M's practice was to ensure that its outside attorneys had neither potential nor actual conflicts of interest. Although Eng made a number of handwritten edits related to the fee provisions, and also edited the paragraph preceding the conflict waiver provision, she did not edit the conflict waiver provision. She ultimately executed the engagement agreement (the Agreement) on March 8, 2010, and sent it to Daly by email.

B. South Tahoe Raises the Conflict of Interest in the Qui Tam Action

Dinkin began actively working for South Tahoe again on March 29, 2010. Between March 2010 and May 2011, Sheppard Mullin billed South Tahoe for 12 hours of work, including telephone conversations and work on employment matters.

In March 2011, Day Pitney, counsel for South Tahoe in the Qui Tam Action, wrote a letter to Sheppard Mullin asserting that Sheppard Mullin had a conflict as a result of its simultaneous representation of J-M and South Tahoe. In response to the Day Pitney letter, Sheppard Mullin took the position that

South Tahoe had agreed to an advance conflict waiver in its engagement agreement with Sheppard Mullin and therefore no conflict existed. Day Pitney's position was that there was an actual conflict. In April 2011, Day Pitney informed Sheppard Mullin that South Tahoe planned to bring a motion to disqualify Sheppard Mullin from the Qui Tam Action.

According to Eng's declaration . . . she first heard about the conflict with South Tahoe on April 20, 2011, which she asserts was about 50 days after Day Pitney first contacted Sheppard Mullin about the conflict. Eng stated that Sheppard Mullin did not inform J-M that counsel for South Tahoe had contacted Sheppard Mullin about a potential disqualification motion because of the conflict until after the disqualification motion was filed.

Eng also stated that she first learned about the results of the March 2010 conflicts check on June 22, 2011, when she read in Sheppard Mullin attorneys' declarations that the conflicts check had revealed South Tahoe as a client. She declared that Sheppard Mullin never requested a conflict waiver from J-M in light of the South Tahoe conflict, and had Sheppard Mullin requested it, J-M would have declined.

C. Sheppard Mullin is Disqualified as Counsel in the Qui Tam Action

South Tahoe's disqualification motion in the Qui Tam Action was heard on June 6, 2011. The district court tentatively ruled that the advance waiver in South Tahoe's engagement agreement with Sheppard Mullin was invalid. In its tentative ruling, the court cited Rule 3-310(C)(3), which bars an attorney from representing clients in adverse positions without the informed written consent of each client. The court referred to the engagement agreement letters between Sheppard Mullin and South Tahoe, and said that "the prospective waivers contained within the 2002 and 2006 letters were ineffective to indicate South Tahoe's informed consent to the conflict at issue here." The court added, "The Court cannot conclude that South Tahoe was in any way close to 'fully informed'" about the conflict with J-M. The court rejected Sheppard Mullin's suggestion that it could drop South Tahoe as a client and remain counsel for J-M in the Qui Tam Action. . . .

[Here the court described Sheppard Mullin's efforts to persuade South Tahoe to consent to the conflict, including offering to pay South Tahoe $250,000 and provide 40 hours of employment work, an offer that South Tahoe rejected.]

On July 14, 2011, the district court granted South Tahoe's motion to disqualify Sheppard Mullin.

D. The Present Action

After Sheppard Mullin was disqualified, J-M took the position that J-M was not required to pay Sheppard Mullin any fees that were outstanding at the time of the disqualification. J-M also demanded that Sheppard Mullin return all fees relating to the Qui Tam Action that J-M had already paid.

In June 2012, Sheppard Mullin filed an action against J-M for specific performance, breach of contract, account stated, services rendered, and quantum meruit. It sought approximately $1.3 million as payment for services rendered to J-M in the Qui Tam Action and related matters. . . .

[Pursuant to Sheppard Mullin's petition to compel arbitration, which J-M had opposed on the ground that the conflict provision was illegal and void as against public policy, the trial court ordered arbitration, finding that J-M had alleged fraud in the inducement and the issue should be presented to the arbitrator.]

E. ARBITRATION

. . . [T]he arbitrators concluded that they need not decide whether Sheppard Mullin's failure to seek. . . . waiver [of the full South Tahoe situation] constituted an ethical violation, and for purposes of their analysis assumed that the ethical violation occurred. The arbitrators rejected J-M's claim for fraudulent concealment, based on their finding that Sheppard Mullin honestly, and in good faith believed that no conflict existed when it undertook JM's representation of the Qui Tam Action.

The arbitrators found the assumed ethical violation did not require automatic fee disgorgement or forfeiture. Instead, they engaged in an equitable weighing of whether the ethical violation was serious or egregious. The arbitrators concluded that Sheppard Mullin's conduct was not so serious or egregious as to make disgorgement or forfeiture of fees appropriate. . . .

DISCUSSION . . .

C. SHEPPARD MULLIN VIOLATED RULE 3-310

Turning to the substance of the case, we determine whether Sheppard Mullin's simultaneous representation of J-M and South Tahoe violated Rule 3-310 of the California Rules of Professional Conduct. . . .

Rule 3-310IC)(3) provides that an attorney "shall not, *without the informed written consent of each client* . . . [r]epresent a client in a matter and at the same time in a separate matter accept as a client a person or entity whose interest in the first matter is adverse to the client in the first matter." (Italics added.) "'Informed written consent' means the client's written agreement to the representation following written disclosure." (Rule 3-310(A)(2).)

. . . [T]he essential facts are not in dispute. Sheppard Mullin partner Jeffrey Dinkin did work for South Tahoe before the parties entered into the Agreement. Sheppard Mullin's conflicts check revealed Dinkin's work for South Tahoe before Sheppard Mullin gave the Agreement to J-M, but Sheppard Mullin concluded that there was no reason to disclose this relationship to J-M. J-M signed the Agreement without knowing that Sheppard Mullin represented South Tahoe in unrelated matters. The parties disagree about whether South Tahoe was a "former" client or a "current" client at the time the Agreement was signed. However, it is undisputed that three weeks after J-M signed the Agreement, Dinkin began working for South Tahoe again, so there is no question that there was an actual conflict at that point. Sheppard Mullin was disqualified from the Qui Tam Action as a result.

Sheppard Mullin argues that it proceeded as required by Rule 3-310(C)(3): "The conflict waiver in the Engagement Agreement waives both current *and* future conflicts. Waivers of current and future conflicts are commonplace and enforced by California and other courts." . . .

What Sheppard Mullin ignores, however, is that Rule 3-310(C)(3) requires *informed* written consent. . . .

Here, the undisputed facts demonstrate that Sheppard Mullin did not disclose *any* information to J-M about a conflict with South Tahoe. The Agreement includes a boilerplate waiver that included no information about any specific potential or actual conflicts. Dinkin was working for South Tahoe while Sheppard Mullin was defending J-M against South Tahoe in the Qui Tam action. It strains credulity to suggest that the Agreement constituted "*informed* written consent" of actual conflicts to J-M, when in fact Sheppard Mullin was silent about any conflict.

Even assuming Sheppard Mullin was not representing South Tahoe at the time it entered into the agreement with J-M, Sheppard Mullin nonetheless began performing additional work for South Tahoe three weeks later. It did not inform either client of this actual conflict. Because "waiver must be informed, a second waiver may be required if the original waiver insufficiently disclosed the nature of a subsequent conflict."

[The court distinguished two California cases cited by Sheppard Mullin. Both cases involved the law firm Heller, Ehrman, White & McAuliffe (Heller). In the first case, Zador Corp. v. Kwan,[32] a corporation purchased a parcel of property through its agent. Subsequently, another party sued both the corporation and the agent. The corporation, a long-time client of Heller, retained Heller to represent it in the lawsuit. The agent also asked Heller to represent him. Heller agreed to represent the agent only so long as there was no present, actual conflict between the corporation and the agent, and if the interests of the corporation became inconsistent with the agent's interests, the corporation would continue to represent the corporation. Heller encouraged the agent to seek independent counsel concerning the waiver. The agent agreed to the waiver, including an agreement not to seek disqualification of Heller if an actual conflict arose. However, when the corporation named the agent as a cross-defendant, the agent unsuccessfully sought disqualification. The California Court of Appeal held that disqualification was not required because the agent provided informed consent.

In the second case, Visa U.S.A. Inc. v. First Data Corp.,[33] a data development company retained Heller to represent it in a patent infringement action. The company was aware that Heller had a longstanding relationship with a credit card company. Heller advised the data company that although there were no current conflicts involving the credit card company, it would only

---

32. 37 Cal.Rptr.2d 754 (Cal. Ct. App. 1995).
33. 241 F.Supp.2d 1100 (N.D. Cal. 2003).

agree to represent the data company if it agreed that Heller could represent its longstanding client in any future disputes, including litigation. The data company agreed and signed an engagement letter to that effect. One year later the credit card company sued the data company for trademark infringement. A federal district court in California denied a disqualification motion, holding that the data company's advance waiver was sufficiently informed, even though it did not specifically state the precise nature of the future conflict. It held that a second waiver in an unrelated litigation was required only if the waiver did not sufficiently disclose the nature of the conflict that later arose.]

Zador and *Visa* stand in sharp contrast to the facts here. Unlike Heller in *Zador* and *Visa*, Sheppard Mullin did not disclose the circumstances regarding a potential or actual conflict with South Tahoe to either J-M or South Tahoe. The Sheppard Mullin attorneys on the Qui Tam Action were aware the firm had a relationship with South Tahoe, and even sought advice from firm counsel as to whether it had to be disclosed before J-M signed the Agreement. The conflict waiver provision in the Agreement did not mention South Tahoe. Instead, it broadly waived all current and future conflicts with any client. . . .

The facts here therefore are not analogous to *Zador* and *Visa*, because Sheppard Mullin (1) failed to inform J-M about any potential or actual conflict with South Tahoe, and (2) did not obtain J-M's informed, written consent to continued representation despite the actual conflict that occurred while Sheppard Mullin was working for J-M and South Tahoe at the same time. Written consent to all potential and actual conflicts in the absence of any knowledge about the existence of such conflicts cannot comply with the requirement of "informed written consent" in Rule 3-310(C). . . .

D. RULE 3-310 IS AN EXPRESSION OF PUBLIC POLICY CENTRAL TO THE ATTORNEY-CLIENT RELATIONSHIP, THE VIOLATION OF WHICH WARRANTS FINDING THE AGREEMENT UNENFORCEABLE.

[The court held that the contract was unenforceable because it violated the public policies embodied in the California Rules of Professional Conduct. It further found that, as a result of Sheppard Mullin's violation of Rule 3-310, it was not entitled to attorney fees during the time that it simultaneously represented both South Tahoe and J-M. This portion of the court's opinion was reversed on appeal. Although the California Supreme Court found that South Tahoe was a current client when Sheppard Mullin initially accepted the representation of J-M, the court disagreed that equitable fee forfeiture required Sheppard Mullin to forfeit all fees, concluding that "a more robust factual record" might justify compensation "for the many thousands of hours of legal work it performed on J-M's behalf," particularly if the law firm could establish that it was "legitimately confused about whether South Tahoe was J-M's current client when it took on J-M's defense." 6 Cal. 5th at 95.]

NOTES AND QUESTIONS

1. Sheppard Mullin had potentially impermissible conflicts of interest affecting both South Tahoe and J-M. Explain the nature of both conflicts, using the Model Rule provisions.

2. Both South Tahoe and J-M signed engagement agreements with similar waivers of both current and future conflicts. When the court in the qui tam action disqualified Sheppard Mullin, it found that South Tahoe's waiver was ineffective. We'll come back to that shortly. For now, let's focus on the J-M waiver, which was the subject of Sheppard Mullin's efforts to recover unpaid legal fees and J-M's claim that Sheppard Mullin should return fees that had already been paid. On what basis did the court in the contract action find that Sheppard Mullin violated California Rule 3-310(C)(3)? Focus on which specific provision of the California rule was not satisfied. Does the text of Rule 1.7 contain a similar provision?

3. Consider Comment [22] to Rule 1.7:

   > Whether a lawyer may properly request a client to waive conflicts that might arise in the future is subject to the test of paragraph (b). The effectiveness of such waivers is generally determined by the extent to which the client reasonably understands the material risks that the waiver entails. The more comprehensive the explanation of the types of future representations that might arise and the actual and reasonably foreseeable adverse consequences of those representations, the greater the likelihood that the client will have the requisite understanding. Thus, if the client agrees to consent to a particular type of conflict with which the client is already familiar, then the consent ordinarily will be effective with regard to that type of conflict. *If the consent is general and open-ended, then the consent ordinarily will be ineffective, because it is not reasonably likely that the client will have understood the material risks involved. On the other hand, if the client is an experienced user of the legal services involved and is reasonably informed regarding the risk that a conflict may arise, such consent is more likely to be effective, particularly if, e.g., the client is independently represented by other counsel in giving consent and the consent is limited to future conflicts unrelated to the subject of the representation.* In any case, advance consent cannot be effective if the circumstances that materialize in the future are such as would make the conflict nonconsentable under paragraph (b).[34]

   The controversy surrounding advance waivers is centered on the italicized portion of the comment, which describes "general and open-ended" waivers, that is, consent that purports to cover a wide range of conflicts, without reference to specifics, such as the identity of the other client or the nature of the conflict. Did either of the prior California cases, *Zador* or *Visa*, involve a general, open-ended waiver? Why were these courts' refusal to disqualify Heller unsurprising?

---

34. Emphasis added.

A. Conflicts Among Current Clients   **131**

4. J-M signed a general, open-ended waiver. In doing so, it was represented by independent counsel, Eng, in signing the waiver provision.[35] Assuming that J-M was an experienced user of litigation services, then the fact that it was independently represented and that the consent was limited to conflicts unrelated to the subject of the qui tam litigation, suggest that a court in a Model Rules state would be more likely to find that the general open-ended waiver signed by J-M was effective. But is it clear that a court following the approach outlined in Comment [22] would find that Shephard Mullin complied with Rule 1.7? Consider the fact that at the time it agreed to represent J-M, Sheppard Mullin knew of its relationship to South Tahoe and could have disclosed those specific facts to J-M as part of the waiver provision. Should it matter, in this respect, whether South Tahoe was a current or a former client at the time Sheppard Mullin agreed to represent J-M?

5. In many situations involving general, open-ended waivers, all the law firm knows is that it wants to retain the ability to represent future, unknown clients who want to sue the client being asked to sign the advance waiver. Like Sheppard Mullin, the law firm will readily agree not to accept representation when "the subject is related to the subject of the representation" or when the firm otherwise has material confidential information of the client. *Sheppard* did not involve a typical general, open-ended waiver because Sheppard Mullin already knew of specific facts and circumstances that it deliberately did not disclose to J-M. But what about the general, open-ended wavier signed by South Tahoe? The qui tam court rejected the validity of that waiver when it granted South Tahoe's motion to disqualify Sheppard Mullin. The validity of South Tahoe's waiver was not an issue in the contract case involving J-M, but did the *Sheppard* court give any indication whether it would have upheld that waiver on the ground that Sheppard Mullin had no knowledge of the J-M representation when it asked South Tahoe to sign its waiver? Subsequent to *Sheppard*, the California Supreme Court revised its rules to more closely follow the Model Rules. Notably, its comment addressing consent to a future conflict differs from Model Rule Comment [22] in that it does not mention the possibility of a general, open-ended waiver.[36]

6. Courts are split on the validity of broad waivers of future conflicts. *Compare, e.g.*, Celgene Corp. v. KV Pharm. Co., 2008 WL 2937415 (D.N.J. 2008) (disqualification despite advance waiver) *with* Galderma Labs., L.P. v. Actavis Mid Atl. LLC, 927 F.Supp.2d 390 (N.D. Tex. 2013) (rejecting *Celgene* and approving general, open-ended waiver).

---

35. "Independent counsel" refers to a lawyer who is independent of the lawyer who has the conflict, in this case Sheppard Mullin. A client company's in-house lawyer typically satisfies this requirement.

36. *See, e.g.*, Cal. Rules of Prof'l Conduct, R. 1.7, cmt [9].

7. The trial court in the qui tam action rejected Sheppard Mullin's offer to "drop South Tahoe as a client and remain counsel for J-M in the Qui Tam Action." Courts generally agree that lawyers should not be able to drop one client "like a hot potato" so they can represent another client.[37] As a result, a law firm that attempts to convert a current client into a former client by withdrawing from the representation will be treated as if the client is still current. An exception is made when the conflict has been "thrust upon" a law firm, through no fault of its own, as when a client is acquired by an adversary being sued by another client in litigation.[38] In that case, the law firm is permitted to withdraw from one of the representations in order to avoid the conflict.[39] Conflicts arising from law firm mergers are generally not treated under the "thrust upon" exception because they arise from voluntary actions of the two firms.

8. Like *Simpson*, *Sheppard* was not a disciplinary case. Unlike *Simpson*, the *Sheppard* court looked to the state disciplinary rules to determine that Sheppard Mullin acted improperly. That determination, however, was insufficient to deny the law firm recovery of its remaining legal fees under a quantum meruit basis or to require it to return the fees it had already been paid. But the court also found that Sheppard Mullin's misconduct constituted a "clear and serious violation of the conflicts rule," which is a prerequisite to total or partial fee forfeiture under general fiduciary law. *See* RLGL §37. Similarly, in disqualification cases, courts usually refer to the applicable disciplinary rules, but they also invoke doctrines unique to the disqualification context, in which courts recognize both a client's interest in being represented by counsel of its choice, and the interest of courts and adversaries in not unduly disrupting or delaying the proceedings. For example, although the disciplinary rule requires a client's actual consent to a conflict, courts might not grant disqualification when the client has impliedly waived the conflict by failing to raise it in a timely manner.[40] Similarly, some courts will not disqualify a law firm for an ethics violation unless the violation threatens the integrity of the action.[41]

---

37. *See, e.g.*, Picker International, Inc. v. Varian Associates, Inc., 670 F. Supp. 1363 (N.D. Ohio 1987), aff'd 869 F.2d 578 (Fed. Cir. 1989).

38. *See, e.g.*, N.Y. City Bar Association, Formal Op. 2005-05 (citing cases applying this concept).

39. The "thrust upon" exception is largely codified in D.C. *See* D.C. Rules of Prof'l Conduct, R. 1.7(d) (lawyer need not withdraw when unforeseeable conflict arises, except when there is a significant risk of adverse effect on the lawyer's representation of one or more of the clients, i.e., for directly adverse conflicts that are not also material limitation conflicts).

40. *See, e.g.*, State ex rel. Swanson v. 3M Co., 845 N.W.2d 808, 818 (Minn. 2014) (finding that waiver by delay in asserting right to disqualification does not preclude attorney discipline for violating ethics rule).

41. *See, e.g.*, Board of Education v. Nyquist, 590 F.2d 1241, 1246 (2d Cir. 1979) (ethical violations do not warrant disqualification unless they "taint" the proceedings or otherwise create "a substantial threat to the integrity" of the judicial process).

9. Even when a client has previously agreed to an advance waiver that is likely to be upheld, many law firms will not seek to enforce the waiver, in deference to that client. Similarly, law firms will often turn down new matters when they are likely to create a so-called "business conflict," i.e., a conflict with the desires of an existing client that do not rise to the level of a conflict of interest under the rules of professional conflict. An example would be a company that insists that its law firm not represent its primary competitor in any matter. Is it appropriate for lawyers to take such business considerations into account in deciding which client matters to accept or reject?

b. Directly Adverse Conflicts in Transactions

As we have seen, the classic directly adverse conflict occurs when a lawyer sues one current client on behalf of another current client, even when the client being sued is represented by the lawyer in a wholly unrelated matter. Putting aside matters in which a lawyer or law firm represents clients in the same transaction (because, like representing multiple parties in the same litigation, these representations typically present a material limitation conflict), under what circumstances are clients directly adverse outside of litigation?

A straightforward application of the rule in the transactional context occurred in Mylan, Inc. v. Kirkland & Ellis LLP, 2015 WL 12733414 (W.D. Pa. 2015). Here the court preliminarily enjoined a law firm from representing a pharmaceutical company in a "hostile takeover attempt" to buy the parent holding company of a pharmaceutical subsidiary that was simultaneously represented by the law firm. Whether the two representations were related was a matter of dispute; however, even if they were unrelated, the court had no trouble finding that the hostile takeover attempt was directly adverse to the takeover target, which was resisting the solicitor's attempt to take control of the target.[42]

Short of a hostile takeover attempt, it is unclear when parties to a transaction will be considered directly adverse to each other. Comment 7 to Model Rule 1.7 provides:

> Directly adverse conflicts can also arise in transactional matters. For example, if a lawyer is asked to represent the seller of a business in negotiations with a buyer represented by the lawyer, not in the same transaction but in another, unrelated matter, the lawyer could not undertake the representation without the informed consent of each client.

---

42. The law firm was not representing the takeover target itself, but rather the parent-target's subsidiary, The question was therefore raised whether representation directly adverse to a corporate parent should be treated as directly adverse to a client subsidiary. In this case the court found that it should, and therefore enjoined the law firm from continuing the adverse representation. We consider this aspect of the *Mylan* case in a later chapter addressing the application of the conflicts rules in the corporate family context. *See infra* Chapter 11: Conflicts of Interest in Entity Representation.

This comment was cited with approval in Carnegie Companies, Inc. v. Summit Properties, Inc., 918 N.E.2d 1052 (Ohio 2009). Here, the court disqualified a law firm representing a seller being sued by a buyer because the law firm was representing the buyer in an unrelated matter at the time the lawsuit was filed—the classic directly adverse conflict in litigation. However, because there was an issue involving an implied waiver, the court also addressed the fact that well before the lawsuit, the law firm had represented the seller in its negotiations to sell the property to the buyer, at the same time that the law firm was representing the buyer in an unrelated environmental matter. In finding that this representation constituted a directly adverse conflict, the court cited with approval the state equivalent of Comment 7.

Direct adversity in transactional matters is rarely litigated. As a result, *Carnegie Companies* is one of the few cases (along with *Mylan*) indicating when courts will find a directly adverse conflict in an unrelated transactional matter.[43] Carl Pierce criticized Comment 7, questioning its equation of representing a buyer in negotiations with a willing seller with representing an adverse party in litigation.[44] He argued that in these situations, it is not clear that there is likely to be "sufficient adversity [such] that the client [being represented by the lawyer in a matter unrelated to the buy-sell transaction] will feel so betrayed that the client-attorney relationship will be so impaired that the lawyer will not be able to effectively represent the client."[45] As he explained, one reason for distinguishing such transactions from litigation is the extent to which, although the parties have differing interests in a transaction, they may also have a commonality of interest not typically present in adverse litigation.[46] According to Pierce, aside from transactions such as buyer-seller or lender-borrower, there will be an even greater commonality of interest in some negotiations, such as when a lawyer represents one client in forming a partnership with a client represented by the lawyer in an unrelated matter.

---

43. Keep in mind that if the matters are related, e.g., the lawyer is representing both buyer and seller in the same transaction, then it does not matter whether we characterize the relationship as directly adverse, because there will inevitably be a material limitation conflict requiring both a determination of consentability and obtaining both clients' informed consent. When the matters are unrelated, however, the characterization does matter, because absent direct adversity, the lawyer need not obtain the informed consent of the clients.

44. Carl A. Pierce, Ethics 2000 and the Transactional Practitioner, 3 Tenn. J. Bus. Law 7, 13 (2002).

45. *Id.*

46. *Id.* An opinion of the New York City Bar Association concludes, as does Comment 7, that a directly adverse conflict exists "where the lawyer represents one party in a negotiated transaction involving another client the lawyer represents in an unrelated matter." Assoc. of Bar of New York City, Formal Op. 2001-02. It should be noted however, that the New York rule in effect at the time the opinion was issued defined all conflicts to include simultaneous representation of two clients in matters involving "differing interests," which was broadly defined to include "every interest that will adversely affect either the judgment or the loyalty of a lawyer to a client, whether it be a conflicting, inconsistent, diverse, or other interest." New York has since adopted a rule based on Model Rule 1.7; however, New York continues to use the term "differing interests" instead of "directly adverse" in its version of Rule 1.7(a)(1). N.Y. Rules of Prof'l Conduct, R. 1.7(a).

If the parties do not necessarily perceive their relationship as adversarial, then Pierce questions whether the parties' consent should be necessary for the lawyer to proceed.

3. Imputation of Conflicts Among Associated Lawyers

Model Rule 1.7 applies to individual lawyers, not law firms. Nevertheless, under Model Rule 1.10(a), the conflicts of individual lawyers are imputed to other firm lawyers. With respect to current client conflicts, the rule generally provides that "[w]hile lawyers are associated in a firm,[47] none of them shall knowingly represent a client when any one of them practicing alone would be prohibited from doing so by [Rule 1.7]." So, for example, when the Sheppard Mullin litigators seeking to represent J-M in the qui tam action discovered that other firm lawyers were representing South Tahoe in unrelated labor-and-employment matters, the litigators should have said to themselves: "The labor-and-employment lawyers representing South Tahoe could not individually undertake to represent J-M in litigation directly adverse to their client, South Tahoe; their conflict is generally imputed to us under Rule 1.10(a); therefore, unless there is an available exception, we cannot represent J-M in that litigation." Comment [2] provides the rationale for the general imputation rule:

> The rule of imputed disqualification stated in paragraph (a) gives effect to the principle of loyalty to the client as it applies to lawyers who practice in a law firm. Such situations can be considered from the premise that a firm of lawyers is essentially one lawyer for purposes of the rules governing loyalty to the client, or from the premise that each lawyer is vicariously bound by the obligation of loyalty owed by each lawyer with whom the lawyer is associated.

The first premise—that the clients of individual firm lawyers are considered to be clients of "the firm," and not just of the individual lawyer working on the case—is reflected in the language in opinions such as *Sheppard*, which the court described as a case in which Sheppard Mullin (the law firm) was disqualified from the qui tam litigation "because, without obtaining informed consent from either client, *Sheppard Mullin* represented J-M, the defendant in the litigation, while simultaneously represented an adverse party in that case, [South Tahoe]."[48]

Absent the informed consent of both clients, there is only one exception to the imputation rule for current client conflicts under Rule 1.10, and that exception applies only to conflicts involving a lawyer's personal interests, not conflicts between multiple current clients. We turn now to a discussion of conflicts between lawyer and client.

---

47. ["Firm" is defined as "a lawyer or lawyers in a law partnership, professional corporation, sole proprietorship or other association authorized to practice law; or lawyers employed in a legal services organization or the legal department of a corporation or other organization." MR Rule 1.0(c). *See also* MR 1.10, cmt [1].—Ed.]

48. Emphasis added.

B. CONFLICTS BETWEEN LAWYER AND CLIENT

1. Personal Interest Conflicts

Material limitation conflicts arise not only with respect to the differing interests of multiple clients, but also when "there is a significant risk that the representation of one or more clients will be materially limited . . . by a personal interest of the lawyer." Comment [10] explains:

> The lawyer's own interests should not be permitted to have an adverse effect on representation of a client. For example, if the probity of a lawyer's own conduct in a transaction is in serious question, it may be difficult or impossible for the lawyer to give a client detached advice.[49] Similarly, when a lawyer has discussions concerning possible employment with an opponent of the lawyer's client, or with a law firm representing the opponent, such discussions could materially limit the lawyer's representation of the client.[50] In addition, a lawyer may not allow related business interests to affect representation, for example, by referring clients to an enterprise in which the lawyer has an undisclosed financial interest.[51]

Personal interest conflicts are not limited to a lawyer's financial interests. For example, a lawyer was disciplined for continuing to represent a pregnant woman in placing her expected child for adoption after the lawyer and his wife had decided to adopt the child.[52] Lawyers have also been disciplined for representing a client with whom the lawyer had a romantic or sexual interest, particularly in cases involving matrimonial litigation.[53] Model Rule 1.8(j) now contains a rule governing lawyers having sexual relations with a client. That rule has not, however, been adopted in all jurisdictions, in which case MR 1.7(a)(2) will apply. Conflicts may also arise out of a lawyer's ideological or altruistic interests, for example, when a lawyer is drafting a client's will that includes a substantial bequest to a charitable organization with which the lawyer has a close relationship.[54]

In the business law context, personal interest conflicts may arise when a lawyer serves on a corporate client's board of directors; for example, when the lawyer is asked to opine on matters involving actions of the directors. *See* MR 1.7, cmt [35]. If the risk of a material limitation conflict is significant, then the

---

49. [*See, e.g.,* In re Enron Corp. Securities, Derivative & ERISA Litigation, 235 F.Supp.2d 549, 668, n.103 (S.D.Tex. 2002) (discussing a serious conflict of interest that arose when a company's longtime law firm investigated a whistleblower complaint that accused the law firm itself of being complicit in management fraud).—ED.]

50. [*See, e.g.,* D.C. Ethics Op. 367 (2014) (Representation of Client by Lawyer Seeking Employment with Entity or Person Adverse to Client, or Adversary's Lawyer).—ED.]

51. [*See, e.g.,* State Bar of Nevada, Standing Comm. on Ethics and Prof. Resp., Formal Op. 45 (2011) (lawyer referred clients to medical-management business owned by lawyer).—ED.]

52. In re Swihart, 517 N.E.2d 792 (Ind. 1988).

53. *See, e.g.,* Bourdon's Case, 565 A.2d 1052 (N.H. 1989).

54. *See, e.g.,* Md. Ethics Op. 2015-2 (lawyer must obtain client's informed consent if client has not determined the amount to give).

client's informed consent should be obtained before the lawyer agrees to serve as a board member. In any event, as specific conflicts arise, the lawyer will need either to cease to act as a director or obtain the client's consent, assuming the conflict is consentable.[55]

An individual lawyer's personal interest conflicts are generally *not* imputed to other associated lawyers. Rule 1.10(a)(1) provides that the general imputation rule does not apply when "the prohibition is based upon a personal interest of the disqualified lawyer and does not present a significant risk of materially limiting the representation of the client by the remaining lawyers in the firm." According to Comment [2], the rationale is that personal interest conflicts typically do not present questions of either client loyalty or the protection of confidential client information; moreover, there is generally no reason to assume that the personal interests of one lawyer will materially limit the representation of a client by another firm lawyer. For example, if one lawyer would be conflicted because of strong personal or political belief about the subject of the representation, there is little risk that another firm lawyer will be similarly affected. However, there are some circumstances in which the risk of material limitation is significant. Consider, for example, a lawyer who owns a practice with no partners and a single lawyer-employee. If the lawyer-owner has a substantial economic or other interest in a matter, there may be a significant risk that the lawyer-employee will know about that interest and be tempted to favor, either consciously or unconsciously, the lawyer-owner's interest. How might a similar situation arise in a large law firm?

2. Business and Other Financial Transactions with a Client

Rule 1.8 provides specific rules for recurring conflicts of interest involving current clients. One of the most frequently invoked rules is the one governing business or financial transactions between a lawyer and a client. Common situations include client transactions with a business in which a lawyer has a financial interest, such as a real estate lawyer who owns the title insurance company that will provide title insurance to the client buyer,[56] and lawyers acquiring stock in a client company, either in lieu of a fee or as an investment opportunity. The following case provides an example of the latter and illustrates both how lucrative such investments can be and why the client may subsequently regret the transaction.

---

55. For a more detailed description of the problems that might confront lawyers serving in this "dual role," as well as suggesting measures to minimize ethical violations, *see* ABA Formal Ethics Op. 98-410 (1998) (including list of secondary sources, some of which have urged prohibiting the practice).

56. If the lawyer has referred the client to the title insurance company, then the referral itself creates a personal interest conflict under MR 1.7(a)(2). The transaction between the title insurance company and the buyer is governed by MR 1.8(a).

Passante v. McWilliam
62 Cal. Rptr. 2d 298 (Cal. Ct. App. 1997)

SILLS, P.J.

As someone once said, if you build it they will come. And by the same token, if you make a baseball card that can't be counterfeited, they will buy it. Which brings us to the case at hand.

In 1988 the Upper Deck Company was a rookie baseball card company with an idea for a better baseball card: one that had a hologram on it. Holograms protect credit cards from counterfeiting, and the promoters of the company thought they could protect baseball cards as well. By the 1990's the Upper Deck would become a major corporation whose value was at least a quarter of a billion dollars. Collecting baseball cards, like baseball itself, is a big business.

But the outlook wasn't brilliant for the Upper Deck back in the summer of 1988. It lacked the funds for a $100,000 deposit it needed to buy some special paper by August 1, and without that deposit its contract with the major league baseball players association would have been jeopardized.

The Upper Deck's corporate attorney, Anthony Passante, then came through in the clutch. Passante found the money from the brother of his law partner, and, on the morning of July 29, had it wired to a company controlled by one of the directors. That evening, the directors of the company accepted the loan and, in gratitude, agreed among themselves that the corporate attorney should have three percent of the firm's stock. The rest is history. Instead of striking out, the Upper Deck struck it rich.

At this point, if we may be forgiven the mixed metaphor, we must change gears. No good deed goes unpunished. Anthony Passante never sought to collect the inchoate gift of stock, and later, the company just outright reneged on its promise. Passante sued for breach of oral contract, and the jury awarded him close to $33 million — the value of three percent of the Upper Deck at the time of the trial in 1993.

The trial judge, however, granted a judgment notwithstanding the verdict, largely because he concluded that Passante had violated his ethical duty as a lawyer to his client. There was no dispute that Passante did not tell the board that it might want to consult with another lawyer before it made its promise. Nor did Passante advise the board of the complications which might arise from his being given three percent of the stock.

The board had a clear moral obligation to honor its promise to Passante. He had, as the baseball cliché goes, stepped up to the plate and homered on the Upper Deck's behalf. And if this court could enforce such moral obligations, we would advise the company even yet to pay something in honor of its promise.

But the trial judge was right. If the promise was *bargained for*, it was obtained in violation of Passante's ethical obligations as an attorney. If, on the other hand, it was not bargained for — as the record here clearly shows — it was gratuitous. It was therefore legally unenforceable, even though it might have moral force. We must therefore, with perhaps a degree of reluctance, affirm the judgment of the trial court. . . .

DISCUSSION . . .

. . . [I]f the stock promise was truly bargained for, then [Passante] had an obligation to the Upper Deck, as its counsel, to give the firm the opportunity to have separate counsel represent it in the course of that bargaining. The legal profession has certain rules regarding business transactions with clients. Rule 3-300 of the California Rules of Professional Conduct . . . forbids members from entering "a business transaction with a client" without first advising the client "in writing that the client may seek the advice of an independent lawyer of the client's choice."

Here it is undisputed that Passante did not advise the Upper Deck of the need for independent counsel in connection with its promise, either in writing or even orally. Had he done so *before* the Upper Deck made its promise, the board of directors might or might not have been so enthusiastic about his finding the money as to give away three percent of the stock. In a business transaction with a client, notes our Supreme Court, a lawyer is obligated to give "his client 'all that reasonable advice against himself that he would have given him against a third person.'" *Bargaining* between the parties might have resulted in Passante settling for just a reasonable finder's fee. Independent counsel would likely have at least reminded the board members of the obvious — that a grant of stock to Passante might complicate future capital acquisition.

For better or worse, there is an inherent conflict of interest created by any situation in which the corporate attorney for a fledgling company in need of capital accepts stock as a reward for past service. As events in this case proved out, had the gift of 3 percent of the company's stock been completed, it would have made the subsequent capital acquisition much more difficult.[57]

Passante's rejoinder to the ethics issue is, as we have noted, to point to the evidence that the stock was virtually thrust at him in return for what he had done. The terms were totally dictated by the Upper Deck board. And that is it, precisely. There was no bargaining. . . .

NOTES AND QUESTIONS

1. Model Rule 1.8(a) governs business and financial transactions with clients. It is more stringent than the California rule cited in *Passante*, which required only that the lawyer advise the client "in writing that the client may seek the advice of an independent lawyer of the client's choice." Model Rule 1.8(a) provides:

---

57. [As described in an omitted portion of the opinion, after Passante arranged for the emergency loan, the company was still in need of financing. A prior investor agreed to reinvest in the company, but only on the condition that Passante, with whom he had had a prior dispute, "would not participate as an owner of the company." Another director agreed to give Passante his 3 percent interest from the director's share, after the investor "cool[ed] off" and everything was "smooth again." Shortly after the company shares were redistributed, but before the director provided Passante with his 3 percent interest, Passante was fired as corporate attorney. — Ed.]

A lawyer shall not enter into a business transaction with a client or knowingly acquire an ownership, possessor, security or other pecuniary interest adverse to a client unless:

(1) the transaction and terms on which the lawyer acquires the interest are fair and reasonable to the client and are fully disclosed and transmitted in writing in a manner that can be reasonably understood by the client;

(2) the client is advised in writing of the desirability of seeking and is given a reasonable opportunity to seek the advice of independent legal counsel on the transaction; and

(3) the client gives informed consent, in a writing signed by the client, to the essential terms of the transaction and the lawyer's role in the transaction, including whether the lawyer is representing the client in the transaction.

As *Passante* indicates, rules like this are used not only in lawyer discipline cases, but also in actions by a client to void the transaction. This is yet another aspect of general fiduciary law, in which self-dealing by a fiduciary gives rise to a presumption of undue influence and makes the transaction voidable at the election of the beneficiary.

2. According to Comment [1], the rationale for Rule 1.8(a) is that "[a] lawyer's legal skill and training, together with the relationship of trust and confidence between lawyer and client, create the possibility of overreaching when the lawyer participates in a business, property, or financial transaction with a client, for example a loan or sales transaction or a lawyer investment on behalf of a client." Given the risk of overreaching, why doesn't the rule simply prohibit such self-dealing transactions, rather than merely subject them to a series of conditions? The potential benefits *to lawyers* are obvious. Are there also potential benefits *for clients*? Was there a potential benefit to the Upper Deck of permitting it to engage in a financial transaction of some sort with Passante, for example, agreeing to give him 3 percent of the stock if he was able to secure for them a $100,000 loan critical to the success of the company?

3. Consider whether and how Passante could have complied with the conditions set forth in Rule 1.8(a). What would be his most difficult challenge? What is the relevance of the fact that at the time he sought to cash in on his shares, they were worth close to $33 million? What were they worth at the time the company promised to give them to him?

4. For a time beginning in the 1990s, it was common practice for lawyers representing start-up companies to acquire an equity investment in the company. This practice may be waning, but it still occurs. Some clients demand that the lawyer make an investment as a signal of the lawyer's belief in and commitment to the success of the company. Others do so as a means of persuading the lawyer to introduce them to the lawyer's venture capital connections. Or it may be as simple as a cash-poor client who

B. Conflicts Between Lawyer and Client **141**

has no other means of paying for the lawyer's services. *Passante* and Rule 1.8(a) address the ethical issues that arise in connection with the *transaction* itself, i.e., the risk to the client that the transaction will be unfair. Arguably, the greatest challenge for a lawyer receiving stock in lieu of a cash fee is establishing that the lawyer's fee is reasonable when the lawyer does not know either the full range of legal services that the lawyer will provide or the value of the stock the lawyer is receiving. A 2000 ABA ethics opinion addresses the ethics of equity billing and provides suggestions as to how the lawyer can establish the reasonableness of the transaction, including working with the client to determine a reasonable fee for her services (i.e., what would a reasonable flat fee be for the services the lawyer is likely to provide) and then accept stock worth approximately that amount at the time of transaction, preferably by using "the amount per share that cash investors, knowledgeable about its value, have agreed to pay for their stock about the same time."[58]

5. But the risk of an unfair transaction is not the only risk to the client. What about the risk of being *represented* by a lawyer who is a personal investor in the client company? Entrepreneurs typically believe that "the interests of an attorney who holds stock in. . . . client are *aligned* with the company's because both seek to increase the company's value for the shareholders."[59] But there are many ways in which the lawyer's personal interest in the investment may limit the lawyer's ability to exercise independent judgment on the client's behalf. For example, if the issuance of stock is contingent on obtaining a certain level of financing, the lawyer may have an interest in securing a quick financing deal, perhaps on terms that an independent lawyer would deem unfavorable. Or the lawyer may be reluctant to provide an investor with the full disclosure required by law for fear of killing the deal. And what about the difficulty of replacing a lawyer who is a co-owner, when the shares were issued in lieu of yet-to-be-performed legal services and are not easily transferable?[60] If Passante did what was required to satisfy the requirements of Rule 1.8(a), what, if any, additional action was he required to take to satisfy the requirements of Rule 1.7?[61]

---

58. ABA Formal Ethics Op. 00-418 (2000). The Opinion acknowledged that the stock may turn out to be worth either vastly more or vastly less than its current value, and acknowledged that this contingency should be taken into account. For an extensive description and critique of lawyer equity investments, *see* John S. Dzienkowski & Robert J. Peroni, The Decline in Lawyer Independence: Lawyer Equity Investments in Clients, 81 Tex. L. Rev. 405 (2002).

59. Young J. Kim & Jeffrey L. Braker, Taking Stock in Your Client: Strengthening the Client Relationship and Avoiding Pitfalls, 1 Bus. Law News 1, 23 (2008).

60. *See, e.g., id.*

61. The 2000 ABA ethics opinion described the ongoing conflict that arises from the lawyer's personal interest in the representation and how that conflict should be addressed under Rule 1.7. ABA Formal Ethics Op. 00-418 (2000). This opinion was issued before Model Rule 1.7 was amended in 2002; however, the substance of the rule is the same, except that the rule now requires that the client's informed consent to the conflict be confirmed in writing.

6. Aside from lawyers acquiring an equity interest in clients, Rule 1.8(a) applies in a wide variety of settings. Sometimes the lawyer-client transaction is unrelated to the representation, as when the lawyer seeks a loan from a client, offers to loan money or guarantee a loan to the client, or buys or sells land or other property in a transaction with a client. Sometimes the lawyer provides or has an ownership interest in an entity that provides law-related services, such as title insurance, estate planning, accounting, investment advice, or financial planning. When the services are provided to a client, Rule 1.8(a) applies. In addition, Model Rule 5.7 determines when lawyers providing law-related services are governed by the rules of professional conduct, regardless of whether the services are provided to clients or nonclients.

3. Other Specific Conflicts Rules

In addition to Rule 1.8(a), which deals with business and financial transactions with clients, Model Rule 1.8 contains a number of other specific rules applying the general principles of Rule 1.7 in commonly recurring situations. Some of them create per se prohibitions on a lawyer's conduct, such as soliciting substantial gifts from a client or preparing an instrument giving the lawyer a substantial gift, as in a will.[62] Lawyers are also prohibited from making an agreement giving the lawyer literary or media rights based on information relating to the representation,[63] providing certain types of financial assistance to a litigation client (including most gifts or loans for living expenses),[64] and engaging in sexual relations with a client unless a consensual relationship existed before the representation began.[65] Other rules address the use of client information to the client's disadvantage,[66] accepting compensation from someone other than the client,[67] participating in an aggregate settlement involving the claims of multiple clients,[68] prospectively limiting or settling claims for a lawyer's liability,[69] and acquiring a proprietary interest in the subject of a lawsuit.[70]

Under Rule 1.8(k), all of the 1.8 specific rules are applicable to lawyers associated in practice, except the prohibition on sexual relations with a client. In other words, if one lawyer in a firm is prohibited from drafting a will or providing financial assistance to a litigation client, then all associated lawyers

---

62. MR 1.8(c).
63. MR 1.8(d).
64. MR 1.8(e).
65. MR 1.8(j).
66. MR 1.8(b).
67. MR 1.8(f). This rule applies not only in the insurance defense context, but also when a company agrees to provide counsel to an employee, as in *Kramer*.
68. MR 1.8(g).
69. MR 1.8(h).
70. MR 1.8(i).

are under a similar ban. Similarly, a lawyer may not engage in a business transaction with a client represented by another lawyer in the firm without complying with the conditions enumerated in Rule 1.8(a).

C. CONFLICTS IN CRIMINAL CASES: THE CONSTITUTIONAL STANDARDS

In *Kramer*, we saw how material limitation conflicts often arise when a lawyer represents co-defendants in civil litigation. Such conflicts also arise when a lawyer represents multiple defendants in a criminal case. In such cases, the lawyer needs to be aware not only of the applicable rules of professional conduct, but also the defendants' Sixth Amendment right to the effective assistance of counsel. The following case illustrates the U.S. Supreme Court's approach to determining when a lawyer's conflict of interests results in a violation of the defendant's Sixth Amendment rights. As you read the case, ask yourself, first, whether the lawyers complied with their obligations under the rules of professional conduct and, second, how the constitutional standards differ from the professional conduct rules.

Cuyler v. Sullivan
446 U.S. 335 (1980)

Mr. Justice POWELL delivered the opinion of the Court.

The question presented is whether a state prisoner may obtain a federal writ of habeas corpus by showing that his retained defense counsel represented potentially conflicting interests.

I

Respondent John Sullivan was indicted with Gregory Carchidi and Anthony DiPasquale for the first-degree murders of John Gorey and Rita Janda. The victims, a labor official and his companion, were shot to death in Gorey's second-story office at the Philadelphia headquarters of Teamsters' Local 107....

Two privately retained lawyers, G. Fred DiBona and A. Charles Peruto, represented all three defendants throughout the state proceedings that followed the indictment. Sullivan had different counsel at the medical examiner's inquest, but he thereafter accepted representation from the two lawyers retained by his codefendants because he could not afford to pay his own lawyer. At no time did Sullivan or his lawyers object to the multiple representation. Sullivan was the first defendant to come to trial. The evidence against him was entirely circumstantial, consisting primarily of [Francis] McGrath's testimony. At the close of the Commonwealth's case, the defense rested without presenting any evidence. The jury found Sullivan guilty and fixed his penalty at life imprisonment. Sullivan's post-trial motions failed, and the

Pennsylvania Supreme Court affirmed his conviction by an equally divided vote. Sullivan's codefendants, Carchidi and DePasquale, were acquitted at separate trials.

Sullivan then petitioned for collateral relief. . . . He alleged, among other claims, that he had been denied effective assistance of counsel because his defense lawyers represented conflicting interests. . . .

DiBona and Peruto had different recollections of their roles at the trials of the three defendants. DiBona testified that he and Peruto had been "associate counsel" at each trial. Peruto recalled that he had been chief counsel for Carchidi and DePasquale, but that he merely had assisted DiBona in Sullivan's trial. DiBona and Peruto also gave conflicting accounts of the decision to rest Sullivan's defense. DiBona said he had encouraged Sullivan to testify even though the Commonwealth had presented a very weak case. Peruto remembered that he had not "want[ed] the defense to go on because I thought we would only be exposing [the defense] witnesses for the other two trials that were coming up." Sullivan testified that he had deferred to his lawyers' decision not to present evidence for the defense. But other testimony suggested that Sullivan preferred not to take the stand because cross-examination might have disclosed an extramarital affair. Finally, Carchidi claimed he would have appeared at Sullivan's trial to rebut McGrath's testimony about Carchidi's statement at the time of the murders.

[After the Pennsylvania Supreme Court affirmed Sullivan's conviction and the denial of collateral relief, Sullivan sought habeas corpus relief in federal court. The Third Circuit reversed the district court's rejection of his petition, and the U.S. Supreme Court granted the state's petition for certiorari.]

IV

We [now address] Sullivan's claim that he was denied the effective assistance of counsel guaranteed by the Sixth Amendment because his lawyers had a conflict of interest. The claim raises two issues expressly reserved in *Holloway v. Arkansas.* The first is whether a state trial judge must inquire into the propriety of multiple representation even though no party lodges an objection. The second is whether the mere possibility of a conflict of interest warrants the conclusion that the defendant was deprived of his right to counsel.

A

In *Holloway,* a single public defender represented three defendants at the same trial. The trial court refused to consider the appointment of separate counsel despite the defense lawyer's timely and repeated assertions that the interests of his client conflicted. This Court recognized that a lawyer forced to represent codefendants whose interests conflict cannot provide the adequate legal assistance required by the Sixth Amendment. Given the trial court's failure to respond to timely objections, however, the Court did not consider whether the alleged conflict actually existed. It simply held that the trial court's error unconstitutionally endangered the right to counsel.

Holloway requires state trial courts to investigate timely objections to multiple representation. But nothing in our precedents suggests that the Sixth Amendment requires state courts themselves to initiate inquiries into the propriety of multiple representation in every case. Defense counsel have an ethical obligation to avoid conflicting representations and to advise the court promptly when a conflict of interest arises during the course of the trial. Absent special circumstances, therefore, trial courts may assume either that multiple representation entails no conflict or that the lawyer and his clients knowingly accept such risk of conflict as may exist. . . . Unless the trial court knows or reasonably should know that a particular conflict exists, the court need not initiate an inquiry.

Nothing in the circumstances of this case indicates that the trial court had a duty to inquire whether there was a conflict of interest. The provision of separate trials for Sullivan and his codefendants significantly reduced the potential for a divergence in their interests. No participant in Sullivan's trial ever objected to the multiple representation. . . . Finally, as the Court of Appeals noted, counsel's critical decision to rest Sullivan's defense was on its face a reasonable tactical response to the weakness of the circumstantial evidence presented by the prosecutor. . . .

B

Holloway reaffirmed that multiple representation does not violate the Sixth Amendment unless it gives rise to a conflict of interest. Since a possible conflict inheres in almost every instance of multiple representation, a defendant who objects to multiple representation must have the opportunity to show that potential conflicts impermissibly imperil his right to a fair trial. But unless the trial court fails to afford such an opportunity, a reviewing court cannot presume that the possibility for conflict has resulted in ineffective assistance of counsel. Such a presumption would preclude multiple representation even in cases where "'[a] common defense . . . gives strength against a common attack.'"

In order to establish a violation of the Sixth Amendment, a defendant who raised no objection at trial must demonstrate that an actual conflict of interest adversely affected his lawyer's performance. In *Glasser v. United States*, for example, the record showed that defense counsel failed to cross-examine a prosecution witness whose testimony linked Glasser with the crime and failed to resist the presentation of arguably impermissible evidence. The Court found that both the omissions resulted from counsel's desire to diminish the jury's perception of a codefendant's guilt. . . . Since this actual conflict of interest impaired Glasser's defense, the Court reversed his conviction.

Dukes v. Warden presented a contrasting situation. Dukes pleaded guilty on the advice of two lawyers, one of whom also represented Dukes' codefendants on an unrelated charge. Dukes later learned that this lawyer had sought leniency for the codefendants by arguing that their cooperation with the police induced Dukes to please guilty. Dukes argued in this Court that his lawyer's conflict of interest had infected his plea. We found "'nothing in the record . . . which would indicate that the alleged conflict resulted in ineffective assistance of counsel and did in fact render the plea in question involuntary and unintelligent.'" Since Dukes did not identify an actual lapse in representation, we affirmed the denial of the habeas corpus relief.

Glasser established that unconstitutional multiple representation is never harmless error. Once the Court concluded that Glasser's lawyer had an actual conflict of interest, it refused "to indulge in nice calculations as to the amount of prejudice" attributable to the conflict. The conflict itself demonstrated a denial of the "right to have the effective assistance of counsel." Thus, a defendant who shows that a conflict of interest actually affected the adequacy of his representation need not demonstrate prejudice in order to obtain relief. But until a defendant shows that his counsel actively represented conflicting interests, he has not established the constitutional predicate for his claim of ineffective assistance.

C

The Court of Appeals granted Sullivan relief because he had shown that the multiple representation in this case involved a possible conflict of interest. We hold that the possibility of conflict is insufficient to impugn a criminal conviction. In order to demonstrate a violation of his Sixth Amendment rights, a defendant must establish that an actual conflict of interest adversely affected his lawyer's performance. Sullivan believes he should prevail even under this standard. He emphasizes Peruto's admission that the decision to rest Sullivan's defense reflected a reluctance to expose witnesses who later might have testified for the other defendants. The petitioner, on the other hand, points to DiBona's contrary testimony and to evidence that Sullivan himself wished to avoid taking the stand. Since the Court of Appeals did not weigh these conflicting contentions under the proper legal standard, its judgment is vacated and the case is remanded for further proceedings consistent with this opinion.

[Justice Brennan wrote a concurring opinion in which he stated that a trial court must affirmatively advise defendants "that joint representation creates potential hazards which the defendants should consider before proceeding with the representation." In the absence of such advice, he would have required that where there is "a significant possibility of conflict," the defendant "is entitled to a presumption that his representation in fact suffered." Justice Marshall wrote a separate opinion, concurring in part and dissenting in part. He agreed with Justice Brennan that the trial court must advise the defendant of the dangers of multiple representation, but disagreed that with such advice, the defendant must "demonstrate that his attorney's trial performance differed from what it would have been if the defendant had been the attorney's only client." He would have held that when "an actual, relevant conflict of interests existed . . . the conviction must be reversed."]

NOTES AND QUESTIONS

1. Assume that Model Rule 1.7 applied to the lawyers' decision to represent all three of the criminal defendants. Did the lawyers comply with that rule?

2. The Court did not refer to the lawyers' obligations under applicable professional conduct rules, but only to the requirements for effective assistance of counsel under the Sixth Amendment. How do those requirements differ from those under Rule 1.7? What is the justification for applying constitutional standards that are more difficult to meet than the professional conduct rules?

3. In the absence of a conflict of interest, the standard for establishing ineffective assistance of counsel requires that the defendant demonstrate both "serious attorney error" and "prejudice," where prejudice is demonstrated by a showing that "there is a reasonable probability that but for counsel's unprofessional errors, the result of the proceeding would have been different."[71] In what respect does the *Cuyler* standard make it easier for defendants to establish ineffective assistance of counsel when they allege a conflict of interests? Is it likely that Sullivan would meet that standard upon remand to the lower court for additional findings?[72]

4. In *Holloway*, the defendants did not need to demonstrate either an actual conflict or an adverse effect on the lawyer's performance. Why wasn't the *Holloway* standard available to Sullivan?

5. Federal Rule of Criminal Procedure 44(c)(2), which was proposed but not enacted when *Cuyler* was decided, requires the judge to follow the procedure outlined in Justice Brennan's concurring opinion: in cases of joint representation, "[t]he court must promptly inquire about the propriety of joint representation and must personally advise each defendant of the right to effective assistance of counsel, including separate representation," and "[u]nless there is good cause to believe that no conflict of interest is likely to arise, the court must take appropriate measures to protect each defendant's right to counsel." The rule applies only in federal court, not in state court. If the state trial court judge had made such an inquiry in *Cuyler*, how do you expect Sullivan would have responded?

6. Concerned that a convicted defendant may subsequently raise an ineffective assistance of counsel claim, prosecutors will usually bring a perceived conflict to the attention of the trial judge and might even file

---

71. Strickland v. Washington, 466 U.S. 668, 669 (1984). We return to a discussion of the *Strickland* standards in Chapter 7, in the context of an ineffective assistance of counsel claim based on a defense lawyer's refusal to permit the defendant to give perjured testimony. *See infra* Chapter 7: Limits of Zealous Representation I: Litigation.

72. Three years later, Sullivan finally prevailed when the Third Circuit affirmed a judgment finding ineffective assistance of counsel based on counsel's failure to call Carchidi as a witness to testify in Sullivan's trial. Sullivan v. Cuyler, 723 F.2d 1077 (3d Cir. 1983).

Chapter 5 Conflicts of Interest: Current Clients

a motion to disqualify joint counsel. Defense counsel often respond by alleging that such prosecutors are acting strategically to remove an effective defense lawyer. Does the government have a legitimate interest in the enforcement of rules designed to protect the defendants themselves?

7. In United States v. Schwartz,[73] the trial judge provided detailed advice to jointly represented police co-defendants, including Schwartz, concerning the various ways in which defense counsel might not advance a defense favorable to one defendant because of its adverse impact on the other defendant, as well as the potential adverse effect of the law firm's personal interest in maintaining a lucrative contract with the police union, which had interests that might differ from those of the individual defendant officers. After receiving the advice of independent counsel, both defendants insisted that they wanted to keep their lawyers. Schwartz, who was convicted and subsequently represented by new counsel, raised an ineffective assistance of counsel claim. The Second Circuit reversed the conviction, holding that Schwartz's lawyer had an actual conflict, that it adversely affected his performance, and that Schwartz had not effectively waived his Sixth Amendment right to effective assistance of counsel because even if the waiver was knowing and intelligent, the conflict was so serious as to be nonwaiveable, precisely the argument the government had made in seeking to disqualify Schwartz's lawyer at trial. Given the result in *Schwartz*, should courts require criminal defendants to be represented by conflict-free counsel, at least when the court is aware of potentially serious conflicts?

Review Problems

5-1 A lawyer represented a recently incorporated sand processing company. The sand processing business involves significant start-up costs and large operating expenses, and there is no revenue until sales begin. The company was significantly undercapitalized and had substantial debt and ongoing cash-flow problems. Despite these problems, the lawyer genuinely believed that the company would do well. The lawyer also represented a businesswoman who was looking for good long-term investments. She had heard that the sand processing company was looking for investors and, knowing that the lawyer represented the company, she asked him to represent her in making the investment. He responded that because he represented the company, he could not advise her whether the investment was a sound one, but that if she had decided on her own to make the investment, he would consider representing both her and the company in the transaction. Issues to be decided include how many shares of stock she will receive in return for her investment and whether the stock will be voting stock. Under what circumstances, if any, may the lawyer represent both parties in the transaction?

---

73. 283 F.3d 76 (2d Cir. 2002).

5-2 A legal services office is representing a class of female prison inmates in custody at the state prison, which is suing the state on the ground that their facility does not have programs and services equivalent to those provided the male inmates at a separate facility. After the court ruled that the state had violated the plaintiffs' equal protection rights, it ordered the state to construct a permanent new in-state facility and to provide a temporary facility for the plaintiffs while the permanent facility is being built. In negotiating with the plaintiffs, the state has offered to provide a temporary facility on the grounds of a state residential home for mentally disabled children (the School). There are other sites available, but the state has stated its clear preference for using this site, and if negotiations fail, it will seek a court order to build the temporary facility on the grounds of the School. Other lawyers at the legal services office are representing a class of the children who reside at the School. That class is suing the state on grounds unrelated to the female inmate class action. The lawyers representing the class of children are seeking to intervene in the female inmates' class action in order to oppose housing the female inmates on the grounds of the School. The state has filed a motion to disqualify the legal services lawyers representing the class of female inmates on the ground that there is a conflict of interest with the lawyers' representation of the School children. Is the motion likely to succeed?

5-3 A lawyer is representing a department store in litigation against one of its suppliers. One of the lawyer's partners has been approached by the department store's landlord, which wants to sue the store for unpaid rent. The subject matter of the two lawsuits is unrelated. May the partner accept the representation? Would your answer differ if the lawyer and the partner agree to establish screening measures to prevent the lawyers in each case from sharing information with each other?

5-4 What if the engagement letter between the law firm and the department store in Problem 5-3 had a provision that the department store agreed that the law firm could represent another client in a matter in which it did not represent the department store, even if the interests of the other client are adverse to the department store, including the appearance on behalf of another client in litigation, provided that the other matter is not substantially related to the law firm's representation of the department store?

5-5 Same facts as in Problem 5-3, except that the department store's landlord has requested the partner to represent the landlord in renegotiating the terms of the lease between the landlord and the department store. May the partner accept the representation?

5-6 A hair and nails salon owner retained a lawyer from time to time to assist him in various matters, including dealings with his landlord, his neighbors, and the municipality. The owner decided to move his salon to a different location and mentioned to the lawyer that he needed cash so that he could buy the property and not have to deal with a landlord. He was having trouble securing a bank loan at a reasonable rate of interest, and the lawyer suggested looking for investors in the business. The owner asked if the lawyer would be interested in becoming his partner. The owner proposed terms for the transaction, which included making the lawyer a minority partner and having her contribute her legal services in forming the partnership, in addition to making a cash contribution. Once the partnership was formed, the lawyer would continue to charge for legal services at a discounted rate. May the lawyer agree to become a partner in the owner's business?

5-7 A husband and wife were charged with several offenses in connection with an armed robbery of a warehouse. Both defendants were charged with conspiracy to commit aggravated robbery. The husband was also charged with aggravated robbery, second degree kidnapping, aggravated motor vehicle theft, second degree burglary, and felony theft. According to the indictment, the husband and another man carried out the armed robbery, while the wife was alleged to have joined in the planning and to have agreed to provide the husband with an alibi. The husband and wife called a well-known criminal defense lawyer and asked her to represent them both. When the lawyer suggested that perhaps they should be separately represented, they responded that they had done some research and determined that, while she was expensive, this lawyer had the best reputation in the area for criminal defense work, and that they could not afford two top lawyers. May the lawyer represent them both? If she did, and they were both convicted, would either or both of them have a claim for ineffective assistance of counsel?

CHAPTER 6

CONFLICTS OF INTEREST: FORMER CLIENTS, PROSPECTIVE CLIENTS, AND GOVERNMENT LAWYERS

Model Rules 1.9, 1.10, 1.11, 1.18

When the interests of a current client conflict with the interests of either another client, a third person, or the lawyer's own interests, conflict of interest doctrine requires the lawyer to consider all the likely ways in which the representation of the current client may be compromised. What happens once the representation is over? We have already seen that the lawyer's duties to a former client are not the same as the duties to a current client,[1] but neither is the former client a complete stranger. And what about a prospective client who consults the lawyer in contemplation of forming an attorney-client relationship, but the relationship is never formed?

A previous chapter addressed the lawyer's duty of confidentiality, including attorney-client privilege and the professional rule of confidentiality.[2] As we have seen, lawyers owe a robust duty of confidentiality to both former and prospective clients.[3] With respect to the duty to avoid conflicts of interest, however, this chapter demonstrates that a lawyer's duty to former and prospective clients is narrower and consists primarily (but not entirely) of a duty to avoid representations that risk violations of the duty of confidentiality. In addition, a lawyer's duty to a former government client is even more circumscribed.

---

1. For example, the section in Chapter 2 on terminating the lawyer-client relationship discusses both ABA Formal Ethics Opinion 18-491 (2018), which advised that lawyers must inform current but not former clients about material errors committed during the representation, and *Manoir-ElectroAlloys*, which addressed the application of directly adverse conflicts, including in unrelated matters, to current but not former clients.
2. *See supra* Chapter 4: Privilege and Confidentiality.
3. *See id.* at n. 19 (discussing MR 1.9(c) and 1.18(b)).

A. FORMER CLIENT CONFLICTS

1. The Individual Private Lawyer in a Stable Firm[4]

Model Rule 1.9(a) provides that "[a] lawyer who has formerly represented a client in a matter shall not thereafter represent another person in the same or a substantially related matter in which that person's interests are materially adverse to the interests of the former client unless the former client gives informed consent, confirmed in writing." And, as we know, Rule 1.10(a) generally imputes the disqualification of an individual lawyer to other, associated lawyers.[5] The following case involves a former representation provided by Richard Fine, a partner in the law firm Schwartz & Freeman, in a business transaction involving the three shareholders of NPD Research, Inc. ("NPD"). It was not Fine, but other Schwartz & Freeman lawyers whose disqualification was sought when they later represented the plaintiff in an antitrust lawsuit against NPD. The majority opinion quickly disposed of the imputation question, distinguishing previous cases recognizing an exception to the imputation rule when an individual lawyer changes jobs, and it is the new firm that is opposed to the former client.[6] As a result, the court focused its analysis on the application of the substantial relationship test, which is the key to determining disqualification of an individual private lawyer. The court relied on the common law of lawyer disqualification, but as you will see, the test it applied is very close to the test set forth in Model Rule 1.9(a).

Analytica, Inc. v. NPD Research, Inc.
708 F.2d 1263 (7th Cir. 1983)

Posner, Circuit Judge.

Two law firms, Schwartz & Freeman and Pressman and Hartunian, appeal from orders disqualifying them from representing Analytica, Inc. in an antitrust suit against NPD, Inc. . . .

John Malec went to work for NPD, a closely held corporation engaged in market research, in 1972. His employment agreement allowed him to, and he did, buy two shares of NPD stock, which made him a 10 percent owner. It also

---

4. A stable firm is one in which the lawyer with the alleged conflict was with the same firm during both the former and current representations.

5. *See supra* Chapter 5: Conflicts of Interest: Current Clients.

6. The edited version of the opinion that appears here does not contain either the portion of the majority opinion that imputed Fine's conflict to the other Schwartz & Freeman lawyers or a lengthy dissenting opinion that would not have imputed the conflict. These aspects of the opinion are discussed in a later section of this chapter on the exceptions to the imputation rule for migratory lawyers with former client conflicts.

A. Former Client Conflicts 153

gave him an option to buy two more shares. He allowed the option to expire in 1975, but his two co-owners, in recognition of Malec's substantial contributions to the firm (as executive vice-president and manager of the firm's Chicago office), decided to give him the two additional shares—another 10 percent of the company—anyway and they told Malec to find a lawyer who would structure the transaction in the least costly way. He turned to Richard Fine, a partner in Schwartz & Freeman. Fine devised a plan whereby the other co-owners would each transfer one share of stock back to the corporation, which would then issue the stock to Malec together with a cash bonus. Because the stock and the cash bonus were to be deemed compensation for Malec's services to the corporation, the value of the stock, plus the cash, would be taxable income to Malec (the purpose of the cash bonus was to help him pay the income tax that would be due on the value of the stock), and a deductible business expense to the corporation. A value had therefore to be put on the stock. NPD gave Fine the information he needed to estimate that value—information on NPD's financial condition, sales trends, and management—and Fine fixed a value which the corporation adopted. Fine billed NPD for his services and NPD paid the bill. . . .

While the negotiations over the stock transfer were proceeding, relations between Malec and his co-owners were deteriorating, and in May 1977 he left the company and sold his stock to them. His wife, who also had been working for NPD since 1972, left NPD at the same time and within a month had incorporated Analytica to compete with NPD in the market-research business. She has since left Analytica; Mr. Malec apparently never had a position with it.

In October 1977, several months after the Malecs had left NPD and Analytica had been formed, Analytica retained Schwartz & Freeman as its counsel. Schwartz & Freeman forthwith complained on Analytica's behalf to the Federal Trade Commission, charging that NPD was engaged in anticompetitive behavior that was preventing Analytica from establishing itself in the market. When the FTC would do nothing, Analytica decided to bring its own suit against NPD, and it authorized Schwartz & Freeman to engage Pressman and Hartunian as trial counsel. The suit was filed in June 1979 and charged NPD with various antitrust offenses, including abuse of a monopoly position that NPD is alleged to have obtained before June 1977.

[NPD moved to disqualify both firms representing Analytica. The judge disqualified both firms and ordered Schwartz & Freeman to pay NPD's fees and expenses. Analytica did not appeal the order of disqualification. It was unclear whether the law firms had standing to appeal the order of disqualification; however, because Schwartz & Freeman had standing to appeal the order to pay fees and costs, the court concluded it was required to consider the validity of the disqualification order.]

For rather obvious reasons a lawyer is prohibited from using confidential information that he has obtained from a client against that client on behalf of another one. But this prohibition has not seemed enough by itself to make clients feel secure about reposing confidences in lawyers, so a further prohibition has evolved: a lawyer may not represent an adversary of his former client if the subject matter of the two representations is "substantially related," which means: if the lawyer could have obtained confidential information in the first representation that would have been relevant in the second. It is irrelevant whether he actually obtained such information and used it against his former client, or whether—if the lawyer is a firm rather than an individual practitioner—different people in the firm handled the two matters and scrupulously avoided discussing them. . . .

Schwartz & Freeman's Mr. Fine not only had access to but received confidential financial and operating data of NPD in 1976 and early 1977 when he was putting together the deal to transfer stock to Mr. Malec. Within a few months, Schwartz & Freeman popped up as counsel to an adversary of NPD's before the FTC, and in that proceeding and later in the antitrust lawsuit advanced contentions to which the data Fine received might have been relevant. Those data concerned NPD's profitability, sales prospects, and general market strength—all matters potentially germane to both the liability and damage phases of antitrust suit charging NPD with monopolization. The two representations are thus substantially related, even though we do not know whether any of the information Fine received would be useful in Analytica's lawsuit (it might just duplicate information in Malec's possession, but we do not know his role in Analytica's suit), or if so whether he conveyed any of it to his partners and associates who were actually handling the suit. If the "substantial relationship" test applies, however, "it is not appropriate for the court to inquire into whether actual confidences were disclosed[.]" . . .

Schwartz & Freeman argues, it is true, that Malec rather than NPD retained it to structure the stock transfer, but this is both erroneous and irrelevant. NPD's three co-owners retained Schwartz & Freeman to work out a deal beneficial to all of them. All agreed that Mr. Malec should be given two more shares of the stock; the only question was the cheapest way of doing it; the right answer would benefit them all. The principals saw no need to be represented by separate lawyers, each pushing for a bigger slice of a fixed pie and a fee for getting it. Not only did NPD rather than Malec pay Schwartz & Freeman's bills (and there is no proof that it had a practice of paying its officers' legal expenses), but neither NPD nor the co-owners were represented by counsel other than Schwartz & Freeman. Though Millman, an accountant for NPD, did have a law degree and did do some work on the stock-transfer plan, he was not acting as the co-owners' or NPD's lawyer in a negotiation in which Fine was acting as Malec's lawyer. As is common in closely held corporations, Fine was counsel to the firm, as well as to all of its principals, for the transaction. If the position taken by Schwartz & Freeman prevailed, a corporation that used only one lawyer to counsel it on matters of shareholder compensation would run the risk of the lawyer's later being deemed to have represented a single shareholder rather than the whole firm, and the corporation would lose the protection of the lawyer-client relationship. Schwartz & Freeman's position thus could force up the legal expenses of owners of closely held corporations.

But it does not even matter whether NPD or Malec was the client. In Westinghouse's antitrust suit against Kerr-McGee and other uranium producers, Kerr-McGee moved to disqualify Westinghouse's counsel, Kirkland & Ellis, because of a project that the law firm had done for the American Petroleum Institute, of which Kerr-McGee was a member, on competition in the energy industries. Kirkland & Ellis's client had been the Institute rather than Kerr-McGee but we held that this did not matter; what mattered was that Kerr-McGee had furnished confidential information to Kirkland & Ellis in connection with the law firm's work for the Institute. *Westinghouse Elec. Corp. v. Kerr-McGee Corp.* As in this case, it was not shown that the information had actually been used in the antitrust litigation. . . . The connection between the representation of a trade association of which Kerr-McGee happened to be a member and the representation of its adversary thus was rather tenuous; one may doubt whether Kerr-McGee really thought its confidences had been abused by Kirkland & Ellis. If there is any aspect of the *Kerr-McGee* decision that it is subject to criticism, it is this. The present case is a much stronger one for disqualification. If NPD did not retain Schwartz & Freeman—though we think it did—still it supplied Schwartz & Freeman with just the kind of confidential data that it would have furnished a lawyer that it had retained; and it had a right not to see Schwartz & Freeman reappear within months on the opposite side of a litigation to which that data might be highly pertinent.

We acknowledge the growing dissatisfaction . . . with the use of disqualification as a remedy for unethical conduct by lawyers. The dissatisfaction is based partly on the effect of disqualification proceedings in delaying the underlying litigation and partly on a sense that current conflict of interest standards, in legal representation as in government employment, are too stringent, particularly as applied to large law firms—though there is no indication that Schwartz & Freeman is a large firm. But we cannot find any authority for withholding the remedy in a case like this. . . . NPD thought Schwartz & Freeman was its counsel and supplied it without reserve with the sort of data—data about profits and sales and marketing plans—that play a key role in a monopolization suit—and lo and behold, within months Schwartz & Freeman had been hired by a competitor of NPD's to try to get the Federal Trade Commission to sue NPD; and later that competitor, still represented by Schwartz & Freeman, brought its own suit against NPD. We doubt that anyone would argue that Schwartz & Freeman could resist disqualification if it were still representing NPD, even if no confidences were revealed, and we do not think that an interval of a few months ought to make a critical difference.

The "substantial relationship test" test has its problems, but conducting a factual inquiry in every case into whether confidences had actually been revealed would not be a satisfactory alternative, particularly in a case such as this where the issue is not just whether they have been revealed but also whether they will be revealed during a pending litigation. Apart from the difficulty of taking evidence on the question without compromising the confidences themselves, the only witnesses would be the very lawyers whose firm was sought to be disqualified (unlike a case where the issue is what confidences a lawyer received while at a former law firm), and their interest not only in retaining a client but in denying a serious breach of professional ethics might outweigh any felt obligation to "come clean." While "appearance of impropriety" as a principle of professional ethics invites and maybe has undergone uncritical expansion because of its vague and open-ended character, in this case it has meaning and weight. For a law firm to represent one client today, and the client's adversary tomorrow in a closely related matter, creates an unsavory appearance of conflict of interest that is difficult to dispel in the eyes of the lay public — or for that matter the bench and bar — by the filing of affidavits, difficult to verify objectively, denying that improper communication has taken place or will take place between the lawyers in the firm handling the two sides. Clients will not repose confidences in lawyers whom they distrust and will not trust firms that switch sides as nimbly as Schwartz & Freeman.

NOTES AND QUESTIONS

1. Once again, we have a situation in which a lawyer failed to clarify who the lawyer was representing. Confusion as to the identity of a client is common in situations involving an entity and an individual constituent,[7] particularly in the case of closely held corporations. Usually, it is a constituent who is seeking to establish an attorney-client relationship with an entity lawyer, but here it was the entity, NPD, claiming that Fine had represented it, as well as Malec, a shareholder. What factors persuaded the court that Fine represented NPD in the transaction?

2. After NPD established that Fine had previously represented it in the transaction with Malec, it then had to satisfy the "substantial relationship" test for former client conflicts. This test requires, for both the former and the current representations, a clear understanding of the identity of the parties (including which party the lawyer represents or represented) and the subject matter of the representations. It may be

---

7. Individual constituents of an entity such as a corporation include officers, directors, employees, and shareholders. We address ethical issues in entity representation in a later chapter. *See infra* Chapter 9: Who's My Client?

helpful to diagram the successive representations in the following manner, using *Analytica* as an example:

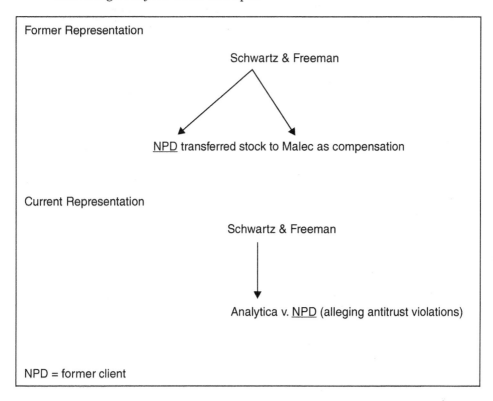

With this diagram in mind, Rule 1.9(a) requires answering the following questions:
- Is the subject matter of the current representation the same or *substantially related* to the subject matter of the former representation?
- Is the current representation *materially adverse* to the former client?
- Has the former client given its *informed consent* to the lawyer's role in the current representation?

3. The *Analytica* court was concerned that Schwartz & Freeman might disclose or use NPD's confidential client information for the benefit of its new client, Analytica, in the antitrust lawsuit. Rule 1.9(c) would prohibit Schwartz & Freeman from doing so. Why isn't the duty of confidentiality sufficient to protect NPD against misuse of its confidential information? And if the goal is a prophylactic rule to prevent lawyers from putting themselves in a position to misuse confidential information, why not simply prohibit *all* representations adverse to a former client?

4. The "substantial relationship" test is a compromise between the two extremes suggested in the previous note. It provides for some prophylactic protection of confidentiality, but it limits disqualification to the

same or substantially related matters, thereby acknowledging the legitimate interests of the both the lawyer and the new client. (What are those interests?) How is the substantial relationship test defined in both *Analytica* and in Rule 1.9(a)? Be sure to read Comment [3], which was added as part of the ABA's "Ethics 2000" revisions in 2002[8] and which was derived from common law cases involving disqualification at the behest of a former client. *Analytica* was decided in 1983, the year that the Model Rules, including Rule 1.9(a), were first adopted. Believe it or not, the Model Code had *no* provision directly addressing former client conflicts. Rather, the prophylactic rule now embodied in Rule 1.9(a) evolved in disqualification cases, in which courts often invoked the Model Code's general admonition to lawyers to avoid the "appearance of impropriety."[9]

5. The difference in the precise language used to describe the substantial relationship test in *Analytica* and in Comment [3] concerns the probability that the lawyer obtained confidential information in the former representation that could be used to the disadvantage of the former client in the current representation. Consider the following scenario, which is commonly used to illustrate the application of the substantial relationship test:

> A lawyer represented a husband in his business and financial affairs. That representation is over. Subsequently, the wife asks the lawyer to represent her in a divorce from the husband.

Assuming that one of the issues in the divorce will be the allocation of the couple's assets, including assets from the husband's business and financial affairs, it is likely that the lawyer obtained confidential information from the husband that will be useful to the wife in the current representation, particularly if the prior representation was recent. But what if the subject matters of the two representations were less obviously related to each other? For example, what if the lawyer had previously represented the husband in the sale of a condominium he owned prior to the marriage? It may be unlikely that the lawyer acquired confidential information of the husband that would be relevant in the current divorce, but isn't it *possible* that the lawyer did so? The lawyer could have learned that the husband had an offshore bank account or that he had a child from a previous relationship that he has not disclosed to the wife. Is that mere possibility sufficient to establish a substantial relationship under the test as it is literally articulated in *Analytica*? Do you think that the court intended a literal interpretation of that test or is it

---

8. The ABA Ethics 2000 Commission was formed in 1997 to conduct a comprehensive review of the Model Rules. It recommended extensive revisions, most of which were adopted by the ABA in 2002. The author of this casebook was the Chief Reporter to the Commission.

9. Model Code, Canon 9 (1969).

more likely that the court intended an interpretation closer to the test articulated in Comment 3?

6. How did the *Analytica* court know that Fine "not only had access to but received confidential financial and operating data of NPD in 1976 and early 1977 when he was putting together the deal to transfer stock to Mr. Malec" and that "[t]hose data concerned NPD's profitability, sales prospects, and general market strength"? Was it obvious that NPD would have disclosed this type of information in the process of determining how to best structure the transfer of two shares of stock to Malec? The parties (and their current lawyers) typically play a significant role in assisting the court to determine both the nature of the former and current representations and whether it is likely that information obtained in the former representation is relevant to material issues in the current representation. When the two matters are not obviously related, the former client will typically authorize some use of its confidential information in order to educate and persuade the judge on the disqualification question. In turn, the trial judge may authorize limited discovery to assist in making the factual determinations necessary to determine whether two matters are substantially related. *See, e.g., State v. 3M Co.*, 2016 Minn. Dist. LEXIS 1 (2016) (following submission of affidavits and limited discovery, court engaged in a detailed analysis of the specific types of client information the lawyers were exposed to in a former representation and an explanation of how this information was material to the factual and legal issues in the current representation).

7. Comment [3] also notes that "[i]nformation acquired in a prior representation may have been rendered obsolete by the passage of time, a circumstance that may be relevant in determining whether two representations are substantially related." Thus even in the hypothetical involving the prior representation of a husband in his business and financial affairs, if that representation occurred many years ago, it may be unlikely that any confidential information obtained at that time will be relevant in the current divorce matter.

8. Lawyers who were formerly in-house counsel for a company, or who otherwise had represented the company in a series of related matters, will often have extensive knowledge of the company's practices in those types of matters, for example, the company's litigation strategies and the psychological profiles of the personnel involved. This type of knowledge is sometimes called "playbook" information, and courts struggle to determine when the information is sufficiently advantageous to the new client that disqualification is required. Comment [2] cautions that "a lawyer who recurrently handled a type of problem for a former client is not precluded from later representing another client in a factually distinct problem of that type," and Comment [3] adds that "[i]n the case of an organizational client, general knowledge of the client's policies and

practices ordinarily will not preclude a subsequent representation; on the other hand, knowledge of specific facts gained in a prior representation that are relevant to the matter in question ordinarily will preclude such a representation." Compare, for example, Watkins v. TransUnion, LLC, 869 F.3d 514 (7th Cir. 2017), in which a lawyer who had defended a credit reporting agency in Fair Credit Reporting Act cases was not disqualified from representing FCRA claimants against the agency because the current claims did not turn on the facts of any specific prior litigation in which the lawyer represented the agency, with Farris v. Fireman's Fund Insurance Co., 14 Cal.Rptr.3d 618 (Cal. Ct. App. 2004), in which a lawyer who had previously handled coverage claims for an insurance company was disqualified from representing a policy holder in a bad faith claim against the company because he had played a role in shaping the coverage and settlement policies at issue in the case.

9. Confidentiality is not the only concern underlying the substantial relationship test. It is disloyal to appear adverse to a former client in the same or a substantially related matter, even when there is no substantial risk of disclosing confidential information. For example, Comment [1] explains that "a lawyer could not properly seek to rescind on behalf of a new client a contract drafted on behalf of the former client," as when representing the wife in a divorce proceeding would involve invalidating a prenuptial agreement previously drafted by the lawyer on behalf of the husband.[10] The comment further explains that "a lawyer who has represented multiple clients in a matter [cannot] represent one of the clients against the others in the same or a substantially related matter after a dispute arose among the clients in that matter, unless all affected clients give informed consent," even though the expectation is that the joint clients would have shared information concerning the joint representation.[11]

10. In *Analytica*, the court held that even if NPD had not been a client of Schwartz & Freeman, it would have been entitled to disqualification under the so-called *Westinghouse* doctrine. Under this doctrine, when a party furnishes confidential information to a lawyer representing another party, in a matter in which both parties have a significant interest, the lawyer has a common law fiduciary duty not to use or disclose those confidences to third parties.[12] Thus, in close

---

10. *See* Price v. Price, 733 N.Y.S.2d 420 (N.Y. App. Div. 2001).

11. *See, e.g.*, Brennans, Inc. v. Brennan's Restaurants, Inc., 590 F.2d 168 (5th Cir. 1979) (lawyer who formerly represented family businesses could not represent one group against another after split that failed to specify which group would have control of family business trademarks; court rejected lawyer's argument that as former joint clients, family businesses would have shared information and therefore disqualification was unnecessary).

12. For example, a law firm that serves as underwriters' counsel in a securities offering and acquires confidential information of the issuer during a due diligence review of the issuer may owe a common law fiduciary duty to the issuer; if so, the lawyer may not subsequently represent a client attempting a hostile takeover of the issuer.

cases, when it is unclear whether an attorney-client relationship has been formed, the party supplying confidential information is entitled to have the lawyer's fiduciary duty protected through a motion to disqualify. This disqualification doctrine is not reflected in the disciplinary rules.

2. The Individual Private Lawyer Who Migrates to Another Firm

In imputing Fine's conflict to the other Schwartz & Freeman lawyers, the *Analytica* court acknowledged an exception to the imputation rule when an individual lawyer changes jobs. When this happens, two questions arise: first, whether the individual lawyer is personally disqualified, and second, if so, whether the new firm can avoid disqualification by "screening" the disqualified lawyer from the representation. In this section we cover the first question, as illustrated in one of the earliest cases to recognize an imputation exception for individual migratory lawyers. As with *Analytica*, this case was decided before the adoption of a disciplinary rule specifically addressing former client conflicts. Model Rule 1.9(b) was drafted to reflect the result in this and similar cases.

Silver Chrysler Plymouth, Inc. v. Chrysler Motors Corp.
518 F.2d 751 (2d Cir. 1975)

MOORE, Circuit Judge:

An action is pending before Judge Weinstein in the Eastern District of New York. . . . It awaits trial. The controversy alleged therein essentially is whether Silver Chrysler's dealership agreement with Chrysler was for five years (the term specified in a written lease executed between the parties in 1968) as asserted by Chrysler or for twenty-five years as alleged by Silver Chrysler on the basis of a 1967 agreement. . . . This brief recital of the nature of the action is required only as a background to the issue on this appeal, which is disqualification of counsel.

Chrysler for many years has been represented by the law firm of Kelley Drye Warren Clark Carr & Ellis (Kelley Drye) and its predecessors, which also represents Chrysler in this action. Although many other law firms represent Chrysler on various matters throughout the country, only Kelley Drye is listed on Chrysler's annual reports as "Counsel." Silver Chrysler is represented by the firm of Hammond & Schreiber, P.C. Dale Schreiber of that firm had been employed as an associate by Kelley Drye, and while there worked on certain Chrysler matters. Because of this fact Kelley Drye by motion sought to disqualify both Schreiber and his firm from representing Silver Chrysler in this action. In support of, and in opposition to, the motion respectively, the parties submitted voluminous affidavits, copies of pleadings in cases in which

Schreiber had allegedly worked, and extensive memoranda of law. With this material before him and after oral argument, the Judge proceeded to analyze the motion on the theory that the "[d]ecision turns on whether, in the course of the former 'representation,' the associate acquired information reasonably related to the particular subject matter of the cases on which Schreiber was claimed to have worked and the law as it appears in this Circuit from decided cases" and in a comprehensive opinion . . . concluded that "disqualification of plaintiff's counsel is not warranted." From this decision Chrysler appeals.

. . . [W]e recognize "our responsibility to preserve a balance, delicate though it may be, between an individual's right to his own freely chosen counsel and the need to maintain the highest ethical standards of professional responsibility."

Upon graduation from law school in 1965, Dale Schreiber was hired by Kelley Drye to commence work in September 1965. He worked at the firm briefly before accepting a position as a law clerk to a federal judge. His work at Kelley Drye began again in September 1966 and continued to February 1969.

Kelley Drye is one of New York's larger law firms, having had at the time some 30 partners and 50 associates. Several of New York's firms have well over 100 associates and over 50 partners. Many firms hire a dozen or more law graduates each year and it has now become the practice to hire for summer work (usually between their second and third years at law school) a substantial number of law students. These "summer associates" most frequently perform tasks assigned to them by supervising associates or partners. Many of the summer students do not return to the same firms with which they have been associated or even remain in New York City. Even after an initial association with a firm upon graduation, it is not uncommon for young lawyers to change their affiliation once or even several times. It is equally well known that the larger firms in the metropolitan areas have hundreds (collectively thousands) of clients. It is unquestionably true that in the course of their work at large law firms, associates are entrusted with the confidences of some of their clients. But it would be absurd to conclude that immediately upon their entry on duty they become the recipients of knowledge as to the names of all the firm's clients, the contents of all files relating to such clients, and all confidential disclosures by client officers or employees to any lawyer in the firm. Obviously such legal osmosis does not occur. The mere recital of such a proposition should be self-refuting. And a rational interpretation of the Code of Professional Responsibility does not call for disqualification on the basis of such an unrealistic perception of the practice of law in large firms.

Fulfilling the purpose of the disqualification remedy, "namely the need to enforce the lawyer's duty of absolute fidelity and to guard against the danger of inadvertent use of confidential information," does not require such a blanket approach. Nor are such broad measures required to maintain "in the public mind, a high regard for the legal profession." Thus, while this Circuit has recognized that an inference may arise that an attorney formerly associated with a firm himself received confidential information transmitted by a client to the firm, that inference is a rebuttable one. . . . The importance of not unnecessarily constricting the careers of lawyers who started their practice of law at large firms simply on the basis of their former association underscores the significance of this language.

[The court discussed a number of cases in which the "substantial relationship" test had been applied to disqualify lawyers who had personally represented the former client.]

In contrast to the foregoing decisions, quite a different situation is presented here. Schreiber was not counsel for Chrysler in the sense that the disqualified attorneys were in those cases. Although Kelley Drye had pervasive contacts with Chrysler, Schreiber's relationship cannot be considered co-extensive with that of his firm. The evidence submitted to Judge Weinstein on the motion was admittedly somewhat conflicting. By affidavits submitted by the head of the litigation department at Kelley Drye, Chrysler sought to show not only the purportedly "substantially related" cases upon which Schreiber worked, but also the extensive amount of Chrysler-dealer litigation in the office and in which Schreiber was concededly not involved. Schreiber responded by affidavit, detailing his responsibilities in Chrysler matters upon which he recalled working. Schreiber also obtained, amongst other things, supporting affidavits of Clark J. Gurney (the associate who handled the bulk of Chrysler dealer matters) and Hugh M. Baum, two former colleagues at Kelley Drye (presently employed elsewhere).

Judge Weinstein was well aware of the tests to be applied. He examined . . . an antitrust action and Schreiber's principal Chrysler case while at Kelley Drye, and concluded that the case was not substantially related to this litigation. As to other matters that Schreiber recalled working on, the judge was entitled to conclude that they also were not substantially related. . . . With respect to still others . . . there was ample basis for crediting Schreiber's denial of having worked on them and concluding that Schreiber's involvement was, at most, limited to brief, informal discussions on a procedural matter or research on a specific point of law. The affidavits of Gurney and Baum provided support for such a conclusion. In this respect we do not believe that there is any basis for distinguishing between partners and associates on the basis of title alone—both are members of the bar and are bound by the same Code of Professional responsibility. But there is reason to differentiate for disqualification purposes between lawyers who become heavily involved in the facts of a particular matter and those who enter briefly on the periphery for a limited and specific purpose relating solely to legal questions. In large firms at least, the former are normally the more seasoned lawyers and the latter the more junior. This is not to say that young attorneys in large firms never become important figures in certain matters but merely to recognize that some of their work is often of a far more limited variety. Under the latter circumstances the attorney's role cannot be considered "representation" . . . so as to require disqualification. The cases and the Canons on which they are based are intended to protect the confidences of former clients when an attorney has been in a position to learn them. To apply the remedy when there is no realistic chance that confidences were disclosed would go far beyond the purpose of these decisions. Chrysler was in a position here conclusively to refute Schreiber's position that his role in these cases had been non-existent or fleeting. Through affidavits of those who supervised Schreiber on particular matters or perhaps through time records, the issue was capable of proof. Chrysler instead chose to approach the matter in largely conclusory terms.[13] We cannot realistically subscribe to the contention that proof submitted for this limited purpose, by time records or otherwise, would have necessitated disclosure of any confidences entrusted to Kelley Drye.

Judge Weinstein also concluded that Schreiber had rebutted any inference, arising merely from his former association with Kelley Drye, that he possessed confidences that can be used against Chrysler in this lawsuit. We think the district judge was plainly correct. There may have been matters within the firm which, had Schreiber worked on them, would have compelled disqualification here. But Schreiber denied having been entrusted with any such confidences. He was supported in this respect by the affidavits of Gurney and Baum. This was sufficient. . . .

Order AFFIRMED.

NOTES AND QUESTIONS

1. Rule 1.9(a), which applies to a lawyer who personally represented a former client, presumes that the lawyer received confidential information that will be of use to a new client whose position is materially adverse to the former client in the same or a substantially related matter. The presumption is based on the type of information that a lawyer in that position would normally have obtained. The rule may be overinclusive because there will be occasions in which the lawyer did not in fact receive such confidential information. Nevertheless, the presumption is *irrebuttable* because we do not want to put former clients in the position of having to reveal the confidences disclosed in order to disqualify the lawyer.

2. Although Schreiber was only an associate while he was at Kelley Drye, he admittedly "represented" Chrysler in some matters; however, the court found that these matters were not substantially related to the pending dealer litigation brought by Silver Chrysler. The court also found that other lawyers at Kelly Drye represented Chrysler in matters

---

13. [Fn. 8 in Original] Example from a Kelley Drye (Chrysler) affidavit:

"[Schreiber] obtained unmeasurable confidential information regarding the practices, procedures, methods of operation, activities, contemplated conduct, legal problems, and litigations of [Chrysler]." . . .

that *were* substantially related to the pending case, but that Schreiber himself had not "represented" Chrysler in these cases. If the Model Rules had been in effect at the time, the court would have concluded that Schreiber was not personally disqualified under Rule 1.9(a).

3. At this point, if the Model Rules had been in effect, the court would have turned to Rule 1.9(b), which was adopted to reflect the result in cases like Silver Chrysler. Rule 1.9(b) provides:

> A lawyer shall not knowingly represent a person in the same or a substantially related matter in which *a firm with which the lawyer formerly was associated had previously represented a client*
> (1) whose interests are materially adverse to that person; and
> (2) about whom the lawyer had acquired information protected by Rules 1.6 and 1.9(c) that is material to the matter;
> unless the former client gives informed consent, confirmed in writing. (Emphasis added.)

Under this rule, there is a *presumption* that while at the lawyer's former firm (Kelley Drye), a lawyer like Schreiber knew all of the confidential information known by the other lawyers who personally represented the former client. Unlike the presumption in Rule 1.9(a), however, this is a *rebuttable presumption*. Thus under paragraph (2), the lawyer (Schreiber) is permitted to introduce evidence, including his own affidavit, that he did not learn material confidential information concerning the substantially related matters. What is the basis for the initial presumption that Schreiber knew everything other Kelly Drye lawyers knew during his period of association with that firm? And what is the basis for permitting him to rebut that inference under Rule 1.9(b), while continuing to maintain an *irrebuttable presumption* when Rule 1.9(a) applies?

4. Richard Fine in *Analytica* clearly represented the former client (NPD), in which case *Rule 1.9(a)* would apply to his individual disqualification in the subsequent case; as a result, he would not be permitted to rebut the presumption that he received confidential information that could be used to the disadvantage of NPD. Dale Schreiber performed *no work* on some of the substantially related former Chrysler cases; as a result, *Rule 1.9(b)* clearly applies, and Schreiber would be permitted to rebut the presumption that he received material confidential information. But what about the cases in which Schreiber performed *some work*, but claims that he billed only several hours doing legal research on peripheral matters? By virtue of that work, did he "represent" Chrysler in those matters (in which case under Rule 1.9(a) he would not be permitted to rebut the presumption that he received material information)? What if he claims that he billed 20 hours or even 30 hours but that he nevertheless did not learn any confidential Chrysler information that would be material to the pending dealer litigation? Does the Rule 1.9 Comment provide any guidance in determining, in these situations, which rule applies? Does *Silver Chrysler*?

3. The New Law Firm of the Individual Migratory Lawyer: Rebuttable or Irrebuttable Presumption?

Assume that Schreiber himself was not going to work on the *Silver Chrysler* litigation at his new law firm. If he was not personally disqualified, then there was nothing to impute, and other firm lawyers were free to undertake the representation of Silver Chrysler Plymouth without any concern about either obtaining Chrysler's consent or screening Schreiber from the representation. But what if Schreiber *was* personally disqualified? This was the case in *Analytica*, where Fine was disqualified, and his disqualification was imputed to the other Schwartz & Freedman lawyers. In the following opinion, from the same court that decided *Analytica* (and in the same year), the court held that a law firm could screen a personally disqualified lawyer in order to avoid imputation of the conflict, over the objection of the former client.

Schiessle v. Stephens
717 F.2d 417 (7th Cir. 1983)

COFFEY, Circuit Judge.

The plaintiff, Eleanor Schiessle, appeals from an order of the United States District Court for the Northern District of Illinois, Eastern Division, disqualifying her co-counsel, the law firm of Ross, Hardies, O'Keefe, Babcock & Parsons in this antitrust action. . . .

Eleanor Schiessle commenced this action in August 1979 against eighteen defendants, including Arthur Swanson, Carl Swanson and Paul Swanson . . . alleging that various acts taken by the defendants to condemn and to redevelop property owned by the plaintiff in Rosemont, Illinois, violated, inter alia, federal antitrust law. The plaintiff retained the law firm of Ross, Hardies, O'Keefe, Babcock & Parsons (Ross) to represent her in this action, and Tobin Richter, a partner in the Ross firm, appeared on behalf of Schiessle in proceedings before the district court. On August 14, 1979, prior to an official appearance being filed on behalf of the Swansons, Michael King, at that time a partner at the Antonow & Fink law firm, contacted Attorney Richter by phone asking that the lawsuits be dismissed as to the Swanson defendants. [Richter refused to do so. Subsequently a different law firm filed an appearance on behalf of the Swansons until October 19, 1979, when that law firm withdrew, and attorneys Goldberg and Kocian of the Antonow & Fink firm were substituted as counsel for the Swansons.]

Attorney King left the Antonow & Fink law firm and joined the Ross law firm as a partner on October 1, 1979. Attorney King changed firms prior to the withdrawal [of the Swansons' first counsel of record] and the substitution of Antonow & Fink[.] [Nearly two years later, the Antonow & Fink law firm informed Richter that if Schiessle refused to dismiss the Swansons, the firm would move to disqualify the Ross firm as counsel for the plaintiff.]

The Ross firm refused to dismiss the Swansons and filed a motion with the district court in September of 1981, requesting a declaration of qualification as counsel for the plaintiff. In conjunction with that motion, the Ross firm filed affidavits of Attorneys King and Richter. In his affidavit, Attorney King averred that although he did some work on the present action on behalf of the Swansons during his affiliation with Antonow & Fink, he never filed either an appearance on behalf of the Swansons or an answer, nor did he conduct any "detailed investigation into the case." In fact, according to King, he never met the Swansons. With regard to his contact with his case after he left the Antonow & Fink firm, he averred:

> "Since the time I joined Ross, Hardies, I have, of course, not worked on the *Schiessle* case, have not filed an appearance, have not discussed the merits of the case, nor have I informed anyone of any conversations or information, if any, which occurred during my time at Antonow & Fink. At this time, I know nothing of the merits of the case, have not worked on the case, have billed no time to Mrs. Schiessle, met Mrs. Schiessle, nor participated in any discussion of the merits of the case with her.
>
> "Notwithstanding that I would not recognize the Swansons or Mrs. Schiessle if she walked into my office, I will continue as I have in the past to have absolutely no contact with the case."

The Swanson defendants responded by filing a cross-motion for disqualification of the Ross firm. Attached to the Swansons' cross-motion was an affidavit of Attorney Goldberg of the Antonow & Fink firm reciting (1) that during August and September of 1979 Michael King was the Antonow & Fink "partner in charge" of representing the Swansons in the antitrust lawsuit; (2) that on "four separate occasions [King] had conversations with Paul Swanson concerning [the] lawsuit;" and (3) that King had "numerous conferences concerning this lawsuit and the Swansons with other attorneys of Antonow & Fink."

On June 29, 1982, the district court granted the defendants' cross-motion and disqualified the Ross firm as counsel for the plaintiff Schiessle. . . . The district court . . . concluded that because the representation of the Swansons by the Ross firm (King's present firm) involved the identical antitrust lawsuit, the court would irrebuttably presume that confidences were shared between King and the other members of the Ross firm. . . .

Questions of ethical propriety like those presented in this appeal have been addressed by this court within the past year. In those cases we noted two important considerations invoked in motions to disqualify counsel and emphasized the delicacy of the balance that must be maintained between them: the sacrosanct privacy of the attorney-client relationship (and the professional integrity implicated by that relationship) and the prerogative of a party to proceed with counsel of its choice. . . .

The analysis outlined in our prior decisions concerning attorney disqualification comprises three steps. First, we must determine whether a substantial relationship exists between the subject matter of the prior and present representations. If we conclude that a substantial relationship does exist, we must next ascertain whether the presumption of shared confidences with respect to the prior representation has been rebutted.[14] If we conclude this presumption has not been rebutted, we must then determine whether the presumption of shared confidences has been rebutted with respect to the present representation. Failure to rebut this presumption would also make the disqualification proper.

In the case at bar, there is no dispute that the subject matter of the prior and present representations are substantially related — indeed the subject matter is identical as it concerns the same antitrust litigation. . . .

The second step in our analysis requires us to ascertain whether the presumption of shared confidences which arises from our determination that the representations are substantially related has been rebutted with respect to the prior representation. In other words, we must determine whether the attorney whose change of employment created the disqualification issue was actually privy to any confidential information his prior law firm received from the party now seeking disqualification of his present firm. The evidence presented to rebut this presumption must "clearly and effectively" demonstrate that the attorney in question had no knowledge of the information, confidences and/or secrets related by the client in the prior representation. In the case at bar, the affidavit of Attorney Goldberg of the Antonow & Fink firm stands uncontradicted. . . . Accordingly, we conclude that Attorney King has not rebutted the presumption of shared confidences with respect to his involvement in the case while he was a partner at Antonow & Fink.

Lastly, the district court must determine whether the presumption of shared confidences has been rebutted with respect to the present representation. In other words, the court must determine whether the knowledge of the "confidences and secrets" of the Swansons which King brought with him has been passed on to or is likely to be passed on to members of the Ross firm. In [a prior case] we held that the presumption of shared confidences could be rebutted by demonstrating that "specific institutional mechanisms" . . . had been implemented to effectively insulate against any flow of confidential information from the "infected" attorney to any member of his present firm. Such a determination can be based on objective and verifiable evidence presented to the trial court and must be made on a case-by-case basis. Factors appropriate for consideration by the trial court might include, but are not limited to, the size and structural divisions of the law firm involved, the likelihood of contact between the "infected" attorney and the specific attorneys responsible for the present representation, the existence of rules which prevent the "infected" attorney from access to relevant files or other information

---

14. [In footnote 2 of the opinion, the court distinguished *Analytica*, in which it held that the presumption of shared confidences was irrebuttable, on the ground that the exception for cases in which a lawyer changed jobs was not available. As the *Analytica* court put it: "The exception is inapplicable here: the firm itself changed sides." — ED.]

pertaining to the present litigation or which prevent him from sharing in the fees derived from such litigation.

We hold that the district court erred in relying on an irrebuttable presumption to find that confidences and secrets had been shared between King and other members of the Ross firm because our [previous opinions] make it clear that the presumption of shared confidences can be rebutted. However, we reach the same conclusion as the district court that the Ross firm must be disqualified from representing Schiessle because: (1) Attorney King obviously had knowledge of the Swansons' case . . . and (2) no evidence exists in the record establishing that the Ross firm has "institutional mechanisms" in effect insulating King "from all participation in and information about [the] case." It should also be noted that counsel for the plaintiff informed the court at oral argument that the Ross firm was without "formal institutional[ized] . . . screening" insulating Attorney King from the members of the firm representing Schiessle. . . .

The order of the district court is AFFIRMED.

NOTES AND QUESTIONS

1. As in *Analytica*, the *Schiessle* court did not rely on a rule of professional conduct, but rather adopted a common law test for disqualification. Its common law test consists of three steps. The first two steps are used to determine the personal disqualification of the migratory lawyer (Attorney King), and, if the lawyer is disqualified, then the third step is used to determine if that disqualification will be imputed to the lawyer's new firm (the Ross law firm). How do the Seventh Circuit's first two steps differ from the analysis under Model Rules 1.9(a) and (b) to determine King's personal disqualification? Under what circumstances might these different tests result in different results on the question whether the migratory lawyer is personally disqualified?

2. It is the willingness of a jurisdiction to adopt a "third step" that is most likely to determine whether the migratory lawyer's new firm will be disqualified. This step allows the new firm to avoid the imputation of the migratory lawyer's personal disqualification through the use of "institutional measures" designed to screen the "infected" lawyer from the representation. Under the Model Code, which had no separate rule for former client conflicts, if any lawyer was required to decline employment under a disciplinary rule, no associated lawyer could accept that employment.[15] And until 2009, Model Rule 1.10 required the same result for lawyers in private practice like Attorney King.[16]

---

15. Model Code, DR 5-105(D).

16. Model Rule 1.11, however, has always provided for nonconsensual screening as a means to avoid imputed disqualification in the case of a former government lawyer. The conflict rules for former government lawyers are discussed in a later section in this chapter.

Analytica was decided by the Seventh Circuit in the same year that it decided *Schiessle*. Why wasn't Schwartz & Freeman given an opportunity to rebut the presumption that Fine would share his confidences with the lawyers representing Analytica? Ross, King's new law firm, was given that opportunity, but failed to satisfy the court that the presumption had been rebutted. Why?

3. In 2009, the ABA amended Rule 1.10 to add the following additional exception[17] to the general rule, which otherwise imputes conflicts arising under both 1.7 and 1.9:

> (2) The prohibition is based upon rule 1.9(a), or (b), and arises out of the disqualified lawyer's association with a prior firm, and
>> (i) the disqualified lawyer is timely screened from any participation in the matter and is apportioned no part of the fee therefrom;
>> (ii) written notice is promptly given to any affected former client to enable the former client to ascertain compliance with the provisions of this Rule, which shall include a description of the screening procedures employed; a statement that review may be available before a tribunal; and an agreement by the firm to respond promptly to any written inquiries or objections by the former client about the screening procedures; and
>> (iii) certifications of compliance with these Rules and with the screening procedures are provided to the former client by the screened lawyer and by a partner of the firm, at reasonable intervals upon the former client's written request and upon termination of the screening procedures.

The term "screened" is defined in Rule 1.0(k) as "the isolation of a lawyer from any participation in a matter through the timely imposition of procedures within a firm that are reasonably adequate under the circumstances to protect information that the isolated lawyer is obligated to protect under these Rules or other law."

4. Even prior to 2009, a number of states had adopted screening measures in their professional conduct rules. According to a 2015 chart prepared by the ABA, 30 jurisdictions have lateral screening rules similar to the new ABA rule, three have a rule that limits screening to situations where the migratory lawyer was not substantially involved in the matter at the former firm, and 18 continue to have rules that do not permit any screening to avoid imputation of the conflict.[18] New York is one of the jurisdictions that does not permit screening for lateral lawyers in its rules of professional conduct; nevertheless, New York courts continue

---

17. Remember that the first exception, added in 2002, was for personal interest conflicts. *See supra* Chapter 5: Conflicts of Interest: Current Clients.

18. *See* ABA, State Adoption of Lateral Screening Rule, at https://www.americanbar.org/groups/professional_responsibility/policy/rule_charts/.

to address disqualification of a migratory lawyer's new firm on a case-by-case basis, sometimes denying disqualification when screening measures have been timely implemented.[19]

5. Virtually all jurisdictions have adopted a rule similar to Rule 1.9(b), which permits a migratory lawyer to rebut the presumption that while that lawyer was associated with a *former firm*, the lawyer learned confidential information known by other lawyers who actually represented the former client. In other words, in that context, rebutting the presumption that lawyers in a law firm share information is not controversial. And yet, if the migratory lawyer is personally disqualified (because he or she has been unable to rebut that presumption), it continues to be controversial whether to permit the *new firm* to rebut the presumption that the migratory lawyer has shared or will share the information that the lawyer has with the other lawyers in the firm who will be representing the new client. What is the difference in the two contexts that could justify a willingness to adopt a rebuttable presumption for information sharing among lawyers in the *former firm* but an unwillingness to adopt the same rebuttable presumption for information sharing in the *new firm*? Does it matter that in one instance, the question is historical (what happened at the former firm), while in the other instance the question is both historical (what has happened already in the new firm) and a matter of prediction (what will happen as the representation progresses)? Consider also the ability of the former client to counter any affidavits submitted by the migratory lawyer and other new firm lawyers, first, on the question of what information the migratory lawyer likely received at the former firm (Rule 1.9(b)), and second, on the question of what information the migratory lawyer has shared or is likely to share at the new firm (Rule 1.10(a)(2)).

6. If there are indeed differences between the two contexts (information sharing at the former firm and information sharing at the new firm), then what policy considerations nevertheless justify the willingness of a majority of jurisdictions to permit firms to justify nonconsensual screening to avoid imputation of a former client conflict in case of a migratory lawyer? Do these policy justifications justify extension of nonconsensual screening in situations not currently covered by the rule, that is, current client conflicts or former client conflicts in the absence of a migratory lawyer (e.g., *Analytica*)?

7. What should the Ross firm have done to rebut the presumption of shared confidences when King joined the law firm? Consider the comment to Rule 1.10, as well as the comment to Rule 1.0(k), both of which

---

19. *See* Fallyn B. Reichert, "Screening" New York's New Rules—Laterals Remain Conflicted Out, 31 Pace L. Rev. 464 (2011).

provide a more detailed description of the type of institutional measures required under those rules. Also consider the following description of measures taken by a new law firm in yet another Seventh Circuit case, in which the court held that the measures were sufficient to rebut the presumption of shared confidences in that firm:

> The types of institutional mechanisms that have been determined to protect successfully the confidentiality of the attorney-client relationship include: (1) instructions, given to all members of the new firm, of the attorney's recusal and of the ban on exchange of information; (2) prohibited access to the files and other information on the case; (3) locked case files with keys distributed to a select few; (4) secret codes necessary to access pertinent information on electronic hardware; and (5) prohibited sharing in the fees derived from such litigation. Moreover, the screening devices must be employed "as soon as the 'disqualifying event occurred.'" . . .
>
> In this case, the defendants have rebutted the presumption of shared confidences by describing the timely establishment of a screening process. When Mr. Weiner [the disqualified lawyer] joined the firm he was denied access to the relevant files, which were located in a different office, under the control of David Kula, the partner handling the case. Mr. Weiner and all employees of the firm were admonished not to discuss any aspect of the case, and all were subject to discipline. In addition, Mr. Weiner was not allowed to share in the fees derived from this case. The defendants also submitted the affidavit of David Kula, the attorney representing them. . . . The affidavit describes the procedures that were put in effect from December 15, 1989, the date that Mr. Weiner joined the firm. Mr. Weiner's new office was in Scariano's downtown Chicago building, and Mr. Kula's office was located in the firm's Chicago Heights office; each came to the other office only for specific business. Mr. Kula maintained the files for this case in his private office. When it implemented specific screening procedures, the firm required all members and employees of the firm to read and sign the memorandum describing the internal rules. Mr. Kula affirmed that "all of the admonitions of the screening memo have been adhered to by all the attorneys and all support staff employed by this firm." We conclude, as did the district court, that the Scariano law firm successfully rebutted the presumption of shared confidences by proving that the screening procedures were timely employed and fully implemented.[20]

B. PROSPECTIVE CLIENT CONFLICTS

As we have seen, a lawyer owes the same duty of confidentiality to former and prospective clients, and that duty is virtually co-extensive with the lawyer's confidentiality obligation to current clients.[21] However, with respect to conflicts of interest, the lawyer's duty to former clients is significantly narrower than the obligation to current clients, and the duty to prospective clients is narrower still.

---

20. Cromley v. Board of Education, 17 F.3d 1059, 1065-66 (7th Cir.1994), *cert. denied*, 513 U.S. 816 (1994).

21. MR 1.18(b). *See supra* Chapter 4: Privilege and Confidentiality, at n. 19.

Model Rule 1.18(c) provides that, without obtaining informed consent, a lawyer "shall not represent a client with interests materially adverse to those of a prospective client in the same or substantially related matter *if the lawyer received information from the prospective client that could be significantly harmful to that person in the matter.*"[22] In other words, unlike Rule 1.9(a), the presumption that the lawyer received material confidential information that could be used against the prospective client is rebuttable. And if an individual lawyer is disqualified under Rule 1.18(c), the conflict will *not* be imputed to other firm lawyers, even in the absence of a migratory lawyer, as long as "the lawyer who received the information took reasonable measures to prevent exposure to more disqualifying information than was reasonably necessary to determine whether to represent the prospective client" and the disqualified lawyer is timely screened with written notice to the prospective client. MR 1.18(d)(2). In the alternative, the lawyer may proceed after obtaining the informed consent of both the prospective client and the current client. Model Rule 1.18(d)(1). Can you see why consent of the current client is also required?

In the digital age, lawyers and law firms face increasing challenges in their use of firm websites as a marketing tool. The following article describes what can go wrong and what lawyers can do to avoid unwanted obligations to website users, as either clients or prospective clients.

Eileen Libby

---

www.warning.law: Websites May Trigger Unforeseen Ethics Obligations to Prospective Clients
97 A.B.A.J. 22 (2011)

After David Walsh lost his job as a cashier at a large warehouse store, he typed "employment lawyer" into an Internet search engine and generated a list of local firms.

The firm websites conveniently listed the names of their lawyers and provided contact information, including e-mail addresses. Walsh randomly e-mailed several of the firms saying that he was looking for a plaintiffs employment lawyer to represent him in a wrongful termination suit against the store, which he identified in the e-mail. He also attached a file with correspondence he exchanged with the store's human resource department. It turns out that one of the lawyers to whom Walsh sent the e-mail represents the store as outside counsel. Now what?

This hypothetical scenario is likely to occur with great frequency now that websites have become a common means for lawyers to communicate with the public in efforts to generate new business. Indeed, lawyer websites have replaced business cards and Yellow Pages advertising for their "branding"

---

22. MR 1.18(c) (emphasis added).

potential. Embedding certain words on a law firm website as HTML text makes it attractive to Internet search engines, thus increasing webpage traffic that may result in more business.

Lawyers and potential clients appear to be going online at similar rates. As early as 2001, 77 percent of law firms already had an online presence, according to Greenfield/Belser Ltd., a brand design firm in Washington, D.C., that focuses on professional services marketing. In 2010, nearly 84 percent of lawyers said their firm had a website, according to the ABA's Legal Technology Survey Report.

Meanwhile, a 2009 study by the Pew Research Center in Washington found that 74 percent of all Americans use the Internet, and of those, 81 percent go online to research products or services.

Given these statistics, lawyers with websites have good reason to be apprehensive about uninvited communications that could inadvertently lead to the formation of lawyer-client relationships, conflicts of interest and breaches of confidentiality. Under Rule 1.18 (Duties to Prospective Client) of the ABA Model Rules of Professional Conduct, for instance, "A lawyer who has had discussions with a prospective client shall not use or reveal information in the consultation," except under certain circumstances involving former clients.

Rule 1.18 also generally prohibits a lawyer from representing a client "with interests materially adverse to those of a prospective client in the same or a substantially related matter" if the lawyer received information from the prospective client that could be significantly harmful to the affected client. . . .

But what particular circumstances cause Rule 1.18 or related ethics provisions to kick in as a result of online communications between a lawyer and a prospective client?

The ABA Standing Committee on Ethics and Professional Responsibility explored that question in Formal Opinion 10-457 (Lawyer Websites), issued Aug. 5, 2010. The opinion recognizes the growing use of websites by lawyers. "A lawyer website can provide to anyone with Internet access a wide array of information about the law, legal institutions and the value of legal services," states the opinion. Websites also serve as an effective marketing tool for lawyers, the opinion notes.

But the opinion cautions that "the obvious benefit of this information can diminish or disappear if the website visitor misunderstands or is misled by website information and features." For lawyers, online marketing can give rise to problems when website visitors interpret material posted as general information to apply to specific situations, or when visitors make unanticipated inquiries or unexpectedly provide confidential information. Websites that invite inquiries, such those with "contact us" or "click here for a free consultation" buttons, can be especially problematic.

Lawyers are "well-advised to consider that a website-generated inquiry may have come from a prospective client," states the opinion, and they should pay special attention to including appropriate warnings that effectively limit, condition or disclaim any obligations to website visitors. "Such warnings or statements may be written so as to avoid a misunderstanding by the website visitor that (1) a client-lawyer relationship has been created, (2) the visitor's information will be kept confidential, (3) legal advice has been given, or (4) the lawyer will be prevented from representing an adverse party."

The key, concludes the ethics committee's opinion, is that "limitations, conditions or disclaimers of lawyer obligations will be effective only if reasonably understandable, properly placed and not misleading. This requires a clear warning in a readable format whose meaning can be understood by a reasonable person." And, the opinion notes, "The appropriate information should be conspicuously placed to assure that the reader is likely to see it before proceeding." . . .

A number of state bar opinions also have tackled the issue of online communications, and several have concluded that lawyer websites should contain "click-through" (also called "click-wrap") or pop-up disclaimers that require a prospective client to assent to the terms of the disclaimer before being permitted to submit the information to the lawyer's site.

This approach was taken in Virginia Legal Ethics Opinion 1842 (Sept. 30, 2008), which states that one way to avoid an inference that an attorney-client relationship has been established or that information submitted to a law firm's website will be kept confidential is to include a disclaimer on the website warning against disclosure of confidential or sensitive information and also warning that the firm has no duty to maintain the confidentiality of any submitted information.

Florida Bar Opinion 07-03 (Jan. 16, 2009) concluded that a person seeking legal services who sends information unilaterally to a lawyer has no reasonable expectation of confidentiality regarding that information. Thus, the lawyer who receives that information has no conflict of interest if already representing or later asked to represent an adversary, and may use or disclose the information. Again, a careful lawyer will post a statement on the website stating that the lawyer does not intend to treat as confidential information sent to the lawyer via the website, and that such information could be used against the person by the lawyer in the future.

Other states agree. New York City Bar Association Ethics Opinion 2001-1 (March 1, 2001) states that a lawyer is not disqualified from representing an existing client when the lawyer receives an unsolicited e-mail from an adverse party, but that the lawyer may not use or disclose that information if the lawyer's website has not adequately disclosed that the law firm will not treat such communications as confidential. According to San Diego County Bar Association Ethics Opinion 2006-1 (2006), a lawyer does not owe a duty of confidentiality to a person who sends unsolicited information to the lawyer and may use such information in representing an existing client. California Formal Ethics Opinion 2005-168 (2005) has gone so far as to conclude that a lawyer may invite people to provide information to the lawyer via e-mail or another form of electronic communication via the lawyer's website with no duty of confidentiality attaching if the lawyer provides a clear disclaimer that he or she will not treat the information provided as confidential.

Effective disclaimers in lawyer websites are particularly important for online visitors who may be inexperienced in using legal services, states the ABA ethics opinion.

"It would be prudent to avoid any misunderstanding," states the ethics committee, "by warning visitors that the legal information provided is general and should not be relied on as legal advice, and by explaining that legal advice cannot be given without full consideration of all relevant information relating to the visitor's individual situation."

Acknowledging a lawyer's duty to avoid conflicts of interest with respect to prospective clients creates the possibility of strategic behavior. For example, if there are a limited number of well-known divorce lawyers in a community, one of the spouses might make an appointment with each one to discuss the possibility of forming a lawyer-client relationship, for the purpose of ensuring that the other spouse will then be precluded from hiring any of those lawyers.[23] Comment [2] to Rule 1.18 defines a prospective client as one who "consult[s] with a lawyer about the possibility of forming a client-lawyer relationship with respect to a matter." A spouse who is acting strategically to "taint" the lawyer pool is not consulting the lawyer for the purpose of deciding whether to retain that lawyer.[24] Of course, it might be difficult to prove that the consulting spouse was acting strategically rather than conducting good faith interviews to determine which lawyer to retain. If the spouse had already retained a lawyer before interviewing the others, that would be evidence of bad faith. And it would be unethical for a lawyer to advise the spouse to engage in such "taint-shopping."[25]

C. FORMER GOVERNMENT LAWYERS

When a lawyer has previously served as a public officer or employee of the government, including but not limited to legal representation, both the individual lawyer's disqualification and the disqualification of the lawyer's new firm are governed by Model Rule 1.11. Rule 1.11(a) provides that the individual lawyer "shall not . . . represent a client in connection with a matter in which the lawyer participated personally and substantially as a public officer or employee unless the appropriate government agency gives its informed consent, confirmed in writing, to the representation."

---

23. In an episode of the TV show *The Sopranos*, Carmella Soprano learns that her husband Tony has "tainted" the pool of divorce lawyers by interviewing a number of them, thereby preventing her from hiring any of them. *See The Sopranos:* "Unidentified Black Males" (HBO television broadcast May 2, 2004).

24. *See* MR 1.18, cmt [2] ("[A] person who communicates with a lawyer for the purpose of disqualifying the lawyer is not a 'prospective client.'")

25. It is professional misconduct for a lawyer to "engage in conduct involving dishonesty, fraud, deceit or misrepresentation," MR 8.4(c), either directly or through the acts of another, *see* MR 8.4(a).

Rule 1.11(a) differs from Rule 1.9 in a number of respects. First, and perhaps most important, it is not limited to representation *adverse* to a former client, but includes representation that may further the interests of the former government client. For example, in a leading case, Armstrong v. McAlpin,[26] a former assistant director of the SEC's Enforcement Division, Altman, had responsibility over an SEC investigation and litigation concerning McAlpin, who had allegedly looted millions of dollars from his company. Altman left the SEC and joined the Gordon Hurwitz firm, which was representing the trustee of McAlpin's former company. The trustee had been charged with recovering misappropriated property and was suing McAlpin in civil litigation. Gordon Hurwitz determined that it would be inappropriate for Altman to personally work on the case but that it could screen Altman from any participation to avoid the imputation of the conflict to the lawyers working on the case. In an en banc opinion, the Second Circuit upheld the district court's refusal to disqualify the law firm. The opinion predated adoption of the Model Rules; however, the result would be the same under Model Rule 1.11(a).

If case law now codified in Model Rule 1.9(a) had applied, then Altman would not have been personally disqualified, because the representation was not materially adverse to the SEC.[27] Under Rule 1.11(a), however, whether the representation was adverse or not is irrelevant. According to Comment [4], the reason for this aspect of the disqualification rule in the case of a former government official is the risk that "power or discretion vested in th[e] agency might be used for the special benefit of the [new] client." In other words, "[a] lawyer should not be in a position where benefit to the other client might affect performance of the lawyer's professional functions on behalf of the government." In this respect, Rule 1.11(a) is *broader* than Rule 1.9.

In two other respects, however, Rule 1.11(a) is *narrower* than Rule 1.9. First, the lawyer must have "personally and substantially" participated in the matter. Second, the disqualification applies only with respect to "a matter," which is defined narrowly to include only a "judicial or other proceeding, application, request for a ruling or other determination, contract, claim, controversy, investigation, charge, accusation, arrest or other particular matter involving a specific party or parties."[28] As a result, a former IRS lawyer will not be disqualified even when the new representation involves taking a position adverse to the current IRS interpretation of rules that the individual IRS lawyer drafted, because drafting regulations or legislation is not a "particular matter involving a specific party or parties." Similarly, with respect to two distinct matters, the fact that the former government lawyer is likely to have learned confidential information about the government that could be used to its detriment in the new matter is not a sufficient basis for disqualification, because Rule 1.11(a)

---

26. 625 F.2d 433 (2d Cir. 1980), *vacated on other grounds*, 449 U.S. 1106 (1981).

27. Even in the absence of Rules 1.9 and Rule 1.11, a lawyer like Altman might have to be disqualified on the basis of statutes or government regulations regarding conflict of interest of former government officials. *See* MR 1.11, cmt [1].

28. MR 1.11(e)(1).

is limited to participation in "the matter," and not a "substantially related" matter. Here, however, there is some wiggle room. Comment [10] provides that "a 'matter' may continue in another form" and that "[i]n determining whether two particular matters are the same, the lawyer should consider the extent to which the matters involve the same basic facts, the same or related parties, and the time elapsed." For example, in *Armstrong*, the company trustee might have been pursuing not only McAlpin, but also another former company official who was tangentially involved but not a target of the former SEC investigation. Arguably a civil lawsuit against that official would involve the same "matter" because the prior investigation involved the same basic facts and parties during the same time period.

As for imputation, the disqualification of the individual lawyer will not be imputed to the lawyer's new firm when the lawyer is timely screened, with notice to the appropriate government agency. *See* MR 1.11(a). Unlike the exception in Rule 1.10(a), the ability to avoid imputation through screening a former government lawyer is accepted in all jurisdictions. *Armstrong* was the leading case to recognize screening, and it was decided even before the Model Rules were adopted. How do jurisdictions that refuse to recognize a screening exception in the case of lawyers moving between private firms justify recognizing such an exception for firms that employ a former government lawyer, as was true under the Model Rules prior to 2009?

According to a leading treatise, the concern was that, if their individual conflicts were imputed to their new firms, many former government lawyers would be "Typhoid Marys," that is, firms would fear to hire them for fear of being conflicted out of too many matters. This was deemed to be a problem "especially acute with respect to government lawyers" with a "negative impact on the public: the government will find it more difficult to attract and promote the most qualified and talented young lawyers to government service—often at far less remuneration than they could earn in private practice—if the result is that the more responsibility the government lawyer is given, the more difficult it will be for the lawyer ever to move on to other legal work."[29] Some critics object to what is sometimes described as the "revolving door," whereby private practice lawyers enter government service and then reenter the private sector, using their special knowledge and contacts to provide an arguably unfair advantage for their new clients.[30]

Review Problems

6-1 A labor lawyer represented a Philadelphia company that transported petroleum products along the east coast of the United States by tug and barge. The company competes in the marine transportation business with

---

29. Hazard et al., 1 The Law of Lawyering §15.03 (2019-20 Supp.).

30. *See, e.g.*, Robert H. Mundheim, Conflict of Interest and the Former Government Employee: Rethinking the Revolving Door, 14 Creighton L. Rev. 707 1981 (a revolving door proponent describes and responds to its critics).

other tug and/or barge companies, including a number of companies based in New York. The lawyer represented the company in all of its negotiations with the union representing its employees and gained considerable information about its labor costs. After many years, the company became dissatisfied with the lawyer's representation and terminated the relationship. The lawyer was immediately approached by one of the company's New York competitors, which sought to retain her to represent them in their upcoming negotiations with their union, which was not the same union as was involved with the Philadelphia company. The Philadelphia company heard about this and demanded that the lawyer refuse to accept the representation. When the lawyer confirmed that she would accept the representation, the Philadelphia company filed a lawsuit seeking to enjoin the lawyer from representing the New York company in its labor negotiations with the union representing its employees. In its complaint, the Philadelphia company alleges that labor costs are a particularly sensitive area in the competition among companies in the marine transportation business. The New York company disagrees and claims that information about another company's labor costs would not be useful in negotiations between a different company and a different union. Is the Philadelphia company likely to succeed in its efforts to prevent the lawyer from representing the New York company?

6-2 Same fact as in Problem 6-1 except: What if it was not the lead lawyer who had represented the Philadelphia company who was approached by the New York company, but rather an associate in the labor department who had not worked on any matters for the Philadelphia company and claims that he has no confidential information concerning that company? Would it make a difference if the New York company did not approach the associate until after he had left his original firm and joined an entirely different firm that had never represented the Philadelphia company?

6-3 Further to Problem 6-2, assume that the associate had billed several hours working on a single labor matter for the Philadelphia company while he was at the lead lawyer's firm. He says that all he did was research some legal issues that are no longer relevant. May he represent the New York company in its labor negotiations after he joins his new law firm?

6-4 Again, from Problem 6-1: What if it is the lead lawyer herself who left her initial law firm and joined an entirely new law firm that has never represented the Philadelphia company but has been longtime labor counsel to the New York company. The lawyer will not work on any labor matter for the New York company, and before the lawyer joined the new firm, the new firm instituted screening measures to isolate the lawyer from any such work on behalf of the New York company. If the Philadelphia company files a lawsuit seeking to enjoin any lawyer in the new firm from representing the New York company in its upcoming labor negotiations with its union, is the lawsuit likely to succeed?

6-5 A woman approached a well-known business lawyer and told him that she had a tentative deal to partner with a local savings and loan association to offer an entirely new type of consumer loan to local residents. Unknown to the woman, the lawyer's partner was representing a company that was interested in developing a similar type of loan but had not yet found a local lender to partner with. The business lawyer declined the representation, citing a potential conflict of interest. May the business lawyer tell his partner the name of the savings and loan association that has expressed an interest in this type of loan? Under what circumstances, if any, may the partner continue to represent the company interested in developing a similar type of loan?

6-6 A lawyer recently left her position as an assistant attorney general in the office of the state's attorney general. While she was there, other lawyers were investigating a drug company for its role in improperly inducing physicians to prescribe an addictive drug. She did not actively work on the investigation, but she did sit in on several witness interviews as part of her training in interviewing techniques. After she left the state attorney general's office, a patient sued a physician for medical malpractice for improperly prescribing the same addictive drug. The drug company in question is the sole manufacturer of this drug. The complaint alleges that the physician accepted cash payments from the drug company based on the amount of drugs he prescribed. The lawyer joined the law firm representing the plaintiff. May she work on that case? May other lawyers work on the case if she is timely and effectively screened?

CHAPTER 7

LIMITS OF ZEALOUS REPRESENTATION I: LITIGATION

Model Rules 3.1, 3.3, 3.4[1]

As we know, Model Rule 1.3 provides that a lawyer must act with reasonable diligence in representing a client.[2] This rule requires the lawyer to "act with commitment and dedication to the interests of the client and with zeal in advocacy upon the client's behalf," taking "whatever *lawful and ethical* measures are required to vindicate a client's cause or endeavor."[3] The purpose of this and the next chapter is to explore the boundaries of what a lawyer may do on behalf of a client, that is, what are the "lawful and ethical" limits of zealous representation?[4] We begin with litigation because the rules of professional conduct and other law have historically focused on the lawyer's obligations to others in the litigation setting; it is only recently that courts and commentators have begun to explore whether transactional and other nonlitigating lawyers are or ought to be governed by a different set of norms.

Before we consider the limitations on what lawyers can do to advance their clients' positions in litigation, we need to understand the particular characteristics of the Anglo-American adversary system of justice, which is used in both federal and state courts. As its name suggests, this system is widely adopted in common law countries, whereas civil law systems more typically embrace what is known as an "inquisitorial system." Both systems

---

1. Also relevant are Model Rules 4.1, 4.2, and 4.3. These rules also apply in transactions and will be discussed in the next chapter. *See* Chapter 8: Limits of Zealous Representation II: Transactions.
2. *See supra* Chapter 3: Competence and Diligence; Control and Communication; Fees.
3. MR 1.3, cmt [1] (emphasis added).
4. Whereas the earlier Canons and Model Code embraced the concept of "zealous" advocacy on a client's behalf, the Model Rules downplay that term in favor of the less emotive requirement of "diligent" representation. Comment [1] appears to relegate zealous representation to advocacy, presumably in a litigation setting, although this is unclear. Whatever its treatment in ethical codes, many lawyers continue to view themselves as zealous advocates of their client's cause, whether in litigation or in transactions.

have adopted reforms bringing them closer together, but the animating spirit of each has distinctively different features.

A. THE ANGLO-AMERICAN ADVERSARY SYSTEM OF JUSTICE

Consider the following brief description of the Anglo-American adversary system, as contrasted with the inquisitorial system.

Edward F. Barrett

The Adversary System and the Ethics of Advocacy
37 Notre Dame L. Rev. 479, 479-80 (1962)

"The purpose of a lawsuit is," indeed, "to arrive at the truth of the controversy, in order that justice may be done." Undoubtedly the courts of the Spanish Inquisition and the Supreme Court of the United States would alike assent to this. It is at least another of those "decencies of civilization that no one would dispute." However, given the idea and given also the inescapably human features of a lawsuit, how can the truth of the matter in dispute between the parties be most practically arrived at in order that justice (not justice in the abstract but justice according to law) may be done? We have no archangel on the bench. The jury is not drawn from a venire of Cherubim or Seraphim. The litigants, their lawyers and their witnesses are not saints. The trial of a lawsuit is a very human thing.

Our adversary system is frankly based on the pragmatic assumption that the truth of the controversy between the parties to a lawsuit stands a reasonably fairer chance of coming out when each side fights as hard as it can to see to it that all the evidence most favorable to it and every rule of law supporting its theory of the case are before the court. In this legal combat each litigant is entitled to an advocate professionally bound, on the one hand, to exhibit in his client's cause "entire devotion, warm zeal and the utmost skill," and on the other hand equally obligated as an officer of the court to discharge his trust "within and not without the bounds of the law," honorably resisting even in the heat of battle, the temptation to win by foul means or by "any manner of fraud or chicane." . . .

Quite different are the basic assumptions of our adversary system from those of the so-called inquisitorial method pursued elsewhere. There it is believed that the truth of the controversy in a lawsuit is more likely to emerge through the independent inquiry of paid public officials owing no partisan allegiance to either side of the dispute. In the quest for the truth the main reliance is upon the competence, thoroughness and fairness of the public inquisitors. The advocate's role, so prominent with us, is secondary or auxiliary. Less value is placed on his contentious contributions. With us, however, much more is hoped for from the battle of the advocates in the total process of getting at the truth. Indeed, Lord Macaulay, no less a lawyer than a historian, once declared with his usual flair for antithesis and paradox that we obtain the fairest decision "when two men argue as unfairly as possible on opposite sides" for then "it is certain that no important considerations will altogether escape notice."

In the following excerpts from an essay he published shortly after retiring from the bench, Judge Marvin Frankel, a federal trial court judge in the Southern District of New York, affirmed and elaborated on Barrett's basic description of the adversary system, while offering a strong critique of some of its features.

Marvin E. Frankel

Partisan Justice
11-19 (1980)

The "adversary system," as we call it, is not merely borne as a supposedly necessary evil. It is cherished as an ideal of constitutional proportions, not only because it embodies the fundamental right to be heard, but because it is thought (often) to be the best assurance of truth and sound results. Decisions of the Supreme Court give repeated voice to this concept. We are taught to presume as a vital premise that "partisan advocacy on both sides," according to rules often countenancing partial truths and concealment, will best assure the discovery of truth in the end. We are not so much as slightly rocked in this assumption by the fact that other seekers after truth have not emulated us. . . .

Like any sweeping proposition, the claim that our adversary process is best for truth seeking has qualifications and limits recognized by its staunchest proponents. While it would not be essential, we have again the high authority of Supreme Court pronouncements noting that lawyers in the process are often expected, with all propriety, to help block or conceal rather than pursue the truth. These endeavors are commonly justified in the service of interests that outweigh truth finding — interests in privacy, personal dignity, security, autonomy, and other cherished values. The problem of how to weigh the competing values is, obviously, at the heart of the concerns to be addressed in these chapters. Nobody doubts that there are ends of diverse kinds, at diverse times and places, more worthy than the accurate discovery or statement of facts; that there are even occasions, not easily defined with unanimity, when a lie is to be preferred. One way to state the thesis of this book is to say, recognizing the complex relativities of life, that the American version of the adversary process places too low a value on truth telling; that we have allowed ourselves too often to sacrifice truth to other values that are inferior or illusory. But the elaboration of the position is best postponed until after we have described how the process works and how its actors perform.

The quality of private initiative and private control is, in its degree, the hallmark of the American judicial process. While the administration of justice is designated as the public's business and the decision-makers are public people (whether full-time judges or the lay judges who sit in jury boxes), the process is initiated, shaped, and managed by the private contestants in civil matters and by the government and non-government lawyer-contestants in criminal matters. The deciders, though commissioned to discover the truth, are passive recipients, not active explorers. They take what they are given. They consider the questions raised by counsel, rarely any others. Issues not joined are not resolved, though they might have led to wiser, fairer dispositions than those reached. The parties, almost always the lawyers or those under their direction, investigate the facts, interview possible witnesses, consult potential experts to find opinions most agreeable to their causes, decide what will be told and what will not be told. The judges and jurors almost never make inquiries on their own, and are not staffed or otherwise equipped to do so. The reconstructions of the past to be given in the courtroom are likely to be the sharply divergent stories told by partisans, divergent from each other and from the actual events supposed to be portrayed. If history can never reproduce the past with total fidelity, one wonders often whether we could not miss by margins much narrower than those marked in courtrooms. . . .

The system rests, we must always remember, on the assumption that we can accurately re-create the facts so that our rules of law, democratically evolved, will work just results. If the rule is that the signer of the note must pay, it works acceptably only if we correctly identify the signer. If we fail to make the identification, or, worse yet, falsely identify one who really did not sign, the result will be an injustice. . . .

The simple point to be stressed, here and throughout, is that many of us trained in the learned profession of the law spend much of our time subverting the law by blocking the way to the truth. The subversion is not for the most part viewed as a pathology; rather, if somewhat paradoxically, it follows from the assigned roles of counsel in the very system of law which thus finds its purposes thwarted.

The games we play about fact finding are, of course, an old story and an old source of professional worry and efforts toward reform. During the last half-century or so, much as been done through rules of "discovery" to cut down on concealment and surprises at trial. The idea is to allow demands for information before trial and to require responses from the adverse party. The device has on the whole worked substantial improvements. Predictably, however, it has been turned — and twisted — to adversary uses. Lawyers react characteristically by demanding as much as possible and giving as little as possible. What is not demanded is not given. It remains as true as ever that if a lawyer fails to ask the right question, the adversary will cheerfully refrain from disclosing what might be vital or decisive information. The discovery process itself, with rules that frequently are (or are made to be) intricate and abstruse, becomes the occasion for expensive contests, producing libraries full of opinions. Where the object always is to beat every plowshare into a sword, the discovery procedure is employed variously as weaponry. A powerful litigant in a complex case may impose costly, even crushing, burdens by demands for files, pretrial testimony of witnesses, and other forms of discovery. An approximately converse ploy has also been evolved to make the procedure a morass rather than the revelatory blessing it was meant to be. A litigant may contrive to dump truckloads of [unsorted] files on the party demanding discovery, hoping, often not in vain, that the searcher will be so exhausted that the damaging items will be overlooked or never reached.

The key point at every stage, which will bear recalling from time to time, is that the single uniformity is always adversariness. There are other goods, but the greatest is winning. There are other evils, but scarcely any worse than losing. Every step of the process, and any attempt to reform it, must be viewed in this light until or unless the adversary ethic comes to be changed or subordinated. . . . Every idea for improved procedures must be imaginatively pretested to foresee its evolving shapes under the fires of adversary zeal.

Because the route of a lawsuit is marked by a running battle all the way, the outcome is nothing like the assuredly right result imagined in our dream that "justice will out." In that dream, neither eloquence nor lawyers' techniques nor cunning has much place. The person who is "right" should win. But that is very far from assured in the kind of contest we've been considering. Where skill and trickery are so much involved, it must inevitably happen that the respective qualities of the professional champions will make a decisive difference. Where sheer power and endurance may count, the relative resources of clients become vital. Describing the tendency of the enterprise as the major forces propel it, two students of the American legal system were led to conclude: "In an ideal adversary system, the less skillful antagonist is expected to lose, which under the laissez-faire notion is the proper outcome."

If that is, fortunately, an exaggeration, it describes a probability high and uncertain enough to be harrowing.

NOTES AND QUESTIONS

1. Using both the Barrett and the Frankel excerpts, describe the hallmarks of both the adversary and inquisitorial systems, stressing the roles to be played by the judge, the jury (where applicable),[5] and the parties or their lawyers.

---

5. Juries are used less frequently in civil law countries and in common law countries outside the United States. In instances where there is no right to jury trial, the judge performs the functions that a jury would otherwise have performed.

2. Assuming that a lawsuit is a search for truth, what is the argument that the adversary system is superior to the inquisitorial system as a means of ascertaining truth? In addition to the points made in the above excerpts, consider the following description of an arbiter deciding a dispute without the aid of the advocates:

> What generally occurs in practice is that at some early point a familiar pattern will seem to emerge from the evidence; an accustomed label is waiting for the case and, without awaiting further proofs, this label is promptly assigned to it. It is a mistake to suppose that this premature cataloguing must necessarily result from impatience, prejudice or mental sloth. Often it proceeds from a very understandable desire to bring the hearing into some order and coherence, for without some tentative theory of the case there is no standard of relevance by which testimony may be measured. But what starts as a preliminary diagnosis designed to direct the inquiry tends quickly and imperceptibly to become a fixed conclusion, as all that confirms the diagnosis makes a strong impact on the mind, while all that runs counter to it is received with diverted attention.
>
> An adversary presentation seems the only effective means for combatting this natural human tendency to judge too swiftly in terms of the familiar that which is not yet fully known. The arguments of counsel hold the case, as it were, in suspension between two opposing interpretations of it. While the proper classification of the case is thus kept unresolved, there is time to explore all of its peculiarities and nuances.[6]

3. On what basis does Judge Frankel dispute the effectiveness of the adversary system, including the role of partisan advocates, as a vehicle for ascertaining truth?

4. One response to Judge Frankel might be to quote the following from another former district judge in the Southern District of New York, Judge Simon Rifkind: "Of course the process I have described is subject to human frailty. Sometimes the poorer cause prevails. That is a price worth paying for the long-range benefits of the system."[7] Judge Rifkind might elaborate that, although the weaknesses identified by Judge Frankel may cause us to question whether the truth has been obtained in individual cases, the adversary system is, in the long run, most likely to produce truthful results. Do you agree? How might Judge Frankel respond to that argument?

5. Judge Rifkind supported the use of the adversary system as the most effective means of ascertaining truth. However, he also suggested "[w]ith some trepidation," that "in actual practice the ascertainment of the truth is not necessarily the target of the trial, that values other than

---

6. Lon L. Fuller & John D. Randall, Professional Responsibility: Report of the Joint Conference of the ABA and AALS, 44 A.B.A. J. 1159, 1160 (1958).

7. Simon H. Rifkind, The Lawyer's Role and Responsibility in Modern Society, 30 The Record 534, 538 (1975).

truth frequently take precedence, and that, indeed, courtroom truth is a unique species of the genus truth, and that it is not necessarily congruent with objective or absolute truth, whatever that may be."[8] He concluded: "[T]he object of a trial is not the ascertainment of truth but the resolution of a controversy by the principled application of the rules of the game. In a civilized society these rules should be designed to favor the just resolution of a controversy; and in a progressive society they should change as the perception of justice evolves in response to greater ethical sophistication."[9] Would Judge Frankel disagree that, under the Anglo-American adversary system, values other than truth sometimes take precedence? What are some of those values? How might Judge Frankel disagree with Judge Rifkind's conclusions about the object of the trial and the nature of the "rules of the game" that constrain the litigants?

6. Judge Frankel did not suggest abandoning the adversary system in favor of an inquisitorial system. Do you think it likely that an inquisitorial system could be adopted in the United States? For a discussion of the comparative advantages and disadvantages of the adversarial and the inquisitorial systems in the criminal context, both conceptually and as practiced in different national systems, *see* Robert P. Mosteller, Failures of the American Adversarial System to Protect the Innocent and Conceptual Advantages in the Inquisitorial Design for Investigative Fairness, 36 N.C.J.Int'l L. & Com. Reg.319 (2011).[10]

7. In the excerpt provided above, it is far from clear how Judge Frankel would reform the adversary system as it is currently practiced. We could change "the rules of the game," including rules of procedure and evidence, as well as rules of professional conduct, or we could attempt to change the adversary ethic, which has elsewhere been described as "one-sided partisan zeal."[11] What difficulties does Judge Frankel see in changing formal rules, for example, the rules of discovery?[12] What

---

8. *Id.*

9. *Id.*

10. Mosteller argued that recent DNA evidence clearly establishing the innocence of many defendants convicted of crimes such as murder and rape has exposed the weaknesses of the adversarial system in a world of unequal resources and prosecutorial power in the plea-bargaining system. For a similar argument, *see* Keith A. Findley, Adversarial Inquisitions: Rethinking the Search for Truth, 56 N.Y.L. Sch. L. Rev. 911 (2012).

11. David Luban, The Adversary System Excuse, in The Good Lawyer: Lawyers' Roles and Lawyers' Ethics 83 (David Luban ed., 1983).

12. For a recent example of potential reforms to the federal rules governing discovery, *see* Fed. Jud. Ctr., Mandatory Initial Discovery Pilot Project: Overview, https://www.fjc.gov /content/321837/mandatory-initial-discovery-pilot-project-overview (last visited Mar. 8, 2021) (describing three-year pilot project requiring parties in certain district courts cases to respond to a series of standard discovery requests before undertaking other discovery).

about attempts to change the adversary ethic? Is it possible for lawyers to become somewhat less adversarial?[13]

8. Judge Frankel suggested various specific reforms in other parts of his book, including changes to the rules of professional conduct he considered as a member of the Kutak Commission that drafted the Model Rules (some of which were not adopted). We will discuss some of these reform proposals as we address the limits on adversary zeal as they are reflected in the rules that govern the conduct of advocates in the adversary system. We now turn to those limitations as they apply to pleadings, affirmative statements of law or fact, failure to disclose adverse law or fact, witness perjury, and fairness to opposing parties and counsel.

B. LIMITS ON ADVERSARY ZEAL

1. Pleadings in Civil and Criminal Cases

Model Rule 3.1 provides in part that "[a] lawyer shall not bring or defend a proceeding, or assert or controvert an issue therein, unless there is a basis in law and fact for doing so that is not frivolous, which includes a good faith argument for an extension, modification or reversal of existing law." As Comment [1] notes, "[T]he law, both procedural and substantive, establishes the limits within which an advocate must proceed."

For civil trials, most courts adopt rules similar to the Federal Rules of Civil Procedure. As you may recall from your first-year course in Civil Procedure, Rule 11 governs the filing of pleadings, including a complaint or an answer.[14] It requires that every such pleading must be signed by an attorney of record (or a party personally, if unrepresented), and that by presenting such a document to the court, the attorney

---

13. In an effort to curb the worst excesses of the adversary ethic, including harassment of opposing lawyers, clients, and witnesses, a number of courts and bar associations have adopted so-called "civility codes," as part of a broader "civility movement." *See, e.g.,* Josh O'Hara, Note, Creating Civility: Using Reference Group Theory to Improve Inter-Lawyer Relations, 31 Vt. L. Rev. 965, 965-74 (2007). Such codes are typically aspirational, although several jurisdictions have made them mandatory. *See, e.g.,* David A. Grenardo, A Lesson in Civility, 32 Geo. J. Legal Ethics 135, 151 (2019). Civility codes have been criticized as either ineffective or elitist. *See, e.g.,* O'Hara, *supra* at 974-79. In any event, courts have the inherent power to sanction many instances of outrageous lawyer behavior. *See, e.g.,* Bedoya v. Aventura Limousine & Transp. Serv., 861 F. Supp. 2d 1346, 1370 (S.D. Fla. 2012) (lawyer's "consistent course of disrespectful, unprofessional conduct" toward opposing counsel could not be directly sanctioned because it occurred in another forum, but nevertheless formed the basis for disqualification of the lawyer in the pending proceeding).

14. Rule 11 also governs written motions or other papers presented to a court.

certifies to the best of the [attorney's] knowledge, information and belief, formed after an inquiry reasonable under the circumstances:

(1) it is not being presented for any improper purpose, such as to harass, cause unnecessary delay, or needlessly increase the cost of litigation;

(2) the claim, defenses, and other legal contentions are warranted by existing law or by a nonfrivolous argument for extending, modifying, or reversing existing law or for establishing new law;

(3) the factual contentions have evidentiary support or, if specifically so identified, will likely have evidentiary support after a reasonable opportunity for further investigation or discovery; and

(4) the denials of factual contentions are warranted on the evidence or, if specifically so identified, are reasonably based on belief or a lack of information.

NOTES AND QUESTIONS

1. Consider the application of these rules to the following scenarios:
   a. A lawyer is representing a physician sued by a former patient for medical malpractice. The complaint contains a specific allegation that the physician was drunk when she performed an operation on the patient and that, as a result, the physician botched the surgery. The physician has admitted to the lawyer that she was drunk when she performed the operation, but insists that her performance was not affected. The lawyer believes that the allegation is based on a statement by a nurse who is apparently claiming that the physician was drunk. The lawyer is also convinced that the nurse will not make a good witness and that his testimony will not hold up well on cross-examination. In filing an answer on the physician's behalf, may the lawyer deny both that the physician was drunk and that she botched the operations?
   b. Let's look now at this problem from the point of view of the lawyer representing the patient, with respect to the initial filing of the complaint. Assume that the only basis that the patient has for believing that the physician was drunk is that while he was in the recovery room, he thinks he overheard some nurses whispering about the physician having been drinking before she performed the operation. Is the lawyer obligated to conduct an investigation before filing a complaint alleging that the physician was drunk? What if the lawyer interviewed the nurses in attendance, and they all denied having said the physician was drunk or having any information to that effect?
   c. One final variation: Assume that, although the patient is extremely unhappy with the results of his surgery, he has no idea what might have gone wrong. His lawyer obtained his hospital records, but there is nothing in them suggesting physician or other hospital error. Nevertheless, the patient appears to be sincere in his conviction that there must have been some medical malpractice. The lawyer believes that if a lawsuit on the patient's behalf is filed,

formal discovery could possibly reveal some evidence of medical malpractice, although this is highly unlikely. May the lawyer file a complaint against the physician and the hospital alleging that as a result of some unknown error by the physician or other hospital staff, the patient suffered physical injuries? If there is *any* possibility that formal discovery might uncover some legal wrongdoing, shouldn't the rules allow the patient his "day in court" to attempt to prove his case? What are the countervailing concerns that underlie the requirements in Model Rule 3.1 and Rule 11 that the lawyer act as a form of gatekeeper with respect to the client's access to the courts?

2. Now we need to consider lawyers who represent defendants in criminal cases. Rule 11 of the Federal Rules of Criminal Procedure provides: "A defendant may plead not guilty, guilty, or (with the court's consent) nolo contendere."[15] Consider the application of this rule, along with Model Rule 3.1, to the following variation on the scenarios we examined in connection with pleading in civil lawsuits.

   a. A lawyer represents a criminal defendant charged with assault. He confessed to the lawyer that he assaulted the complaining witness, as charged. In addition, he has numerous prior convictions for assault. Based on the lawyer's investigation, the lawyer has no doubt that the defendant committed the offense, but believes that the alleged victim will make a poor witness at trial and will not hold up well on cross-examination. The jury will probably not be permitted to learn about the defendant's prior convictions. May the lawyer assist the defendant in entering a plea of not guilty? Be sure to refer to both Model Rule 3.1 and Rule 11 of the Federal Rules of Criminal Procedure.

   b. Prior to the adoption of the Model Rules, Disciplinary Rule 7-102(A)(2) of the Model Code provided that a lawyer may not "[k]nowingly advance a claim or defense that is unwarranted under existing law, except that he may advance such claim or defense if it can be supported by good faith argument for an extension, modification or reversal of existing law." Would the result differ under this rule?

3. When asked how they can defend someone they know is guilty of criminal conduct, some criminal defense lawyers make arguments based on the following exchange between the famous English writer Samuel Johnson and his biographer, James Boswell:

   Boswell: But what do you think of supporting a cause which you know to be bad?

---

15. Fed. R. Crim. P., R. 11(a)(1). A plea of nolo contendere is a plea where the defendant neither admits nor disputes a charge. It has the same immediate effect as a guilty plea, but may have different collateral effects.

Johnson: Sir, you do not know it to be good or bad till the judge determines it. You are to state facts clearly: so that your *thinking*, or what you call *knowing*, a cause to be bad must be from reasoning, must be from supposing your arguments to be weak and inconclusive. But, sir, that is not enough. An argument which does not convince yourself may convince the judge to whom you urge it; and if it does convince him, why then, sir, you are wrong and he is right. It is his business to judge; and you are not to be confident in your opinion that a cause is bad, but to say all you can for your client, and then hear the judge's opinion.[16]

The dialogue may sound familiar, as it presents yet another justification for the adversary system. But how is it relevant to determining the lawyer's role in assisting a client to enter a plea? Criminal defense lawyers sometimes argue that they never "know" that a defendant is guilty of the offense charged. Is this a viable interpretation of either the Federal Rules of Criminal Procedure, the Model Rules, or the Model Code provisions? If not, why not? What would such an interpretation mean for interpreting other Model Rules, such as Rule 1.2(d), which provides that "[a] lawyer shall not counsel a client to engage in conduct that the lawyer knows is criminal or fraudulent"? The Model Rules define the terms "knowingly," "known," or "knows" as "actual knowledge of the fact in question."[17] They also state that "[a] person's knowledge may be inferred from circumstances."[18] We will revisit this question when we consider the rules regulating the lawyer's role in presenting a client's perjured testimony.

4. The truth-seeking function of a criminal trial is clearly undermined when a lawyer is permitted to assist a criminal defendant in entering a plea of not guilty even though the lawyer knows that the defendant committed the crime charged. Where would Judge Frankel stand on this issue?

2. Lawyer Misrepresentation to a Court or Other Tribunal

Our typical view of a lawyer addressing a court or jury involves the lawyer making arguments in support of the client's position. In addition, however, lawyers routinely make statements of fact or law purportedly based on the lawyer's personal knowledge. This occurs not only when the lawyer submits an affidavit or a declaration, but also when the lawyer summarizes the testimony of the witnesses or tells the court about a scheduling conflict. Model Rule 3.3(a)(1) provides that "[a] lawyer shall not knowingly . . . make a false statement of fact or law to a tribunal or fail to correct a false statement

---

16. James Boswell, The Life of Samuel Johnson 345 (Random House 1992) (1791).
17. MR 1.0(f).
18. *Id.*

of material fact or law previously made to the tribunal by the lawyer." Rule 1.0(m) defines tribunal as "a court, an arbitrator in a binding arbitration proceeding or a legislative body, administrative agency or other body acting in an adjudicative capacity."

The rationale for this rule is straightforward. Judges (and other adjudicators) rely on lawyers to supply accurate information about a case and should not have to second guess the word of a lawyer who is purportedly speaking on the basis of personal knowledge. Note that the rule prohibits *all* knowingly false statements of fact and law, but requires correction of a previous false statement, when the lawyer later comes to know of its falsity, only when the statement is "material." For example, the lawyer may have described her client as being 60 years old and only later learn that the client was actually 62 years old. If the client's age is not a material fact, Rule 3.3 does not require the lawyer to correct the previous false statement. Can you see why the rule distinguishes between knowingly making false statements and knowingly failing to correct a false statement previously made?

Model Rule 4.1 applies to statements made to adversaries and other third persons, as well as statements to mediators, and to legislatures or administrative agencies not acting in an adjudicative capacity. Unlike Rule 3.3, Rule 4.1 prohibits knowingly false statements by a lawyer only when such statements are material.[19] We'll address the differences between Rules 3.3 and 4.1 in a later chapter.[20]

The comment to Rule 3.3 elaborates on what constitutes knowingly making or failing to correct a false statement. It provides that "an assertion purporting to be on the lawyer's own knowledge, as in an affidavit by the lawyer or in a statement in open court, may properly be made only when the lawyer knows the assertion is true or believes it to be true on the basis of a reasonably diligent inquiry." It further provides that "[t]here are circumstances where failure to make a disclosure is the equivalent of an affirmative misrepresentation." These provisions complicate the application of Rule 3.3 in two ways.

First, we might ask how a lawyer can "knowingly" make a false statement when the lawyer *believes it to be true*, but has not made a reasonably diligent inquiry. Or when the lawyer has no idea whether the statement is true or false. The answer appears to be that by making a statement to a tribunal purportedly based on personal knowledge, without qualification, a lawyer implies that the lawyer believes the statement to be true and that the lawyer has made reasonable inquiries, where necessary.[21] Again, courts need to rely on lawyers

---

19. MR 4.1(a).

20. *See infra* Chapter 8: Limits of Zealous Representation II: Transactions. Prior to the 2002 amendments, Rule 3.3(a)(1) provided, as does Rule 4.1, that the prohibition applied only to knowingly making or failing to correct false statements of material fact. Some states have retained the original provision.

21. Making a reasonable inquiry presumably includes reasonably relying on the inquiry of another, for example, a partner signing a brief in which much of the underlying research was done by a responsible associate.

to make unqualified affirmative representations only when they reasonably believe them to be accurate.[22] Keep in mind that this rule does not apply to pleadings, where the lawyer is not making allegations or denials based on the lawyer's own personal knowledge, nor does it apply to evidence the lawyer presents[23] or to arguments the lawyer makes based on the evidence.[24]

Second, we might ask under what circumstances a lawyer's *failure to disclose* is the equivalent of making a false statement. It is difficult to predict when courts will find an affirmative false statement as a result of a failure to disclose. However, there are some recurring situations in which courts have made such findings, such as the death of a client during settlement negotiations, secret agreements between opposing parties, a client's use of a false identity, and the submission of incomplete records.[25] The common link appears to be that by engaging in certain conduct, the lawyer is impliedly making representations that the lawyer knows are false. For example, in the case of the death of a client during settlement negotiations, an ABA formal opinion explained that prior to the client's death, the lawyer expressly acted on behalf of an identified client; afterward, however, the lawyer was no longer acting on behalf of that client and might not have had any client at all. Continuing the negotiations, without disclosing the material fact of the client's death, operated as a false representation that the lawyer was still acting on behalf of that client.[26]

Newly admitted lawyers should be aware of a case in which a junior lawyer was reprimanded by a judge for knowingly failing to correct a false statement to the court made by a senior lawyer in the presence of the junior lawyer. Although the junior lawyer had done nothing more than introduce himself to the judge as representing the petitioner at the start of a hearing on an ex parte

---

22. In one case, for example, a lawyer was disciplined for telling a magistrate judge that a suspect had previously "pulled a gun" on a deputy sheriff, when in fact all he had done was to have a gun in his possession. The court rejected the lawyer's argument that she had not intended to deceive the judge, stating: "If an attorney does not know if an assertion is true or cannot point to a reasonably diligent inquiry to ascertain the truth of the statement, the attorney can remain silent, profess no knowledge, or couch the assertion in equivocal terms so the court can assess the assertion's probative value." In re Dodge, 108 P.2d 362, 367 (Idaho 2008).

23. *See* MR 3.3(a)(3), discussed later in this chapter.

24. *See* ABA, Criminal Justice Standards for the Defense Function, Standard §4-7.8(a) (4th ed. 2017) ("[i]n closing argument to a jury . . . defense counsel may argue all reasonable inferences from the evidence in the record" but "[d]efense counsel should not knowingly misstate the evidence in the record, or argue inferences that counsel knows have no good-faith support in the record"). For a fascinating debate as to whether and when a lawyer should be permitted to advance a "false case,"*see* Harry Subin, The Criminal Lawyer's "Different Mission": Reflections on the "Right" to Present a False Case, 1 Geo. J. Legal Ethics 125 (1987); John Mitchell, Reasonable Doubts Are Where You Find Them: A Response to Professor Subin's Position on the Criminal Lawyer's Different Mission, 1 Geo. J. Legal Ethics 339 (1987); Harry Subin, Is This Lie Necessary? Further Reflections on the Right to Present a False Defense, 1 Geo J. Legal Ethics 689 (1988).

25. *See* Trial Conduct: Candor Toward Tribunals, 61.301 ABA/BLAW Law. Man. on Prof. Conduct .20.60.20 (ABA/BLAW) (2021).

26. ABA Formal Ethics Op. 95-397 (1995) (explaining that death of a client terminates the lawyer-client relationship).

motion for temporary custody, he then sat quietly while the judge questioned the senior lawyer, who was falsely reporting a conversation the junior lawyer had had with another person.[27]

As for false statements of law, judges are understandably upset when lawyers misquote precedent, cite authority that has been repealed or overruled (without appropriate disclosure), or cite an apparently exhaustive list of supporting authorities without including an important adverse authority.[28]

3. Failure to Disclose Adverse Law or Facts

Model Rule 3.3(a)(2) provides that "[a] lawyer shall not knowingly . . . fail to disclose to the tribunal legal authority in the controlling jurisdiction known to the lawyer to be directly adverse to the position of the client and not disclosed by opposing counsel." In other words, lawyers are required to disclose adverse law when opposing counsel has not done so and the undisclosed adverse law is clearly material to the court's decision.

There is no analogous rule for material adverse facts. Except in ex parte proceedings, discussed below, an advocate is free to remain silent even when the advocate knows that opposing counsel has failed to discover possibly dispositive evidence, such as the defendant physician's admission, in the earlier hypothetical, that she was drunk when she operated on the plaintiff patient.

When, exactly, does a lawyer need to disclose adverse legal authority? Does it matter if the lawyer reasonably believes that the authority is distinguishable? And what is the basis for distinguishing between adverse law and adverse facts? The following opinion addresses some of these questions.

Tyler v. State
47 P.3d 1095 (Alaska Ct. App. 2001)

MANNHEIMER, Judge.

On May 18, 2001, this court ordered attorney Eugene B. Cyrus to show cause why sanctions should not be imposed on him . . . for his conduct in this appeal. Having considered Mr. Cyrus's response, we conclude that Mr. Cyrus should be fined.

[David A. Tyler had twice been convicted of misdemeanor DWI-driving while intoxicated when he entered a no contest plea to a third DWI charge. Because this constituted his third DWI offense within five years, his no contest plea to the third offense caused him to be convicted of felony DWI. On appeal,[29] his attorney, Cyrus, conceded that Tyler was guilty of the most recent

---

27. *See* Daniels v. Alander, 844 A.2d 182 (Conn. 2004).

28. *See* RLGL §111, cmt b (first two examples described as "direct misstatement"; third example described as an "implicit misrepresentation").

29. [Under the terms of his no contest plea, Tyler purportedly reserved the right to litigate the validity of his pleas to the two prior DWI charges. —ED.]

DWI charge, but argued that he had not knowingly waived his right to counsel before he pleaded no contest[30] to the earlier cases, that his two prior DWI convictions were therefore invalid and should be set aside, and therefore his current DWI offense should be reduced to a misdemeanor. The State moved to dismiss the appeal on the ground that the validity of Tyler's two prior DWI pleas was not dispositive of Tyler's case, which was a prerequisite to the appellate court having jurisdiction to hear the appeal. The State's argument was that even if Tyler had not knowingly waived his right to counsel, he would not be entitled to an acquittal of the two prior charges but would face trial on the charges if he withdrew his pleas. If convicted, the State argued that he would still be a third offender for purposes of the current offense and his felony DWI conviction would remain valid. Cyrus contended, however, "that the present state of the law does not permit such a relation back," i.e., that even if he was reconvicted on both charges, these two convictions would no longer be "prior" and therefore his current conviction would have to be deemed a misdemeanor rather than a felony.]

Although the three cases cited by Mr. Cyrus [in support of his contention] do not involve or address this legal issue, the Alaska Supreme Court has in fact addressed this very issue in a slightly different setting. The case is *McGhee v. State.* . . .

Neither Mr. Cyrus nor the State's attorney cited *McGhee* in their pleadings. We found the case ourselves. And, having found it, we concluded that it provided the answer to Tyler's appeal [as the State had argued]. . . .

When the parties submitted their pleadings on this issue, neither Mr. Cyrus nor the State's attorney alerted us to *McGhee v. State*, the Alaska Supreme Court decision that addresses this re-conviction issue in the context of an administrative revocation of a driver's license for a third-offense DWI.[31] The State's attorney apparently did not find the *McGhee* case when he researched the State's motion to dismiss Tyler's appeal-for if the State's attorney had found *McGhee,* he doubtless would have cited it. But Mr. Cyrus plainly knew of the supreme court's decision in *McGhee*: he was the attorney who represented McGhee in the supreme court.

---

30. Under a no contest plea, a defendant does not admit or deny guilt but does not contest the charges. The right of the defendant to enter a no contest plea, as well as the collateral consequences of such a plea (such as the ability of an adversary to use it as proof of the facts charged in a civil lawsuit) differ from state to state.

31. [In *McGhee*, the defendant was challenging an increase in the period of his driver's license revocation following his third conviction for DWI. The defendant had successfully challenged his prior convictions and was allowed to withdraw them. After he was convicted again on both charges, the defendant challenged his revocation enhancement on the ground that one of his "prior" convictions was no longer prior. The Alaska Supreme Court rejected this argument, holding that "the temporary set-aside of the prior DWI requires no alteration of the original [license] revocation." McGhee v. State, 951 P.2d 1215, 1217 (Alaska 1998).—Ed.]

Alaska Professional Conduct Rule 3.3(a)(3)[32] declares that a lawyer shall not knowingly "fail to disclose . . . legal authority in the controlling jurisdiction" if the lawyer knows that his legal authority is "directly adverse to the position of the [lawyer's] client" and if this authority has "not [been] disclosed by opposing counsel." *McGhee* was decided by our supreme court, so it is "legal authority in the controlling jurisdiction." Mr. Cyrus knew about the *McGhee* decision, and he knew that the State's attorney had not brought *McGhee* to our attention. The remaining question is whether Mr. Cyrus knew that *McGhee* was "directly adverse" to his legal position—directly adverse to his contention that Tyler would have to be treated as a "first offender" even if he was reconvicted of the two prior DWIs.

. . . [O]ur dismissal of Tyler's appeal . . . is clearly premised on our conclusion that *McGhee* is, in fact, directly adverse to Mr. Cyrus's legal position. However, it would be unfair to judge Mr. Cyrus's ethical duties in hindsight. Obviously, Mr. Cyrus had not read our decision when he wrote his brief. The question is whether, at the time Mr. Cyrus wrote his brief, he knew that *McGhee* was directly adverse to his position.

(A) MR. CYRUS'S RESPONSE TO OUR ORDER TO SHOW CAUSE

In his response to our order to show cause, Mr. Cyrus asserts that he did not tell us about the *McGhee* decision because he believed that *McGhee* did not control the outcome of Tyler's case. Mr. Cyrus contends that "*McGhee* is unique because of its fact pattern" and, because of this, he did not believe (and still does not believe) that *McGhee* was "controlling authority" in Tyler's case. To back up his argument, Mr. Cyrus points out that at least one superior court judge shared his views concerning *McGhee*. . . .

[The court discussed another superior court case in which Cyrus also represented a defendant convicted of third offense DWI, where Cyrus employed the same tactics he used in *Tyler*. In arguing to the superior court that the defendant's felony conviction should be reduced to a misdemeanor, neither Cyrus nor the State mentioned *McGhee*. The superior court judge, Judge Hensley, discovered *McGhee* on his own, but he concluded that it was factually distinguishable.]

To summarize: Mr. Cyrus offers two defenses to our order to show cause. First, he argues that even though we relied on *McGhee* when we dismissed Tyler's appeal, we were wrong to do so. . . . Second, Mr. Cyrus argues that even if this court was right when we concluded that *McGhee* was dispositive of Tyler's appeal, this conclusion was reasonably debatable. Based on [Judge Hensley's analysis] Mr. Cyrus points out that competent attorneys and judges might reasonably conclude that *McGhee* was factually distinguishable from Tyler's case—and that, therefore, *McGhee* did not control the outcome

---

32. [Like Model Rule 3.3, Alaska Rule 3.3 has since been amended, and the identical duty to disclose adverse law now appears as Rule 3.3(a)(2). —ED.]

of Tyler's appeal. Mr. Cyrus argues that if reasonable attorneys conclude that *McGhee* was not controlling authority in Tyler's appeal, he was under no obligation to cite the case in his brief.

Of the two defenses advanced by Mr. Cyrus, this second one is clearly the stronger. Judge Hensley's decision . . . shows that Mr. Cyrus was not alone in thinking that *McGhee* should be limited to an administrative context and should not be viewed as controlling authority in criminal cases that raise the same re-conviction issue.

[The court concludes that Cyrus "might reasonably have concluded that the *McGhee* decision did not control the outcome of Tyler's appeal."]

But Mr. Cyrus's defense to our order to show cause also hinges on his assertion that Professional Conduct Rule 3.3(a)(3) only requires attorneys to reveal "controlling" court decisions and statutes. This is not correct.

(B) As Used in Professional Conduct Rule 3.3(a)(3), "Directly Adverse" Is Not Synonymous with "Controlling" or "Dispositive"

Fortified by Judge Hensley's decision. . . . Mr. Cyrus argues that "if attorneys could [reasonably] disagree as to [whether *McGhee* was] controlling authority," then his failure to cite *McGhee* cannot constitute a violation of Professional Conduct Rule 3.3(a)(3). The problem with Mr. Cyrus's argument is that Rule 3.3(a)(3) does not speak of an attorney's failure to cite "controlling authority." Instead, it speaks of an attorney's failure to cite authority in the "controlling jurisdiction" if that authority is *directly adverse* to the [lawyer's] position."

McGhee was decided by our state supreme court, so it clearly constitutes "authority in the controlling jurisdiction." The next question is whether *McGhee* was "directly adverse" to Mr. Cyrus's position in Tyler's appeal. The legislative history of Professional Conduct Rule 3.3(a)(3) and the commentaries on the rule show that "directly adverse" does not mean "controlling." It refers to a broader range of cases and statutes.

[The court traced a series of ABA ethics opinions, court opinions in other jurisdictions, and secondary sources, concluding that Rule 3.3(a)(3) and its predecessors had consistently been interpreted to require disclosure when "the omitted authorities 'would be considered important by the judge sitting on the case,' or whether the judge might consider himself 'misled' if he remained unaware of them."]

(C) Using This Definition of "Directly Adverse," Did Mr. Cyrus Know That McGhee Was Directly Adverse to the Position He Was Advancing in Tyler's Appeal?

Turning to the facts of Tyler's appeal, and using the test explained in the previous section, it is evident that the supreme court's decision in *McGhee* was "directly adverse" to the position that Mr. Cyrus was arguing in Tyler's appeal.

McGhee is the only Alaska Supreme Court decision (to our knowledge) that addresses the question raised in Tyler's appeal—the effect of a withdrawn plea and a re-conviction of DWI when a defendant faces harsher penalties if the defendant is found to be a repeat offender. The result reached in *McGhee* is the opposite of the result that Mr. Cyrus advocated in Tyler's appeal. And, although the matter was obviously debatable, one could reasonably interpret *McGhee* as being directly inconsistent with, or at least substantially undercutting, the argument that Mr. Cyrus was making in Tyler's case. Further, even if Mr. Cyrus thought that *McGhee* was distinguishable because of its procedural context, Tyler's appeal involved a novel issue on which there was a dearth of authority, and *McGhee* was the only Alaska decision that came close to addressing this issue.

Given these circumstances, *McGhee* was "directly adverse" to Mr. Cyrus's position for purpose of Professional Conduct Rule 3.3(a)(3). In the words of ABA Formal Ethics Opinion 280, *McGhee* is a decision "which would reasonably be considered important" by this court, a decision "which the court should clearly consider in deciding [Tyler's] case." . . .

In Great Britain, barristers are under "an unquestioned obligation" to cite to all relevant law, both favorable and unfavorable. Professional Conduct Rule 3.3(a)(3) does not impose such a broad duty on Alaska attorneys. But although our state's duty of disclosure is narrower, enforcement of this duty remains important.

The process of deciding appeals involves the joint efforts of counsel and the court. As the Supreme Court of New Jersey has noted, "[i]t is only when each branch of the profession performs its function properly that justice can be administered to the satisfaction of both the litigants and society." Only then can an appellate court "[develop] a body of decisions . . . that will be a credit to the bar, the courts[,] and the state."

When a lawyer practicing before us fails to disclose a decision of the Alaska Supreme Court (or one of our own published decisions) that is directly adverse to the lawyer's position, the lawyer's conduct will, at the very best, merely result in an unneeded expenditure of judicial resources—the time spent by judges or law clerks in tracking down the adverse authority. At worst, we will not find the adverse authority and we will issue a decision that fails to take account of it, leading to confusion in the law and possibly unfair outcomes for the litigants involved. This potential damage is compounded by the fact that our decision, if published, will be binding in future cases. . . .

We acknowledge that Professional Conduct Rule 3.3(a)(3) has not previously been interpreted by the appellate courts of this state. Given that fact, Mr. Cyrus might plausibly have been unaware of the definition of "directly adverse," and he might honestly have thought that Rule 3.3(a)(3) only required him to cite adverse authority if that authority unquestionably controlled the litigation. But, as we have explained here, the American Bar Association and various courts and commentators have adhered to a broader definition of "directly adverse" for more than half a century. While Mr. Cyrus's misunderstanding of the rule may be a mitigating circumstance, it does not justify his conduct.

[Cyrus was ordered to pay a $250 fine.]

NOTES AND QUESTIONS

1. What if the State had cited *McGhee* in its motion to dismiss Tyler's appeal, but failed to cite the superior court decision in which Judge Hensley had distinguished *McGhee* as applying only to administrative decisions, not criminal cases? Are decisions by a different judge in a parallel court "legal authority in a controlling jurisdiction" if they are not binding on the judge hearing the motion? Although courts have reached differing conclusions on this question,[33] *Tyler* strongly suggests that lawyers should err on the side of citing contrary authority within the same jurisdiction.

2. The adversary system presupposes that each advocate has a duty of "one-sided partisan zeal" and that it is up to opposing counsel to make arguments and produce evidence beneficial to the opposing party. The duty to disclose adverse law constitutes an exception to "one-sided partisan zeal." What is the basis for this exception, and why isn't a similar exception made for material adverse fact? Comment [4] to Rule 3.3 says only that "[t]he underlying concept is that legal argument is a discussion seeking to determine the legal premises properly applicable to the case." Is this comment helpful?

3. Does *Tyler* offer any insight on the basis for recognizing a duty to disclose adverse law but not adverse facts? What are the consequences of a tribunal making incorrect findings of law or fact? The *Tyler* court expressed concern that failure to disclose adverse law might result in "possibly unfair outcomes for the litigants involved," which of course is precisely the concern we have about failure to disclose a critical adverse fact. Are there other consequences of the failure to disclose adverse law that are of even greater concern to the court?

4. What role does the lawyer's duty of confidentiality play in forming these rules? Rule 1.6 protects *all* information relating to the representation of a client, regardless of its source and even when the information is a matter of public record.[34] Rule 3.3(c) provides that the duties of disclosure recognized in this rule "apply even if compliance requires

---

33. *Compare* Smith v. Scripto-Tokai Corp., 170 F.Supp.2d 533 (W.D.Pa. 2001) (Rule 3.3 violated when lawyer failed to cite adverse trial court decision from a different federal district court within state), *with* Estate of Carambio, 951 A.2d 947 (N.J. 2008) (no violation when lawyer failed to cite contrary decision by different trial judge, both because the opinion was unpublished and because the decision was not binding authority).

34. *See supra* Chapter 4: Privilege and Confidentiality.

disclosure of information otherwise protected by Rule 1.6." Is there any basis for distinguishing disclosure of adverse law and adverse fact that takes into consideration the extent of the impact of such disclosure on the duty of confidentiality? One federal district court justified the duty to disclose adverse law on the ground that it helps courts avoid legal errors without harming the lawyer-client relationship "because the law does not 'belong' to a client, as privileged factual information does."[35] Does this make sense to you?

5. As a member of the Kutak Commission that drafted the 1983 Model Rules, Judge Frankel considered a proposal that would have required disclosure of facts known to the lawyer that "'would probably have a substantial effect on the determination of a material issue.'"[36] Judge Frankel acknowledged the proposal's "'radical' character," but was impressed that "it [was] advanced as a respectable subject for debate; and (more problematically) because it may be a harbinger of times not too distant."[37] Neither the ABA nor any state has adopted a rule generally requiring the disclosure of material adverse facts; however, the Federal Judicial Center has instituted a Mandatory Initial Discovery Pilot Project, in which several federal district courts require the parties in civil cases to respond to a series of standard discovery requests before undertaking other discovery.[38] The study is designed to determine whether requiring such initial disclosures will reduce the cost and delay of civil litigation, but it may also assist in the search for truth by assuring that the parties have access to basic information about evidence known to the opponent.

6. Although there is no general duty to reveal adverse facts, Rule 3.3(d) provides that "[i]n an ex parte proceeding, a lawyer shall inform the tribunal of all material facts known to the lawyer that will enable the tribunal to make an informed decision, whether or not the facts are adverse." Comment [14] explains that in ex parte proceedings, such as an application for a temporary restraining order, "there is no balance of presentation by opposing advocates" and yet "[t]he judge has an affirmative responsibility to accord the absent party just consideration." Should this rule apply when there has been notice and an opportunity to be heard, but neither the opposing party nor opposing counsel appears at the proceeding? In a class action when the parties submit a settlement agreement for the court's approval?[39]

---

35. Smith v. Scripto-Tokai Corp., 170 F.Supp.2d 533, 539 (W.D. Pa. 2001) (quoting Geoffrey C. Hazard, Jr. & W. William Hodes, The Law of Lawyering §29.11 (3d ed. 2001)).

36. Frankel, *supra*, at 83. The proposal would not have required disclosure of adverse facts on behalf of a criminal defendant.

37. *Id.*

38. *See supra* n.12.

39. *See* N.Y. City Bar Ass'n Comm. on Prof'l Ethics, Formal Op. 2019-1 (2019) (discussing state ethics opinions supporting either narrow or broad interpretation of what constitutes an "ex parte proceeding" for purposes of Rule 3.3(d)).

4. Client and Other Witness Perjury

Model Rule 3.3(a)(3) provides that "[a] lawyer shall not knowingly . . . offer evidence that the lawyer knows to be false. If a lawyer, the lawyer's client, or a witness called by the lawyer, has offered material evidence and the lawyer comes to know of its falsity, the lawyer shall take reasonable remedial measures, including, if necessary, disclosure to the tribunal. A lawyer may refuse to offer evidence, other than the testimony of a defendant in a criminal matter, that the lawyer reasonably believes is false."

If ever there were an exception to the adversary's ordinary duty of "one-sided partisan zeal," a rule prohibiting a lawyer from knowingly presenting false evidence appears to be the least in need of justification. As Comment [5] explains, the duty to "refuse to offer evidence that the lawyer knows is false, regardless of the client's wishes . . . is premised on the lawyer's obligation as an officer of the court to prevent the trier of fact from being misled by false evidence." Not to mention that, in most cases, to do so would be to commit, or at least assist, a criminal act. None of us will be surprised to learn that lawyers have been disciplined for submitting a fabricated subpoena,[40] permitting a client to give a false affidavit,[41] or offering into evidence a physician's report knowing that the report had been altered in significant aspects.[42]

In a civil case, when the lawyer knows in advance that testimony will be false, including the client's own testimony, the lawyer may not offer that testimony. If the lawyer is surprised by false evidence offered by either the client or a witness called by the lawyer, and the evidence is material, then the lawyer must take "reasonable remedial measures, including, if necessary, disclosure to the tribunal." MR 3.3(a)(3). These requirements apply not only at trial or pretrial hearings, but also in "an ancillary proceeding conducted pursuant to the tribunal's adjudicative authority, such as a deposition." *Id.* at cmt [1]. Reasonable remedial measures include remonstrating with the client and seeking the client's agreement to withdraw or correct the false evidence. If the attorney's withdrawal will not undo the effect of the false evidence, then "the advocate must make such disclosure to the tribunal as is reasonably necessary to remedy the situation, even if doing so requires the lawyer to reveal information that otherwise would be protected by Rule 1.6." *Id.* at cmt [10].

The rule does not apply to testimony by an adversary or an adversary's witness, where the lawyer may elicit and then demonstrate the falsity of the testimony, as an effective means of establishing the witness's lack of credibility.

---

40. *See* In re Steele, 868 A.2d 146 (D.C. 2005) (fabricated subpoena offered in motion to vacate dismissal of client's case, in order to excuse lawyer's failure to appear at pretrial conference).

41. *Cf.* Patsy's Brand, Inc. v. I.O.B. Realty, Inc., 2002 WL 59434 (S.D.N.Y. 2002) (lawyers sanctioned under Rule 11; although client insisted affidavit was true, "no reasonable lawyer would believe it" in light of evidence clearly indicating that client's statements were false).

42. *See* In re Watkins, 656 So.2d 984 (La. 1995).

As for evidence that the lawyer reasonably believes, but does not know, is false, the lawyer has discretion to refuse to offer the evidence, except for the testimony of a defendant in a criminal case, where a defendant has a constitutional right to testify.

The constitutional rights of a criminal defendant complicate the application of Rule 3.3(a)(3), even when the lawyer knows that the defendant will or has offered material false evidence. These rights include the right to testify and the right to the effective assistance of counsel. In the following U.S. Supreme Court case, the Justices all agreed that the defendant's constitutional rights had not been violated when the defense lawyer threatened to tell the court if the defendant gave testimony the lawyer knew was perjured; however, as at least one of the Justices recognized, the factual posture of this case was unusual, leaving many "areas of uncertainty" that would be difficult to resolve.

Nix v. Whiteside
475 U.S. 157 (1986)

Chief Justice BURGER delivered the opinion of the Court.

We granted certiorari to decide whether the Sixth Amendment right of a criminal defendant to assistance of counsel is violated when an attorney refuses to cooperate with the defendant in presenting perjured testimony at his trial.

I

A

Whiteside was convicted of second-degree murder by a jury verdict which was affirmed by the Iowa courts. The killing took place on February 8, 1977, in Cedar Rapids, Iowa. Whiteside and two others went to one Calvin Love's apartment late that night, seeking marihuana. Love was in bed when Whiteside and his companions arrived; an argument between Whiteside and Love over the marihuana ensued. At one point, Love directed his girlfriend to get his "piece," and at another point got up, then returned to his bed. According to Whiteside's testimony, Love then started to reach under his pillow and moved toward Whiteside. Whiteside stabbed Love in the chest, inflicting a fatal wound.

Whiteside was charged with murder. . . . Gary L. Robinson . . . was appointed and immediately began an investigation. Whiteside gave him a statement that he had stabbed Love as the latter "was pulling a pistol from underneath the pillow on the bed." Upon questioning by Robinson, however, Whiteside indicated that he had not actually seen a gun, but that he was convinced that Love had a gun. No pistol was found on the premises; shortly after the police search following the stabbing, which had revealed no weapon, the victim's family had removed all of the victim's possessions from the apartment. Robinson interviewed Whiteside's companions who were present during the stabbing, and none of them had seen a gun during the incident. Robinson advised Whiteside that the existence of a gun was not necessary to establish the claim of self-defense, and that only a reasonable belief that the victim had a gun nearby was necessary even though no gun was actually present.

Until shortly before trial, Whiteside consistently stated to Robinson that he had not actually seen a gun, that that he was convinced that Love had a gun in hand. About a week before trial, during preparation for direct examination, Whiteside for the first time told Robinson and his associate . . . that he had seen something "metallic" in Love's hand. When asked about this, Whiteside responded: "[I]n Howard Cook's case there was a gun. If I don't say I saw a gun, I'm dead." Robinson told Whiteside that such testimony would be perjury and repeated that it was not necessary to prove that a gun was available but only that Whiteside reasonably believed that he was in danger. On Whiteside's insisting that he would testify that he saw "something metallic" Robinson told him, according to Robinson's testimony:

> "[W]e could not allow him to [testify falsely] because that would be perjury, and as officers of the court we would be suborning perjury if we allowed him to do it; . . . I advised him that if he did so that it would be my duty to advise the Court of what he was doing and that I felt he was committing perjury; also, that I probably would be allowed to attempt to impeach that particular testimony."

Robinson also indicated that he would seek to withdraw from the representation if Whiteside insisted on committing perjury.

Whiteside testified in his own defense at trial and stated that he "knew" that Love had a gun and that he believed Love was reaching for a gun and he had acted swiftly in self-defense. On cross-examination, he admitted that he had not actually seen a gun in Love's hand. Robinson presented evidence that Love had been seen with a sawed-off shotgun on other occasions, that the police search of the apartment may have been careless, and that the victim's family had removed everything from the apartment shortly after the crime. Robinson presented this evidence to show a basis for Whiteside's asserted fear that Love had a gun.

The jury returned a verdict of second-degree murder, and Whiteside moved for a new trial, claiming that he had been deprived of a fair trial by Robinson's admonitions not to state that he saw a gun or "something metallic." The trial court held a hearing, heard testimony by Whiteside and Robinson, and denied the motion. The trial court made specific findings that the facts were as related by Robinson.

The Supreme Court of Iowa affirmed respondent's conviction. [The Iowa court concluded that not only were Robinson's actions permissible, but were required.] The court commended "both Mr. Robinson and [his associate] for the high ethical manner in which this matter was handled."

[Whiteside petitioned for a writ of habeas corpus. The District Court denied the writ. The Eighth Circuit reversed and directed that the writ of habeas corpus be granted.]

II . . .

B

In *Strickland v. Washington*, we held that to obtain relief by way of federal habeas corpus on a claim of a deprivation of effective assistance of counsel under the Sixth Amendment, the movant must establish both serious attorney error and prejudice. To show such error, it must be established that the assistance rendered by counsel was constitutionally deficient, in that "counsel made errors so serious that counsel was not functioning as 'counsel' guaranteed the defendant by the Sixth Amendment." To show prejudice, it must be established that the claimed lapses in counsel's performance rendered the trial unfair so as to "undermine confidence in the outcome" of the trial. . . .

Under the *Strickland* standard, breach of an ethical standard does not necessarily make out a denial of the Sixth Amendment guarantee of assistance of counsel. When examining attorney conduct, a court must be careful not to narrow the wide range of conduct acceptable under the Sixth Amendment so restrictively as to constitutionalize particular standards of professional conduct and thereby intrude into the state's proper authority to define and apply the standards of professional conduct applicable to those it admits to practice in its courts. In some future case challenging attorney conduct in the course of a state-court trial, we may need to define with greater precision the weight to be given to recognized canons of ethics, the standards established by the state in statutes or professional codes, and the Sixth Amendment, in defining the proper scope and limits on that conduct. Here we need not face that question, since virtually all of the sources speak with one voice.

C

We turn next to the question presented: the definition of the range of "reasonable professional" responses to a criminal defendant client who informs counsel that he will perjure himself on the stand. We must determine whether, in this setting, Robinson's conduct fell within the wide range of professional responses to threatened client perjury acceptable under the Sixth Amendment.

In *Strickland*, we recognized counsel's duty of loyalty and his "overarching duty to advocate the defendant's cause." Plainly, that duty is limited to legitimate, lawful conduct compatible with the very nature of a trial as a search for truth. Although counsel must take all reasonable lawful means to attain the objectives of the client, counsel is precluded from taking steps or in any way assisting the client in presenting false evidence or otherwise violating the law. This principle has consistently been recognized in most unequivocal terms by expositors of the norms of professional conduct since the first Canons of Professional Ethics were adopted by the American Bar Association in 1908. . . .

These principles have been carried through to contemporary codifications of an attorney's professional responsibility. Disciplinary Rule 7-102 of the Model Code of Professional Responsibility (1980) entitled "Representing a Client Within the Bounds of the Law," provides:

"(A) In his representation of a client a lawyer shall not. . . .

(4) Knowingly use perjured testimony or false evidence." . . .

(7) Counsel or assist his client in conduct that the lawyer knows to be illegal or fraudulent."

This provision has been adopted in Iowa, and is binding on all lawyers who appear in its courts. The more recent Model Rules of Professional Conduct (1983) similarly admonish attorneys to obey all laws in the course of representing a client:

"RULE 1.2 Scope of Representation . . .

(d) A lawyer shall not counsel a client in conduct that the lawyer knows is criminal or fraudulent . . . ."

Both the Model Code of Professional Responsibility and the Model Rules of Professional Conduct also adopt the specific exception from the attorney-client privilege[43] for disclosure of perjury that his client intends to commit or has committed. DR 4-101(C)(3) (intention of client to commit a crime); Rule 3.3 (lawyer has duty to disclose falsity of evidence even if disclosure compromises client confidences). Indeed both the Model Code and the Model Rules do not merely *authorize* disclosure by counsel of client perjury; they *require* such disclosure.

These standards confirm that the legal profession has accepted that an attorney's ethical duty to advance the interests of his client is limited by an equally solemn duty to comply with the law and standards of professional conduct; it specifically ensures that the client may not use false evidence. This special duty of an attorney to prevent and disclose frauds upon the court derives from the recognition that perjury is as much a crime as tampering with witnesses or jurors by way of promises and threats, and undermines the administration of justice. . . .

It is universally agreed that at a minimum the attorney's first duty when confronted with a proposal for perjurious testimony is to attempt to dissuade the client from the unlawful course of conduct. . . .

The commentary [to Model Rule 3.3] also suggests that an attorney's revelation of his client's perjury to the court is a professionally responsible and acceptable response to the conduct of a client who has actually given perjured testimony. Similarly, the Model Rules and the commentary, as well as the Code of Professional Responsibility adopted in Iowa, expressly permit withdrawal from representation as an appropriate response of an attorney when the client threatens to commit perjury. Withdrawal of counsel when this situation arises at trial gives rise to many difficult questions including possible mistrial and claims of double jeopardy.

---

43. [Was the Court correct in using the term "attorney-client privilege" here? — ED.]

The essence of the brief amicus of the American Bar Association reviewing practices long accepted by ethical lawyers is that under no circumstances may a lawyer either advocate or passively tolerate a client's giving false testimony. This, of course, is consistent with the governance of trial conduct in what we have long called "a search for truth." The suggestion sometimes made that "a lawyer must believe his client, not judge him" in no sense means a lawyer can honorably be a party to or in any way give aid to presenting known perjury.

D

Considering Robinson's presentation of respondent in light of these accepted norms of professional conduct, we discern no failure to adhere to reasonable professional standards that would in any sense make out a deprivation of the Sixth Amendment right to counsel. Whether Robinson's conduct is seen as a successful attempt to dissuade his client from committing the crime of perjury, or whether seen as a "threat" to withdraw from representation and disclose the illegal scheme, Robinson's representation of Whiteside falls well within accepted standards of professional conduct and the range of reasonable professional conduct acceptable under *Strickland*. . . .

The Court of Appeals' holding that Robinson's "action deprived [Whiteside] of due process and effective assistance of counsel" is not supported by the record since Robinson's action, at most, deprived Whiteside of his contemplated perjury. Nothing counsel did in any way undermined Whiteside's claim that he believed the victim was reaching for a gun. Similarly, the record gives no support for holding that Robinson's action "also impermissibly compromised [Whiteside's] right to testify in his own defense by conditioning continued representation . . . and confidentiality upon [Whiteside's] *restricted* testimony." The record in fact shows the contrary: (a) that Whiteside did testify, and (b) he was "restricted" or restrained only from testifying falsely and was aided by Robinson in developing the basis for the fear that Love was reaching for a gun. Robinson divulged no client communications until he was compelled to do so in response to Whiteside's post-trial challenge to the quality of his performance. We see this as a case in which the attorney successfully dissuaded the client from committing the crime of perjury. Paradoxically, even while accepting the conclusion of the Iowa trial court that Whiteside's proposed testimony would have been a criminal act, the Court of Appeals held that Robinson's efforts to persuade Whiteside not to commit that crime were improper, *first*, as forcing an impermissible choice between the right to counsel and the right to testify; and, *second*, as compromising client confidences because of Robinson's threat to disclose the contemplated perjury.

Whatever the scope of a constitutional right to testify, it is elementary that such a right does not extend to testifying *falsely*. . . .

The paucity of authority on the subject of any such "right" may be explained by the fact that such a notion has never been responsibly advanced; the right to counsel includes no right to have a lawyer who will cooperate with planned perjury. A lawyer who would so cooperate would be at risk of prosecution for suborning perjury, and disciplinary proceedings, including suspension or disbarment.

Robinson's admonitions to his client can in no sense be said to have forced respondent into an *impermissible* choice between his right to counsel and his right to testify as he proposed for there was no *permissible* choice to testify falsely. For defense counsel to take steps to persuade a criminal defendant to testify truthfully, or to withdraw, deprives the defendant of neither his right to counsel nor the right to testify truthfully. . . . When an accused proposes to resort to perjury or to produce false evidence, one consequence is the risk of withdrawal of counsel.

On this record, the accused enjoyed continued representation within the bounds of reasonable professional conduct and did in fact exercise his right to testify; at most he was denied the right to have the assistance of counsel in the presentation of false testimony. Similarly, we can discern no breach of professional duty in Robinson's admonition to respondent that he would disclose respondent's perjury to the courts. The crime of perjury in this setting is indistinguishable in substance from the crime of threatening or tampering with a witness or juror. A defendant who informed his counsel that he was arranging to bribe or threaten witnesses or members of the jury would have no "right" to insist on counsel's assistance or silence. Counsel would not be limited to advising against that conduct. An attorney's duty of confidentiality, which totally covers the client's admission of guilt, does not extend to a client's announced plans to engage in future criminal conduct. In short, the responsibility of an ethical lawyer, as an officer of the court and a key component of a system of justice, dedicated to a search for truth, is essentially the same whether the client announces an intention to bribe or threaten witnesses or jurors or to commit or procure perjury. No system of justice worthy of the name can tolerate a lesser standard.

The rule adopted by the Court of Appeals, which seemingly would require an attorney to remain silent while his client committed perjury, is wholly incompatible with the established standards of ethical conduct and the laws of Iowa and contrary to professional standards promulgated by this State. . . . Since there has been no breach of any recognized professional duty, it follows that there can be no deprivation of the right to assistance of counsel under the *Strickland* standard.

E

We hold that, as a matter of law, counsel's conduct complained of here cannot establish the prejudice required for relief under the second strand of the *Strickland* inquiry. Although a defendant need not establish that the attorney's deficient performance more likely than not altered the outcome in order to establish prejudice under *Strickland*, a defendant must show that "there is a reasonable probability that, but for counsel's unprofessional errors, the result of the proceeding would have been different." According to *Strickland*, "[a] reasonable probability is a probability sufficient to undermine confidence in the outcome." The *Strickland* Court noted that the "benchmark" of an ineffective-assistance claim is the fairness of the adversary proceeding, and that in judging prejudice and the likelihood of a different outcome, "[a] defendant has no entitlement to the luck of a lawless decisionmaker."

Whether he was persuaded or compelled to desist from perjury, Whiteside has no valid claim that confidence in the result of his trial has been diminished by his desisting from the contemplated perjury. Even if we were to assume that the jury might have believed his perjury, it does not follow that Whiteside was prejudiced. . . .

Reversed.

Justice BRENNAN, concurring in the judgment.

This Court has no constitutional authority to establish rules of ethical conduct for lawyers practicing in the state courts. Nor does the Court enjoy any statutory grant of jurisdiction over legal ethics. . . .

I join Justice Blackmun's concurrence because I agree that respondent has failed to prove the kind of prejudice necessary to make out a claim under *Strickland v. Washington*.

Justice BLACKMUN, with whom Justice BRENNAN, Justice MARSHALL, and Justice STEVENS join, concurring in the judgment.

How a defense attorney ought to act when faced with a client who intends to commit perjury at trial has long been a controversial issue. But I do not believe that a federal habeas corpus case challenging a state criminal conviction is an appropriate vehicle for attempting to resolve this thorny problem. When a defendant argues that he was denied effective assistance of counsel because his lawyer dissuaded him from committing perjury, the only question properly presented to this Court is whether the lawyer's actions deprived the defendant of the fair trial which the Sixth Amendment is meant to guarantee. Since I believe that the respondent in this case suffered no injury justifying federal habeas relief, I concur in the Court's judgment. . . .

Whether an attorney's response to what he sees as a client's plan to commit perjury violates a defendant's Sixth Amendment rights may depend on many factors: how certain the attorney is that the proposed testimony is false, the stage of the proceedings at which the attorney discovers the plans, or the ways in which the attorney may be able to dissuade his client, to name just three. The complex interaction of factors, which is likely to vary from case to case, makes inappropriate a blanket rule that defense attorneys must reveal, or threaten to reveal, a client's anticipated perjury to the court. Except in the rarest of cases, attorneys who adopt "the role of the judge or jury to determine the facts," pose a danger of depriving their clients of the zealous and loyal advocacy required by the Sixth Amendment.

I therefore am troubled by the Court's implicit adoption of a set of standards of professional responsibility for attorneys in state criminal proceedings. . . . The signal merit of asking first whether a defendant has shown any adverse prejudicial effect before inquiring into his attorneys performance is that it avoids unnecessary federal interference in a State's regulation of its bar. Because I conclude that the respondent in this case failed to show such an effect, I join the Court's judgment that he is not entitled to federal habeas relief.

Justice STEVENS, concurring in the judgment.

Justice Holmes taught us that a word is but the skin of a living thought. A "fact" may also have a life of its own. From the perspective of an appellate judge, after a case has been tried and the evidence has been sifted by another judge, a particular fact may be as clear and certain as a piece of crystal or a small diamond. A trial lawyer, however, must often deal with mixtures of sand and clay. Even a pebble that seems clear enough at first glance may take on a different hue in a handful of gravel.

As we view this case, it appears perfectly clear that respondent intended to commit perjury, that his lawyer knew it, and that the lawyer had a duty — both to the court and to his client, for perjured testimony can ruin an otherwise meritorious case — to take extreme measures to prevent the perjury from occurring. The lawyer was successful and, from our unanimous and remote perspective, it is now pellucidly clear that the client suffered no "legally cognizable prejudice."

Nevertheless, beneath the surface of this case there are areas of uncertainty that cannot be resolved today. A lawyer's certainty that a change in his client's recollection is a harbinger of intended perjury — as well as judicial review of such apparent certainty — should be tempered by the realization that, after reflection, the most honest witness may recall (or sincerely believe he recalls) details that he previously overlooked. Similarly, the posttrial review of a lawyer's pretrial threat to expose perjury that had not been committed — and, indeed, may have been prevented by the threat — is by no means the same as review of the way in which such a threat may actually have been carried out. Thus, one can be convinced — as I am — that this lawyer's actions were a proper way to provide his client with effective representation without confronting the much more difficult questions of what a lawyer must, should, or may do after his client has given testimony that the lawyer does not believe. The answer to such questions may well be colored by the particular circumstances attending the actual event and its aftermath.

Because Justice Blackmun has preserved such questions for another day, and because I do not understand him to imply any adverse criticism of this lawyer's representation of his client, I join his opinion concurring in the judgement.

NOTES AND QUESTIONS

1. *Whiteside* illustrates yet another remedy for unethical conduct on the part of a lawyer — overturning a criminal conviction on the ground that the lawyer's unethical conduct constituted the ineffective assistance of counsel, in violation of the defendant's constitutional rights.[44] The general standard for proving an ineffective assistance of counsel claim was established in Strickland v. Washington, 466 U.S. 668 (1984). As *Whiteside* explains, *Strickland* requires the defendant to establish: (1) "serious attorney error"; and (2) "prejudice." With respect to serious attorney error, the *Whiteside* court asked "whether, in this setting, Robinson's conduct fell within the wide range of professional responses to threatened client perjury acceptable under the Sixth Amendment." As for prejudice, the Court asked "whether the claimed lapses in counsel's performance rendered the trial so unfair so as to 'undermine confidence in the outcome' of the trial."

2. All the Justices agreed that Robinson's conduct did not violate the *Strickland* standard. The majority addressed both parts of the *Strickland* test, but the concurring Justices preferred to rely solely on the lack of prejudice. Ordinarily, prejudice is established when "there is a reasonable probability that but for counsel's unprofessional errors, the result of the proceeding would have been different." Here, however, all the Justices agreed that even if the jury might have believed Whiteside's perjured testimony, "legally cognizable prejudice" was not established because the inability to present perjured testimony would not undermine public confidence in the fairness of the proceeding.

3. As for "serious attorney error," on what basis did the majority opinion find that Robinson's conduct was "within the wide range of professional responses to threatened client perjury acceptable under the Sixth Amendment"? Do you agree with the Blackmun concurring opinion that the majority opinion "implicit[ly] adopt[ed] a set of standards of professional responsibility for attorneys in state criminal proceedings"? The majority opinion began by stating that "[w]hen examining attorney conduct, a court must be careful not to narrow the wide range of conduct acceptable under the Sixth Amendment so restrictively as to constitutionalize particular standards of professional conduct and thereby intrude into the state's proper authority to define and apply the standards of professional conduct applicable to those it admits to practice in its courts." Is there other language in the majority opinion that appears to undermine this statement, leading to the concerns expressed in Justice Blackmun's concurring opinion?

---

44. This remedy was also illustrated in Cuyler v. Sullivan, in which a criminal defendant sought to overturn his criminal conviction because of his lawyers' conflict of interest. *See supra* Chapter 5: Conflict of Interest: Current Clients.

4. Although the Blackmun opinion suggests that there are many factors that determine whether a client's intended perjury violates the defendant's constitutional rights, it is the Stevens concurrence that focuses explicitly on the unusual factual posture in which the issue reached the Court in *Whiteside*—one in which "it appears perfectly clear that respondent intended to commit perjury [and] that his lawyer knew it." Why were those facts "perfectly clear" here? What if Whiteside had insisted it was true that he saw a gun, despite the fact that he had earlier said only that he was convinced that Love had a gun? Don't witnesses sometimes recall details that they had earlier forgotten? And what if Whiteside had never previously said that he was convinced Love had a gun, such that it made no sense for him to take the stand at all if he couldn't give the testimony that Robinson believed would be perjured? How do these different facts alter the application of the *Strickland* standard?

5. Rule 3.3 does not apply a different standard of "knows" for purposes of the testimony of a criminal defendant, but might courts adopt a stricter standard as a matter of constitutional law? In State v. McDowell,[45] the Wisconsin Supreme Court said that "[a]bsent the most extraordinary circumstances, such knowledge [that a criminal defendant client intends to testify falsely] must be based on the client's expressed admission of intent to testify untruthfully."[46]

6. What can a trial court judge do when a defense lawyer communicates that he believes his client intends to or has given perjured testimony? In Nguyen v. Knowles,[47] a federal district court judge held that the defendant's rights were violated when he was excluded from an ex parte conference between his lawyer and the judge concerning the lawyer's belief that the defendant's testimony would be perjured. The lawyer's only basis for his belief was that the defendant had changed his version of the facts, which the court held did not establish that he had a "firm factual basis" for believing his client would testify falsely. What if the lawyer told the court that his client had admitted to him that the testimony would be false? May the judge take the lawyer's word for it? What if the judge questions the defendant, and the defendant denies having made that admission? A District of Columbia Court of Appeals decision requires an evidentiary hearing before an independent judge,[48] but most courts have rejected such a requirement on grounds of "judicial economy and the need to avoid disclosure of client confidences during the attorney-client relationship."[49]

---

45. 681 N.W.2d 500 (Wis. 2004).

46. *Id.* at 504. *See also* United States v. Midgett, 342 F.3d 321 (4th Cir. 2003).

47. 2010 U.S. Dist. LEXIS 89894 (E.D. Cal. 2010), aff'd, 2010 U.S. Dist. LEXIS 97816 (E.D. Cal. 2010).

48. *See* Witherspoon v. United States, 557 A.2d 587, 592-93 (D.C. 1989).

49. Raymond J. McKoski, Prospective Perjury by a Criminal Defendant: It's All about the Lawyer, 44 Ariz. St. L.J. 1575, 1633 (2012).

7. In *Nguyen*, instead of excluding the defendant from testifying at all, the trial court agreed with the defense lawyer that the defendant would present his testimony in a "narrative manner." This alternative approach has been adopted by several states as an appropriate remedial measure, after the lawyer has remonstrated with the defendant and advised him of the risk of perjury, and the lawyer's withdrawal is not a viable option.[50] The lawyer elicits only the defendant's name and then "essentially, ask[s] him a very large leading question, such as, Can you tell us what happened on June 3rd, 1998, at 6:30 a.m. and let[s] him speak in narrative fashion."[51] In closing argument, the lawyer may not refer to any facts known to be false. What are the advantages and disadvantages of this approach? What alternative course might the court take when defense counsel communicates the defendant's intent to commit perjury? Some courts require defense counsel to proceed with the usual examination of the defendant as a witness.[52]

8. Whiteside's lawyer knew in advance of his client's intent to perjure himself. Should the lawyer have sought to withdraw from the representation? Jurisdictions that require the defendant to testify in the narrative fashion typically do so only if the lawyer has been unable to withdraw. If the defendant tells replacement counsel of his intent to commit perjury, then that lawyer will similarly attempt to withdraw. And if the defendant recognizes that in order to testify in the normal fashion, he will need to lie first to his new lawyer, then what will have been accomplished? If the goal of Rule 3.3 is to prevent perjured testimony, then having the lawyer withdraw accomplishes little. But might the goal be to prevent a lawyer from actively participating in such perjury? Is this a worthwhile goal?[53]

---

50. *See, e.g.*, D.C. Rules of Prof'l Conduct, R. 3.3(b) ("When the witness who intends to give evidence that the lawyer knows to be false is the lawyer's client and is the accused in a criminal case, the lawyer shall first make a good-faith effort to dissuade the client from presenting the false evidence; if the lawyer is unable to dissuade the client, the lawyer shall seek leave of the tribunal to withdraw. If the lawyer is unable to dissuade the client or to withdraw without seriously harming the client, the lawyer may put the client on the stand to testify in a narrative fashion, but the lawyer shall not examine the client in such manner as to elicit testimony which the lawyer knows to be false, and shall not argue the probative value of the client's testimony in closing argument."). *See also* Tenn. Rules of Prof'l Conduct, R. 3.3(b); Mass. Rules of Prof'l Conduct, R. 3.3(e).

51. *Ngyuen, supra*, 2010 U.S. LEXIS 89894, at *18. Some courts permit the defense lawyer to play a greater role, for example, asking specific questions on direct except when the lawyer knows that the answer to that question will be perjurious, in which case the lawyer must ask an open-ended question. *See* McKoski, *supra* n. 49, at 1623-24 (2012).

52. *See, e.g.*, Coleman v. State, 621 P.2d 869 (Alaska 1980).

53. Raymond McKoski argued that witness perjury, particularly by an interested party, is an expected feature of the adversary system, but that skilled cross-examination is expected to assist the jury in ferreting out such perjury. *See* McKoski, *supra* n. 49 at 1577 ("A defendant's perjured testimony is not the concern; it occurs all the time. The concern is the lawyer's knowing participation in the client's deception.")

B. Limits on Adversary Zeal 213

9. The *Whiteside* Court stated on several occasions that the defense lawyer's obligation to prevent client perjury is no different than the obligation to prevent the client from bribing or threatening a witness or juror. Indeed, Rule 3.3(b) expressly requires a lawyer to take "reasonable remedial measures, including, if necessary, disclosure to the tribunal" when the lawyer knows that any person, including the client, "intends to engage, is engaging or has engaged in criminal or fraudulent conduct related to the proceeding." There is little debate over Rule 3.3(b),[54] and yet there continues to be disagreement concerning the best means of addressing client perjury in the context of a criminal defendant. Contrary to the majority's view in *Whiteside*, is there arguably a significant difference between preventing bribing or threatening a witness or juror and permitting the defendant to give perjured testimony?

10. Criminal defense lawyers often say that the problem of client perjury rarely arises. Some take the position that they never "know" the testimony will be perjured (relying on Samuel Johnson's famous quote). Others say they can almost always persuade the defendant not to testify, either because the testimony will not be believed or because, regardless of any perjured testimony, the defendant is subject to impeachment by evidence of a prior conviction or other prejudicial evidence. Still others avoid gaining knowledge by refusing to ask the defendant what happened. Rather, they will ask questions indirectly, such as what the defendant believes the prosecution will say happened. Is "deliberate ignorance" a defensible strategy? Don't lawyers need to know as much as possible about the case in order to effectively defend against a criminal charge?

11. According to a 1972 anonymous survey of the District of Columbia criminal defense bar, "90% of those surveyed would call the perjurious criminal defendant to the witness stand and conduct the defense as if the client had testified truthfully."[55] The lawyers were not asked to provide the reason why they did so, but it is possible that they were simply ignoring the existence of the client perjury rule.[56]

12. In an earlier chapter, we saw that another U.S. Supreme Court case, Cuyler v. Sullivan,[57] provides for a more relaxed standard for

---

54. For example, Massachusetts prohibits a criminal defense lawyer from disclosing either intended or completed client perjury, but requires the lawyer to disclose a criminal defendant's participation in bribing or harming a juror or witness. *See* Mass. Rules of Prof'l Conduct, R. 3.3(b), (e). *But see* D.C. Rules of Prof'l Conduct, R. 3.3 & cmt [8] (rule contains no equivalent of MR 3.3(b), but comment explains that lawyer may be permitted under D.C. Rule 1.6(c) to disclose a client's involvement in bribing or intimidating a witness).

55. Jay Sterling Silver, Truth, Justice, and the American Way: The Case Against the Client Perjury Rules, 47 Vand. L. Rev. 423, n.311 (1994) (citing Friedman, Professional Responsibility in D.C.: A Survey, 1972 Res Ipsa Loquitur 60).

56. *Id.* at 423, n. 311.

57. 446 U.S. 335 (1980). *See supra* Chapter 5: Conflicts of Interest: Current Clients.

establishing ineffective assistance of counsel claims when the defendant is alleging impermissible conflicts of interest. There the Court held that when the defendant establishes the existence of an *actual conflict* (as opposed to Rule 1.7's "significant risk" of material limitation), prejudice is presumed if the defendant further establishes that the actual conflict *adversely affected the lawyer's conduct*. In other words, the defendant need not meet the ordinary test of prejudice, which is the reasonable probability that the outcome would have been different. The *Cuyler* standard is more relaxed than the *Strickland* standard,[58] but both are harder to meet than the standard for lawyer discipline. What justifies a higher bar to establish ineffective assistance of counsel than professional misconduct?

5. Fairness to Opposing Party and Counsel

Model Rule 3.4 contains a list of prohibited conduct for lawyers operating as advocates within the adversary system. As Comment [1] explains: "The procedure of the adversary system contemplates that the evidence in a case is to be marshalled competitively by the contending parties. Fair competition in the adversary system is secured by prohibitions against destruction or concealment of evidence, improperly influencing witnesses, obstructive tactics in discovery procedure and the like."

Some prohibitions expressly track substantive law. For example, Rule 3.4(a) provides that a lawyer shall not "unlawfully obstruct another party's access to evidence or unlawfully alter, destroy or conceal a document or other material having potential evidentiary value." Other rules do so implicitly, for example, Rule 3.4(b) (prohibiting falsification of evidence), Rule 3.4(c) (knowingly disobeying an obligation under the rules of a tribunal), and Rule 3.4(d) (making frivolous discovery request or failure to make reasonably diligent effort to comply with proper discovery request). Other rules impose obligations regardless of whether they are prohibited by other law. For example, Rule 3.4(f) prohibits a lawyer from requesting persons other than a client not to volunteer information to the other party, with certain exceptions.

Advocates need to be familiar with applicable rules of civil and criminal procedure, especially the extensive and detailed rules governing the conduct of discovery in civil cases. Violation of a discovery obligation may subject a lawyer to discipline, but as a practical matter, the lawyer is at greater risk of litigation sanctions, either at the request of the opposing party or by sua sponte action of the court. An area of recent concern is the lawyer's ability to limit an opposing party's access to evidence on a client's social media

---

58. *Cuyler* was decided before *Strickland*. Since *Strickland* was decided, the Supreme Court has confirmed that there is a lesser burden for defendants claiming ineffective assistance of counsel based on a conflict than for defendants claiming other grounds of ineffectiveness. *See* Burger v. Kemp, 483 U.S. 776 (1987).

accounts. Lawyers have been sanctioned for advising a client to destroy post-ings of photos and other damaging information,[59] but ethics opinions gener-ally approve advising a client to maintain strict privacy and to delete postings if the relevant information is properly preserved for use in pending or antici-pated litigation.[60]

Aside from Rule 3.4, the most important professional conduct rules addressing fairness to opposing parties and counsel are Rule 4.1 (Truthfulness in Statements to Others), Rule 4.2 (Communications with Person Represented by Counsel), and Rule 4.3 (Dealing with Unrepresented Person). Because these rules apply equally to transactional lawyers, we will address them in that context in the following chapter.

Review Problems

7-1 A young woman was accused of shoplifting when a security officer observed her leaving the store without having paid for a $2.00 store item she was holding in her hand. When questioned by the security officer, the woman emptied her pockets and revealed that she had a ten-dollar bill there. She con-fessed to her criminal defense lawyer that she had stolen the item and that the reason she didn't pay for it with the ten-dollar bill was that she needed that money to buy school supplies for her daughter at another store. May the defense attorney remind the jury that the woman had made no attempt to conceal the item and that she had the means to pay for it and then argue for an acquittal based on the woman having "accidently" walked out of the store with the item?

7-2 A lawyer is representing a man accused of negligence in a two-car crash. The plaintiff, who was the driver of the other car, was rendered unconscious as a result of the accident and therefore was unable to take the name of the sole bystander witness, who had left by the time the police came. The man got the witness's contact information, and his lawyer subsequently interviewed her. She was adamant that she had a clear view of the accident and that the man was clearly speeding at the time of the crash. The man's lawyer will not call the witness to testify at trial. The plaintiff's lawyer is unaware of the exis-tence of the witness and when taking the man's deposition, failed to ask if the man was aware of any witnesses to the crash. Must the man's lawyer disclose the existence of the witness to either the plaintiff or the court?

7-3 A plaintiff sued a defendant under a state unfair trade practices act for mislabeling a food product. The defendant moved to dismiss the complaint for failure to state a claim. On the morning that the defendant's motion was to be heard, lawyers who had not appeared as part of the original complaint made an appearance for the plaintiff. The judge expressed concern about the appearance of new counsel at this late hour and indicated that she was con-sidering rejecting the amended complaint on that ground. The plaintiff's new

---

59. *See, e.g.,* Allied Concrete Co. v. Lester, 736 S.E.2d 699 (Va. 2013).
60. *See, e.g.,* Fla. Ethics Op. 14-1 (2016); Phila. Ethics Op. 2014-5 (2014).

lawyers argued that they should be permitted to enter their appearance. The defendant's lawyer remained silent even though he was aware of a state rule of civil procedure permitting additional lawyers to appear on behalf of a party without securing the court's permission. Neither the plaintiff's new lawyers nor the judge had mentioned the rule. Was it proper for the defendant's lawyer to remain silent and not disclose the existence of the court rule?

7-4 A nonprofit rural water system corporation filed a federal lawsuit in the Northern District of Iowa (in the Eighth Circuit) against a city alleging violation of a federal statute that protects rural water associations indebted to the United States from encroachment on their service by an adjacent municipality annexing portions of its service area. The city filed a motion for summary judgment, arguing that the corporation had lost the protection of the statute when it paid off its loans immediately prior to the time when the city annexed portions of its service area. In its brief, the city had cited no legal authorities that directly addressed this question. The lawyer for the corporation filed a brief that cited a decision of the Colorado Supreme Court on a comparable issue that was favorable to the corporation. The lawyer was aware of but did not cite a recent decision of the Sixth Circuit Court of Appeals holding that a party that has paid off or bought out its government loans may not assert the protections of the statute. The lawyer believed that there were facts in the Sixth Circuit opinion that made it factually distinguishable from the facts in the current case. Is the lawyer subject to discipline for failing to cite the Sixth Circuit opinion? What if the opinion was from the Eighth Circuit? From a district court in the Southern District of Iowa?

7-5 The department of motor vehicles determined that a woman was an habitual traffic violator and suspended her license for five years. Three years later, the woman was driving a motor vehicle when she was stopped for making an illegal turn. She was charged in a criminal case with driving a motor vehicle while her license was suspended. The woman retained a lawyer to represent her and, in discussing the case with her, the woman never claimed that she had not been driving the car that day. The lawyer considered that whether the woman was driving was irrelevant because the defense was based solely on the argument that the notice of suspension was sent to the woman at the wrong address. While that case was pending, the lawyer filed on the woman's behalf a petition for a probationary license, which is available after at least three years has passed since the time of suspension. At the hearing on this petition, the judge asked the woman, "Have you driven an automobile in the last three years?" The woman answered "No." The lawyer attended the hearing as the woman's counsel and was present in the courtroom during that exchange. The lawyer took no steps to correct the woman's testimony. Is the lawyer subject to discipline? Would your answer differ if the lawyer called the woman to testify in the criminal case that she never received the notice of suspension and, on cross-examination, she denied having driven the car that day, claiming that her sister was driving the car?

CHAPTER 8

LIMITS OF ZEALOUS REPRESENTATION II: TRANSACTIONS

Model Rules 1.2(d), 1.6, 4.1, 4.2, 4.3

In Chapter 4, we considered the saga of the law firm of Singer Hutner and its client O.P.M. The company was engaged in a pattern of fraudulent conduct, including falsifying computer leases in order to obtain bank loans. The law firm's lawyers closed loans and issued legal opinions, relied on by lenders, that O.P.M. had title to the computers and that the leases were lawful. Despite subsequent allegations by the company's president, Myron Goodman, that the law firm partner in charge was a "knowing, although reluctant principal," the law firm insisted that prior to June 1980, none of the lawyers had any idea that O.P.M. was engaged in fraud.

In June 1980, Goodman indicated to a senior firm lawyer that he "might have done something wrong in his stewardship of the company—something he could not set right because it involved millions of dollars more than he could raise." He refused, however, to give the lawyer a detailed account of his wrongdoing. An in-house accountant discovered evidence of lease fraud and wrote a letter to one of the Singer Hutner lawyers. The evidence was conflicting whether the accountant delivered the letter to Singer Hutner, but a contemporaneous law firm memo stated that the accountant told them "that O.P.M. had perpetrated a multimillion-dollar fraud and that the opinion letters Singer Hutner had drawn up to obtain loans for O.P.M. had been based upon false documents." The memorandum also stated that the accountant's lawyer told them that, according to the accountant, O.P.M.'s survival depended upon continuing the same types of activities.

In Chapter 4, we used the O.P.M. saga to discuss the limits of the lawyer's obligation of confidentiality, including Model Rules provisions permitting, but not requiring lawyers to disclose confidential information when necessary to prevent, rectify, or mitigate substantial economic harm resulting from

217

a client crime or fraud. In this chapter, we begin by revisiting the O.P.M. saga in order to highlight limitations on what lawyers in transactional practice may do when advising, counseling, or assisting their clients to achieve their goals.

A. LAWYER DISCIPLINE: KNOWINGLY COUNSELING OR ASSISTING A CLIENT'S CRIME OR FRAUD

1. Active Counseling or Assisting

Model Rule 1.2(d) provides that "[a] lawyer shall not counsel a client to engage, or assist a client, in conduct that the lawyer knows is criminal or fraudulent, but a lawyer may discuss the legal consequences of any proposed course of conduct with a client and may counsel or assist a client to make a good faith effort to determine the validity, scope, meaning, or application of the law." Rule 1.0(d) defines "fraud" as "conduct that is fraudulent under the substantive or procedural law of the applicable jurisdiction and has a purpose to deceive."[1] Rule 1.0(f) defines "knowingly," "known," or "knows" as "actual knowledge of the fact in question," and further states that "[a] person's knowledge may be inferred from circumstances."

In most cases of lawyer discipline under Rule 1.2(d), it is obvious that the lawyer knew that the client was engaging in criminal or fraudulent conduct. For example, in In re Siegel,[2] corporate counsel was disciplined for engaging with a company executive in a fraudulent scheme involving unrecorded cash sales of corporate merchandise, with the proceeds being turned over to the company executive. Similarly, in In re Feeley,[3] a lawyer was disciplined for helping a client forge checks for payment of the client's bond and legal fees. The client had directed the lawyer to create online checks under a name that was not the client's and was otherwise not known to the lawyer; the lawyer then deposited those checks in his clients' trust account after the client signed them in the name of the fictitious account holder. And in People v. Gifford,[4] a case involving lawyer counseling, a lawyer was disciplined for advising a client to offer his ex-wife real estate in exchange for favorable testimony in a pending criminal case.

But in other cases, the lawyer's "knowledge" may be less clear. Did the Singer Hutner senior partner "know" that Goodman had committed fraud when Goodman confessed that "he might have done something wrong in his stewardship of the company—something that he could not set right because it involved millions of dollars more than he could raise"? And even if he knew

---

1. This definition excludes "constructive fraud," in which the cause of action is treated as fraud even though deceptive intent is lacking.

2. 471 N.Y.S.2d 591 (N.Y. App. Div. 1984).

3. 581 S.E.2d 487 (S.C. 2003).

4. 76 P.3d 519 (Colo. O.P.D.J. 2003).

that Goodman had committed past fraud, did he know that the fraud was continuing? The Singer Hutner lawyers denied reading the accountant's letter claiming that the fraud was ongoing, but the lawyers' story was that "Goodman snatched the letter unopened from Reinhard's hand or seized it from the top of the desk." Even if this was true, and they didn't actually read the letter, what was the significance of this clearly bizarre behavior? And if they had read the letter, couldn't they claim that it was the accountant's word against Goodman's? Under what is commonly referred to as the "willful blindness" or "blind eye" doctrine, knowledge may be imputed to a lawyer who is "aware of the highly probable existence of a material fact but does not satisfy himself that it does not in fact exist."[5]

A leading professional responsibility treatise provides the following explanation of the "knowledge" requirement adopted in Rule 1.2(d):

> As Rule 1.0(f) states, a person's belief or knowledge "may be inferred from circumstances." Actually, it would have been more accurate to say that a person's belief or knowledge may *only* be inferred from circumstances. . . .
>
> This method of proof has enormous practical significance. Even where a violation requires proof of "knowledge," the circumstances may be such that a disciplinary authority will infer that a lawyer *must* have known. In such a case the lawyer will be legally chargeable as if actual knowledge had been proved. In terms of what can be proved, the "knows" standard thus begins to merge with the "should have known" standard, because it will sometimes be impossible to believe that a lawyer lacked the requisite knowledge, unless he deliberately tried to evade it. But one who knows enough to try to evade legally significant knowledge already knows too much. . . .
>
> As all lawyers who are honest with themselves know . . . occasions arise when doubts about a client turn into a suspicion and then a moral certainty that a client is lying or engaged in ongoing fraud or crime. Although his professional role may require a lawyer to take a detached attitude of unbelief, the law of lawyering does not permit a lawyer to escape all accountability by suspending as well his intelligence and common sense. See, for example, Model Rule 3.3(a)(3). . . .
>
> A lawyer may try to persuade himself that he is not absolutely sure whether his client is committing perjury. Or he may try to tell himself that he is not absolutely sure that his client is committing fraud in a negotiation. But all authorities agree — even those who take the most unqualified positions on the duty of a lawyer zealously to serve his clients — that there comes a point where only brute rationalization, moral irresponsibility, and pure sophistry can support the contention that the lawyer does not "know" what the situation is. That is the deep significance of Model Rule 1.2(d). . . .
>
> Apart from moral bases of responsibility, lawyers must also consider the problem of "what a lawyer knows" from the pragmatic viewpoint of self-protection, as intimated above. After the fact, a lawyer's conduct will be assessed

---

5. *See, e.g.,* Nancy J. Moore, Mens Rea Standards in Lawyer Disciplinary Codes, 23 Geo. J. Legal Ethics 1, 24 (2010). The doctrine was developed in criminal law, but is also applied in disciplinary actions. ABA Formal Ethics Op. 20-491 (2020) discusses "willful blindness" in transactional settings, particularly those involving terrorism funding or money laundering. *See infra* notes 9 and 10 and accompanying text.

according to a legal standard that assumes a lawyer *can* know the truth of a situation, even if he cannot be absolutely sure. Even the criminal law, after all, does not require absolute certainty; it requires only a conclusion that is beyond a reasonable doubt. . . . Moreover, the law takes account of a lawyer's legal training and experience in assessing his state of mind. A lawyer is an adult, a man or woman of the world, not a child. He is also better educated than most people, more sophisticated and more sharply sensitized to the legal implications of a situation. The law will make inferences as to a lawyer's knowledge with those considerations in mind.

Looking forward into his professional conduct as it proceeds, a lawyer must imagine how his conduct will appear to others looking back at it later. And he must imagine the inferences that will be drawn as to what he must have known at the time. In pragmatic terms, that is what a lawyer knows.[6]

The treatise authors assume that "knows" is interpreted the same way regardless whether the issue is client perjury under Rule 3.3(a)(3) or a client's commission of a transactional crime or fraud under Rule 1.2(d). But given that the client perjury issue is raised most frequently in criminal defense cases, where the defendant's constitutional right to testify is at stake, is this necessarily so? And, with respect to civil litigation or transactions, should courts interpret and apply the requirement of a lawyer's "knowledge" differently in the context of future or ongoing transactions, as opposed to litigation concerning a client's completed conduct? After all, lawyers in transactions are helping to shape conduct that has yet to occur. Indeed, in many situations, the lawyer's services, such as a legal opinion, are necessary before the transaction can be effectuated. In addition, there is no judge to serve as a neutral decisionmaker after hearing the evidence and arguments of the opposing advocates.[7]

Case law offers some support for a relatively expansive interpretation of the knowledge requirement under Rule 1.2(d) in transactional settings. For example, a Maryland estates lawyer was disciplined under that rule for knowingly notarizing a forged signature on a document that he did not personally file on the public record, but which his client later filed. The court explained that the knowledge-of-filing requirement was satisfied because "[e]xecuting false estate planning documents and filing them on the public records *or knowing the high probability or necessity that those false documents are going to be filed* and relied on in the future as truthful and accurate violates this Rule."[8]

A recent ABA ethics opinion adopted a similar approach to the knowledge requirement of Rule 1.2(d), articulating a "duty to inquire further" when "facts known to the lawyer establish a high probability that a client seeks to use the lawyer's services for criminal or fraudulent activity."[9] Focusing on concerns

---

6. Geoffrey C. Hazard, Jr. et al., The Law of Lawyering §1.24 (4th ed., 2020-2 Supp).

7. *See, e.g.*, W. Bradley Wendel, Professionalism as Interpretation, 99 Nw. U. L. Rev. 99, 1167, 1199 (2005).

8. Attorney Grievance Comm'n of Maryland v. Coppola, 419 Md. 370, 394 (2011).

9. ABA Formal Ethics Op. 20-491 (2020) (referring to the "willful blindness" or "conscious avoidance of facts" doctrines developed in criminal law).

A. Lawyer Discipline: Knowingly Counseling or Assisting a Client's Crime or Fraud

that a client or prospective client might seek a transactional lawyer's assistance in terrorist financing or money laundering,[10] the Committee emphasized the necessity of the lawyer conducting an inquiry to find out whether a highly suspicious request was in fact "above board" in order to avoid assisting in criminal or fraudulent activity. Even when not required by Rule 1.2(d), the Committee concluded that other rules including those requiring competent and diligent representation, may trigger a duty to inquire.

2. Failure to Disclose

Model Rule 4.1(b) provides that a lawyer "shall not knowingly . . . fail to disclose a material fact when disclosure is necessary to avoid assisting a criminal or fraudulent act by a client, unless disclosure is prohibited by Rule 1.6." As the Comment suggests, this rule "is a specific application of the principle set forth in Rule 1.2(d) and addresses the situation where a client's crime or fraud takes the form of a lie or misrepresentation." For an example of a Rule 4.1(b) violation, consider a lawyer who submitted a loan application on behalf of himself and his client with the loan to be repaid from the proceeds of the client's workers' compensation case, without disclosing that the client had filed for bankruptcy.[11]

The Singer Hutner lawyers undoubtedly believed that by withdrawing from the representation when they did, they would not be assisting in O.P.M.'s ongoing fraudulent conduct. But the Rule 4.1 Comment explains that although "[o]rdinarily, a lawyer can avoid assisting a client's crime or fraud by withdrawing from the representation . . . [s]ometimes it may be necessary for the lawyer to give notice of the fact of withdrawal and to disaffirm an opinion, document affirmation or the like."[12] And "[i]f the lawyer can avoid assisting a client's crime or fraud only by disclosing this information, then . . . the lawyer is required to do so, unless the disclosure is prohibited by Rule 1.6."[13]

This rule is complicated and convoluted. First, it requires the lawyer to understand when failure to disclose constitutes assisting in criminal or fraudulent conduct. The Singer Hutner lawyers apparently understood that if they continued to close loans for O.P.M. knowing that they were fraudulent, they would be acting improperly. But when is withdrawing from a representation insufficient to avoid assisting a client's ongoing criminal or fraudulent activity? The reference in the comment to withdrawing or disaffirming "an

---

10. For an extensive discussion of the possible use of lawyers to assist in money laundering and terrorist financing, *see generally* Am. Bar Ass'n Task Force on Gatekeeper Regulation and the Profession, Voluntary Good Practices for Lawyers to Detect and Combat Money Laundering and Terrorist Financing (2010).

11. *See* In re Cantrell, 619 S.E.2d 434 (S.C. 2005). The significance of the bankruptcy filing is that the proceeds of the workers' compensation case would be part of the bankruptcy estate and thus available for distribution to all creditors, who typically receive only a percentage of what they are owed when the debt is discharged.

12. MR 4.1, cmt [3].

13. *Id.*

opinion, document, affirmation or the like" gives us a clue to what the drafters had in mind. Consider the Singer Hutner lawyers who had given legal opinions that O.P.M. had title to the computers and that the leases were lawful, but who learned of the O.P.M. fraud shortly before the scheduled closing of a particular loan transaction. If the bank was likely to continue to rely on the law firm's opinion, even after the firm withdrew from the representation, then the lawyers' failure to disaffirm their opinion itself might constitute assisting in the client's criminal or fraudulent activity, under substantive law.[14] Engaging in a "noisy withdrawal"[15] might be sufficient to avoid such assistance, in which case the ABA has taken the position that doing so does not constitute an impermissible disclosure of confidential information, even in jurisdictions that have no exception in Rule 1.6 to prevent economic crimes or fraud.[16]

So far so good. But what if even a "noisy withdrawal" is insufficient to avoid assisting the client's misconduct? After noting that it is sometimes necessary to disaffirm "an opinion, document, affirmation or the like," the comment goes on to say that "[i]n extreme cases substantive law may require a lawyer to disclose information relating to the representation to avoid being deemed to have assisted the client's crime or fraud." In the absence of such disclosure, the comment assumes that the lawyer will violate not only substantive law, but also Rule 1.2(d). And yet, Rule 4.1(b) requires disclosure only when permitted by Rule 1.6 (thereby converting Rule 1.6's permissive disclosure to mandatory disclosure under Rule 4.1(b)).

---

14. A 1992 formal ABA opinion addressed a hypothetical situation involving installation contracts that a lawyer comes to learn are fraudulent. The opinion explained that the lawyer's "'assistance' would stem in material part from an invited, and assumed, reliance by the bank on [the lawyer's] prior representations about the enforceability of the client's installation contracts, and, by extension, about the client's financial situation generally." ABA Formal Ethics Op. 92-366 (1992).

15. Neither the Model Rules nor the Comments speak of a "noisy withdrawal," which is the term now commonly used to describe giving notice of the fact of withdrawal and disaffirming a prior opinion or document. For what may be the earliest use of this term, *see* Geoffrey C. Hazard, Jr., Rectification of Client Fraud: Death and Revival of a Professional Norm, 33 Emory L.J. 271, 307 (1984). Geoffrey Hazard was the Reporter for the Kutak Commission, which had initially drafted a confidentiality exception to prevent or rectify client fraud. According to Hazard, the "notice of withdrawal" provision in the Comment was proposed by the Commission and accepted by a prominent opponent of the confidentiality exception, as a compromise that permitted lawyers to extricate themselves from their unwitting involvement in client fraud. *Id.* For another early use of the term, *see* Ronald D. Rotunda, The Notice of Withdrawal and the New Model Rules of Professional Conduct: Blowing the Whistle and Waving the Red Flag, 63 Or. L. Rev. 455, 481 (1984) ("noisy notice of withdrawal"). New York, which has not adopted ABA Model Rule 1.6(b)(2) or (3), expressly permits the lawyer "to withdraw a written or oral opinion or representation previously given by the lawyer and reasonably believed by the lawyer still to be relied upon by a third person, where the lawyer has discovered that the opinion or representation was based on materially inaccurate information or is being used to further a crime or fraud." N.Y. Rules of Prof'l Conduct, R. 1.6(b)(3).

16. *See* ABA Formal Ethics Op. 92-366 (1992). The ABA opinion was written at a time when Model Rule 1.6 had no exception to prevent or rectify merely economic harm. Although Model Rule 1.6(b)(2) and (3) now permit such disclosure in some circumstances, the opinion is still of value in jurisdictions like Rhode Island that continue to follow the original Model Rule.

Under what circumstances would current Rule 1.6 prohibit disclosure reasonably necessary to prevent economic harm resulting from a client crime or fraud? If failure to disclose would implicate the lawyer in a client's misconduct, what justifies limiting the lawyer's ability to make the disclosures necessary to avoid the assistance that Rule 1.2(d) prohibits?[17]

3. Knowingly Counseling or Assisting Other Wrongful Client Acts

Both Rules 1.2 and 4.1(b) prohibit lawyer involvement in client crimes or frauds. But what about lawyer involvement in other wrongful acts by a client, such as violation of a court order, breach of fiduciary duty, or tortious interference with contractual relations?[18] According to the Restatement, "[a] lawyer's counseling or assisting a client that does not constitute a crime or fraud or violation of a court order is not subject to professional discipline . . . even if the client or lawyer would be subject to other remedies, such as damages in a civil action by an injured third person."[19] The Restatement justifies including counseling or assisting a client to violate a court order by referencing decisional law treating such violations as equally wrongful as client crimes and frauds. These decisions rely either on circumstances where a client's violation of a court order constitutes criminal contempt, or on Model Rule 8.4(d), which prohibits "conduct prejudicial to the administration of justice." In a later section of this chapter, we consider the possibility that the lawyer, as well as the client, may be liable for damages when the lawyer counsels or assists in wrongful client conduct, including but not limited to client crimes and frauds.

Why do you think that, outside of advocacy before a tribunal, disciplining a lawyer for counseling and assisting client wrongdoing is limited to criminal and fraudulent conduct? Several jurisdictions have expanded the prohibition in Rule 1.2(d) to include counseling or assisting a client in conduct that the lawyer knows is "illegal,"[20] and one jurisdiction also prohibits "preparation of a written instrument containing terms the lawyer knows are expressly prohibited by law."[21] Does the term "illegal" include preparing a contract with a term that the lawyer knows is unenforceable?[22]

---

17. There is nothing in the legislative history of Rule 4.1 that addresses what appears to be an inconsistency between Rule 1.2(d) and Rule 4.1(b).

18. Commentators disagree whether mere breach of contract is a legal "wrong." Proponents of the theory of "efficient breach" argue that we should expect a party to breach a contract and pay damages when that is cheaper than performing under the contract. Opponents of such a theory argue that parties are morally obligated to honor a contract because of having made a promise to do so.

19. RLGL, §94, cmt c.

20. Three such jurisdictions are Michigan, New Jersey, and Ohio.

21. *See* N.J. Rules of Prof'l Conduct, R. 1.2(d).

22. Ohio narrowly defines "illegal" to denote "criminal conduct or a violation of an applicable statute or administrative regulation." Ohio Rules of Prof'l Conduct, R. 1.0(e). Neither Michigan nor New Jersey defines the term.

If a client or a lawyer includes a term known to be unenforceable, then presumably the reason for doing so is an expectation that an opposing party who is uninformed as to the law will comply with the term. Is this conduct fraudulent under Rule 1.2(d)? What about Rule 8.4(c), which prohibits a lawyer from engaging in conduct involving dishonesty? Consider a lawyer drafting consumer contracts on behalf of a company doing business nationally, when the lawyer knows that some, but not all states refuse to enforce particular contract provisions, such as an agreement to a shorter statute of limitations than is otherwise provided by state law. May the lawyer include such a provision in the contracts that will be governed by the laws of the states that refuse to enforce such provisions?

B. LAWYER DISCIPLINE: LAWYER INTERACTIONS WITH PERSONS OTHER THAN CLIENTS

1. Truthfulness in Statements to Others

Rule 4.1(a) provides that "in the course of representing a client a lawyer shall not knowingly . . . make a false statement of material fact or law to a third person." Note the difference between this rule and Rule 3.3(a)(1), which prohibits the lawyer advocate from knowingly making *any* false statement of fact to a court or other tribunal.[23] Some states have retained the approach of the former Model Code and omit the materiality requirement in Rule 4.1(a).[24]

As with Rule 3.3(a)(1), "knowingly making a false statement" includes both false statements and statements that are misleading because of a material omission. Comment [1] to Rule 4.1 states that "[m]isrepresentations can also occur by partially true but misleading statements or omissions that are the equivalent of affirmative false statements." Consider this comment in the context of the following case.

The Florida Bar v. Joy
679 So.2d 1165 (Fla. 1996)

PER CURIAM . . .

Since approximately 1985, Joy represented Joel Cantor (J. Cantor) and his father Irwin (I. Cantor) in personal and business matters. In 1988, Joy developed a friendship with and eventually began to represent Sam Cohen. In 1990, J. Cantor, I. Cantor and Cohen became shareholders in Morrison Court, Inc. (Morrison Court), a corporation engaged in purchasing and managing

---

23. *See supra* Chapter 7: Limits of Zealous Representation I: Litigation.
24. These states include Minnesota, New York, North Dakota, and Virginia.

B. Lawyer Discipline: Lawyer Interactions with Persons Other Than Clients

real estate. Shortly after incorporation, Morrison Court purchased the Morrison Court Apartments (Apartments) from G & O Properties (G & O) and gave mortgages to both G & O and the Resolution Trust Corporation (RTC). In July 1991, the Apartments were destroyed by fire. Midland Risk Insurance Company (Midland Risk), denied payment of Morrison Court's claim due to suspicions of arson. In September 1991, J. Cantor, on behalf of Morrison Court, retained Joy to pursue Morrison Court's claim against Midland Risk. . . .

In August 1993, Joy, on behalf of Morrison Court, entered a settlement agreement with Midland Risk, the RTC, and G & O in which Midland Risk would pay a total of $1,250,000 in settlement of Morrison Court's claims. The agreement required Midland Risk to pay $750,000 to the RTC in satisfaction of its first mortgage and $500,000 to Joy's law firm's trust account for the benefit of Morrison Court and G & O. The $500,000 check was made payable to Joy's trust account "on behalf of Morrison Court, Inc. and G & O Properties." The letter of transmittal accompanying the check stated that Joy could not disburse the funds to Morrison Court and G & O until they had reached an agreement.

Following the agreement, Joy and the Cantors discussed the possibility of moving the $500,000 from Joy's trust account to another trust or escrow account in order to protect it from Morrison Court's creditors, such as G & O. . . . Without telling either [of the Cantors], Joy withdrew the $500,000 from his trust account and deposited it in an interest-bearing account in his wife's name as trustee for the benefit of 2311 MC Corporation, a nonexistent corporation. Joy then told G & O's lawyer that he had disbursed the funds from his trust account. . . .

Finally, in September 1993, the parties reached a final settlement and the $500,000 was disbursed. . . .

[The referee found Joy in violation of several disciplinary rules including the Florida equivalent of Model Rules 4.1 and 8.4(c) (prohibiting engaging in "conduct involving dishonesty, fraud, deceit or misrepresentation").]

. . . [T]he most damning evidence against Joy involves his handling of the $500,000 and his attempts to mislead G & O's lawyer. Joy concedes that the original check for the money was made payable to his law firm's trust account "on behalf of Morrison Court, Inc. and G & O Properties," and that the transmittal letter accompanying the check stated that Joy could not disburse the funds to either Morrison Court or G & O until the two had reached an agreement. Joy's transfer of the $500,000 into an interest-bearing account in his wife's name for the benefit of a non-existent corporation violated the terms of the escrow agreement. . . .

Joy not only violated his fiduciary obligation under the escrow agreement, he did so with the intent of bettering his client's negotiating position with respect to G & O. Despite Joy's argument to the contrary, we agree with the referee when he said:

> Relative to Respondent's transfer of the escrow funds into the account in his wife's name, as trustee, Respondent wrote a letter to Smith, counsel for G & O . . . [in which Respondent] represented to Smith that the

funds held in his Trust Account had been disbursed from his Trust Account. Respondent failed to disclose to Smith that the funds had been deposited into an interest-bearing account in the name of his wife, Madeline Joy, as Trustee, for the benefit of 2311 MC Corp. Respondent's statement to Smith regarding his disbursement of the funds from his Trust Account therefore amounted to a half-truth.

Respondent intended for Smith to misinterpret his statement to mean that he had disbursed the funds directly to his client, Morrison Court, and that he no longer had control over the funds. . . .

Further evidence of Respondent's intent to mislead Smith into believing that he had disbursed the funds to his client can be found in Respondent's failure to correct Smith's misunderstanding that the funds had been disbursed to Morrison Court, which misunderstanding was repeatedly stated in Smith's letters to Respondent. Respondent clearly intended for Smith to interpret his statement to mean that he had disbursed the funds to Morrison Court as an attempt to maximize his client's negotiating position.

Whether the escrow funds were still secure in Respondent's Trust Account and available for distribution by Respondent, as escrow agent, to G & O should a settlement agreement have been reached, was clearly a material fact relative to the settlement negotiations. Respondent, therefore, intentionally made a false statement or misrepresentation by omission to Smith about a material fact, the disbursement of the escrow funds

[The court suspended Joy for 91 days and thereafter for an indefinite period until he could demonstrate proof of rehabilitation.]

NOTES AND QUESTIONS

1. The opinion does not say on what basis Joy argued that the referee's findings were incorrect. Perhaps he argued that his statement that he had disbursed the funds from his trust account was literally true. On what basis did the referee conclude that Joy knowingly made a false statement?

2. Joy also appeared to be arguing that any false statement he made was not material. He didn't pocket the funds, and he didn't actually disburse them to Morrison Court, his client. Rather, he merely transferred the funds to another trust account in his wife's name (albeit for the benefit of a fictitious company), where they remained available for disbursement when the parties finally settled their disagreement. And the funds were in fact disbursed when a settlement agreement was reached. So how did the court conclude that Joy made a false statement of material fact?

3. Read the comment to Rule 4.1. What would the result in the case have been if Joy made the following statements during negotiations between Morrison Court and G & O regarding the allocation of the Midland funds?

    a. "My client has a strong claim to at least 80% of those funds" (when in fact Joy believed that Morrison Court's claim was weak).

B. Lawyer Discipline: Lawyer Interactions with Persons Other Than Clients

b. "My client is willing to agree to 50% of the funds in order to settle the dispute" (when in fact the client had told Joy that it would settle for 40% of the funds).

c. "We have an expert who will testify in a court proceeding that my client is entitled to 80% of the funds" (when Joy knows either that no expert has been hired or that the expert will testify that the client is entitled to less than 80% of the funds).

4. ABA Formal Ethics Op. 06-439 (2006) describes Comment [2] to Rule 4.1 as permitting "as 'posturing' or 'puffing,' . . . statements upon which parties to a negotiation ordinarily would not be expected justifiably to rely [as] distinguished from false statements of material facts." As such, Rule 4.1(a) does not require total honesty and candor in negotiations. Professor James White defended this position on two grounds, both of which acknowledge a range of different community expectations for negotiators, who may or may not be lawyers. The first ground recognizes the "paradoxical nature of the negotiator's responsibility":

> On the one hand the negotiator must be fair and truthful; on the other he must mislead his opponent. Like the poker player, a negotiator hopes that his opponent will overestimate the value of his hand. Like the poker player, in a variety of ways he must facilitate his opponent's inaccurate assessment. The critical difference between those who are successful negotiators and those who are not lies in the capacity both to mislead and not to be misled.[25]

Thus, White argued that "a careful examination of the behavior of even the most forthright, honest and trustworthy negotiators will show them actively engaged in misleading their opponents about their true positions." His second ground is that what constitutes acceptable negotiating techniques varies according to the circumstances (e.g., negotiating with terrorists, bargaining between labor and management, and bargaining between parties to a business deal) and according to the background of the negotiators (e.g., "the costs of conformity to ethical norms are less in a small community" than in a "large and heterogeneous community [where] one will not have confidence either about the norms that have been learned by the opposing negotiator or about his conformance to those norms").[26]

5. Federal district court judge Alvin Rubin strongly disagreed with the proposition that lawyer negotiators should be judged by the standards of conduct of other negotiators:

> It is scant comfort to observe here, as apologists for the profession usually do, that lawyers are as honest as other men. If it is an

---

25. James J. White, Machiavelli and the Bar: Ethical Limitations on Lying in Negotiation, 1980 Am. Bar F. Res. J. 926, 927 (1980).

26. *Id.* at 927-29.

inevitable professional duty that they negotiate, then as professionals they can be expected to observe something more than the morality of the marketplace . . . .[27]

The lawyer must act honestly and in good faith. Another lawyer, or a layman, who deals with a lawyer should not need to exercise the same degree of caution that he would if trading for reputedly antique copper jugs in an oriental bazaar. It is inherent in the concept of an ethic, as a principle of good conduct, that it is morally binding on the conscience of the professional, and not merely a rule of the game adopted because other players observe (or fail to adopt) the same rule.[28]

Which of these two views do you prefer? Why?

6. In Fire Insurance Exchange v. Bell,[29] the Indiana Supreme Court held that a personal injury plaintiff could proceed to trial on his fraud claim against the insurance company's lawyer, which was based on the lawyer's knowingly false statement that the insurance policy limit was only $100,000. The court rejected the defendant's argument that the plaintiff's lawyer, a trained advocate with access to discovery, was not entitled to rely on a statement by his adversary's lawyer. The court explained that "[a] lawyer's representations have long been accorded a particular expectation of honesty and trustworthiness":

The reliability of lawyers' representations is an integral component of the fair and efficient administration of justice. The law should promote lawyers' care in making statements that are accurate and trustworthy and should foster the reliance upon such statements by others.

Can you reconcile the court's view of the importance of a lawyer's trustworthiness with the position taken in the comment to Rule 4.1 on a lawyer's right to adhere to "generally accepted conventions in negotiations"? Might this court favor amending that comment to reflect Judge Rubin's view?

7. What may or must a lawyer for a buyer do upon discovering that the seller's lawyer made a material error, in the buyer's favor, in memorializing the agreed-upon terms in a final draft? Most authorities agree that the lawyer should disclose the drafting error, with or without first consulting the client, but their reasoning differs. ABA Informal Opinion 86-1518 concluded that lawyer disclosure is impliedly authorized to further the representation; therefore, a lawyer is permitted to disclose without first obtaining the client's permission.[30] Although the opinion

---

27. Alvin B. Rubin, A Causerie on Lawyers' Ethics in Negotiation, 35 La. L. Rev. 577, 578-79 (1975). *See also* Reed Elizabeth Loder, Moral Truthseeking and the Virtuous Negotiator," 8 Geo. J. Legal Ethics 45, 93-102 (1994) (rejecting assumption that negotiation is inherently deceptive and that the profession must accept "convention" as a governing principle).

28. Rubin, *supra* n. 27 at 589. White explicitly acknowledged lawyer negotiators' common practice of "hunting for the rules of the game as the game is played in that particular circumstance." White, *supra* n. 25, at 929.

29. 643 N.E.2d 310 (Ind. 1994).

30. ABA Informal Ethics Op. 86-1518 (1986).

did not address the lawyer's duty to disclose, it clearly favored disclosure on the ground that permitting the client to capitalize on the "scrivener's error" would raise a "serious question" whether the lawyer violated Rules 1.2(d), 4.1(b), and 8.4(c). Gregory Duhl agreed, but he relied on contract law providing that "a contract containing a scrivener's error will not be enforced, but will be rewritten to reflect the parties' actual agreement."[31] Nathan Crystal made an argument based on the comment to Model Rule 4.1 to the effect that nondisclosure may be tantamount to a material misrepresentation.[32] David Luban concluded that the reasoning underlying ABA Informal Opinion 86-1518 is extremely weak and that the Model Rules probably do not authorize disclosure over the client's objection unless failure to disclose would constitute "contractual fraud by omission," of which he was doubtful.[33] Nevertheless, Luban disclosed that a "distinguished mergers-and-acquisitions partner at a New York law firm"[34] told Luban that he had disclosed the error under similar circumstances, that he believes "every M&A partner he knows in every large law firm in New York would do the same," and that "fair dealing with others is part of the discretion that goes with the lawyer's role."[35] How would you interpret the Model Rules to apply in this scenario? Should lawyers have discretion to make such disclosures? Should they be required to do so?

2. Communication with Person Represented by Counsel

Model Rule 4.2 provides that "[i]n representing a client, a lawyer shall not communicate about the subject of the representation with a person the lawyer knows to be represented by another lawyer in a matter, unless the lawyer has the consent of the other lawyer or is authorized to do so by law or a court order." According to the comment, the purpose of the rule is to "contribute[] to the proper functioning of the legal system by protecting a person who has chosen to be represented by a lawyer in a matter against possible overreaching by other lawyers who are participating in the matter, unless the lawyer has the consent of the other lawyer or is authorized to do so by law or a court order."[36]

---

31. Gregory M. Duhl, The Ethics of Contract Drafting, 14 Lewis & Clark L. Rev. 989, 1003 (2010) (citing Restatement (Second) of Contracts §155 (1981)).

32. Nathan M. Crystal, The Lawyer's Duty to Disclose Material Facts in Contract or Settlement Negotiations, 87 Ky. L. J. 1055, 1085 (1998-99). At the time Crystal was writing, the ABA had not yet enacted the current disclosure provisions of Model Rule 1.6(b)(2) and (3); therefore, disclosures permitted (and therefore required) under Rule 4.1(b) would be rare. *See id.* at 1083.

33. David Luban, Fiduciary Legal Ethics, Zeal, and Moral Activism, 33 Geo. J. Legal Ethics 275, 292-95 (2020).

34. *Id.* at 292.

35. *Id.* at 295.

36. MR 4.2, cmt [1].

Virtually all of the cases and ethics committee opinions interpreting and applying this rule do so in the context of litigation, mostly when the represented person is an opposing party. Indeed, the Model Code version of the rule prohibited contact of a represented "party," thereby raising the question whether the rule applied at all in the context of a business transaction.[37] Model Rule 4.2 expressly includes all represented "persons," and the comment emphasizes that "[t]his Rule applies to communications with *any* person who is represented by counsel concerning the matter to which the communication relates."[38] Nevertheless, transactional lawyers are often unaware of the application of the rule to their type of business practice. The following article describes some of the circumstances in which business lawyers need to be sensitive to the rule and some of the issues that arise in both litigation and transactional practice. Although the authors focus on the California equivalent of the Model Rule, that rule is similar to Model Rule 4.2. One of the differences is that, like the Model Code, the California rule then in effect spoke of communication with a represented "party."

Neil J. Wertlieb & Nancy T. Avedissian

Ex Parte Communications in a Transactional Practice
The State Bar of California, Business Law News (2009)

You are sitting at your desk when your secretary announces that your most active client is on the phone. You take the call, looking forward to hearing about her next big M&A deal. After some pleasantries, the client announces that she also has on the line the counterparty with whom she is negotiating a term sheet. The client informs you that the counterparty is also represented by counsel, but your client explains that they are trying to hammer out some of the key business terms before they incur significant legal costs. The client then proceeds to ask for your input on how to best structure the deal.

Sounds familiar, right? But do you also hear the sound of alarm bells ringing? This all-too-common occurrence may result in a violation of the California Rules of Professional Conduct (CRPC)—specifically CRPC Rule [4.2],[39] which prohibits communication by an attorney with a represented party without the

---

37. *See* ABA, A Legislative History: The Development of the ABA Model Rules of Professional Conduct, 1982-2013, 559 (2013) (discussing change from "parties" to "persons" as intending to show that the rule applies to more than just the parties formally named in a proceeding).

38. MR 4.2, cmt [2] (emphasis added).

39. [The authors cite Rule 2-1000 of the California Rules of Professional Conduct, which was in effect at the time the article was written. Since then, California has adopted a Model Rule format and numbering system, so that the current citation would be to California Rule 4.2. Unlike Rule 2-1000, however, California Rule 4.2 expressly applies to communications with a represented "person."—Ed.]

consent of the party's attorney. The rule relating to such *ex parte* communications does not appear to be of obvious importance to many transactional attorneys. In fact, the term itself suggests that the rule is more relevant to our colleagues, the litigators, than to us deal lawyers. However, the rule prohibiting such communication does indeed apply to transactional attorneys, and violations of the rule can carry consequences including disqualification and discipline.

The rule aims to protect a represented party from possible overreaching by an attorney who may take advantage of the opportunity to gain a better deal for his or her client. It is not difficult to anticipate other potential mishaps, such as interference with the attorney-client relationship and inadvertent disclosure of confidential or privileged information. In the above example, however, many transactional attorneys would not hear alarm bells ringing, and even for those who do, they may feel that terminating the discussion to prevent a violation is awkward at best and may demonstrate a lack of cooperativeness to the client and other parties to a transaction. . . .

The Basic Rule . . .

CRPC Rule [4.2] is not limited to the litigation context, and the rule expressly applies to transactional matters as well. However, terminating the telephone call in the example above or ceasing a friendly conversation with someone seated across a conference table simply because the person's attorney steps out for a bathroom break may not be second nature to most transactional attorneys. Therefore, it is important to note that the rule applies not just to communications "which are intentionally improper, but, in addition, [communications] which are well intentioned but misguided."

What Types of Communications Are Covered?

Generally, any form of communication is covered by CRPC Rule [4.2]. The most common forms of communication include in-person meetings, traditional or electronic correspondence, and telephonic communication. For most transactional attorneys, the telephone call described above presents a real-life scenario. For purposes of CRPC Rule [4.2], it is not relevant that the client initiated the call or that the advice given is impartial—the attorney's participation in the discussion is a violation of the rule. Similarly, when an attorney dials into a conference call and it becomes evident that some parties are participating with their counsel while others are not, the ethical attorney should either drop off the line or request that all represented parties get their counsel on the line. While parties are assembling and engaging in small talk, it may also be advisable to email or call opposing counsel to either invite them to the call or obtain their consent to the *ex parte* communication.

The foregoing hypothetical conference call raises an interesting question: is it a permissible alternative for the attorney to stay on the call and just listen without speaking? Would that constitute prohibited communication? There is no clear answer to these questions. Although the attorney's conduct might not technically qualify as "communication with a party," it does put the attorney in the position of possible obtaining confidential information from the represented party or otherwise gaining an unfair advantage. . . .

"Directly or Indirectly"

CRPC Rule [4.2] expressly extends to both direct and indirect communications. Clearly the use by an attorney of an intermediary or agent to communicate with a represented party could be a prohibited form of indirect communication. Interestingly, the prohibition might even extend to the use of the client as an intermediary of the attorney. In such a situation, there is a tension between improper indirect communications with a represented party, on the one hand, and encouraging principal-to-principal communications on the other hand. In most business transactions, having the principals get together to discuss and agree upon material business terms is necessary, beneficial, and cost effective. However, if the content of a communication between principals originates with or is directed by the attorney (who either scripts the principal's questions or conveys his or her own thoughts or positions through the principal), then the communication may be improper. The attorney may confer with and advise a client with respect to a principal-to-principal communication, but the attorney may not direct the conversation. There is no bright line test, but generally reviewing, commenting on, or proofing letters and emails at the request of a client is probably acceptable, but ghostwriting them may not be.

The prohibition on indirect communication may also extend to providing a represented party with copies of correspondence sent to the party's attorney. For example, separately sending a represented party copies of correspondence you sent to his or her counsel (e.g., to incite the party to "light-a-fire" under counsel) would be an example of behavior in violation of the rule. Likewise, sending a represented party a "courtesy copy" of email correspondence without consent may also be prohibited.

"Subject of the Representation"

There is little guidance regarding this specific element of CRPC Rule [4.2]. . . . The exact scope of what constitutes the subject matter of the representation . . . may be somewhat elusive in certain matters. Consider a situation where an attorney represents the issuer in a private placement,[40] and the lead investor is represented by counsel. Absent consent by such counsel, the attorney must direct all communications with respect to the private placement through counsel. Suppose sometime after closing of the investment,

---

40. [A private placement is the sale of securities not to the public, but rather to a limited number of chosen investors. — Ed.]

the issuer needs shareholder consent for a proposed corporate action. Is the subject matter sufficiently different that the issuer's attorney can now communicate directly with the investor without going through counsel? On the one hand, a corporate action is a different matter than an investment in the issuer. On the other hand, the representation may be in connection with all matters relating to the investor's interests in the issuer, not just the initial investment. The attorney must use common sense and his or her reasonable judgment to make the determination. Often the prudent course of action is to inquire, either of the party or (if known) counsel, whether the party is represented by counsel with respect to the particular matter proposed to be discussed. . . .

"KNOWS TO BE REPRESENTED" . . . "IN THE MATTER"

A violation of Rule [4.2] requires that the attorney know that the contacted party is represented in the particular matter that is the subject of the communication. Although the authorities appear to be split as to whether constructive knowledge is sufficient,[41] knowledge can be established using an objective standard based on circumstantial evidence to determine if the attorney had reason to believe that a party was represented but failed to obtain counsel's consent prior to initiating contact. In such cases, an attorney ought to inquire about the existence and nature of a representation to confirm his or her understanding. . . . If the attorney is unsure, it is prudent to ask the party whether or not the party is represented before initiating any communication regarding the matter. . . .

The fact that an attorney knows a party will likely retain counsel for a particular matter but has not yet done so does not mean that the attorney is barred from communicating with the party. . . . Conversely, a representation is not perpetual, "forever excluding other attorneys from contacting [a] former [party]." Once a representation has concluded and an attorney does not have any reason to believe there is a continuing representation, communication is permitted. It is not always clear, however, when a transactional representation has ended. As a practical matter, in many instances a transactional representation has ended once the deal has closed, your fees have been paid, the closing dinner has occurred, and the closing sets have been distributed. However, where there are post-closing obligations and survival provisions, and especially where the notice provisions in the principal transactional document call for copies to be sent to counsel, the attorney should assume that the relationship continues for post-closing disputes. In such a case, the attorney should not communicate with a party without at least inquiring as to the current status of the representation. . . .

---

41. [Constructive knowledge exists when the law presumes a person's knowledge because a reasonable investigation would have revealed the relevant facts. — ED.]

"Consent of the Other Lawyer"

Consent is the cornerstone of compliance with CRPC Rule [4.2]. However, consent of the represented party is not sufficient. Consent must be obtained from opposing counsel before the attorney may communicate with the represented party. . . . The rule does not expressly require that consent be documented, but as an evidentiary matter, it is good practice to confirm a consent in writing.

The rule also does not expressly address whether consent can be implied from facts and circumstances, and there appears to be no authority specifically addressing this issue. Consent may well be implied by the joint presence of counsel and the represented party on a conference call or at a meeting, and transactional practitioners (if they think about it at all) could assume that such implied consent is sufficient to permit direct communication. However, failure to expressly address the issue in such circumstances might mean that the existence of proper consent could be subsequently disputed and/or reviewed.

Also consider standard notice provisions in agreements, which contractually mandate that notices and other communications under such agreements to be directed to a party (often, but always, with copies to counsel). If consent were not implied by the existence of such provision, the attorney providing notice under the agreement might need to choose between a potential violation of CRPC Rule [4.2] or a breach of the contractual mandate. . . . At a minimum, the attorney should copy counsel on such notices, even if it is not expressly required by the agreement.

Exceptions

CRPC Rule [4.2] recognizes three exceptions where communications with a represented party are permissible without the consent of counsel: (i) contact with a public officer, board, committee, or body; (ii) communications initiated by a represented party seeking advice or representation from an independent attorney (not opposing counsel); and (iii) communications otherwise authorized by law. . . .

Consequence of Failure to Comply

Improper communications with a represented party can lead to consequences even for transactional lawyers. The State Bar of California may discipline an attorney for a violation of Rule [4.2]. While we have found no instance in the transactional context, a violation in a litigation context typically results in a three-month suspension of the attorney's license to practice law. Whether an attorney can be disqualified from representing the client rests with a trial court (if applicable). Normally, a technical violation alone may not warrant disqualification unless it "led to the disclosures of confidential communications protected by the attorney-client privilege . . . or created an unfair advantage, or impacted . . . the integrity of the judicial system." . . . It may be . . . that disqualification is most relevant where the transactional matter also involves or results in litigation. . . .

NOTES AND QUESTIONS

1. Why does the rule prohibit sending a represented person a "courtesy copy" of a letter, including copying the person on an email directed to the person's lawyer? What about using "Reply All" to respond to an email sent to you by the opposing lawyer with a copy to his or her client? Given the opposing lawyer's knowledge of the communication, how could the opposing party be harmed? A recent New Jersey ethics committee opinion concluded that a lawyer who copies clients on emails to opposing counsel may not complain when opposing counsel responds using "Reply All," although it acknowledged that other jurisdictions addressing the question have reached a contrary result.[42] The Committee acknowledged that a lawyer who received a letter from opposing counsel, on which opposing counsel's client had been copied, could not respond by writing a letter to both opposing counsel and her client, but analogized email exchanges as a more informal means of communication, more like a telephone conference call in which both opposing counsel and the opposing client participated. Why do you think some ethics committees have taken a contrary approach, disapproving use of the "Reply All" function in this context?

2. How would you answer the authors' question whether in the hypothetical conference call, the lawyer can avoid violating the rule by staying on the call and listening without speaking?

3. Why isn't it sufficient to get the consent of the represented person? What if the lawyer seeks to ensure that the consent is informed by advising the represented person of the risks of communicating outside the presence of his or her lawyer? Sometimes the contact is initiated by represented persons frustrated by their inability to get their own lawyer to respond. What should a lawyer do when a represented person insists that she simply cannot get her lawyer to answer her questions about the purpose of a particular provision in a contract she is being asked to sign?

4. The text of both the former and the current California rule differs from the Model Rule by using the language "directly or indirectly" to prohibit a lawyer from attempting to circumvent the rule by using an intermediary, such as an investigator or other nonlawyer employee to communicate with the represented person. The result is the same under the Model

---

42. *See* N.J. Advisory Comm'n on Prof'l Ethics, Op. No. 739 (Mar. 10, 2021).

Rules because of Rule 8.4(a), which says it is "professional misconduct for a lawyer to . . . violate or attempt to violate the Rules of Professional Conduct, knowingly assist or induce another to do so, or do so through the acts of another." As with the California rule, it is unclear what role the lawyer may play in advising the client concerning a "principal-to-principal" communication. The comment to Model Rule 4.2 states that "[p]arties to a matter may communicate directly with each other, and a lawyer is not prohibited from advising a client concerning a communication that the client is legally entitled to make."[43] For an opinion that appears to approve of a broader role for the lawyer than is suggested in this article, *see* ABA Formal Ethics Op. 11-461 (2011) (lawyer may provide "substantial assistance" to a client concerning issues and strategies for communicating with a represented adversary, and it doesn't matter whether the client initiated the idea of having such a communication).

5. The California rule recognizes three separate exceptions, whereas the Model Rule expressly includes only one of those exceptions—for communications "authorized . . . by law or a court order."[44] However, the two other exceptions recognized in California would also be included in the Model Rule. Contacts "with a public officer, board, committee, or body" are undoubtedly "authorized by law," and "communications initiated by a represented party seeking advice or representation from an independent attorney" are not even prima facie prohibited by the Model Rule, because the communicating lawyer is not "representing a client" in making the communication.

6. In litigation, one of the most frequent questions concerning the application of Rule 4.2 is whether a lawyer may contact a current or former employee of a represented entity. That question is addressed in Chapter 10: Privilege and Confidentiality Revisited.

3. Communication with an Unrepresented Person

Model Rule 4.3 provides:

> In dealing on behalf of a client with a person who is not represented by counsel, a lawyer shall not state or imply that the lawyer is disinterested. When the lawyer knows or reasonably should know that the unrepresented person misunderstands the lawyer's role in the matter, the lawyer shall make reasonable efforts to correct the misunderstanding. The lawyer shall not give legal advice to an unrepresented person, other than the advice to secure counsel, if the lawyer knows or reasonably should know that the interests of such a person are or have a reasonable possibility of being in conflict with the interests of the client.

---

43. MR 4.2, cmt [4]. *See also* MR 8.4, cmt [1] (rule "does not prohibit lawyer from advising a client concerning action the client is legally entitled to take").

44. The California rule does not expressly include a "court order," but a court-authorized communication is clearly "authorized by law."

In Sin Ho Nam v. Quichocho, a case we discussed in Chapter 2, Quichocho was a lawyer representing himself and a co-owner when he drafted a lease and explained its terms to Nam, the lessee. The court held that Nam was entitled to have the jury decide whether, under these circumstances, an attorney-client relationship existed between Quichocho and him. If there was no attorney-client relationship, then Quichocho was dealing with Nam as an unrepresented person. Let's consider what Quichocho's obligations would have been under Rule 4.3.

Because Quichocho was a co-owner of the property, it may have been unlikely that Nam viewed him as disinterested. But assume that Quichocho had no direct financial interest in the transaction, but was merely a lawyer representing the property owner. What does it mean to say that a lawyer representing another party is disinterested? How might Quichocho have stated or implied he was disinterested?

Even if a lawyer does nothing affirmatively to state or imply disinterest, the rule contemplates that there will be circumstances where the lawyer knows or reasonably should know that the unrepresented person misunderstands the lawyer's role. Would it have been enough if Nam had asked questions about the meaning or the need for particular provisions? In In re Faraone,[45] a buyer informed the unrepresented sellers that the mortgage would remain in their names in order for him to avoid paying transfer taxes, but that he would assume the mortgage payments.[46] The sellers then asked the buyer's lawyer how they would be protected if the buyer failed to make mortgage payments. That questioning was deemed sufficient to give rise to a Rule 4.3 violation when the lawyer failed to advise the sellers to seek legal counsel, although there was no suggestion that they believed the lawyer was representing both parties. How did the sellers' question indicate a misunderstanding of the lawyer's role? What if the sellers had merely asked what a particular legal term meant? Would that indicate a misunderstanding of the lawyer's role?

The *Faraone* court assumed that, once the lawyer became aware that the sellers misunderstood his role, what was required was for him to advise them that they should seek their own legal counsel. But if they refused, was he then prohibited from answering their questions? Rule 4.3 prohibits a lawyer from giving *legal advice*, other than the advice to secure counsel, if the interests of the unrepresented person are likely to conflict with the lawyer's client. Obviously, the interests of a buyer and seller of real estate are in conflict. Does that mean that the lawyer in a sales transaction can never answer an unrepresented person's questions? The comment suggests not. It says that "[t]his Rule does not prohibit a lawyer from negotiating the terms of a transaction or settling a dispute with an unrepresented person," and "[s]o long as the lawyer

---

45. 722 A.2d 1 (Del.1998).

46. The buyer's scheme was clearly fraudulent, but let's assume for the moment that it was lawful.

has explained that the lawyer represents an adverse party and is not representing the person, the lawyer may inform the person of the terms on which the lawyer's client will enter into an agreement or settle a matter, prepare documents that require the person's signature *and explain the lawyer's own view of the meaning of the document or the lawyer's view of the underlying legal obligations.*"[47] Nevertheless, in *Faraone*, would it have been possible for the lawyer to answer the sellers' question without giving them legal advice? Perhaps it was for that reason that the court concluded that merely asking the question indicated their confusion over the lawyer's role.

In Chapter 2, we also briefly discussed a North Carolina case in which the buyer's lawyer in a residential real estate transaction may have also represented the seller when the lawyer prepared the deed as an accommodation to his client.[48] The court cited a North Carolina State Bar opinion ruling that a buyer's lawyer may ethically prepare such a deed, without creating a lawyer-client relationship, provided the lawyer makes specific disclosures and clarifies her role. With respect to preparing the deed, the opinion states that the lawyer must "inform Seller that she will prepare the deed consistent with the specifications in the purchase agreement, if any, but, in the absence of such specifications, she will prepare a deed that will protect the interests of her client and, therefore, Seller may desire to seek legal advice."[49]

C. LAWYERS' LIABILITY FOR AIDING AND ABETTING A CLIENT'S CRIME OR FRAUD OR OTHER TORTIOUS CONDUCT

Under Section 56 of the Restatement, lawyers are subject to general law; if a nonlawyer would be civilly liable for engaging in certain activities, then a lawyer who engages in the same activities in the same circumstances is also liable. For example, in Fire Insurance Exchange v. Bell,[50] a case discussed in an earlier section of this chapter, an insurance company's lawyer was personally sued for fraudulent misrepresentation on the basis of his own materially false statement to a personal injury plaintiff concerning the amount of insurance available to cover the plaintiff's losses. Similarly in Vega v. Jones, Day, Reavis & Pogue,[51] a shareholder in an acquired corporation sued the law firm Jones Day, which had represented the acquiring corporation, alleging that the law firm committed fraud when it actively concealed material facts after expressly undertaking to disclose a financing transaction that substantially lowered

---

47. MR 4.3, cmt [2] (emphasis added).
48. Johnson v. Schultz, 691 S.E.2d 701 (N.C. 2010).
49. N. C. St. B. Formal Ethics Op. 10 (2004).
50. 643 N.E.2d 310 (Ind. 1994).
51. 17 Cal.Rptr.3d 26 (Cal. Ct. App. 2004).

the value of the acquiring company's stock. Thus, lawyers who themselves knowingly make materially false statements, including omissions that are the equivalent of affirmative false statements, may be liable to the defrauded victims.

In addition to primary liability, lawyers have been sued for aiding and abetting a client's wrongful conduct. The Restatement (Third) of Torts: Liability for Economic Harm provides that aiding and abetting another's tortious conduct requires a plaintiff to establish that the defendant knew that the other's conduct constituted a breach of duty and gave substantial assistance or encouragement to the other so to conduct himself.[52] In the following case in which a lawyer was alleged to have aided and abetted his client's breach of fiduciary duty to the plaintiffs, consider the court's discussion of the dual requirements of "knowledge" and "substantial assistance."

Chem-Age Industries, Inc. v. Glover
652 N.W.2d 756 (S.D. 2002)

KONENKAMP, Justice.

[Glover was a lawyer who had represented Dahl, a businessman, for many years. Dahl had persuaded investors Pederson and Shepard to invest in a start-up firm, Chem-Age Industries, which Glover incorporated after Pederson and Shepard requested that the business be incorporated. Pederson and Shepard agreed to serve as incorporators and corporate directors, and Dahl served as chief executive officer. Glover notarized the signatures of Pederson and Shepard on articles of incorporation, although the documents were not signed in his presence, as required. Pederson arranged for Dahl to use a credit card issued by the company, which Dahl proceeded to use extensively for personal expenses. Dahl also used the credit card to charge a desk as a "gift" to Glover. The investors sued Dahl and Glover, among others, on several theories, including an allegation that Glover knowingly aided and abetted Dahl's breach of fiduciary duty to them. The following excerpt addresses that allegation.]

[] AIDING AND ABETTING BREACH OF FIDUCIARY DUTY . . .

Dahl, as the operating officer of the corporation, owed a fiduciary duty to the company and its investors. . . . For summary judgment purposes, the evidence that Dahl breached his fiduciary duties to the corporation and the investor-directors remains wholly uncontradicted. He used corporate funds for personal

---

52. Restatement (Third) of Torts: Liab. for Econ. Harm § 28 (2020). The plaintiff must first prove that another party committed a tort against the plaintiff, and also that, as a result of the combined conduct of the other party and the defendant, the plaintiff suffered economic loss.

expenditures; he failed to deliver promised stock issues; he sold corporate assets and kept the proceeds. Now the question is whether his lawyer may be subject to liability for assisting Dahl in his breach of fiduciary duties.

Holding attorneys liable for aiding and abetting the breach of a fiduciary duty in rendering professional services poses both a hazard and a quandary to the legal profession. One the one hand, overbroad liability might diminish the quality of legal services, since it would impose "self protective reservations" in the attorney-client relationship. Attorneys acting in a professional capacity should be free to render advice without fear of personal liability to third persons if the advice later goes awry. On the other hand, the privilege of rendering professional services not being absolute, lawyers should not be free to substantially assist their clients in committing tortious acts. To protect lawyers from meritless claims, many courts strictly interpret the common law elements of aiding and abetting the breach of a fiduciary duty.

The substantial assistance requirement carries with it a condition that the lawyer must actively participate in the breach of a fiduciary duty. Merely acting as a scrivener for a client is insufficient. A plaintiff must show that the attorney defendant rendered "substantial assistance" to the breach of duty, not merely to the person committing the breach.[53] In [an earlier Oregon case], the lawyer facilitated [the majority partners'] squeeze-out [of the minority partner], not just by providing legal advice and drafting documents, but by sending letters containing misrepresentations and helping to amend by-laws eliminating voting requirements that protected the minority shareholder's interest.

Another condition to finding liability for assisting in the breach of a fiduciary duty is the requirement that the assistance be "knowing." Knowing participation in a fiduciary's breach of duty requires both knowledge of the fiduciary's status as a fiduciary and knowledge that the fiduciary's conduct contravenes a fiduciary duty. Although in some instances actual knowledge may be required, constructive knowledge[54] will often suffice. Constructive knowledge is adequate when the aider and abettor has maintained a long-term or in-depth relationship with the fiduciary.

In accordance with these principles, we hold that to establish a cause of action for aiding or assisting in the breach of a fiduciary duty, a plaintiff must prove that (1) the fiduciary breached an obligation to plaintiff; (2) defendant

---

53. [Fn. 13 in Original] It has been suggested that an element of wrongful intent should be included as part of the "substantial assistance" requirement. One example of wrongful intent would be when a lawyer aids and abets the breach of a fiduciary duty in furtherance of the lawyer's own self-interest. The receipt of legal fees may be a basis for concluding that an attorney "participated" in the client's breach of fiduciary duty for the attorney's own financial gain. In most instances, however, the receipt of normal legal fees in this circumstance would not constitute a personal financial interest in the matter. Although not an element in providing aiding and abetting the breach of a fiduciary duty, certainly these are circumstances to consider in gauging a lawyer's alleged knowing participation and substantial assistance.

54. ["Constructive knowledge" is knowledge that a person is presumed to have of facts that would have been discovered with the exercise of reasonable care. — ED.]

substantially assisted the fiduciary in the achievement of the breach; (3) defendant knew that the fiduciary's conduct constituted a breach of that duty; and (4) damages were sustained as a result of the breach.

Glover recounts that shortly after incorporation, Dahl told him that the two investors, Pederson and Shepard, had decided not to proceed and that the business would be solely controlled by Dahl as a proprietorship. Because no shares were issued, Glover took the position that the company had no official existence. But we think that what Glover actually knew and what he should have known are questions of credibility. After all, Glover notarized Pederson's and Shepard's signatures on corporate documents without having them in his presence. If he did not know his client was in the midst of a swindle, he certainly knew that Dahl had several questionable investment schemes in the past, leaving unhappy investors in his wake. Thus his decision to notarize these signatures may or may not have been an altogether innocuous act. Perhaps if Glover had met with Pederson and Shepard at that time, instead of simply notarizing their signatures unseen, and heard their expectations, he could have disabused them of any misunderstanding or encouraged them to seek independent legal advice. Pederson and Shepard allege that this was part of a pattern in which Glover allowed Dahl to use his legal services as a means to allow Dahl to misappropriate investor funds. The creation of a corporation with the assistance of an attorney gave a patina of authenticity to Dahl's otherwise rogue activities. Moreover, Glover listed himself as registered agent[55] for the company. Pederson and Shepard claim that they began investing more heavily once they learned the company had been incorporated and an attorney was onboard. They say that they felt reassured upon incorporation that the business would proceed with all the formalities required of corporations.

Four months after the business was incorporated, Glover received a "gift" of office furniture from Dahl, bought with the company credit card. Glover claimed he did not know how the furniture was paid for. Accepting such a "gift" from a client like Dahl, who Glover knew had longstanding financial problems, raises a question of constructive knowledge and exposes the problem of improper, personal financial gain in assisting Dahl.

We think it also significant that Glover assisted Dahl in selling assets that were obtained with investor funds in the corporation. In a meeting with the investors and their lawyer, Glover was present when Dahl assured the investors that upon the sale, they would be receiving their money back. The next month, with Glover's help, the company's assets were sold to a Wisconsin business. Dahl and Glover had taken the position that Chem-Age Industries, Inc., was not a corporation but a proprietorship owned solely by Dahl. Yet Glover helped to arrange the sale of Chem-Age assets through another entity: "Byron

---

55. [A registered agent is a business or individual designated to receive service of process when a business agent is a party in a legal action.—ED.]

Dahl d/b/a BMD Associates, a South Dakota sole proprietorship." Glover testified that he did not know the relationship between BMD and Chem-Age.

Although Glover may not have taken any active role in defrauding the investor-directors and may not have owed any direct fiduciary duty to them, Dahl did owe such a duty, and a material question of fact exists on whether Glover substantially assisted Dahl in breach that duty. It may be that Glover, as much as Pederson and Shepard, was duped by Dahl's conniving business dealings, but that is for a jury to decide.

NOTES AND QUESTIONS

1. Victims of O.P.M.'s fraudulent conduct sued Singer Hutner for aiding and abetting that fraud. The case never went to trial, because Singer Hutner settled the claims for $10 million.[56] Most of the reported aiding and abetting lawsuits filed against lawyers appear to be for assisting a client's breach of fiduciary duty, as in *Chem-Age*. It is unclear why this is so. Perhaps the reason is that fraud claims are more difficult to prove because they are limited to knowingly false representations and require greater particularity in pleading, whereas a client's breach of fiduciary duty covers a much broader spectrum of client misconduct. A prerequisite to an aiding and abetting a breach of fiduciary duty claim is the existence of a fiduciary relationship between the client and the plaintiff and the lawyer's knowledge of such relationship. A fiduciary relationship is a "relationship of trust and confidence where one party (the principal) places control over her property or affairs with another (the fiduciary), and the fiduciary agrees to act in the principal's benefit with respect to her property or affairs."[57] In *Chem-Age*, the court acknowledged that "Dahl, as the operating officer of the corporation, owed a fiduciary duty both to the corporation and to its investors." Other fiduciary relationships include "professional relationships between partners in general and limited partnerships, employers and employees, trustees and beneficiaries, bankruptcy trustees and debtor corporations, and joint venturers in a business transaction."[58]

2. Recall that Rule 1.2(d) prohibits any knowing "assistance" in a client's crime or fraud. Tortious aiding and abetting liability, however, requires "substantial assistance," regardless of whether the defendant is a lawyer or a layperson. According to the Restatement (Third) of Torts: Liability for Economic Harm, "'substantial assistance' means active participation," not merely the "passive receipt of benefits from a tort,

---

56. *See* Stuart Taylor, Jr., Ethics and the Law: A Case History, The New York Times at 52 (Jan. 9, 1983), at https://www.nytimes.com/1983/01/.09/magazine/ethics-and-the-law-a-case-history.html.

57. Arthur B. Laby, Resolving Conflicts of Duty in Fiduciary Relationships, 54 Am. U. L. Rev. 75, 79 (2004).

58. Katerina P. Lewinbuk, Let's Sue All the Lawyers: The Rise of Claims Against Lawyers for Aiding and Abetting a Client's Breach of Fiduciary Duty, 40 Ariz. St. L. J. 135, 151 (2008).

C. Lawyers' Liability for Aiding and Abetting a Client's Crime **243**

or a decision not to report wrongdoing," unless the defendant had a fiduciary or other legal duty to the plaintiff.[59] Glover was not himself a fiduciary to the plaintiffs, and he owed them no direct legal duty; therefore, his active assistance was necessary to establish aiding and abetting liability.

3. The *Chem-Age* court notes that when lawyers are sued for aiding and abetting a client's breach of fiduciary duty to another, "many courts strictly interpret the common law elements of aiding and abetting the breach of a fiduciary duty." Why is this so? Some courts have suggested that the same concerns exist when a lawyer is sued for aiding and abetting a client's fraud, whereas others limit this concern to aiding and abetting a breach of fiduciary duty. Should courts distinguish between the two causes of action for purposes of aiding and abetting liability? The Restatement (Third) of Torts: Liability for Economic Harm does not make any such distinction in a comment explaining that "[Substantial] ordinarily means something more than routine professional services provided to the primary wrongdoer."[60]

4. Under *Chem-Age*, what is required for a lawyer to render "substantial assistance" to a client's breach of fiduciary duty? In referring to an earlier Oregon case, the court emphasized that the lawyer did more than merely "provid[e] legal advice and draft[] documents." Why isn't providing legal advice and drafting documents sufficient if a lawyer knows that doing so is necessary to complete a transaction that constitutes the breach of fiduciary duty? What did Glover do that could be found to have constituted "substantial assistance"? The court referenced several acts, including Glover's role in incorporating the company. How is that different than drafting documents?

5. What about the "knowledge" requirement? Here the court held that actual knowledge is not necessarily required, but that "constructive knowledge" will often suffice. Under this doctrine, a person is deemed to have *constructive knowledge* of facts that would have been discovered by a reasonable investigation. According to the *Chem-Age* court, under what circumstances will constructive knowledge suffice to establish a lawyer's liability for aiding and abetting a client's breach of fiduciary duty? Were those circumstances present in *Chem-Age*? Was there sufficient evidence of actual knowledge? One commentator states that "under the clear majority approach, *actual knowledge* of the primary tortfeasor's unlawful conduct is essential for liability."[61] Nevertheless, it appears that courts consider the lawyer's knowledge in relation to the lawyer's substantial assistance, i.e., "[w]here there is a minimal showing of assistance, courts generally require a greater showing of knowledge."[62]

---

59. *See* Restatement (Third) of Torts: Liability for Econ. Harm §28, cmt. d (2020).

60. *Id.*

61. Douglas R. Richmond, A Primer on Lawyer Liability for Aiding and Abetting Clients' Misconduct, 25 Prof. Law. 20, 22 (2008) (emphasis added).

62. *Id.* at 21.

6. Strict interpretation of the "substantial assistance" requirement is designed to avoid liability for aiding and abetting client misconduct when a lawyer in good faith provides routine legal services to a client. Some courts have gone so far as to say that a lawyer has a "qualified privilege" such that the lawyer cannot be held liable for aiding and abetting a client's breach of fiduciary duty to a third party unless the lawyer was acting outside the scope of the attorney-client relationship. This approach was adopted in Reynolds v. Schrock,[63] in which Schrock's lawyer, Markley, helped to negotiate and draft a settlement agreement in a property dispute between Schrock and Reynolds, who co-owned two parcels of land. Pursuant to the agreement, Reynolds was to transfer his interest in one property to Schrock. They would then jointly sell the second property, with the proceeds going to Reynolds. If the sale of the second property was less than $500,000, Schrock would owe Reynolds the difference and would grant Reynolds a security interest in the first property to guarantee payment of that debt. After Reynolds transferred his interest in the first property, Markley (Schrock's lawyer) advised Schrock that the agreement did not expressly require Schrock to retain the first property in anticipation of subsequently creating a security interest in favor of Reynolds. Without telling Reynolds, Schrock immediately sold the first property to a third party, before the second property was sold. Markley assisted her in that sale, asking the escrow officer to keep the transaction confidential. Schrock then revoked her consent to the sale of the second property.[64] Citing cases like *Chem-Age*, in which courts have recognized that "'substantial assistance' means something more than the provision of routine professional services," the Reynolds court, "exercising its common-law authority to define tortious conduct," recognized a qualified immunity for lawyers acting within the scope of the attorney-client relationship, that is, for "actions of the kind that permissibly may be taken by lawyers in the course of representing their clients." Such an immunity would not extend to conduct unrelated to the representation, to actions taken in the lawyer's self-interest and contrary to the clients' interest, or to actions that fall within the "crime or fraud" exception to the attorney-client privilege. In applying the test to Markley's conduct, the court held that there was no evidence from which a reasonable jury could find that Markely acted outside the scope of the lawyer-client relationship of Schrock and thus the trial court properly granted Markley's motion for summary judgment. Would the plaintiffs in *Chem-Age* survive a summary judgment motion under the *Reynolds* standard?

---

63. 142 P.2d 1062 (Or. 2006).

64. There is no cause of action for aiding and abetting a breach of contract. Moreover, advising or assisting another to breach a contract is actionable as tortious interference with contract only under limited circumstances. *See* Restatement (Third): Liab. for Econ. Harm. §17 (2020).

7. The *Reynolds* court explained that qualified immunity was necessary to prevent "a third party's claim against the lawyer that puts the lawyer at odds with the client [and] will compromise the lawyer-client relationship" by subjecting the lawyer to "divided loyalties." Isn't the same concern present when a lawyer is alleged to have aided and abetted a client's crime or fraud? If so, then why did the *Reynolds* court state that there is no qualified immunity for actions by a lawyer that aid and abet a client's crime or fraud? Several recent Texas Supreme Court cases have held that lawyers are immune from liability to third parties even when the underlying claim is fraud, as long as the lawyer's conduct occurred while the lawyer was providing legal services to the client. The initial case involved actions taken in connection with representing a client in litigation,[65] but the doctrine was subsequently extended to transactional representations in which the client and nonclient positions are similarly adversarial.[66]

D. LAWYERS' LIABILITY TO NONCLIENTS FOR NEGLIGENCE

Historically, nonclients were not permitted to sue a lawyer for negligence because such liability was limited to persons in privity of contract with the lawyer. Most jurisdictions have eliminated a strict privity requirement in negligence suits brought by third parties; nevertheless, courts continue to be reluctant to authorize such actions except in limited circumstances. For example, under Section 51 of the Restatement, the circumstances in which a lawyer owes a duty of care to a nonclient include when

> 1) "the lawyer or (with the lawyer's acquiescence) the lawyer's client invites the nonclient to rely on the lawyer's opinion or provision of other legal services," and "the nonclient is not, under applicable tort law, too remote from the lawyer to be entitled to protection";[67] or when
> 2) "the lawyer knows that a client intends as one of the primary objectives of the representation that the lawyer's services benefit the nonclient," "such a duty would not significantly impair the lawyer's performance of obligations to the client," and "the absence of such a duty would make enforcement of those obligations to the client unlikely."[68]

Consider whether either or both of these exceptions are recognized in the following opinion, which includes negligent misrepresentation, as well as professional malpractice, as a basis for the lawyer's liability.

---

65. Cantey Hanger, LLP v. Byrd, 467 S.W.3d 477 (Tex. 2015).

66. Haynes & Boone, LLP v. NFTD, LLC, 631 S.W.3d 65 (Tex. 2021). In *Cantey*, the Texas Supreme Court had expressly declined to address the applicability of the immunity doctrine in a nonlitigation setting. 467 S.W.3d at 482, n.6.

67. RLGL §51(2)(a).

68. *Id*. at §51(2)(b).

246 Chapter 8 Limits of Zealous Representation II: Transactions

---

Greycas, Inc. v. Proud
826 F.2d 1560 (7th Cir. 1987)

POSNER, Circuit Judge.

Theodore S. Proud, Jr., a member of the Illinois bar who practices law in a suburb of Chicago, appeals from a judgment against him for $833,760, entered after a bench trial. The tale of malpractice and misrepresentation that led to the judgment begins with Proud's brother-in-law, Wayne Crawford, like Proud a lawyer but one who devoted most of his attention to a large farm that he owned in downstate Illinois. The farm fell on hard times and by 1981, Crawford was in dire financial straits. He had pledged most of his farm machinery to lenders, yet now desperately needed more money. He approached Greycas, Inc., the plaintiff in this case, a large financial company headquartered in Arizona, seeking a large loan that he offered to secure with the farm machinery. He did not tell Greycas about his financial difficulties or that he had pledged the machinery to other lenders, but he did make clear that he needed the loan in a hurry. Greycas obtained several appraisals of Crawford's farm machinery but did not investigate Crawford's financial position or discover that he had pledged the collateral to other lenders, who had perfected their liens in the collateral. Greycas agreed to lend Crawford $1,367,966.50, which was less than the appraised value of the machinery.

The loan was subject, however, to an important condition, which is at the heart of this case: Crawford was required to submit a letter to Greycas, from counsel whom he would retain, assuring Greycas that there were no prior liens on the machinery that was to secure the loan. Crawford asked Proud to prepare the letter, and he did so, and mailed it to Greycas, and within 20 days of the first contact between Crawford and Greycas the loan closed and the money was disbursed. A year later Crawford defaulted on the loan; shortly afterward he committed suicide. Greycas then learned that most of the farm machinery that Crawford had pledged to it had previously been pledged to other lenders.

The machinery was sold at auction. The Illinois state court that determined the creditors' priorities in the proceeds of the sale held that Greycas did not have a first priority on most of the machinery that secured its loan; as a result Greycas has been able to recover only a small part of the loan. The judgment it obtained in the present suit is the district judge's estimate of the value that it would have realized on its collateral had there been no prior liens, as Proud represented in his letter.

That letter is the centerpiece of the litigation. Typed on the stationery of Proud's firm and addressed to Greycas, it identifies Proud as Crawford's lawyer and states that, "in such capacity, I have been asked to render my opinion in connection with" the proposed loan to Crawford. It also states that "this opinion is being delivered in accordance with the requirements of the Loan Agreement" and that

> I have conducted a U.C.C., tax, and judgment search with respect to the Company [i.e., Crawford's farm] as of March 19, 1981, and except as hereinafter noted all units listed on the attached Exhibit A ("Equipment") are free and clear of all liens or encumbrances other than Lender's perfected security interest therein which as recorded March 19, 1981 at the Office of the Recorder of Deeds of Fayette County, Illinois.

The reference to the lender's security interest is to Greycas's interest; Crawford, pursuant to the loan agreement, had filed a notice of that interest with the recorder. The excepted units to which the letter refers are four vehicles. Exhibit A is a long list of farm machinery—the collateral that Greycas thought it was getting to secure the loan, free of any other liens. . . .

Proud never conducted a search for prior liens on the machinery listed in Exhibit A. His brother-in-law gave him the list and told him there were no liens other than the one that Crawford had just filed for Greycas. Proud made no effort to verify Crawford's statement. The theory of the complaint is that Proud was negligent in representing that there were no prior liens, merely on his brother-in-law's say-so. Proud *was* negligent in failing to conduct a search, but we are not clear why the *misrepresentation* is alleged to be negligent rather than deliberate and hence fraudulent, in which event Greycas's alleged contributory negligence would not be an issue (as it is, we shall see), since there is no defense of contributory or comparative negligence to a deliberate tort, such as fraud. Proud did not merely say "There are no liens": he said, "I have conducted a U.C.C., tax, and judgment search"; and not only is this statement, too, a false one, but its falsehood cannot have been inadvertent, for Proud knew he had not conducted such a search. The concealment of his relationship with Crawford might also support a charge of fraud. But Greycas decided, for whatever reason, to argue negligent misrepresentation rather than fraud. It may have feared that Proud's insurance policy for professional malpractice excluded deliberate wrongdoing from its coverage, or may not have wanted to bear the higher burden of proving fraud, or may have feared that an accusation of fraud would make it harder to settle the case—for most cases, of course, are settled, though this one has not been. In any event, Proud does not argue that either he is liable for fraud or he is liable for nothing.

He also does not, and could not, deny or justify the misrepresentation; but he argues that it is not actionable under the tort law of Illinois, because he had no duty of care to Greycas. . . . He argues that Greycas had an adversarial relationship with Proud's client, Crawford, and that a lawyer has no duty of straight dealing to an adversary, at least none enforceable by a tort suit. In so arguing, Proud is characterizing Greycas's suit as one for professional malpractice rather than negligent misrepresentation, yet elsewhere in his briefs he insists that the suit was solely for negligent misrepresentation—while Greycas insists that its suit charges both torts. Legal malpractice based on a false representation, and negligent misrepresentation by a lawyer, are such similar legal concepts, however, that we have a great difficult both in holding them apart in our minds and in understanding why the parties are quarreling over the exact characterization. . . . So we shall discuss both.

Proud is undoubtedly correct in arguing that a lawyer has no general duty of care toward his adversary's client. . . . The tort of malpractice normally refers to a lawyer's careless or otherwise wrongful conduct toward his own client. Proud argues that Crawford rather than Greycas was his client, and although this is not so clear as Proud supposes—another characterization of the transaction is that Crawford undertook to obtain a lawyer for Greycas in the loan transaction—we shall assume for purposes of discussion that Greycas was not Proud's client.

Therefore if malpractice just meant carelessness or other misconduct toward one's own client, Proud would not be liable for malpractice to Greycas. But in *Pelham v. Griesheimer*, the Supreme Court of Illinois discarded the old common law requirement of privity of contract for professional malpractice; so now it is possible for someone who is not the lawyer's . . . client to sue him for malpractice. The court in *Pelham* was worried, though about the possibility of a lawyer's being held liable "to an unlimited and unknown number of potential plaintiffs," so it added that "for a nonclient to succeed in a negligence action against an attorney, he must prove that the primary purpose and intent of the attorney-client relationship itself was to benefit or influence the third party." That, however, describes this case exactly. Crawford hired Proud not only for the primary purpose, but for the sole purpose, of influencing Greycas to make Crawford a loan. The case is much like *Brumley v. Touche, Ross & Co.*, where a complaint that an accounting firm had negligently prepared an audit report that the firm knew would be shown to an investor in the audited corporation and relied on by that investor was held to state a claim for professional malpractice. In *Conroy v. Andeck Resources '81 Year-End Ltd.*, in contrast, a law firm that represented an offeror of securities was held not to have any duty of care to investors. The representation was not intended for the benefit of investors. Their reliance on the law firm's using due care in the services it provided in connection with the offer was not invited.

All this assumes that *Pelham* governs this case, but arguably it does not, for Greycas, as we noted, may have decided to bring this as a suit for negligent misrepresentation rather than professional malpractice. . . .

The claim of negligent misrepresentation might seem utterly straightforward. It might seem that by addressing a letter to Greycas intended (as Proud's counsel admitted at argument), to induce reliance on the statements in it, Proud made himself prima facie liable for any material misrepresentations, careless or deliberate, in the letter, whether or not Proud was Crawford's lawyer, or for that matter anyone's lawyer. Knowing that Greycas was relying on him to determine whether the collateral for the loan was encumbered and to advise Greycas of the results of his determination, Proud negligently misrepresented the situation, to Greycas's detriment. But merely labeling a suit as one for negligent misrepresentation rather than professional malpractice will not make the problem of indefinite and perhaps excessive liability, which induced the court in *Pelham* to place limitations on the duty of care, go away. So one is not surprised to find that courts have placed similar limitations on suits for negligent misrepresentation—so similar that we are led to question whether . . . these really are different torts, at least when both grow out of negligent misrepresentations by lawyers. . . .

There is no serious doubt about the existence of a causal relationship between the misrepresentation and the loan. Greycas would not have made the loan without Proud's letter. Nor would it have made the loan had Proud advised it that the collateral was so heavily encumbered that the loan was as if unsecured, for then Greycas would have known that the probability of repayment was slight. . . .

Proud argues, however, that his damages should be reduced in recognition of Greycas's own contributory negligence, which, though no longer a complete defense in Illinois, is a partial defense, renamed "comparative negligence." It is as much a defense to negligent misrepresentation as to any other tort of negligence. . . . If Greycas was careless in deciding whether to make the loan, this implies that a reasonable investigation by Greycas would have shown that the collateral for the loan was already heavily encumbered; knowing this, Greycas would not have made the loan and therefore would not have suffered any damages.

But we think it too clear to require a remand for further proceedings that Proud failed to prove a want of due care by Greycas. . . .

The law normally does not require duplicative precautions unless one is likely to fail or the consequences of failure (slight though the likelihood may be) would be catastrophic. One UCC search is enough to disclose prior liens, and Greycas acted reasonably in relying on Proud to conduct it. Although Greycas had much warning that Crawford was in financial trouble and that the loan might not be repaid, that was a reason for charging a hefty interest rate and insisting that the loan be secured; it was not a reason for duplicating Proud's work. It is not hard to conduct a UCC lien search; it just requires checking the records in the recorder's office for the county where the debtor lives. So the only reason to backstop Proud was if Greycas should have assumed that he was careless or dishonest; and we have just said that the duty of care does not require such an assumption. Had Proud disclosed that he was Crawford's brother-in-law this might have been a warning signal that Greycas could ignore only at its peril. To go forward in the face of a known danger is to assume the risk. But Proud did not disclose his relationship to Crawford. . . .

A final point. The record of this case reveals serious misconduct by an Illinois attorney. We are therefore sending a copy of this opinion to the Attorney Registration and Disciplinary Commission of the Supreme Court of Illinois for such disciplinary action as may be deemed appropriate in the circumstances.

Affirmed.

NOTES AND QUESTIONS

1. Judge Posner suggested that Greycas might have been viewed as Proud's client, along with Crawford. Why did Judge Posner see this as a possibility? What could Proud have done to avoid such a finding?

2. Courts limit lawyers' liability for aiding and abetting liability based largely on their concern that such liability creates divided loyalties between lawyer and client. Is this an even greater concern when a non-client sues a lawyer for negligence? What additional concern did Judge Posner give as a rationale for limiting a lawyer's negligence liability to nonclients? Are either or both these concerns reflected in the Restatement formulations of the "invitation to rely" and "third-party beneficiary" exceptions to the traditional privity requirement? Does Greycas recognize either or both of these exceptions?

3. The third-party beneficiary exception is applied primarily to cases involving beneficiaries of a will drafted by a lawyer on behalf of the testator, an exception recognized in all but a handful of states.[69] Why is this a particularly compelling situation in which to recognize the drafting lawyer's potential liability to will-beneficiary nonclients? Despite the need for such an exception, courts often limit liability to circumstances where the beneficiary can prove the client's intent by sufficient evidence to warrant construction or reformation of the document under trusts and estates law.[70] For example, assume that a will fails to name a charity as a beneficiary, but the charity has two witnesses who will testify that shortly before the will was signed, the testator assured them that he would make a substantial gift to the charity in his will. Why are many courts reluctant to recognize the charity's right to sue the lawyer for negligence when the will drafted by the attorney fails to provide for such a gift? How is this situation different from a lawsuit based on the lawyer's negligence in failing to have the requisite number of witnesses to the signing of a will naming the charity as a beneficiary?

4. Courts strictly construe the third-party beneficiary exception to exclude nonclients who are merely incidental rather than intended beneficiaries. When a lawyer representing a seller in a residential real estate transaction prepares a deed for the seller making the buyer a grantee of the property, should the buyer be able to sue the lawyer for negligently drafting the deed to the buyer's detriment?

5. A third privity exception recognized under the Restatement covers lawyers representing a limited category of fiduciaries, such as trustees, executors, and guardians, when the lawyer's negligence permits the

---

69. States that continue to apply a strong privity requirement in wills cases are Maryland, Nebraska, New York, Ohio, and Texas.

70. *See* RLGL §51, cmt f.

client to breach a fiduciary duty owed to the nonclient, but only when "the nonclient is not reasonably able to protect its rights" and "such a duty would not significantly impair the performance of the lawyer's obligations to the client."[71] A comment to the rule states explicitly that this exception "does not apply when the client is a partner in a business partnership, a corporate officer or director, or a controlling stockholder," thereby excluding a negligence cause of action in most of the reported cases involving aiding and abetting a client's breach of fiduciary duty.

Review Problems

8-1 A lawyer has represented a title company for many years. To save on legal fees, the title company has explained to the lawyer that it plans to have a nonlawyer employee draft deeds following general instructions for deed drafting from the lawyer. The title insurance company will indicate to the parties that the lawyer drafted the deed, although the lawyer will not review the deed until after it has been executed by the seller and the closing has occurred, but prior to the recording of the deed. The lawyer is concerned that the title company is misrepresenting the lawyer's role. May the lawyer participate in the title company's plan?

8-2 A lawyer represented a husband in divorce negotiations. No legal action had been filed, and the parties were attempting to come to an amicable resolution before filing a joint petition for divorce. The lawyer prepared a financial statement for the husband, based on information supplied by the husband. If the statement was filed in court, it would have to be certified by the lawyer as to accuracy of the statement. When the lawyer provided the statement to the wife's lawyer, she believed it to be accurate. Subsequently, the lawyer learned that the husband had materially misrepresented his assets. When the husband refused to permit the lawyer to correct the financial statement, the lawyer withdrew without doing more. Is the lawyer subject to discipline for failing to take any further action with respect to the husband's false financial statement?

8-3 A plaintiff brought an eviction action against a company and its subsidiary. The company offered to settle with the plaintiff. In exchange for the plaintiff releasing both company and its subsidiary, the company alone would pay the plaintiff the settlement amount. Before agreeing to release the subsidiary, the plaintiff's lawyer said to the lawyer representing both the company and the subsidiary, "I don't know of any reason that we could have pierced the corporate veil between the company and its subsidiary, do you?" The lawyer for the company and subsidiary responded, "There isn't anything. These two companies are totally separate." Later, the plaintiff's lawyer learned contradictory facts suggesting a strong likelihood that the two companies had failed to observe corporate formalities, in which case the corporate veil between them might have been pierced, thereby subjecting the subsidiary to damages.

---

71. RLGL §51(4).

Seeking to rescind the settlement, the plaintiff's lawyer is claiming that the statement by the lawyer for the company and subsidiary was fraudulent, i.e., that the statement was knowingly false and that the plaintiff's lawyer had relied upon it. The company's lawyer is defending himself by arguing that she gave a legal opinion and that, in any event, she was unaware of facts establishing the basis for piercing the corporate veil. In fact, she had not investigated the issue and did not know one way or another whether such facts existed. Did the lawyer for the company and subsidiary commit fraud? Is she subject to discipline?

8-4 A company lawyer is negotiating with a lawyer representing a prospective hire, who is a friend of and had been recommended for the position by a current manager employed by the company. Although the parties have substantially negotiated the terms of employment, the prospective hire's lawyer keeps delaying the finalization and signing of the contact and refuses to explain why. The company lawyer is concerned that the prospective hire is using the negotiations with the company as a basis for negotiating with a different company. May the company lawyer ask the manager to contact the prospective hire informally and see if she can find out if he is negotiating with a different company?

8-5 A successful professional baseball player proposed marriage to his girlfriend. Several weeks before the wedding, she met with his lawyer, who presented her with a draft premarital agreement, which provided that upon dissolution of the marriage, she would have no claim on any of his property or earnings acquired either before or during the marriage. The lawyer said she should take the draft agreement home with her and review its provisions. He further explained that she was free to consult with independent counsel, although he did not actively encourage her to do so. Without reading the draft, she asked him to explain to her what the provisions meant, and he did so. He correctly explained that under applicable state law, she was entitled to a share of his property and earnings acquired during the marriage, and that by signing the agreement, she would be waiving her right to claim that share. He also truthfully stated that the baseball player had said that he would not marry her unless she signed the agreement. She took the agreement home, but did not review it. Without hiring independent counsel, she signed the agreement. Is the baseball player's lawyer subject to discipline?

8-6 A law firm represented an ERISA[72] fiduciary who defrauded various ERISA plans out of millions of dollars. The plans subsequently sued both the fiduciary and the law firm. The lawsuit against the law firm alleged that it had aided and abetted both fraud and breach of fiduciary duty. The complaint alleged that the law firm's fees for representing the fiduciary were paid directly from the ERISA plans' accounts, which necessarily alerted the law firm to the breach of fiduciary duty. The complaint further alleged that the law firm had assisted the client's breach by accepting stolen funds in payment

---

72. The Employee Retirement Income Security Act of 1974 (ERISA) is a federal law that establishes minimum standards for pension plans in private industry.

D. Lawyers' Liability to Nonclients for Negligence 253

of its fees. The law firm has filed a motion to dismiss on the basis that even if the allegations were true, the plaintiffs had not stated an adequate basis for suing the law firm for aiding and abetting its client's fraud or breach of fiduciary duty. Is the motion to dismiss likely to succeed?

8-7 A lawyer represented a property developer who had purchased a tract of undeveloped land. The developer had hired an engineer to perform soil percolation tests to determine the suitability of soil for a septic system. The township required two successful percolation tests for municipal approval of a septic system. The engineer provided two reports. The first report revealed that of 22 tests, only one had been successful. The second showed that of eight tests, only one had been successful. The developer listed the property with a real estate broker. At the request of the developer, the lawyer sent the broker a two-page document consisting of one page from each of the engineer's reports. Read together, the two pages appeared to describe a single series of seven tests, two of which were successful. The document became part of the broker's sales packet. When the property didn't sell, the broker bought the property himself. One year later, the broker listed the property for sale and found an interested buyer. The broker gave the potential buyer a sales packet, which included the composite report. After providing a substantial down payment, the potential buyer insisted on conducting its own soil tests before completing the sale. When these soil tests revealed the same disappointing results as the original tests, the potential buyer refused to close on the sale, demanding the return of its down payment. The potential buyer is suing the developer's lawyer for negligence in providing a misleading report concerning the percolation tests. The lawyer has filed a motion to dismiss on the ground that she owed no duty to the potential buyer. Is the motion to dismiss likely to succeed?

PART II

REPRESENTING ENTITIES

CHAPTER 9

WHO'S MY CLIENT?

Model Rule 1.13

So far, we've been assuming either that the client is an individual person or that when the client is a company, there is no special problem in determining such issues as client identity or which individuals properly speak on behalf of the company. But sometimes representing entities rather than individuals complicates a lawyer's ability to comply with such core duties as communication, confidentiality, loyalty, and respecting the rights of others. In Part II of this casebook, we reexamine the core duties we explored in Part I in view of the difficulties that frequently arise when lawyers represent entities such as corporations, partnerships, and limited liability companies.

Model Rule 1.13(a) provides that "[a] lawyer employed or retained by an organization represents the organization acting through its duly authorized constituents." Although this rule appears to state a simple truism, there is in fact a great deal of complexity in identifying both who is the client and to whom the lawyer owes various duties, including fiduciary duties typically owed only to clients, but sometimes owed to nonclients, including the individual constituents of an organizational client.[1]

What's at stake here? A lot. Identifying a lawyer-client relationship is often critical to determining who can sue a lawyer for malpractice or disqualify a lawyer from representing another client. And even when it's clear that the organization alone is the client, lawyers still need to know which individuals within the organization have the right to direct the lawyer's conduct and to whom the lawyer should address important communications. In this chapter we address these questions of *client identity*, *control*, and *communication*. In the next few chapters, we address the core duties of *confidentiality* and *loyalty*, as well as the *limits of loyal representation*, for lawyers engaged in entity representation.

---

1. The term "constituent" refers to individuals such as "[o]fficers, directors, employees and shareholders" and persons who hold equivalent positions in organizations other than corporations. *See* MR 1.13, at cmt [1]. We use the term "entity" and "organization" interchangeably.

A. CLIENT IDENTIFICATION

1. Large, Publicly Held Corporations

Model Rule 1.13(a) is easiest to apply when a lawyer represents a large, publicly held corporation, where there is a clear separation of ownership (shareholders) and control (officers, directors, and employees). At the time this rule was first adopted in 1983, the Kutak Commission had to choose between two theories of representing organizations — the "entity theory" and the "group theory." Under the entity theory chosen by both the Kutak Commission and the ABA House of Delegates, the lawyer represents the fictional entity itself, as Rule 1.13(a) describes. Although the entity can only act through its "duly authorized constituents," the lawyer ordinarily owes duties only to the entity itself, and not to its individual constituents. As a result, it is typically only the entity that can sue the lawyer for malpractice or seek the lawyer's disqualification from representing other clients.

Under the alternative "group theory," the "entity *shares* a lawyer with certain leading individuals within, such as officers and directors."[2] When the interests of everyone are aligned, this form of joint representation may work well. But when there is disagreement among the leading individuals, as there often is, it makes more sense to say that the lawyer's primary duty is to the organization, recognizing that there is a hierarchy of individuals within the organization, each of whom also owes duties of loyalty to that organization.[3]

Under Rule 1.13(a), a lawyer representing the organization does not *necessarily* represent individual constituents; however, Rule 1.13(g) provides that the organization's lawyer "may *also* represent any of its directors, officers, employees, members, shareholders or other constituents," subject to complying with the conflict of interest rules.[4] Corporate lawyers often undertake to represent both the corporation and one or more constituents, and when they do, they should look directly to Rule 1.7 to determine whether and how they are permitted to do so.[5] But as we have already seen, lawyers all too often end up representing persons they did not intend to represent, and this sometimes happens when a corporate lawyer inadvertently represents an individual constituent, typically one whose interests are or may be adverse to the interests of the corporation itself. This happens less frequently in large, publicly held corporations than in closely held corporations or other smaller entities, but it happens often enough that even lawyers for these entities must be careful in their dealings with individual constituents. The following case illustrates problems that can arise when corporate lawyers get sloppy.

---

2. Geoffrey C. Hazard, Jr. et al., 1 The Law of Lawyering §18.03 (2016-1 Supp).

3. For a justification of the entity theory by reference to the law of principal and agent, in which the entity is the principal and individuals such as officers and directors are co-agents of the entity, along with the lawyer, *see id.* at p. 18-13.

4. MR 1.13(g) (emphasis added).

5. *See infra* Chapter 11: Conflicts of Interest in Entity Representation.

Plaintiff E.F. Hutton & Company, Inc. ("Hutton"), a national brokerage firm, sued John D. Brown, Jr., its former Houston regional vice-president, alleging negligence and breach of fiduciary duty. Brown moved to disqualify a New York law firm and a Houston law firm from representing Hutton on the ground that they previously represented Brown, as well as Hutton, at SEC and bankruptcy hearings concerning the collapse of Westec Corporation. An individual named John Hurbrough had approached Brown seeking a substantial loan from Hutton to be secured by Westec common stock. Brown authorized the loan on Hutton's behalf. Shortly after the loan was completed, the SEC suspended trading in Westec stock. Brown and other Hutton personnel were asked to testify before the SEC, in a formal investigation into trading in Westec stock, and then at public hearings instituted by Westec's trustee in bankruptcy. Federal securities law imposes both criminal and civil liability for extending credit in violation of certain margin requirements, and under federal bankruptcy law, the trustee is obligated to identify fraud, misconduct, mismanagement, and other violations of law in order to identify causes of action available to the bankruptcy estate. Any claims against both Hutton and Brown depended on whether Brown knew when he authorized the Hurbrough loan that the proceeds would be used to purchase the Westec shares that served as collateral for the loan.

Members of the New York and Houston law firms accompanied Brown to the SEC hearing and a member of the Houston firm also accompanied Brown to the bankruptcy hearing. Ultimately, Hurbrough sued Hutton, seeking a declaration that the loan agreement was unenforceable. Several months later, Hutton terminated Brown's employment and initiated this lawsuit. The trial court granted Brown's motion to disqualify, and Hutton filed a motion to reconsider.

E.F. Hutton & Company v. Brown
305 F. Supp. 371 (S.D. Tex. 1969)

NOEL, District Judge. . . .

[] THE SEC INVESTIGATIVE HEARING . . .

Pursuant to regulation, the hearings were non-public: only the witness, his attorney, and representatives of the Texas State Securities Board and the SEC were allowed in the hearing room. . . .

On the day before the hearing, the New York partner and associate flew from New York to Houston. On arrival they went directly to Brown's office. They and Brown discussed the Westec situation generally, and the Hurbrough loan transaction in particular. . . . In the course of the meeting, the partner informed Brown that he would accompany him to the hearing.

The next morning, both lawyers again met briefly with Brown, after which the partner accompanied him to the hearing. [The SEC's examining attorney] said to Brown, "I see you are accompanied by [the partner] here this morning. Is he your counsel in this proceeding?" Brown answered, "Yes."

Brown's answer was unexpected, if affidavits filed by the New York partner and the associate are to be believed. In those affidavits, both the partners and the associate claim that during their conference the evening before the hearing, Brown was specifically informed of the New York firm's position as counsel only for Hutton. They also allege that Brown agreed to explain their firm's position to the examining officer if he was asked whether the partner represented him individually.

Brown submitted his supplemental affidavit to deny these allegations. . . .

The official transcript of the SEC hearing states that the New York partner appeared as "Counsel for John D. Brown."

[] THE BANKRUPTCY HEARING

. . . [C]ounsel for the trustee approached the Houston partner in August 1967 and requested that Hutton produce Brown and two other Hutton employees for examination. . . . [Brown] requested the New York partner to be present in Houston during the examinations. On the day before Brown was due to testify, the New York partner flew to Houston. On arrival, he met briefly with the Houston partner and Brown. The next morning, the New York partner and the Houston partner accompanied Brown to the hearing.

As soon as Brown had been sworn, the Special Master informed him that the SEC was participating, and warned him that the facts developed at the hearing could constitute violations of the securities laws. He then advised Brown of his right to counsel and of his privilege against self-incrimination. . . . After Brown had indicated that he understood these warnings, the following colloquy took place:

The Master: "Do I understand correctly that you are represented by counsel of your choice here this morning?"
The Witness: "Yes, sir."
The Master: "Namely, [the Houston partner] and [the New York partner]?"
The Witness: "Correct." . . .

[] FINDINGS AND CONCLUSIONS

Brown bases his motion to disqualify chiefly on undisputed record evidence. The official transcript of the SEC hearing reveals that the New York partner entered an appearance as counsel for Brown, not for Hutton. The official transcript of the bankruptcy hearing reveals that both the New York and Houston partners entered appearances for Brown, not for Hutton. At each hearing Brown identified counsel as his counsel, not as Hutton's, and counsel stood mute.

An attorney's appearance in a judicial or semi-judicial proceeding creates a presumption that an attorney-client relationship exists between the attorney and the person with whom he appears. This presumption shifts to Hutton, the party denying the existence of the relationship, the burden of persuasion. When the relationship is also evidenced by the entry of a formal appearance by the attorney on behalf of the person with whom he appears, the presumption becomes almost irrebuttable, for the entry of a formal appearance quite properly has been called "record evidence of the highest character." In this case, the Court finds that Hutton's opposition has failed to overcome the presumption that the New York and Houston partners represented Brown when he testified in the SEC and bankruptcy investigations.

[Hutton argued that counsel represented only Hutton at both hearings, citing evidence of the company's long-standing relationship with the two law firms.] These are inapposite, for Brown does not assert that counsel did not represent Hutton at the two hearings. His motion is based on the proposition that counsel represented him as well. Hutton and its counsel are in error if they believe that an attorney cannot ever represent two clients with respect to a single matter. Attorneys frequently represent more than one party to a single transaction. Ordinarily there is nothing improper in such a practice so long as the attorney discloses the consequences of the joint representation to all of his clients, and all parties as well as the attorney consent.

The remaining evidence marshaled by Hutton is also insufficient to overcome the presumption. Brown admits that he cannot recall ever conversing with either firm about representing him personally, or paying either firm a fee. But the relation of attorney and client may be implied from the conduct of the parties. . . . The Court takes judicial notice that it is not uncommon for corporate counsel to represent an individual corporate officer when he is sued as a result of actions he has taken within the ambit of his official duties. When this occurs, corporate counsel becomes counsel for the individual officer as well, even if the corporation pays all of his fee. If the officer is a party to a proceeding, and corporate counsel appear on his behalf, an implied relationship between them arises.

Hutton asserts, however, that a relationship of attorney and client could not have been created by counsel's appearances with Brown, for at the time of the two hearings, Hutton's and Brown's interests were identical. And, since counsel's fiduciary duties to Hutton required that they be present on its behalf, and Brown was present only as Hutton's spokesman, this Court should not find that counsel represented Brown as well.

There are several fallacies in this reasoning. First, it is not accurate to say, as Hutton does, that the SEC and the Westec trustee were investigating only Hutton, and not Brown, who appeared solely as Hutton's spokesman. . . . Brown testified for himself as well as for Hutton. Secondly, Hutton's assertion that because Brown's interests at the two investigatory hearings coincided with Hutton's, he had no need for individual counsel at all, is without merit. . . .

This brings the Court to Hutton's last cluster of arguments in opposition to Brown's motion, all of which are directed to the proposition that Brown could not have believed that corporate counsel were representing *him*.

[Hutton argued the following: (1) it was Brown himself who asked the Houston firm to represent Hutton in the controversy with Hurbrough; (2) his only contact with either firm occurred when he was functioning as an officer of Hutton; (3) at the hearings he testified only about what he had done as an officer of Hutton; and (4) before the SEC hearing, the New York partner and associate informed Brown that their firm represented only Hutton.]

In asking the Court to consider all the circumstances when determining whether Brown believed counsel to be his attorneys, Hutton has proposed a proper inquiry. Brown's reasonable understanding of his relation with the attorneys is the controlling factor here. But when all circumstances are considered, it becomes clear that the transcripts of the two hearings reflect Brown's understanding of his relation with counsel accurately.

[The court noted that when Brown appeared at the SEC hearing, he was aware that if criminal violations were discovered, "his freedom, but not Hutton's would be in jeopardy." Similarly, when he appeared at the bankruptcy hearing, he knew that the trustee intended to bring civil lawsuits against persons and companies suspected of violating securities law in dealing with Westec stock.]

In this atmosphere it would seem reasonable and natural for Brown to have assumed that the New York partner represented him as well as Hutton when the partner accompanied him to the hearing before the SEC examiner; and that the New York and Houston partners represented him as well as Hutton when they accompanied him to his examination by counsel for the Westec trustee. His prior contact with counsel, when he was acting only for Hutton, was not significant. When he was called by the trustees and the SEC to give testimony, he was subjected to the possibility of civil liability and criminal prosecution. These possible consequences—more severe in their potential impact upon him than upon Hutton—were acutely pressing.

The reasonableness of Brown's assumption is not destroyed by the coincidence that Hutton, for some of the same reasons as he, needed to be represented by counsel at the hearings. Hutton and Brown agree that at the time of the two hearings, both they and counsel believed their interests to be identical. Certainly in these circumstances, Brown's awareness that counsel were representing Hutton could not have caused him to doubt that they were representing him as well.

The only other event urged by Hutton as establishing that Brown could not have understood counsel's appearances as appearances for him is the conversation alleged by the New York partner and associate to have occurred the evening before the SEC appearance. . . .

[T]he Court is impressed by the fact that after hearing Brown testify they were his counsel at the SEC hearing, New York counsel did not attempt to correct the record; and, that Brown gave the same answer as to his being represented by New York counsel when asked at the bankruptcy hearing four months later, although he had conferred further with the counsel after they had had a full opportunity to reflect on his testimony at the SEC hearing and to be certain that he not make the same mistake at the bankruptcy hearing, indeed if such a mistake had been made at the SEC hearing. Therefore the Court is not persuaded that Brown agreed with New York counsel at a conference held in Houston on the evening before his appearance at the SEC hearing, to testify that New York counsel represented Hutton only. The Court will assume arguendo but not find that the conference transpired precisely as New York counsel now contend; but nevertheless, the Court finds from Brown's reply given to the SEC examiner the day following the alleged conference and from his testimony before the Special Master in bankruptcy four months later, that Brown did not then appreciate the distinction between his individual and representative capacity. He continued to believe that counsel would represent his interests, as well as Hutton's.

The Court thus finds that nothing advanced by Hutton has rebutted the presumption raised by counsel's appearances with Brown at the SEC and bankruptcy hearings. . . .

[The court then determined that the New York and Houston firms should be disqualified, even if Brown understood that any information he conveyed to the lawyers would be disclosed to Hutton.]

NOTES AND QUESTIONS

1. One reason that client identity issues are less frequent in large, publicly held corporations, as opposed to smaller entities, is that the hierarchy of constituents is more clearly understood. Employees report to officers, who in turn report to the board of directors. Employees, officers, and directors tend to better understand the concept of entity representation and, as a result, individuals are less likely to assume that when they interact with the entity lawyer, the lawyer is representing them personally, particularly when, as apparently was the case in *Hutton*, the entity lawyer had not expressly represented the constituent on prior occasions. Further, it is not uncommon for corporate counsel to prepare individual officers and employees for testimony at a deposition or other proceeding in which the corporation is a party or otherwise has an interest. And yet, ordinarily, it would be understood that they do so as lawyers for the corporation itself, and not for the individual witness. So why did the court in *Hutton* conclude that the New York and Houston lawyers represented both Hutton and Brown at the hearings in which he testified?

2. At one point in the opinion, you may have believed that the court was going to resolve the conflicting affidavits as to what the lawyers said to Brown about who they represented—and to resolve that conflict by crediting Brown's account. But the court did not do so. Instead, it said that it was willing to assume that the lawyers' account was correct, but that it didn't matter. How could the court find individual representation if the lawyers in fact advised Brown that they represented only the corporation?

3. What was the relevance of the nature of these hearings, which differed from the typical lawsuits in which a corporate lawyer accompanies an individual constituent to a deposition?

264   Chapter 9 Who's My Client?

4. For a discussion of the ethical issues facing company lawyers defending a deposition of a company employee, including whether the lawyer should treat such employees as unrepresented persons or jointly represented clients, *see* Lawrence J. Fox, Defending a Deposition of Your Organizational Client's Employee: An Ethical Minefield Everyone Ignores, 44 S. Tex. L. Rev. 185 (2002).

2. Closely Held Corporations

A closely held corporation is one where the company's stock is held by a small number of shareholders and is not publicly traded.[6] Typically, these corporations have more informal business structures, and the shareholders are active in controlling the operation of the business, including holding senior management positions and seats on the board, if any. As a result, these shareholders are less likely than the constituents of a publicly held corporation to view their individual interests as separate from those of the company.

Consider the following two judicial opinions addressing the question of client identification in the context of a small, closely held corporation. Both cases involved a motion to disqualify on behalf of a former or current 50 percent shareholder. In the first case, the court found that the shareholder did not reasonably believe that the corporation's lawyer had previously represented him in any matter related to the current lawsuit. In the second case, however, the court found to the contrary that the 50 percent shareholder did reasonably believe that the corporation's lawyer had represented him in the matter that was the subject of the current lawsuit. See if you can understand why the courts reached different results in these two cases.

Bobbitt v. Victorian House, Inc.
545 F. Supp. 1124 (N.D. Ill. 1982)

SHADUR, District Judge.

Richard A. Bobbitt ("Bobbitt") sues Victorian House, Inc. ("Victorian House") and its President Albert Morlock ("Morlock"), primarily seeking dissolution of Victorian House and an accounting of corporate funds allegedly misapplied by Morlock. Bobbitt has moved to disqualify defendants' attorney John C. Stiefel ("Stiefel") and his law firm . . . from representing defendants. For the reasons stated in this memorandum opinion and order that motion is denied.

Bobbitt has owned one-half of Victorian House's outstanding shares since its inception and has been a member of its board of directors since at least July 27, 1978. Stiefel has represented Victorian House since about December 1976. Although not articulated in precisely these terms, Bobbitt's claim is dual in nature:

---

6. Some closely held corporations trade their stock publicly at times, but this is done infrequently.

1. Stiefel assertedly represented the Victorian House incorporators (including Bobbitt) before the corporation was formed.
2. Bobbitt contends he later gave confidential information to Stiefel in his capacity as counsel to Victorian House.

As a result Stiefel's presence in this action allegedly constitutes a conflict of interest.

During the past several years our Court of Appeals has dealt with a number of variations on the theme of lawyer disqualification. In doing so, it has stated this test for determining if a conflict of interest exists in the face of prior representation . . . :

> Initially, the trial judge must make a factual reconstruction of the scope of the prior legal representation. Second, it must be determined whether it is reasonable to infer that the confidential information allegedly given would have been given to a lawyer representing a client in those matters. Finally, it must be determined whether that information is relevant to the issues raised in the litigation pending against the former client.

First, however, it must be decided whether "prior legal representation" of Bobbitt was present at all.

As to the undisputed Stiefel representation — that involving Victorian House itself — the problem is relatively straightforward. Normally a corporate director talking to corporate counsel should understand anything he told that attorney was "known by the corporation." Thus there should normally be no conflict of interest when a director sues a corporation represented by its general corporate counsel, because anything the director would previously have told that attorney would ordinarily have been communicated to him as lawyer for the corporation. In other words, no conflict exists simply because there was no prior representation. . . .

Analysis is somewhat more complex as to a small close corporation with only a few shareholders and directors. There it may be more difficult to draw the line between individual and corporate representation. But representing such a corporation does not inherently mean also acting as counsel to the individual director-shareholders. Rather the question must be determined on the individual facts of each case.

This Court has found only a single case dealing with closely parallel facts. In *Wayland v. Shore Lobster & Shrimp Corp.* . . . the court rejected a like disqualification claim in these terms:

> However, Wayland has presented no support, and we have found none, for the proposition that a law firm which acts as counsel to a close corporation acts as counsel to individual shareholders simply by suggesting amendments to a shareholder agreement or by drafting and negotiating on behalf of the corporation [a] severance agreement with departing shareholders. . . . Wayland has pointed to no instance where the firm has represented any shareholder as an individual. Furthermore, Wayland's argument that the firm must be disqualified because it may have been exposed to confidential information from Wayland while he was employed at Shore is unpersuasive since, in the circumstances of Proskauer's representation, it is clear

that the firm was representing the corporation and thus Wayland could not have reasonably believed or expected that any information given to the firm would be kept confidential from the shareholders or from the corporation as an entity. . . .

At least after Victorian House was formed the situation was substantively the same as in *Wayland*, for Bobbitt looked to Stiefel as his personal counsel in only three minor instances (two of them trivial indeed), none of which was in any way related to this action:

1. They had a single meeting in 1977 involving Bobbitt's general estate tax considerations (for a $40 fee).
2. Stiefel handled a medical insurance claim in July 1977, which was settled in May 1978 with Prudential Insurance.
3. About April 1978 Stiefel reviewed an apartment lease for Bobbitt (one telephone call to the lessor may have been involved).

To that extent Stiefel represented Bobbitt as an individual and Bobbitt could have expected any communications were confidential. But . . . an attorney should be disqualified only if matter he might have discussed with his former client would in some way be relevant to the current action. That is clearly not so here.

That leaves the claim in Bobbitt's initial affidavit that Stiefel represented the incorporators (including Bobbitt) before Victorian House's incorporation. At his deposition, Bobbitt shifted to the position that Stiefel was "consulted" before incorporation and another attorney actually took care of the incorporation. More importantly Stiefel's claimed consultation was only as to *corporate* matters.

Bobbitt's original affidavit also said:

In the course of this aforementioned representation, during late 1974 and 1975, Stiefel and the plaintiff met privately and during those meetings, Stiefel received confidential information covering the finances and economic goals of Bobbitt and had access to his confidential records and Stiefel participated in and was party to, various decisions concerning this confidential information.

[At his deposition, Bobbitt conceded that there was nothing in the documents he showed Stiefel that was not something the other shareholders, including Morlock, already knew.]

Thus Bobbitt's deposition makes plain his use of the term "confidential" was in the sense of non-public. There is no evidence whatever he discussed confidential matters with Stiefel that he expected would not be revealed to Morlock or Victorian House (in fact his testimony was precisely the opposite). Both Bobbitt's motion and his original affidavit seriously overstated the situation to Stiefel's detriment (or more accurately to defendants, for it is their right to representation of their choice that would have been impaired by a successful disqualification motion). This Court concurs in the *Wayland* analysis and finds it fully applicable here.

Rosman v. Shapiro
653 F. Supp. 1441 (S.D.N.Y. 1987)

SPRIZZO, District Judge.

In 85 Civ. 7154 (Action I), Alexander Rosman brings suit against Zvi Shapiro and R.S. Filtomat, USA, Inc. ("Filtomat") seeking, *inter alia*, an accounting of the profits of Filtomat and monetary damages. In a related action . . . (Action II), Filtomat and Shapiro bring suit against Rosman, Zvi Livni, and Filtration Ltd., ("Filtration") for, *inter alia*, breach of contract. Presently before the Court is Rosman's motion to disqualify the attorneys representing Shapiro and Filtomat in both actions. Specifically, Rosman seeks to disqualify the law firm of Yisraeli and Yerushalmi ("Y & Y") and the attorneys who have appeared in both actions as of counsel to Y & Y. . . .

I. BACKGROUND

A. THE DISPUTE BETWEEN THE PARTIES

Filtration, a defendant in Action II, is an Israeli corporation engaged in the manufacture of water filters and other filtration products. It is undisputed that in July of 1984 Rosman and Shapiro entered into an agreement with Filtration ("the Agreement") for the marketing and distribution of Filtration's products in the United States. This agreement provided, *inter alia*, that Rosman and Shapiro would create a corporation, Filtomat, through which Filtration's products would be distributed.

In accordance with the Agreement, Rosman and Shapiro did create Filtomat, as a Delaware corporation. For the purposes of the instant motion, it is undisputed that Rosman and Shapiro are the sole shareholders in Filtomat, each owning 50% of Filtomat's shares of stock.

Following the formation of Filtomat, a dispute arose between Shapiro and Filtration over the terms of the Agreement. Shapiro asserted that the Agreement provided that Filtomat had the *exclusive* right to distribute Filtration's products in several regions of the United States. Filtration, on the other hand, denied that allegation.

This dispute between Shapiro and Filtration eventually led to strained relations between Shapiro and his partner Rosman. Rosman took the position that Filtration's interpretation of the Agreement was correct; that is, that Filtomat did not have any exclusive distribution rights. . . .

B. Y & Y'S INVOLVEMENT

In July and August of 1985, following the execution of the Agreement, Rosman and Shapiro jointly consulted with Y & Y seeking legal advice with respect to Filtomat's contractual relationship with Filtration, the same subject which is the focus of the dispute in the two actions before the Court. According to Shapiro, although he believed that the Agreement already gave

Filtomat exclusive distribution rights, he was willing to alter the existing contractual relationship between the parties if a new agreement favorable to Filtomat could be reached. It was in the context of Rosman and Shapiro's efforts to reach this new agreement with Filtration that Shapiro and Rosman sought legal advice from Y & Y.

There is little dispute about the substance of Shapiro and Rosman's meetings with Y & Y. Rosman and Shapiro met with Itzhak Zisman, an attorney with Y & Y in Tel Aviv, Israel to discuss the possibility of drafting a new agreement between Filtomat and Filtration. . . . At this meeting, it is undisputed that Rosman, Shapiro, and Zisman extensively discussed the existing contractual relationship between Filtomat and Filtration.

In August, 1985, Rosman again met with Zisman, this time without Shapiro, to further discuss Filtomat's relationship with Filtration. . . . Rosman also instructed Zisman to prepare a draft agreement between Filtration and Filtomat.

Following this meeting, the relationship between Shapiro and Rosman deteriorated and, in early September, the complaints in the two instant action were filed. . . .

II. Discussion

As the above-stated facts make clear, Rosman and Shapiro jointly consulted Y & Y for legal advice concerning Filtomat's contractual relationship with Filtration. Moreover, it is clear that Y & Y now represents Shapiro against Rosman in two actions before the Court and that both actions focus on the identical issues discussed during the prior consultations. Based on these facts, Rosman seeks to disqualify Y & Y. . . .

At the outset, the Court rejects Shapiro and Filtomat's argument that disqualification . . . is inappropriate because Y & Y only represented the corporate entity, Filtomat, and that Y & Y never represented Rosman as an individual. For purposes of this disqualification motion, the Court must protect Rosman's reasonable expectations of confidentiality. Thus, the Court may find that an attorney-client relationship existed between Rosman and Y & Y if Rosman reasonably believed Zisman was acting as his counsel.

It is clear that Rosman reasonably believed that Zisman was representing him. Although, in the ordinary corporate situation, corporate counsel does not necessarily become counsel for the corporation's shareholders and directors, whereas here, the corporation is a close corporation consisting of only two shareholders with equal interests in the corporation, it is indeed reasonable for each shareholder to believe that the corporate counsel is in effect his own individual attorney.

This is especially true in this case because both Rosman's uncontradicted affidavit, and the shareholder agreement, creating Filtomat, demonstrate that both Rosman and Shapiro treated Filtomat as if it were a partnership rather than a corporation. In short, it would exalt form over substance to conclude that Y & Y only represented Filtomat, solely because Rosman and Shapiro chose to deal with Filtration through a corporate entity.[7]

Although Y & Y did previously represent Rosman, it does not follow that disqualification of Y & Y pursuant to Canon 4 [of the Code of Professional Responsibility].

[The court rejected disqualification to prevent a breach of confidentiality because "Rosman could not have reasonably expected that any information imparted to Y & Y would have been withheld from Shapiro during the course of that representation because Y & Y represented Shapiro and Rosman jointly." However, the court agreed with Rosman's argument that Y & Y should be disqualified pursuant to Canon 9, which provided "that attorneys 'should avoid even the appearance of professional impropriety'" because "[a] client reasonably expects that an attorney will remain loyal to his interests in matters on which that attorney previously represented him" and that expectation was worthy of protection in this case. In other words, when a lawyer jointly represents two clients and the interests of the clients become antagonistic, "'their lawyer must be absolutely impartial between them, which . . . usually means that he may represent none of them.'"]

NOTES AND QUESTIONS

1. The *Bobbitt* court rejected Bobbitt's request to disqualify Stiefel based on its findings that: (1) Stiefel did not represent Bobbitt in connection with the incorporation of Victorian House; and (2) while he did represent Bobbitt on three personal matters after incorporation, these matters were not substantially related to the current dispute. Remember that Bobbitt was suing both the corporation and Morlock alleging that Morlock had misapplied corporate funds. Why did the court conclude that Stiefel did not represent Bobbitt in connection with the incorporation of Victorian House? Was it inevitable that the court would reach that result? Consider the implications of the court's findings that there was nothing in the documents Bobbitt disclosed to Stiefel in their pre-incorporation meetings that Bobbit did not intend to keep confidential from Morlock. In an earlier chapter, we noted that according to the Rule 1.9 comment, loyalty, as well as confidentiality, is an important value

---

7. [Fn. 8 in Original] . . . [T]he cases relied upon by Shapiro and Filtomat with respect to this issue do no more than establish the general proposition that in a close corporation, the issue of corporate versus individual representation must be decided on a case by case basis. *See, e.g., Bobbitt, supra* . . . *Wayland v. Shore Lobster & Shrimp Corp.* . . . Neither of those cases, however, involved the situation presented here, i.e., a close corporation, consisting of only two 50% shareholders, created solely to facilitate the transaction which is the focus of the dispute in the two instant actions. Although there does not appear to be any case directly on point, this case is more closely analogous to the cases cited by Rosman, wherein courts have disqualified counsel from representing one spouse against the other when that counsel previously served as corporate counsel to the family corporation.

underlying the prohibition against representation adverse to a former client; as a result, the fact that joint clients share information does not relieve the lawyer from the obligation not to subsequently represent one of the former joint clients in a matter adverse to the other joint client.[8] Is the *Bobbitt* court's treatment of information sharing among potentially joint clients reconcilable with this comment?

2. If the court found that Stiefel *did* represent Bobbitt in connection with the incorporation of Victorian House, does it necessarily follow that the court would have disqualified Stiefel?

3. Bobbitt also contended that after incorporation, "he later gave confidential information to Stiefel in his capacity as counsel to Victorian House." If Bobbitt was referring to a matter other than the three clearly personal representations, the court does not specifically describe that matter. It does, however, refer to the *Wayland* opinion, in which a lawyer may have suggested amendments to a shareholder agreement or negotiated and drafted on behalf of the corporation a severance agreement with departing shareholders. Assume that Bobbitt was alleging that he discussed with Stiefel amending a shareholder agreement or negotiating and drafting a severance agreement between the corporation and Bobbitt. How might the *Bobbitt* court have responded?

4. Why did the *Rosman* court reach a different result in determining that both Rosman and Shapiro had a lawyer-client relationship with Y & Y? In answering this question, pay close attention to the footnote in which the court expressly mentions and distinguishes cases like *Bobbitt* and *Wayland*.

5. Some courts have held that the absence of an attorney-client relationship between a close corporation's lawyer and one of its shareholders does not preclude a finding that the lawyer owed fiduciary duties to the shareholder. In Fassihi v. Sommers, Schwartz, Silver, Schwartz & Tyler, P.C.,[9] the court held that a corporate lawyer who assisted one of two 50 percent shareholders to terminate the other shareholder's interest might have had a fiduciary duty to the ousted shareholder based on a determination that, because of the lawyer's close interaction with that shareholder, he "repose[d] faith, confidence, and trust in [the lawyer's] judgment and advice."[10] In Baker v. Wilmer Cutler Pickering Hale & Dorr LLP,[11] the court went even further and held that a corporate lawyer may have had a fiduciary duty to the minority shareholders in light of significant protections for them in the company's operating agreement, even if these shareholders had no dealings with the lawyers

---

8. *See supra* Chapter 6: Conflicts of Interest: Former Clients, Prospective Clients, and Government Lawyers.

9. 309 N.W.2d 645 (Mich. Ct. App. 1981).

10. *Id.* at 648.

11. 81 N.E.3d 782 (Mass. App. 2017).

and even if their interests conflicted with the corporate client's interests. Other courts have rejected the view that a corporate lawyer owes fiduciary duties to nonclient constituents.[12] Courts rejecting such a duty typically cite the inevitability of conflicts between the corporate client and its shareholders, as well as the practical difficulties of having to protect shareholders with interests different from each other.[13] Are these concerns similar to those expressed in cases such as *Chem-Age*, in which courts have limited the circumstances in which third persons may sue a lawyer for aiding and abetting a client's breach of fiduciary duty?[14]

6. For an example of a case in which the majority shareholders' breach of fiduciary duty to a minority shareholder was also contrary to the interests of the corporate client, consider In re Kinsey,[15] where a lawyer who assisted majority shareholders to form a new corporation to take advantage of a business opportunity was found to have violated the lawyer's duty to the corporate client because the new corporation would be competing for business with the existing corporation. Violations of the lawyer's duty to the corporate client may result not only in professional discipline, but also in a legal malpractice award to the corporation.[16]

7. Potential ambiguities in determining who a lawyer represents is not limited to individual constituents. In Kirschner v. K&L Gates,[17] a law firm was retained by a special committee of the board of directors to investigate allegations of fraud against the chief executive officer (CEO) and his senior managers. The retention agreement specified that the law firm would represent the special committee, and not the corporation; however, the court held that the law firm represented the corporation itself, and therefore the corporation could sue the law firm for malpractice in failing to detect the massive fraud. The reasons for rejecting the provision in the retention agreement included statements in other documents indicating that the special committee had been authorized to retain counsel to conduct the investigation *on behalf of the company* and Delaware corporate law, which provided that a special committee

---

12. *See, e.g.,* Rice v. Strunk, 670 N.E.2d 1280 (Ind. 1996); Egan v. McNamara, 467 A.2d 733 (D.C. 1983). *See also* RLGL §96, cmt g ("A lawyer representing only the organization has no duty to protect one constituent from another, including from a breach by one constituent of such fiduciary duties, unless the interests of the lawyer's client organization are at risk.")

13. *See generally* Matthew J. Rossman, The Descendants of *Fassihi:* A Comparative Analysis of Recent Cases Addressing the Fiduciary Claims of Disgruntled Stakeholders Against Attorneys Representing Closely-Held Entities, 38 Ind. L. Rev. 177 (2005).

14. *See supra* Chapter 8: Limits of Zealous Representation II: Transactions.

15. 660 P.2d 660 (Or. 1983).

16. *See, e.g.,* Murphy & Demory, Ltd. v. Admiral Daniel J. Murphy, U.S.N. (Ret.), Cir. Ct. of Fairfax County (Virginia) Chancery No. 128219 (June 6, 1994) (legal malpractice award based on lawyers' assisting one of two shareholders in his efforts to take control of company or divert business to a new company).

17. 46 A.3d 737 (Pa. Super. 2012).

could be created only by action of the board and that such a committee acted with the authority of the board to manage the company in accordance with the duties of the board, including fiduciary duties to both the shareholders and the company. According to the court, the fact that the special committee consisted of independent board members who had been appointed by the minority shareholders to protect their interests did not give the special committee the authority to retain counsel to protect the interests of those shareholders, as opposed to the interests of the corporate entity.

3. General and Limited Partnerships, Limited Liability Companies

The application of the entity theory has been more problematic with respect to partnerships than to corporations. Common law treated partnerships not as a collective whole, but rather as a collection of individuals in which "[t]he rights and liabilities of a partnership are the rights and liabilities of the partners, and are enforceable by and against them individually."[18] The original partnership statutes were unclear, and while the revised statutes typically define a partnership as an entity distinct from its partners, the aggregate theory continues to govern certain aspects of a partnership such as the personal liability of all the partners.[19]

Because these prior authorities treated a partnership as an "aggregate" or group of individuals, initially it was unclear whether Model Rule 1.13 applied to partnerships as well as corporations. In 1991, the ABA Committee on Ethics and Professional Responsibility issued Formal Ethics Opinion 91-361, which clarified that the rule applied to partnerships, in part because they were now generally viewed as "separate jural enti[ties] having distinct rights and duties." Nevertheless, this view has not been endorsed in all jurisdictions. New York, for example, continues to treat partnerships as having no existence separate from the individual partners; as a result, under New York law lawyers representing partnerships are considered to have lawyer-client relationships with all the general partners.[20]

Even in jurisdictions recognizing general partnerships as an aggregation of individual partners, limited partnerships are usually treated more like corporations. Limited partnerships consist of a general partner, who oversees and runs the business, and limited partners, who are investors who do not manage the business. The general partner has unlimited liability for the partnership's debt, whereas limited partners have limited liability up to

---

18. 1 Lindley, Partnership 61 (5th ed. (Audenried Am. Ed.) 1891).

19. *See* Bromberg & Ribstein on Partnership §1.03[B] (Christine Hurt et al. eds., 2d ed. Supp. 2018).

20. Might this explain the significance of the *Rosman* court's statement that "both Rosman and Shapiro treated Filtomat as if it were a partnership rather than a corporation"?

the amount of their investment. Although the limited partnership lawyer may represent both the partnership and the general partner, the lawyer will not have a lawyer-client relationship with the limited partners. Nevertheless, some courts find that the partnership lawyer owes a duty to the limited partners, based on the fiduciary duty owed by the general partner to the limited partners.[21]

A limited liability company (LLC) combines attributes of both corporations and partnerships. Like corporations, none of the owners (known as "members") have personal liability for the company's debts; however, like partnerships, the entity itself is not taxed, and both income and losses "flow through" to the members. Beyond these basic elements, the members are free to design the company's structure, which could have the corporate attributes of centralized management and free transferability of interests, or the partnership attributes of equal management and no transferability of interests.

In addition to limited liability companies, state laws provide for other business entities such as a limited liability partnership (LLP) and a limited liability limited partnership (LLLP). With the exception of a general partnership, which can be formed under common law (and without the intention or awareness of the partners), all these different forms of business entities — corporations, close corporations, limited partnership, and limited liability entities — are governed by state statutes, which can vary significantly from state to state.

Even when a particular business is recognized as an "entity" pursuant to Rule 1.13, the "reasonable expectations" test applies, and lawyers must take care not to inadvertently form lawyer-client relationships with individual constituents.

4. Other Formal and Informal Associations

Comment [1] to Rule 1.13 states that the rule applies not only to corporations, but also to "unincorporated associations." ABA Opinion 91-361 referenced this language in its determination that the rule applies to partnerships, and courts have also applied the rule to such unincorporated associations as trade associations, labor unions, business trusts, and joint ventures, particularly when such associations are recognized as separate legal entities.

But what about informal associations such as a neighborhood or tenants' association? A comment to the Restatement states that "[a]n organization client may also be an informal entity such as a social club or an informal group that has established an investment pool"; however, the Restatement cites no legal authority supporting that position. Several commentators have

---

21. *See, e.g.*, Arpadi v. First MSP Corp., 628 N.E.2d 1335 (Ohio 1994) (because general partner owes fiduciary duty to limited partners, partnership attorney's duty to general partner must extend to limited partners).

Chapter 9 Who's My Client?

observed that granting such informal associations entity status, for purposes of Rule 1.13, is problematic when the group lacks the "attributes of a well-structured organization."[22]

B. CONTROL

You will recall that Rule 1.13(a) provides that a lawyer may be "employed or retained by an organization" and that the organization "act[s] through its duly authorized constituents." Who are the constituents who are "duly authorized" to retain or discharge a lawyer, determine the scope of the representation, sign a fee agreement, and direct the lawyers during the course of the representations? The answers to these questions are determined not by the law governing lawyers, but rather by applicable organizational law and by internal governance documents authorized by such organizational law. For example, in the absence of an agreement to the contrary, each general partner typically has an equal right under partnership statutes to manage the partnership, including the right to retain and direct a lawyer. And if the partners disagree on such matters, in the absence of an agreement to the contrary, the views of a majority of the partners governs. But many partnership agreements provide that a managing partner has the right to make certain decisions, in which case the lawyer must take direction from that partner only.[23]

For an example of the complications that can arise for the lawyer when there is an internal dispute among an organization's constituents, consider the following ethics opinion.

Legal Ethics Committee of the D.C. Bar

Representation of Closely Held Corporation in Action Against Corporate Shareholder
Op. 216 (1991)

APPLICABLE RULE

- Rule 1.13(a) (Organization as Client)

A and B were each 50% shareholders of C, a close corporation organized under Maryland law which did business in the District of Columbia.

---

22. Paul R. Tremblay, Counseling Community Groups, 17 Clinical L. Rev. 389, 426 (2010). *See also* Nancy J. Moore, Forming Start-Up Companies: Who's My Client, 88 Fordham L. Rev. 1699 (2000) (arguing against recognizing entity status for a group of founders forming start-up companies).

23. *See, e.g.*, Richter v. Van Amberg, 97 F.Supp.2d 1255, (D.N.M. 2000) (finding that the partnership agreement gave the managing partner the authority to convey partnership real property and incur debt without the other partner's consent; profits would be distributed at the discretion of the managing partner).

C had a banking relationship with U, which also extended personal loans to A and B, individually. A and B have defaulted on their loan payments to U. C has filed an action in the District of Columbia against U, alleging a wrongful termination of the banking relationship.

Following the filing of C's action against U, U obtained a judgment against A and, as the result of a Sheriff's execution sale, U became the owner of A's 50% interest in C. A, however, maintains that he is still President of C, since C's two shareholders, B and U, are deadlocked and a majority vote is needed to remove him. U has filed an action in the Maryland courts to dissolve C because of a shareholder deadlock. This action is still pending.

B's widow, who has succeeded to B's interest in C, wishes to maintain C's action against U. U, of course, wishes to discontinue the action. The question in this Inquiry is whether C's corporate lawyer, retained when C was controlled by A and B, may continue to represent C in its action against U, now one of its 50% shareholders, and in U's action to dissolve C.

DISCUSSION

The Inquiry is governed by Rule 1.13 of the District of Columbia Rules of Professional Conduct. Under Rule 1.13(a), "[a] lawyer employed or retained by an organization represents the organization acting through its duly authorized constituents." This rule embodies the well-established principle that a lawyer retained by a corporation, or by any other organization recognized as a separate legal entity, represents the entity....

The principle that a lawyer representing a corporation represents the entity and not its individual shareholders or other constituents applies even when the shareholders come into conflict with the entity. Courts have generally held, therefore, that a corporation's lawyer is not disqualified from representing the corporation in litigation against its constituents. A different result may sometimes be required where the shareholders of a closely held corporation reasonably might have believed they had a personal lawyer-client relationship with the corporation's lawyer. This is not the case, however, since under the circumstances U, the bank, could not reasonably believe it has or had a personal lawyer-client relationship with C's lawyer.

Since C's lawyer is not disqualified from continuing to represent C in its litigation with one of its 50% shareholders, the question arises how the lawyer is to carry out his ethical duties in this representation. On the one hand, the corporate lawyer owes a duty of loyalty to the corporation, as distinct from its owners and managers, and he or she must act in the best interests of the corporation as an entity.

On the other hand, the lawyer must normally follow the direction of those duly appointed or elected to act on behalf of the corporation. Rule 1.13 expressly recognizes that a lawyer represents an organization such as a corporation "through its duly authorized constituents." Comment [4] further states that "[w]hen constituents of the organization make decisions for it, the decisions ordinarily must be accepted by the lawyer even if their utility or prudence is doubtful."

The difficulty here is that the corporation's President, A, may continue to hold office only because of the shareholder deadlock; moreover, because of his own dispute with U, A may have reason to disregard the corporation's interest in determining the corporation's course of action in its dispute with U. These difficulties notwithstanding, the corporation's lawyer may continue to take direction from A until the dispute over control of the corporation is resolved by the courts or the parties. If, however, the lawyer should become convinced that A's decisions are clearly in violation of A's own fiduciary duties to the corporation, the lawyer may be forced to seek guidance from the courts as to who is in control of the corporation, there being no higher authority within the corporation to whom the lawyer can turn. Throughout the representation, the lawyer must continue to recognize that the interests of the corporation must be paramount and that he must take care to remain neutral with respect to the disputes between the present shareholders, B and U, and between A and U. See ABA Opinion 86 (1932) ("In acting as the corporation's legal adviser [an attorney] must refrain from taking part in any controversies or factual differences which may exist among stockholders as to its control."). . . .

NOTES AND QUESTIONS

1. For a similar opinion in the context of a partnership, *see* State Bar of Calif., Standing Comm. on Prof. Resp. and Conduct, Formal Op. No. 1994-137, which addressed a limited partnership in which the two general partners disagreed whether to file a lawsuit against a lender. The agreement provided that one general partner was to oversee the daily operation of the partnership, but that the other general partner must approve "major decisions." They disagreed whether the decision to file a lawsuit was such a major decision. The committee characterized the disagreement not as a "conflict of interest, because the lawyer has only one client, the partnership," but rather as a "conflict of authority within the partnership over who oversees and instructs the partnership's lawyer." If neither the partnership agreement nor applicable law answers the question as to which general partner had the authority to instruct the lawyer, the lawyer was advised to attempt to work with the partners to resolve their dispute. If the dispute was not resolved, the lawyer was permitted to withdraw because the dispute rendered it unreasonably difficult for the lawyer to continue representing the partnership effectively.

2. If the lawyer in the California opinion described above was convinced that it was in the best interest of the partnership to file the lawsuit, should the lawyer have resolved the dispute in favor of the partner who was instructing the lawyer to do so?

C. COMMUNICATION

As we learned in Chapter 3, Model Rule 1.4 requires a lawyer to keep a client informed about its legal affairs. Because the duty of communication exists primarily to enable the client to participate in decision-making, ordinarily the lawyer representing an entity should communicate with one or more constituents who will participate in the decision-making process. This might be the constituent who retained the lawyer or another constituent designated to communicate with the lawyer.

As Comment [3] states, "[w]hen constituents of the organization make decisions for it, the decisions ordinarily must be accepted by the lawyer even if their utility or prudence is doubtful." Under Model Rule 1.13(b), however, when the lawyer knows that the entity is likely to be substantially harmed by the conduct of a constituent that is either a violation of legal obligation to the entity (such as a CFO who is embezzling from the company) or a violation of law that might be imputed to the entity (such as a CEO who refuses to correct materially false financial statements filed with the SEC), then the lawyer is obligated to "proceed as is reasonably necessary in the best interest of the organization." This will usually entail communicating the information to a higher authority in the organization. This type of communication is commonly known as "reporting up" and is discussed further, along with SEC regulations requiring more extensive "reporting up" for certain lawyers representing public companies, in a subsequent chapter.[24]

So far, we've been discussing communication with the entity client, as required by Rule 1.4. If an individual constituent is not involved in decision-making, and has not been designated as someone to whom the lawyer should communicate as an entity representative, then Rule 1.6 generally prohibits the entity lawyer from communicating information relating to the representation to that individual. This is so even though these individuals are themselves entity agents for some purposes — that is, they are insiders, not outsiders.[25] Under Rule 1.6, however, a lawyer may be impliedly authorized to disclose information to these individuals when necessary to carry out the representation. For example, a lawyer retained to conduct an internal investigation is impliedly authorized to reveal information necessary to conduct interviews with a wide range of individual officers or employees. Similarly, a lawyer is ordinarily authorized to disclose information to constituents who are entitled to obtain that information: for example, to partners (including both general and limited partners) who do not themselves manage the partnership but are entitled under partnership law to request and receive information relating to the business of the partnership.[26]

---

24. *See infra* Chapter 12: Corporate Wrongdoing.
25. *See infra* Chapter 10: Privilege and Confidentiality Revisited.
26. *See, e.g.,* Bromberg & Ribstein on Partnership §6.06 (Christine Hurt et al. eds., 2d ed. Supp. 2018).

Rule 1.13(f) imposes an additional duty of communication for entity lawyers. Under that rule, "[i]n dealing with an organization's directors, officers, employees, members, shareholders or other constituents, a lawyer shall explain the identity of the client when the lawyer knows or reasonably should know that the organization's interests are adverse to those of the constituents with whom the lawyer is dealing." This rule is analogous to the lawyer's obligations under Rule 4.3 in communicating with unrepresented persons who may misunderstand the lawyer's role[27] and is cited most frequently in connection with internal investigations. In conducting such investigations, lawyers are commonly urged not only to clarify that the lawyer is not representing (and cannot represent) a potentially adverse constituent, but also that "such person may wish to obtain independent representation."[28]

NOTES AND QUESTIONS

1. In Rice v. Strunk,[29] a partnership agreement designated Cobin as the managing partner of a general partnership, which owned and managed certain apartments. The partnership had a property management agreement with Rice, the second of the three general partners, to manage and lease the apartments. Several months before the closing of a partnership refinancing, which required each of the three partners to personally guarantee a $2,300,000 loan, Cobin informed Strunk, the partnership lawyer, that he was planning to replace Rice as the property manager. Cobin also instructed Strunk not to tell Rice about this development until after the closing, because Rice would not agree to participate in the refinancing if he knew he would lose his position as property manager. Rice subsequently sued Strunk for malpractice and fraud, and the Supreme Court of Indiana affirmed summary judgment for Strunk on both counts. Can you explain how the court likely explained its findings? Was Strunk justified in obeying Cobin's instruction not to inform Rice that he was going to be replaced as property manager?

2. You may recall that in *Hutton*, the first contact the New York lawyers had with Brown was during an internal investigation, when the New York associate interviewed Brown with respect to his role in the loan to Hurbrough. What should the associate have said to Brown prior to beginning the interview? Does it make a difference what information the associate had with respect to the potential illegality of the Hurbrough loan?

---

27. *See supra* Chapter 8: Limits of Zealous Representation II: Transactions.
28. MR 1.13, cmt [10].
29. 670 N.E.2d 120 (Ind. 1996).

D. CONTACTING A REPRESENTED ENTITY

In Chapter 8, we discussed Model Rule 4.2, which prohibits a lawyer representing a client from communicating about the subject matter of the representation with a person known to be represented by another lawyer, without that lawyer's consent. Comment [7] explains how the rule is applied when the person contacted is an entity, that is, which constituents may not be contacted as representatives of the entity itself. Because this issue raises questions similar to those raised in considering which constituents' communications are protected under the entity's attorney-client privilege, we postpone a discussion of Comment [7] until the following chapter on privilege and confidentiality.

Review Problems

9-1 A law firm was retained by a mutual life insurance company to assist it in reorganizing itself as a stock insurance corporation. Subsequently, the individual policy holders filed a lawsuit against both the mutual life insurance company and the stock insurance corporation alleging that its officers committed fraud in inducing the policy holders to agree to the reorganization. Counsel for the policy holders filed a motion to disqualify the law firm representing both defendants, claiming that the law firm represented the policy holders themselves when it acted to assist the mutual life insurance company in reorganizing as a corporation. Under state law, a mutual life insurance company is a cooperative enterprise in which the policy holders constitute the members for whose benefit the company is organized, maintained, and operated. Is the motion for disqualification likely to succeed? What additional evidence might have a bearing on the answer to this question?

9-2 A woman and her twin sister are equal co-owners of a catering business. The woman retained a lawyer to organize the business. After the business was formed, the lawyer continued to act for the business in negotiating contracts with suppliers and drafting contracts with various employees. The lawyer has also represented the woman in the purchase of her condominium and in her divorce. Recently, the woman became less involved in the business and after several disagreements with the sister, she consulted the lawyer and asked him to explain how she can best protect her interests in the dissolution of the business. She has asked him not to inform her sister about the consultation. May the lawyer represent her in this matter? Must or may he inform the sister about the woman's plan? What if instead of consulting the lawyer, the woman initiated a lawsuit against both the business and the sister alleging breach of fiduciary duty? May the lawyer represent the business and the sister in defending against that lawsuit? With respect to all of these questions, does it matter whether the business is a public corporation, a private closely held corporation, or a partnership?

9-3 A man and his brother were the two managing members of a limited liability company (LLC). The man brought a collection action in his individual capacity against the LLC to recover monies loaned to the LLC. Both the man and his brother were personally represented by separate counsel, and each retained yet another lawyer to represent the LLC. Each managing member also filed a motion to disqualify the LLC counsel retained by the other. How should the court rule on the disqualification motions? What if a provision of the LLC's operating agreement provides that "[n]otwithstanding any other provision of this Agreement, during the period that any portion of the [man's] loan is outstanding, in the event of a disagreement between the Managers regarding any matter affecting the Company, the decision of [the man] shall control with respect to such matter"?

CHAPTER 10

PRIVILEGE AND CONFIDENTIALITY REVISITED

Model Rules 1.6, 3.4(f), 4.2, cmt [7], 4.3, 4.4(a)

You will recall from Chapter 4 that the lawyer's duty of confidentiality encompasses three separate doctrines: (1) attorney-client privilege; (2) work product immunity; and (3) the professional duty of confidentiality. In this chapter we revisit two of these doctrines—attorney-client privilege and the professional duty of confidentiality—in the context of lawyers representing entities. In addition, we revisit the no-contact rule discussed in Chapter 8 as applied to lawyers who want to contact constituents of a represented entity.

As we learned in the preceding chapter, the difficulties in these areas arise from the fact that fictional entities can only speak and be spoken to through their individual constituents. As we will see, particularly with respect to the attorney-client privilege, courts often struggle in determining which constituent's communications to the lawyer (and vice versa) are protected for purposes of the legal doctrines addressed in this chapter.

A. ATTORNEY-CLIENT PRIVILEGE

1. Basic Doctrinal Approaches

Remember that prima facie protection of the attorney-client privilege requires: (1) a communication; (2) made between privileged persons; (3) in confidence; (4) for the purpose of obtaining or providing legal assistance for the client.[1] The difficulty in entity representation is determining which constituent communications to the lawyer are from the client (or prospective client) and when the sharing of otherwise privileged information among different constituents will waive the privilege. Courts have taken several different doctrinal

---

1. *See supra* Chapter 4: Privilege and Confidentiality.

approaches, ranging from a narrow "control group" test to a broad "subject matter" test. In 1981, the United States Supreme Court decided Upjohn Co. v. United States, excerpted below, in which it rejected the control group test for federal courts applying the federal common law privilege. Although the Court did not articulate a separate test, the approach it adopted is similar to the broad subject matter test that some courts had adopted prior to *Upjohn*. The following two opinions, including *Upjohn*, describe the basic approaches that different courts have adopted, as well as the policy concerns underlying these different approaches. Note that the first case, Consolidated Coal Co. v. Bucyrus-Erie Co., was decided one year *after* the Supreme Court decision in *Upjohn*. You are asked to read it first because it provides an excellent overview of the state of the law prior to *Upjohn*.

Consol. Coal Co. v. Bucyrus-Erie Co.
432 N.E.2d 250 (Ill. 1982)

UNDERWOOD, Justice:

[Consolidated Coal Co. sued Bucyrus-Erie Co. ("B-E"), a wheel excavator manufacturer, to recover damages from the collapse of an excavator located in a mine. The trial court denied B-E's claims of attorney-client privilege and work product protection in resisting the plaintiff's request to produce various documents. An appellate court upheld the trial court, and B-E appealed to the Illinois Supreme Court. The documents at issue included a "metallurgical report" prepared by a B-E employee, Richard Sailors, and notes of interviews conducted by in-house counsel with various other B-E employees. Sailors's supervisor had requested the report, and the supervisor transferred it to the legal department after it was made. With respect to the attorney-client privilege claim, the appellate court ruled that the privilege did not apply because of the lack of an allegation that the documents came from members of B-E's "control group."]

The question of who speaks for a corporation on a privileged basis has created considerable confusion and conflict in the Federal system and has frequently been the subject of law review commentaries. B-E urges that we abandon the "control group" test first adopted in Illinois by the appellate court [in 1964]. This test was recently rejected by the [U.S.] Supreme Court as the governing test in the federal courts. *Upjohn v. United States.* . . .

In the Federal system prior to *Upjohn*, three major tests had emerged. The most widely adopted control-group test was first announced in *City of Philadelphia v. Westinghouse Electric Corp.* (E. D. Pa. 1962) . . . at a time when one Federal court had held that the attorney-client privilege was not available to corporations. . . .

This test focuses on the status of the employee within the corporate hierarchy:

> "[I]f the employee making the communication, of whatever rank he may be, is in a position to control or even to take a substantial part in a decision about any action which the corporation may take upon the advice of the attorney, or if he is an authorized member of a body or group which has that authority, then, in effect, he is (or personifies) the corporation when he makes his disclosure to the lawyer and the privilege would apply. In all other cases the employee would be merely giving information to the lawyer to enable the latter to advise those in the corporation having the authority to act or refrain from acting on the advice."

This approach was subsequently followed by the Third, Sixth and Tenth Circuits, as well as several district courts outside these circuits. In addition, several States have incorporated this test in their rules of evidence.

The Seventh Circuit, in *Harper & Row Publishers, Inc. v. Decker* . . . adopted a broader approach for determining when a corporation could claim the attorney-client privilege. The *Harper & Row* test, sometimes referred to as the "subject matter" or "scope of employment" test, is said to focus on why an attorney was consulted rather than with whom he communicated. Under the *Harper & Row* test, "an employee of a corporation, though not a member of its control group, is sufficiently identified with the corporation so that his communication to the corporation's attorney is privileged where the employee makes the communication at the direction of his superiors in the corporation and where the subject matter upon which the attorney's advice is sought by the corporation and dealt with in the communication is the performance by the employee of the duties of his employments."

Finally, the Eighth Circuit, in *Diversified Industries, Inc. v. Meredith* . . . , responding to one of the criticisms of the subject matter test—that a corporation could protect much information by simply directing all their employees to channel business reports to corporate attorneys—announced a modified version of the *Harper & Row* test:

> "[T]he attorney-client privilege is applicable to an employee's communication if (1) the communication was made for the purpose of securing legal advice; (2) the employee making the communication did so at the direction of his corporate superior; (3) the superior made the request so that the corporation could secure legal advice; (4) the subject matter of the communication is within the scope of the employee's corporate duties; and (5) the communication is not disseminated beyond those persons who, because of the corporate structure, need to know its contents."

Under this modified subject matter approach, any communication in which the employee functioned merely as a "fortuitous" or "bystander" witness would not be privileged. The *Harper & Row* court had implicitly recognized this same limitation.

All of the above tests have been criticized and additional tests have been proposed. . . . The broader tests have been criticized as shielding too much relevant information from discovery, whereas the principal criticism of the control-group test is that it frustrates the purpose of the attorney-client privilege by failing to take into account modern "corporate realities." While the

Supreme Court rejected this test as inadequate, it declined to articulate an alternative standard to govern future cases in the Federal courts.

Whether a narrow or broad test should prevail depends, it seems to us, on the value to be accorded the two competing policies. . . .

The purpose of the attorney-client privilege is to encourage and promote full and frank consultation between a client and legal advisor by removing the fear of compelled disclosure of information. Under some circumstances, however, the privilege poses an absolute bar to the discovery of relevant and material evidentiary facts, and in the corporate context, given the large number of employees, frequent dealings with lawyers and masses of documents, the "zone of silence grows large." That result, in our judgment is fundamentally incompatible with this State's broad discovery policies looking to the ultimate ascertainment of the truth. Its potential to insulate so much material from the truth-seeking process convinces us that the privilege ought to be limited for the corporate client to the extent reasonably necessary to achieve its purpose. As Dean Wigmore admonished:

> "[T]he privilege remains an exception to the general duty to disclose. Its benefits are all indirect and speculative; its obstruction is plain and concrete ***. It is worth preserving for the sake of a general policy, but it is nonetheless an obstacle to the investigation of the truth. It ought to be strictly confined within the narrowest possible limits consistent with the logic of its principles."

The control-group test appears to us to strike a reasonable balance by protecting consultations with counsel by those who are the decisionmakers or who substantially influence corporate decisions and by minimizing the amount of relevant factual material which is immune from discovery. We note, too, that the burden of showing facts which give rise to the privilege rests on the one who claims the exemption. Moreover, the claimant must show certain threshold requirements in order to avail itself of the privilege, including a showing that the communication originated in a confidence that it would not be disclosed, was made to an attorney acting in his legal capacity for the purpose of securing legal advice or services, and remained confidential. Although the control-group test has been noted for its predictability and ease of application, we believe it is necessary to elaborate on those individuals whom we believe should be considered as members of the corporate control group.

In many of the cases in which the control-group test was adopted, the party claiming the privilege either presented no evidence which indicated that the particular employee had any actual authority to make a judgment or decision or, as in the present case, conceded that none of the employees whose statements were alleged to be privileged were a part of their control group. Some courts have indicated that the labels or titles of the employees are not determinative; rather, the actual duties or responsibilities delegated to these individuals determine their status as decisionmakers. Nevertheless, as a practical matter, the only communications that are ordinarily held privileged under this test are those made by top management who have the ability to make a final decision, rather than those made by employees whose positions are merely advisory. We believe that an employee whose advisory role to top management in a particular area is such that a decision would not normally be made without his advice or opinion, and whose opinion in fact forms the basis of any final decision by those with actual authority, is properly within the control group. However, the individuals upon whom he may rely for supplying information are not members of the control group. Thus, if an employee of the status described is consulted for the purpose of determining what legal action the corporation will pursue, his communication is protected from disclosure. This approach, we think, better accommodates modern corporate realities and recognizes that decisionmaking within a corporation is a process rather than a final act.

While B-E has conceded that Richard Sailors was not a member of its control group in the usual sense, we must consider whether he qualifies for that group as we have defined it. [Sailors was a materials development engineer at the time he prepared the "metallurgical report," which was one of the documents B-E sought to protect under the attorney-client privilege.]

In October 1976, he was contacted by a superior and asked to examine pieces of the machine in question which were in B-E's possession and render an opinion. There is conflict in the record as to which superior contacted him. B-E's attorney's affidavit indicated that Lennart Hansson, who was B-E's engineer in charge of overseeing technical aspects of litigation involving mining machinery, requested Sailors' assistance; Sailors stated in his deposition that he was contacted by Tom Learmont, B-E's director of engineering-mining machinery whose responsibilities including supervising several chief engineers. In our judgment, it is clear that Sailors was not a member of B-E's corporate control group. As one of several engineers within his department, he supplied information to those whose opinions were sought and relied upon by others such as Hansson who occupied an advisory role and substantially contributed to decisionmaking. It is this fact which is critical, for it seems clear that Sailors' role was one of supplying the factual bases upon which were predicated the opinions and recommendations of those who advised the decisionmakers. While those who directly advise the decisionmakers could, conceivably, come within the control group, it is evident that Sailors did not.

Accordingly, we hold that Sailors' report is not privileged and must be made available to Consolidation for inspection.

Upjohn Co. v. United States
449 U.S. 383 (1981)

Justice Rehnquist delivered the opinion of the Court. . . .

I

Petitioner Upjohn Co. manufactures and sells pharmaceuticals here and abroad. In January 1976 independent accountants conducting an audit of one of Upjohn's foreign subsidiaries discovered that the subsidiary made payments to or for the benefit of foreign government officials in order to secure government business. The accountants so informed petitioner, Mr. Gerard Thomas, Upjohn's Vice President, Secretary and General Counsel. Thomas is a member of the Michigan and New York Bars, and has been Upjohn's General Counsel for 20 years. He consulted with outside counsel and R.T. Parfet, Jr., Upjohn's Chairman of the Board. It was decided that the company would conduct an internal investigation of what were termed "questionable payments." As part of this investigation the attorneys prepared a letter containing a questionnaire which was sent to "All Foreign General and Area Managers" over the Chairman's signature. The letter began by noting recent disclosures that several American companies made "possibly illegal" payments to foreign government officials and emphasized that the management needed full information concerning any such payments made by Upjohn. The letter indicated that the Chairman had asked Thomas, identified as "the company's General Counsel," "to conduct an investigation for the purpose of determining the nature and magnitude of any payments made by the Upjohn Company or any of its subsidiaries to any employee or official of a foreign government." The questionnaire sought detailed information concerning such payments. Managers were instructed to treat the investigation as "highly confidential" and not to discuss it with anyone other than Upjohn employees who might be helpful in providing the requested information. Responses were to be sent directly to Thomas. Thomas and outside counsel also interviewed the recipients of the questionnaire and some 33 other Upjohn officers or employees as part of the investigation.

On March 26, 1976, the company voluntarily submitted a preliminary report to the Securities and Exchange Commission on Form 8-K disclosing certain questionable payments. A copy of the report was simultaneously submitted to the Internal Revenue Service, which immediately began an investigation to determine the tax consequences of the payments. Special agents conducting the investigation were given lists by Upjohn of all those interviewed and all who had responded to the questionnaire. On November 23, 1976, the Service issued a summons pursuant to 26 U.S.C. § 7602 demanding production of:

> "All files relative to the investigation conducted under the supervision of Gerard Thomas to identify payments to employees of foreign governments and any political contributions made by the Upjohn Company or any of its affiliates since January 1, 1971 and to determine whether any funds of the Upjohn Company had been improperly accounted for on the corporate books during the same period.
>
> "The records should include but not be limited to written questionnaires sent to managers of the Upjohn Company's foreign affiliates, and memorandums or notes of the interviews conducted in the United States and abroad with officers and employees of the Upjohn Company and its subsidiaries."

The company declined to produce the documents specified in the second paragraph on the grounds that they were protected from disclosure by the attorney-client privilege and constituted the work product of attorneys prepared in anticipation of litigation. On August 31, 1977, the United States filed a petition seeking enforcement of the summons under §§7402(b) and 7604(a) in the United States District Court for the Western District of Michigan. That court adopted the recommendation of a Magistrate who concluded that the summons should be enforced. Petitioners appealed to the Court of Appeals for the Sixth Circuit which rejected the Magistrate's finding of a waiver of the attorney-client privilege, but agreed that the privilege did not apply "[t]o the extent that the communications were made by officers and agents not responsible for directing Upjohn's actions in response to legal advice . . . for the simple reason that the communications were not the 'client's.'" The court reasoned that accepting petitioners' claim for a broader application of the privilege would encourage upper-echelon management to ignore unpleasant facts and create too broad a "zone of silence." Noting that Upjohn's counsel had interviewed officials such as the Chairman and President, the Court of Appeals remanded to the District Court so that a determination of who was within the "control group" could be made. . . .

II

Federal Rule of Evidence 501 provides that "the privilege of a witness . . . shall be governed by the principles of the common law as they may be interpreted by the courts of the United States in light of reason and experience." The attorney-client privilege is the oldest of the privileges for confidential communications known to the common law. Its purpose is to encourage full and frank communication between attorneys and their clients and thereby promote broader public interests in the observance of law and administration of justice. The privilege recognizes that sound legal advice or advocacy serves public ends and that such advice or advocacy depends upon the lawyer's being fully informed by the client. As we stated last Term. . . . "The lawyer-client privilege rests on the need for the advocate and counselor to know all that relates to the client's reasons for seeking representation if the professional mission is to be carried out." . . . [W]e recognized the purpose of the privilege to be "to encourage clients to make full disclosure to their attorneys." This rationale for the privilege has long been recognized by the Court. Admittedly complications in the application of the privilege arise when the client is a corporation, which in theory is an artificial creature of the law, and not an individual; but this Court has assumed that the privilege applies when the client is a corporation, and the Government does not contest the general proposition.

The Court of Appeals, however, considered the application of the privilege in the corporate context to present a "different problem," since the client was an inanimate entity and "only the senior management, guiding and integrating the several operations, . . . can be said to possess an identity analogous to the corporation as a whole." . . . Such a view, we think, overlooks the fact that the privilege exists to protect not only the giving of professional advice to those who can act on it, but also the giving of information to the lawyer to enable him to give sound and informed advice. The first step in the resolution of any legal problem is ascertaining the factual background and sifting through the facts with an eye to the legally relevant. See ABA Code of Professional Responsibility, Ethical Consideration 4-1:

> "A lawyer should be fully informed of all the facts of the matter he is handling in order for his client to obtain the full advantage of our legal system. It is for the lawyer in the exercise of his independent professional judgment to separate the relevant and important from the irrelevant and unimportant. The observance of the ethical obligation of a lawyer to hold inviolate the confidences and secrets of his client not only facilitates the full development of facts essential to the proper representation of the client but also encourages laymen to seek early legal assistance."

In the case of the individual client the provider of information and the person who acts on the lawyer's advice are one and the same. In the corporate context, however, it will frequently be employees beyond the control group as defined by the court below — "officers and agents . . . responsible for directing [the company's] actions in response to legal advice" — who will possess the information needed by the corporation's lawyer. Middle-level — and indeed lower-level — employees can, by actions within the scope of their employment, embroil the corporation in serious legal difficulties, and it is only natural that these employees would have the relevant information needed by corporate counsel if he is adequately to advise the client with respect to such actual or potential difficulties. This fact was noted in *Diversified Industries, Inc. v. Meredith*:

> "In a corporation, it may be necessary to glean information relevant to a legal problem from middle management or non-management personnel as well as from top executives. The attorney dealing with a complex legal problem 'is thus faced with a "Hobson's choice". If he interviews employees not having "the very highest authority", their communications to him will not be privileged. If, on the other hand, he interviews *only* those employees with the "very highest authority", he may find it extremely difficult, if not impossible, to determine what happened.'"

The control group test adopted by the court below thus frustrates the very purpose of the privilege by discouraging the communication of relevant information by employees of the client to attorneys seeking to render legal advice to the client corporation. The attorney's advice will also frequently be more significant to noncontrol group members than to those who officially sanction the advice, and the control group test makes it more difficult to convey full and frank legal advice to the employees who will put into effect the client corporation's policy.

The narrow scope given the attorney-client privilege by the court below not only makes it difficult for corporate attorneys to formulate sound advice when their client is faced with a specific legal problem but also threatens to limit the valuable efforts of corporate counsel to ensure their client's compliance with the law. In light of the vast and complicated array of regulatory legislation confronting the modern corporation, corporations, unlike most individuals, "constantly go to lawyers to find out how to obey the law," particularly since compliance with the law in this area is hardly an instinctive matter. The test adopted by the court below is difficult to apply in practice, though no abstractly formulated and unvarying "test" will necessarily enable courts to decide questions such as this with mathematical precision. But if the purpose of the attorney-client privilege is to be served, the attorney and client must be able to predict with some degree of certainty whether particular discussions will be protected. An uncertain privilege, or one which purports to be certain but results in widely varying applications by the courts, is little better than no privilege at all. The very terms of the test adopted by the court below suggest the unpredictability of its application. The test restricts the availability of the privilege to those officers who play a "substantial role" in deciding and directing a corporation's legal response. Disparate decisions in cases applying this test illustrate its unpredictability.

The communications at issue were made by Upjohn employees to counsel for Upjohn acting as such, at the direction of corporate superiors in order to secure legal advice from counsel. . . . Information, not available from upper-echelon management, was needed to supply a basis for legal advice concerning compliance with securities and tax laws, foreign laws, currency regulations, duties to shareholders, and potential litigation in each of these areas. The communications concerned matters within the scope of the employees' corporate duties, and the employees themselves were sufficiently aware that they were being questioned in order that the corporation could obtain legal advice. The questionnaire identified Thomas as "the company's General Counsel" and referred in its opening sentence to the possible illegality of payments such as the ones on which information was sought. A statement of policy accompanying the questionnaire clearly indicated the legal implications of the investigation. . . . Pursuant to explicit instructions from the Chairman of the Board, the communications were considered "highly confidential" when made, and have been kept confidential by the company. Consistent with the underlying purposes of the attorney-client privilege, these communications must be protected against compelled disclosure.

The Court of Appeals declined to extend the attorney-client privilege beyond the limits of the control group test for fear that doing so would entail severe burdens on discovery and create a broad "zone of silence" over corporate affairs. Application of the attorney-client privilege to communications such as those involved here, however, puts the adversary in no worse position than if the communications had never taken place. The privilege only protects disclosure of communications; it does not protect disclosure of the underlying facts by those who communicated with the attorney:

> "[T]he protection of the privilege extends only to *communications* and not to facts. A fact is one thing and a communication concerning that fact is an entirely different thing. The client cannot be compelled to answer the question,

'What did you say or write to the attorney?' but may not refuse to disclose any relevant fact within his knowledge merely because he incorporated a statement of such fact into his communication to his attorney."

Here the Government was free to question the employees who communicated with Thomas and outside counsel. Upjohn has provided the IRS with a list of such employees, and the IRS has already interviewed some 25 of them. While it would probably be more convenient for the Government to secure the results of petitioner's internal investigation by simply subpoenaing the questionnaires and notes taken by petitioner's attorneys, such considerations of convenience to do not overcome the policies served by the attorney-client privilege. . . .

Needless to say, we decide only the case before us, and do not undertake to draft a set of rules which should govern challenges to investigatory subpoenas. Any such approach would violate the spirit of Federal Rule of Evidence 501. While such a "case-by-case" basis may to some slight extent undermine desirable certainty in the boundaries of the attorney-client privilege, it obeys the spirit of the Rules.

NOTES AND QUESTIONS

1. Use the following problem to work through the various doctrinal approaches to the corporate attorney-client privilege. Consider the pre-*Upjohn* approaches, including the original control group test and the two subject matter tests described in *Consolidated Coal*. Then consider the U.S. Supreme Court's approach in *Upjohn* itself and the modified control group test now in use in Illinois.

> Paul was injured in an accident involving a car he was driving and a truck owned by a department store. According to a statement made by Ed, the driver of the truck, at the scene of the accident, the truck's brakes suddenly failed, causing him to lose control of the truck and veer into the next lane, colliding with Paul's car. Following any incident in which someone is seriously injured, a deputy general counsel in the legal department of the corporation that owns the department store routinely conducts an investigation to determine the cause of the accident. Carrie, the deputy general counsel, conducted such an investigation and interviewed the following employees: (1) Ed, the truck driver; (2) Sally, a passenger in the truck, who was herself a truck driver and who was assisting Ed in making deliveries that day; and (3) Derek, the head of the deliveries department, who supervised not only the drivers but also the maintenance of the delivery trucks. Derek reports to the vice-president for operations. The primary purpose of interviewing Ed and Sally was to ascertain the circumstances of the accident, including how fast Ed was driving, whether he was paying attention to the road, and whether he may have been distracted by anything, including any interactions between him and Sally. Carrie interviewed Derek, with respect to policies and procedures concerning the maintenance of the trucks and the maintenance history of the truck Ed was driving. After the interviews, Carrie prepared a memorandum summarizing the interview statements.

One year later, Paul filed a personal injury lawsuit against the corporation that owns the department store. Discovery began months later. Paul's attorney deposed Ed, Sally, and Derek, but none of them had a clear memory of the subjects on which they were questioned. Paul's attorney has demanded that the corporation produce any memoranda recording prior statements of any of these employees. Analyze the likelihood of the success of Paul's attorney's demand for production of the memorandum over the objection of the corporation that the memoranda are protected by the corporation's attorney-client privilege. Are there additional facts you would need to know?

2. Having worked through the doctrine, let's now consider the policy considerations that underlie the different approaches. What do you think was the basis for the original control group test? Why did the U.S. Supreme Court reject that approach? Why did the Illinois Supreme Court reject *Upjohn* in favor of a modified control group test?[2] Consider the difficulty Paul's attorney faced when he was eventually able to depose Ed, Sally, and Derek. As for any attempt on his part to interview them informally soon after the accident, keep in mind that Rule 4.2's no-contact rule applies to some corporate employees, as we shall see in a subsequent section.[3] And even if the no-contact rule does not apply, how likely is it that these employees would agree to meet informally with Paul's lawyer?[4]

3. Even under the broader subject matter or *Upjohn* approaches, only top management or persons authorized by management are entitled to *assert* the privilege, and the same persons are the only ones capable of *waiving* the privilege.

4. What if one or more of the employees identified in the problem above had left the company and were *former employees* at the time they communicated with the company's deputy general counsel? Under the control group test, even the statements of a former CEO are not protected, because the former CEO is not *currently* in a position to make decisions on behalf of the company. In jurisdictions applying the subject matter test or *Upjohn*, three approaches have emerged: (1) treat the former employee like any other third-party witnesses who do not speak as agents of the company; (2) apply the privilege to the attorney's purely information-gathering communications but not to pre-deposition counseling; and (3) extend the privilege to former employees to the same extent as current employees.[5] Regardless of the approach taken to statements made to the entity's lawyer by former employees after they leave

---

2. More states have adopted *Upjohn* or some variation of the subject matter test, but seven states continue to use a control group test; some states have not firmly adopted a test for the corporation's attorney-client privilege. *See* Types of Practice, Corporate, Privilege/Confidentiality, 91:2201 ABA/BLAW Law. Man. on Prof. Conduct .20.30.20 (ABA/BLAW) (2020).

3. *See infra* at C.

4. *See* MR 3.4(f) (permitting lawyer to request client's employees to refrain from voluntarily giving relevant information to another party).

5. *See generally* Heath Henley, The Attorney-Client Privilege and Former Employees: History, Principle, and Precedent, 3 Belmont L. Rev. 229, 246-51 (2016).

the company, any statements made while they were employed remain fully protected by the privilege to the extent they would be protected if they remained current employees.

5. Although corporate shareholders are not ordinarily entitled to access communications protected by the attorney-client privilege, a court may withhold protection of the privilege in proceedings brought by shareholders against the entity's directors or officers alleging that they breached their fiduciary duties to the entity.[6] The same considerations may apply when the proceeding is brought by a member or other constituent of a noncorporate entity against those who manage the entity and when a minority shareholder sues a majority shareholder for breach of fiduciary duty.[7] For a discussion of the factors courts consider in determining whether to apply the organizational fiduciary exception to the privilege, *see* RLGL §85 (noting that this exception is analogous to the "fiduciary-lawyer" exception in which a beneficiary of a trust may obtain privileged communications in a proceeding alleging a breach of fiduciary duties by the trustee or similar fiduciary). Is it a problem that as a result of the shareholder derivative action and similar cases, a CEO consulting the general counsel seeking legal advice might fear that the conversation will not be privileged if the CEO is subsequently sued for breach of fiduciary duties to the company? Isn't the purpose of the corporate privilege to encourage candid and open conversations with counsel?

6. Regardless of whether an individual constituent's statements to a lawyer will be covered by the entity's attorney-client privilege, an entity lawyer interviewing such a constituent must ensure that the individual does not misunderstand the lawyer's role. This topic will be addressed in Chapter 11: Conflicts of Interest in Entity Representation.

7. Special problems may arise when the privilege issue concerns in-house counsel, who sometimes function as a lawyer and other times as a businessperson. This topic will be address in Chapter 13 In-House Counsel.

2. Application of Privilege to Third-Party Agents and Consultants

As we know, the privilege applies to communications between privileged persons, and privileged persons include not only the client, but also agents of the clients who facilitate communications between them.[8] For individual clients, such agents include language translators and other persons whose presence is reasonably necessary to facilitate the communication, such as the parent of a young child or an assistant who types a letter from a businessperson to the

---

6. *See, e.g.*, Garner v. Wolfinbarger, 430 F.2d 1093 (5th Cir. 1970) (shareholder derivative action).

7. *See, e.g.*, Frederick R. Ball, The Attorney-Client Privilege in Director and Shareholder Litigation, 89 Ill. B. J. 537 (2001).

8. *See supra* Chapter 4, Privilege and Confidentiality.

lawyer. Consultants such as investment bankers and other financial advisors and public relations consultants are typically viewed as noncommunicative agents and therefore are not included as privileged persons, unless as in the following case, they facilitate the client's communication with the lawyer. With respect to entity clients, however, the picture has become more complicated in recent years, as businesses are increasingly using nonemployees for assistance not only in the regular course of business, but also in the entity's various legal matters. The following cases illustrate two different approaches courts have taken to the use of outside agents and consultants. The first was a putative class action alleging securities fraud with respect to various alleged material misrepresentations and omissions concerning the 2013 launch by BlackBerry Limited ("BlackBerry") of its Z10 smartphone, thereby artificially inflating its stock price for a period of time. A dispute arose concerning documents BlackBerry withheld from production on the grounds they were protected by the attorney-client privilege and/or the work product doctrine.

Pearlstein v. Blackberry Ltd.
2019 WL 2281280 (S.D.N.Y. 2019)

KATHERINE H. PARKER, United States Magistrate Judge . . .

[After a March 19, 2019 court decision addressing BlackBerry's privilege designations, the Magistrate Judge directed BlackBerry to review the court's decision and inform the plaintiffs which documents it still believed were privileged. This opinion addresses the parties' dispute over 27 of 40 documents pertaining to upcoming depositions.]

The 27 documents fall into only . . . three categories and comprise variations of only 10 email chains. Nineteen of the communications are between and among BlackBerry employees, BlackBerry's outside counsel, and BlackBerry's financial advisor, JP Morgan. . . .

As to [this] category of documents, Plaintiffs argue that they are not privileged and that any privilege was waived by virtue of BlackBerry's financial advisors at JP Morgan being included in the communications. They are wrong on both counts. Seventeen of the documents are requests by BlackBerry employees for legal review of draft talking points for a September 2012 earnings call.[9] As discussed in this Court's prior Opinion, BlackBerry's communications to its counsel requesting comment on draft talking points are properly withheld as privileged. . . .

Although this Court recognized in its earlier opinion that including a third party in an otherwise privileged communication generally results in a waiver of privilege, there are exceptions. "An agent, such as a financial advisor, may

---

9. [An earnings call is a teleconference or webcast in which management of a public company discusses with analysts, investors, and other participants the company's financial results during a given reporting period. —ED.]

have communications with an attorney that 'are covered by the attorney-client privilege if the financial advisor's role is limited to helping a lawyer give effective advice by explaining financial concepts to the lawyer.'" In contrast to this Court's holding that by including a public relations consultant on certain communications BlackBerry had waived privilege, including its financial advisors at JP Morgan did not waive privilege as to the communications at issue. To start, there can be no dispute that JP Morgan was BlackBerry's agent. Additionally, there can be no dispute that all communications between JP Morgan and BlackBerry and BlackBerry's counsel were intended to remain strictly confidential. Indeed, JP Morgan and BlackBerry entered into a non-disclosure agreement, which this Court has examined, requiring JP Morgan to maintain confidentiality of all information it received from BlackBerry. In contrast, the public relations consultant included in some of BlackBerry's communications with its in-house counsel was not retained via a formal agreement and had no contractual confidentiality obligations to BlackBerry. Also, unlike the public relations consultant whose advice was not needed by the attorneys to provide effective legal advice, JP Morgan was included in the communications to provide BlackBerry's outside counsel with information about certain strategic and transactional matters about which it had expertise so that BlackBerry's counsel could give effective legal advice about what could be said publicly about those matters. It is clear from review of the documents *in camera* that it was legal, not business advice being requested or conveyed in the communications. In similar circumstances, courts have found including a financial advisor in the communication did not result in a waiver of privilege.

The two other communications that included JP Morgan were requests from JP Morgan to BlackBerry's outside counsel to review a July 2013 presentation concerning potential strategic alternatives that JP Morgan was preparing to present to BlackBerry's board of directors. This communication, in which JP Morgan, as BlackBerry's agent, was seeking legal advice for BlackBerry, is clearly privileged.

The cases cited by Plaintiffs are distinguishable. *See United States v. Ackert* (case did not involve communications between and among a company, its outside counsel and financial advisor regarding legal advice; instead, it involved a communication between a company's in-house lawyer and an investment banker who had made a pitch to the company so lawyer could gather information about the proposed deal and render legal advice to the company). . . .

In Re Copper Market Antitrust Litigation
200 F.R.D. 213 (S.D.N.Y. 2001)

SWAIN, District Judge.

Plaintiffs Viacom Inc. and Emerson Electric Co. ("Plaintiffs") move to compel the production of documents listed on the privilege log (the "Privilege Log") produced by non-party Robinson Lerer & Montgomery ("RLM") in response to a subpoena issued from this Court on March 9, 2000. For the reasons set forth below, Plaintiffs' motion is denied.

FACTUAL BACKGROUND

This motion arises out of multi-district litigation pending in the Western District of Wisconsin. On about September 27, 1999, Plaintiffs brought an action against Sumitomo Corporation ("Sumitomo") [and other companies] alleging that the defendants conspired to manipulate global copper prices. By the subpoena dated March 9, 2000, Plaintiffs requested that RLM produce documents relating to RLM's public relations consulting work for Sumitomo. . . .

The signal event giving rise to the underlying antitrust litigation occurred during a deposition conducted in April 1995 by the Commodities Futures Trading Commission ("CFTC"), when Yasuo Hamanaka ("Hamanaka"), then head of Sumitomo's Non-Ferrous Metals Division, disclosed that he had executed an unauthorized power of attorney relating to hundreds of millions of dollars in copper trading. Anticipating a CFTC investigation and other litigation, Sumitomo retained RLM, a "crisis management" public relations firm, on or about May 23, 1996, to handle public relations matters arising from the copper trading scandal.

Sumitomo hired RLM because it had no prior experience in dealing with issues relating to publicity arising from high profile litigation, and because Sumitomo lacked experience in dealing with the Western media. Only two of the three executives in Sumitomo's Corporate Communications Department had English language facility and those individuals' English language skills were not sufficiently sophisticated for media relations. Working largely out of Sumitomo's Tokyo headquarters with Sumitomo's Corporate Communications Department, RLM acting as Sumitomo's agent and its spokesperson when dealing with the Western press on issues relating to the copper trading scandal. The chief object of RLM's engagement was damage control, i.e., the management of press statements in the context of anticipated litigation "to ensure that they do not themselves further damage the client." "RLM's primary goal in representing Sumitomo was to help the Company make the statements it needed to make, but to do so within the necessary legal framework—all with the realization, indeed the expectation, that each such statement might subsequently be used by Sumitomo's adversaries in litigation." In the course of providing its services to Sumitomo, RLM conferred frequently with Sumitomo's outside counsel, Paul, Weiss, Rifkind, Wharton & Garrison ("Paul Weiss").

RLM dealt with the western press on Sumitomo's behalf, while Sumitomo's internal Corporate Communications Department dealt with the Japanese press. RLM's public relations duties included preparing statements for public release and internal documents designed to inform Sumitomo employees about what could and could not be said about the scandal. RLM's duties also included drafting, in collaboration with Sumitomo's counsel, public relations documents, press releases, talking points, and Questions and Answers ("Q and As") to be used as a framework for press inquiries. The press releases were intended for different audiences, including regulators and other parties with whom Sumitomo anticipated litigation. RLM prepared many drafts of the documents, incorporating legal advice from Paul Weiss and Sumitomo in-house counsel. All documents prepared by RLM relating to legal issues arising from the CFTC investigation or the Hamanaka scandal were vetted with Sumitomo's in-house counsel and/or outside counsel. RLM had the authority to make decisions on behalf of Sumitomo concerning its public relations strategy.

RLM was the functional equivalent of an in-house public relations department with respect to Western media relations, having authority to make decisions and statements on Sumitomo's behalf, and seeking and receiving legal advice from Sumitomo's counsel with respect to the performance of its duties. . . .

RLM has asserted both attorney-client privilege and work-product immunity with respect to . . . 583 communications listed on the Privilege Log [provided by RLM with instructions from Paul Weiss]. . . . Plaintiffs contend that the attorney-client privilege is inapplicable because RLM, a third party, was involved in the communications as to which the privilege is asserted. . . . They further assert that any privilege that may be applicable to the documents listed on the Privilege Log has been waived by disclosure of the information to RLM, a third party. . . .

DISCUSSION . . .

The *Upjohn* Court based its holding that the communications at issue were privileged on determinations that the communications had been made to Upjohn's counsel by its employees acting at the direction of their corporate superiors; that the information was needed to supply a basis for legal advice concerning potential litigation relating to the subject matter of the communications; that the communications concerned matters within the scope of the employees' corporate duties; and that the employees were aware that the communications were for the purpose of rendering legal advice for the corporation. . . . The Supreme Court's functional approach in *Upjohn* thus looked to whether the communications at issue were by the Upjohn agents who possessed relevant information that would enable Upjohn's attorney to render sound legal advice.

In *In re Bieter Co.*, the Eighth Circuit applied these principles to a claim of attorney-client privilege with respect to communications with a consultant who had been retained by a real estate development company, finding that the consultant's confidential communications to the company's attorneys were protected by the attorney-client privilege. The court held that in determining whether a corporation's communications were protected by the attorney-client privilege, there was no reason to distinguish between persons on the corporation's payroll and the consultant.

In *Bieter*, a real estate partnership had hired a consultant to assist in a real estate development. The venture failed and the real estate partnership commenced litigation. Because the consultant was involved in the subject matter of the litigation arising from the failed real estate venture, the court in *Bieter* determined that the consultant was "precisely the sort of person with whom a lawyer would wish to confer confidentially in order to understand [the real estate firm's] reasons for seeking representation." In sum, the Eighth Circuit asked whether the consultant's relationship to the company was one of the kind that justified application of the attorney-client privilege and found that, because the consultant was involved in the activities which were the subject matter of the ensuing litigation and because the consultant possessed the information required by the attorney for informed advice, the consultant's confidential communications to counsel were protected.

The Court finds persuasive the reasoning of the *Bieter* court. *Upjohn* teaches that the attorney-client privilege "exists to protect not only the giving of professional advice to those who can act on it but also the giving of information to the lawyer to enable him to give sound and informed advice." The Supreme Court in *Upjohn* looked to whether the corporation's agents possess the information needed by the corporation's attorneys in order to render informed legal advice. In applying the principles set forth by the Supreme Court in *Upjohn*, there is no reason to distinguish between a person on the corporation's payroll and a consultant hired by the corporation if each acts for the corporation and possess the information needed by attorneys in rendering legal advice. These principles, although articulated in the context of corporate employee relationships, inform this Court's analysis of RLM's ability to assert the attorney-client privilege with respect to communications with Sumitomo's inside and outside counsel, and Sumitomo's disclosure of privileged information to RLM. . . .

RLM was, essentially, incorporated into Sumitomo's staff to perform a corporate function that was necessary in the context of the government investigation, actual and anticipated private litigation, and heavy press scrutiny obtaining at the time. Sumitomo retained RLM to deal with public relations problems following the exposure of the copper trading scandal. Sumitomo's internal resources were insufficient to cover the task. RLM's public relations duties included preparing statements for public release and internal documents designed to inform Sumitomo employees about what could and could not be said about the scandal. RLM possessed authority to make decisions on behalf of Sumitomo concerning its public relations strategy. The legal ramifications and potential adverse use of such communications were material factors in the development of the communications. In formulating communications on Sumitomo's behalf, RLM sought advice from Sumitomo's counsel and was privy to advice concerning the scandal and attendant litigation.

In addition, RLM's communications concerned matters within the scope of RLM's duties for Sumitomo, and RLM employees were aware that the communications were for the purpose of obtaining legal advice from Paul

Weiss and/or Sumitomo's in house attorneys. Under the principles set out in *Upjohn*, RLM's independent contractor status provides no basis for excluding RLM's communications with Sumitomo's counsel from the protection of the attorney-client privilege.

The Court therefore finds that, for purposes of the attorney-client privilege, RLM can fairly be equated with . . . Sumitomo for purposes of analyzing the availability of the attorney-client privilege to protect communications to which RLM was a party concerning its scandal-related duties. . . .

The Court finds unpersuasive Plaintiffs' argument that third-party consultants come within the scope of the privilege only when acting as conduits or facilitators of attorney-client communications. The case law cited by Plaintiffs arises in a factual context that is readily distinguishable from this case. *See, e.g., United States v. Kovel* (privilege applies to communications of a third-party made at the request of an attorney or the client where the purpose of the communication was to put in usable form information obtained from the client). . . . For example, in *United States v. Ackert* . . ., a recent case following the reasoning in *Kovel* and relied upon by Plaintiffs, the court determined that communications between an investment banker and an attorney made for the purpose of providing information to the attorney so that he could better advise his client were not privileged. In so finding, the court held that the communications with the third-party investment banker did not serve to facilitate or translate communications with the attorney's client. Moreover, in *Ackert*, the investment banker was neither the attorney's client nor an agent of the client.

By contrast, in this case RLM is the functional equivalent of a Sumitomo employee. Accordingly, the analysis set forth in *Kovel* and its progeny concerning whether the privilege applies to communications made to third parties for the purpose of facilitating attorney-client communications is inapposite.[10]

NOTES AND QUESTIONS

1. *Pearlstein* illustrates the "third party as agent" test for applying the privilege to representatives of either the client or the attorney: *Copper Market* illustrates the "functional equivalents" test, which is limited

---

10. [Fn. 4 in Original] By letter dated January 10, 2001, Plaintiffs asserted that *Calvin Klein Trademark Trust v. Wachner, et al* . . . further supports their position. That case has superficial similarities to the instant matter in that it concerns whether documents and testimony from a public relations company (RLM in that case also) were entitled to protection. *Calvin Klein* differs, however, from this case in that in *Calvin Klein*, RLM was hired by the client's attorneys to assist them in their representation of the plaintiff and there was no suggestion that RLM performed business functions for the client or entered into communications with counsel for that purpose. Thus, the court's analysis focused on whether RLM served the "translator" function discussed in *Kovel*. As explained herein, RLM was retained by Sumitomo and was the functional equivalent of a Sumitomo employee.

A. Attorney-Client Privilege   **299**

to representatives of the client.[11] *Copper Market* also explicitly distinguishes between the two tests, as they have been applied in the Second Circuit.

2. The "third party as agent" test derives from the Second Circuit's opinion in United States v. Kovel,[12] which is discussed in *Copper Market*. There the court applied the attorney-client privilege to an accountant employed by a law firm to assist the law firm in understanding the tax document supplied by the client to the law firm. The court analogized the accountant to an interpreter translating a client speaking in a foreign language. Some courts, like the *Ackert* court, have narrowly confined *Kovel* to a translator-like function, where a nonlawyer assists counsel to understand the client's own communications to the attorney.[13] Other courts have more broadly applied *Kovel* to include "third parties who provide services that merely *facilitate* the attorney's ability to render legal advice."[14] Did the magistrate judge in *Pearlstein* take a narrow or broad approach in finding that JP Morgan's presence and participation did not waive BlackBerry's attorney-client privilege? How did she distinguish the court's earlier finding that the presence of BlackBerry's public relations firm waived the privilege for communications that would otherwise have been protected? Could BlackBerry have avoided waiver of the privilege if it had restructured its relationship with the public relations firm in a manner more like its relationship with JP Morgan?

3. What does it mean to say that a third-party independent contractor functions as the equivalent of a company employee? The length of the association is apparently not a critical factor because RLM, the "crisis management" public relations firm in *Copper Market*, was not retained for an indefinite or extended time period, but only for the limited purpose of addressing public relations issues arising in a particular high-profile lawsuit. Could the company in *Ackert* have taken advantage of the "functional equivalents" test by arguing its applicability there? What about the public relations firm in *Pearlstein*? Not all jurisdictions have adopted the "functional equivalents" test, citing both the uncertainty of who is covered and concern for the expansion of the scope of the corporate privilege.[15]

---

11. *See generally* Michele DeStefano Beardslee, The Corporate Attorney-Client Privilege: Third-Rate Doctrine for Third-Party Consultants, 62 SMU L. Rev. 727 (2009).

12. 296 F.2d 918 (2d Cir. 1961).

13. In *Ackert*, the court concluded that "the privilege protects communications between a client and an attorney, not communications that prove important to an attorney's legal advice to a client." United States v. Ackert, 169 F.3d 136, 139 (2d Cir. 1999).

14. Beardslee, *supra* n. 11 at 747. One of the cases Beardslee cites is United States v. Alvarez, 519 F.2d 1036, 1046 (3d Cir. 1975), in which the court applied the attorney-client privilege to a criminal defendant's communications with a psychiatrist hired by the defendant's lawyer to assist the lawyer in developing an insanity defense.

15. *See, e.g.*, BSP Software, LLC v. Motio, Inc., 2013 WL 3456870 (N.D. Ill. 2013).

3. Application of Privilege After Changes in Entity Control

In Commodity Futures Trading Comm'n v. Weintraub, 471 U.S. 343 (1985), the U.S. Supreme Court held that a trustee in bankruptcy holds the right to waive the privilege on behalf of the entity. In doing so, it analogized the appointment of a bankruptcy trustee to the more common shifts of management that occur as a result of changes in the composition of the board or executive officers:

> [W]hen control of a corporation passes to new management, the authority to assert and waive the corporation's attorney-client privilege passes as well. New managers installed as a result of a takeover, merger, loss of confidence by shareholders, or simply normal succession, may waive the attorney-client privilege with respect to communications made by former officers and directors. Displaced managers may not assert the privilege over the wishes of current managers, even as to statements that the former might have made to counsel concerning matters within the scope of their corporate duties.

Id. at 349. Under the entity theory of client identity, this position makes perfect sense because a former manager would have previously had control of the privilege only as a result of the manager's role as a corporate representative; having left the corporation, or assumed a nonmanagement role, the former manager no longer has the right to act on the entity's behalf, at least with respect to asserting or waiving the privilege.

A more complicated situation arises with respect to communications between management and the entity's lawyer pertaining specifically to the negotiations leading to a transfer of control of an entity, such as a merger. Courts in New York and Delaware have taken different approaches to this question, as illustrated in the following two cases.

Tekni-Plex, Inc. v. Meyner and Landis
674 N.E.2d 663 (N.Y. 1996)

KAYE, Chief Judge.

Central to this appeal, involving a dispute over a corporate acquisition, are two questions. *First,* can long-time counsel for the seller company and its sole shareholder continue to represent the shareholder in the dispute with the buyer? And *second,* who controls the attorney-client privilege as to pre-merger communications? We conclude that counsel should step aside, and that the buyer controls the privilege as to some, but not all, of the pre-merger communications.

A. FACTS

Tekni-Plex, Inc., incorporated under the laws of Delaware in 1967, manufactured and packaged products for the pharmaceutical and other industries. For nearly 20 years, from 1967 to 1986, Tekni-Plex had 18 shareholders and was managed by a five-member Board of Directors. Appellant Tom Y.C. Tang was both a director and a shareholder of the company.

In 1986, Tang became the sole shareholder of Tekni-Plex. From that time until the corporation's sale in 1994, Tang was also the president, chief executive officer and sole director of Tekni-Plex.

Appellant Meyner and Landis (M&L), a New Jersey law firm, was first retained as Tekni-Plex counsel in 1971. During the ensuing 23 years, M&L represented Tekni-Plex on various legal matters, including environmental compliance. As the record indicates, M&L in the mid-1980's assisted Tekni-Plex in securing an environmental permit for the operation of a laminator machine at its Somerville, New Jersey, plant. Similarly, the law firm apparently assisted the company in an investigation by the New Jersey Department of Environmental Protection into Tekni-Plex's compliance with environmental laws. Additionally, during this period M&L represented Tang individually on several personal matters.

In March 1994, Tang and Tekni-Plex entered into an Agreement and Plan of Merger (the Merger Agreement) with TP Acquisition Company (Acquisition), whereby Tang sold the company to Acquisition for $43 million. M&L represented both Tekni-Plex and Tang personally. The two instant lawsuits grow out of that transaction.

Acquisition was a shell corporation created by the purchasers solely for the acquisition of Tekni-Plex. Under the Merger Agreement, Tekni-Plex merged into Acquisition, with Acquisition the surviving corporation, and Tekni-Plex ceased its separate existence. Tekni-Plex conveyed to Acquisition all of its tangible and intangible assets, rights and liabilities. Acquisition in return paid Tang the purchase price "in complete liquidation of Tekni-Plex" and all of Tang's shares in Tekni-Plex—the only shares outstanding—were cancelled.

The Merger Agreement contained representations and warranties by Tang concerning environmental matters, including that Tekni-Plex was in full compliance with all applicable environmental laws and possessed all requisite environmental permits. It further provided for indemnifications of Acquisition by Tang for any losses incurred by Acquisition as the result of misrepresentation or breach of warranty by either Tang or Tekni-Plex. Acquisition, in turn, agreed to indemnify Tang and Tekni-Plex for any similar losses suffered by them.

Following the transaction, Acquisition changed its name to "Tekni-Plex, Inc." (new Tekni-Plex). In June 1994, new Tekni-Plex commenced an arbitration against Tang, alleging breach of representations and warranties contained in the Merger Agreement regarding the former Tekni-Plex's (old Tekni-Plex) compliance with environmental law.

Among other things, new Tekni-Plex claimed that Tang falsely represented that a laminator machine at the Somerville facility did not emit volatile organic compounds (VOCs). New management, however, allegedly learned that the machine did indeed emit VOCs into the air. . . . New Tekni-Plex also contended that Tang and old Tekni-Plex had taken steps to conceal from Acquisition the emission of VOCs at the Somerville facility.

Tang retained M&L to represent him in the arbitration. New Tekni-Plex moved to disqualify the law firm from representing Tang, but the arbitrator concluded that he lacked authority to rule on the motion. [New Tekni-Plex went to the N.Y. Supreme Court, a trial court, for an order disqualifying M&L. The court held that M&L should be disqualified from representing Tang in the arbitration and further enjoined M&L from disclosing to Tang any information obtained from old Tekni-Plex and to return to new Tekni-Plex all of its files concerning its prior representation of old Tekni-Plex. The Appellate Division affirmed.]

We agree with the courts below that, in the circumstances presented, M&L should be disqualified from representing Tang in the arbitration. As for confidential communications between old Tekni-Plex and M&L generally during the law firm's prior representation of the corporation on environmental compliance matters, authority to assert the attorney-client privilege passed to the corporation's successor management. Moreover, because the record fails to establish that M&L also represented Tang individually on these matters, the exception to the privilege for co-clients who subsequently become adversaries in litigation is inapplicable. Thus, the Appellate Division correctly concluded that M&L should be enjoined from disclosing the substance of these communications to Tang and directed the law firm to return the files relating to this representation to new Tekni-Plex.

New Tekni-Plex, however, does not control the attorney-client privilege with regard to discrete communications made by either old Tekni-Plex or Tang individually to M&L concerning the acquisition — a time when old Tekni-Plex and Tang were joined in an adversarial relationship to Acquisition. Consequently, new Tekni-Plex cannot assert the privilege in order to prevent M&L from disclosing the contents of such communications to Tang. Nor is new Tekni-Plex entitled to the law firm's confidential communications concerning its representation of old Tekni-Plex with regard to the acquisition.

B. The Applicable Ethics Principles

Attorneys owe fiduciary duties of both confidentiality and loyalty to their clients. The Code of Professional Responsibility thus imposes a continuing obligation on attorneys to protect their clients' confidences and secrets. . . .

In accordance with these duties, the Code precludes attorneys from representing interests adverse to a former client on matters substantially related to the prior representation. . . . Under [the New York equivalent to MR 1.9(a)], a party seeking disqualification of its adversary's lawyer must prove: (1) the existence of a prior attorney-client relationship between the moving party and opposing counsel, (2) that the matters involved in both representations are substantially related, and (3) that the interests of the present client and former client are materially adverse. Satisfaction of these three criteria by the moving party gives rise to an irrebuttable presumption of disqualification. . . .

C. Disqualification of Counsel

New Tekni-Plex, as the party seeking M&L's disqualification, thus has the burden of satisfying the three-pronged test for disqualification by establishing that (1) it assumed the role of M&L's "former client," (2) the matters involved in both representations are substantially related, and (3) the interests of M&L's present client Tang are materially adverse to the interests of the former client. We next consider each of these elements.

1. Is New Tekni-Plex a "Former Client" of M&L? It is undisputed that M&L represented old Tekni-Plex for over 20 years on a variety of legal matters. As counsel to the corporation, the law firm's duties of confidentiality and loyalty ran to old Tekni-Plex on these matters. Concomitantly, the attorney-client privilege attached to any confidential communications that took place between M&L and Tekni-Plex corporate actors in the course of this representation. The power to assert or waive the privilege, moreover, belonged to the management of old Tekni-Plex, to be exercised by its officers and directors.

Appellants (Tang and M&L) argue that the purchase of old Tekni-Plex by Acquisition did not transfer the corporation's attorney-client relationship to the newly formed entity. According to appellants, the transaction effected nothing more than a transfer of assets, with old Tekni-Plex expiring upon the merger, there being no "former client" still in existence. In support of this contention, appellants point out that, under the Merger Agreement, Acquisition was designated the surviving corporation, old Tekni-Plex explicitly ceased to exist and all of the outstanding shares of stock in old Tekni-Plex were liquidated. They further note that, for tax purposes, the transaction was deemed a sale of assets.

When ownership of a corporation changes hands, whether the attorney-client relationship transfers as well to the new owners turns on the practical consequences rather than the formalities of the particular transaction. [The U.S. Supreme Court decision in Commodity Futures Trading Comm'n. v. Weintraub] establishes that, where efforts are made to run the pre-existing business entity and manage its affairs, successor management stands in the shoes of prior management and controls the attorney-client privilege with respect to matters concerning the company's operations. It follows that, under such circumstances, the prior attorney-client relationship continues with the newly formed entity.

By contrast, the mere transfer of assets with no attempt to continue the pre-existing operation generally does not transfer the attorney-client relationship. Thus in [a federal district court case], the court held that the FDIC, which had purchased the assets of a bank and was appointed receiver for the purpose of liquidation, did not assume the role of former client to the bank's counsel. In denying the FDIC's motion to disqualify the bank's prior attorney from representing the bank's former officers against the FDIC, the court explained that, unlike *Weintraub*, in the case before it "[t]here [was] no thought or effort to reconstitute the entity or to run it at all."

Here, appellants emphasize that old Tekni-Plex merged into Acquisition and ceased to exist as a separate legal entity. That Acquisition, rather than old Tekni-Plex, was designated the surviving corporation, however, is not dispositive. Acquisition was a mere shell corporation, created solely for the purpose of acquiring old Tekni-Plex. Following the merger, the business of old Tekni-Plex remained unchanged, with the same products, clients, suppliers and non-managerial personnel. Indeed, under the Merger Agreement, new Tekni-Plex possessed all of the rights, privileges, liabilities and obligations of old Tekni-Plex, in addition to its assets. Certainly, new Tekni-Plex is entitled to access to any relevant pre-merger legal advice rendered to old Tekni-Plex that it might need to defend against those liabilities or pursue any of these rights.

As a practical matter, then, old Tekni-Plex did not die. To the contrary, the business operations of old Tekni-Plex continued under the new managers. Consequently, control of the attorney-client privilege with respect to any confidential communications between M&L and corporate actors of old Tekni-Plex concerning these operations passed to the management of new Tekni-Plex. An attorney-client relationship between M&L and new Tekni-Plex necessarily exists.

Thus, the first of the three prongs for disqualification is established: new Tekni-Plex is a "former client" of M&L.

2. Is There a Substantial Relationship Between the Current and Former Representations? M&L previously assisted old Tekni-Plex on at least two matters that are substantially related to its current representation of Tang in the arbitration. First, the record indicates that M&L represented old Tekni-Plex during negotiation of the Merger Agreement. That Agreement contains representations and warranties that are the subject of the arbitration.

Second, the record evidences that M&L counseled old Tekni-Plex concerning environmental compliance and assisted the company in obtaining the permit for the laminator machine at the Somerville facility. The alleged misrepresentations made by old Tekni-Plex and Tang relate to that permit and the corporation's compliance with environmental laws.

There is thus a substantial relationship between the current and former representations.

3. Are the Interests of M&L's Present Client Materially Adverse to the Interests of Its Former Client? The arbitration claim pits Acquisition's interest as the purchaser against Tang's interest as the selling shareholder. Furthermore, the Merger Agreement provides that Tang is responsible for indemnifying Acquisition for any misrepresentation or breach of warranty made by either Tang or old Tekni-Plex. Plainly the parties contemplated a unity of interest between old Tekni-Plex and Tang should a dispute arise between the buyer and seller regarding the representations and warranties. Thus, to the extent the arbitration relates to the merger negotiations—as opposed to corporate operations—Tang and old Tekni-Plex remain on the same side of the table. The interest of M&L's former client old Tekni-Plex is aligned with the interest of the law firm's present client Tang—both in opposition to the buyer. . . .

The dispute here, however, . . . goes beyond the merger negotiations. It also involves issues relating to the law firm's longstanding representation of the acquired corporation on matters arising out of the company's business operations—namely, M&L's separate representation of old Tekni-Plex prior to the merger on environmental compliance matters. Any environmental violations will negatively affect not only the purchasers, but also the business interests of the merged corporation. In this regard, the interests of M&L's current client Tang are adverse to the interests that new Tekni-Plex assumed from old Tekni-Plex.

Indeed, M&L's earlier representation of old Tekni-Plex provided the firm with access to confidential information conveyed by old Tekni-Plex concerning the very environmental compliance matters at issue in the arbitration. M&L's duty of confidentiality with respect to these communications passed to new Tekni-Plex; yet its current representation of Tang creates the potential for the law firm to use these confidences against new Tekni-Plex in the arbitration.

Under the circumstances, the appearance of impropriety is manifest and the potential conflict of interest apparent. M&L should therefore be disqualified from representing Tang in the arbitration.

D. CONFIDENTIAL COMMUNICATIONS

As a final matter, we must determine whether M&L was properly enjoined from revealing to Tang any confidential communications obtained from old Tekni-Plex and whether new Tekni-Plex won the confidences created during the law firm's prior representation of old Tekni-Plex. For analytical purposes, the attorney-client communications must be separated into two categories: general business communications and those relating to the merger negotiations.

1. General Business Communications. As explained above, the management of new Tekni-Plex continues the business operations of the pre-merger entity. Control of the attorney-client privilege with regard to confidential communications arising out of those operations—including any pre-merger communications between old Tekni-Plex and M&L relating to the company's environmental compliance—thus passed to the management of new Tekni-Plex. As a result, new Tekni-Plex now has the authority to assert the attorney-client privilege to preclude M&L from disclosing the contents of these confidential communications to Tang. Likewise, ownership of the law firm's files regarding its pre-merger representation of old Tekni-Plex on environmental compliance matters passed to the management of new Tekni-Plex. This conclusion comports with new Tekni-Plex's right to invoke the pre-merger attorney-client relationship should it have to prosecute or defend against third-party suits involving the assets, rights or liabilities that it assumed from old Tekni-Plex.

Appellants urge that because Tang and old Tekni-Plex were co-clients of M&L, none of the communications made by corporate actors to the law firm are confidential from Tang. Generally, where the same lawyer jointly represents two clients with respect to the same matter, the clients have no expectation that their confidences concerning the joint matter will remain secret from each other, and those confidential communications are not within the privilege in subsequent adverse proceedings between the co-clients. While M&L jointly represented Tang and old Tekni-Plex during the acquisition, with respect to the environmental compliance matters the record before us establishes only M&L's representation of the corporation.

We note that some courts have held that, in the case of a close corporation, corporate representation may be individual representation as well. Here, the record indicates that at least some of M&L's representation of old Tekni-Plex on the environmental matters at issue took place before Tang became the corporation's sole shareholder and manager. Whether corporate counsel also functioned as Tang's individual attorney on the environmental matters involved factual questions not addressed by the trial court or Appellate Division. . . .

2. Communications Relating to the Merger Negotiations. As to the other category of attorney-client communications between old Tekni-Plex and M&L—those relating to the merger transaction—new Tekni-Plex did not succeed to old Tekni-Plex's right to control the attorney-client privilege. New Tekni-Plex's misrepresentation and breach of warranty claims do not derive from the rights it inherited from old Tekni-Plex but from the rights retained by the buyer, Acquisition, with respect to the transaction. Under the Merger Agreement, moreover, the rights of old Tekni-Plex with regard to disputes arising from the merger transaction remain independent from—and, indeed, adverse to—the rights of the buyer. During this dispute stemming from the merger transaction, then, new Tekni-Plex cannot both pursue the rights of the buyer (Acquisition) and simultaneously assume the attorney-client rights that the buyer's adversary (old Tekni-Plex) retained regarding the transaction.

This conclusion is especially compelling here, where at the time of the acquisition the seller corporation was solely owned and managed by one individual, Tang. "As corporate stock ownership is concentrated into fewer and fewer hands, the distinction between corporate entity and shareholders begins to blur" and "[i]n the case of a sole owner corporation, they may merge." To allow new Tekni-Plex access to the confidences conveyed by the seller company to its counsel during the negotiations would, in the circumstances presented, be the equivalent of turning over to the buyer all of the privileged communications of the seller concerning the very transaction at issue. The parties here, moreover, recognized the community between the selling shareholder and his corporation and expressly provided that it be preserved in any subsequent dispute regarding the acquisition.

Indeed, to grant new Tekni-Plex control over the attorney-client privilege as to communications concerning the merger transaction would thwart, rather than promote, the purposes underlying the privilege. The attorney-client privilege encourages "full and frank communication between attorneys and their clients and thereby promote[s] broader interests in the observance of law and administration of justice." Where the parties to a corporate acquisition agree that in any subsequent dispute arising out of the transaction the interests of the buyer will be pitted against the interests of the sold corporation, corporate actors should not have to worry that their privileged communications with counsel concerning the negotiations might be available to the buyer for use against the sold corporation in any ensuing litigation. Such concern would significantly chill attorney-client communication during the transaction.

Thus, while generally "parties who negotiate a corporate acquisition should expect that the privilege of the acquired corporation would be incidents of the sale," the agreement between the parties here contemplated that, in any dispute arising from the merger transaction, the rights of the acquired corporation, old Tekni-Plex, relating to the transaction would remain independent from and adverse to the rights of new Tekni-Plex.

In light of the facts of this particular transaction and the structure of the underlying agreement, new Tekni-Plex is without authority to assert the attorney-client privilege to preclude M&L from revealing to Tang the contents of communications conveyed by old Tekni-Plex concerning the merger transaction. Similarly, new Tekni-Plex does not control M&L's files relating to its prior representation of old Tekni-Plex during the acquisition. Of course, nothing in our decision today prevents new Tekni-Plex from obtaining through the normal course of discovery any non-confidential documents, or confidential documents for which the privilege has been waived, to which it is entitled.

Great Hill Equity Partners IV, LP v. SIG Growth Equity Fund I, LLLP
80 A.3d 155 (Del. Ch. 2013)

STRINE, Chancellor.

The plaintiffs, Great Hill Equity Partners IV, LP, Great Hill Investors LLC, Freemont Holdco, Inc., and BlueSnap, Inc. (for clarity, collectively the "Buyer"), have filed this suit alleging that the defendants, former shareholders and representatives of Plimus, Inc. (for clarity, collectively the "Seller"), fraudulently induced the Buyer to acquire Plimus, Inc. ("Plimus") in September 2011. Plimus was the surviving corporation in the merger.

After the Buyer brought this suit in September 2012—a full year after the merger—it notified the Seller that among the files on the Plimus computer systems that the Buyer acquired in the merger, it had discovered certain communications between the Seller and Plimus's then-legal counsel at Perkins Coie regarding the transaction. During that year, the Seller had done nothing to get these computer records back, and there is no evidence that the seller took any steps to segregate these communications before the merger or excise them from the Plimus computer systems, the control over which was passing to the Buyer in the merger. It is also undisputed that the merger agreement lacked any provision excluding pre-merger attorney-client communications from the assets of Plimus that were transferred to the Buyer as a matter of law in the merger, and the merger was intended to have the effects set forth in the Delaware General Corporation Law ("DGCL"). Nonetheless, when the Seller was notified that the Buyer had found pre-merger communications on the Plimus computer system, the Seller asserted the attorney-client privilege that belonged to Plimus for communications regarding the negotiation of the merger agreement. Before the court is a motion by the Buyer seeking to resolve this privilege dispute and determine, among other things, that the surviving corporation owns and controls any pre-merger privilege of Plimus or, alternatively, that the Seller has waived any privilege otherwise attaching to these pre-merger communications.

The question before the court is thus an issue of statutory interpretation in the first instance. Section 259 of the DGCL provides that following a merger, "all property, rights, privileges, powers and franchises, and all and every other interest shall be thereafter as effectually the property of the surviving or resulting corporation. . . . " Nonetheless, the Seller contends that the statutory term "all . . . privileges" does not include the attorney-client privilege, and claims that the Seller still retains control over that particular subset of Plimus's privileges, or, as shall be seen, at least the portion of that subset consisting of attorney-client communications regarding the merger negotiations.

At oral argument, the Seller suggested without citation that the General Assembly actually intended the "privilege" referred to in § 259 of the DGCL to include only certain property rights, and that it did not extend to privileges established by a rule of evidence. But, when asked, the Seller was not able to cite any legislative history that supported its narrow reading of the statute, and the court has not been able to find any evidence for its suggested interpretation in the leading treatises. Most importantly, the Seller's reading is not a plausible interpretation of the plain statutory language. That language uses the broadest possible terms to make sure that "all" assets of any kind belong to the surviving corporation after a merger. The Seller's attempt to interpret the word "privileges" to mean "property rights" ignores the reality that the word "property" is already specifically used in the statute, as is the term "rights"—and then these terms are expanded still further to include "all and every other interest." The definition of "all" is well known, and means "the whole amount, quantity, or extent of." There is a presumption that the General Assembly carefully chose particular language when writing a statute, and this court will not construe the statute to render that language mere surplusage if another interpretation is reasonably possible. The term "privilege" is commonly defined as "a right or immunity granted as a peculiar benefit, advantage, or favor," and one of the most obvious examples is the attorney-client privilege. To indulge the Seller's argument would conflict with the only reasonable interpretation of the statute, which is that *all* means *all* as to the enumerated categories, and that this includes *all* privileges, including the attorney-client privilege.

In the face of the statutory language, the Seller cites to two cases in support of its argument, which it claims stand for the proposition that the former stockholders of a selling corporation retain the selling corporation's privileges as to any attorney-client communications regarding the negotiation of the merger. In particular, the Seller relies on a decision of the New York Court of Appeals, *Tekni-Plex, Inc. v. Meyner & Landis*, which dissected the privileges belonging to a Delaware corporation that was sold in a merger into two categories, and held that only one category, *i.e., less than all*, passed to the surviving corporation in the merger. *Tekni-Plex* held that the privilege over attorney-client communications regarding general business operations did pass to the surviving corporation in the merger. But then the Court of Appeals innovated and, without citing § 259 of the DGCL, concluded that the pre-merger attorney-client communications regarding the merger negotiations did not pass to the surviving corporation for policy reasons related to its analysis of New York attorney-client privilege law. The Seller also cites *Postorivo v. AG Paintball Holdings, Inc.*, a decision of this court that applied *Tekni-Plex*. But in *Postorivo*, the court did not take a stand on whether *Tekni-Plex* would be correct under Delaware law, because it was not necessary to do so under the facts of that case. There, the court was applying New York law to an asset purchase agreement that excluded certain assets, rather than a merger that included all assets, and the parties had agreed that under the specific contractual terms of their transaction, the seller retained the attorney-client privilege over communications relating to the negotiation of the transaction. Thus, as was the case in *Tekni-Plex*, *Postorivo* did not even cite § 259 of the DGCL.

The Buyer answers the Seller's arguments about these cases with a dispositive response: it points out that the General Assembly's statutory determination leaves no room for judicial improvisation. The Buyer contends that under the plain terms of § 259 of the DGCL, the attorney-client privilege — like all other privileges — passes to the surviving corporation in the merger as a matter of law. Thus, the Buyer argues, this court must enforce the statute. The court agrees. If the General Assembly had intended to exclude the attorney-client privilege, it could easily have said so. Instead, the statute uses the broadest possible language to set a clear and unambiguous default rule: *all privileges* of the constituent corporations pass to the surviving corporation in a merger. Tellingly, the Seller admits that the attorney-client privilege has transferred to the surviving corporation for at least some purposes, and the Seller conceded at oral argument that the surviving corporation would, in fact, be able to access and use these same documents if it was necessary to defend itself against a third party. But this concession means that the seller, like the Court of Appeals in *Tekni-Plex*, is not allowing the surviving corporation to receive "all" of the "privileges" of Plimus in the merger, but only the subset that the judiciary has deemed acceptable to transfer. Thus, "all . . . privileges" in §259 of the DGCL would become "all . . . privileges, minus judicially-created exceptions." Whatever the case may be in other states, members of the Delaware judiciary have no authority to invent a judicially-created exception to the plain words "all . . . privileges" and usurp the General Assembly's statutory authority.

The Seller claims that giving effect to § 259 of the DGCL will create serious public policy issues. But, as has long been recognized by the Delaware Courts, when the General Assembly has addressed an issue within its authority with clarity, there is no policy gap for the court to fill. If a valid statute is not ambiguous, the court will apply the plain meaning of the statutory language to the facts before it. . . .

Of course, parties in commerce can — and have — negotiated special contractual agreements to protect themselves and prevent certain aspects of the privilege from transferring to the surviving corporation in the merger. The Buyer submitted several excerpts from private company merger transactions that contained provisions excluding pre-merger attorney-client communications regarding the negotiation of the transaction from the assets to be transferred to the surviving corporation and explicitly acknowledging that the attorney-client privilege for those documents would belong solely to the seller after the merger. Furthermore, one of the cases cited by the Seller demonstrates that parties already know how to protect themselves from this situation. In *Postorivo*, the transactional agreements specifically retained the attorney-client privilege for communications regarding the negotiation of the transaction, so that particular element of the privilege did not pass to the surviving corporation as an incident of the sale. The question in that case, rather, was whether a selling party that *had* contractually negotiated to retain the privilege waived the rights it had preserved by contract through its failure to take steps to ensure that the privileged information did not actually pass into the possession of the buyer.

Notably, in the immediate wake of *Postorivo* and *Tekni-Plex* — and before the parties began negotiating this transaction — several articles were written encouraging practitioners to take privilege issues into account when negotiating a merger agreement. . . . Thus, the answer to any parties worried about facing this predicament in the future is to use their contractual freedom in the manner shown in prior deals to exclude from the transferred assets the attorney-client communications they wish to retain as their own. Here, by contrast, the Seller did not carve out from the assets transferred to the surviving corporation any pre-merger attorney-client communications, and this court will not unilaterally read such a carve out into the parties' contract. Absent such an express carve out, the privilege over all pre-merger communications — including those relating to the negotiation of the merger itself — passed to the surviving corporation in the merger, by plain operation of clear Delaware statutory law under § 259 of the DGCL.

NOTES AND QUESTIONS

1. The New York and Delaware courts agreed that when control of an entity is transferred, as in mergers and certain types of other transactions, control of the attorney-privilege is transferred with respect to general communications concerning the business of the entity. The

question then arises as to what sorts of transactions result in a change of control of the entity. If certain discrete assets have been sold, such as a patent, but the selling entity continues to exist and is not controlled by the buyer, then control of the privilege does *not* transfer, even as to communications relating to that asset.[16] When, however, the "practical consequences" of the transaction are the transfer of the entity itself, including its ongoing business, then courts generally agree with the *Tekni-Plex* court that control of the entity (and the privilege) has been transferred, regardless of whether the transaction is labeled a merger or a sale of assets. Some courts have been willing to apply the "practical consequences" approach to the sale of a particular business unit, as when Wells Fargo sold its insurance business, including all of the "assets, information, and goodwill" of such business, although Wells Fargo continued as an ongoing entity with respect to all of its other businesses.[17]

2. The New York and Delaware courts also agreed that parties who are negotiating a "transformational transaction"[18] may provide in the transaction documents that the seller will retain control of the attorney-client privilege with respect to the seller's communications to its lawyer concerning those negotiations. As the Delaware court noted in its opinion, parties to such transactions frequently agree to such a provision, as they have been urged to do by various commentators. Other commentators, however, have argued that control of the privilege should *not* be transferable by contract, but rather should be determined solely by courts in view of the balance of the public interests involved.[19]

3. The New York and Delaware courts apparently disagreed, however, on the question of what the default rule should be with respect to communications concerning the transaction when the parties have failed to address the issue. Ignoring the Delaware statute, the New York court concluded that the purpose of the privilege is best served by permitting the seller to retain control of the privilege for communications concerning the transaction by which control is transferred. Why did the court come to that conclusion? Would the court permit the parties to agree by contract that the *buyer* will obtain control of the privilege for those communications?

---

16. *See, e.g.,* Applied Asphalt Technologies v. Sam B. Corp., 2015 WL 427070 (D. Utah 2016).

17. *See* USI Insurance Services, LLC v. Ryan, 2014 WL 3054278 (N.D. Ind. 2014) (holding that control of the insurance business, including control of the attorney-client privilege, passed to the buyer).

18. *See generally* Grace M. Giesel, Control of the Attorney-Client Privilege After Mergers and Other Transformation Transactions: Should Control of the Privilege Be Alienable by Contract?, 48 Seton Hall L. Rev. 309, 330-37 (2018).

19. *See, e.g., id.* (arguing by analogy to decisions refusing to allow the parties to determine by contract the existence of a common interest privilege and decisions refusing to enforce contractual extension of a statute of limitations prior the accrual of a cause of action).

4. If the New York court had addressed the impact of Section 259 of the DGLC, would it have reached the same result that it did? At least one court has interpreted the result in *Tekni-Plex* to depend on the court's finding that the parties had agreed that the seller would retain control of the privilege and that the *Tekni-Plex* court did not adopt a default rule different than that adopted in Delaware.[20] Are you persuaded by the Delaware court's discussion of the statute? Would either the New York or the Delaware court permit the parties to agree that the seller would retain control of the privilege even as to general communications, such as the communications in *Tekni-Plex* concerning the company's environmental issues at its Somerville plant?

5. What is the significance of the presence or absence of a joint representation of both the entity and a shareholder manager like Tang in *Tekni-Plex*? What would have been the result, for example, if M&L had represented both old Tekni-Plex and Tang with respect to the company's environmental issues? And what would the result have been in *Great Hill* if Perkins & Coie had been representing both the seller and either a sole shareholder or one of the entity's top management personnel during the acquisition negotiations?

B. PROFESSIONAL RULE OF CONFIDENTIALITY

Recall that, unlike the narrow prima facie protection of information under the attorney-client privilege, the professional rule of confidentiality, under Model Rule 1.6, broadly protects all "information relating to the representation of a client."[21] As a result, an entity lawyer has a prima facie duty not to voluntarily disclose not only communications (confidential or otherwise) from any current or former constituent, but also information learned from any other source.

Clearly, the prohibition under Rule 1.6 applies to a lawyer's disclosures outside of the entity. But what about communications within the entity? As noted earlier in connection with the lawyer's duty of communication with an entity client, if a constituent is not involved in decision-making, and has not been designated as someone to whom the lawyer should communicate as an entity representative, then Rule 1.6 generally prohibits the entity lawyer from communicating information relating to the representation to those individuals.[22] Of course, the lawyer may be expressly or impliedly authorized to discuss confidential information with constituents in order to carry out the

---

20. *See* In re Hechinger Investment Company of Delaware, Inc., 285 B.R. 601 (Bankr. D. Del. 2002). For a contrary interpretation of *Tekni-Plex*, *see* Orbit One Communications, Inc. v. Numerex Corp., 255 F.R.D. 98, 105, n.6 (S.D.N.Y. 2008) (concluding that supporting language in transaction agreement "was not central to the court's legal analysis").

21. *See supra* Chapter 4: Privilege and Confidentiality.

22. *See supra* Chapter 9: Who's My Client?

representation, as when the lawyer provides background information to constituents being interviewed as part of an investigation of alleged wrongdoing. *See* MR 1.13, cmt [2]. In addition, as we will discuss in a future chapter, Rule 1.13(b) requires the lawyer to report certain information about corporate wrongdoing "up the ladder," and Rule 1.13(c) permits the lawyer in some circumstances to disclose such information *outside* the organization even when not otherwise authorized by an exception under Rule 1.6.[23]

C. CONTACTING A REPRESENTED ENTITY

In Chapter 8, we discussed Model Rule 4.2, which prohibits a lawyer representing a client from communicating about the subject matter of the representation with a person represented by another lawyer, without that lawyer's consent. Comment [7] of that rule addresses its application to represented entities. As with the attorney-client privilege, the problem is to identify *which* constituents of an entity cannot be contacted without the permission of the entity's lawyer. The following opinion of the State Bar of Wisconsin's Professional Ethics Committee explains the comment, as well as the policy considerations underlying the comment.

Professional Ethics Committee of the State Bar of Wisconsin

Contact With Current and Former Constituents of a Represented Organization
Ethics Opinion E-07-01 (July 1, 2007)

This opinion discusses the extent to which SCR 20:4.2 prohibits contact with current and former constituents of an organization when the organization is represented with respect to a matter. The opinion also discusses the obligations under the Rules of Professional Conduct of lawyers seeking to contact constituents of represented organizations and the obligations of lawyers representing organizations.

SCR 20:4.2 Communication with Person Represented by Counsel reads:

> In representing a client, a lawyer shall not communicate about the subject of the representation with a person the lawyer knows to be represented by another lawyer in the matter, unless the lawyer has the consent of the other lawyer or is authorized to do so by a court order.

As is apparent, the language of the rule itself does not provide explicit guidance with respect to constituents (for example, employees, officers, agents) of a represented organization. Paragraph [7] of the comment to the rule, however, provides as follows:

---

23. *See infra* Chapter 12: Corporate Wrongdoing.

[7] In the case of a represented organization, this Rule prohibits communications with a constituent of the organization who supervises, directs or regularly consults with the organization's lawyer concerning the matter or has the authority to obligate the organization with respect to the matter or whose act or omission in connection with the matter may be imputed to the organization for purpose of civil or criminal liability. Consent of the organization's lawyer is not required for communication with a former constituent. If a constituent of the organization is represented in the matter by his or her own counsel, the consent by that counsel to a communication will be sufficient for purposes of this Rule. Compare Rule 3.4(g). In communicating with a current or former constituent of an organization, a lawyer must not use methods of obtaining evidence that violate the legal rights of the organization. See Rule 4.4.

The comment to SCR 20:4.2 thus provides specific guidance with respect to the question at hand. Before discussing the parameters of allowable contact with current and former constituents of represented organizations, the Professional Ethics Committee believes some background information regarding the history and purpose of SCR 20:4.2 is appropriate. . . .

1. HISTORY AND PURPOSE OF SCR 20:4.2

Wisconsin's current SCR 20:4.2 and comment are identical to ABA Model Rule 4.2 and comment.[24] The ABA Model Rule and its comment were amended in 2002 as part of the ABA's Ethics 2000 revision of the Model Rules of Professional Conduct. Like the current Rule 4.2, the prior Model Rule . . . itself contained no reference to constituents of a represented organization but rather addressed the issue in the comment.

The 2002 amendments to the comment were significant and reflected the ABA's intention to clarify the language and provide better guidance. In particular, the ABA removed language from the comment prohibiting contact with constituents having "managerial responsibility," which had frequently been criticized as "vague and overly broad." Language prohibiting contact with constituents "whose statements may constitute an admission on the part of the organization" also was removed. This is because this language originally was intended to protect those jurisdictions that still maintained the old evidentiary rule that statements by an agent bound the principal, in the sense that when such statements of an agent are admitted into evidence, the principal may not introduce other evidence to contradict the statement. Modern evidence rules, however, while permitting an employee's statement to be admitted as an exception to the hearsay rule, do not bind the employer, who is free to introduce evidence contradicting the employee's statement. Accordingly, that language in the old comment often was misinterpreted to prevent contact with any constituent whose statement may constitute a nonbinding admission. Finally, a sentence was added to the comment to clarify that

---

24. [In fact, the text of the Wisconsin rule differs very slightly from the text of the Model Rule, which approves communications "authorized . . . by *law or* a court order." (Emphasis added.)—ED.]

Rule 4.2 does not prohibit contact with former constituents of an organization, regardless of the position the former constituent once occupied.

Thus, the changes made by the ABA have narrowed the rule's prohibition with respect to constituents of a represented organization. As will be discussed later in this opinion, this is in keeping with the pronounced trend in case law and ethics opinions.

Although often invoked in the context of litigation, SCR 20:4.2 is a disciplinary rule and proscribes conduct that can subject a lawyer to professional discipline. The purpose behind the disciplinary rule is to "contribute to the proper functioning of the legal system by protecting a person who has chosen to be represented by a lawyer in a matter against possible overreaching by other lawyers who are participating in the matter, interference by those lawyers with the client-lawyer relationship and the uncounseled disclosure of information relating to the representation." Put more succinctly, the "[p]urpose of the rule is to protect the attorney-client relationship from intrusion by opposing counsel."

Applying this rule to the representation of an individual is relatively simple. Defining the parameters of the attorney-client relationship with respect to a represented organization proves more difficult. It is clear that when a lawyer represents an organization, the client is the organization itself. It is also clear that an organization acts only through its constituents, some of whom should be afforded the protections of SCR 20:4.2. In determining just which constituents should be protected by SCR 20:4.2, courts have attempted to balance many competing interests. One court described the factors to be balanced as follows:

> Many competing policies must be considered when deciding how to interpret the no-contact rule as applied to organizational clients: protecting the attorney-client relationship from interference, protecting represented parties from overreaching by opposing lawyers; protecting against the inadvertent disclosure of privileged information; balancing on the one hand an organization's need to act through agents and employees, and protecting those employees from overreaching and the organization from the inadvertent disclosure of privileged information, and on the other hand the lack of any such protection afforded an individual, whose friends, relatives, acquaintances and co-workers may generally all be contacted freely; permitting more equitable and affordable access to information pertinent to a legal dispute; promoting the court system's efficiency by allowing investigation before litigation and informal information-gathering during litigation; permitting a plaintiff's attorney sufficient opportunity to adequately investigate a claim before filing a complaint in accordance with Rule 11; and enhancing the court's truth-finding role by permitting contact with potential witnesses in a manner that allows them to speak freely.

In balancing these interests, courts have formulated a variety of tests. On one end of the spectrum is an outright ban on contact with any constituent of a represented organization. The advantage of such a bright-line test is clarity and certainty, but this comes at a high cost; an opposing party might have to resort to filing suit to begin to gather information about the viability of a possible claim, or simply be without the means to informally gather information in transactional or certain administrative proceedings without formal discovery. This involves great expense when compared to informal interviews and clogs the courts with potentially baseless claims. It also gives organizations almost complete control over information in a matter and thus a great advantage over individuals, whose friends, colleagues, and associates are not protected by SCR 20:4.2. . . .

[C]ourts seek to interpret Rule 4.2 to protect those within the organization who act on behalf of an organization in connection with a matter, that is, those who direct and consult with the organization's lawyer or whose act or omission serves as a basis for the matter in question. These decisions also recognize that Rule 4.2 is not meant to protect an organization from the disclosure or discovery of potentially damaging facts. As one court stated, "[p]reventing the disclosure of unfavorable facts merely because they happen to have occurred in the workplace is not a legitimate organizational interest for purposes of applying Rule 4.2." Thus the rule's protection extends to those constituents who may be said to personify the organization as a "client" in a matter, but ordinarily does not extend to constituents of an organization who simply possess relevant facts. . . .

IV. OBLIGATIONS OF LAWYER CONTACTING CURRENT OR FORMER CONSTITUENT NOT COVERED BY SCR 20:4.2

Although SCR 20:4.2 does not prohibit contact with some current and all former constituents of an organization, that does not mean that lawyers contacting such constituents are free from all constraint. Comment [7] to SCR 20:4.2 states, "In communicating with a current or former constituent of an organization, a lawyer must not use methods of obtaining evidence that violate the legal rights of the organization."

SCR 20:4.4(a) provides as follows:

> In representing a client, a lawyer shall not use means that have no substantial purpose other than to embarrass, delay or burden a third person, or use methods of obtaining evidence that violate the legal rights of such a person.

Comment [1] to SCR 20:4.4 provides:

> Responsibility to a client requires a lawyer to subordinate the interest of others to those of the client, but that responsibility does not imply that a lawyer may disregard the rights of third persons. It is impractical to catalogue all such rights, but they include legal restrictions on methods of obtaining evidence from third persons and unwarranted intrusions into privileged relationships, such as the client-lawyer relationship.

Comment [9] to SCR 20:4.2 states: "In the event the person with whom the lawyer communicates is not known to be represented by counsel in the matter, the lawyer's communications are subject to Rule 4.3."

SCR 20:4.3 provides as follows:

> In dealing on behalf of a client with a person who is not represented by counsel, a lawyer shall inform such person of the lawyer's role in the matter. When the lawyer knows or reasonably should know that the unrepresented person

misunderstands the lawyer's role in the matter, the lawyer shall make reasonable efforts to correct the misunderstanding. The lawyer shall not give legal advice to an unrepresented person, other than the advice to secure counsel, if the lawyer or reasonably should know that the interests of such a person are or have a reasonable possibility of being in conflict with the interests of the client.

These two rules thus impose the obligation to inform an unrepresented person of the lawyer's role in the matter and to avoid seeking privileged information. Reported decisions and ethics opinions also have cautioned lawyers seeking to informally contact current and former constituents of represented organizations to observe certain guidelines when making such contacts. Some decisions go beyond these two rule-based proscriptions and set forth other guidelines for lawyers in these circumstances.

One of the purposes of imposing such guidelines is to protect the organization's privileged information. In *Upjohn Co. v. United States*, the U.S. Supreme Court held that attorney-client privilege may attach to communications with any employee of a corporation, not simply high-ranking management. A lawyer is thus forbidden by SCR 20:4.4 from seeking to induce disclosure of information protected by the privilege when contacting any constituent of a represented organization. . . .

In the wake of *Upjohn*, it was argued that the scope of Rule 4.2 should be extended to all constituents who may be in possession of privileged information, but courts and ethics opinions have rejected such an interpretation as overly broad and unnecessary to protect organizations. As one court noted, if a lawyer violates an organization's attorney-client privilege, the court may disqualify him or her from further participation in the case . . . and, under certain circumstances, may exclude improperly obtained evidence or take other appropriate measures to achieve justice and ameliorate the effect of improper conduct. Thus, protections such as protective orders, disqualification motions, and motions for sanctions are available to organizations. . . .

Thus if a constituent who witnessed an act that serves as a basis for a suit against an organization is interviewed about the matter by the organization's lawyer, and is not otherwise protected by SCR 20:4.2, opposing counsel may contact the constituent with respect to factual information about the matter. There are, however, ethical duties placed on lawyers who seek to contact such a constituent. . . .

V. OBLIGATIONS OF LAWYERS REPRESENTING ORGANIZATION

Lawyers representing organizations also have obligations relative to constituents who may be contacted by opposing counsel. These obligations reflect the lawyer's role of representing the organization itself, as opposed to representing the organization's constituents.

1) A lawyer representing an organization may not assert blanket coverage of all current and former constituents of an organization by SCR 20:4.2 unless the lawyer *actually* represents each and every constituent of the organization. . . .

2) Lawyers for organizations may appear on behalf of the organization when a constituent is deposed, but that does not mean that the lawyer represents that constituent as an individual. . . .

3) SCR 20:3.4(f) permits a lawyer representing an organization in a matter to *request* that employees or agents of the client refrain from voluntarily giving relevant information to another party. It is important to note that this rule does not allow a lawyer to forbid constituents from speaking to the other side. That being said, this rule would permit a lawyer for an organization to contact employees and ask that they not speak to the lawyer representing a client adverse to the organization. The lawyer should be careful to choose language that makes plain that such request is not an order. This rule also applies only to current employees. . . .

VI. IN-HOUSE COUNSEL

Finally, the committee wishes to comment on the status of organizations with permanent in-house counsel. The fact in itself that an organization has in-house counsel, or regularly retains outside counsel, does not render the organization represented with respect to a specific matter. "Similarly, retaining counsel for all matters that might arise would not be sufficiently specific to bring the rule into play. In order for the prohibition to apply, the subject matter of the representation needs to have crystallized between the client and the lawyer."

A lawyer does not violate SCR 20:4.2 by contacting in-house counsel for an organization that is represented by outside counsel in a matter. The retention of outside counsel does not normally transform counsel for an organization into a represented constituent and contact with a lawyer does not raise the same policy concerns as contact with a lay person. . . .

NOTES AND QUESTIONS

1. Let's return to the problem involving Paul, who was injured when a truck owned by a department store crashed into his car.[25] Before filing a lawsuit against the corporation that owned the department store, Paul's lawyer would like to informally interview Ed, Sally, and Derek. Assume that each of them is currently employed by the corporation. Which, if any, of the employees may Paul's lawyer contact informally to discuss what they know about the accident? What if one of these constituents is a former employee?

2. How is Comment [7] to Rule 4.2 different from either the control group, subject matter, or *Upjohn* approaches to determining which constituent's communications with the corporation's lawyer are protected by the corporation's attorney-client privilege? Most jurisdictions have

---

25. *See supra* Note 1 following *Upjohn*.

adopted the Ethics 2000 amendments reflected in Comment [7], regardless of which approach the jurisdiction takes to determining the scope of an entity's attorney-client privilege. Why isn't Comment [7] more closely aligned with a jurisdiction's approach to entity privilege, particularly in jurisdictions that adopt the narrow control group test?

3. As for any current or former employee whom Paul's lawyer is permitted to contact informally, what guidelines does the Wisconsin ethics opinion provide that Paul's lawyer should follow in conducting these interviews?

4. Once the corporation's in-house lawyers become aware that Paul's lawyer might attempt to informally contact one or more of the employees whose statements had been obtained, is there anything the corporation's lawyers can do to minimize the risk of Paul's lawyer obtaining information that would be harmful to the corporation? May an in-house lawyer instruct those employees not to voluntarily speak with Paul's lawyer? *See* MR 3.4(f). In addition to the disciplinary rules, the in-house lawyers should also be aware of substantive law, including obstruction of justice statutes.[26]

Review Problems

10-1 A corporation retained a law firm to conduct an investigation into allegations of dumping toxic waste into a city reservoir. A law firm lawyer interviewed a number of employees, including the employee who physically disposed of the toxic waste, that employee's supervisor, under whose direction the employee allegedly acted, and a whistleblowing employee who claims to have observed the dumping. Are these statements protected by the corporation's attorney-client privilege?

10-2 Same facts as above. The law firm reported to the corporation's CEO that the employee who dumped the waste appears to have acted contrary to the supervisor's instructions and therefore advised the CEO to cooperate with the government by identifying the employee as a "rogue" employee who acted contrary to company policy. To do so, the CEO would need to turn over to the government the statements of both the supervisor and the employee, as well as the statement of the whistleblower. Assuming that any or all of the statements are privileged, may the CEO disclose them to the government without first obtaining the consent of either the corporation's board of directors or the individuals who made the statements?

10-3 A company sued a manufacturing corporation for infringing its trademark in a clothes dryer that uses steam to reduce wrinkles. When the company requested that the manufacturer produce communications between

---

26. *See, e.g.,* John K. Villa, Corporate Counsel Guidelines §3:29 (2020) ("[A] corporation in a criminal investigation should not instruct its employees to refuse to talk to federal or state law enforcement officers or prosecutors. Otherwise, the company and any officer who gave such instructions could face obstruction of justice charges.").

its lawyers and its outside advertising agencies relating to the purportedly infringing dryer, the manufacturer claimed that the communications were protected by the attorney-client privilege. The manufacturer claimed that the communications contained a discussion of legal advice provided by the manufacturer's lawyers that was critical for the advertising agencies to understand how the product could be lawfully marketed. It further argued that the advertising agencies were not third parties, but de facto employees of the company. The manufacturer had to approve all marketing materials before they were publicly disseminated. Is the claim of privilege likely to succeed?

10-4 A man was the president and controlling shareholder of a New York corporation ("Corporation") that had one other shareholder. The man retained a law firm to restructure the corporation and sell a percentage of those shares to an unrelated corporate entity ("Entity"). The engagement agreement stated that the law firm was representing only the Corporation, and not the individual shareholders. Nevertheless, the law firm drafted all of the agreements, including agreements signed by the man in his individual capacity, and the man alleges that the law firm also provided legal advice to him regarding his personal liability for the representations and warranties contained in the merger agreement with the unrelated Entity. The unrelated Entity was a Delaware corporation. After the merger, the law firm represented the newly formed entity ("New Entity") which had been organized under Delaware law. The man subsequently demanded that the law firm provide him with all documents relating to the reorganization and merger, so that he could investigate the possibility of suing the law firm and the New Entity[27] for malpractice and fraud, respectively, on behalf of himself and the New York Corporation. The law firm refused, claiming that the documents were privileged and that the privilege was owned by the newly formed entity ("New Entity"). The man filed an action in a New York state court seeking access to the documents. What arguments are available to the man and to the law firm as to who owns the privilege concerning the law firm's representation during the reorganization and merger?

---

27. The New Entity would be liable for the wrongdoing of the old Entity, which no longer has its own corporate existence.

CHAPTER 11

CONFLICTS OF INTEREST IN ENTITY REPRESENTATION

Model Rules 1.7, 1.9, Rule 1.13(g)

You will recall from Chapter 5 that Model Rule 1.7, the general rule governing current client conflicts of interest, identifies two types of conflicts — directly adverse and material limitation. Both types of conflicts can apply to lawyers representing entities. The most common conflicts arise when a lawyer represents both a company and one of its constituents. These are usually *material limitation* conflicts, which are permissible (with the requisite informed consent) so long as the clients' interests are generally aligned; however, if the clients' interests become adversarial, the lawyer may need to withdraw from both representations. *Directly adverse* conflicts arise when a law firm sues a current corporate client; they may also arise when a lawyer represents a client adverse to an affiliate of an entity client. These latter situations are commonly known as "corporate family" conflicts.

A. CURRENT CLIENTS: SIMULTANEOUSLY REPRESENTING AN ENTITY AND A CONSTITUENT

The following opinion illustrates the material limitation conflicts that commonly arise when a lawyer or law firm represents both an entity client and one or more of its individual constituents. The district court opinion reproduced below was reversed on appeal, but not because the appellate court disagreed with the trial court's conclusion that the representation violated California state ethics rules. The trial court relied on rules that predated California's recent adoption of a version of the Model Rules. As you read the case, substitute the Model Rules for the California Rules and see if you reach the same result.

United States v. Nicholas
606 F. Supp.2d 1109 (C.D. Cal. 2009)

ORDER SUPPRESSING PRIVILEGED COMMUNICATIONS

CORMAC J. CARNEY, District Judge.

INTRODUCTION

The California Rules of Professional Conduct protect clients, promote public confidence in the legal profession, and ensure the fair administration of justice. The most fundamental of these rules is a lawyer's duty of undivided loyalty to his client. A lawyer must do everything legally possible to protect a client. A lawyer can never assume a position adverse to the client or disclose client confidences without the client's knowing, intelligent, and voluntary consent in writing. Unfortunately, in this case, a law firm breached its duty of loyalty to a client in several respects.

In May 2006, Irell & Manella LLP ("Irell") undertook three separate, but inextricably related, representations of Broadcom Corporation ("Broadcom") and its Chief Financial Officer, Defendant William J. Ruehle. More specifically, Irell represented Broadcom in connection with the company's internal investigation of its stock option granting practices. At the same time, Irell also represented Mr. Ruehle in connection with two shareholder lawsuits filed against him regarding those same stock option granting practices. Prior to undertaking these representations of clients with adverse interests, Irell failed to obtain Mr. Ruehle's informed written consent.

In June of 2006, Irell lawyers met with Mr. Ruehle at his office to discuss the stock option granting practices at Broadcom. During this meeting, Mr. Ruehle told the Irell lawyers about Broadcom's stock option granting practices and his role in them. Before questioning Mr. Ruehle, however, the Irell lawyers never disclosed to him that they were representing only Broadcom at the meeting, not him individually, and that whatever he said to them could be used against him by Broadcom or disclosed by the company to third parties. Subsequently, Broadcom directed Irell to disclose statements Mr. Ruehle made to the Irell lawyers about Broadcom's stock option granting practices to Broadcom's outside auditors, Ernst & Young, as well as to the Securities Exchange Commission ("SEC") and the United States Attorney's Office (the "Government"). Prior to making these disclosures, Irell never obtained Mr. Ruehle's consent.

The Government now argues that it can use Mr. Ruehle's statements to the Irell lawyers against him at the trial in this criminal case. The Government is mistaken. Mr. Ruehle's statements to the Irell lawyers are privileged attorney-client communications. Mr. Ruehle reasonably believed that the Irell lawyers were meeting with him as his personal lawyers, not just Broadcom's lawyers. Mr. Ruehle had a legitimate expectation that whatever he said to the Irell lawyers would be maintained in confidence. He was never told, nor did he ever contemplate, that his statements to the Irell lawyers would be disclosed to third parties, especially not the Government in connection with criminal charges against him. Irell had no right to disclose Mr. Ruehle's statements, and Irell breached its duty of loyalty when it did so. Accordingly, the Court must suppress all evidence reflecting Mr. Ruehle's statements to the Irell lawyers regarding stock option granting practices at Broadcom.

But the Court has a further obligation in this case. The Court must also ensure the fair administration of justice and promote the public's confidence in the legal profession. By failing to comply with its duties under the Rules of Professional Conduct, Irell compromised these important principles. The Court simply cannot overlook Irell's ethical misconduct in this regard and must refer Irell to the State Bar for appropriate discipline.

BACKGROUND

Both Broadcom and Mr. Ruehle had long-standing relationships with Irell. Beginning in 2002, Irell represented both Broadcom and Mr. Ruehle personally in several securities-related actions ("Warrants Litigation"). Irell represented Mr. Ruehle in a deposition taken in connection with the Warrants Litigation. In the course of this representation, Irell informed Mr. Ruehle in writing of the potential for conflicts inherent in dual representation and obtained Mr. Ruehle's informed written consent to proceed with the representation. The Warrants Litigation concluded at the end of 2005.

In the spring of 2006, after a series of articles related to the stock option granting practices both at Broadcom and other corporations, Broadcom was aware that it might be investigated by the Government or sued on the basis of its stock option granting practices. In mid-May 2006, Broadcom retained Irell to investigate its stock option granting practices on behalf of the corporation. Shortly thereafter, on May 25, 2006, a group of shareholders filed a derivative action against Mr. Ruehle and other current and former officers of Broadcom ("Derivative Action") concerning the corporation's stock option granting practices. On May 26, 2006, an amended complaint was filed in *Jin v. Broadcom Corp., et al* ("Jin Action"), naming Mr. Ruehle personally and asserting substantially similar claims regarding stock option practices at Broadcom. In addition to its representation of Broadcom in connection with the internal investigation, Irell accepted individual representation of Mr. Ruehle in both the Jin Action and the Derivative Action, accepting service on his behalf and appearing as counsel of record until September 2006. . . .

On June 1, 2006, Mr. Heitz and Mr. Lefler met with Mr. Ruehle and interviewed him regarding Broadcom's stock option granting practices. The Irell lawyers did not tell Mr. Ruehle that they were not his lawyers. The Irell lawyers did not suggest that Mr. Ruehle might want to consult with his own lawyer before speaking with him. After their meeting, Mr. Heitz had subsequent conversations with Mr. Ruehle in June 2006 about Broadcom's stock option granting practices and never disclosed to Mr. Ruehle in any of these conversations that his statements to him would be disclosed to third parties.

On June 13, 2006, the SEC commenced its investigation of the stock option granting practices at Broadcom. Throughout June and July, 2006, Mr. Ruehle continued to receive legal advice from Irell. . . .

In August of 2006, at Broadcom's direction, Irell disclosed the substance of Mr. Ruehle's interviews with Mr. Heitz and Mr. Lefler to Broadcom's outside auditors, Ernst & Young. Thereafter, again at Broadcom's direction, Irell disclosed the same information to the SEC and the United States Attorney's Office in connection with their investigations of stock option granting practices at Broadcom. . . . Ruehle did not consent to any of these disclosures.

Mr. Ruehle first learned that the Government intended to use his statements to Irell against him when the FBI Form FD-302 memoranda were produced to him in December 2008 in connection with the Government's criminal case. Mr. Ruehle promptly objected and asserted that his conversations with Irell were privileged communications. . . . The Court held an evidentiary hearing on February 23, 24, and 25, 2009 to determine whether Mr. Ruehle's statements to the Irell lawyers were subject to the attorney-client privilege.

ANALYSIS

A. MR. RUEHLE'S STATEMENTS TO THE IRELL LAWYERS ARE PRIVILEGED ATTORNEY-CLIENT COMMUNICATIONS . . .

There is no serious question in this case that when Mr. Ruehle met with the Irell lawyers on June 1, 2006, Mr. Ruehle reasonably believed that an attorney-client relationship existed, he was communicating with his attorneys in the context of this relationship for the purpose of obtaining legal advice, and that any information he provided to Irell would remain confidential. Mr. Ruehle testified that he understood Irell would be representing him in both the Jin Action and the Derivative Action. Prior to his initial meeting with the Irell lawyers, Mr. Ruehle received an email from Broadcom's General Counsel, Mr. Dull, on which an Irell litigation partner was copied, confirming that Irell would be representing him personally in both litigations. In the days leading up to their June 1, 2006 interview, the Irell lawyers frequently updated Mr. Ruehle on the progress of their investigation of the stock option practices at Broadcom. But more than mere progress reports, Mr. Heitz discussed his strategy for defending the corporation and its directors and summarized the fact-finding that would be necessary to support that strategy. In these emails, which were sent to Mr. Ruehle individually, as opposed to the entire board of directors, Mr. Heitz asked Mr. Ruehle to review and obtain specific information and advised him how this information would be relevant to preparing a defense. The evidence establishes that Mr. Ruehle had a reasonable belief that an attorney-client relationship existed prior to his initial interview with the Irell lawyers on June 1, 2006.

Second, Mr. Ruehle testified that he believed that the interviews were being conducted to gather information in preparation for the litigations and for the purpose of obtaining legal advice. Mr. Ruehle was first asked by the Irell lawyers to schedule a meeting with them in an email that he received 4 minutes after he received an email from Mr. Dull informing Mr. Ruehle that Irell would be representing him personally in the pending litigations. Mr. Ruehle was never advised that he should have another lawyer present at the meeting to represent his interests. Based on these communications, Mr. Ruehle reasonably understood the Irell lawyers to be gathering facts and information for his defense against the claims asserted against him as well as for the company's own internal investigation.

Finally, Mr. Ruehle intended his statements to be confidential, and he had no reason to suspect that his conversations with the Irell lawyers would be disclosed to third parties. . . . He knew he was being personally investigated regarding Broadcom's stock option granting practices, and he would never have agreed to provide information that Irell could then turnover to the Government should it commence a criminal investigation of him.[1]

The Government nevertheless suggests that because the Irell lawyers supposedly gave Mr. Ruehle an *Upjohn* warning, his statements to the Irell lawyers are not privileged communications. A so-called *Upjohn* warning or "Corporate Miranda" is ordinarily given to inform a "constituent member o[f] an organization that the attorney represents the organization and *not* the constituent member." The warning is intended to make clear to the individual being interviewed that the corporation, and not the individual employee, is the client and therefore "controls the privilege and the confidentiality of the communication." An *Upjohn* warning apprises a corporate employee that no attorney-client relationship exists, and any communication between the lawyer and the individual may be disclosed to third parties at the corporation's discretion. In this case, the Government's reliance on the alleged *Upjohn* warning is misplaced.

As an initial matter, the Court has serious doubts whether any *Upjohn* warning was given to Mr. Ruehle. Mr. Ruehle did not remember being given any warning, no warning is referenced in Mr. Lefler's notes from the meeting, and no written record of the warning even exists. But even if an *Upjohn* warning were provided to Mr. Ruehle, the substance of the warning Mr. Heitz testified he gave is woefully inadequate under the circumstances. Mr. Heitz

---

1. [Fn. 6 in Original] The Government argues that Mr. Ruehle knew that Irell would make some disclosure to Ernst & Young in connection with its investigation, and therefore Mr. Ruehle knew that his statements were not confidential. This argument is unpersuasive. Mr. Ruehle never understood that Irell might disclose statements adverse to Mr. Ruehle's interests to the Government for use in a criminal case against him.

testified that he advised Mr. Ruehle on June 1, 2006 that he and Mr. Lefler were interviewing him on behalf of Broadcom in connection with their investigation of Broadcom's stock option granting practices. Mr. Heitz further testified that he never told Mr. Ruehle that he and Mr. Lefler were not Mr. Ruehle's lawyers or that Mr. Ruehle should consult with another lawyer. Most importantly, neither Mr. Heitz nor Mr. Leflar ever told Mr. Ruehle that any statements he made to them could be shared with third parties, including the Government in a criminal investigation of him. . . .

Perhaps most critically, however, whether an *Upjohn* warning was or was not given is irrelevant in light of the undisputed attorney-client relationship between Irell and Mr. Ruehle. An *Upjohn* warning is given to a non-client to advise the employee that he is not communicating with his personal lawyer, no attorney-client relationship exists, and any communication may be revealed to third parties if disclosure is in the best interest of the corporation. Here, Mr. Ruehle was represented by Irell in litigation related to the identical subject matter as Irell's internal investigation on behalf of Broadcom. An oral warning, as opposed to a written waiver of the clear conflict presented by Irell's representation of both Broadcom and Mr. Ruehle, is simply not sufficient to suspend or dissolve an existing attorney-client relationship and to waive the privilege. An oral warning to a current client that no attorney-client relationship exists is nonsensical at best—and unethical at worst.

B. Irell Breached Its Duty of Loyalty to Mr. Ruehle

The most fundamental aspect of the attorney-client relationship is the duty of undivided loyalty owed by a lawyer to his client, and ultimately all of the ethical rules are derived from this fundamental principle. . . . Simply put, a lawyer cannot, consistent with the duty of loyalty, "jettison[ ] one client in favor of another." All clients are equal under the Rules of Professional Conduct, and no lawyer can sacrifice the interests of one client for those of another.

In this case, Irell committed at least three clear violations of its duty of loyalty to Mr. Ruehle. First, Irell failed to obtain Mr. Ruehle's informed written consent to Irell's simultaneous representation of Mr. Ruehle individually in the Jin Action and Derivative Action, on the one hand, and Broadcom in its internal investigation on the other hand. Under the Rules of Professional Conduct, a lawyer may not simultaneously represent two clients whose interests actually or potentially conflict without each client's informed written consent. . . .

By the spring of 2006, Broadcom was acutely aware of the possibility that it might be investigated or sued on the basis of its stock option granting practices. At the time Irell accepted representation of Broadcom and Mr. Ruehle in May 2006, Irell knew or should have known that Broadcom's interests and Mr. Ruehle's interests conflicted and were adverse to each other. If there were any wrongdoing committed in connection with Broadcom's stock option practices, Broadcom might contend that Mr. Ruehle was responsible for it and that he acted without the knowledge and approval of the company. In these circumstances, Irell had a clear duty to disclose to Mr. Ruehle the potential conflict of interest created by the dual representation and obtain Mr. Ruehle's informed written consent to that conflict. Irell readily admits, however, that it did not apprise Mr. Ruehle of that conflict, nor did it obtain his written waiver of the conflict.[2]

Second, Irell breached its duty of loyalty to Mr. Ruehle, a current client, by interrogating him for the benefit of another client, Broadcom. . . . [I]t is a clear violation of that duty for the attorney to assume a position adverse or antagonistic to the client without the latter's free and intelligent consent, given with full knowledge of all the facts and circumstances." . . .

The Fourth Circuit addressed a similar ethical issue in *In re Grand Jury Subpoena*. In that case, a law firm undertook an investigation on behalf of a corporation, but did not represent the officers. Before interviewing the corporation's officers, however, the lawyers told the corporate officers that the firm did not represent the officers currently, but assured the corporate officers that the firm could represent them individually. The Fourth Circuit, seemingly incredulous that such assurances were given, noted that it did not implicitly accept "the watered-down '*Upjohn* warnings' the investigating attorneys" provided to the corporate officers. The Fourth Circuit went on to note that it "would be hard pressed to identify how investigating counsel could robustly investigate and report to management or the board of directors of a publicly-traded corporation with the necessary candor if counsel were constrained by ethical obligations to individual employees." . . .

Absent informed written consent and waiver of the conflict of interest, Irell should not have interviewed Mr. Ruehle on behalf of Broadcom alone. . . . When Irell interviewed Mr. Ruehle about the stock option granting practices at Broadcom, it should have known that in the course of the interview, Mr. Ruehle might provide incriminating evidence about his role in those practices. Irell should never have permitted Mr. Ruehle, let alone encouraged him, to disclose his role without full knowledge of the consequences. . . . By sacrificing the interests of Mr. Ruehle in favor of those of Broadcom, Irell breached its duty of loyalty to him.

Finally, Irell disclosed Mr. Ruehle's privileged communications to third parties without his consent. . . .

Irell's ethical breaches of the duty of loyalty are very troubling. Mr. Ruehle's confidential and privileged information has been disclosed to numerous third parties, most notably the Government in connection with its criminal prosecution against him. The Government's case against Mr. Ruehle is a serious one, and Mr. Ruehle faces a significant prison sentence if convicted on

---

2. [Fn. 8 in Original] Even if Mr. Heitz did give Mr. Ruehle an *Upjohn* warning, such a warning would not suffice to waive the conflict of interest created by the dual representation. The oral warning Irell claims to have given Mr. Ruehle was not sufficient to apprise him of the potential consequences of the dual representation. . . .

all counts charged in the indictment. It must be disconcerting to Mr. Ruehle to know that his own lawyers at Irell disclosed his confidential and privileged information to the Government, lawyers whom Mr. Ruehle trusted and believed would never do anything to hurt him. And now the Court has had to intervene and suppress relevant evidence in the Government's case against Mr. Ruehle. . . . Irell should not have put the parties and the Court in this position. The Rules of Professional Conduct are not aspirational. The Court is at a loss to understand why Irell did not comply with them here. Because Irell's ethical misconduct has compromised the rights of Mr. Ruehle, the integrity of the legal profession, and the fair administration of justice, the Court must refer Irell to the State Bar for discipline. Mr. Ruehle, the Government, and the public deserve nothing less.

NOTES AND QUESTIONS

1. The district court's decision to suppress evidence of Ruehle's communications to Irell on the ground they were protected by the attorney-client privilege was reversed on appeal. United States v. Ruehle, 583 F.3d 600 (9th Cir. 2009). The Ninth Circuit upheld the district court's factual finding that when the June 1, 2006 interview took place, Ruehle reasonably believed that Irell represented him individually with respect to the ongoing civil lawsuits. It disagreed, however, that Ruehle reasonably believed that the communications were confidential, finding that Ruehle understood that communications made in the course of the internal investigation would be disclosed to Ernst & Young, the outside auditors, in order to persuade them of the integrity of Broadcom's financial statements to the public. In footnote 6 to the district court's opinion, reproduced above as footnote 1, the court had rejected the government's argument on this point, finding that Ruehle "never understood that Irell might disclose statements adverse to Mr. Ruehle's interests to the Government for use in a criminal case against him." Given that the Ninth Circuit did not disagree with this factual finding, why did it nevertheless reject the district court's conclusion on the question of privilege?

2. The Ninth Circuit did not address the district court's findings that the Irell lawyers acted unethically, although it rejected the premise that violations of a state rule of professional conduct provide an adequate basis for a federal court to suppress evidence that is otherwise admissible. Focusing on the conflicts of interest question, do you agree that the Irell lawyers acted unethically? How? Analyze their conduct under the Model Rules, including conflict identification, the consentability of the conflict(s) and the lawyers' failure to obtain informed consent. Be sure to address both Irell's joint representation of Ruehle and Broadcom in the civil lawsuits, as well as their representation of Ruehle in those lawsuits while they were simultaneously representing Broadcom

in the internal investigation. As for the latter, both the district court and the Ninth Circuit appeared to agree that Ruehle probably understood that Irell did not represent him in the internal investigation. So how could the June 1 interview of Ruehle—which occurred in the course of the internal investigation—constitute a conflict of interest?

3. The Ninth Circuit held that federal law, not state law, determines the protection of the attorney-client privilege, including whether there is a *"personal* attorney-client *privilege."* 583 F.3d at 607. It then noted that "[s]everal other circuits have adopted some form of tailored test for [determining personal privilege in] joint-representation scenarios." The Third Circuit, for example, has adopted what the Ninth Circuit characterized as "extraordinary requirements" for establishing a personal attorney-client privilege when both the executive and the corporation assert dual representation. *Id.* at 608, n.7. In these situations, the Third Circuit limits executives' ability to assert privilege with a five-prong test, which includes requirements that the executives demonstrate that they made it clear to counsel that they sought advice in their individual rather than representative capacities, that counsel agreed to communicate with them in their individual capacities, and that the substance of their communications did not concern matters within the company or general affairs of the company. *See* In re Bevill, Bresler & Schulman Asset Mgmt. Corp., 805 F.2d 120, 123 (3d Cir. 1986). Why do you think the *Bevill* court adopted such a stringent test in corporate joint representation situations? The *Bevill* court stated that the purpose of the test was to clarify that "any privilege that exists as to a corporate officer's role and functions within a corporation belongs to the corporation, not the officer." 805 F.2d at 123-24. Is that a sufficient explanation?

4. The Ninth Circuit explicitly declined to decide the propriety of adopting the *Bevill* court's specialized test for assertion of the privilege by a jointly represented executive given "Irell's long-standing representation of Ruehle as an individual before the instant case arose and in light of the planned disclosure . . . to the third-party auditor." 583 F.3d at 608, n.7. The significance of the planned disclosure to the auditor has already been explained as a fact that contradicted Ruehle's assertion that he believed his communications were confidential. But why did the Ninth Circuit believe that Irell's long-standing representation of Ruehle as an individual is a factor that could undermine the appropriateness of a *Bevill* test in this case?

5. Is it permissible for corporate counsel to jointly represent the corporation and an executive in a *Bevill* jurisdiction? If such a joint representation is permitted, what sorts of disclosure would be necessary to satisfy the informed consent requirement?

6. When joint representation is permissible, who can effectively consent on behalf of the entity? Under Rule 1.13(g), "[i]f the organization's

consent to the dual representation is required by Rule 1.7, the consent shall be given by an appropriate official of the organization other than the individual who is to be represented, or by the shareholders." What happens in a two-shareholder close corporation when the shareholder who is president of the corporation and, as such, ordinarily authorized to retain counsel for the corporation, wants to be individually represented by the same attorney who will be representing the corporation in an action against both by the other shareholder? One ethics opinion concluded that the president could consent on behalf of the organization, not as a duly-authorized officer, because of his self-interest, but as a shareholder, because the rule requires disinterest only on the part of an officer. *See* California Formal Ethics Op. 1999-153 (acknowledging that the decision could be complicated when a majority shareholder owes fiduciary duties to a minority shareholder). For a contrary result, *see* Campellone v. Cragon, 910 So.2d 363 (Fla. Dist. Ct. App. 2005) (upholding a trial court decision that the majority shareholder could not consent to the dual representation of herself and the corporation because of her self-interest, and the only other shareholder would not consent).

The reason that courts like *Bevill* adopt tailored tests for determining individual privilege in joint representations is concern for protecting the corporation's interest in retaining control of the privilege. Another, less controversial situation in which courts have expressed concern for protecting the corporation involves joint representation in a shareholder derivative lawsuit. The following opinion illustrates this concern:

Musheno v. Gensemer
897 F. Supp. 833 (M.D. Pa. 1995)

CALDWELL, District Judge.

We are considering the Plaintiffs' motion to disqualify Defendants' counsel.

I. INTRODUCTION

The Plaintiffs are shareholders of Keystone Heritage Group, Inc. ("Keystone"). They instituted this action by filing a writ of summons on January 6, 1994, in the Dauphin County Court of Common Please, against Keystone, Lebanon Valley National Bank ("LVNB"), and the board of directors of Keystone and LVNB ("Directors"). The claims arise from two loans made by LVNB to Gelder, Luttrell & Associates ("GLA"). Plaintiffs contend that the loans were made in violation of the National Bank Act, 12 U.S.C. §21 *et seq.*, which limits the amount of money a bank can lend to a single customer.

On January 21, 1994, Plaintiffs' counsel sent a letter of demand to Defendant Lesher requesting that Keystone take action against the individuals responsible for losses sustained as a result of illegal loans to GLA. On February 22, 1994, the Directors appointed an independent committee to investigate Plaintiffs' demands. This group was composed of two non-defendant Directors. . . . The committee conducted an investigation and concluded that it would not be in Keystone's best interest to pursue legal action against the Directors named in Plaintiffs' writ of summons.

After the committee's recommendation was accepted by Keystone, the parties moved forward in the state court action, engaging in pre-complaint discovery. [The case was removed by defendants to federal court.] The complaint contains seven claims, all arising from losses sustained in connection with the allegedly improper loans to GLA.

[The claims included claims of negligence, self-dealing, willful misconduct, and/or recklessness, breach of fiduciary duty, fraud, and conspiracy.]

The law firm of Drinker, Biddle & Reath ("Drinker") entered an appearance in state court on behalf of Keystone and the Directors. Plaintiffs seek to disqualify Drinker from continuing in its dual representation. They claim there is a conflict of interest in the representation of both Keystone and its Directors, and that such representation violates the Model Rules of Professional Conduct. The Directors contend that, at this stage of the litigation, there is no conflict of interest, and that it is premature to disqualify counsel from representing Keystone because Keystone's interests are aligned with those of its Directors, i.e., to have this action dismissed.

II. LAW AND DISCUSSION

A. DISQUALIFICATION

The Plaintiffs' suit appears to be a shareholder derivative action. In a derivative action, suit is brought on behalf of a corporation, by its shareholders. The defendants are generally corporate officers and directors, as well as the corporation itself. However, the corporation is merely a "nominal" defendant, and in fact stands to receive a substantial benefit if the plaintiffs/shareholders are successful. Thus the corporation is in the anomalous position of being both a plaintiff and a defendant.

We are faced with the question of whether, within the confines of the Model Rules of Professional Conduct, an attorney or law firm can engage in the joint representation of both a corporation and its officers/directors in a derivative action. This issue has, to some extent, produced a split in authority. Early decisions adopted the position that, at least in the absence of a breach of trust, joint representation was permissible.

However, more recent decisions, beginning with *Lewis v. Shaffer Stores Co.*, 218 F. Supp. 238 (S.D.N.Y. 1963), have identified numerous problems with dual representation. In *Lewis*, the shareholders of a corporation brought a derivative action against the corporation and its board of directors. After counsel entered an appearance on behalf of the corporation and its Directors, the shareholders sought to disqualify the law firm from representing the corporation. The court stated that

> [t]he interests of the officer, director and majority stockholder defendants in this action are clearly adverse, on the face of the complaint, to the interests of the stockholders of [the corporation] other than defendants. I have no doubt that [the attorneys] believe in good faith that there is no merit to this action. Plaintiff, of course, vigorously contends to the contrary. The court cannot and should not attempt to pass upon the merits at this stage. Under all the circumstances, including the nature of the charges, and the vigor with which they are apparently being pressed and defended, I believe that it would be wise for the corporation to retain independent counsel, who have had no previous connection with the corporation, to advise it as to the position it should take in this controversy. . . .

Finally, in *Bell Atlantic Corp. v. Bolger*, 2 F.3d 1304 (3d Cir. 1993), the Third Circuit was faced with a factual scenario similar to the present action. After the settlement of consumer fraud claims brought by the Pennsylvania Attorney General against Bell Atlantic, a group of shareholders made a demand on Bell Atlantic's board to seek recovery from those responsible for causing the losses. The board formed a special committee, which included independent counsel, to investigate the allegations. The committee recommended that the board reject the demand as not in the corporation's best interest. The committee's recommendation was adopted, and the shareholders instituted a derivative action against Bell Atlantic and its directors. After the shareholders and the directors reached a proposed settlement, a second group of shareholders filed suit and objected to the settlement terms. The district court denied their objections and approved the settlement.

On appeal the court addressed the issue of whether the settlement was invalid based on the fact that counsel represented both the corporation and its directors in the derivative action. The court first conducted an historical overview of the law in this area, citing what it identified as a "representative observation" of one commentator:

> There is some conflict as to the propriety of an attorney or law firm simultaneously representing a corporation and its officers and directors in a stockholders' derivative action. But the modern view is that it is generally improper due to conflict of interests for counsel to attempt to represent the corporation, on whose behalf the action has been instituted, while also representing the individuals charged with harming the corporation for their wrongful conduct.

However, the court noted that "'independent counsel may not be required if the derivative claim is obviously or patently frivolous.'" The court then turned to the Model Rules of Professional Conduct to determine whether dual representation was appropriate.

Pursuant to MRPC 1.13, "[a] lawyer employed or retained by an organization represents the organization acting through its duly authorized constituents," and when "representing an organization may also represent any of its directors, officers, employees, members, shareholders or other constituents, subject to the provisions of Rule 1.7." In *Bell Atlantic*, the court relied upon the commentary to Rule 1.13, which provides, in relevant part that:

> The question can arise whether counsel for the organization may defend [a derivative] action. The proposition that the organization is the lawyer's client does not alone resolve the issue. Most derivative actions are a normal incident of an organization's affairs, to be defended by the organization's lawyer like any other suit. *However, if the claim involved serious charges of wrongdoing by those in control of the organization, a conflict may arise between the lawyer's duty to the organization and the lawyer's relationship with the board.* In those circumstances, Rule 1.7 governs who should represent the directors and the organization.

([E]mphasis added.) Applying this standard to the facts before it, the court determined that "serious charges of wrongdoing have not been levelled against the individual defendants," and that Plaintiffs alleged only a breach of the fiduciary *duty of care*, not a breach of the directors' *duty of loyalty*. Thus, the court held that independent counsel was not required, and affirmed the district court's approval of the settlement. The underlying rationale for the court's decision in *Bell Atlantic* conclusively establishes that Keystone must retain independent counsel in the present case.

Like the shareholders in *Bell Atlantic*, the Plaintiffs' demand to the bank, to pursue an action against the Directors, was investigated by an independent committee and determined not to be in the best interest of the corporation. In *Bell Atlantic*, the court relied on this fact in reaching its decision, stating that

> [t]his suggests a relative (though not complete) convergence of the individual and the corporate interests in defending and settling the litigation. Although not dispositive, it is important that early in the litigation, independent counsel, after undertaking an exhaustive investigation, determined the corporation's interest were more in line with those of the defendants than the plaintiffs.

In the present case, the Directors focus on this language in arguing that the interest of Keystone and its directors are not in conflict at this point in the litigation because the independent committee determined that Keystone should not pursue legal action. However, the Directors ignore the remainder of the quote from *Bell Atlantic*, which provides that

> [o]f greater significance, however, is the absence of allegations of fraud, intentional misconduct, or self-dealing. *We have no hesitation in holding that—except in patently frivolous cases—allegations of directors' fraud, intentional misconduct, or self-dealing require separate counsel.*

([E]mphasis added.) In this case, unlike *Bell Atlantic*, the Plaintiffs claims that the Directors committed fraud . . . by concealing the fact that they exceeded the legal lending limit, and self-dealing . . . by engaging in willful misconduct that was contrary to Keystone's interests and favorable to their own. Additionally, there is no evidence that the Plaintiffs' claims are "patently frivolous." Thus, under the standard set forth in *Bell Atlantic*, Keystone must retain independent counsel.

The Directors' sole argument in opposition to Plaintiffs' motion is that disqualification is premature because the business judgment rule[3] will likely result in dismissal of Plaintiffs' action. They contend that the disqualification motion should be postponed until a motion to dismiss, based on the business judgment rule, is decided. [In a previous decision, a federal district] court held that:

> There is no conflict of interest requiring disqualification in the narrow instance when one law firm represents a derivatively sued corporation and its individually sued directors and the law firm initially files a motion to dismiss on behalf of its clients, does not otherwise participate in the lawsuit, and withdraws from representation of either the corporation or the individual directors when either the motions are overruled or when it becomes necessary to participate in the defense of the corporation and the individual directors. At this stage of the proceedings, when the court must make a determination on whether as a matter of law the defendants should be in the lawsuit, unless it can be shown that an actual conflict exists or that certain confidences are being jeopardized, I think the client's right to select the counsel of his choice outweighs any potential conflict of interest.

[This] decision is not without merit. Keystone will be forced to incur additional cost to retain independent counsel and disqualifying Drinker impinges upon Keystone's right to select its own counsel. However, we believe the factual situation in the case at bar dictates that independent counsel be retained by the bank. There is a clear divergence of interests between Keystone and its directors on the face of Plaintiffs' complaint, which weighs against joint representation. Additionally, permitting Drinker to represent two clients with conflicting interests, even if only until a motion to dismiss is decided, could result in substantial difficulty for all parties and the court. Finally, there exists a chance that confidences obtained from one client could be used to the detriment of the other, particularly if the motion to dismiss is denied. In our view the potential for harm requires that Keystone retain independent counsel. . . .

B. Retention of Independent Counsel

Although not expressly raised by the parties, we will briefly address the manner in which Keystone is to select independent counsel. This issue has produced varying results. At least one court appointed counsel for the corporation itself. Other courts have declined to appoint counsel, or direct the corporation how to do so, irrespective of the fact that the directors who were defendants were involved in the decision-making process. However we believe the most suitable procedure was adopted by the court in [a prior decision].

In that case, the corporation appointed an ad hoc committee of two nondefendant directors, and indicated that, upon court order, it would have the

---

3. [Under the business judgment rule, a board of directors is presumed to act rationally and in good faith and therefore cannot be sued on the ground that a different decision would have been better for the corporation. —Ed.]

ad hoc committee select independent counsel. The court, without approving or disapproving of the corporation's proposal, determined that the corporation should

> resolve this problem as it would any other issue as to which the existence of interested directors renders the usual corporate decision-making process unavailable. . . . It is the duty of the directors, in this as in other matters, to act in the corporation's best interest. If they are disqualified from acting on this or on any other matter, then it is for them, in the first instance, to devise a method to accommodate the need to continue the corporate enterprise while refraining from participating in any corporate decision in which they might have a personal interest. They act, or fail to act, at their peril.

We also will not appoint counsel, nor will we dictate how Keystone chooses its new attorneys. Rather, Keystone should select independent counsel in the manner it would act in any other circumstance where a conflict of interest exists.

NOTES AND QUESTIONS

1. The *Nicholas* court expressed no concern over Irell's dual representation of both Broadcom and Ruehle in the two civil lawsuits that had been filed against them based on Broadcom's stock option granting practices. One was clearly a shareholder derivative action and the other, the Jin Action, was probably a direct action by Broadcom shareholders. The difference between the two is that in the shareholder derivative action, the lawsuit is brought on behalf of the corporation itself; therefore, any monetary damages from the individual defendants would be paid to the corporation, not to the plaintiff shareholders. In a direct action, the shareholders sue on their own behalf, and the corporation is a real and not a nominal defendant; therefore, monetary damages can be recovered from both the corporation and the individual defendants and will go directly to the plaintiff shareholders. The *Nicholas* court was not confronted with any objection to Irell's dual representation in either of these civil lawsuits, but what if the plaintiffs in those two actions had moved to disqualify the firm from representing both clients? The opinion in *Musheno* strongly suggests that the court would be more concerned with dual representation in the derivative action than in the direct action. Indeed dual representation is common in direct actions, whereas courts are inclined to prohibit it in most derivative actions. What is the reason for this difference in approaches to the two types of actions? With respect to a motion to disqualify, there is an initial distinction based on the standing (or lack of standing) of the plaintiff shareholders to object. Why is standing less of a problem in a shareholder derivative action than in a direct action?
2. Putting aside the question of standing, why are courts more troubled by dual representation in derivative actions than in direct actions? For

each type of action, consider what is at stake for the corporation and who is determining what is in the best interest of the corporate client.

3. Unlike *Nicholas*, where the court was concerned about the effect of the representation on the individual executive (Ruehle), the court in *Musheno* was concerned with the effect of the dual representation on the *corporation*, because of the self-interest of the defendant directors. As the *Musheno* court recounted, the plaintiffs' counsel, before filing the lawsuit, had sent a letter demanding that the corporation take action against the individual directors alleged responsible for corporate losses as a result of the illegal loans. The directors appointed an "independent committee," meaning a committee composed of "independent" directors,[4] to investigate these demands. The committee conducted the investigation and concluded that it was not in the corporation's best interest to pursue legal action against the defendant directors.[5] If an independent committee had investigated and determined where the corporation's best interest lay, then why did the court nevertheless prohibit the dual representation, thereby forcing the corporation to retain a separate, "independent" attorney?

4. According to the *Musheno* court, dual representation in a shareholder derivative action is generally prohibited, but there are exceptions to that rule, including when the allegations are "obviously or patently frivolous" and when the lawsuit alleges mismanagement rather than "serious charges of wrongdoing by those in control of the organization."[6] How can a court determine whether the allegations are "obviously or patently frivolous" at the outset of the litigation? And why do courts distinguish between negligence and more serious wrongdoing? Can't negligence result in just as much harm to the corporation as fraud?

5. Once the court determines that disqualification is appropriate, it must then decide who selects the new, "independent" attorney to represent the corporation. Some courts permit the board of directors to select the new counsel, including the participation of the defendant directors; others

---

4. Directors are deemed independent when they are neither officers nor employees and do not otherwise have any operational responsibilities or significant relationship with the company's management. This does not necessarily mean that they are not in a practical sense beholden to either management or the interested directors who were probably responsible for their selection for a prestigious and potentially lucrative board position.

5. For a discussion of the requirements for filing a shareholder derivative action, *see* 5 Charles A. Wright et al., Fed. Prac. & Proc. Civ. 23.1 (3d ed. 2021).

6. Officers and directors owe the corporation both a duty of care and a duty of loyalty. The duty of care requires action in good faith, on an informed basis; under the "business judgment rule," good faith and informed decisions are protected from second guessing by judges and juries. However, the business judgment rule does not apply to allegations of breach of the duty of loyalty, which applies when there is a conflict of interest, a lack of good faith, or a failure to exercise business judgment. *See generally* Ronald J. Columbo, Law of Corp. Offs. & Dirs. Rts., Duties & Liabs. §§2.1 (duty of care), 3.1 (duty of loyalty) (2020-2021).

hold that the decision should be made in the same manner as other issues where some directors have a conflict of interest, which under corporate law would probably require selection by independent directors; and at least two courts have made the selection themselves. What are the pros and cons of each approach? Which one did the *Musheno* court follow?

6. When dual representation is prohibited, courts usually permit the conflicted attorney to continue representing the individual defendant directors, even when the attorney had previously served as corporate counsel. Why shouldn't the attorney continue to represent the corporation, rather than the individual directors?

7. Several commentators have argued that the prohibition on dual representation in derivative actions may be warranted for publicly held corporations but not for private, closely held companies. Their arguments are based on several distinctive features of closely held companies, including the following: (1) the defendant directors are likely to be the majority shareholders; (2) it is unlikely that there are independent directors; and (3) the plaintiff shareholders typically have a greater stake in the litigation because they own more shares that the typical plaintiff shareholders when the corporation is publicly held. The first two factors suggest that retaining "independent" counsel is less likely to make a difference in how the lawsuit is litigated on behalf of a closely held company, whereas the third factor suggests that the plaintiff shareholder in a closely held company has a greater incentive to pursue the best result for the corporation and to monitor attorneys' fees.[7] Do you find these arguments persuasive?

B. CURRENT CLIENTS: CORPORATE FAMILY CONFLICTS

Businesses are often organized as interrelated corporations. A parent company may wholly or partially own one or more subsidiaries, and partial ownership may be based on greater or lesser ownership.[8] Two corporations may be affiliated as "sister corporations" when they have a common parent. These "corporate families" can be incredibly large, and the membership may change frequently as a result of mergers and acquisitions. What happens when a law firm representing either a parent or an affiliate wants to undertake representation adverse to another member of the same corporate family?

---

7. *See generally* Robert J. Riccio, Conflicts of Interest in Derivative Litigation Involving Closely Held Corporations: An All or Nothing Approach to the Requirement of "Independent" Corporate Counsel, 31 J. of Legal Prof., 337 (2007).

8. The term "subsidiary" is sometimes limited to companies that are wholly owned by a parent, with the term "affiliate" used to denote lesser ownership. Some courts and commentators, however, use the term "subsidiary" to include any significant ownership by a parent and may also use the term "affiliate" more generally to denote all of the various forms of interrelated ownership.

Comment [34] to Model Rule 1.7 states that "[a] lawyer who represents a corporation or other organization does not, by virtue of that representation, necessarily represent any constituent or affiliated organization, such as a parent or subsidiary." Ordinarily, then, "the lawyer for an organization is not barred from accepting representation adverse to an affiliate in an unrelated matter." Nevertheless, such representation will be prohibited in three circumstances: (1) "the circumstances are such that the affiliate should also be considered a client of the lawyer"; (2) "there is an understanding between the lawyer and the organizational client that the lawyer will avoid representation adverse to the client's affiliates"; or (3) the lawyer's obligations to either the organizational client or the new client are likely to limit materially the lawyer's representation of the other client." The last circumstance is most likely to arise when the matters are related rather than unrelated and when the company being sued is an affiliate of a corporation that is a major client of the law firm, in which the lawyer may have what has previously been described as a "punch-pulling" conflict.[9]

The following case illustrates questions that arise with respect to the first two circumstances, that is, when an affiliate should also be considered a client of the lawyer and what to do when there are ambiguities in interpreting a written engagement that purports to address the lawyer's ability to undertake representation adverse to a client's affiliate.

GSI Commerce Solutions, Inc. v. BabyCenter, L.L.C.
618 F.3d 204 (2d Cir. 2010)

WINTER, Circuit Judge:

CSI Commerce Solutions, Inc. ("GSI") appeals from Judge Rakoff's order granting a motion by BabyCenter, LLC ("BabyCenter"), a wholly-owned subsidiary of Johnson & Johnson, Inc. ("J&J"), to disqualify Blank Rome, LLP, as GSI's counsel. The court concluded that the doctrine forbidding concurrent representation without consent applies because the relationship between BabyCenter and J&J, which Blank Rome represents in other matters, is so close that the two are essentially one client for disqualification purposes. . . .

---

9. As you may recall, a "punch-pulling" conflict occurs when a lawyer may be tempted to pull its punches on behalf of a new client because of a desire not to displease the person or company being sued. *See supra* Chapter 5: Conflicts of Interest: Current Clients. Although the affiliate being sued is not itself a law firm client, the long-standing client has a financial interest in avoiding harm to members of its corporate family, and it is not in the law firm's interest to upset that long-standing client.

BACKGROUND

A) ATTORNEY-CLIENT RELATIONSHIP BETWEEN JOHNSON & JOHNSON AND BLANK ROME

J&J entered into an Engagement Agreement with Blank Rome in 2004. The agreement, contained in a letter to J&J ("2004 Letter"), describes the scope of Blank Rome's representation as limited to compliance matters involving J&J and J&J affiliates "in connection with the European Union . . . Data Protection Directive and potential certification to the U.S. Safe Harbor." The bulk of the agreement concerns two provisions purporting to waive certain conflicts of interest. The first provision addresses Blank Rome's concurrent representation of Kimberly-Clark in a specific patent matter "adverse to [J&J's] corporate affiliate, McNeil PPC, Inc." Specifically, it sets out the Rules of Professional Conduct applicable to attorneys representing an enterprise with diverse operations and concludes that Blank Rome is free to continue to represent Kimberly-Clark in that matter so long as J&J agrees to waive the conflict. The second provision in the 2004 Letter to J&J seeks a prospective waiver of all conflicts arising out of Blank Rome's representation of Kimberly-Clark in patent matters adverse to J&J and affiliates. The prospective waiver provision provides: . . .

> Specifically, this letter seeks confirmation that, should our representation of Kimberly-Clark in connection with patent-related proceedings involve Johnson & Johnson, or any other entity related to Johnson & Johnson, Johnson & Johnson consents, and will not object to our continuing representation of Kimberly-Clark in connection with these proceedings. . . .

A final part of the 2004 Letter summarizes the terms of the two waivers and directly asks J&J to acknowledge that "you are aware of the conflict of interests that results from our representation of Kimberly-Clark and Johnson & Johnson but that notwithstanding that conflict . . . you consent to our representation of Johnson & Johnson and our simultaneous continued representation of Kimberly-Clark." Blank Rome also attached a standard Addendum, which provides in relevant part:

> Unless otherwise agreed to in writing or we specifically undertake such additional representation at your request, we represent only the client named in the engagement letter and not its affiliates, subsidiaries, partners, joint venturers, employees, directors, officers, shareholders, members, owners, agencies, departments or divisions. . . .

In 2005, Blank Rome sent another letter to J&J ("2005 Letter") seeking to amend the terms of the Engagement Agreement. The 2005 Letter first explains that Blank Rome had increased its representation of generic drug manufacturers in patent-related matters. It specifically notes that the firm's representation of these new clients could lead to conflicts with its existing clients, such as J&J,

that are known as branded drug manufacturers. The 2005 Letter then states: "The Addendum to our current engagement letter stipulates that we represent only [J&J], and not its affiliates, subsidiaries, partners, divisions and joint venturers." However the Letter goes on to request the following waiver from J&J:

> Specifically, this letter seeks confirmation that, should our representation of generic drug manufacturers in connection with patent-related proceedings involve Johnson & Johnson, or any other entity related to Johnson & Johnson, Johnson & Johnson consents, and will not object, to our continuing representation of the generic drug manufacturers in connection with these proceedings. . . .

A final part of the 2005 Letter specifically asks J&J to acknowledge: "you [J&J] provide your prospective consent to our [Blank Rome's] representation of generic drug manufacturers in patent-related proceedings involving Johnson & Johnson and its affiliates and subsidiaries."

Pursuant to this Engagement Agreement, "Blank Rome advised J&J on a variety of privacy matters, much of which was related to J&J affiliates. In particular, Jennifer Daniels, a partner at Blank Rome, provided affiliates with privacy-related services, including the preparation of policies and procedures, guidance documents and training materials. In 2006, Ms. Daniels represented BabyCenter in a privacy-related matter. Blank Rome did not, however, advise J&J with regard to the E-Commerce Services Agreement ("E-Commerce Agreement") between BabyCenter and GSI, which is the subject of the current litigation. It also appears that Blank Rome received no confidential information relevant to that agreement during its representation of J&J or, separately, BabyCenter.

B) J&J's RELATIONSHIP WITH BABYCENTER

BabyCenter is a wholly-owned subsidiary of J&J that operates as an online media company. BabyCenter hosts a variety of websites in the United States and abroad that focus on pregnancy and early childhood development. Until January 2009, BabyCenter also hosted an online retail store offering baby-care and related products.

BabyCenter relies on J&J for a variety of business services, including accounting, audit, cash management, employee benefits, finance, human resources, information technology, insurance, payroll, and travel services and systems. It also substantially relies on J&J's legal department either to provide legal services or to secure outside counsel. Stuart Wilks, a member of the J&J legal department, serves as "Board Attorney" to BabyCenter. J&J's legal department participated in the negotiation of the E-Commerce Agreement between BabyCenter and GSI. J&J lawyers have also been involved from the beginning in the dispute between BabyCenter and GSI. Indeed, J&J's legal department has dealt directly with Blank Rome in attempting to resolve the present dispute.

Finally, it appears that J&J exercises some management control over Baby-Center's business decisions, although the extent of this control is not clear from the record. BabyCenter is a limited liability company. Its sole member is BC Acquisition group, which is itself a wholly-owned subsidiary of J&J. J&J structures affiliates into groups of companies. BabyCenter belongs to the Consumer Healthcare Group and its operations are supervised by the Consumer Healthcare Group Operating Committee, which is composed mainly of J&J employees.

C) BABYCENTER & GSI COMMERCE SOLUTIONS

BabyCenter and GSI entered into the aforementioned E-Commerce Agreement in August 2006, pursuant to which GSI agreed to run the day-to-day operations of BabyCenter's online store in return for a percentage of sales revenue. [The agreement provides that if a dispute arises, the parties will attempt to resolve it through first mediation and then arbitration.]

When BabyCenter closed its online store in 2009, GSI accused it of wrongfully terminating the E-Commerce Agreement. Specifically, it argued that the five-year term of service in the agreement had not expired at the time the store closed. James Smith, a Blank Rome partner, notified BabyCenter on December 1, 2008 of GSI's demand for mediation on its claim. Daniels, the Blank Rome partner who had worked with J&J and affiliates on privacy matters, contacted J&J's legal department the same day to inform J&J of the dispute. [When mediation failed, BabyCenter refused to go to arbitration so long as Blank Rome represented GSI.] On the same day, J&J informed Blank Rome of its opposition to Blank Rome's representation of GSI.

[The district court granted BabyCenter's motion to disqualify Blank Rome.]

DISCUSSION . . .

We have not previously considered whether, and under what circumstances, representation adverse to a client's corporate affiliate implicates the duty of loyalty owed to the client. However, the issue has been addressed by the ABA and also has been discussed extensively in other courts.

The ABA's Model Rules of Professional Conduct provide that a "lawyer who represents a corporation or other organization does not, by virtue of that representation, necessarily represent any constituent or affiliated organization, such as a parent or subsidiary." This statement embodies what is often termed the "entity theory" of representation. However, an attorney may not accept representation adverse to a client affiliate if "circumstances are such that the affiliate should also be considered a client of the lawyer. . . ." The ABA discussed this subject further in a 1995 Opinion Letter [Formal Opinion 95-390], concluding that "whether a lawyer represents a corporate affiliate of his client . . . depends not upon any clearcut per se rule but rather upon the particular circumstances."

Many courts have reached the conclusion that the bar to concurrent representation applies if a firm's representation adverse to a client's corporate affiliate "reasonably diminishes the level of confidence and trust in counsel held by [the client]." Put another way, these courts focus on the reasonableness of the client's belief that counsel cannot maintain the duty of undivided loyalty it owes a client in one matter while simultaneously opposing that client's corporate affiliate in another.

We agree that representation adverse to a client's affiliate can, in certain circumstances, conflict with the lawyer's duty of loyalty owed to a client, a situation that we shall refer to as "a corporate affiliate conflict."

The factors relevant to whether a corporate affiliate conflict exists are of a general nature. Courts have generally focused on: (i) the degree of operational commonality between affiliated entities, and (ii) the extent to which one depends financially on the other. As to operational commonality, courts have considered the extent to which entities rely on a common infrastructure. Courts have also focused on the extent to which the affiliated entities rely on or otherwise share common personnel such as managers, officers and directors. In this respect, courts have emphasized the extent to which affiliated entities share responsibilities for both the provision and management of legal services. This focus on shared or dependent control over legal and management issues reflect the view that neither management nor in-house legal counsel should, without their consent, have to place their trust in outside counsel in one matter while opposing the same counsel in another.

As to financial interdependence, several courts have considered the extent to which an adverse outcome in the matter at issue would result in substantial and measurable loss to the client or its affiliate. Courts have also inquired into the entities' ownership structure. Some have even suggested that an affiliate's status as a wholly-owned subsidiary of the client may suffice to establish a corporate affiliate conflict. However, we agree with the ABA that affiliates should not be considered a single entity for conflicts purposes based solely on the fact that one entity is a wholly-owned subsidiary of the other, at least when the subsidiary is not otherwise operationally integrated with the parent company.

However, the record here establishes such substantial operational commonalty between BabyCenter and J&J that the district court's decision to treat the two entities as one client was easily within its ample discretion. First, BabyCenter substantially relies on J&J for accounting, audit, cash management, employee benefits, finance, human resources, information technology, insurance, payroll, and travel services and systems. Second, both entities rely on the same in-house legal department to handle their legal affairs. The member of J&J's in-house legal department who serves as "board lawyer" for BabyCenter helped to negotiate the E-Commerce Agreement between BabyCenter and GSI that is the subject of the present dispute. Moreover, J&J's legal department has been involved in the dispute between GSI and BabyCenter since it first arose, participating in mediation efforts and securing outside counsel for BabyCenter. Finally, BabyCenter is a wholly-owned subsidiary of J&J, and there is at least some overlap in management control.

When considered together, these factors show that the relationship between the two entities is exceedingly close. That showing in turn substantiates the view that Blank Rome, by representing GSI in this matter, "reasonably diminishes the level of confidence and trust in counsel held by" J&J. . . .

GSI argues that, with the Engagement Letter, J&J and Blank Rome dispositively waived the corporate affiliate conflict.

We agree that a law firm may ordinarily accept representation involving a corporate affiliate conflict if the client expressly consents. . . .

However, Blank Rome failed to obtain J&J's consent to the instant corporate affiliate conflict. Although certain provisions of the Engagement Agreement may constitute a waiver by J&J of certain corporate affiliate conflicts, they do not waive the conflict at issue here. Specifically, the wavier is strictly limited to matters involving patent litigation and, even then, only to matters brought by either Kimberly-Clark or a generic drug manufacturer. Thus, because these provisions acknowledge Blank Rome's continuing duty to avoid conflicts arising out of its representation of J&J and third parties, and because the instant matter does not fall into the narrow category of cases waived by those provisions, Blank Rome did not contract around the corporate affiliate conflict at issue here.

GSI argues that the waiver provisions simply do not address Blank Rome's authority to accept representation that might raise a corporate affiliate conflict. Rather, it argues, the conflicts addressed in the waivers arise only if a J&J affiliate is a Blank Rome client in its own right at the time the law firm accepts representation adverse to that affiliate. If the affiliate is not separately a Blank Rome client at that time, GSI argues, the waiver provisions imply no limitation on the firm's ability to accept the adverse representation.

GSI argues that the Engagement Agreement gives Blank Rome carte blanche to accept representation adverse to J&J affiliates that are not separately Blank Rome clients. This argument relies entirely on the clause that states: "Unless otherwise agreed to in writing or we specifically undertake such additional representation at your request, we represent only the client named in the engagement letter and not its affiliates, subsidiaries, partners, joint venturers, employees, directors, officers, shareholders, members, owners, agencies, departments or divisions."

We are unpersuaded. The waiver provisions unambiguously state that the contemplated conflicts arise out of Blank Rome's representation of J&J and third parties in matters adverse to J&J affiliates, and not out of some separate representation of those affiliates. The 2004 Letter states: "you [J&J] are aware of the conflicts of interest that results from our representation of Kimberly-Clark and *Johnson & Johnson* but that notwithstanding *that* conflict of interest . . . you [J&J] consent to our representation of Johnson & Johnson and our simultaneous continued representation of Kimberly-Clark," (emphasis added). The 2005 Letter similarly provides: "[I]t is our belief that, if a conflict did exist, we would be permitted, subject to the consent being given via this letter, to represent Johnson & Johnson, while remaining available to represent the generic drug manufacturers in future patent-related proceedings involving *Johnson & Johnson* or any of its affiliates, subsidiaries or divisions." (Emphasis added). The plain language of the Engagement Agreement thus contradicts GSI's argument that the waivers do not address corporate affiliate conflicts.

And because the waiver provisions do address corporate affiliate conflicts, GSI's construction of the Addendum also fails. If the broadly-worded, standard language of the Addendum actually waives all corporate affiliate conflicts, then there is no possible purpose served by the non-standard waiver provisions waiving only certain corporate affiliate conflicts. Adopting GSI's construction of the Addendum as waiving all such conflicts would render the more specific and more limited waiver provisions meaningless. We cannot accept such a construction. "The rules of contract construction require us to adopt an interpretation which gives meaning to every provision of the contract." Also, "specific language in a contract will prevail over general language where there is an inconsistency between two provisions." Because GSI's construction of the broadly-worded, standard language of the Addendum would strip the remainder of the Engagement Agreement of any meaning, it violates basic canons of construction of contract law.

In any event, the relevant language in the Addendum states that Blank Rome represents only the named client and not unnamed "affiliates, subsidiaries, partners, joint venturers, employees, directors, officers, shareholders, members, owner, agencies, departments, or division." Construed as a waiver of all corporate affiliate conflicts involving the entities listed therein, this clause would raise a serious ethical problem. Specifically, Blank Rome cannot, consistent with its duty of loyalty to J&J, sue unincorporated departments or divisions of J&J. GSI conceded as much at oral argument but could not then explain why that same language grants Blank Rome authority to accept representation adverse to the other entities listed therein, such as affiliates. This troublesome aspect of GSI's construction only illustrates how hard GSI is straining to work a broad waiver into language that simply is not plain enough or clear enough to support it. There is, therefore, no waiver of the present corporate affiliate conflict.[10]

NOTES AND QUESTIONS

1. As the *GSI* court notes, some courts treat an affiliate's status as a wholly owned subsidiary of the client as sufficient to establish a corporate affiliate conflict. According to one court cited in the opinion, the justification

---

10. [Fn. 4 in Original] We of course need not and do not address issues that might arise with regard to a blanket waiver, without specifying types of claims or parties, of corporate affiliate conflicts.

B. Current Clients: Corporate Family Conflicts

for this result is that "the liabilities of a [wholly owned] subsidiary corporation directly affect the bottom line of the corporate parent." This fact could justify treating the entities as one client or, even if the affiliate is not a client, could justify a finding that representation adverse to the nonclient affiliate is "directly adverse" to the corporate parent, thereby creating a current conflict under Rule 1.7(a)(1). ABA Formal Opinion 95-390 rejected this approach, reasoning that "the immediate impact is on the affiliate, and only derivatively upon the client."[11] The *GSI* court agreed with the ABA that affiliates are not a single entity based solely on the fact that one is a wholly owned subsidiary of the other, but might it be receptive to the recognition of a "directly adverse" conflict based on the economic effect on the client of a substantial economic loss by its affiliate?

2. Blank Rome had attached to the 2004 Letter a standard Addendum providing in part that "[u]nless otherwise agreed to in writing or we specifically undertake such additional representation at your request, we represent only the client named in the engagement letter and not its affiliates, subsidiaries, partners, joint venturers, employees, directors, officers, shareholders, members, owners, agencies, departments or divisions." Why wasn't this provision sufficient to warrant a finding that Blank Rome did not represent BabyCare for purposes of the conflicts analysis? Is the answer that Blank Rome had in fact undertaken to represent J&J affiliates, including BabyCare, in privacy-related matters?

3. Blank Rome made substantial efforts to contract around the corporate affiliate conflicts problem. Where did it go wrong? How should the 2004 Letter and Addendum have been worded differently?

4. The Addendum included a disclaimer involving not only J&J affiliates, but also its "departments or divisions." A dissenting opinion to ABA Formal Opinion 95-390 used a hypothetical involving the relationships between Ford Motor Co. and Jaguar, a wholly owned subsidiary, and between Ford and Lincoln Mercury, which is a division of Ford. A division is a part of a business entity. It can operate under a different name and have its own financial statements, but it is not separately incorporated. According to the dissenting opinion, the majority would treat a lawsuit against Lincoln Mercury as a lawsuit against Ford itself, while simultaneously treating a lawsuit against Jaguar as a lawsuit against Ford only if the particular circumstances warranted treatment of the

---

11. The ABA Opinion was not unanimous. Several dissenting opinions vigorously objected to the majority's finding that a "directly adverse" conflict does not arise merely because representation adverse to an affiliate will cause substantial economic harm to the client. The majority insisted that any such harm was "indirect" rather than "direct." The dissenters did not limit their interpretation to wholly owned subsidiaries. For a court decision accepting the dissenters' approach, *see* JPMorgan Chase Bank ex rel. Mahonia Ltd. v. Liberty Mutual Insurance Co., 189 F.Supp.2d 20 (S.D.N.Y. 2002) (disqualifying a law firm from pursuing a $183 million claim against a 95 percent owned subsidiary which accounted for approximately 90 percent of the parent client's business).

entities as a single organization for conflicts purposes. The dissenting opinion is correct that this is precisely the distinction that the ABA opinion and a majority of courts would make. Do you understand why? Do you agree that the distinction is an appropriate one? The dissenting opinion argues that "[this] result exalts form over substance." Does it?

C. FORMER CLIENTS: THE ACCOMMODATION CLIENT

One of the risks of jointly representing an entity and a constituent is that if the clients' interests become adverse, the conflict will become nonconsentable or one of the clients will withdraw its consent to the joint representation. If the lawyer is forced to withdraw from representing one client, then under Model Rule 1.9(a), the lawyer will also be forced to withdraw from representing the other client if the continuing representation will be materially adverse to the former client, unless the former client gives its informed consent to the continuing representation.

In many instances, the entity lawyer undertakes to represent the constituent, typically an executive such as William Ruehle in the *Nicholas* case, as an accommodation to the entity client. When the parties' positions become adverse, the entity wants to continue with its regular counsel and believes that it is entitled to do so. The following article describes the development of a controversial doctrine that recognizes the entity's ability to maintain its regular counsel, even absent an express waiver by the former constituent client.

Douglas R. Richmond

Accommodation Clients
35 Akron L. Rev. 59 (2001)

Lawyers sometimes represent more than one client in a matter. A lawyer may represent a second client as an accommodation to the lawyer's regular client to avoid duplication of effort and the accompany expense. For example, a lawyer may regularly represent an organization and, in a case in which the organization and one of its officers are named as defendants, also represent the officer. If a conflict later develops between the organization and the officer, the lawyer may seek to withdraw from the officer's representation but continue to represent the organization on the theory that the officer was a mere "accommodation client" who understood and impliedly consented to this arrangement. . . . "Accommodation client" status is most likely to be claimed where the lawyer has long represented the regular client, the accommodation client's representation is of limited duration or scope, and the accommodation client allegedly has no reasonable expectation that the lawyer will keep his confidences from the regular client.

C. Former Clients: The Accommodation Client   **347**

Accommodation clients typically are the creation of lawyers facing possible disqualification in litigation, although professional discipline and malpractice liability may also be concerns. They are also the creation of courts who believe that slavish adherence to conflict of interest rules sometimes produces unfair results in disqualification disputes. Ethics rules do not distinguish between "primary" clients and accommodation clients. Clients are clients. Or are they? . . .

The case most often cited to support an accommodation client theory is *Allegaert v. Perot*, decided by the Second Circuit. Winthrop Allegaert was the trustee in bankruptcy of Walston, once a large Wall Street brokerage firm. He moved to disqualify two law firms, Weil, Gotshal and Leval, Hawes, who represented some of the defendants in a preference action brought by Allegaert. The preference action arose out of Walston's realignment with another struggling brokerage, DGF, in what amounted to a joint venture. Weil, Gotshal and Leva, Hawes had represented DGF and other interested parties related to DGF in the Walston-DGF realignment. Weil, Gotshal and Leva, Hawes had thereafter represented Walston in a derivative action known as *Nella Walston*, which was substantially similar to the case at bar. In both cases Allegaert alleged that payments made by Walston to DGF were unlawful preferences, and that DGF had otherwise defrauded and looted DWI through their alignment. Allegaert based his disqualification motion on Weil, Gotshal's and Leva, Hawers' representation of Walston in the *Nella Walston* litigation. The district court declined to disqualify the law firms and Allegaert took an interlocutory appeal. . . .

The [*Allegaert*] court reasoned that the substantial relationship test [developed under the former ABA Model Code for former client conflicts] did not apply because Walston knew that information given to Weil, Gotshal and Leva, Hawes "would certainly be conveyed to their primary clients, i.e., DGF and its affiliates, in view of the realignment agreement." Neither Walston nor anyone associated with it reasonably could have believed that Weil, Gotshal and Leva, Hawes would withhold from DGF and its affiliates information shared with the law firms by Walston. Walston always had the law firm of Shearman & Sterling as its own counsel and, with the exception of the *Nella Walston* litigation, Weil, Gotshal and Leva, Hawes always represented DGF and its affiliates. . . .

The court thus affirmed the district court's decision not to disqualify the law firms. . . .

Several courts have followed *Allegaert*, and some of those courts have gone beyond the issue of client confidences to examine the problems posed by lawyers' duty of loyalty under Canon 5 [of the former ABA Model Code] and Rule 1.9, which the *Allegaert* court did not reach. . . .

A Pennsylvania federal court embraced the accommodation client concept in *In re Rite Aid Corp. Securities Litigation*. In March 1999, pharmacy giant Rite Aid announced disappointing earnings and, when its stock price fell dramatically as a result, it was sued by shareholders in several class actions. The suits initially named as defendants Rite Aid and its CEO, Martin Grass. Rite Aid's General Counsel, Elliot Gerson, retained Alan Davis of the law firm of Ballard Spahr to represent both Rite Aid and Grass. At the same time he retained Davis and Ballard Spahr, Gerson had also retained the law firm of Wilmer Cutler & Pickering to represent Grass personally after the *Wall Street Journal* published an article indicating that Grass had entered into several transactions involving Rite Aid that benefitted him and his family.

Davis memorialized his representation of Rite Aid and Grass in an engagement letter to Gerson. Davis explained to Gerson in the engagement letter that while there did not appear to be a conflict of interest that would prevent Ballard Spahr from representing both the company and Grass, it was possible that such a conflict might arise in the future. If it did, Davis wrote, it was "understood" that Grass would retain separate counsel and that Ballard Spahr would continue to represent Rite Aid. . . .

In October 1999, Davis learned that Grass and Bergonzi [another Rite Aid executive jointly represented by Davis] had engaged in conduct that apparently breached their fiduciary duties to Rite Aid. Davis told Gerson that he and his firm could no longer represent Bergonzi and Grass. He also advised Bergonzi that he could no longer represent him and urged him to replace Ballard Spahr with personal counsel. Bergonzi heeded Davis' advice. Finally, Davis told Wilmer Cutler of the conflict and that Ballard Spahr could no longer represent Grass.

The litigation proceeded and, for more than one year, Grass did not object to Ballard Spahr's continued representation of Rite Aid. Davis finally settled the case on behalf of Rite Aid in November 2000, but that settlement did not encompass any of the individual defendants or Rite Aid's accountants. Grass and Bergonzi objected to the settlement, arguing that the settlement was "the fruit of a tree poisoned by the allegedly unethical participation of Ballard Spahr in its negotiation and consummation." They also moved to disqualify Ballard Spahr, although Bergonzi later withdrew from the dispute, leaving Grass to press the motion alone.

Grass argued that Ballard Spahr, which had previously represented him in the litigation, had taken a position adverse to him by negotiating the partial settlement favoring Rite Aid, and that the firm did so without his consent. Thus, Ballard Spahr clearly violated Rule 1.9(a) and should be disqualified. The *Rite Aid* court disagreed.

The *Rite Aid* court pronounced that "Rite Aid was clearly the 'primary' client." This was particularly so because Ballard Spahr represented Grass through Rite Aid; the company engaged Ballard Spahr on Grass's behalf, and the firm typically communicated with Grass through Gerson or in his presence. Ballard Spahr did not drop Grass as a client to represent a more desirable client in Rite Aid; any change in position was occasioned by Grass.

The court bolstered its conclusion that Ballard Spahr did not violate Rule 1.9(a) by looking to the *Restatement (Third) of the Law Governing Lawyers*, which countenances similar conduct by describing a client such as Grass as an "accommodation client." Comment (i) to Section 132 of the Restatement provides:

Withdrawal from representing an "accommodation" client. With the informed consent of each client . . . a lawyer might undertake representation of another client as an accommodation to the lawyer's regular client, typically for a limited purpose in order to avoid duplication of services and consequent higher fees. If adverse interests later develop between the clients, even if the adversity relates to the matter involved in the common representation, circumstances might warrant the inference that the "accommodation" client understood and impliedly consented to the lawyer's continuing to represent the regular client in the matter. Circumstances most likely to evidence such an understanding are that the lawyer has represented the regular client for a long period of time before undertaking representation of the other client, that the representation was to be of limited scope and duration, and that the lawyer was not expected to keep confidential from the regular client any information provided to the lawyer by the other client. . . . The lawyer bears the burden of showing that circumstances exist to warrant an inference of understanding and implied consent. . . .

The *Rite Aid* court believed that the dispute before it was analogous to the situation described in the *Restatement* comment. It therefore deemed Grass to be an "accommodation client," and inferred that he had consented to Ballard Spahr's continued representation of Rite Aid after it had stopped representing him because of potential conflicts of interest.

Leaving aside Grass's accommodation client status, it was also apparent that he had consented to Ballard Spahr's continued representation of Rite Aid. The nature and scope of Ballard Spahr's engagement could not have been clearer. Davis' engagement letter to Gerson made it "pellucid that Ballard Spahr would in the event of a conflict between Rite Aid and Grass, cease to represent Grass but continue to represent Rite Aid." The court was unmoved by Grass's claim that he never saw the letter, because his decision to engage counsel through Gerson bound him to the letter's terms and as Rite Aid's CEO he was constructively on notice of its contents. . . .

A Texas court rejected the accommodation client concept in *Insurance Co. of North America v. Westergren.* The attorney whose conduct was challenged in *Westergren,* James Harris, argued that he could represent a contractor in litigation against a surety, INA, even though he had earlier represented INA in substantially related matters in which the contractor was also a party. Harris argued that there was no conflict of interest because his representation of INA was "merely an accommodation or pro forma relationship." . . . The trial court denied INA's motion to disqualify Harris based on the lack of an attorney-client relationship and INA appealed.

The appellate court acknowledged Harris' accommodation or pro forma representation argument, but concluded that he shared an attorney-client relationship with INA. While the duties or specifics of the relationship might be disputed, the court could "find nothing in the disciplinary rules which permits a pro forma representation of a client." The *Westergren* court thus held that the trial court erred in failing to disqualify Harris. . . .

In an effort to address [similar issues in a case involving Time Warner and two other companies], the [law] firm submitted a declaration by Cornell Law School Professor Charles W. Wolfram. Relying on *Allegaert* and the *Restatement*

(Third) of the Law Governing Lawyers, Professor Wolfram opined that Time Warner was "a 'non-primary' or 'accommodation' client, that only 'primary' clients may seek disqualification of counsel affected with conflicts, and in any case, that a lawyer representing a non-primary client 'can drop the accommodation client (like a hot potato, or otherwise) and file suit against the former accommodation client.'" Professor Wolfram did not [address the ethical propriety of the firm's conduct]. Rather he stated only that disqualification is an inappropriate remedy when the aggrieved client is an accommodation client. . . .

The Second Circuit's decision in *Allegaert v. Perot* does not broadly authorize the recognition of accommodation clients as a new subcategory of clients. The case should be limited to its fact, as several courts have recognized. Additionally, the case was decided by the application of Canon 4 of the Model Code, which specifically deals with client confidences, rather than under the broader Model Rule 1.9(a). While certainly intended to protect client confidences, Rule 1.9(a) also safeguards public confidence in the legal system and a client's broader expectation of his lawyer's loyalty. The *Allegaert* court did not address lawyers' duty of loyalty in successive representations. . . .

A lawyer may take on the representation of a second client in a matter at the request of a regular client. That means only that the lawyer represents co-clients. There is not a category of inferior clients known as accommodation clients to whom lawyers owe diminished professional duties. The *Restatement*'s apparent creation of such a breed of client is at best an ill-considered description of some attorney-client relationships that are characterized by unusual facts or defined by well-crafted engagement letters.

There is no need for the potential confusion the accommodation client moniker creates. A lawyer who wishes to avoid a disqualifying conflict in the representation of multiple clients often can avoid trouble by obtaining the client's consent, and by detailing the scope and nature of his representation of each client in a clear and thorough engagement letter. If a lawyer does these things and is thus able to continue to represent a favored client after withdrawing from the representation of a second client, that does not retroactively transform the second client into an "accommodation client." The second client is nothing more than a former client who has waived the lawyer's conflict of interest. The second client has, for whatever reason, decided that nay advantage to be gained by insisting on his lawyer's loyalty is outweighed by other considerations. . . .

There clearly are cases of dual representation where the disqualification of the clients' common lawyer would be unfair to one of the clients, to the lawyer, or both. A lawyer's professional discipline and exposure to malpractice liability in cases of dual representation can also be unfair. And, these cases may involve one client who has a long-time relationship with the lawyer, a situation where the lawyer's representation of the second client is limited in duration or scope, and circumstances in which the second client does not expect that the lawyer will keep his confidences inviolate. That does not mean, however, that the "accommodation client" is anything less than an ordinary client, or should be treated differently under ethics rules or the law of lawyering. Courts deciding disqualification motions in such cases can avoid any threatened unfairness by examining the facts and applying established legal principles. A court that believes a disqualification motion has been filed to gain some sort of tactical advantage in the case can always exercise its discretion to deny the motion for that reason. To create a new breed of client — the accommodation client — in an effort to avoid unfairness is unnecessary and confusing. Worse yet it is imprudent, because it makes it too easy to excuse lawyers' ethical failures. Clients' expectations of confidentiality and loyalty are worthy of protection in all representations.

Lawyers can head off the problems that accommodation client status is intended to avoid or mitigate by crafting appropriate engagement letters or by obtaining appropriate waivers. If a lawyer fails to explain matters to his clients or fails to memorialize his agreements with his clients, he ought to expect that there may be unfortunate consequences.

NOTES AND QUESTIONS

1. Richmond criticizes the Restatement comment as "ill-considered." What exactly is he objecting to in the comment? Is it merely the use of the terms "primary client" and "accommodation client" or is there more? For example, Richmond concludes that lawyers can solve the "accommodation client" problem, such as Rite Aid's desire to have Ballard Spahr continue to represent it even when Grass was forced to hire a new lawyer, by "crafting appropriate engagement letters or by obtaining appropriate waivers." Isn't this also required under the Restatement comment, which requires "the informed consent of each client" before a lawyer "undertake[s] representation of another client as an accommodation to the lawyer's regular client"? What exactly is the "informed consent" that the Restatement is referencing here and how does it differ from the "appropriate engagement letters" or "appropriate waivers" that Richmond is recommending?

2. The *Rite Aid* court deemed Grass to be an "accommodation client" and would have denied the disqualification motion on that ground alone. It also found, however, that Grass had consented to Ballard Spahr's continued representation of Rite Aid as a result of an engagement letter to Gerson, Rite Aid's general counsel, which made it "pellucid that Ballard Spar would, in the event of a conflict between Rite Aid and Grass, cease to represent Grass but continue to represent Rite Aid." How did Grass argue that he was not bound by this waiver? Why did the court disagree with Grass's argument? The issue arose in the context of a disqualification motion. Does that context matter?

3. What Richmond is recommending is an advance waiver of a future conflict. We encountered advance waivers in Chapter 5 and learned that

courts do not always enforce them.[12] Try your hand at drafting the type of waiver Richmond might approve for Grass to sign at the time Ballard agreed to represent him as an accommodation to Rite Aid. Is that waiver likely to be upheld? For an example of an advance waiver that was upheld by a court, without relying on the "accommodation client" doctrine, *see* Zador Corp., N.V. v. Kwan, 37 Cal. Rptr.2d 754 (Cal. Ct. App. 1995).[13]

Review Problems

11-1 A lawyer and her law firm have been regular outside counsel to a large, publicly held corporation for several years. The lawyer, a college classmate of the CEO, was initially retained by the CEO, who had recently joined the corporation and who had previously retained either the lawyer or other lawyers in her firm to represent him in various personal matters (including matters involving real estate, trusts and estates, and his divorce) and to represent various companies that he was involved with. The lawyer recently learned that the SEC is conducting an investigation into an allegation that the corporation's recent financial statements were false and misleading. The CEO is not an accountant, but he certified the accuracy of the financial statements. The CEO has requested the lawyer to conduct an internal investigation in order to better represent the corporation in its dealings with the SEC, which will likely interview the CEO, as well as the accountants who prepared the statements, but at a later date. Who will the lawyer be representing in this interview? How should the lawyer prepare for her upcoming interview with the CEO?

11-2 A law firm was retained by Company X, a large insurance company, to organize and incorporate Company Y, a holding company, the primary holding of which was Company X, 95 percent of which is owned by Company Y. The law firm has continued to represent Company Y in a variety of matters, including capital market transactions, securities filings, and bank financings, but has not represented Company X since the reorganization. The law firm has also represented a large bank for many years. Recently the bank retained the law firm to investigate the liability of Company X to the bank on $183 million in surety bonds guaranteeing the obligations of a now-bankrupt company. When the lawyer representing Company X learned of the representation, she called the firm lawyer representing the bank and complained that the law firm needed the consent of Company Y to the law firm's representation of the bank in litigation adverse to its subsidiary, Company X. The lawyer ignored the complaint, continued representing the bank and initiated a lawsuit against Company X. Company X has filed a motion to disqualify the law firm from representing the bank without the informed consent of Company Y, which opposes the representation. Is the motion likely to succeed? Is there additional information you would want to obtain before answering this question?

---

12. *See supra* Chapter 5: Conflicts of Interest: Current Clients.

13. This case was discussed in the *Sheppard* opinion on the propriety of advance waivers; there the court distinguished *Zador* from the facts in *Sheppard*. *See id.*

CHAPTER 12

CORPORATE WRONGDOING

Model Rules 1.2(d), 1.6, 4.1, 1.13, 5.2

In Chapter 8, we explored the limits of zealous representation in transactions. These limitations take into consideration the interests of third persons who might suffer financial harm as a result of a client's crime or fraud. All of the limitations discussed in that chapter, including Model Rules 1.2(d), 1.6, and 4.1, apply equally to clients who are entities. When the client is an entity, however, there is *also* concern that the client itself may be harmed as a result of the misconduct of individual entity constituents. In this chapter, we explore the obligations of an entity lawyer to protect the entity from such internal harm. In particular, we address two sources of authority that address the lawyer's obligation or permission to either "report up" or "report out" when reasonably necessary to prevent substantial harm to the client. These sources of authority are Model Rule 1.13, which was revised in 2003, and the SEC regulations adopted pursuant to the Sarbanes-Oxley legislation, which were briefly mentioned in Chapter 1. Both the MR 1.13 amendments and the SOX legislation and regulations were adopted in response to massive corporate scandals resulting in harm both to the public and to the shareholders of the companies involved.

A. REPORTING UP

We begin by examining the complaint in an action brought by the SEC against a corporation's general counsel. The SOX regulations were not yet in effect, and the general counsel was charged with violation of an SEC rule prohibiting officers and directors of public companies from failing to disclose a material fact to company accountants or causing another person to do so. The SEC sought to enjoin the lawyer from future violations and to obtain civil monetary penalties from him. We will not be concerned with the particular SEC rule that was the basis for this complaint. Rather, after quickly reviewing the lawyer's obligations to third persons under the duties discussed in Chapter 8, we explore what *additional* obligations such a lawyer owes to the client itself under both Model Rule 1.13 and the SOX regulations. The lawyer in question settled the action, without admitting or denying the SEC's allegations, agreeing to pay a $50,000 civil penalty and consenting to an injunction against similar securities law violations.[1]

COMPLAINT

SEC v. Isselmann
No. CV 04-1350 (D. Or. Sept. 23, 2004)[2] . . .

DEFENDANT

6. Isselmann, age 35, resides in Portland, Oregon, and is licensed to practice law in the State of Oregon. He served as General Counsel of ESI from May 2000 until his resignation in August 2003.

FACTUAL ALLEGATIONS

7. ESI is an Oregon corporation with its principal place of business in Portland. The Company makes manufacturing equipment for electronics and other high technology companies. ESI common stock is registered with the Commission pursuant to Section 12(g) of the Exchange Act and trades on the Nasdaq National Market.

8. In order to meet external expectations that ESI would be profitable, the Company's CFO and Controller engaged in a scheme to fraudulently inflate ESI's financial results for its quarter ended August 31, 2002. ESI's CFO and Controller reduced expenses and increased ESI's bottom line by $1 million by secretly and unilaterally deciding to eliminate vested retirement and severance benefits in ESI's Asian offices (which included primarily Japan, but also Taiwan and Korea). This accounting transaction violated generally accepted accounting principles because ESI could not legally eliminate the benefits as it had purported to do. The accounting transaction enabled the CFO and the Controller to avoid a loss and report a profit in line with external expectations.

9. Isselmann was not involved, present, or consulted when the CFO and the Controller made the accounting decision described above.

10. On September 17, 2002, Isselmann participated in a meeting with ESI's Audit Committee[3] and auditors to review the quarterly financial results,

---

1. *See Isselmann*, Litigation Release No. 18,896 (Sept. 23, 2004), available at http://www.sec.gov/litigation/litreleases/lr18896.htm.

2. Available at http://www.sec.gov/litigation/complaints/comp18896b.pdf.

3. [An audit committee is one of the most important committees of a company's board of directors. It is in charge of overseeing financial reporting and disclosure. U.S. publicly traded companies must have a qualified audit committee to be listed on a stock exchange. Committee members must be independent outside directors, and the committee must include at least one member who is a financial expert.—ED.]

including the financial impact of eliminating the retirement and severance benefits. During the meeting, ESI's CFO told the Audit Committee that the Japanese benefits were not legally required and that the decision to eliminate them had been approved by legal counsel. During the same discussion, Isselmann identified ESI's legal counsel in Japan, causing an Audit Committee member to believe that outside legal counsel had reviewed the decision. Although Isselmann was unaware that the CFO had decided to eliminate the benefits in order to fraudulently inflate ESI's financial results, and did not question the CFO about his statements, Isselmann was aware that at that time he had not reviewed or approved the decision to eliminate benefits nor had he, as General Counsel, sought any outside legal review of the case. At the conclusion of the meeting, the Audit Committee approved the inclusion of the $1 million transaction relating to the benefits in ESI's financial results for the quarter.

11. During the same time frame, Isselmann was informed that ESI's auditors had been told that the elimination of the benefits had legal support. In connection with the auditors' review of ESI's quarterly financial results, ESI provided the auditors with a written memorandum stating that the benefits had been eliminated because ESI was under "no legal obligation" to pay them and that the change was approved by ESI's CFO and CEO. Isselmann subsequently received a copy of this memorandum and was told that it had been written for the auditors. However, Isselmann did not speak directly with the auditors and did not inform them that he had not reviewed the retirement benefits issue and that he had not retained outside counsel to do so.

12. On October 3, 2002, Isselmann sought legal advice from ESI's counsel in Japan on whether ESI could eliminate the benefits.

13. On October 7, 2002, the outside counsel informed Isselmann in writing that ESI could not unilaterally eliminate its retirement and severance benefits in Japan and that if ESI wanted to terminate the benefits it was required to first consult with and obtain the consent of ESI's Japanese employees. As Isselmann was aware, ESI had neither consulted the Japanese employees nor obtained their consent to the elimination of their retirement benefits. Despite the contradiction with information Isselmann had been told had been written for ESI's auditors, Isselmann did not speak directly with the auditors. Nor did Isselmann provide the information to the Audit Committee, despite the fact that they had questioned the legal review of the matter.

14. ESI's Disclosure Committee[4] met on October 7, 2002 to review and ensure the accuracy of ESI's quarterly report to the Commission on Form

---

4. [A disclosure committee is a committee of either the board of directors or management, and its purpose is to assist management and the audit committee to prepare the disclosures required under SEC rules. Public companies are not required to have a disclosure committee, but they have become more common following the enactment of Sarbanes-Oxley and the adoption of the SOX regulations. It is not clear from the *Isselmann Complaint* whether the ESI Disclosure Committee was a management committee or a committee of the board of directors. —ED.]

10-Q. Isselmann, other ESI officers and employees, ESI's external auditors, and its Portland-based outside corporate counsel attended the meeting, which had been arranged by Isselmann. During the meeting, Isselmann tried to raise the issue of the termination of the Asian retirement benefits. However, the CFO objected and, as a result, Isselmann provided no further detail and did not provide the written legal advice to the participants in the meeting. After the meeting, Isselmann spoke with the CFO and provided him with a copy of the written legal advice. The CFO subsequently signed the Form 10-A, which included the $1 million increase to the bottom line resulting from the elimination of the benefits.

15. On October 15, 2002, ESI filed its Form 10-Q, reporting net income of $158,000 and earnings per share of $0.01 for the quarter. Before the Form 10-Q was filed with the Commission, an Audit Committee member questioned Isselmann about the language describing the elimination of the benefits and the $1 million accounting entry. Isselmann failed to convey the legal advice to the Audit Committee member in response. As a result, the Form 10-Q was not changed.

16. On March 31, 2003, Isselmann learned that the CFO (who had been promoted to CEO in December 2002) had eliminated the accrued liability for the benefits late at night after learning of an accounting error that negatively impacted earnings. On the night of March 31, 2003, Isselmann reported to ESI's outside counsel his suspicions that the CFO had engaged in misconduct. The next day, Isselmann informed the Audit Committee.

17. On April 1, 2003, after receiving the written legal advice, the Audit Committee commenced an internal investigation. In August 2003, following the completion of an internal investigation by its Audit Committee, ESI restated its financial results for the quarter ended August 31, 2002. The previously recorded accounting transaction was reversed and the accrued liability of $1 million for the payment of Asian retirement and severance benefits was restored.

NOTES AND QUESTIONS

1. ESI's CFO and Controller allegedly fraudulently inflated ESI's publicly reported earnings, and as a result, investors in the company who bought shares at an artificially inflated price suffered harm when the stock price fell after discovery of the fraud. What duties did Isselmann, as ESI's general counsel, owe to these third-party investors? What, if any, remedies are available to the investors to recover compensation from Isselmann? Review the materials in Chapter 8 to answer this question.
2. The allegedly fraudulent scheme posed risks of substantial harm not only to the third-party investors, but also to ESI itself, which could have been charged by the SEC or by private investors with violations of the Securities Acts, as well as common law crimes or frauds. Engaging in fraudulent schemes to artificially inflate share prices was the

basis for earlier corporate scandals that ultimately sent companies like Enron and WorldCom into bankruptcy. In addition to duties of competence and diligence under Model Rules 1.1 and 1.3, Model Rule 1.13(b) imposes a special duty on organization lawyers to protect the organization from harm as a result of the misconduct of insiders like ESI's CFO and Controller. The first sentence of Model Rule 1.13(b) provides:

> If a lawyer for an organization knows that an officer, employee or other person associated with the organization is engaged in action, intends to act or refuses to act in a matter related to the representation that is a violation of a legal obligation to the organization, or a violation of law that reasonably might be imputed to the organization, and that is likely to result in substantial injury to the organization, then the lawyer shall proceed as is reasonably necessary in the best interest of the organization.

This first sentence describes both the circumstances that *trigger* the lawyer's obligation to act to protect the organization and the general *action* that the lawyer is then required to take. The trigger provision contains three requirements pertaining to: (1) the lawyer's scienter; (2) the nature of the legal violation; and (3) the level of threatened harm to the organization. Assuming the truth of the SEC's allegations, was the MR 1.13(b) trigger met in this case? Be sure to consider all three requirements. If the trigger was met, when did this happen? At the meeting with ESI's Audit Committee on September 17, 2002? When Isselmann received a copy of the written memorandum that had been sent to the auditors? When Isselmann received information from ESI's outside counsel in Japan?

3. Once the trigger is met, the general action that the lawyer is required to take is to "proceed as is reasonably necessary in the best interest of the organization." The second sentence of MR 1.13(b), as amended in 2003, further provides:

> Unless the lawyer reasonably believes that it is not necessary in the best interest of the organization to do so, the lawyer shall refer the matter to higher authority in the organization, including, if warranted by the circumstances, to the highest authority that can act on behalf of the organization as determined by applicable law.

Comments [4] and [5] provide further guidance. Could Isselmann have reasonably believed that "reporting up" was not necessary? Assuming Isselmann was required to "report up," to whom was he required to report? The possibilities include the CFO, the CEO, the Audit Committee, the full Board of Directors, and the shareholders.

4. If the "trigger" conditions are not met, then a lawyer like Isselman is not *required* to take any reporting-up action under Model Rule 1.13(b). Is the lawyer *permitted* to do so? What are the potential consequences of a lawyer's inaction in such a situation?

5. What if Isselmann was not the general counsel, but rather was a deputy general counsel or even an assistant general counsel (reporting to an associate or deputy general counsel) when he learned that the CFO had

falsely stated that outside counsel had approved his actions? The duties of a subordinate lawyer are addressed in Model Rule 5.2.

Let's turn now to the "reporting-up" provisions of the SEC regulations adopted pursuant to the Sarbanes-Oxley legislation.

OUTLINE OF SEC'S "REPORTING UP" REGULATIONS
17 C.F.R. PART 205[5]

§205.3 (Issuer as client)

(b)(1): "If an attorney, appearing and practicing before the Commission in the representation of an issuer, becomes aware of evidence of a material violation by the issuer or by any officer, director, employee, or agent of the issuer, the attorney shall report such evidence to the issuer's chief legal officer (or the equivalent thereof) or to both the issuer's chief legal officer and its chief executive officer (or the equivalents thereof) forthwith. . . ."

Relevant definitions include:

Appearing and practicing before the Commission means: "(i) Transacting any business with the Commission, including communications in any form; (ii) Representing an issuer in a Commission administrative proceeding or in connection with any Commission investigation, inquiry, information request, or subpoena; (iii) Providing advice in respect of the United States securities laws or the Commission's rules or regulations thereunder regarding any document that the attorney has notice will be filed with or submitted to, or incorporated into any document that will be filed with or submitted to, the Commission, including the provision of such advice in the context of preparing, or participating in the preparation of any such document; or (iv) Advising an issuer as to whether information or a statement, opinion, or other writing is required under the United States securities laws or the Commission's rules or regulations. . . ." It does not include an attorney who: "(i) Conducts the activities [above] other than in the context of providing legal services to an issuer with whom the attorney has an attorney-client relationship; or (ii) Is a non-appearing foreign attorney." §205.2(a)

Issuer means: A company, government, or political subdivision, agency, or instrumentality of a government that offers stocks, bonds, options, or other securities registered under the Securities Exchange Act of 1934 to raise funds from investors, or proposes to do so. Basically, publicly held companies or private companies planning an initial public offering (IPO). §205.2(h)

---

5. Quotation marks indicate verbatim sections of the regulations. Otherwise, the material represents a summary of the complex regulations.

Evidence of a material violation means: "credible evidence, based upon which it would be unreasonable, under the circumstances, for a prudent and competent attorney not to conclude that it is reasonably likely that a [violation of federal or state securities law or material breach of fiduciary duty], has occurred, is ongoing, or is about to occur." §205.2(e), (i).

(b)(2) "The chief legal officer (or the equivalent thereof) [CLO] shall cause such inquiry into the evidence of a material violation as he or she reasonably believes is appropriate to determine whether the material violation described in the report has occurred, is ongoing, or is about to occur . . . and advise the reporting attorney of the basis for such determination. Unless the [CLO] reasonably believes that no material violation has occurred, is ongoing, or is about to occur, he or she shall take all reasonable steps to cause the issuer to adopt an appropriate response, and shall advise the reporting attorney thereof. In lieu of causing an inquiry under this paragraph (b), a [CLO] may refer a report of evidence of a material violation to a qualified legal compliance committee under paragraph (c)(2) of this section [QLCC] if the issuer has duly established a [QLCC] prior to the report of evidence of a material violation."

A QLCC is an optional board committee comprised of at least one member of the audit committee and two or more additional independent directors, which has established a detailed set of procedures as outlined in the SEC regulations. §205.3(c)(2).

An appropriate response means a response as a result of which the reporting attorney reasonably believes: "(1) "That no material violation . . . has occurred, is ongoing, or is about to occur; (2) That the issuer has, as necessary, adopted appropriate remedial measures, including appropriate steps or sanctions to stop any material violations that are ongoing, to prevent any material violation that has yet to occur, and to remedy or otherwise appropriately address any material violation that has already occurred and to minimize the likelihood of its recurrence; or (3) That the issuer, with the consent of the issuer's board of directors . . . has retained or directed an attorney to review the reported evidence of a material violation and either: (i) Has substantially implemented any remedial recommendations made by such attorney after a reasonable investigation . . . ; or (ii) Has been advised that such attorney may . . . assert a colorable defense on behalf of the issuer . . . in any investigation [or proceeding] related to the reported evidence of a material violation." §205.2(b)

(b)(3) "Unless an attorney who has made a report under paragraph (b)(1) of this section reasonably believes that the chief legal officer or the chief executive officer of the issuer . . . has provided an appropriate response within a reasonable time, the attorney shall report the evidence of a material violation to: (i) The audit committee . . . ; (ii) Another committee [consisting solely of independent directors]; or (iii) The issuer's board of directors (if the issuer's board of directors has no committee consisting solely of [independent directors])."

(b)(6) "An attorney shall not have any obligation to report evidence of a material violation . . . if: (i) The attorney was retained or directed by the issuer's [CLO] . . . to investigate such evidence . . . and: (A) The attorney reports the results of such investigation to the [CLO] . . . ; and (B) Except where the attorney and the [CLO] each reasonably believes that no material violation has occurred, is ongoing, or is about to occur, the [CLO] reports the results of the investigation to the issuer's board of directors, [an applicable committee], or a [QLCC]; or (ii) The attorney . . . [will] . . . assert a colorable defense on the part of the issuer . . . in any investigation or judicial or administrative proceeding relating to such evidence . . . and the [CLO] provides reasonable and timely reports . . . to the issuer's board of directors [or other applicable committee]."

(b)(9) "An attorney who does not reasonably believe that the issuer has made an appropriate response within a reasonable time to the [attorney's] report . . . shall explain his or her reasons therefor to the [CLO, the CEO,] and the directors to whom the attorney has reported the evidence. . . ."

§205.5 (Responsibilities of a subordinate attorney)

"(a) An attorney who appears and practices . . . on a matter under the supervision or direction of another attorney (other than under the direct supervision or direction of the [CLO]) is a subordinate attorney.

(b) A subordinate attorney shall comply with this part notwithstanding that the subordinate attorney acted act the direction of or under the supervision of another person.

(c) A subordinate attorney complies with §205.3 if the subordinate attorney reports to his or her supervising attorney . . . evidence of a material violation of which the subordinate attorney has become aware. . . ."

NOTES AND QUESTIONS

1. Like MR 1.13, the SOX "reporting up" regulations contain both a *trigger* and the *action* required once that trigger is met. Was the SOX trigger met under the SEC allegations against Isselmann? Consider the same three requirements that we identified as critical under MR 1.13 pertaining to: (1) the lawyer's scienter; (2) the nature of the legal violation; and (3) the level of threatened harm to the organization.

2. How is the SOX trigger different than the trigger under MR 1.13? When MR 1.13 was being amended in 2003, consideration was given to changing the scienter requirement to "knows or reasonably should

know," but that change was rejected. Would that have made the scienter requirement under MR 1.13 the same as under the SOX regulations? Which do you think is the right approach?

3. Consider the definition of the phrase "evidence of a material violation." In the SEC's initial proposal, the trigger was met when a lawyer "'reasonably . . . believe[d]' that a material violation of law 'has occurred, is occurring, or is about to occur.'"[6] The SEC's official comments asserted that the standard was objective, but a group of academics disagreed.[7] Can you see why? The definition was rewritten to take the professors' concerns into account, but the professors objected yet again, not only because they viewed the standard as "incomprehensible," but also because they believed that the use of the double negative had the practical effect of establishing a knowledge standard,[8] similar to that contained in MR 1.13(b). Do you agree? Is there a substantive difference between the adopted standard and the standard proposed by the academics, in which a lawyer would be required to report up when "confronted with information that a prudent and competent attorney, acting reasonably under the same circumstances, would conclude was credible evidence of a material violation by the issuer"?[9]

4. All lawyers representing organizations are governed by MR 1.13, but not all such lawyers are covered under the SOX regulations. Which lawyers must comply with the SEC regulations? Was Isselmann one of them? What about a litigator who is asked to review a proposed description of pending litigation for purposes of a document to be filed with the SEC?

5. Once the trigger was met, what action would Isselmann have been required to take under the SOX regulations?

6. What if Isselmann was not the general counsel, but rather was a deputy general counsel or even an assistant or associate general counsel (reporting to either the associate or deputy general counsel) when he learned that the CFO was falsely stating that outside counsel had approved his actions?

B. REPORTING OUT

If Isselmann had reported his concerns to the board of directors, is there any indication in the SEC complaint whether the board would have stopped the CFO and Controller from fraudulently inflating the company's publicly

---

6. Susan P. Koniak, When the Hurlyburly's Done: The Bar's Struggle with the SEC, 103 Colum. L. Rev. 1236, 1271 (2003) (citing Implementation of Standards of Professional Conduct for Attorneys, Securities Act Release No. 33-8150, 67 Fed. Reg. 71,670, 71, 704 (proposed Dec. 2, 2002)).

7. *Id.* at 1272-73. Professor Koniak was one of the drafters of these comments. *Id.*

8. *Id.* at 1275.

9. *Id.* at 1275, n.128.

reported earnings? What if the board refused to act? In some states, Isselmann might have been *required* to disclose ESO's intended criminal or fraudulent conduct, under that state's version of Rule 1.6, in order to protect investors from suffering substantial economic harm as a result of ESO's conduct.[10] Under Model Rule 1.6, Isselmann was *permitted* but not required to do so. And in California and some other states, disclosure is *prohibited* except when the threatened harm is death or serious bodily harm.[11]

But what about the potential harm to be suffered by ESI itself? Model Rule 1.13(c) addresses the obligation or permission of lawyers like Isselmann to disclose the intended or ongoing violations, even when the lawyer is prohibited from making such disclosures under Rule 1.6. What may or must Isselmann have done under MR 1.13(c) if ESI's board of directors refused to act? What qualifications to MR 1.13(c) are made under MR 1.13(d)? Would MR 1.13(d) have applied to Isselmann? What is the basis for the MR 1.13(d) limitations? Are they justified, or do they essentially gut the lawyer's permission to report out?

Commentators have observed that, as a practical matter, MR 1.13(c) will rarely provide any protection for publicly held companies, but that it might be highly effective in closely held companies. Can you see why that would be? What can the lawyer for a closely held company do that is difficult for a lawyer for a publicly held company to do?

Let's turn now to the "reporting out" provisions of the SEC's SOX regulations. The following materials provide both the permissive disclosure provision that was adopted in the SEC's final regulations and a mandatory "noisy withdrawal" rule that was proposed but never adopted. The SEC had proposed the mandatory "noisy withdrawal" provision as part of the initial draft rules submitted for public comment. However, after receiving uniformly negative comments (except from a group of academics), the SEC provided time for additional comments.[12] Nothing more has been done with that proposal.

**OUTLINE OF SEC'S "REPORTING OUT" REGULATIONS
17 C.F.R. PART 205**

Adopted regulation
§ 205.3 (Issuer as client)

(d)(1) "Any report under this section . . . or any response thereto . . . may be used by an attorney in connection with any investigation, proceeding, or litigation in which the attorney's compliance with this part is in issue."

---

10. *See supra* Chapter 4: Privilege and Confidentiality.

11. *See id.*

12. *See generally* Koniak, *supra* n. 6 at 1269-73. Professor Koniak was one of the academics who supported the mandatory "noisy withdrawal" provision.

(d)(2) "An attorney . . . may reveal to the Commission, without the issuer's consent, confidential information related to the representation to the extent the attorney reasonably believes necessary: (i) To prevent the issuer from committing a material violation that is likely to cause substantial injury to the financial interest or property of the issuer or investors; (ii) To prevent the issuer, in a Commission investigation or administrative proceeding from committing perjury . . . that is likely to perpetrate a fraud upon the Commission; or (iii) To rectify the consequences of a material violation by the issuer that caused, or may cause, substantial injury to the financial interest or property of the issuer or investors in the furtherance of which the attorney's services were used."

Proposed but never adopted provision
67 Fed. Reg. 71688-71690 (Dec. 2, 2002)

§ 205.3 (Issuer as client)

Notice to the Commission where there is no appropriate response within a reasonable period of time.

(d)(1) "Where an attorney who has reported evidence of a material violation . . . does not receive an appropriate response . . . and the attorney reasonably believes that a material violation is ongoing or is about to occur and is likely to result in a substantial injury to the financial interest or property of the issuer or of investors:

(i) An attorney retained by the issuer shall:

(A) Withdraw forthwith from representing the issuer, indicating that the withdrawal is based on professional considerations;

(B) Within one business day of withdrawing, give written notice to the Commission of the attorney's withdrawal, indicating that the withdrawal was based on professional considerations; and

(C) Promptly disaffirm to the Commission any opinion, document, affirmation, representation, characterization, or the like in a document filed with or submitted to the Commission . . . that the attorney has prepared or assisted in preparing and that the attorney reasonably believes is or may be materially false or misleading;

(ii) An attorney employed by the issuer shall:

(A) Within one business day, notify the Commission in writing that he or she intends to disaffirm some opinion, document, affirmation [as described above];

(B) Promptly disaffirm to the Commission in writing, any such opinion, affirmation, representation, characterization, or the like; and

(iii) The issuer's [CLO] shall inform any attorney retained or employed to replace the attorney who has withdrawn that the previous attorney's withdrawal was based on professional considerations."

(d)(2) "Where an attorney who has reported evidence of a material violation . . . does not receive an appropriate response . . . and the attorney reasonably believes that a material violation has occurred and is likely to have resulted in substantial injury to the financial interest or property of the issuer or of investors but is not ongoing:

(i) An attorney retained by the issuer may: [proceed as is outlined in section (d)(1)(i)];

(ii) An attorney employed by the issuer may: [proceed as is outlined in section (d)(1)(ii)]; and

(iii) [Same as (d)(1)(iii)."

NOTES AND QUESTIONS

1. How do the adopted SEC "reporting out" regulations differ from Model Rules 1.6, 1.13(c), and 3.3(a)(3)? Are there circumstances in which a lawyer would be prohibited from disclosing under the Model Rules but permitted to disclose under the SOX regulations?

2. Consider a lawyer who is prohibited from disclosing under state rules of professional conduct but is permitted to disclose under the SOX regulations. This will occur most often in states like California that prohibit any disclosures designed to prevent or rectify merely economic harm.[13] Is a lawyer who discloses information pursuant to SOX subject to discipline by the state? Another section of the SOX regulations provides that "[a]n attorney who complies in good faith with provisions of this part shall not be subject to discipline or otherwise liable under inconsistent standards imposed by any state."[14] A Washington State Bar Association "Interim Formal Ethics Opinion" took the position that its then-existing rule permitting significantly less disclosure than is permitted under SOX was not "inconsistent" with the SOX regulations because disclosure pursuant to the federal regulation was merely *permissive*; therefore, a lawyer could comply with *both* state and federal law by maintaining confidentiality. In response, the SEC argued that the federal regulation preempted the Washington State rule because it was clear that the federal mandate was to give lawyers the ability to disclose in appropriate circumstances.[15] Before the issue could be resolved, Washington State amended its version of Rule 1.6 to permit more disclosure. A more recent North Carolina ethics opinion endorsed the SEC's position, concluding that North Carolina lawyers may disclose pursuant to SOX even when the North Carolina Rules of Professional Conduct prohibit disclosure.[16]

---

13. *See supra* Chapter 4: Privilege and Confidentiality.

14. 17 C.F.R. §205.6.

15. *See* Roger C. Cramton et al., Legal and Ethical Duties of Lawyers after Sarbanes-Oxley, 49 Vill. L. Rev. 725, 799-802 (2004).

16. *See* N.C. State Bar, 2005 Formal Ethics Op. 9.

B. Reporting Out   365

3. How does the proposed-but-never-adopted version of Section 205.3(d) differ from both the SEC's adopted rule and the Model Rules?

4. Entity lawyers who are considering reporting either up or out, when permitted (or even required) to do so, may realistically fear they will be discharged by management. The Sarbanes-Oxley legislation offers some whistleblower protection to in-house counsel, but this protection applies only to lawyers under the jurisdiction of the SEC.[17] For a discussion of the ability of in-house lawyers to sue under state law for retaliatory discharge if fired or demoted because they either refused to act unethically or acted pursuant to their ethical responsibilities, see *infra* Chapter 13: In-House Counsel.

5. The SOX regulations, including the proposed mandatory "noisy withdrawal" provision, have been described as efforts to strengthen the securities lawyer's "gatekeeping" function. A gatekeeper is a reputational intermediary that uses its "reputational capital, acquired over many years and many clients, . . . to assure the accuracy of statements or representations that it either makes or verifies."[18] Auditors[19] are professionals whose services consist primarily of gatekeeping, whereas "the attorney is primarily an advocate or a transaction engineer and only sometimes a gatekeeper."[20] Some have argued that the lawyer's typical role is inconsistent with that of a gatekeeper; therefore, lawyers should not be expected or required to perform a gatekeeper function.[21] John Coffee has argued that lawyers can successfully perform a significant gatekeeping role, but only when "the attorney is playing a clearly defined professional role that the client has invited" because "[o]therwise, the attorney is risking professional disaster and will predictably resist."[22] As a result, Coffee is skeptical that lawyers would report misconduct to the SEC under the proposed mandatory "noisy withdrawal" provision, but he has supported other minimum standards that the SEC could adopt, such as requiring a lawyer who is principally responsible for drafting a document or report filed with the SEC to certify "(1) that such attorney believes the statements made in the document or report to be true and accurate in all material respects, and (2) that such

---

17. *See* 18. U.S.C. §1514A.

18. John C. Coffee, Jr., Gatekeeper Failure and Reform: The Challenge of Fashioning Relevant Reforms, 84 B.U. L. Rev. 301, 308 (2004). The term was first used to describe investment bankers as gatekeepers. *See* Ronald J. Gilson & Ranier H. Kraakman, The Mechanisms of Market Efficiency, 70 Va. L. Rev. 549, 613-21 (1984).

19. Auditors review and verify the accuracy of financial records, including corporate financial statements.

20. Coffee, *supra* n. 18 at 309.

21. *See, e.g.,* Jill E. Fisch & Kenneth M. Rosen, Is There a Role for Lawyers in Preventing Future Enrons?, 48 Vill. L. Rev. 1097, 1097 (2003).

22. Coffee, *supra* n. 18 at 354-55.

attorney is not aware of any additional material information whose disclosure is necessary in order to make the statements made . . . not misleading."[23] Do you agree with the opponents of mandating lawyers as gatekeepers that the result will be that clients are likely to stop confiding in their lawyers, resulting in even more illegality?

C. LAWYER LIABILITY

1. Liability to the Client Entity

Apart from MR 1.13(b) or the SOX regulations, lawyers have a common law duty to exercise reasonable care to avoid causing harm to their clients. As a result, if a lawyer knows or reasonably should know that a constituent is either breaching a duty to the entity or engaging in illegal conduct that will be imputed to the entity, the lawyer has a common law duty to act reasonably in the best interest of the entity. Failure to do so might result in either a legal malpractice action or an action for aiding and abetting a breach of fiduciary owed by a constituent to the entity.

Aside from any difficulties in proof, there is a potential legal obstacle to recovery by an entity client against the lawyer or the law firm — the doctrine of *in pari delicto*. This doctrine provides that a plaintiff who participated equally with a defendant in wrongdoing cannot pursue an action against the defendant. A classic example involving an individual client is a plaintiff who, following the negligent advice of the defendant-lawyer, lied under oath: a court will likely conclude that the client knew it was wrong to lie under oath; therefore, both client and lawyer were equally at fault. As a result, the court will dismiss the lawsuit under the doctrine of *in pari delicto*.[24]

In the context of a business-entity client, the plaintiff company's "wrongdoing" is based on imputing the offending constituent's knowledge or conduct to the company itself, using basic agency principles, including principles permitting injured third parties to sue the company based on the constituent's misconduct.[25] Consider the following two cases, in which the same judge reached different results in separate lawsuits against two different law firms that represented the same client with respect to the same wrongdoing.

---

23. *Id.* at 355-56.

24. *See* Paula Schaefer, In Pari Delicto Deconstructed: Dismantling the Doctrine That Protects the Business Entity's Lawyer from Malpractice Liability, 90 St. John's L. Rev. 1003, 1004 (2016).

25. *See, e.g.,* Restatement (Third) of Agency §§5.03 (2006) (imputing facts an agent knows to the principal if knowledge of facts is material to agent's duties to principal), 7.03 (principal's direct and vicarious liability for harm caused by agent to third persons).

C. Lawyer Liability

Peterson v. Winston & Strawn LLP
729 F.3d 750 (7th Cir. 2013)

Easterbrook, Chief Judge

Ever since Gregory Bell's mutual funds, known as the Lancelot or Colossus group (collectively "the Funds"), folded in late 2008, their trustee in bankruptcy has been seeking assets from solvent third parties. Last year we considered the Trustee's claims against the Funds' auditor. This appeal concerns the Trustee's claim, on behalf of two Funds, against one of their law firms. . . .

The Funds invested most of their money in ventures run by Thomas Petters, who claimed to be operating as a commercial factor—that is, a lender financing other businesses' inventory. A factor advances money to purchase inventory, takes a security interest in the inventory, and is repaid as the inventory is sold. The Funds' offering circulars told their investors that the Funds would verify the inventory's existence and ensure that repayments were made to a "lockbox"—that is, made directly to financial institutions that would ensure the money's proper application.

The Funds did not keep these promises and could not do so, because Petters was running a Ponzi scheme in which new investments were used to pay off older investments rather than to finance an operational business. Peters has been convicted of fraud. Bell concedes that he learned of, and joined, Petters's scam early in 2008; Bell pleaded guilty to fraud. But both Bell and the Funds' Trustee maintain that until 2008, Bell was ignorant of the Ponzi scheme. The events in question concern years during which, we must assume (because this suit was resolved on the pleadings), Bell honestly if incompetently thought Petters's businesses legitimate.

The Funds hired Winston & Strawn in 2005 to revise their offering circular (the "Confidential Information Memorandum") shown to persons thinking about investing in the Funds. According to the Trustee's complaint, Bell told the law firm that Petters refused to allow the Funds to verify the existence of inventory and that repayments did not come through lockboxes. The law firm prepared a revised offering circular, which the Funds started using in 2006; this circular, like the 2003 version, represents that the Funds will verify the existence of inventory and ensure that factors use lockboxes. The Trustee contends that the law firm committed malpractice, but the district court, invoking the doctrine of *in pari delicto*, dismissed the suit after concluding that Bell's knowledge was at least as great as the law firm's.

The Trustee has no greater rights against the law firm than the Funds themselves had, and the law firm maintains that the Funds had none because Bell (and thus the Funds) knew as much as the law firm did about Petters's activities. One potential problem with this perspective is that people and corporations often hire law firms for advice about what to do. Suppose we take it as established that Bell had learned of Petters's scheme by 2005. He and the Funds might well have needed to know what should happen next.

If a law firm gave incompetent advice, it could not defend by asserting that Bell already knew the facts. The fault would not be equal, because Bell would have hired the law firm for legal expertise rather than factual information. Similarly, if Bell had been indicted for securities fraud and supplied a law firm with facts showing that the prosecution was untimely, and the law firm failed to invoke the statute of limitations, it could not defend a malpractice suit by observing that Bell knew all the facts. When the goal of hiring a professional adviser is to cope with the consequence of known facts, the parties' equal access to the facts is beside the fact.

Nonetheless, the Trustee's complaint was properly dismissed, because it does not plausibly allege that the law firm violated any duty to the Funds. The Trustee does not contend that Winston & Strawn should have provided better, or even different, legal advice. Instead he contends that it should have done two things on learning that Petters would not allow verification of inventory and did not use a lockbox: The law firm should have alerted the Funds' directors and should have revealed the truth in the 2006 offering circular.

The latter step would not have offered a benefit to the Funds (as opposed to their investors); to the contrary, it probably would have precipitated the Funds' immediate collapse. The Trustee has stepped into the shoes of the Funds, *not* of their investors, who may (or may not) have independent claims based on the contents of the 2006 circular. Lancelot Investors Fund and Lancelot Investment Management (of which Bell was the sole principal) issued that circular and thus vouched for the truth of the statements it contained. Winston & Strawn did not sign the documents or warrant the truth of its contents. As administrator of the Funds' estate, the Trustee is in no position to collect from the law firm on the theory that factual representations in the 2006 circular were false, when the Funds represented them to be true.

As for the Trustee's assertion that the law firm should have alerted the Funds' directors, the initial problem is that the law firm was not hired to blow the whistle on Bell, and the Trustee does not identify any rule of Illinois law (which governs here) treating failure to do so as a tort. The SEC's rules sometimes require disclosure or "noisy withdrawal," but the Funds were established in the Cayman Islands, and the Trustee does not contend that federal law governs the law firm's responsibilities. Rule 1.13 of the Illinois Rules of Professional Responsibility, which does apply (because the law firm rendered its services in Illinois), sometimes requires a lawyer to report to the highest corporate authority—which may well have been Bell, but we'll assume that the board is a higher authority. And we can assume, without deciding, that Rule 1.13 required the law firm to do more than it did. The problem for the Trustee is that no court in Illinois has held that failure to report a corporate manager's acts to the board of directors exposes a law firm to damages for malpractice. Rules of professional conduct are enforced through the disciplinary mechanism rather than by awards of damages. The Trustee does not argue otherwise.

Nor does the complaint plausibly allege that alerting the directors would have made a difference. The offering circular says that the four directors appointed Bell's firm, Lancelot Investment Management, to be responsible for conducting all of the Funds' investment-management operations. Thus Bell was as firmly in charge of the Funds as he was of his advisory firm — and we said exactly that [in the opinion involving the Trustee's action against the Funds' auditor]. [That opinion] rejects the Trustee's argument that Bell's knowledge should not be imputed to the Funds because he was acting adversely to their interests. The Trustee repeats that argument, which fares no better the second time.

One of the four directors lived in Hong Kong and the other three in the Bahamas. Nothing in the complaint suggests that any of the four ever exercised any responsibility over the Funds other than to delegate all powers and duties to Bell. The Trustee might have bolstered his claim by conducting an investigation into the four directors' careers and learning how they had responded if or when other firms with which they were affiliated had encountered troubled investments or balky borrowers (Petters's ventures fit both descriptions). But the Trustee conceded at oral argument that he had not conducted any pre-filing investigation, and he did not ask for discovery in order to learn whether the directors were independent of Bell in any realistic sense.

This is equally true with respect to the "loan acquisition officer," a position that the 2006 circular said would be created. The Trustee does not know whether the job was filled — or, if it was, what the incumbent learned from Bell or Petters — and seems remarkably uncurious about those subjects. This makes it hard to advance a plausible claim that the law firm had a duty to bypass Bell and present the facts about Petters to the "loan acquisition officer."

The complaint and briefs stop with the assertion that the directors had a legal duty to ride herd on Bell and thus would have done so. That may be a correct statement of their duties, but the Trustee has not offered anything to make plausible a contention that the directors would have fulfilled them, even if the law firm had a duty to bypass Bell. Given the plausibility standard added to federal pleading law . . . , this complaint was properly dismissed.

Peterson v. Katten Muchin Rosenman LLP
792 F.3d 789 (7th Cir. 2015)

EASTERBROOK, Circuit Judge

[T]he Trustee appointed to marshal the assets of Lancelot Investors Fund and other entities in bankruptcy (collectively "the Funds") has filed multiple suits against solvent entities that, the Trustee maintains, failed to detect the peril the Funds were in and help curtail their risks.

This appeal concerns the Trustee's contention that Katten Muchin Rosenman LLP committed legal malpractice during the six years it advised the

Funds how to structure their transactions with entities controlled by Thomas Petters. As we recount in other opinions we have cited, the Funds loaned money to the Petters vehicles, which in turn supposedly financed some of Costco's inventory. Petters insisted that the Funds not contact Costco; doing that, he said, would upset his favorable business relations with it.

Security for the Funds' advances was supposed to come in two forms; paperwork showing the inventory Petters furnished and Costco's undertaking to pay, and a "lockbox" bank account into which Costco would deposit its payments for the Funds to draw on, eliminating any risk that Petters would put his hand into the till. That is how the Funds described the arrangement to their own investors. Yet Costco never put a penny into the account; all of the money came from a Petters entity. Gregory Bell, who established and managed the Funds, asserts that Petters told him that Costco had insisted on paying one of Petters's vehicles. [H]owever, Bell (and the Funds) lied to investors about the arrangements and asserted that the money came directly from Costco. The actual setup left the Funds at Petters's mercy—and he had no mercy, just as he never had any dealings with Costco. When Petters's Ponzi scheme collapsed, so did the Funds.

The Trustee's complaint contends that Katten violated its duty to its clients by not telling Bell that the actual arrangement (no checks with Costco, no money directly from Costco) posed a risk that Petters was not running a real business. Katten had been engaged to structure transactions, the Trustee asserts, and part of that duty entails telling the client what contractual devices are appropriate to the situation. The complaint focuses on two periods: first, a time during 2003 when principal contracts were being negotiated and signed; second, a time during 2007 when Petters fell behind in payments to the lockbox (he asserted that Costco was late paying him) and the Funds consulted Katten about what to do. According to the complaint, in 2003 Katten did not advise the Funds to ask for additional protections—the Trustee believes that Katten's lawyers did not recognize the risk from the combination of no contacts and no direct payments, plus the potential that the paperwork purporting transactions with Costco had been forged. The complaint also alleges that in 2007 Katten advised the Funds to defer the due dates on the payments, and that no other change was necessary, even though the delay coupled with the other indicators should have alerted any competent transactions lawyer to the possibility of fraud, and the lawyer should have counseled the client to obtain better security.

The district court dismissed the complaint under Fed.R.Civ.P. 12(d)(6) for failure to state a claim on which relief may be granted. Instead of taking the complaint on its own terms, the district court's opinion narrates the events from the law firm's perspective. Katten maintains, and the opinion states, that Bell knowingly by-passed verification with Costco in order to obtain a higher interest rate from Petters. Thus the Funds knowingly took a risk and cannot blame a law firm for failing to give business advice.

There are three problems with this decision. First, it rests on a factual view extrinsic to the complaint and therefore is not an appropriate use of

Rule 12(b)(6). The complaint alleges that Bell attributed the Funds' high return at least in part to the lack of direct verification with Costco and that he told some would-be investors about this tradeoff, but it does not allege that Bell was indifferent to legal advice concerning how to curtail risks given the no-contact constraint.

Second, the decision does not engage the complaint's main contention—not that Katten was supposed to do something about Petters's no-direct-contact edict, but that Katten had to alert its client to the risk of allowing repayments to be routed through Petters, drafting and negotiating any additional contracts necessary to contain that risk. As the complaint depicts matters, Bell did not appreciate the difference between funds from Costco and funds from Petters. A competent transactions lawyer should have appreciated that the former arrangement offers much better security than the latter and alerted its client. If a client rejects that advice, the lawyer does not need to badger the client; but the complaint alleges that the advice was not offered, leaving the client in the dark about the degree of the risk it was taking.

The third problem is that the decision does not identify any principle of Illinois law that sharply distinguishes between business advice and legal advice. It is hard to see how any such bright line could exist, since one function of a transactions lawyer is to counsel the client how different legal structures carry different levels of risk, and then to draft and negotiate contracts that protect the client's interests. A client can make a business decision about how much risk to take; the lawyer must accept and implement that decision. But it is in the realm of legal advice to tell a client that the best security in a transaction such as this one is direct verification with Costco plus direct deposits to a lockbox; the second-best is direct deposits to a lockbox; and worse is relying wholly on papers over which Petters had complete control, for they may be shams with forged signatures by Costco managers who have never heard of Petters. Knowing degrees of risk presented by different legal structures, a client *then* can make a business decision; but it takes a competent lawyer, who understands how the law of secured transactions works (and who also knows what's normal in the world of commercial factoring that Petters claimed to practice), to ensure that the client knows which legal devices are available and how they affect risks.

The district court did not cite any Illinois statute or decision holding that a transactions lawyer never needs to supply a client with legal information that affects the degree of business risk attached to a transactions. Nor does Katten's brief in this court. Our own search did not turn up any such case. . . .

We take the point that a transactions lawyer's task is to propose, draft, and negotiate contractual arrangements that carry out a client's business objective, not to tell the client to have a different objective or to do business with a different counterparty. A lawyer is not a business consultant. But within the scope of the engagement a lawyer must tell the client which different legal forms are available to carry out the client's business, and how (if at all) the risks of that business differ with the different legal forms. Even if Bell was determined to do business with Petters, the Fund's lawyers still could have explained how to structure the transactions in a less risky way, and if Petters refused to cooperate then Bell might have reconsidered lending the Funds' money to his operations. The Trustee alleges that Katten did not offer any advice about how relative risks correspond to different legal devices, and its complaint states a legally recognized claim for relief. Whether the law firm has a defense—and whether any neglect on its part caused injury—are subjects for the district court in the first instance.

The judgment is reversed, and the case is remanded for proceedings consistent with this opinion.

NOTES AND QUESTIONS

1. What explains the difference in the result in these two cases? Is it likely that the lawyers representing the Trustee in *Katten* changed their pleading strategy in response to the result in *Winston Strawn*? Are you persuaded by Judge Easterbrook's reasoning in *Winston Strawn*?

2. Review the SEC complaint against Isselmann. Isselmann was an in-house lawyer, and companies dissatisfied with their in-house lawyers rarely sue them for malpractice.[26] Assume that Isselmann was an outside lawyer and that the SEC allegations formed the basis of a malpractice complaint filed by ESI against Isselmann and his hypothetical law firm for failure to alert higher authorities in the company concerning the suspected misconduct of ESI's CFO and Controller in fraudulently inflating ESI's publicly reported earnings. Would such a lawsuit be more similar to the facts in *Winston & Strawn* or to the facts in *Katten*?

3. Assume that an ESI complaint would be governed by the precedent in *Winston & Strawn*. In that case, Judge Easterbrook concluded that there was no evidence that the Funds' directors would have acted to protect the Funds even if Winston & Strawn had alerted them to Bell's misconduct. Is the evidence on causation different in the case against Isselmann? If so, can you frame an argument that might permit ESI to withstand a motion to dismiss against Isselmann and his hypothetical law firm even under the more restrictive opinion in *Winston & Strawn*?

4. Some courts have not applied the *in pari delicto* defense when the plaintiff is a trustee in bankruptcy. These courts find that the so-called "adverse interest" exception to the doctrine applies. Under this

---

26. There are several reasons for the scarcity of legal malpractice lawsuits against in-house counsel, including the requirement in some states that an employer indemnify an employee for expenses or losses incurred in the discharge of their duties, *see, e.g.*, Cal. Lab. Code §2802 (2016), or, in the absence of such a requirement, the existence of a negotiated indemnification agreement. In any event, in-house counsel rarely has malpractice insurance (for which the company would undoubtedly have to pay), and may not have sufficient assets to warrant a lawsuit.

exception, knowledge of a constituent is not imputed to the company when the constituent acts solely out of self-interest against the interest of the company (as, for example, when a constituent embezzles from the company). For example, in FDIC v. O'Melveny & Myers, 969 F.2d 744 (9th Cir. 1992), the court held that a law firm's alleged negligence in failing to detect insider misconduct resulting in false statements in a memo to potential investors did not benefit the company because "conduct aggravating a corporation's insolvency and fraudulently prolonging its life does not benefit that corporation." 969 F.2d at 750. In a subsequent opinion, the court held that, even if the corporation benefitted from insider misconduct and, therefore, the corporation itself would be denied a recovery, "there is little reason to impose the same punishment on a trustee, receiver or similar innocent entity" because that would deny a recovery to "the wrongdoer's innocent creditors," who are the real victims of the fraud when the company is insolvent. FDIC v. O'Melveny & Myers, 61 F.3d 17, 19 (9th Cir. 1995).

5. Most courts reject both of the *O'Melveny* arguments. First, with respect to corporate benefit, courts commonly find that adverse interest does not apply "when the agent acts for both himself and the principal, though his primary interest is inimical to the principal." Oppenheimer-Palmieri Fund, L.P. v. Peat Marwick Main & Co., 802 F. Supp. 804, 817 (E.D.N.Y. 1992). As a result, even the temporary benefit of prolonging the corporation's life constitutes a benefit sufficient to avoid the adverse interest exception. *See. e.g.*, In re Greater Southeast Community Hospital Corp., 353 B.R. 324, 368 (Bankr. D.D.C. 2006) (finding that even acts that are "ultimately injurious" to a company may provide "an immediate benefit to the [company] at the expense of innocent third parties," comparing the harm suffered by the company to the harm suffered by an imprisoned robber as "the price of having enjoyed the temporary benefit of his ill-gotten gains").[27] Second, with respect to the applicability of the *in pari delicto* defense in cases involving trustees, receivers and other innocent parties, most courts agree with Judge Easterbrook that such parties have no greater rights than the companies themselves have. Peterson v. Winston & Strawn, 729 F.3d at 751. For an extensive review of the *in pari delicto* defense in lawyer malpractice cases, as well as an argument to narrow the applicability of the defense in such cases, *see* Paula Schaeffer, *In Pari Delicto* Deconstructed: Dismantling the Doctrine that Protects the Business Entity's Lawyer from Malpractice Liability, 90 St. John's L. Rev. 1003 (2016).

---

27. *See also* Kirschner v. KPMG LLP, 938 N.E. 941 (N.Y. 2010) ("So long as the corporate wrongdoer's fraudulent conduct enables the business to survive — to attract investors and customers and raise funds for corporate purposes — this test is not met.").

2. Liability to Others for Violating Securities Laws

Chapter 8 addressed a lawyer's liability to others based on common law fraud and other wrongdoing in the representation of clients, including a lawyer's primary liability for his or her own false representations, as well as aiding and abetting a client's fraud or breach of fiduciary duty. The principles discussed in that chapter apply both to individual clients and to entity clients.

This section addresses a lawyer's liability to others based on violations of securities laws statutes, principally Section 10(b) of the federal Securities Exchange Act of 1934, which prohibits various forms of fraud or deceit in connection with the purchase and sale of securities issued by public companies.

In Central Bank of Denver v. First Interstate Bank of Denver,[28] the U.S. Supreme Court held that Section 10(b) does not provide for aiding and abetting liability in lawsuits brought by private parties. As a result, these parties began to assert theories of liability based on primary violations, even when the defendants were secondary actors such as lawyers and accountants.[29] Following *Central Bank of Denver*, there was a split in authority among the federal circuit courts of appeal concerning the circumstances under which secondary actors can be primary violators of SEC Rule 10b-5's prohibition against making false or misleading statements. The majority of circuit courts followed the "bright line" test illustrated in the following opinion. This opinion also addresses a lawyer's primary liability for a "scheme" to defraud investors under a different provision of Rule 10b-5.

Pacific Inv. Management Co. LLC v. Mayer Brown LLP
603 F.3d 144 (2d Cir. 2010)

JOSE A. CABRANES, Circuit Judge: . . .

Plaintiffs-appellants, Pacific Investment Management Company LLC and RH Capital Associates (jointly, "plaintiffs") appeal from a judgment of the Southern District of New York (Gerard E. Lynch, *Judge*) dismissing their claims against defendants-appellees Mayer Brown LLP ("Mayer Brown"), a law firm, and Joseph P. Collins ("Collins"), a former partner at Mayer Brown. Plaintiffs alleged that defendants violated federal securities laws in the course of representing the now-bankrupt brokerage firm Refco Inc. ("Refco"). . . .

This case arises from the 2005 collapse of Refco, which was once one of the world's largest providers of brokerage and clearing services in the international derivatives, currency, and futures markets. According to plaintiffs,

---

28. 511 U.S. 164 (1994).

29. The term "secondary actor" is used in reference to parties such as lawyers, accountants, and bankers who are not employed by the company whose securities are the subject of alleged securities fraud.

Mayer Brown served as Refco's primary outside counsel from 1994 until the company's collapse. Collins, a partner at Mayer Brown, was the firm's primary contact with Refco and the billing partner in charge of the Refco account. Refco was a lucrative client for Mayer Brown and Collins' largest personal client.

As part of its business model, Refco extended credit to its customers so that they could trade on "margin"—*i.e.*, trade in securities with money borrowed from Refco. In the late 1990s, Refco customers suffered massive trading losses and consequently were unable to repay hundreds of millions of dollars of margin loans extended by Refco. Concerned that properly accounting for these debts as "write-offs" would threaten the company's survival, Refco, allegedly with the help of defendants, arranged a series of sham transactions designed to conceal the losses.

Specifically, plaintiffs allege that Refco transferred its uncollectible debts to Refco Group Holdings, Inc. ("RGHI")—an entity controlled by Refco's Chief Executive Officer—in exchange for a receivable purportedly owed from RGHI to Refco. Recognizing that a large debt owed to it by a related entity would arouse suspicion with investors and regulators, Refco, allegedly with the help of defendants, engaged in a series of sham loan transactions at the end of each quarter and each fiscal year to pay off the RGHI receivable. It did so by loaning money to third parties, who then loaned the same amount to RGHI, which in turn used the funds to pay off Refco's receivable. Days after the fiscal period closed, all of the loans were repaid and the third parties were paid a fee for their participation in the scheme. The result of these circular transactions was that, at the end of financial periods, Refco reported receivables owed to it by various third parties rather than the related entity RGHI.

Mayer Brown and Collins participated in seventeen of these sham loan transactions between 2000 and 2005, representing both Refco and RGHI. According to plaintiffs, defendants' involvement included negotiating the terms of the loans, drafting and revising the documents relating to the loans, transmitting the documents to the participants, and retaining custody of and distributing the executed copies of the documents.

Plaintiffs also allege that defendants are responsible for false statements appearing in three Refco documents: (1) an Offering Memorandum for an unregistered bond offering in July 2004 ("Offering Memorandum"), (2) a Registration Statement for a subsequent registered bond offering ("Registration Statement"), and (3) a Registration Statement for Refco's initial public offering of common stock in August 2005 ("IPO Registration Statement"). Each of these documents contained false or misleading statements because they failed to disclose the true nature of Refco's financial condition, which had been concealed, in part, through the loan transactions described above.

Defendants allegedly participated in the creation of the false statements contained in each of the documents identified above. Collins and other Mayer Brown attorneys allegedly reviewed and revised portions of the Offering Memorandum and attended drafting sessions. Collins and another Mayer

Brown attorney also personally drafted the Management Discussion & Analysis ("MD & A") portion of the Offering Memorandum, which, according to plaintiffs, discussed Refco's business and financial condition in a way that defendants knew to be false. The Offering Memorandum was used as the foundation for the Registration Statement, which was substantially similar in content. According to plaintiffs, defendants further assisted in the preparation of the Registration Statement by reviewing comment letters from the Securities and Exchange Commission ("SEC") and participating in drafting sessions. Finally, plaintiffs allege that defendants were directly involved in reviewing and drafting the IPO Registration Statement because they received, and presumably reviewed, the SEC's comments on that filing.

Both the Offering Memorandum and the IPO Registration Statement note that Mayer Brown represented Refco in connection with those transactions. The Registration Statement does not mention Mayer Brown. None of the documents specifically attribute any of the information contained therein to Mayer Brown or Collins.

Plaintiffs, who purchased securities from Refco during the period that defendants were allegedly engaging in fraud, commenced this action after Refco declared bankruptcy in 2005. They asserted claims for violation of §10(b) of the Exchange Act and Rule 10b-5 promulgated thereunder. . . .

The District Court dismissed plaintiffs' claims against Mayer Brown and Collins pursuant to Fed.R.Civ.P. 12(b)(6). With respect to plaintiffs' claim that defendants violated Rule 10b-5(b) by drafting and revising portions of Refco's public documents, the Court found that no statements in those documents were attributed to defendants and that plaintiffs had therefore alleged conduct akin to aiding and abetting, for which securities laws provide no private right of action. The District Court also dismissed plaintiffs' Rule 10b-5(a) and (c) claims for "scheme liability. . . ."

Section 10(b) [of the Exchange Act] makes it unlawful "for any person, directly or indirectly, . . . [t]o use or employ, in connection with the purchase or sale of any security . . . , any manipulative or deceptive device or contrivance in contravention of such rules and regulations as the [SEC] may prescribe." Rule 10b-5, promulgated thereunder, provides as follows:

> It shall be unlawful for any person, directly or indirectly, by the use of any means or instrumentality of interstate commerce, or of the mails or of any facility of any national securities exchange,
>> (a) To employ any device, scheme, or artifice to defraud,
>> (b) To make any untrue statement of a material fact or to omit to state a material fact necessary in order to make the statements made, in the light of the circumstances under which they were made, not misleading, or
>> (c) To engage in any act, practice, or course of business which operates or would operate as a fraud or deceit upon any person. . . .

The Supreme Court has held that, to maintain a private damages action under §10b and Rule 10b-5,

A plaintiff must prove (1) a material misrepresentation or omission by the defendant; (2) scienter; (3) a connection between the misrepresentation or omission and the purchase or sale of a security; (4) reliance upon the misrepresentation of omission; (5) economic loss; and (6) loss causation. . . .

This appeal raises primarily two issues regarding the scope of Rule 10b-5 liability in private actions: (1) whether defendants can be liable under Rule 10b-5(b) for false statements that they allegedly drafted, but which were not attributed to them at the time the statements were disseminated; and (2) whether the allegations in the complaint are sufficient to state a claims for "scheme liability" under Rule 10b-5(a) and (c).

I. Plaintiffs' Rule 10b-5(b) Claim

Plaintiffs assert that the District Court erred in holding that attorneys who participate in the drafting of false statements cannot be liable in a private damages action if the statements are not attributed to those attorneys at the time of dissemination. Along with the SEC as *amicus curiae*, plaintiffs argue that attribution is one only means by which attorneys and other secondary actors can incur liability for securities fraud. They urge us to adopt a "creator standard" and hold that a defendant can be liable for creating a false statement that investors rely on, regardless of whether that statement is attributed to the defendant at the time of dissemination. According to the SEC, "[a] person creates a statement . . . if the statement [1] is written or spoken by him, or [2] if he provides the false or misleading information that another person then puts into the statement, or [3] if he allows the statement to be attributed to him."

Defendants respond that, under our precedents, attorneys who participate in the drafting of false statements cannot be liable absent explicit attribution at the time of dissemination. Without attribution, defendants contend, secondary actors do not commit a primary violation of Rule 10b-5(b) and their conduct amounts, at most, to aiding and abetting. . . .

A. History of the Attribution Requirement

The distinction between primary liability under Rule 10b-5 and aiding and abetting became especially important after the Supreme Court's 1994 decision in *Central Bank of Denver, N.A. v. First Interstate Bank of Denver.* . . . That case involved the issuance of bonds by a public building authority and plaintiffs' allegations that Central Bank of Denver, the indenture trustee for the bond issues, aided and abetted the issuer in committing securities fraud by agreeing to delay an independent appraisal of the real property securing the bonds. After reviewing the text and history of §10(b), the Supreme Court concluded that "the 1934 [Exchange Act] does not itself reach those who aid and abet a §10(b) violation." To hold otherwise, it explained, would be "to impose . . . liability when at least one element critical for recovery under 10b-5 is absent: reliance."

Despite holding that Rule 10b-5 liability does not extend to aiders and abettors, the Supreme Court acknowledged that "secondary actors" could, in some circumstances still be liable for fraudulent conduct. Specifically, the Court explained that

> [a]ny person or entity, including a lawyer, accountant, or bank, who employs a manipulative device or makes a material misstatement (or omission) on which a purchaser or seller of securities relies may be liable as a primary violator under 10b-5, assuming *all* of the requirements for primary liability under Rule 10b-5 are met. In any complex securities fraud, moreover, there are likely to be multiple violators. . . .

We considered the effect of *Central Bank* on private securities litigation against secondary actors in *Shapiro v. Canto.* . . . *Shapiro* involved claims against the accounting firm Deloitte & Touche and its predecessor-in-interest for alleged complicity in the deceptive conduct of a limited partnership. We held that plaintiffs failed to state a claim for a primary violation of securities laws against Deloitte & Touche because

> [a]llegations of "assisting," "participating in," "complicity in" and similar synonyms used throughout the complaint all fall within the prohibitive bar of *Central Bank*. A claim under §10(b) must allege a defendant has made a material misstatement or omission indicating an intent to deceive or defraud in connection with the purchase or sale of a security.

The principle that *Central Bank* requires the attribution of false statements to the defendant at the time of dissemination first appeared in our 1998 decision in *Wright v. Ernst & Young LLP. Wright.* . . . involved claims against the accounting firm Ernst & Young and allegations that the firm orally approved a corporation's false and misleading financial statements, which were subsequently disseminated to the public.

We explained that after *Central Bank*, courts had generally adopted either a "bright line" test or a "substantial participation" test to distinguish between primary violations of Rule 10b-5 and aiding and abetting:

> Some courts have held that a third party's review and approval of documents containing fraudulent statements is not actionable under Section 10(b) because one must make the material misstatement or omission in order to be a primary violator. . . .

> Other courts have held that third parties may be primarily liable for statements made by others in which the defendant had significant participation.

We noted that, in *Shapiro*, we had followed the "bright line" approach. We therefore held that "a secondary actor cannot incur primary liability under [Ruble 10b-5] for a statement not attributed to that actor at the time of its dissemination." *Wright* also made clear that attribution is necessary to satisfy the reliance element of a private damages action under Rule 10b-5. Because the misrepresentations on which plaintiffs' claims were based were not attributed to Ernst & Young, we held that the complaint failed to state a claim under Rule 10b-5. . . .

B. Creator Standard v. Attribution Standard

Plaintiffs and the SEC urge us to adopt a "creator" standard that would require us to hold that a defendant can be liable for *creating* a false statement that investors rely on, regardless of whether that statement is attributed to the defendant at the time of dissemination. They argue that their proposed standard is consistent with the law of the Circuit. They distinguish *Wright* and [another prior case] on the ground that the defendants in those cases were not alleged to have created the false statements in question, but rather, merely reviewed false statements created by others. Plaintiffs and the SEC contend that, notwithstanding the broad language that suggests attribution is always required, these cases are best read as holding that a defendant can be liable if he or she creates a false or misleading statement *or* allows a false statement to be attributed to him or her. Their position finds some support in *dicta* from one of our recent cases . . . (describing *Wright* as holding that "under *Central Bank*, a defendant 'cannot incur primary liability' for a statement neither made by him *nor* 'attributed to [him] at the time of its dissemination.'"(emphasis added)). . . .

Notwithstanding the *dicta* in [that opinion], we reject the creator standard for secondary actor liability under Rule 10b-5. An attribution requirement is more consistent with the Supreme Court's guidance on the question of secondary actor liability. Furthermore, a creator standard is indistinguishable from the "substantial participation" test that we have disavowed since *Wright*, and it is incompatible with our stated preference for a "bright line" rule.

Accordingly, secondary actors can be liable in a private action under Rule 10b-5 for only those statements that are explicitly attributed to them. The mere identification of a secondary actor as being involved in a transaction, or the public's understanding that a secondary actor "is at work behind the scenes" are alone insufficient. To be cognizable, a plaintiff's claim against a secondary actor must be based on that actor's own "articulated statement," or on statements made by another that have been *explicitly* adopted by the secondary actor. . . .

C. Application of the Attribution Requirement

Applying the attribution standard to the alleged false and misleading statements in this case, we conclude that the District Court properly dismissed plaintiffs' Rule 10b-5(b) claims against Mayer Brown and Collins. No statements in the Offering Memorandum, the Registration Statement, or the IPO Registration Statement are attributed to Collins, and he is not even mentioned by name in any of those documents. Accordingly, plaintiffs cannot show reliance on any of Collins' statements.

The Offering Memorandum and the IPO Registration Statement note that Mayer Brown, among other counsel, represented Refco in connection with those transactions but neither document attributes any particular statements to Mayer Brown. Mayer Brown is not identified as the author of any portion of the documents. Nor can the mere mention of the firm's representation of Refco be considered an "articulated statement" by Mayer Brown adopting Refco's statements as its own. Absent such attribution, plaintiffs cannot show reliance on any statements of Mayer Brown.

II. Plaintiffs' Rule 10b-5(a) and (c) Claims ("Scheme Liability")

The District Court dismissed plaintiffs' Rule 10b-5(a) and (c) claims on the ground that the Supreme Court's decision in *Stoneridge* [*Investment Partners, LLC v. Scientific-Atlanta, Inc.*] foreclosed plaintiffs' theory of "scheme liability." We agree. . . .

In *Stoneridge*, plaintiffs sought to hold two companies liable for their participation in sham transactions that allowed an issuer of securities to overstate its revenue. Although the defendants' conduct was deceptive and enabled the issuer to conceal the misrepresentations in its financial statements, the Supreme Court found that the essential element of reliance was absent. It explained that

> [defendants'] deceptive acts were not communicated to the public. No member of the investing public had knowledge, either actual or presumed, of [defendants'] acts during the relevant times. [Plaintiffs], as a result, cannot show reliance upon any of [defendants'] actions except in an indirect chain that we find too remote for liability.

Like the defendants in *Stoneridge*, Mayer Brown and Collins are alleged to have facilitated sham transactions that enabled Refco to conceal the true state of its financial condition from investors. As in *Stoneridge*, plaintiffs were not aware of those transactions and, in fact, plaintiffs explicitly disclaim any knowledge of defendants' involvement. . . .

Plaintiffs attempt to distinguish *Stoneridge* by arguing that (1) defendants' deceptive conduct was communicated to the public; (2) defendants' conduct made it "necessary or inevitable" that Refco would misstate its finances; and (3) defendants' conduct occurred in the "investment sphere."[30]

As explained above, plaintiffs admit that they were unaware of defendants' deceptive conduct or "scheme" at the time they purchased Refco securities. Under *Stoneridge*, it does not matter that those transactions were "reflected" in Refco's financial statements. The Supreme Court explicitly rejected the argument that "investors rely not only upon the public statements relating to a security but also upon the transactions that those statements reflect." Accordingly, the fact that the sham transactions (or "scheme") allegedly facilitated by Mayer Brown and Collins rendered Refco's public financial disclosures false or misleading does not materially distinguish this case from *Stoneridge*. . . .

---

30. [In *Stoneridge*, the Court noted that the deceptive transactions "took place in the marketplace for goods and services, not in the investment sphere." Stoneridge Inv. Partners, LLC v. Sci.-Atlanta, Inc., 552 U.S. 148, 166 (2008). —Ed.]

Furthermore, nothing about Mayer Brown's or Collins' actions made it necessary or inevitable that Refco would mislead investors. As the District Court aptly noted, unlike in *Stoneridge*, "the Mayer Brown defendants were not even the counter-party to the fraudulent transactions; they merely participated in drafting the documents to effect those transactions. We therefore agree that, "[a]s was the case in *Stoneridge*, it was Refco, not the Mayer Brown Defendants, that filed fraudulent financial statements; nothing the Mayer Brown defendants did made it necessary or inevitable for Refco to record the transactions as it did."

Finally, the fact that defendants' conduct arguable occurred in the "investment sphere" is not dispositive or materially relevant. Although *Stoneridge* acknowledged the dangers of expanding liability to "the whole marketplace in which the issuing company does business," the Court's opinion was primarily focused on whether investors were aware of, and relied on, the defendants' own conduct. . . .

For the foregoing reasons, we agree with the District Court that plaintiffs' Rule 10b-5(a) and (c) claims for "scheme liability" are foreclosed by the Supreme Court's decision in *Stoneridge*. . . .

B.D. PARKER, JR., Circuit Judge, concurring. . . .

[O]ur sibling circuits have debated sharply whether an attribution requirement is necessary under *Central Bank of Denver*. . . . In an amicus brief submitted in this case, the SEC takes the position that a creator standard is fully consistent with *Central Bank of Denver*. Moreover, it argues that an attribution requirement would prevent the securities laws from deterring individuals who make false statements anonymously or through proxies. The SEC also observes that private plaintiffs who bring securities claims already face significant hurdles—they must prove that the defendants knew the falsity of their statements, and as a result of the Private Securities Litigation Reform Act, must "state with particularity facts giving rise to a strong inference that the defendant acted with the required state of mind." The Appellants in our case argue with some force against a result that shields Mayer Brown from damages in a circumstance where the partner responsible for the misleading statements was criminally convicted and received a prison term of seven years.

In light of the importance of the existence [or not] of an attribution requirement to the securities laws, the bar, and the securities industry, this case could provide our full Court, as well as, perhaps, the Supreme Court, with an opportunity to clarify the law in this area.

NOTES AND QUESTIONS

1. Amendments to the Private Securities Litigation Reform Act of 1995 make it clear that the SEC continues to have the authority to seek injunctive relief or certain money penalties against aiders and abettors

382 Chapter 12 Corporate Wrongdoing

of primary violations of the Exchange Act or any rule or regulation promulgated thereunder. These lawsuits are referred to as "enforcement actions."

2. In an omitted portion of the *Pacific Investment* opinion, the court noted that its prior opinion in In re Scholastic Corp. Securities Litigation, 252 F.3d 63 (2d Cir. 2001), might have resulted in "uncertainty or ambiguity with respect to when attribution is required." In that case, the Second Circuit "held that a corporate officer could be liable for misrepresentations made by the corporation, notwithstanding the fact that none of the statements at issue were specifically attributed to him." *Pacific Investment*, 603 F.3d at 154. The defendant in *Scholastic* was the vice president for finance and investor relations and was primarily responsible for the company's communications with investors. He was involved in "the drafting, producing, reviewing and/or disseminating of the false and misleading statements issued by the company." Despite this "uncertainty or ambiguity," the *Pacific Investment* court noted that because the appeal did not involve claims against corporate insiders, "we intimate no view on whether attribution is required for such claims." 603 F.3d at 158, n.6. Nevertheless, the court stated that "[t]here may be justifiable basis for holding that investors rely on the role corporate executives play in issuing public statements even in the absence of explicit attribution," but that prior case law held that "at least with respect to secondary actor liability, *Scholastic* did not relax *Wright*'s attribution requirement." *Id.* How can a 10b-5(b) claim against a corporate officer not identified as an author of a public statement be reconciled with the attribution requirement? What if the insider defendant is the company's general counsel? Does it matter whether the general counsel is also an officer of the company, as many general counsel are?

3. In a separate lawsuit arising out of the Refco fraud, Collins and Mayer Brown were sued by a private equity firm that had invested more than $450 million in Refco stock through a leveraged buyout.[31] Mayer Brown not only drafted and negotiated the transactional documents, but as part of the equity firm's due diligence leading up to the purchase of Refco securities, Mayer Brown provided information directly to the equity firm and its advisors. Collins made a number of statements directly to the plaintiffs and their counsel, "including informing them that he had 'confirmed with' or was 'advised by' Refco management that there were no related-party transactions and that all material documents were being produced." Thomas H. Lee Equity Fund V, L.P.

---

31. A leveraged buyout is the acquisition of a company by another company using a significant amount of borrowed money to cover the cost of the acquisition. The assets of both the acquired and acquiring companies are often used as collateral for the loans.

v. Mayer Brown, Rowe & Maw LLP, 612 F.Supp.2d 267, 272 (S.D.N.Y. 2009). The district court held that the allegations were insufficient to support liability under Rule 10b-5(b) because, although Collins and Mayer Brown made statements directly to the plaintiffs, they were merely passing along false statements made by Refco, "without any endorsement or representation that Mayer Brown had, itself, verified or adopted the information provided." As a result, the misstatements were attributed to Refco, not to Collins or Mayer Brown. "Even if what the [plaintiffs] were, in fact, relying on was that an attorney would not knowingly convey the false statements of his client because doing so would violate the rules of professional conduct," the district court viewed Second Circuit precedent as requiring attribution to establish a primary violation of Rule 10b-5(b).

4. As the *Pacific Investment* court explained, there was a split in authority at the time of its decision concerning the standards for liability of secondary actors such as lawyers and accountants for primary violations of Rule 10b-5(b). In Janus Capital Group, Inc. v. First Derivative Traders, 564 U.S. 135 (2011), the U.S. Supreme Court appears to have resolved that split in favor of the narrower Second Circuit approach. In *Janus*, a case involving an investment advisor, the Court held that "misstatement liability" under Rule 10b-5(b) extends only to the "*maker* of a statement," which the Court held is "the person or entity with ultimate authority over the statement, including its content and whether and how to communicate it." The Court explicitly rejected the SEC's argument that one who "creates" a statement is the maker of the statement, using by analogy the relationship between a speechwriter and the speaker: "Even when a speechwriter drafts a speech, the content is entirely within the control of the person who delivers it. And it is the speaker who takes credit—or blame—for what is ultimately said." Although the Court did not explicitly mention the Second Circuit's "attribution" test, it noted that "in the ordinary case, attribution within a statement or implicit from surrounding circumstances is strong evidence that a statement was made by—and only by—the party to whom it is attributed." Moreover, commentators have noted that at the time *Janus* was decided, the Supreme Court had declined certiorari in *Pacific Investment*,[32] strongly suggesting both that the *Janus* holding extends to lawyers as well as other secondary actors and that *Janus* constituted an implicit endorsement of the Second Circuit's attribution test.[33]

---

32. 131 S. Ct. 3021 (2011).

33. *See, e.g.,* Gary M. Bishop, A Framework for Analyzing Attorney Liability Under Section 10(b) and Rule 10b-5, 10 U.N.H. L. Rev. 193, 195-96 (2012).

Lorenzo v. SEC
139 S. Ct. 1094 (2019)

Justice BREYER delivered the opinion of the Court. . . .

In this case, we consider whether those who do not "make" statements (as *Janus* defined "make"), but who disseminate false or misleading statements to potential investors with the intent to defraud, can be found to have violated the *other* parts of Rule 10b-5, subsections (a) and (c), as well as related provisions of the securities laws. We believe that they can.

I.

A.

For our purposes, the relevant facts are not in dispute. Francis Lorenzo, the petitioner, was the director of investment banking at Charles Vista, LLC, a registered broker-dealer in Staten Island, New York. Lorenzo's only investment banking client at the time was Waste2Energy Holdings, Inc., a company developing technology to convert "solid waste" into "clean renewable energy."

In a June 2009 public filing, Waste2Energy stated that its total assets were worth about $14 million. This figure included intangible assets, namely, intellectual property, valued at more than $10 million. Lorenzo was skeptical of this valuation, later testifying that the intangibles were a "dead asset" because the technology "didn't really work."

During the summer and early fall of 2009, Waste2Energy hired Lorenzo's firm, Charles Vista, to sell to investors $15 million worth of debentures, a form of "debt secured only by the debtor's earning power, not by a lien on any specific assets."

In early October 2009, Waste2Energy publicly disclosed, and Lorenzo was told, that its intellectual property was worthless, that it had "'"[w]rit[ten] off . . . all [of its] intangible assets,"'" and that its total assets (as of March 31, 2009) amounted to $370,552.

Shortly thereafter, on October 14, 2009, Lorenzo sent two e-mails to prospective investors describing the debenture offering. According to later testimony by Lorenzo, he sent the e-mails at the direction of his boss, who supplied the content and "approved" the messages. The e-mails described the investment in Waste2Energy as having "3 layers of protection," including $10 million in "confirmed assets." The e-mails nowhere revealed the fact that Waste2Energy had publicly stated that its assets were in fact worth less than $400,000. Lorenzo signed the e-mails with his own name, he identified himself as "Vice President—Investment Banking," and he invited the recipients to "call with any questions."

B.

In 2013, the Securities and Exchange Commission instituted proceedings against Lorenzo (along with his boss and Charles Vista). The Commission charged that Lorenzo had violated Rule 10b-5, § 10(b) of the Exchange Act, and § 17(a)(1) of the Securities Act. Ultimately, the Commission found that Lorenzo had run afoul of these provisions by sending false and misleading statements to investors with intent to defraud. As a sanction, it fined Lorenzo $15,000, ordered him to cease and desist from violating the securities laws, and barred him from working in the securities industry for life.

[Lorenzo appealed. He] argued that, in light of *Janus*, he could not be held liable under subsection (b) of Rule 10b(5). The panel agreed. Because his boss "asked Lorenzo to send the emails, supplied the central content, and approved the messages for distribution," it was the boss that had "ultimate authority" over the content of the statement "and whether and how to communicate it." (We took this case on the assumption that Lorenzo was not a "maker" under subsection (b) of Rule 10b-5, and do not revisit the court's decision on this point.)

The Court of Appeals nonetheless sustained (with one judge dissenting) the Commission's finding that, by knowingly disseminating false information to prospective investors, Lorenzo had violated other parts of Rule 10b(5), subsections (a) and (c). . . .

Lorenzo then filed a petition for certiorari in this Court. We granted review to resolve disagreement about whether someone who is not a "maker" of a misstatement under *Janus* can nevertheless be found to have violated the other subsections of Rule 10b-5 and related provisions of the securities law, when the only conduct involved concerns a misstatement.

II.

A.

[Subsection (a) of Rule 10b-5] makes it unlawful to "employ any device, scheme, or artifice to defraud." Subsection (b) makes it unlawful to "make any untrue statement of a material fact." And subsection (c) makes it unlawful to "engage in any act, practice, or course of business" that "operates . . . as a fraud or deceit." . . .

B.

After examining the relevant language, precedent, and purpose, we conclude that (assuming other here-irrelevant legal requirements are met) dissemination of false or misleading statements with intent to defraud can fall within the scope of subsections (a) and (c) of Rule 10b-5. . . . In our view, that is so even if the disseminator did not "make" the statements and consequently falls outside subsection (b) of the Rule.

It would seem obvious that the words in these provisions are, as ordinarily used, sufficiently broad to include within their scope the dissemination of false or misleading information with the intent to defraud. By sending emails he understood to contain material untruths, Lorenzo "employ[ed]" a "device," "scheme," and "artifice to defraud" within the meaning of subsection [a] of the Rule[s]. . . . By the same conduct, he "engage[d] in a[n] act, practice, or course of business" that "operate[d] . . . as a fraud or deceit" under subsection (c) of the Rule. Recall that Lorenzo does not challenge the appeals court's scienter finding, so we take for granted that he sent the emails with "intent to deceive, manipulate, or defraud" the recipients. Under the circumstances, it is difficult to see how his actions could escape the reach of these provisions.

Resort to dictionary definitions only strengthens this conclusion. A "'device,'" we have observed, is simply "'[t]hat which is devised, or formed by design'"; a "'scheme'" is a "'project,'" "'plan[,] or program of something to be done'"; and an "'an artful stratagem or trick.'" By these lights, dissemination of false or misleading material is easily an "artful stratagem" or a "plan," "devised" to defraud an investor under subsection (a). The words "act" and "practice" in subsection (c) are similarly expansive.

These provisions capture a wide range of conduct. Applying them may present difficult problems of scope in borderline cases. Purpose, precedent, and circumstance could lead to narrowing their reach in other contexts. But we see nothing borderline about this case, where the relevant conduct (as found by the Commission) consists of disseminating false or misleading information to prospective investors with the intent to defraud. And while one can readily imagine other actors tangentially involved in dissemination—say, a mailroom clerk—for whom liability would typically be inappropriate, the petitioner in this case sent false statements directly to investors, invited them to follow up with questions, and did so in his capacity as vice president of an investment banking company.

C.

Lorenzo argues that, despite the natural meaning of these provisions, they should not reach his conduct. This is so, he says, because the only way to be liable for false statements is through those provisions that refer *specifically* to false statements. Other provisions, he says, concern "scheme liability claims" and are violated only when conduct other than misstatements is involved. Thus, only those who "make" untrue statements under subsection (b) can violate Rule 10b-5 in connection with statements. . . . Holding to the contrary, he and the dissent insist, would render subsection (b) of Rule 10b-5 "superfluous."

The premise of this argument is that each of these provisions should be read as governing different, mutually exclusive, spheres of conduct. But this Court and the Commission have long recognized considerable overlap among the subsections of the Rule and related provisions of the securities laws. As we have explained, these laws marked the "first experiment in federal regulation of the securities industry." It is "understandable, therefore," that "in declaring certain practices unlawful," it was thought prudent "to include both a general proscription against fraudulent and deceptive practices and, out of an abundance of caution, a specific proscription against nondisclosure" even though "a specific proscription against nondisclosure" might in other circumstances be deemed "surplusage." "Each succeeding prohibition" was thus "meant to cover additional kinds of illegalities — not to narrow the reach of the prior sections." . . .

The idea that each subsection of Rule 10b-5 governs a separate type of conduct is also difficult to reconcile with the language of subsections (a) and (c). It should go without saying that at least some conduct amounts to "employ[ing]" a "device, scheme, or artifice to defraud" under subsection (a) as well as "engag[ing] in a[n] act . . . which operates . . . as a fraud" under subsection (c). . . . (The dissent, for its part, offers no account of how the superfluity problems that motivate its interpretation can be avoided where subsections (a) and (c) are concerned.)

Coupled with the Rule's expansive language, which readily embraces the conduct before us, this considerable overlap suggests we should not hesitate to hold that Lorenzo's conduct ran afoul of subsections (a) and (c), as well as the related statutory provisions. Our conviction is strengthened by the fact that we here confront behavior that, though plainly fraudulent, might otherwise fall outside the scope of the Rule. Lorenzo's view that subsection (b), the making-false-statements provision, *exclusively* regulates conduct involving false or misleading statements would mean those who disseminate false statements with the intent to cheat investors might escape liability under the Rule altogether. But using false representations to induce the purchase of securities would seem a paradigmatic example of securities fraud. We do not know why Congress or the Commission would have wanted to disarm enforcement in this way. And we cannot easily reconcile Lorenzo's approach with the basic purpose behind these laws: "to substitute a philosophy of full disclosure for the philosophy of *caveat emptor* and thus to achieve a high standard of business ethics in the securities industry."

III.

Lorenzo and the dissent make a few other important arguments. They contend that applying subsections (a) or (c) of Rule 10b-5 to conduct like his would render our decision in *Janus* . . . "a dead letter." But we do not see how that is so. In *Janus*, we considered the language in subsection (b), which prohibits the "mak[ing] of any untrue statement of a material fact." We held that the "maker" of a "statement" is the "person or entity with ultimate authority over the statement." And we found that subsection (b) did not (under the circumstances) cover an investment adviser who helped draft misstatements issued by a different entity that controlled the statements' content. We said nothing about the Rule's application to the dissemination of false or misleading information. And we can assume that *Janus* would remain relevant (and preclude liability) where an individual neither makes nor disseminates false information — provided, of course, that the individual is not involved in some other form of fraud. . . .

We do not believe, however, that our decision weakens the distinction between primary and secondary liability. For one thing, it is hardly unusual for the same conduct to be a primary violation with respect to one offense and aiding and abetting with respect to another. John, for example, might sell Bill an unregistered firearm in order to help Bill rob a bank, under circumstances that make him primarily liable for the gun sale and secondarily liable for the bank robbery. . . .

The holding of *Central Bank*, we have said, suggests the need for a "clean line" between conduct that constitutes a primary violation of Rule 10b-5 and conduct that amounts to a secondary violation. Thus, in *Janus*, we sought an interpretation of "make" that could neatly divide primary violators and actors too far removed from the ultimate decision to communicate a statement. The line we adopt today is just as administrable. Those who disseminate false statements with intent to defraud are primarily liable under Rules 10b-5(a) and (c) . . . even if they are secondarily liable under Rule 10b-5(b). Lorenzo suggests that classifying dissemination as a primary violation would inappropriately subject peripheral players in fraud (including him, naturally) to substantial liability. We suspect the investors who received Lorenzo's e-mails would not view the deception so favorably. And as *Central Bank* itself made clear, even a bit participant in the securities markets "may be liable as a primary violator under [Rule] 10b-5" so long as "all of the requirements for primary liability . . . are met."

Lorenzo's reliance on *Stoneridge* is even further afield. There, we held that private plaintiffs could not bring suit against certain securities defendants based on *undisclosed* deceptions upon which the plaintiffs could not have relied. But the Commission, unlike private parties, need not show reliance in enforcement actions. And even supposing reliance were relevant here, Lorenzo's conduct involved the direct transmission of false statements to prospective investors intended to induce reliance—far from the kind of concealed fraud at issue in *Stoneridge*.

As for Lorenzo's suggestion that those like him ought to be held secondarily liable, this offer will, far too often, prove illusory. In instances where a "maker" of a false statement does not violate subsection (b) of the Rule (perhaps because he lacked the necessary intent), a disseminator of those statements, even one knowingly engaged in an egregious fraud, could not be held to have violated the "aiding and abetting" statute. That is because the statute insists there be a primary violator to whom the secondary violator provided "substantial assistance." . . .

That is not what Congress intended. Rather, Congress intended to root out all manner of fraud in the securities industry. And it gave the Commission the tools to accomplish that job. . . .

[Justice Thomas dissented, in an opinion joined by Justice Gorsuch. Justice Kavanaugh took no part in the decision.]

NOTES AND QUESTIONS

1. You may be confused as to why the email Lorenzo sent was not "attributed" to him given that it was sent by him from his own email account and signed by him with his own name. Justice Thomas's dissenting opinion explained that both the emails Lorenzo sent stated that they were sent "[a]t the request" of Lorenzo's boss, who was the owner of the investment banking company.

2. In *Janus*, the defendant was a related but independent company from the mutual fund whose prospectuses were alleged to contain false statements. The defendant served as an investment fund advisor and administrator that was alleged to have participated in the writing and dissemination of the prospectuses. As for the "dissemination" of the prospectuses, the defendant as administrator may have played some role in causing the prospectuses to be filed with the SEC; however, the SEC records reflected that the entity that "filed" the prospectuses was the investment fund itself, not the defendant. Given those facts, do you agree with the *Lorenzo* dissenters that the decision in *Lorenzo* makes *Janus* a "dead letter"? Could the *Janus* plaintiffs have rewritten their complaint to allege the defendant's liability under Rule 10b-5(a) or (c) based on its participation and/or dissemination of the prospectuses? Assume, as did the Supreme Court in *Janus*, that the defendant had the requisite intent to defraud.

3. Analyze the facts alleged in the two cases involving the Refco fraud — *Pacific Investments* and *Thomas H. Lee Equity Fund*,[34] under *Lorenzo*. Would the facts alleged in those cases support liability under 10b-5(a) or (c)?

4. In his dissent, Justice Thomas criticized the majority's use of the hypothetical involving a man who sells a gun to a robber the man knows will use to commit a robbery. Justice Thomas agreed that it makes perfect sense to conclude that the man was a primary violator with respect to the illegal sale of the gun, while simultaneously only a secondary violator with respect to the robbery. But Justice Thomas objected that the hypothetical is inapplicable to Lorenzo's dissemination of his boss's false statement because there were not two distinct illegal acts. Do you agree? Although neither the gun laws nor the robbery laws are covered by Rule 10b-5, using the three sections of that rule as a framework, couldn't the man be charged as a primary violator in the robbery on the ground that he engaged in a "scheme" or "act" to violate the robbery law?

---

34. The *Thomas H. Lee Equity Fund* opinion is described at Note 3 following the *Pacific Investments* opinion.

Review Problems

12-1 A lawyer is employed in-house by a privately held company that manufactures medical devices. Recently, the company began marketing a new device designed to reduce pain from nerve damage. After receiving several complaints from users who claimed that after using the device, their pain intensified, leading to possibly permanent nerve damage, the lawyer conducted an investigation and discovered, from one of the scientists who worked on the device, that the scientist did not fully report the results of various tests in documents submitted to the Food and Drug Administration (FDA) before the FDA approved the device. As a result of the omissions, the documents underreported the number of users who complained of intensified pain and apparent nerve damage. The scientist says he withheld the full results at the direction of the company's CEO. The lawyer confronted the CEO, who insisted that the submitted document was substantially accurate and that any discrepancies in the data are minor. The lawyer believes that the discrepancies are not minor but were required to be reported to the FDA. The CEO instructed the lawyer to do nothing further. What may or must the lawyer do? What potential consequences does the lawyer face if the lawyer does not comply with all applicable legal requirements?

12-2 What if the company in Problem 12-1 is publicly held and the lawyer is drafting the company's annual 10K report to be filed with the SEC, including a letter to auditors about contingent legal liabilities? The letter to the auditors will form the basis of the auditor's report concerning contingent legal liabilities, as part of the 10K report. What may or must the lawyer do? What potential consequences does the lawyer face if the lawyer does not comply with all applicable legal requirements?

12-3 Assume that a pharmaceutical company acquired the majority of the medical device company's publicly traded stock. As part of its due diligence, the pharmaceutical company's executives had extensive discussions with the medical device company's in-house lawyer. After that lawyer had spoken with the medical device company's scientist and the CEO, counsel for the pharmaceutical company told the lawyer that he had heard there were complaints from users of intensified pain and apparent nerve damage after using the device and asked if this information was correct. The lawyer said he would check with the CEO during the lunch break and, after lunch, reported back that there had been a few such complaints but that they were minor and had been reported to the FDA in seeking its approval to market the device. In fact, the lawyer had not spoken with the CEO during the lunch break, but had used the opportunity to decide how she would respond to the question. After the medical device company settled a class action lawsuit for more than $5 million, the pharmaceutical company sued executives of the medical device company, including the in-house lawyer, for violations of SEC Rule 10b-5. Is the lawyer likely to be subject to liability?

CHAPTER 13

IN-HOUSE COUNSEL

Model Rules 1.6, 1.7, 1.8, 1.13, 1.16, 1.18, 2.1

A. THE EVOLVING ROLE OF IN-HOUSE COUNSEL

Until recently, in-house counsel occupied a low-key, secondary role among members of the legal profession. Beginning in the 1970s, all that changed. Today, in-house counsel constitute an increasing percentage of lawyers with growing power and prestige. Moreover, the role of in-house counsel has changed, bringing new tensions and ethical dilemmas, as illustrated throughout this chapter.

1. The Emergence of the Modern In-House Counsel

Mary C. Daly

The Cultural, Ethical, and Legal Challenges in Lawyering for a Global Organization: The Role of General Counsel
46 Emory L.J. 1057, 1059-66 (1997)...

Between 1970 and 1980, there was a forty percent increase in the number of lawyers working in-house; and between 1980 and 1991, there was a thirty-three percent increase. Between 1962 and 1982, the number of salaried lawyers quadrupled.

More important than the percentage growth in number, however, is the accompanying shift in power from outside law firms to the offices of general counsel. For a considerable period of time in recent history, general counsel functioned essentially as conduits between corporate clients and the clients' outside law firms. Their status was that of middle management. Both qualitatively and quantitatively, very little work was performed in-house. As Professor Chayes has observed, "[t]he traditional house counsel was a relatively minor management figure, stereotypically, a lawyer from the corporation's principal outside law firm who had not quite made the grade as partner. The responsibilities of general (corporate) counsel were confined to corporate housekeeping and other routine matters...."

These responsibilities expanded greatly in the 1970s in response to the rising costs of legal services. Corporations increased the size of legal departments for the purpose of redirecting the delivery of routine, predictable services such as consumer credit and commercial loan transactions from outside counsel to their own salaried lawyer-employees.

Over the course of time, an increasing number of highly talented lawyers abandoned corporate law firm practice and sought in-house positions. As the legal fees charged by law firms continued to rise, both corporate financial officers and general counsel perceived the fiscal and professional wisdom of making salaried lawyers responsible for the delivery of nonroutine, complex legal services, particularly those of a transactional character. They "add[ed] value through specialized knowledge of the business." Clients came to expect their general counsel to be "involved in any big strategic issue at the heart of the organization" and to "know very intimately what's going on in the minds of top executives."

As the scope of government regulation increased exponentially at the federal, state, and local level, so did corporate clients' need for lawyers who were well versed in all aspects of their clients' business operations and therefore equipped to advise clients on a daily basis with respect to compliance issues. . . . Corporate clients believed that salaried lawyers could meet this need more effectively and at a far lower cost than outside counsel.

In sum, by the early 1980s, general counsel usually performed four distinct functions. They managed and reviewed the legal services provided to corporate clients by outside counsel; they regularly supplied routine legal services, and on some occasions, directly handled complex transactions and even litigation; they counseled clients and their constituents on regulatory requirements; and they created compliance programs. The assumption and expansion of these functions helped shift power incrementally from outside law firms to corporate legal departments. A significant shift back is most unlikely, especially in light of the importance of the regulatory counseling function. This new generation of in-house lawyers, moreover, frequently offers business as well as legal advice, and its members decidedly reject any notion that their role is limited to counseling clients on purely legal matters. A "can do" attitude characterizes their lawyering. . . .

Emblematic of the change's significance and the altered balance of power is the emergence of a professional identity that champions in-house lawyering as a challenging and rewarding career choice, affirmatively rejecting the second-class status that traditionally stigmatized salaried lawyers. Dissatisfied with their treatment by the American Bar Association (ABA), in-house lawyers in 1982 formed their own professional organization, the American Corporate Counsel Association (ACCA)[1]. . . .

---

1. [In 2003 ACCA became ACC, the Association of Corporate Counsel, a change that was designed to reflect the increasingly global interests of the organization's interests and membership. — ED.]

ACCA's principal importance . . . is its symbolic legitimization of in-house lawyering as valid career option—one no longer associated with deficient legal or interpersonal skills. In Professor Chayes's words, ACCA is an "indication of the growing prestige of corporate counsel." The establishment and continued growth of ACCA reflect an insistent demand by in-house lawyers for the respect of their law firm peers and demonstrate the success of their demand.

Examining ACCA from a sociological perspective, Professor Rosen has questioned Professor Chayes's conclusion: "Rather, I take [ACCA's] development to be an indicator of professional mobilization: The American Corporate Counsel Association is part of a political movement to consolidate and extend inside counsel interests within both business and the profession." Even if Professor Rosen is correct, his view does not alter the importance . . . attach[ed] to ACCA's establishment or growth. Whether ACCA is a "political movement" or an icon of professional legitimation matters less than the phenomenon that it represents: a fundamental and irreversible shift in the power relationship between corporate clients and their traditional legal service providers, large private law firms. General counsel, not law firm partners, are now the "statesmen" to chief executive officers (CEOs), confidently offering business as well as legal advice.

While these changes in growth, prestige, and power were taking place in law departments across the United States, a profound shift was simultaneously occurring in the business and capital markets. Businesses began to reach beyond national borders, offering their products and services to individual and government consumers in all parts of the global village. Worldwide marketing, selling, and purchasing became a matter of financial survival. This shift added a new dimension (and burden) to in-house lawyering. Suddenly, corporate clients needed their general counsel to possess a substantive and procedural familiarity with the laws of other countries and to supervise competently the work of foreign in-house lawyers and outside law firms around the globe.

Operating synergistically, the growth in numbers, prestige, and power of in-house counsel and their globalization of the business and capital markets are presenting general counsel with unique challenges. They must now devise new management structures to oversee the delivery of legal services in foreign countries, integrate lawyers from different legal systems into a single professional community, and educate the clients' professional and administrative staff outside the United States to appreciate the potential contributions of in-house lawyers to the clients' business operations. . . . The importance of these tasks is considerable. According to the 1996 Price Waterhouse Law Department Spending Survey, the general counsel of 240 major U.S. corporations anticipated that their clients' need for international law expertise will grow faster than their need in any other area of the law. . . .

394   Chapter 13 In-House Counsel

NOTES AND QUESTIONS

1. According to Daly, the responsibilities of in-house counsel began to expand greatly when management, in response to the rising cost of legal services, increased the size of corporate legal departments in order to bring more work in-house. It is now up to corporate counsel to determine when to use inside counsel and when to retain outside counsel. This function is known as the "make or buy decision" and applies not only to legal services, but to all aspects of a company's operations. In this respect, purchasing legal services is deemed by management to be part of the company's overall procurement strategy. In turn, general corporate guidelines imposed on ordinary vendors are now being applied to outside legal service providers, to the dismay of outside counsel.[2]

2. A committee of the District of Columbia Bar recently proposed amendments to the D.C. Rules that would limit the ability of lawyers to propose or agree to certain outside counsel guidelines, such as those that provide "overbroad definitions of what constitutes a conflict of interest (sometimes couched as overbroad designation of who is considered the 'client') and demands that would require breaches of lawyers' duties of confidentiality,"[3] for example, requiring outside counsel to inform the client of its representation of a competitor, even in an unrelated matter.[4] Other provisions the amendments would prohibit are "indemnification requirements that are broader than those created by law and covered by existing forms of lawyers' malpractice insurance" and "client demands for ownership of, and control over, the lawyer's work product, coupled with restrictions on any subsequent use of 'information' acquired by the lawyer in the course of the representation."[5] Responding to the argument that these are private matters for negotiation between corporate clients and their outside lawyers, the D.C. Bar committee explained that the outside counsel guidelines in question may unduly limit the ability of other companies (often smaller companies) to retain counsel of their choice[6] and adversely affect outside counsel's independent judgment.[7] The committee did not address outside counsel guidelines

---

2. *See, e.g.*, Anthony Davis & Noah Fiedler, The New Battle Over Conflicts of Interest: Should Professional Regulators—or Clients—Decide What Is a Conflict?, 24 Prof. Law. 38 (2016-2017).

3. D.C. Bar Rules of Professional Conduct Review Committee, Draft Report Proposing Changes to the D.C. Rules of Professional Conduct Relating to Client-Generated Engagement Letters and Outside Counsel Guidelines 4 (Nov. 2020).

4. *Id.* at 13.

5. *Id.* at 4.

6. *Id.* at 7-10 (explaining proposals designed to prohibit overbroad definition of conflicts and unduly broad restrictions on future representation of business competitors).

7. *Id.* at 15 (explaining that proposals designed to prohibit indemnification provisions that make lawyers liable for the effects of client conduct when such liability is not covered by malpractice insurance "likely will have the effect (presumably unintended) of making such lawyers more hesitant and cautious in their advice to clients").

that address corporate social responsibility issues, such as demands for racial and gender diversity.[8]

3. One of the keys to the shift in power from outside to inside counsel is the expertise that corporate general counsel brings not only to the decision *whether* to retain outside counsel, but also to the selection of *which* outside counsel to retain. General counsel's familiarity with both the inefficiencies of law firm practice and factors that enhance the quality of the work provides the corporation with the bargaining power to force law firms to compete with each other (and with nonlawyer service providers)[9] for the corporation's legal business. One of the common features of this landscape is the "beauty contest," in which the corporation interviews several law firms and asks them to provide information on such matters as staffing, legal approach, and fees and costs. When multiple law firms are qualified to do the legal work, qualities such as responsiveness and cost become critical to the corporation.[10] What ethical issues are raised when a law firm agrees to participate in a beauty contest? Are there confidentiality and conflict-of-interest issues that may arise as a result of learning basic information about the prospective representation? How might both the corporation and the competing firms minimize the risks they face?

4. Another important development leading to greater responsibilities of in-house counsel is the increased scope of government regulation, primarily at the federal level. This regulatory expansion includes corporate governance requirements under Sarbanes-Oxley and related legislation, as well as developments in corporate criminal law, such as heightened criminal penalties for corporations, federal sentencing guidelines that provide incentives for internal corporate investigations, and various corporate whistleblower programs.[11]

5. The final development Daly discussed is the impact of the globalization of business, which has led to the need for general counsel to manage the global provision of legal services by providers whose characteristics may differ significantly from the U.S. legal profession. In later sections of her article, Daly explored some of these differences, including

---

8. *See, e.g.* Christopher J. Whelan & Neta Ziv, Law Firm Ethics in the Shadow of Corporate Responsibility, 26 Geo. J. Legal Ethics 153 (2013). For an argument justifying corporate clients' demands for diversity initiatives on the ground that such clients have an ethical obligation to help their law firm "joint venturers" resist the impulse to forgo long-term legitimacy in favor of short-term profits, *see* David B. Wilkins, Do Clients Have Ethical Obligations to Lawyers—Some Lessons from the Diversity Wars, 11 Geo. J. Legal Ethics 855 (1998).

9. Increasingly, law firms are competing for legal business with nonlawyer providers such as accounting firms and legal tech companies. These developments are discussed in Chapter 16: Nonlawyer Ownership, Multidisciplinary Practice, and Alternative Legal Service Providers.

10. *See, e.g.*, Omari Scott Simmons & James D. Dinnage, Innkeepers: A Unifying Theory of the In-House Counsel Role, 41 Seton Hall L. Rev. 77, 107 (2011).

11. *See id.* at 99-106 (also discussing a decision of the Delaware Court of Chancery recognizing directors' duty to monitor through various internal compliance controls).

the multiplicity of different types of professionals who provide what we would call legal services and the manner in which the regulation of legal professionals differs from country to country. Some of these differences are also explored in Chapter 15: Unauthorized Practice of Law and Multijurisdictional Practice and Chapter 16: Nonlawyer Ownership, Multidisciplinary Practice, and Alternative Legal Service Providers.

2. Questioning the "Independence" of Modern In-House Counsel

Two distinguishing features of modern in-house counsel are the multiplicity of roles they play and their "deep and daily understanding of, and involvement in, the corporation's business."[12] Their multiple roles include legal advisor and administrator of the corporation's legal department, as well as business advisor, corporate officer and member of senior management, and compliance designer and/or chief compliance officer.[13] By assuming "organizational responsibilities well beyond those of their external counterparts,"[14] they have unprecedented access to both formal and informal information, which may make them more valuable than outside counsel in many situations.[15]

Despite these advantages, however, commentators have noted the tension that results from the multiplicity of roles corporate counsel are expected to play, a tension that may undermine counsel's ability to maintain the "independence" that is deemed to be the hallmark of the legal professional.[16] Consider the following critical commentary.

Pam Jenoff

Going Native: Incentive, Identity, and the Inherent Ethical Problem of In-House Counsel
114 W.Va. L. Rev. 725, 725-26, 732-43 (2012) . . .

"Going native" is the perhaps politically-incorrect term used in international circles to describe the situation in which a diplomat, having spent too much time in a foreign country, begins to identify more with the local culture than with his own state. This provides a fitting analogy to the attorney who works

---

12. E. Norman Veasey & Christine T. Di Guglielmo, The Tensions, Stresses, and Professional Responsibilities of the Lawyer for the Corporation, 62 Bus. Law. 1, 8 (2006).

13. *Id.* at 5-6. *See also* Simmons & Dinnage, *supra* n. 10, at 112 (describing in-house counsel as the "'Swiss Army Knife' of the legal profession" as a result of their multiple roles).

14. *Id.,* at 112.

15. Veasey & Di Guglielmo, *supra* n. 12, at 8.

16. *See generally id.*

as in-house counsel for a company for many years, operating in the corporate environment, surrounded by co-workers who are all part of the organization.

This "cultural immersion" has serious implications for the attorney's ability to fulfill his ethical obligations. The hallmark of the legal profession is independence — the duty to render advice and to meet the requirements placed upon attorneys with respect to clients, adversaries, tribunals, and society-at-large without interference from external or personal concerns. However, as with the diplomat stationed abroad, an attorney who works within a particular organization for an extended period of time may begin to identify more closely with the host entity and its constituents than his own professional organization.

The conundrum of corporate counsel's independence is further exacerbated by a second problem not present in the diplomatic analogy: incentive. The in-house attorney is financially dependent upon a lone client, and is assessed, compensated, and rewarded based on his ability to satisfy that client's business objectives. This creates an inducement for the attorney to provide advice that is amenable to the company's goals, regardless of whether that is the most legally salient advice. . . .

In-house counsel often claim that their roles mirror that of their counterparts at firms. The tendency of corporate counsel to engage in what Sally Weaver has dubbed "a public incantation of sameness," may be an attempt to remain on equal footing with firm counterparts and avoid the return to the perceived inferior status associated with the role in an earlier era. Alternatively, corporate counsel may feel pressure to accentuate their legal capabilities in order to be seen as valuable and non-redundant of outside attorneys in a climate of leaner budgets and constrained resources.

Notwithstanding these claims, and despite the fact that many of the duties of corporate counsel mirror those of their colleagues at firms, the two positions differ significantly. First, while an attorney at a firm generally works for a number of different clients, in-house counsel has just one — the company which employs him. He has been hired by and owes his job security to that client. This creates much greater dependence upon the satisfaction of the client.

In-house counsel also plays a different role on the food chain than the firm attorney. Whereas in a firm the lawyers are the rainmakers or fee generators who bring in the revenue, in a company the attorneys are back office expense and arguably more expendable. They are therefore under pressure to make themselves relevant and useful. Thus, an in-house attorney needs to be seen as one who facilitates and enables client objectives in order to have merit to the organization which employs him.

While duties of the outside attorney and corporate counsel may overlap, their positions and points of view are entirely different. In-house counsel wear business as well as legal hats and participate in decision-making as officers of the company. This model, under which the attorney participates in formatting business objectives, deviates significantly from the traditional firm-client model whereby the client determines the objectives and the attorney determines the means. As Milton Regan has noted, "if in-house counsel do indeed become integrally involved in the formulating company goals and structuring company operations, it may be unrealistic to insist that they nonetheless remain legal technicians morally unaccountable for the consequences of those activities.". . .

One of an attorney's most fundamental obligations is that of professional independence. . . .

The duty of independence manifests itself in a number of different ways throughout the Rules. First, when acting in an advisory capacity, an attorney must offer independent advice to his client. Rule 2.1 provides, in part, that "[i]n representing a client, a lawyer shall exercise independent professional judgment and render candid advice." As the comments to this rule note, even though the advice may be unpleasant and contrary to what the client wishes to hear, the lawyer must give a candid opinion. Thus, an attorney must be prepared to tell a client "the good, the bad, and the ugly" without fear of the consequences it will have. This often may involve advice that is unpalatable to a client or which may slow, frustrate, or stand in the way of the company's business objectives or the desired means of achieving them.

[The Rules also require attorney independence through Rule 1.7, which prohibits self-interest conflicts, Rule 3.3, which requires candor to a tribunal, and Rule 1.16, which requires withdrawal when continuing the representation will result in a violation of the Rules or other law.]

The Rules and other ethical obligations . . . apply with equal force to attorneys in private practice as well as in-house counsel, and the potential conflicts highlighted are present in their work as well. The question then is why are they any more problematic with respect to in-house counsel? How, if at all, are the ethical conflicts of in-house counsel any different or more complex? In-house counsel, by virtue of their unique placement and point of view, face an independence problem that is without parallel in the firm context in its pervasiveness and scope. In understanding the magnitude of the issue, it is necessary to examine the causes of the problem and the ways in which those causes manifest themselves in counsel's thoughts and actions. . . .

Historically, the scholarship addressing the independence problem of in-house counsel has focused on the issue of incentive. The emphasis is not entirely misplaced, as the structure under which in-house counsel is employed, assessed, and rewarded creates innumerable pressures. . . . Unlike attorneys in private practice who may receive fees from numerous clients, in-house counsel is compensated solely by the company and is dependent upon the client, which employs him for salary and benefits. . . .

Corporate counsel are often compensated with other financial incentives based upon performance and value to the corporation, such as bonuses, which can reflect a significant portion of counsel's total compensation. . . .

Another major piece of the in-house counsel incentive puzzle is stock options. Stock options are granted as incentive for management performance and are intended to align the interests of executive management with those of shareholders for a common goal of maximizing profits. However, this model is problematic with respect to corporate counsel. First, . . . the Model Rules of Professional Conduct make clear that the attorney should be acting without regard for personal interest. Moreover, the attorney's mandate goes beyond that of short-term profit maximization. Counsel needs to give advice about legal liability and long-term legal issues, even where the best course of action for those objectives may be inconsistent with maximizing stock price. The attorney may also, in his capacity as gatekeeper, need to interdict with respect to plans that would increase profits but may be potentially fraudulent or violate the law. Scandals such as Enron highlighted the problem; corporate misconduct was attributed to emphasis by executives to maximize personal profits and attorneys were among those who stood to gain.

Beyond the financial incentives of the in-house attorney's job, there is the inducement of the very job itself. With counsel employed by his lone client, all advice given is under the dangling sword of being fired and losing one's financial security. Even for an attorney who is willing to risk losing his job, there are more significant long term consequences. As Professor Hazard noted, "The ultimate risk is not only being fired, with loss of employment, fringe benefits and pension rights, but the possibility of being professionally blacklisted. . . . Many [corporate officers] will not hesitate in firing a lawyer who gives them a hard time and then bad-mouthing the lawyer afterward.". . .

Recognition of incentive as a cause of the independence problem of in-house counsel is important, but tells only half of the story. By focusing on pecuniary security and wealth maximization as the principal influences on corporate counsel, earlier analysis has failed to take into account the effect that self-perception and organizational dynamics have on the psyche of counsel. More recent scholarship has attempted to explain the independence problem of in-house counsel by utilizing social science, arguing that it is the intangible elements, the environment in which counsel works and the pressures to which he is subjected, that subconsciously alter the lens through which he views his work and his decision-making processes. . . .

Organizational identity pertains to the group or body of which an individual considers himself a member. In the case of in-house counsel, the attorney is situated in the client entity rather than a law firm. Additionally, where an outside attorney generally works for numerous organizations, an in-house counsel works for just one. Moreover, he is likely to work for this one entity for several years, perhaps even an entire career. Thus an attorney may come to identify himself closely as a member of the organization.

The second identity problem is interpersonal, arising from the relationships which counsel forms with others within the corporation. While in-house counsel may work with a limited number of other attorneys, most of his colleagues will be non-lawyer members of the company. Counsel is likely to form long-term working relationships, and perhaps even friendships, with these peer employees. Additionally, the in-house attorney is likely to have very limited contact with other members of the legal profession who are not part of the company, unless he voluntarily seeks out bar or other professional training or activities. Thus the overwhelming majority of counsel's workplace interactions will be with non-lawyer members of the corporate entity. This immersion among non-lawyers lessens in-house counsel's perception of himself as an independent advisor and more closely aligns his outlook with organizational constituents.

The third aspect of identity is the actor problem: in-house counsel acts on behalf of the company and participates in business and strategic decision-making. Thus, the attorney is often asked to defend or opine upon his own decisions, removing objectivity. As Tim Terrell noted, by acting in legal and business capacities for the company, "counsel is often in the uncomfortable position of, in effect, rendering legal advice to himself or herself.". . .

The relative intensity of the identity pressures may vary depending upon the working environment. For example, attorneys who work in smaller legal departments with fewer professional peers or who are imbedded directly within a business unit surrounded entirely by non-legal co-workers may face more intense psychological pressures than those situated in larger legal departments. Similarly, the reporting structures of some companies, whereby the legal department reports to the chief financial officer or other non-legal executive, can also increase the conformity pressures of the law department. Identity pressures may also differ depending on the seniority of an attorney's position, *e.g.*, the general counsel may have more autonomy by virtue of his position within the company and his access to the board of directors than a lower level attorney. . . .

NOTES AND QUESTIONS

1. E. Norman Veasey, former Chief Justice of the Delaware Supreme Court and a law firm senior partner, agreed that there are threats to in-house counsel's independence, but he was optimistic that "courageous" corporate counsel can fulfill the independence obligation. He suggested a number of strategies to assist in this endeavor, including maintaining a regular line of communication with the board of directors, which can "provid[e] a buffer between the general counsel and the CEO," and involving the board in corporate counsel's compensation plan, which should reward "exceptional and professionally independent legal work, as distinct from pure financial performance."[17] And, as Daly noted, ACCA (now ACC)[18] provides support for general counsel's identification with the legal profession as opposed to the corporate entity. Many general counsel also maintain informal networks among their general counsel peers, through which they get advice on issues of common concern.

---

17. Veasey & Di Guglielmo, *supra* n. 12, at 13.
18. *See supra* n. 1.

A. The Evolving Role of In-House Counsel   **401**

2. Jenoff rejected what she called the "man of honor" approach.[19] She also rejected proposals for limited structural reforms, for example, prohibiting nonlegal roles such as serving on the board of directors, eliminating attorney stock options, or having the attorney regularly report directly to the board.[20] Instead, she favored more radical reforms, such as limiting the time corporate counsel can be employed within a company or recognizing a separate status for in-house counsel as a "business legal advisor[]" without the benefit of the attorney-client privilege.[21] The latter proposal is based on the "European model of corporate counsel," in which in-house counsel are not expected to exercise the same degree of independent judgment and, as a result, their communications are not protected by the attorney-client privilege.[22] What are the advantages and disadvantages of each of these approaches? Which do you prefer?

3. Partners in law firms are typically rewarded for the amount of business they bring and maintain within the firm, and some partners work almost exclusively for a single, large client. The firm itself has multiple clients, but if an individual partner is working primarily for only one corporate client, and his or her compensation depends on maintaining (and increasing) the business of that client, is that partner any more "independent" than general counsel for the same corporate client?

4. How do the current Model Rules govern the use of stock options as a form of compensation to in-house counsel? What about what Jenoff identified as the attorney defending his or her own decisions as a corporate actor? For example, consider a company that is contemplating an internal investigation of a series of transactions that general counsel structured and executed. How do the Model Rules apply to general counsel advising the company on initiating the investigation?

5. In recognition of both the actual and perceived lack of independence of in-house counsel, commentators typically recommend that outside counsel be retained to conduct "significant internal investigation[s]," as determined by "the seriousness of the allegations, whether the conduct at issue is alleged to be widespread or systemic, whether senior management or board members potentially are implicated, whether criminal or regulatory authorities are (or are likely to become) involved and whether a shareholder derivative demand has been made."[23] When senior management or board members are potentially implicated, the

---

19. 114 W. Va. L. Rev. at 751.

20. *Id.* at 752.

21. *Id.* at 753-57.

22. *Id.* at 754-57 (citing Case 550/07, Akzo Nobel Chemicals Ltd. & Akcros Chems. Ltd. v. European Comm'n, Opinion of Advocate General Kokott (Apr. 29, 2010), available at http://eurlex.europa.eu/LexUriServ/LexUriServ.do?uri=CELEX:62007CCO550:EN:HTML).

23. Daniel J. Fetterman & Mark P. Goodman, Defending Corp. & Indiv. In Gov. Invest. §3:11 (2020).

independence of in-house counsel is questionable given that their "employment and compensation are directly or indirectly controlled by senior management."[24]

B. DIFFICULTIES IN ESTABLISHING THE ATTORNEY-CLIENT PRIVILEGE

Unlike the European approach, U.S. courts recognize the applicability of the attorney-client privilege to communications between in-house counsel and the corporate client, so long as all of the requirements of invoking the privilege have been met. Nevertheless, the dual role that the modern in-house counsel plays as both legal and business advisor, complicates the corporation's ability to establish those requirements, as illustrated in the following opinion.

Leazure v. Apria Healthcare Inc.
2010 WL 3895727 (E.D. Tenn. 2010)

WILLIAM B. MITCHELL CARTER, United States Magistrate Judge.

Pursuant to the Court's order entered on August 27, 2010, defendant Apria Healthcare, Inc. (Apria) has submitted further documents for an in camera review to determine whether the documents are privileged or must be produced in response to discovery requests. . . . Of particular importance in this case is the role in-house counsel played during the decision making process leading to plaintiff's termination. . . .

It is now generally accepted that communications between and attorney and client of primarily a business nature are outside the scope of the privilege. This issue of the principle nature of the advice given by the attorney, i.e., business or legal, most often arises when in-house counsel offers advice to its corporate employer. *See, e.g., In re Southern Industrial Banking Corp.* (while "the involvement of an attorney in the commercial endeavors of a corporation does not per se vitiate the attorney-client privilege, . . . the participation of general counsel in the business of the corporation likewise does not automatically cloak the business activity with the protection of the attorney-client privilege"); *Puckett v. Arvin/Calspan Field. Serv.* (holding in-house counsel was acting in an administrative capacity during corporation's staff meeting and thus attorney-client privilege did not apply to conversation which occurred during meeting); *Georgia Pacific Corp. v. GAF Roofing Mfg. Corp.* (holding that in-house counsel who acted as negotiator as to certain provisions of a contract between two corporations was acting in a business capacity thereby rendering the attorney-client privilege inapplicable. . . . *See also Amway Corp. v. Proctor & Gamble Co.* ("Where . . . in-house counsel appears as one of many recipients of

---

24. *Id.*

an otherwise business-related memo, the federal courts place a heavy burden on the proponent to make a clear showing that counsel is acting in a professional legal capacity and that the document reflects legal, as opposed to business advice.")...

The documents submitted by Apria raise the always difficult and uncomfortable question of the "hat" in-house counsel wears. Based on the considerations discussed above, I conclude that the documents bearing on the reduction in force (RIF), Apria's selection of the plaintiff as the employee to terminate in the RIF, and the timing of plaintiff's termination in the RIF should be produced. These documents discuss the reasons for plaintiff's selection as the person to be terminated in the RIF, when the RIF should be executed, i.e., when plaintiff should be terminated, and how other employee disciplinary actions shall be approached. These types of considerations are part of the normal process of determining who is to be terminated in a RIF and when and how to carry[] out a RIF; they are normal HR functions.

Apria has simply not prevailed in its burden to show that in-house counsel, Lan Farrell, was providing legal advice and/or legal guidance regarding the RIF and plaintiff's termination in the RIF. The documents submitted by Apria do not, by themselves, indicate her role was one of a legal advisor, and no affidavit has been submitted to explain or clarify her role. Rather, it appears that Lan Farrell's role was that of a business advisor and an active participant and decision-maker in the decision to terminate plaintiff. Based on my conclusion that Lan Farrell was not acting as a legal advisor in relation to the RIF and plaintiff's termination, and based on my conclusion that the documents at issue reflect ordinary business purposes when making a decision to terminate employment in a RIF, I conclude neither the attorney-client privilege nor the work product doctrine applies to [these] documents. . . .

NOTES AND QUESTIONS

1. Assume that Apria included Lan Farrell in the discussions concerning the plaintiff's termination because the company was concerned that the plaintiff would subsequently sue for wrongful termination (as did in fact occur) and wanted to ensure that the process and means used to accomplish the termination adhered to applicable legal guidelines. How might the company have structured Farrell's participation to maximize the likelihood that the attorney-client privilege would apply to communications between Farrell and the other participants?

2. What is the relevance of the magistrate judge's conclusion that Farrell was "an active participant and decision-maker in the decision to terminate plaintiff"? Was this an indicia of Farrell's role as a business rather than legal advisor? If so, why? Is it relevant whether, during the meetings, Farrell was specifically requested to render legal advice concerning the process and means used to accomplish the termination?

3. In Amway Corp. v. Procter & Gamble Co.,[25] an opinion cited by the magistrate judge, the court expressed concern for documents in which "in-house counsel appears as one of many recipients of an otherwise business-related memo."[26] It is not uncommon for a company officer to circulate a draft document to multiple recipients, including in-house counsel, and for counsel (and others) to respond by proposing edits in the document, which is then circulated to all the original recipients. Even if counsel is included because of a concern for potential legal issues, and even if counsel's edits in fact reflect primarily legal concerns, the document with counsel's proposed edits might not be covered by the privilege. Federal district judge Eldon E. Fallon explained this result in a case involving the pharmaceutical company Merck:

> When these simultaneous conveyances for mixed purposes are through an e-mail message that lists the lawyers' names in the header of the e-mail message, [the defendant] Merck is revealing the contents of the single message that may have been conveyed to its lawyer primarily for legal assistance. In that circumstance, the single message could have been withheld as a privileged communication had Merck sent blind copies to the lawyers, instead of electing this format. Through a blind copy, the content of what was communicated to its attorney would have remained confidential after future discovery of the document from the other recipient's files, its purpose would have been primarily legal, and the privilege would have been applicable. Similarly, if Merck had sent a wholly separate e-mail communication with the same materials to the lawyer, the same claim could be successfully made for that single communication even though it otherwise served mixed purposes. In modern vernacular, Merck, in a variety of instances, "could have had a V-8," but it chose another format and manner of document circulation and cannot now be heard to complain about the consequences of those choices. Otherwise, Merck would be able to limit the scope of what adversaries can discover by the way in which it chooses to communicate.[27]

Why should it matter whether counsel is listed as a recipient of an email with a document attached, as opposed to being blind copied on the same email and attachment? If the concern is not that the communication to the lawyer was for a business and not a legal purpose, what requirement of the privilege is not being met?

4. The difficulty in establishing attorney-client privilege for in-house counsel is yet another reason to use outside counsel to conduct significant internal investigations. This is because "[e]ngaging outside counsel . . . signals to the government or to a court that the company's investigation is being conducting in anticipation of future litigation and for the purpose of obtaining legal, rather than business advice, and so

---

25. 2001 WL 1818698 (W.D. Mich. 2001).
26. *Id.* at *5.
27. *In re* Vioxx Products Liability Litigation, 501 F.Supp.2d 789, 805-06 (E.D. La. 2007).

may facilitate claims of privilege and associated work product protections over the information, analysis, and results of the investigation."[28] A particularly egregious example of the abuse of in-house counsel in a calculated effort to avoid future production of harmful corporate documents is the decades-long practice of the tobacco companies funneling scientific research through the legal department.[29]

5. In-house counsel are not always licensed to practice in the jurisdiction where they are physically located. This is because they are often required to switch locations, either within the same corporation or corporate family or when switching jobs from one company to another. For many years, this lack of licensure was ignored because counsel represented only one client and the corporate employer typically knew but did not care about counsel's failure to seek admission in a new state. Recently, most jurisdictions have adopted reforms that permit in-house counsel licensed in one jurisdiction to serve a corporate employer in another jurisdiction. *See infra* Chapter 15: Unauthorized Practice of Law and Multijurisdictional Practice.

C. LAWYERS AS COMPLIANCE OFFICERS

One of the factors Daly cited for the growing prominence of in-house counsel is the increased scope of governmental regulation, which has created the need for routine advice on compliance issues. In addition, recent Delaware cases have held that a corporate board of directors has a duty to take affirmative law compliance measures, including a "responsibility to assure that appropriate information and reporting systems are established by management" to ensure compliance with the key regulatory regimes under which it operates.[30]

Companies use a combination of lawyers and nonlawyers to perform the compliance function. But when lawyers serve in that role, they may or may not be "practicing law." This ambiguity raises various issues, including difficulties in determining when the attorney-client privilege applies and uncertainty concerning the nature of the role of compliance officer, as opposed to practicing lawyer. The following article describes both the role of the compliance officer and the tensions created for lawyers performing that role.

---

28. Fetterman & Goodman, *supra* n. 23 at §3:11.

29. *See* Order Regarding Privilege and the Crime-Fraud Exception and Setting Forth Procedures to Determine Privilege Beginning with the Liggett Documents, State ex rel. Humphrey v. Philip Morris Inc., No. C1-94-8565 (Minn. Dist. Ct., Ramsey County, May 9, 1997) (unredacted version available at http://www.pmdocs.com/core/downloadSearchBlob? IDX=1&FROM=SEARCH&CVSID=5cf3e45177dab8ebe6d92a8396d4e3fc).

30. In re Caremark International Inc. Derivative Litigation, 698 A.2d 959, 969-70 (Del. Ch. 1996); *see also* Stone v. Ritter, 911 A.2d 362 (Del. 2006).

Jennifer M. Pacella

The Regulation of Lawyers in Compliance
95 Wash. L. Rev. 947, 953-58, 963-64, 968-81 (2020)...

The field of compliance was once a "virtually unknown topic," and "not traditionally the exclusive domain of lawyers," but has since emerged as one of the most vibrant sources of employment and research for the legal field as a whole. Two decades ago, compliance could be described as "a bit of a backwater," as a field that was not particularly specialized and did not necessarily attract individuals of any particular skillset—"[c]ompliance officers tended to work in cubicles and performed a sort of glorified bookkeeping task, making sure that forms were filled out and boxes checked." Today, the landscape is extremely different, as the field of compliance and the role of the compliance officer now boast better salaries, expansive and collaborative departments, increased prestige, and provide insight on crucial and strategic decision of an organization. Compliance departments play a crucial role in organizations through their preventative focus. Although "compliance" is often subject to varying definitions, one succinct way to describe it is as "a field that focuses on prospectively ensuring adherence to laws and regulations through the use of monitoring, policies, and other internal controls."

The growth of the compliance function has come about largely as a response to the extraordinary complexity in regulation over recent decades, and has increased in attention with the U.S. Sentencing Commission's amendment of the Federal Sentencing Guidelines in 1991 to include the Organizational and Sentencing Guidelines (OSG). The OSG are based on a "carrots and sticks" model, with the carrot being a significantly reduced fine for organizations that adopt effective compliance programs and the stick being the placement of the organization on probation without any reduced penalty if compliance programs are not adopted. To obtain the carrot of a significantly reduced fine, the OSG lists several steps for a court to consider when determining the effectiveness of a compliance program, which includes procedures for reducing the risk of criminal activity, oversight by high-level individuals; limited discretionary authority granted to any individual likely to be criminally active; communication of the program to all employees; the use of monitoring, auditing, and reporting systems; and disciplinary action for any violations of the program. These steps were intentionally adopted in a general tone to allow organizations some flexibility in tailoring a compliance program specific to their needs.

The focus on compliance has continued steadily since 1991 and was enhanced in the wake of the financial crisis from 2007 to 2009 and the enactment of the Dodd-Frank Wall Street Reform and Consumer Protection Act ("Dodd-Frank") in 2010. Even prior to Dodd-Frank, new regulatory models governing organizations and business were beginning to emerge that laid the groundwork for compliance racing to the forefront. The post Enron-era and the passage of the Sarbanes-Oxley Act of 2002 ("SOX") helped further facilitate a tangible move away from traditional, top-down "command and control" government-dictated regulatory schemes to the "new governance" models focused on self-regulation, self-reporting to government, preventative practices, and generally more collaboration between regulated entities and regulators. New Governance models reflect the collective recognition from regulators and public and private entities that the traditional style of top-down governance, which addresses problems reactively rather than pre-emptively and proactively, was not effective in avoiding large-scale fraud and other violations of the law. . . . The modern-day compliance function can be said to be largely descriptive of the new governance models, specifically given its emphasis on the development of policies, programs, and procedures aimed at detecting red flags and possible and known violations of the law, as well as maintaining focus on self-regulation and self-reporting. In this way, the compliance function's focus is internal, rather than external, thereby encouraging entities to avoid violations altogether, rather than facing government investigation or litigation at a later point. . . . Compliance officers also commonly establish ethics programs to facilitate adherence to laws and take responsibility for the day-to-day implementation and effectiveness of such programs.

Despite the potential for variation in the everyday duties of compliance officers across the board, their core function is to interpret, assess, and facilitate the organization's adherence to the regulations to which it is subject, and to offer advice about such regulations and other pertinent laws and the repercussions of non-compliance, all of which are fitting characteristics of legally trained individuals. Individuals of varied backgrounds and skills may be qualified to work in the compliance field but, as many scholars have noted, a lawyer brings a uniquely advantageous set of skills to the table and many organizations prefer that a lawyer hold the position of compliance officer given their special legal training. . . .

The uptick in lawyers holding compliance positions coincided with an era in which traditional employment prospects for new law school graduates were at an all-time low largely due to the financial crisis, thereby opening up a wave of "J.D. Advantage" or quasi-legal career options in which neither a law degree nor bar passage is required, but is desired. Currently, compliance positions across various industries comprise one of the largest portions of J.D. Advantage jobs. J.D. Advantage jobs reflect "the porousness of legal practice," resulting in numerous employment opportunities for legally-trained persons in various areas of "law and law-related services shared by lawyers *and others*." These expansions in compliance are not limited to any particular industry, as rapid growth in compliance jobs has run the gamut from financial institutions to non-governmental organizations. As a result, while law students have traditionally pursued either a litigation or a transactional track in their studies, they are now increasingly discovering a third option—that of a compliance officer or compliance attorney. . . .

[T]he inevitable question of whether lawyers operating in compliance roles are "practicing law" must be addressed. Although collective instinct may deem such work to be outside the realm of law practice, the title of lawyer, in itself, often leads constituents of an organization to believe, whether the case or not, that an attorney-client relationship has been formed. . . . [E]ven the ABA's Compliance Officer's Deskbook acknowledges that a lawyer who is a compliance officer is likely to expect the substance of their work to be privileged, but it is necessary to be cognizant of the fine lines between law practice and law-related services, the latter of which may not necessarily invoke the privilege or other coveted characteristics of an attorney-client relationship.

The question of attorney-client privilege applicability is a crucial consideration for compliance work given its influence upon the individuals comprising the organization. . . . When the general counsel serves simultaneously as the compliance officer, it is often quite difficult for individuals to know whether or not the privilege applies. The privilege applies only to situations in which the lawyer is providing "legal advice or services" and "will not protect disclosure of non-legal communications where the attorney acts as a business or economic advisor." As courts have made clear, neither the attorney-client privilege nor work-product protections apply to documents or communications produced as part of an internal investigation within an entity's compliance department when that investigation was not conducted for the purpose of receiving or providing legal advice, prior to litigation emerging, or when a non-lawyer carrying out the investigation was not acting as the lawyer's direct agent. . . .

In light of the uncertainty of defining the practice of law and the general consensus among states that, at a minimum, possession of specialized, legal knowledge or judgment is required, it is a reasonable conclusion that the work of a compliance officer or a person engaged in the compliance function does not fit squarely into the "practice of law" for purposes of triggering adherence to all of the ABA's Model Rules of Professional [Conduct]. This is the case because compliance officers are not necessarily trained in law. As previously noted, such individuals need not possess a J.D. or a law license. While possession of a J.D. may be an advantage, it is not a requirement for the job. Further, the definitions of law practice among the states have in common a focus on litigation-related activities, whether the drafting of pleadings, advocacy, or representation in an adjudicative setting. Such activities are not on par with the work of a compliance officer, which is focused on organizational monitoring for red flags to ensure, well in advance of actual violations, that an entity is conforming its behavior to the expectations of the appropriate regulatory agency. . . .

[O]ne way to minimize [potential risk to lawyers serving as compliance officers] is to clearly separate the legal and compliance departments within an organization. There has been extensive scholarly debate as to whether an organization's legal and compliance functions should be departmentalized or operate as separate units, from each other. Various corporate scandals, occurring over the last two decades, and spanning multiple industries, have prompted regulators to favor the separation of the two functions. In particular, the SEC and the Department of Health and Human Services have each required corporations that have engaged in wrongdoing to both establish stand-alone compliance departments, and appoint a chief compliance officer who reports directly to the board of directors, rather than to the general counsel. Regulators commonly believe that a compliance department that is separate from the legal function will allow more autonomy and independence to the former to discover, report, and manage instances of non-compliance because general counsel would not have a chance to filter or safeguard the information before it reaches the board of directors. This regulatory preference towards separation of the two functions is also telling of the inherent differences between a compliance officer and an attorney, especially pertaining to the relationship of these individuals with the organization itself and with regulators; in essence, the compliance officer represents the regulator, rather than the organization it monitors.

NOTES AND QUESTIONS

1. We have already seen how in-house lawyers serving as both legal and business advisors complicates the application of the attorney-client privilege. As Pacella notes, this problem is especially acute for lawyers who serve as compliance officers, a position occupied by lawyers and nonlawyers alike. When General Counsel (GC) also serves as the Chief Compliance Officer (CCO), the company seeking the protection of the privilege has the burden of establishing that communications to or from employees were for the primary purpose of seeking legal advice. For example, in Freescale Semiconductor, Inc. v. Maxim Integrated Products, Inc., 2013 WL 5874139 (W.D. Tex. 2013), the court held that an initial whistleblower communication through an EthicsPoint online portal was not privileged, although it was reviewed by the GC, who was also serving as the CCO, because there was no indication that the employee was seeking legal advice. However, subsequent communications through the same portal were found to be privileged because the GC was seeking additional information in support of an investigation initiated by him for the purpose of rendering legal advice to the company. Communications with a lawyer serving as a compliance officer are less likely to be protected by the privilege when the compliance officer is not part of the legal department and does not hold himself or herself out as a lawyer for the company. *See, e.g.*, U.S. ex rel. Frazier v. IASIS Healthcare Corp., 2012 WL 130332 (D. Ariz. 2010). If the company wants the maximum protection of the attorney-client privilege, shouldn't it merge the compliance and legal functions by either designating the GC as chief compliance officer, or at least have the CCO report to the GC? Why do many companies separate the two functions?

Chapter 13 In-House Counsel

2. For an illustration of some of the consequences of combining the two functions, consider Balla v. Gambro,[31] in which a lawyer who had been serving as general counsel added the position of "manager of regulatory affairs" to his portfolio. That position, which had previously been occupied by a nonlawyer, was the equivalent of a chief compliance officer, reporting to the general counsel. Balla was subsequently fired and when he sued his employer for retaliatory discharge, he argued that he had been fired for his conduct as manager of regulatory affairs and was thus eligible to take advantage of the public policy exception to the at-will employee doctrine. The court disagreed, relying in part on Balla's own testimony that he did not separate the two functions even in his own mind.[32] The ability of in-house counsel to sue for the tort of wrongful discharge is discussed in the next section of this chapter.

3. If the "core function [of compliance]" is to "interpret, assess, and facilitate the organization's adherence to the regulations to which it is subject, and to offer advice about such regulations and other pertinent laws," as Pacella suggested, then why isn't serving as a compliance officer clearly the practice of law? In an omitted portion of the article, Pacella described the acknowledged difficulty of defining the practice of law, "especially as it pertains to rendering legal advice versus non-legal business or strategic advice."[33] Michele DeStefano similarly acknowledged the indeterminacy of the practice-of-law definitions; she concluded that the compliance function "appears to overlap with the traditional job of the corporate attorney" and could be considered the practice of law.[34] An argument in favor of viewing most compliance functions as separate from practicing law is that the particular knowledge and skill of a trained lawyer have not been a prerequisite to serving as a compliance officer, just as nonlawyers have historically occupied such positions as real estate broker and tax accountant, whose work also requires some knowledge of applicable law. We will further explore the ramifications of the indeterminacy of defining the practice of law in Chapter 15: Unauthorized Practice of Law and Multijurisdictional Practice.

4. At the conclusion of the excerpted article, Pacella described the "inherent differences between a compliance officer and an attorney, especially pertaining to the relationship of these individuals with the organization itself and with regulators; in essence, the compliance officer represents

---

31. 584 N.E.2d 104 (Ill. 1991).
32. *Id.* at 112.
33. 95 Wash. L. Rev. at 965.
34. Michele DeStefano, Compliance and Claim Funding: Testing the Borders of Lawyers' Monopoly and the Unauthorized Practice of Law, 82 Fordham L. Rev. 2961, 2979 (2014) (referring not to the part of the job where compliance officers encourage adherence to ethical guidelines that go beyond what the law requires, but rather to "the other part of the compliance officer's job—the part that attempts to interpret new laws and regulations and counsel the client on how to comply with those laws and regulations").

the regulator, rather than the organization it monitors."[35] It is unclear what she meant. Did she mean that the compliance officer is functioning as a legal agent of the regulating agency? This seems doubtful, as the compliance officer is an employee of the company and can be fired by the company, although whistleblower statutes provide some level of protection for the compliance officer. Rather, it would appear that Pacella was referring to the way in which compliance officers, particularly those who are separate from the legal department, view their role within the company. For example, DeStefano described how "compliance officers distinguish what they do from what lawyers do by explaining that lawyers say what you *can* do and compliance officers say what you *should do*."[36] When compliance officers view themselves as the "cop" on the "beat,"[37] this may reflect what Pacella described as "the 'new governance' models focused on self-regulation, self-reporting to government . . . and generally more collaboration between regulated entities and regulators." Other scholars, including Rory Van Loo, have noted a growing tendency for administrative agencies to use legal rules and guidance documents that mandate or encourage private firms to perform a public regulatory function.[38] Of course, as was discussed in the preceding chapter, lawyers themselves have been recruited to perform a similar function as part of the "reporting up" and "reporting out" provisions of SOX.[39]

D. WRONGFUL DISCHARGE

Model Rule 1.16(a)(3) requires a lawyer to withdraw from representation of a client when the lawyer is discharged. This provision reflects the view that "[a] client has a right to discharge a lawyer at any time, with or without cause, subject to liability for payment of the lawyer's services." MR 1.16, Comment [4]. But in-house lawyers are also employees, and at-will employees sometimes have the right under state law to sue for wrongful discharge when they are fired in contravention of a clear public policy, such as for refusing an employer's direction to engage in criminal conduct.[40] So when an

---

35. 95 Wash. L. Rev. at 981.

36. DeStefano, *supra* n. 34, at 2978 (noting that general counsel disagree with this attempted distinction).

37. Geoffrey P. Miller, The Law of Governance, Risk Management, and Compliance 130 (2017) (describing a compliance officer to "a beat cop walking the corridors of the company's organization chart to ensure that rules and regulations are being followed"), cited in Pacella, 95 Wash. L. Rev. at 982, n.169.

38. *See generally* Rory Van Loo, The New Gatekeepers: Private Firms as Public Enforcers, 106 Va. L. Rev 467 (2020) (analyzing the extent to which the world's largest businesses are now required to routinely police other businesses).

39. *See supra* Chapter 12: Corporate Wrongdoing.

40. *See* Restatement (Third) of Employment Law §5.01 (2014).

Chapter 13 In-House Counsel

in-house lawyer is fired allegedly in contravention of a clear public policy, does MR 1.16(a)(3) apply, or will a state recognize such a lawyer's claim for wrongful discharge? The following case discusses the evolution of the case law on this question, as well as the competing public policies at issue.

Crews v. Buckman Laboratories International, Inc.
78 S.W.3d 852 (Tenn. 2002)

WILLIAM M. BARKER, J. . . .

According to the allegations of the complaint, the plaintiff was hired by Buckman in 1995 as associate general counsel in its legal department, and while working in this capacity, she reported to Buckman's General Counsel, Ms. Katherine Buckman Davis. Sometime in 1996, the plaintiff discovered that Ms. Davis, who "held herself out as a licensed attorney," did not possess a license to practice law in the State of Tennessee. The plaintiff became concerned that Ms. Davis was engaged in the unauthorized practice of law, and she discussed her suspicions with a member of Buckman's Board of Directors.[41]

Ms. Davis eventually took and passed the bar exam, but the plaintiff learned some time later that Ms. Davis had to complete the requirements for licensure by taking the Multi-State Professional Responsibility Examination. The plaintiff informed Buckman officials of the continuing problem, and she advised them on how best to proceed. On June 17, 1999, Ms. Davis allegedly entered the plaintiff's office, yelling that she was frustrated with the plaintiff's actions. The plaintiff responded that she also was frustrated with the situation, to which Ms. Davis remarked that "maybe [the plaintiff] should just leave," and she later received a below-average raise for the first time during her tenure at Buckman, despite having been told earlier by Ms. Davis that she was "doing a good job in position of Associate Counsel."

In August, the plaintiff sought legal advice concerning her ethical obligations, and based on this advice, she informed the Board of Law Examiners of Ms. Davis's situation. . . .

The plaintiff then informed Mr. Buckman and the Vice President of Human Resources that "the situation [had become] untenable and that she could not function under those circumstances." They agreed that the plaintiff should be immediately transferred to a position away from Ms. Davis's supervision and that she should eventually leave the company altogether within six to nine months. However, while the plaintiff was "in the midst of working out the

---

41. [Fn. 1 in Original] This Director then requested an opinion from the Board of Professional Responsibility based on a hypothetical scenario mirroring the situation at Buckman. The Board replied that a person without a Tennessee law license may not be employed as general counsel in this state and that the failure to have such a license constitutes the unauthorized practice of law.

new arrangement," Ms. Davis informed her that her services would no longer be needed. . . . Although the plaintiff denied that she had resigned, her computer was confiscated; she was placed on personal leave; and she was given a notice of termination.

On April 10, 2000, the plaintiff filed suit against Buckman in the Shelby County Circuit Court, alleging a common-law action for retaliatory discharge in violation of public policy. [The trial court granted Buckman's motion to dismiss for failure to state a claim, and the Court of Appeals affirmed the dismissal of the complaint.]

The intermediate court listed three primary reasons why in-house counsel could not state a claim for retaliatory discharge in Tennessee: (1) the important public policy of regulating the practice of law "is adequately served by the existing protections of Tennessee's statutes and the Code of Professional Responsibility," and that in-house counsel does not need an action for retaliatory discharge to comply with the Disciplinary Rules; (2) a recognition of such an action would "seriously impair the special relationship of trust between an attorney and his or her client" and "might have the effect of chilling the attorney-client relationship"; and (3) allowing damages as a remedy for retaliatory discharge would have "the effect of shifting to the employer the costs of in-house counsel's adherence to the Disciplinary Rules.". . .

Tennessee has long adhered to the employment-at-will doctrine in employment relationships not established or formalized by a contract for a definite term. Under this "employment at will" doctrine, both the employer and the employee are generally permitted, with certain exceptions, to terminate the employment relationship "at any time for good cause, bad cause, or no cause.". . .

However, an employer's ability to discharge at-will employees was significantly tempered by our recognition . . . of a cause of action for retaliatory discharge. Since that time, we have further recognized that an at-will employee "generally may not be discharged for attempting to exercise a statutory or constitutional right, or for any other reason which violates a clear public policy which is evidenced by an unambiguous constitutional, statutory, or regulatory provisions." Therefore, in contrast to the purposes typically justifying the employment-at-will doctrine, an action for retaliatory discharge recognizes "that, in limited circumstances, certain well-defined, unambiguous principles of public policy confer upon employees implicit rights which must not be circumscribed or chilled by the potential of termination."

This Court has not previously addressed the issue of whether a lawyer may pursue a claim of retaliatory discharge against a former employer. At least initially, we must recognize that this case differs significantly from the usual retaliatory discharge case involving non-lawyer employees. When the discharged employee served as in-house counsel, the issue demands an inquiry into the corporation's expectations as the lawyer's sole employer and client, the lawyer's ethical obligations to the corporation, and the interest of the lawyer — in her character as an employee — in having protections available to other employees seeking redress of legal harm. Therefore, because this issue is one of first impression in this state, it is perhaps helpful to examine how other jurisdictions have addressed it. . . .

Several jurisdictions have grappled with how to balance the competing interests involved in these types of cases. Although the rationales often differed, most of the earlier cases on this subject held that a lawyer could not bring a retaliatory discharge action based upon the lawyer's adherence to his or her ethical duties. This line of cases culminated in *Balla v. Gambro, Inc.*, in which the Illinois Supreme Court reviewed the other cases and set forth several rationales why in-house counsel should not be permitted to assert an action for retaliatory discharge. These rationales included (1) that because "[i]n-house counsel do not have a choice of whether to follow their ethical obligations as attorneys licensed to practice law," lawyers do not need an action for retaliatory discharge to encourage them to abide by their ethical duties; and (2) that recognizing such an action would affect the foundation of trust in attorney-client relationships, which would then make employers "naturally hesitant to rely upon in-house counsel for advice regarding [the employer's] potentially questionable conduct."

In more recent years, however, other states have permitted a lawyer, under limited circumstances, to pursue a claim of retaliatory discharge based upon termination in violation of public policy. The principal case permitting such an action is *General Dynamics Corp. v. Rose*, in which the California Supreme Court rejected the views held by *Balla* and others and established an analytical framework permitting a lawyer to sue for retaliatory discharge. According to this framework, a lawyer is generally permitted to assert a retaliatory discharge action if the lawyer is discharged for following a mandatory ethical duty or engaging in conduct that would give rise to an action by a non-lawyer employee. However, the *General Dynamics* Court cautioned that the lawyer bringing the action could not rely upon confidential information to establish the claim and that any unsuccessful lawyer breaching his or her duty of confidentiality was subject to disciplinary sanctions.

Following California's lead, the Supreme Judicial Court of Massachusetts has also permitted in-house counsel to assert a limited retaliatory discharge action. In *GTE Products Corp. v. Stewart*, the court questioned why the employee's status as an attorney should preclude an action. . . . However, while the *Stewart* Court permitted a limited retaliatory discharge action based upon a lawyer's refusal to violate "explicit and unequivocal statutory or ethical norms," it also restricted the scope of such an action to that in which "the claim can be proved without any violation of the attorney's obligation to respect client confidences and secrets."

Finally, and most recently, the Montana Supreme Court also held that in-house counsel should be permitted to bring retaliatory discharge actions when necessary to protect public policy. In *Burkhart v. Semitool, Inc.*, the court discussed the rationales in favor of adopting such an action and noted that while clients have a right to discharge counsel at any time and for any reason, this right does not necessarily apply to in-house counsel. Instead, the court reasoned that "by making his or her attorney an employee, [the employer] has avoided the traditional attorney-client relationship and granted the attorney protections that do not apply to independent contractors, but do apply to employees. . . ." Moreover, unlike the previous cases recognizing such an action, the *Burkhart* Court permitted lawyers to disclose the employer's confidential information to the extent necessary to establish a retaliatory discharge claim [relying upon a Montana Rule of Professional Conduct identical to current Model Rule 1.6(b)(5)]. . . .

Considering these two general approaches to retaliatory discharge actions based upon termination in violation of public policy, we generally agree with the approaches taken by the courts in *General Dynamics*, *Stewart*, and *Burkhart*. The very purpose of recognizing an employee's action for retaliatory discharge in violation of public policy is to encourage the employee to protect the public interest, and it seems anomalous to protect only non-lawyer employees under these circumstances. Indeed, as cases in similar contexts show, in-house counsel do not generally forfeit employment protections provided to other employees merely because of their status or duties as a lawyer.[42]

Moreover, we must reject the rationales typically set forth by *Balla* and the Court of Appeals in this case to generally deny lawyers the ability to pursue retaliatory discharge actions. *Balla*'s principal rationale was that recognition of a retaliatory discharge action was not necessary to protect the public interest so long as lawyers were required to follow a code of ethics. Indeed, relying on *Balla*, the intermediate court in this case specifically concluded that statutory and ethical proscriptions are sufficient to protect the public policy against the unauthorized practice of law and that in-house counsel do not need incentives, by way of a cause of action for retaliatory discharge, to comply with the Disciplinary Rules.

We respectfully disagree that the public interest is adequately served in this context without permitting in-house counsel to sue for retaliatory discharge. It is true that counsel in this case was under a mandatory duty [under the Tennessee equivalent to MR 5.5(a)] to not aid a non-lawyer in the unauthorized practice of law, and the intermediate court was also correct that lawyers do not have the option of disregarding the commandments of the Disciplinary Rules. This is not to say, however, that lawyers can never choose to violate mandatory ethical duties, as evidenced by the number of sanctions, some more severe than others, imposed upon lawyers by this Court and the Board of Professional Responsibility for such violations.

Ultimately, sole reliance on the mere presence of the ethical rules to protect important public policies gives too little weight to the actual presence of economic pressures designed to tempt in-house counsel into subordinating

---

42. [Fn. 2 in Original] For example, courts have permitted in-house lawyers to sue for age and race discrimination in violation of federal law; to sue for protections under a state "whistleblower" statute; to sue for breach of express and implied employment contracts; and to sue based on implied covenants of good faith and fair dealing.

ethical standards to corporate misconduct. Unlike lawyers possessing a multiple client base, in-house counsel are dependent upon only *one* client for their livelihood. . . .

The pressure to conform to corporate misconduct at the expense of one's entire livelihood, therefore, presents some risk that ethical standards could be disregarded. Like other non-lawyer employees, an in-house lawyer is dependent upon the corporation for his or her sole income, benefits, and pensions; the lawyer is often governed by the corporation's personnel policies and employees' handbooks; and the lawyer is subject to raises and promotions as determined by the corporation. In addition, the lawyer's hours of employment and nature of work are usually determined by the corporation. To the extent that these realities are ignored, the analysis here cannot hope to present an accurate picture of modern in-house practice.

We also reject *Balla*'s reasoning that recognition of a retaliatory discharge action under these circumstances would have a chilling effect upon the attorney-client relationship and would impair the trust between an attorney and his or her client. This rationale appears to be premised on one key assumption: the employer desires to act contrary to public policy and expects the lawyer to further that conduct in violation of the lawyer's ethical duties. We are simply unwilling to presume that employers as a class operate with so nefarious a motive, and we recognize that when employers seek legal advice from in-house counsel, they usually do so with the intent to comply with the law. . . .

Finally, we reject *Balla*'s assertion that allowing damages as a remedy for retaliatory discharge would have the effect of shifting to the employer the costs of in-house counsel's adherence to the ethics rules. The very purpose of permitting a claim for retaliatory discharge in violation of public policy is to encourage employers to refrain from conduct that is injurious to the public interest. Because retaliatory discharge actions recognize that it is the *employer* who is attempting to circumvent clear expressions of public policy, basic principles of equity all but demand that the costs associated with such conduct also be borne by the employer. . . .

If we perceive any shortcomings in the holdings of *General Dynamics* and *Stewart*, it is that they largely take away with one hand what they appear to give with the other. Although the courts in these cases gave in-house counsel an important right of action, their respective admonitions about preserving client confidentiality appear to stop just short of halting most of these actions at the courthouse door. With little imagination, one could envision cases involving important issues of public concern being denied relief merely because the wrongdoer is protected by the lawyer's duty of confidentiality. Therefore, given that courts have recognized retaliatory discharge actions in order to protect the public interest, this potentially severe limitation strikes us as a curious, if not largely ineffective, measure to achieve that goal.

[The Tennessee Disciplinary Rule governing confidentiality did not recognize an exception for disclosing the information necessary to establish a claim in a dispute between a lawyer and client. Therefore, the court adopted a new

D. Wrongful Discharge 417

exception to the Tennessee Rule paralleling the language of the Model Rule exception, now MR 1.6(b)(5).] Nevertheless, while in-house counsel may ethically disclose such information to the extent necessary to establish the claim, we emphasize that in-house counsel "must make every effort practicable to avoid unnecessary disclosure of [client confidences and secrets], to limit disclosure to those having the need to know it, and to obtain protective orders or make other arrangements minimizing the risks of disclosure" [citing a Model Rule comment similar to current Comment [16]].

NOTES AND QUESTIONS

1. For those states that have not yet decided whether in-house lawyers have a right to sue for retaliatory discharge, what are the arguments for and against recognizing such a right?

2. In *Crews*, the Tennessee Supreme Court adopted an exception to its rule of confidentiality to permit lawyers to disclose confidential information when reasonably necessary to establish a claim in a controversy with a client. Model Rule 1.6(b)(5) had already recognized such an exception, and ABA Formal Ethics Opinion 01-424 (2001) interpreted that rule to permit reasonably necessary disclosures in a lawyer's claim for retaliatory discharge. In the *General Dynamics* decision, the California Supreme Court recognized the lawyer's right to bring a retaliatory discharge action, but only if the lawyer could do so without violating confidentiality. Given that California has no equivalent to MR 1.6(b)(5), is the *Crews* court correct that the court appeared to "stop just short of halting most of these actions at the court house door"? Subsequent cases have emphasized that *General Dynamics* sought to protect against the *public* exposure of client secrets, noting that courts have at their disposal "an array of ad hoc measures from their equitable arsenal," including "[t]he use of sealing and protective orders, limited admissibility of evidence, orders restricting the use of testimony in successive proceedings, and, where appropriate, in camera proceedings."[43]

3. Aside from the professional duty of confidentiality, what about the attorney-client evidentiary privilege? The *General Dynamics* court stated that it "reject[ed] any suggestion that the scope of the privilege should be diluted in the context of in-house counsel and their corporate clients"; however, it also noted that "many of the cases in which house counsel is faced with an ethical dilemma will lie outside the scope of

---

43. General Dynamics v. Superior Court, 876 P.2d 487, 504 (Cal. 1994). For a subsequent decision emphasizing this aspect of *General Dynamics*, *see* Fox Searchlight Pictures, Inc. v. Paladino, 106 Cal.Rptr.2d 906, 920-21 (Cal. Ct. App. 2001) (holding that former in-house lawyer does not violate confidentiality when disclosing former employer's confidences to former lawyer's own lawyer in contemplation of wrongful discharge case).

the . . . privilege."[44] What sorts of communications do you think the court had in mind? Were the communications between Crews and her employer protected by the attorney-client privilege? Some jurisdictions have implied that there may be a higher degree of protection for privileged materials than for information protected by the professional rules of confidentiality such as MR 1.6, but have also endorsed the use of equitable measures to protect privileged materials from public disclosure.[45] Perhaps one way of explaining courts' permission for in-house counsel to use otherwise privileged communications to establish their claim is to observe, as the *Crews* court did, that "by making his or her attorney an employee, [the employer] has avoided the traditional attorney-client relationship and granted the attorney protections that do not apply to independent contractors, but do apply to employees."[46]

4. Regardless of whether the former in-house counsel can bring a retaliatory discharge action or disclose confidential or privileged information in establishing the claim, the question arises whether when leaving their position, lawyers may take with them or copy the employer's documents for purposes of defending themselves against a possible charge of wrongdoing or establishing a claim against the employer. Some lawyers have been sanctioned for doing so.[47]

5. Cases like *Crews* and *General Dynamics* recognize a common law cause of action for retaliatory discharge. Recent federal legislation has expanded whistleblower rights and protections, including protection from employer retaliation for providing information and assisting in the investigation of an employer's violation of securities violations under SOX.[48] In Van Asdale v. International Game Technology,[49] the Ninth Circuit held that in-house lawyers can state a claim of retaliatory discharge under SOX. Courts disagree whether the otherwise impermissible taking or copying of the employer's documents constitutes protected activity under whistleblower retaliation statutes.[50]

6. Legislation also provides for whistleblower "bounties" as an inducement for whistleblowers to come forward. The federal False Claims Act, for example, provides that a person who successfully brings a claim

---

44. 876 P2d at 504.

45. *See* Burkhart v. Semitool, Inc., 5 P.3d 1031, 1041 (Mont. 2000).

46. *Crews*, 78 S.W.3d at 859 (quoting Burkhart v. Semitool, Inc., 5 P.3d 1031, 1039 (Mont. 2000)).

47. *See, e.g.*, U.S. ex rel. Frazier v. IASIS Healthcare Corp., 2012 WL 130332 (D. Ariz. 2010).

48. *See* 18 U.S.C. §1513(e) (providing for criminal penalties for retaliating against an informant); §1514A (providing for a federal cause of action for retaliatory discharge).

49. 577 F.3d 989 (9th Cir. 2009).

50. *Compare, e.g.*, Quinlan v. Curtiss-Wright Corp, 204 N.J. 239, 269 (2010) (employing multi-factor test to determine whether employee can take or copy employer documents) *with* Niswander v. Cincinnatti Ins. Co., 529 F.3d 714, 722-23 (6th Cir. 2008) (accessing, copying, and disseminating employer data did not constitute protected activity).

against a company that has filed false claims with the federal government is entitled to a percentage of the amount awarded the government. So far, former in-house lawyers seeking to file such claims have had little success because courts have ruled that their duties of confidentiality under state rules of professional conduct do not permit them to serve in such a capacity.[51] In a jurisdiction that follows MR 1.6, why aren't such lawyers permitted to disclose information given that filing a false claim with the government constitutes a crime or fraud? The SEC regulations under Dodd-Frank similarly provide for whistleblower awards, and because the whistleblower can remain anonymous, even after collecting an award, potential whistleblowers include not only former lawyers, but also current in-house lawyers whose employers may never know of their role in prompting an adverse SEC action.[52]

Review Problems

13-1 A large corporation sought to retain the services of a law firm for a small tax matter. The law firm is hopeful that if the corporation is pleased with the law firm's services, it will retain the law firm for additional services, which the law firm believes it is well-positioned to offer. The partner who had been approached by the corporation did a conflicts check and learned that there were no conflicts under the applicable state rules. When the partner provided the corporation's in-house lawyer with the law firm's standard engagement agreement, however, the in-house lawyer responded by providing the partner with a copy of the corporation's outside counsel guidelines, which the in-house lawyer insisted must be a part of any engagement agreement. The partner was disturbed by one provision of the guidelines, which provided that the law firm agreed that the "client" for purposes of the engagement agreement included "all subsidiaries, affiliates, or parent companies of [the corporation], both as of the date of the signing of this agreement and hereafter, for the duration of the retention of the law firm." Should the partner recommend that the law firm agree to this provision? What are the pros and cons of allowing in-house lawyers to impose such a restrictive provision on outside counsel?

13-2 An in-house lawyer met with the corporation's CEO for her annual review. Pleased with the lawyer's performance, the CEO announced that the lawyer was eligible to participate in the corporation's stock option plan for senior executives. Under this plan, the lawyer would be granted stock options as part of her compensation package. Are there any ethical issues raised as a result of this offer? Does it matter whether the details of the plan are standardized for all participating executives or negotiated on a case-by-case basis? Are there other facts that the lawyer should take into account in deciding how to proceed?

---

51. *See generally* Kathleen Clark & Nancy J. Moore, Financial Rewards for Whistleblowing Lawyers, 56 B.C. L. Rev. 1697, 1703-41 (2015).

52. *See id.* at 1742-52.

13-3 Under a state video gaming statute, the gaming board has discretion to utilize the services of one or more outside testing laboratories to certify certain technical requirements of gaming machines. The board had utilized the services of Lab X, but it was under some pressure from Lab Y to be authorized to provide similar services. Lab X executives arranged to have an "educational meeting" with the board administrator concerning the lab's capabilities. Outside counsel to Lab X were concerned that such a meeting might violate the procedural requirements of the gaming statute if the forthcoming contract proposal requirements were discussed at the meeting. The meeting took place with senior executives of Lab X and the board administrator. After Lab X was granted the exclusive certification contract, Lab Y sued the gaming board to nullify the contract. During the litigation, Lab Y sought in discovery to obtain email messages among the Lab X senior executives who attended the meeting and the corporation's general counsel, whose official title is "Vice President of Government Relations and General Counsel." The subject of the emails was how the senior executives should conduct themselves in the meeting, including but not limited to concerns about avoiding subjects that might violate the gaming statute. Lab X is asserting the attorney-client privilege to protect these emails from discovery. Is the court likely to rule that the emails are privileged? How might general counsel have better ensured that the emails would be protected if there was subsequent litigation challenging the legality of the meeting?

13-4 An in-house lawyer advised the corporation's vice president for human resources that the corporation was engaged in illegal employment practices. When the vice president insisted that the employment practices would continue, the in-house lawyer stated that she would not assist the corporation in implementing the practices, as the vice president was demanding. Shortly thereafter, the corporation's president informed the lawyer that her employment had been terminated, allegedly as part of more widespread layoffs. The lawyer believes that she was terminated because of her refusal to assist the corporation in its illegal employment practices and wants to bring a state law claim against her former employer for wrongful discharge. Will she likely be permitted to bring such a claim?

PART III

REGULATING THE PROFESSION

CHAPTER 14

ADMISSION AND DISCIPLINE

Model Rules 8.1, 8.3, 8.4

In Part III of this casebook, we step back from the ethics issues that arise in the day-to-day practice of law and focus on the manner in which the profession is regulated in the interest of society as a whole. Lawyers are most directly regulated with respect to their admission to practice and their encounters with the lawyer disciplinary system. This chapter briefly describes the process of admission and discipline, highlighting some of the issues that frequently arise, as well as various criticisms of the current system.

A. ADMISSION TO PRACTICE

Most states' highest courts hold that as a matter of state constitutional law, the judiciary has the *inherent power* to regulate lawyers. Courts use this authority not only to adopt binding rules of professional conduct, but also to regulate both admission to practice and the disciplinary process.[1] Both admissions and discipline are typically controlled by boards and committees whose members are appointed by the courts. In the past these boards and committees were staffed exclusively with lawyers; however, courts have recently supported the inclusion of more nonlawyers in all aspects of the regulatory process.

Court-adopted rules govern the requirements for admission to the practice of law. First-time lawyers are typically required to have a J.D. degree from an ABA-accredited law school, pass both a general bar examination and a professional responsibility bar examination, and establish the requisite character and fitness to practice law. Lawyers already licensed in other states may have

---

1. Some state courts further hold that their inherent power to regulate is *exclusive*, i.e., that other branches of state government cannot regulate lawyers in a manner that interferes with the judicial power. As a result, some courts have found state legislation in violation of the state constitution when it threatens the court's regulation of lawyers. *See, e.g.,* Mississippi Bar v. McGuire, 647 So.2d 706 (Miss. 1994) (invalidating state statute providing for automatic disbarment of lawyers for any felony conviction because statute conflicted with court's rules of professional conduct).

relaxed requirements; however, some states exercise their right to limit these relaxed requirements to lawyers licensed in jurisdictions that provide reciprocal benefits to out-of-state lawyers.

1. Educational Requirements

Most states require a J.D. degree from an ABA-accredited law school, but a few permit legal education through law office study[2] or a J.D. from a state-accredited law school.[3] Some jurisdictions will admit graduates from non-accredited law schools if the law school provides a substantially equivalent education to that offered by ABA-accredited schools. This most often occurs with respect to British, Canadian, and other common law countries' law schools, for which ABA-accreditation is unavailable, but it may also include non-ABA-accredited U.S. law schools.

Many foreign-trained lawyers want to take the bar examination and be admitted to practice in the United States, even if their intention is to continue to practice in their home countries. ABA-accredited law schools are increasingly offering special graduate degrees to foreign-trained lawyers, typically in a one-year program of study at the law school. Because the ABA does not accredit either foreign law schools or U.S. graduate programs, most foreign-trained lawyers do not have the option of enrolling in an ABA-accredited program. As a result, some jurisdictions will accommodate these lawyers if they meet certain requirements; for example, earning an LLM degree at an ABA-accredited institution, including courses in certain specified subject areas.

2. Bar Examinations

All states but one require unlicensed applicants to pass a written examination as a condition of licensure.[4] Jurisdictions typically use one or more of the multistate examinations created by the National Conference of Bar Examiners, including the Multistate Bar Exam (MBE), the Multistate Performance Test (MPT), and the Multistate Essay Exam (MEE). The Multistate Professional Responsibility Exam (MPRE), adopted in all states but one, is administered as a separate test, usually taken while students are still in law school. A growing number of states have adopted the Uniform Bar Exam (UBE), which consists

---

2. These states include California, Maine, New York, Vermont, Virginia, Washington, and West Virginia.

3. California has a number of law schools that are accredited by California but not by the ABA. California also permits graduates of non-accredited law schools to apply for admission, but only after passing a special bar examination that is administered after the first year of law school study. *See* Cal. Rules of the State Bar, Title 5, Div. 1, R. 4.55.

4. Wisconsin, the only state not to have adopted the MPRE, exempts graduates of its two law schools from taking the general bar examination. New Hampshire exempts students in an honors program at the University of New Hampshire from taking the general bar examination, but these students must still take and pass the MPRE.

of the MBE, the MEE, and the MPT.[5] States set their own passing score, but use of the multistate exams, particularly the UBE, provides greater flexibility to law graduates who do not know where they will be employed.

There have been numerous challenges to the administration of the bar examinations. States are subject to federal statutes requiring reasonable accommodations to test-takers with disabilities, and a number of applicants have been successful in challenging the reasonableness of the accommodations provided. Civil rights challenges based on a documented gap in performance between white applicants and racial and ethnic minority group applicants have been less successful. During the summer of 2020, a few jurisdictions responded to difficulties in administering either an in-person or an online bar exam as a result of the COVID-19 pandemic by temporarily suspending their bar examination requirement for some law graduates. Citing the minority-white gap in exam performance, as well as challenges to the usefulness of bar exams, some critics continue to call for their permanent elimination.[6]

In January 2018, the National Conference of Bar Examiners (NCBE) formed a testing task force to identify foundational knowledge and skills that should be included on the next generation of the bar exam (the "NextGen Bar Exam") and to determine how and when they should be assessed. The task force issued its final report in the spring of 2021, recommending major changes in the content and format of the exam, including placing greater emphasis on assessing real-world lawyer skills and activities.[7] The NCBE estimates that it will take four to five years to develop and implement the new bar exam.

3. Character and Fitness

All states require that applicants establish the requisite character and fitness to practice law. Typically the process entails completing a detailed questionnaire covering such matters as unlawful conduct (including arrests not resulting in conviction), academic misconduct, employment history (including reason for leaving prior employment), indications of financial irresponsibility, prior misconduct in a licensed occupation, and evidence of current mental or emotional

---

5. The MPRE is administered as a separate test in all jurisdictions that adopt it.

6. *See, e.g.,* Valerie Straus, Why this pandemic is a good time to stop forcing prospective lawyers to take bar exams, Washington Post, July 13, 2020, at https://www.washingtonpost .com/education/2020/07/13/why-this-pandemic-is-good-time-stop-forcing-prospective-lawyers-take-bar-exams/. For a detailed explanation of the performance gap between whites and racial and ethnic minority groups, *see* Jane E. Cross, The Bar Examination in Black and White: The Black-White Bar Passage Gap and the Implications for Minority Admissions to the Legal Profession, 18 Nat'l Black L.J. 63 (2004-2005). For the perspective of the National Conference of Bar Examiners, *see* Douglas Ripkey & Susan Case, A National Look at MBE Performance Differences Among Ethnic Groups, 76 Bar Exam'r no 3., p. 21 (Aug. 2007).

7. National Conference of Bar Examiners, Final Report of the Testing Task Force (April 2021).

instability or drug or alcohol dependency.[8] Based on the answers given, some applicants will be required to be interviewed by and obtain the approval of a character and fitness committee.

The U.S. Supreme Court has rejected the argument that the good character requirement is unconstitutionally vague. *See* Law Students Civil Rights Research Council Inc. v. Wadmond, 401 U.S. 154 (1971). As for applying the standard to specific persons, the Court has held that the basis for rejecting an applicant must have a "rational connection with the applicant's fitness or capacity to practice law" to withstand a due process challenge. *See* Schware v. New Mexico Bd. of Bar Exam'rs, 353 U.S. 292 (1957) (reversing denial of admission based on past membership in the Communist Party and arrests for participating in labor strikes). *See also* Cord v. Gibb, 219 Va. 1019 (1979) (concluding that the applicant's "unorthodox" living arrangement with a man to whom she was not married had no rational connection to her fitness to practice law).

Although most of the reported cases involve conduct that occurred either prior to or unrelated to the applicant's attending law school, some applicants have been denied admission on the basis of law school misconduct, including disciplinary violations for cheating or plagiarism.[9] In one case, a student co-chair of the U.C.L.A. School of Law's moot court board secretly borrowed thousands of dollars of moot court funds, including $1,000 used to pay his sister's bail. Despite repaying all of the money prior to graduation, as well as submitting letters of reference from several law professors and his law firm employer, he was denied admission based on his failure to establish the requisite good character.[10] The following case provides another example of conduct in law school leading to a failure to establish good character.

In Re Application of Burch
975 N.E.2d 1001 (Ohio 2012)

PER CURIAM

Robin Leigh Burch of Cincinnati, Ohio, is a 2010 graduate of the University of Cincinnati College of Law and has applied as a candidate for admission to the bar. This matter is before the court on Burch's application to take the July 2011 bar exam. The Board of Commissioners of Character and Fitness expresses serious concerns about Burch's conduct during law school, including her lack of diligence and failure to abide by law-school rules, her unprofessional conduct, and her failure to accept responsibility for those actions.

---

8. Many jurisdictions use the NCBE to conduct character and fitness investigations, including use of its questionnaire. The current form can be obtained on the NCBE website.

9. *See generally* Caroline P. Jacobson, Current Development, Academic Misconduct and Bar Admissions: A Proposal for a Revised Standard, 20 Geo. J. Legal Ethics 739 (2007).

10. *See* In re Mustafa, 631 A.2d 45 (D.C. App. 1994). Mustafa was subsequently admitted to the bar in California, but seven years later he was disciplined and suspended; one year later, he resigned with charges pending against him.

A. Admission to Practice 427

Believing that Burch needs additional time to mature, the board recommends that Burch's application be disapproved and that she be permitted to apply for the February 2013 bar exam. . . .

As part of the admissions process, Burch was interviewed by different teams of Cincinnati Bar Association Admissions Committee members in June and November 2010. The questions at those interviews focused on a report submitted to the National Conference of Bar Examiners ("NCBE") by the University of Cincinnati College of Law, detailing a number of instances of conduct that officials believed to reflect upon Burch's fitness to practice law, including

(1) failing to comply with requirements in courses taken in the spring of 2008 and fall of 2009, which resulted in her unauthorized withdrawal from the courses and failing grades, and failing to submit an assigned paper and acceptable work in another class, which resulted in her not passing a portion of that class,

(2) making comments in an open courtroom during a judicial externship that were critical of the court process and its participants and were heard by others in the courtroom,

(3) failing to disclose to the dean that she had not completed course work from the previous semester as she sought permission to exceed the credit-hour limit for the last semester of law school, and

(4) signing of an attorney-instructor's name to a court document without authorization.

Expressing concern not only with Burch's conduct, but also with her attitude that the rules did not apply to her, her failure to accept responsibility for her actions, her compulsive need to excuse her behavior, and her difficulty being forthright when asked direct questions, both sets of interviewers recommended that Burch's application be disapproved on her character and fitness.

[After an eight-member review panel heard further testimony and subsequently recommended that Burch be approved, the admissions committee certified Burch's character and fitness. Nevertheless the board exercised its authority to further investigate in light of the concerns expressed in the law-school report to the NCBE, as well as Burch's mental health issues.]

Megan Snyder, a licensed independent social worker and a clinical associate with the Ohio Lawyers Assistance Program ("OLAP"), testified that Burch had been referred to OLAP by the Cincinnati Bar Association. Because Burch had longstanding diagnoses of depression and attention deficit disorder, Snyder did not conduct an independent assessment. Based upon their discussion, however, Burch entered into a two-year mental health-recovery contract and has substantially complied with its requirements. Snyder testified that OLAP has no objection to Burch's being permitted to sit for the bar exam. . . .

Though Burch had minor disagreements with the facts set forth in the law school's report, she stipulated that most of the alleged conduct did occur. The panel found that Burch's testimony gave credence to the concerns of the law school and the admissions committee.

The panel summarized Burch's testimony:

> [S]he vacillated from acknowledging that she had these issues to attempting to justify her right to, for example, not attend class or complete certain assignments because she was paying for law school and if she wanted to spend her time in what she considered more productive activities, she was entitled to do that. She also indicated that she was not aware that there would be such serious consequences for her actions, with the implication being that the consequences were unfair because she had no warning of them. Disturbingly, the applicant did not seem to exhibit any insight into her behavior or to express any recognition that her actions may not have been proper. Although she indicated that she would not conduct herself in this manner when a client's interests were at stake, this was not because she seemed to recognize that her behavior under the circumstances was problematic, but rather that the circumstances of representing a client would necessarily cause her to act responsibly. . . .

As the board observed:

> The difficulty with such vacillation by the applicant is that it fails to recognize that she did not just miss some classes; she repeatedly missed deadlines on significant course assignments and then because she probably would have failed the course, she withdrew from it. She conducted herself in an unprofessional manner during her judicial externship by making untoward comments about court personnel and procedure. And, she without permission signed an attorney's name to a document to be filed with the Court. Moreover, throughout the entire process from her initial interviews through to this panel's hearing, she continued on the one hand to say both "I'm responsible" but followed always by "I was treated too harshly" and "I got on the wrong side of the wrong people." At best, the applicant's attitude makes for an unattractive presentation; at worst it calls into question fitness to undertake professional responsibilities.

Based upon these findings, the panel found that Burch had not proven by clear and convincing evidence that she presently possesses the requisite character and fitness to be admitted to the Ohio bar. Expressing hope that with more time to mature, Burch will one day be able to satisfy this burden, the panel recommended that Burch not be approved for admission, but that she be permitted to apply for the [next] bar exam.

The board adopted the panel's findings of fact and recommendation that Burch's current application be disapproved but recommended that Burch be permitted to apply for the February 2013 bar examination. . . .

Gov. Bar R. I(11)(D)(4) sets forth a number of factors to be considered in assigning weight and significance to an applicant's prior conduct: (a) age of the applicant at the time of the conduct, (b) recency of the conduct, (c) reliability of the information concerning the conduct, (d) seriousness of the conduct, (e) factors underlying the conduct, (f) cumulative effect of the conduct, (g) evidence of rehabilitation, (h) positive social contributions of the applicant since the conduct, (i) candor of the applicant in the admissions process, and (j) materiality of any omissions or misrepresentations.

Despite Burch's protestations, a number of these factors weigh in favor of the panel's and board's findings. Her misconduct did not involve youthful indiscretions. It occurred while she was in law school and contemplating her future admission to the bar. The information submitted by the law school was reliable. Indeed, Burch stipulated that the events had occurred, though she also sought to justify her conduct.

On the surface, Burch's failure to comply with course attendance requirements and assignment deadlines and her unauthorized withdrawal from classes when faced with the prospect of a failing grade appear to harm no one but Burch. Burch claimed that she missed the deadline for one of her writing assignments because she "was not very comfortable with the side [she] was on." She explained, "I really wanted to be on the other side, in reality, probably the losing side, but it was the side I felt much stronger arguing from, personally." But in practice, a lawyer has a duty to diligently represent her clients regardless of their position in the case. Some of those clients will have what the attorney believes to be the weaker legal argument or will have positions that clash with the attorney's personal or political views. But an attorney cannot miss court deadlines simply because a case is difficult to prepare. Burch's inability or unwillingness to follow the rules when compliance was to her own benefit calls into question her ability to comply with the rules and meet deadlines for the benefit of others—particularly her clients—should she be admitted to the bar.

Burch's pattern of reckless conduct is also reflected in her decision to sign her supervising attorney's name to several attorney-designation forms. Burch knew that as an intern, she was not authorized to sign an attorney's name to a document. Despite this knowledge, she testified that she signed the attorney's name because she wanted more responsibility and because it would save her from making a second trip to the courthouse. The attorney reported that Burch "generally completed her assigned tasks on time and in a satisfactory manner" and that she worked diligently. She attributed Burch's poor decisions to eagerness and enthusiasm and believed that she had learned from her mistakes. The panel and board, however, were not convinced—and neither are we.

Burch's critical comments about the court process in an open courtroom and her failure to appreciate the impropriety of signing an attorney's name to a court document are serious because the Rules of Professional Conduct prohibit a lawyer both from engaging in undignified or discourteous conduct that is degrading to a tribunal and knowingly making a false statement or law or fact to a tribunal. See Prof. Conduct. R. 3.5(a)(6) and 3.3(a)(1).

Moreover, Burch's omission of the material fact that she had not completed the coursework for the previous semester when she sought permission to exceed the law school's credit-hour limit exhibits a disturbing lack of candor and maturity in her final semester of law school. . . . Burch's lack of candor and, perhaps more importantly, her continuing failure to recognize that her incomplete coursework from a prior semester might be relevant to the dean's decision on her request to exceed the credit-hour limit demonstrate that she does not currently possess the level of candor that is essential to the practice of law.

Although Burch has been candid with the admissions committee and the board, has substantially complied with her OLAP contract, and has excelled in her recent employment as an in-home tutor, we agree with the board's assessment that these rehabilitative efforts and positive social contributions do not overcome the cumulative effect of Burch's errors in judgment during her law-school career.

Burch may have expressed *some* insight into her behavior and recognized that *some* of her actions—signing an attorney's name to a court document and making inappropriate comments in an open courtroom—may not have been proper. But she does not appreciate how her failure to attend class, the missed deadlines and withdrawal from several classes, and her failure to be candid with the dean of her law school negatively reflect on her fitness to practice law.

Burch's repeated attempt to excuse her conduct and deflect blame from herself with claims that she was treated too harshly, got on the wrong side of the wrong people, and was caught off guard by the law school's reporting of her conduct to the NCBE demonstrate that she does not yet possess the maturity to accept responsibility for her past conduct, to learn from her mistakes, or to make better choices in the future.

[The court found that Burch failed to prove the requisite character and fitness, overrode her objections, adopted the board's finding of fact, and disapproved her application to take the July 2011 bar exam. The court gave her permission to apply for the February 2013 bar exam by timely submitting a new application and submitting an updated report from OLAP.]

NOTES AND QUESTIONS

1. The *Burch* court conceded that Burch had been candid with the admissions committee and the board, although her candor was insufficient to overcome her previous misconduct. Lack of candor in the admissions process can be fatal, even when the underlying facts would not have resulted in rejection. *See, e.g.*, In re Pasyanos, 2005 WL 103065 (Cal Bar Ct. Review Dep't 2005) (finding that failure to disclose a misdemeanor charge in a domestic dispute was a material omission, even when the applicant had already disclosed several other similar incidents, and stating that materiality does not depend whether the fact is "outcome-determinative"). The Ohio Supreme Court's Office of Bar Admission advises that "[t]he vast majority of disapprovals are based upon applicants' failure to disclose relevant information either on applications or during the character and fitness investigations; giving false information or misrepresenting the facts; or other dishonesty or lack of candor during the character and fitness review process."[11] Candor on law school applications is also important to character and fitness committees; as a result, many law schools advise their students to review and amend their law school applications before they file their application to the bar.

---

11. *See* Ohio Supreme Court, Summary of Character and Fitness Process in Ohio, http://www.supremecourt.ohio.gov/Boards/characterFit/CFProcess.pdf.

2. There was no indication that any of Burch's law school misconduct resulted in a law school disciplinary investigation or sanction. Should that matter? What did you think of her argument that her extensive absences from class and late paper submissions hurt only herself and that she would not act in such a manner when client interests were at stake? Did the *Burch* court fail to seriously consider her argument?

3. What was the relevance of the undisputed fact that Burch suffered mental health issues? In an omitted portion of the opinion, the court summarized her psychiatrist's testimony that "with continuing psychotherapy and medication, Burch's prognosis [was] fair" and that "she ha[d] a tendency to be unfocused and to engage in rambling discourse rather than directly answering a question." The psychiatrist concluded his testimony by opining that "her failure to meet deadlines and other responsibilities was more a choice than a result of her mental-health conditions, stating that she was 'more unwilling than unable.'" That testimony did not help Burch's cause. If the treating psychiatrist had concluded that Burch's misconduct was in fact the result of her mental health conditions, how would that conclusion have affected her ability to demonstrate good character? The Ohio Supreme Court's Summary of Character and Fitness Process states that "disability" is a factor that will *not* be considered, "provided that the applicant, though disabled, is able to satisfy the essential eligibility requirements for the practice of law."[12] In examining prior misconduct, Ohio takes into account the "factors underlying the conduct," which presumably includes the fact that mental health issues may have caused or contributed to the conduct; however, that is only one of several factors taken into account. As for mental health generally, the Ohio Supreme Court advises that the board will consider "evidence of a mental or psychological disorder that . . . affects or, *if untreated*, could affect the applicant's ability to practice law in a competent and professional manner."[13] An applicant who is being treated for mental health or substance abuse issues and who, with continuing treatment, is unlikely to engage in misconduct, should not encounter significant difficulties in admission, at least in the absence of prior incidents of serious misconduct.

4. What is the relevance of evidence that an applicant openly espouses racial hatred and bias? Two applicants were denied admission to the bar based on their explicit expressions of racial and ethnic bias. Illinois denied admission to Matthew Hale, the leader of a white supremacist organization, based on a hearing panel's conclusion that he would not abide by an Illinois rule barring racial discrimination by lawyers.[14]

---

12. *Id.*

13. *Id.* (Emphasis added.)

14. *See* Hale v. Comm. on Character & Fitness, 335 F.3d 678 (7th Cir. 2003) (upholding dismissal of Hale's subsequent civil rights action). Hale was subsequently convicted of soliciting an undercover FBI informant to murder a federal judge who ruled against him in a trademark dispute over the name of his white supremacist group.

Rhode Island denied admission to Roger Roots, who had publicly argued the inferiority of the black race and publicly disavowed the illegitimate "regime" of the federal government.[15]

5. Many commentators have been critical of the character and fitness requirement and the manner in which it has been applied. Deborah Rhode argued that character investigations began in earnest only in the 1920s "in response to an influx of Eastern European immigrants" and that such investigations reflected "nativist and ethnic prejudices."[16] She conceded that few applicants are formally denied admission, but expressed concern that "the number deterred, delayed, or harassed has been more substantial."[17] Other commentators have focused their criticism on the weak predictive value of the information obtained during character and fitness inquiries.[18]

B. DISCIPLINE

Once a lawyer is admitted to practice, discipline is limited to violations of a rule of professional conduct. State disciplinary authorities derive their authority from the state's highest court and adopt their own rules of procedure, often borrowing from the ABA Model Rules for Lawyer Disciplinary Enforcement. Disciplinary proceedings are not criminal; therefore a lawyer charged with a violation, typically called a "respondent," is not entitled to the protections afforded a criminal defendant. Nevertheless, the U.S. Supreme Court has held that the respondent must be given adequate notice and an opportunity to be heard.[19] Sanctions include: admonition (private); reprimand (public); probation; suspension for a specified or indefinite period; and disbarment. Courts or disciplinary bodies are sometimes authorized to provide other sanctions or remedies, such as restitution or a requirement that the lawyer take a professional responsibility examination or attend continuing legal education courses.

Some complaints are handled on an informal basis, including the use of diversion programs for lawyers charged with minor offenses that arise from addiction or mental-health issues. These diversion programs typically offer the affected lawyers treatment rather than punishment. When formal charges are instituted, the matter proceeds as in the *Burch* case: a hearing before a panel or committee, whose findings are reviewed by a disciplinary board, whose conclusions are subject to review by the state's highest court.

---

15. In re Roots, 762 A.2d 1161 (R.I. 2000).

16. Deborah L. Rhode, Moral Character as a Professional Credential, 94 Yale L.J. 491, 497 (1985).

17. *Id.* at 493-94.

18. *See e.g.,* Leslie C. Levin, The Folly of Expecting Evil: Reconsidering the Bar's Character and Fitness Requirement, 2014 B.Y.U. L. Rev. 775 (2014); Carrie Menkel-Medow, Private Lives and Professional Responsibilities? The Relationship of Personal Morality in Lawyering and Professional Ethics, 21 Pace L. Rev. 365 (2001).

19. *See* In re Ruffalo, 390 U.S. 544 (1968).

1. Common Grounds for Discipline

The most common grounds for complaints filed against lawyers are for neglect and failure to communicate. These allegations alone may not be sufficient to warrant formal charges, except when there is a pattern of lawyer abuse, typically for neglect. In many instances, neglect of client matters is a symptom of a larger problem involving substance abuse or mental health issues, and these lawyers are often referred to a diversion program.

Common causes of formal charges and subsequent discipline involve mishandling of client funds, other forms of dishonesty, and criminal conduct.

a. Mishandling Client Funds

Mishandling client funds frequently involves unauthorized withdrawals from an attorney's client trust account. Model Rule 1.15 requires lawyers to place funds belonging to clients or others in a trust account, where they will not be "commingled" with the lawyer's own money. The purpose of this requirement is to ensure that the lawyer's creditors cannot reach these funds. In addition to advanced payments for fees and expenses, funds required to be deposited in such accounts include settlement proceeds or proceeds from the sale of a client's property, which the lawyer holds and safeguards pending the deduction of legal fees, expenses, and other allocations, remitting the balance to the client. If there is a dispute concerning the allocation of these funds, including disputes over fees between lawyer and client and disputes over liens asserted by third parties,[20] the lawyer is obligated to keep the disputed fees in the trust account until the matter has been resolved.

Many jurisdictions conduct random audits of lawyers' client trust accounts. If an audit or a client complaint reveals that the lawyer intentionally took or borrowed client funds, the lawyer will almost always be subject to serious sanctions. In some jurisdictions disbarment is either automatic or presumed.[21]

b. Other Forms of Dishonesty

Dishonesty unrelated to mishandling client funds is also a frequent cause of lawyer discipline. Violations involve rules proscribing candor to a tribunal (MR 3.3) or to third persons (MR 3.4(b) and MR 4.1), as well as Model Rule 8.4(c), which makes it professional misconduct for a lawyer to "engage in conduct involving dishonesty, fraud, deceit or misrepresentation." Rule 8.4(c) has been used to fill in a gap in the rules resulting from the lack of a specific rule prohibiting a lawyer from lying to a client. *See, e.g.,* Cunningham v. Ky. Bar Ass'n, 266 S.W.3d 808 (Ky. 2008) (disbarring a lawyer who misled his

---

20. *See* MR 1.15(e) & cmt [4] ("when the third-party claim is not frivolous under applicable law, the lawyer must refuse to surrender the property to the client until the claims are resolved").

21. *See, e.g.* In re Warhaftig, 524 A.2d 398 (N.J. 1987) (knowing misappropriation of client funds requires disbarment even when attorney replaced funds borrowed without client authorization and client suffered no harm).

clients about how he allocated funds from an aggregate settlement, including falsely stating that the defendant and not the lawyer himself had determined what the client would receive, as well as impermissibly sharing legal fees with other lawyers and placing funds other than legal fees in his personal account).

The rule is also frequently applied to a lawyer's conduct outside the practice of law. *See, e.g.*, People v. Rishel, 50 P. 3d 938 (Colo. O.P.D. 2002) (disbarring a lawyer for taking money from others to buy baseball season tickets and then misappropriating the money for his personal use); Supreme Ct. Disciplinary Bd. v. Kress, 747 N.W.2d 530 530 (Iowa 2008) (indefinitely suspending a law professor for altering and manufacturing student evaluations to improve the composite rating of his teaching ability); In re Aboyade, 578 S.E.2d 727 (S.C. 2003) (disbarring a lawyer who falsified her law school transcript to deceive potential employers). Although fraud and deceit necessarily involve knowing dishonesty, courts disagree whether the rule prohibits misrepresentation that is merely negligent. *Compare e.g.*, In re Doughty, 832 A.2d 724 (Del. 2003) (disciplining a lawyer for negligently misrepresenting that his books and records were maintained in accordance with law and that his tax obligations were being met), *with* State ex rel. Okla. Bar Ass'n v. Wilcox, 318 P.3d 1114 (Okla. 2014) (holding that Rule 8.4(c) requires "intent or purpose to deceive" and does not encompass "negligent misrepresentation or failure to apprise another of relevant information").

c. *Criminal Conduct*

Model Rule 8.4(b) provides that it is professional misconduct for a lawyer to "commit a criminal act that reflects adversely on the lawyer's trustworthiness or fitness as a lawyer in other respects." Comment [2] explains that "[m]any kinds of illegal conduct reflect adversely on fitness to practice law, such as offenses involving fraud and the offense of willful failure to file an income tax return." According to the same comment, offenses that would not subject a lawyer to discipline include "offenses concerning some matters of personal morals, such as adultery and comparable offenses that have no specific connection to fitness for the practice of law."

Although offenses committed in the representation of a client are almost always relevant to the lawyer's fitness to practice, offenses committed outside the practice of law are also deemed relevant, particularly when they involve dishonesty or fraud. *See, e.g.*, Attorney Grievance Comm'n v. Bereano, 744 A.2d 35 (Md. 2000) (disbarring a lawyer on the basis of a federal mail fraud conviction arising out of lobbying activities outside the practice of law); Attorney Grievance Comm'n v. Gore, 845 A.2d 1204 (Md. 2004 (disbarring an attorney for repeated failure to pay sales tax for a restaurant he owned). Drug-related offenses also commonly lead to discipline under this rule. *See, e.g.*, Ligon v. Clouette, 378 S.W. 3d 708 (Ark. 2011) (finding that felony possession of methamphetamine was a serious offense warranting more than a mere caution).

Violent crimes often result in lawyer discipline. *See, e.g.*, Fla. Bar v. Bartholf, 775 So.2d 957 (Fla. 2000) (ordering reprimand and probation for a lawyer who assaulted an individual with a golf cart and golf club). Although domestic violence has been found to violate Rule 8.4(b), *see, e.g.*, Iowa Supreme Court Bd. of Prof'l Ethics & Conduct v. Polson, 569 N.W.2d 612 (Iowa 1997) (suspending a lawyer for grabbing his wife by the neck and subsequently violating a no-contact order), some courts have found that absent serious violence, a single act of domestic abuse, unrelated to the lawyer's practice, was insufficient to violate the rule. *See, e.g.*, In re Disciplinary Action Against Stoneburner, 882 N.W.2d 200 (Minn. 2016) (refusing to find a violation based on a lawyer throwing a "soft-sided case" at his wife, hitting her leg, but reversing finding that lawyer had not engaged in conduct "prejudicial to the administration of justice" when he interfered with wife's attempt to call 911 for help). How are crimes of violence, including domestic violence, relevant to a lawyer's fitness to practice?

It is unnecessary that the lawyer be convicted of a crime, or even charged. Indeed, lawyers who have been acquitted of a crime have nevertheless been disciplined, based on the lesser burden of proof outside the context of a criminal proceeding.

2. Failure to Report Another Lawyer's Serious Misconduct

Model Rule 8.3(a) provides that "[a] lawyer who knows that another lawyer has committed a violation of the Rules of Professional Conduct that raises a substantial question as to that lawyer's honesty, trustworthiness or fitness as a lawyer in other respects, shall inform the appropriate professional authority." Rule 8.3(b) provides that disclosure is not required when the information is protected by Rule 1.6. Failure to report may not be among the most common grounds of lawyer discipline, but lawyers have indeed been disciplined under this rule. A well-known example involved an Illinois lawyer who was disciplined under the Model Code's predecessor to this rule. In In re Himmel, 533 N.E.2d 790 (1988), the respondent lawyer had investigated a personal injury lawyer's failure to turn over settlement proceeds to the client and then negotiated a settlement agreement for the client in which the respondent agreed not to initiate any criminal, civil, or attorney disciplinary action against the personal injury lawyer. That case might not be decided the same today because the information was clearly protected under Rule 1.6, and the client was unlikely to consent to disclosure if the agreement not to report was necessary to obtain receipt of her share of the settlement funds.[22] It is unclear whether a lawyer is permitted to negotiate such an agreement. *See, e.g.*, In re Eicher, 661 N.W. 2d 354 (S.D. 2003) (lawyer disciplined for proposing not to appeal trial court decision if opposing counsel withdrew disciplinary complaint).

---

22. Under the Model Code provision adopted in Illinois at the time of *Himmel*, disclosure was not required only when the information was protected under the attorney-client privilege.

Children are often told not to "tattle" on each other. Do you understand why it is important that lawyers be willing to report serious violations of the rules by other lawyers? Consider the following explanation from a Kentucky Bar Association Ethics Opinion:

> In many circumstances, lawyers are in the best position to know of another lawyer's misconduct and to minimize its consequences to others. Not only do lawyers know the standards by which lawyers and judges are expected to conduct themselves, lawyers also work closely with them and may be the first ones actually to observe the acts of misconduct. In many cases, the victim of the misconduct may not even be aware of it. As officers of the legal system, lawyers must take the affirmative responsibility to assure that both the bench and bar maintain the highest standards, and to assure that those who do not conform to these standards are disciplined.[23]

Similarly, a New York court stated that the reporting rule "is critical to the unique function of self-regulation belonging to the legal profession"; as a result, the court permitted a law firm associate to claim breach of an implied contract of employment when his law firm allegedly prevented him from reporting professional misconduct of another associate, under an exception to the at-will employment doctrine.[24]

3. Bias, Prejudice, Harassment, and Discrimination

In 2016, the ABA amended the Model Rules to add a new Rule 8.4(g), which makes it professional misconduct for a lawyer to "engage in conduct that the lawyer knows or reasonably should know is harassment or discrimination on the basis of race, sex, religion, national original, ethnicity, disability, age, sexual orientation, gender identity, marital status or socioeconomic status in conduct related to the practice of law." This rule has been controversial, and as of November 2020, only three jurisdictions — Maine, Vermont, and New Mexico — had substantially adopted it.[25] Many jurisdictions have rules or comments that specifically address bias or prejudice, but they are less comprehensive than the ABA rule. Around 14 jurisdictions have no specific language in either their rules or comments addressing the subject, although lawyers can and have been disciplined under more general rules, such as Model Rule 8.4(d), which prohibits "conduct that is prejudicial to the administration of justice," or a rule modeled on the former Model Code provision subjecting lawyers to discipline for engaging in "any other conduct that adversely reflects on [the lawyer's] fitness to practice law."[26]

---

23. Ky. Bar Assoc. Ethics Opinion E-430 (2010).
24. *See* Wieder v. Skala, 609 N.E.2d 105, 108 (N.Y. 1982).
25. The New Mexico rule is identical to the ABA rule, except that it omits "socioeconomic status" as one of the protected characteristics. The Maine rule is essentially the same, except that it defines "discrimination," "harassment," and "related to the practice of law." The Vermont rule is also essentially the same, varying slightly the list of prohibited characteristics, including adding "or other grounds that are illegal or prohibited under state or federal law."
26. ABA Model Code, DR 1-102(A)(6).

Prior to 2016, the Model Rules addressed bias and prejudice in a comment to Rule 8.4(d). That comment explained that "[a] lawyer who, in the course of representing a client, knowingly manifests by words or conduct, bias or prejudice based upon race, sex, religion, national origin, disability, age, sexual orientation or socioeconomic status, violates paragraph (d) when such actions are prejudicial to the administration of justice."[27] The following case illustrates the application of Rule 8.4(d) to a lawyer who insulted an opponent and her lawyer based on gender and national origin. As you read the case, ask yourself why the ABA believed that it was necessary to adopt Rule 8.4(g) if lawyers were already subject to discipline under Rule 8.4(d).

The Florida Bar v. Martocci
791 So.2d 1074 (Fla. 2001)

PER CURIAM

We have for review a referee's report regarding ethical breaches by respondent Henry John Martocci (Martocci). We have jurisdiction. For the reasons stated herein, we affirm the referee's findings of fact, conclusions of guilt, and recommend discipline.

On April 14, 1999, based on Martocci's representation of Francis Berger in a dissolution of marriage and child custody action and a child dependency action, The Florida Bar filed a two-count complaint against Martocci. In count one, the Bar alleged that, in various instances during the course of the Berger proceedings, Martocci made unethical, disparaging, and profane remarks to belittle and humiliate the opposing party, Florence Berger, and her attorney, Diana Figueroa. The allegation of unethical behavior in count two arose from a confrontation between Martocci and James Paton, the father of Ms. Berger, during the recess of a hearing on May 8, 1998. After a three-day hearing in September 1999, the referee, Judge Cynthia G. Angelos, found Martocci guilty on both counts of violating rule 4-8.4(d) of the Rules Regulating The Florida Bar. The referee made the findings of fact.

Based on testimonial and documentary evidence, the referee made findings as to specific instances of Martocci's misconduct. Regarding count one, the referee found that, in December 1996, Martocci called Ms. Berger a "nut case." After a deposition on May 5, 1998, Martocci referred to Ms. Berger as "crazy" and a "nut case." During another deposition on May 5, 1998, Martocci made demeaning facial gestures and stuck out his tongue at Ms. Berger and Ms. Figueroa. After a hearing on June 24, 1998, upon exiting an elevator, Martocci told Ms. Figueroa that she was a "stupid idiot" and that she should "go back to Puerto Rico." In another incident, on June 19, 1998, during an intermission of a deposition, Ms. Figueroa telephoned the office of Judge

---

27. Standing Committee on Ethics and Professional Responsibility, Draft Proposal to Amend Model Rule 8.4, p. 2 (Dec. 22, 2015).

Edward J. Richardson and reached Pamela Walker, a judicial assistant. After Ms. Figueroa spoke to Ms. Walker, Martocci took the telephone and yelled the word "bitch." Martocci admitted that because the phone was dead when he received it from Ms. Figueroa, he said "son of a bitch" as a frustrated response to missing the opportunity to speak to Ms. Walker. Martocci claims that he did not say these words to anyone in particular. The referee also found that throughout the Berger proceedings Martocci repeatedly told Ms. Figueroa that she did not know the law or the rules of procedure and that she needed to go back to school.

As to the second count, the referee found that on May 8, 1998, during a recess to a hearing in the Berger proceedings, when Mr. Paton entered the courtroom, Martocci said "here comes the father of the nut case." Mr. Paton responded by approaching respondent and saying, "If you have something to say to me, say it to my face, not in front of everyone here in the courtroom." Thereafter, in open court and for all to see, Martocci closely approached Mr. Paton and threatened to beat him. Upon Ms. Figueroa's attempt to intervene, Martocci told her to "go back to Puerto Rico." This confrontation only ended when a bailiff entered the courtroom.

On the basis of such misconduct, the referee recommended the imposition against Martocci of a public reprimand and a two-year period of probation with conditions including an evaluation by Florida Lawyers Assistance for possible anger management or mental health assistance or both. In recommending discipline, the referee noted that the underlying Berger proceedings were difficult cases which caused frustration to all the parties involved, including the presiding judges. The referee also noted that Martocci had a good reputation for representing his clients and had no disciplinary convictions. In aggravation, the referee recognized that, despite Martocci's substantial experience in the practice of law, Martocci engaged in a pattern of unethical misconduct and refused to acknowledge the wrongful nature of his conduct.

In seeking review, Martocci raises four general claims: (1) the findings of fact are clearly erroneous and unsupported by the evidence in the record; (2) even if the findings of fact are correct, they legally do not constitute a violation of rule 4-8.4(d); (3) the referee erroneously shifted to Martocci the burden of proving his innocence; and (4) the public reprimand penalty is excessive, and the misconduct only warrants a private reprimand. . . . Claims one, two and four merit discussion and are analyzed in turn. Review of the record, however, demonstrates that claim three is without merit, and we dispose of it summarily. . . .

Review of the record reveals that there is competent, substantial documentary and testimonial evidence to support the referee's findings of fact and conclusions of guilt. The deposition transcripts in the record alone establish that Martocci engaged in the unprofessional conduct of seeking to belittle and humiliate Ms. Figueroa and Ms. Berger. The record reflects that Martocci: (1) made insulting facial gestures to Ms. Berger and Ms. Figueroa; (2) called Ms. Figueroa a "bush leaguer"; (3) told Ms. Figueroa that depositions are not conducted under "girl's rules"; (4) continually disparaged Ms. Figueroa's knowledge and ability to practice law; and (5) threatened Mr. Paton physically within the courtroom during a recess to a hearing. The entire record is replete with evidence of Martocci's verbal assaults and sexist, racial, and ethnic insults supporting the referee's conclusion that Martocci engaged in patently unethical behavior designed to belittle and humiliate Ms. Berger and Ms. Figueroa and threaten Mr. Paton. . . .

Martocci's second claim is that, even if the referee's findings of fact are correct, Martocci's conduct was not prejudicial to the administration of justice as it did not rise to a level that violated rule 4-8.4(d). In support of this proposition Martocci argues that Florida Bar v. Martocci established a distinction between unprofessional conduct and unethical conduct violating rule 4-8.4(d). In that case, we upheld the referee's conclusion that the Bar did not clearly and convincingly prove that Martocci violated rules 4-8.4(c) and (d), although Martocci used profanity against the opposing attorney and threatened the court reporter. However, we find *Martocci* to be distinguishable from the case before us today.

In *Martocci*, we reasoned that, despite the contrary evidence in the record, there was competent, substantial evidence to support the referee's resolution of the debatable issues in respondent's favor. Likewise, in the present case, because there is competent, substantial evidence supporting the referee's conclusion of guilt, we will not substitute our judgment for that of the referee. Such misconduct clearly prejudiced the administration of justice by further exacerbating relationships between respondent, opposing counsel, and the various judges involved in the already difficult underlying Berger cases.

We previously have admonished members of the Bar to refrain from offensive conduct. Martocci's disrespectful and abusive comments cross the line from that of zealous advocacy to unethical misconduct. Such unethical conduct shall not be tolerated. . . .

NOTES AND QUESTIONS

1. Would Martocci have been disciplined under Rule 8.4(d) if he had not made the references to the Puerto Rican ancestry of Ms. Berger and Ms. Figueroa or to depositions being conducted under "girls' rules"? Rule 4.4(a) of the Model Rules provides that "[i]n representing a client, a lawyer shall not use means that have no substantial purpose other than to embarrass, delay, or burden a third person. . . ." New York has a similar rule[28] and also provides that a lawyer shall not "engage in any . . . conduct that adversely reflects on the lawyer's fitness as a lawyer."[29] If harassing or demeaning conduct is unprofessional even

---

28. N.Y. Rules of Prof'l Conduct, R. 4.4(a) ("In representing a client, a lawyer shall not use means that have no substantial purpose other than to embarrass or harm a third person. . . .").

29. *Id.* at R. 8.4(g).

Chapter 14 Admission and Discipline

when not directed to members of an enumerated group, why have most jurisdictions created rules or comments specifically addressing bias, prejudice, harassment, or discrimination directed toward such group members?

2. One reason to replace the prior comment to Rule 8.4(d) with an entirely new Rule 8.4(g) was to elevate the prohibition against bias and prejudice from the comment to the text. A few jurisdictions do not officially adopt the comments, and in those jurisdictions, prohibiting bias and prejudice in the text of a rule makes sense, that is, to alert lawyers to the possibility that such conduct can be disciplined. But in jurisdictions that adopt the comments, why did the ABA also deem it important to have the prohibition in the text of a rule?

3. If the primary goal of the amendment was to make more prominent the prohibition against bias and prejudice, why didn't the ABA simply move the material in the comment to the text of Rule 8.4(d)?[30] Consider the argument that Martocci made that even if the referee's factual findings were supported, his conduct did not "prejudice the administration of justice." How does that requirement limit the scope of the prohibition?

4. The prior comment to Rule 8.4(d) referred to conduct that "manifests bias or prejudice." Rule 8.4(g) prohibits conduct that constitutes "harassment or discrimination." Why do you think the ABA changed the underlying basis for the prohibited conduct? Are harassment and discrimination adequately defined? (Take a look at Comment [3].) Are they more or less difficult to establish than "bias or prejudice"? What if a male lawyer says to his female adversary, "Chill, babe"? Does it matter if he only said it once? What if a law firm in good faith adopts hiring criteria that turn out to have an adverse impact on a protected group; if the law firm's conduct violates employment discrimination law that contains no mens rea requirement, should the lawyers who adopted the criteria be subject to discipline?

5. The prior comment to Rule 8.4(d) also limited the prohibition to "knowingly" manifesting bias or prejudice, whereas Rule 8.4(g) includes conduct that a lawyer "knows or reasonably should know" is harassment or discrimination. Do you agree that lawyers should be disciplined when they do not know but "reasonably should know" that their conduct is wrongful?

6. Perhaps the most controversial aspect of Rule 8.4(g) is the extension of the prohibition from conduct "in the representation of a client" to conduct "related to the practice of law." What is the justification for

---

30. For an example of a state that has done something like this, *see* Ga. Rules of Prof'l Conduct, R. 8.4(d) (lawyer shall not "engage in conduct that is prejudicial to the administration of justice, including but not limited to, harmful or discriminatory treatment of litigants, jurors, witnesses, lawyers, and others based on race, national origin, gender, religion, disability, age, sexual orientation or socioeconomic status").

extending the prohibition beyond conduct that occurs when a lawyer is representing a client? If an employee believes that a law firm employer has unlawfully discriminated against the employee on the basis of one of the covered characteristics, isn't it sufficient that the employee has an alternative remedy, e.g., a civil lawsuit?[31] And why should we be concerned with harassment or discrimination that occurs in the context of events such as a law firm dinner or a bar association continuing education or networking event?

7. The text of Rule 8.4(g) also states that "[t]his paragraph does not limit the ability of a lawyer to accept, decline or withdraw from a representation in accordance with Rule 1.16." Traditionally, lawyers have been free to refuse to represent a prospective client for any reason. As a result, Rule 1.16 does not address the lawyer's decision to decline a client or a matter, except when the lawyer *must* decline because the representation would violate another rule (such as the rule against conflicts of interest). Does Rule 8.4(g) prohibit a woman lawyer from refusing to represent husbands in a divorce?[32] What about a male lawyer who represents only husbands? Consider both the text of the rule and the statement in comment [5] that a lawyer does not violate the rule "by limiting the scope or subject matter of the lawyer's practice or by limiting the lawyer's practice to members of underserved populations in accordance with these Rules and other law." Does the comment suggest that *refusing* to serve persons who are members of an "underserved population" violates Rule 8.4(g), despite the apparently contradictory language in the text of the rule? Should this be a matter of professional regulation, that is, in the absence of applicable state or federal statutes? The Maine version of this rule states more clearly that "[d]eclining representation, limiting one's practice to particular clients or types of clients, and advocacy of policy positions or changes in the law are not regulated by Rule 8.4(g)."[33]

8. The last sentence of the rule states that "[t]his paragraph does not preclude legitimate advice or advocacy consistent with these Rules." Would this provision justify the decision of a law firm to assign a woman lawyer to represent a man accused of sexually harassing women or a Black

---

31. In New Jersey, a lawyer violates Rule 1.8(g) by engaging in employment discrimination only when there has been a final agency or judicial determination of such discrimination.

32. In Stropnicky v. Nathanson, 1997 Mass. Comm. Against Discrim. LEXIS 12 (1997), attorney Judith Nathanson was found to have violated a state antidiscrimination law for refusing to represent a stay-at-home dad. She justified her "women only" policy on the ground that she was seeking to eliminate gender bias in the court system, noting for example that "wives' attorneys emphasize the value of homemaker services and the limited future earning potential of homemakers re-entering the work force, while husbands' attorneys tend to minimize these issues." The fact that her prospective male client was himself a stay-at-home parent did not persuade her to accept his representation.

33. Maine Rules of Prof'l Conduct, R. 8.4(g)(4).

442   Chapter 14 Admission and Discipline

lawyer to represent a company accused of racial discrimination? In In re Charges of Unprofessional Conduct, 597 N.W.2d 563 (Minn. 1999), a prosecutor was disciplined for filing a motion seeking to prevent a public defender from bringing in a "token African-American public defender to try the case with her," allegedly for the sole reason of buttressing the defendant's argument that his race played a role in his arrest. Should the public defender have been disciplined for bringing in an African-American public defender based solely on his race?

9. In December 2020, a federal district court judge enjoined the enforcement of Pennsylvania's recently added Rule 8.4(g) on the ground that the new provision and comments "consist of unconstitutional viewpoint discrimination in violation of the First Amendment."[34] The Pennsylvania version of the rule made it professional misconduct for a lawyer to, "in the practice of law, by words or conduct, knowingly manifest bias or prejudice, or engage in harassment or discrimination, as those terms are defined in applicable federal, state or local statutes or ordinances, including but not limited to bias, prejudice, harassment or discrimination based upon" the enumerated protected categories. The court rejected the disciplinary board's attempt to focus on harmful *conduct*, emphasizing the inclusion of "the fatal language, 'by words . . . manifest bias or prejudice'"; however, the court also implied that a rule that prohibited "'harassment and discrimination . . . carried out by words'" might have survived a First Amendment challenge.[35] What are the implications of this ruling for the constitutionality of Model Rule 8.4(g)?

10. The Florida Supreme Court, on its own motion, recently amended its rules governing course approval for minimum CLE requirements; this action was taken after the Business Law Section of the Florida Bar adopted a policy requiring a minimum number of "diverse" faculty in CLE programs (defining diversity in terms of membership in "groups based upon race, ethnicity, gender, sexual orientation, gender identity, disability, and multiculturalism"). The newly amended rule prohibits approval of any course submitted by a sponsor "that uses quotas based on race, ethnicity, gender, religion, national origin, disability, or sexual orientation in the selection of course faculty or participants."[36] A dissenting justice believed that the enactment of a rule was unnecessary, and that the court should have sent a letter to the Business Law Section stating that its action might violate U.S. Supreme Court precedent, such as Grutter v. Bollinger, 539 U.S. 306, 334 (2003) and Regents

---

34. *See* Greenberg v. Haggerty, 491 F.Supp.3d 12, 32-33 (E.D. Pa. 2020).
35. *Id.* at 28-29.
36. In re Amendment to Rule Regulating the Florida Bar 6-10.3, 315 So.3d 637 (Fla. 2021). With respect to the Business Law Section policy, the minimum number of "diverse" faculty depended on the number of faculty in any particular program.

of Univ. of Cal. v. Bakke, 438 U.S. 265, 307 (1978).[37] Do you agree with this action by the Florida Supreme Court? What if the Business Law Section changes its policy to make it a goal to achieve a specific number of "diverse" faculty? Many institutional CLE providers, including the ABA, have policies to promote the broader representation of diverse faculty on CLE programs.

Review Problems

14-1 As a member of a state court character and fitness committee, would you be inclined to approve the application of a law graduate who:

(a) In her final year of law school, was reprimanded for plagiarism when she included without attribution 10 word-for-word quotations from a law review that was never cited in her seminar paper? Two of the quotations were more than three paragraphs long.

(b) In his bar application, failed to disclose several financial debts and delinquent payments regarding outstanding student loans totaling $80,000?

(c) Prior to entering law school, organized and led a large-scale international drug smuggling operation involving marijuana? After spending some years as a fugitive abroad, he returned to the United States and illegally sold marijuana until he was indicted, receiving a suspended sentence plus probation, which he completed immediately prior to entering law school.

14-2 A law firm partner discovered that a colleague had falsified expense reports and time sheets when billing a mutual client. When confronted by the partner, the colleague confessed that he had a substance abuse problem but was now in treatment. The colleague has repaid all of the money to the client and has vowed to have his time records and expense requests reviewed by a senior partner prior to submission to any client. Must the partner report the colleague's misconduct to the applicable state disciplinary authority?

14-3 A lawyer represented a client in a contract dispute. The lawyer attended a mediation session with opposing counsel and the judge, but the clients did not attend. In describing the poor result of the mediation session to the client, the lawyer explained that the judge was extremely hostile to him, describing the judge as a "gay, fat, f*g." The client, who was not gay, found the remark offensive, but did nothing until after the case was over. The client was satisfied with the result in the case but disputed the lawyer's bill. In the context of that dispute, the client filed a grievance against the lawyer with the state disciplinary authority and included complaints about both the fees and the remark about the judge. Is the lawyer subject to discipline? Would it matter if the comment about the judge was made privately to a colleague during a bar association dinner honoring the judge? Does it matter whether the judge was ever informed of the comment?

---

37. *Id.* at 638 (Justice Labarga, dissenting).

CHAPTER 15

UNAUTHORIZED PRACTICE OF LAW AND MULTIJURISDICTIONAL PRACTICE

Model Rules 5.5, 8.5

All jurisdictions, either by statute or court regulation, prohibit the unauthorized practice of law (UPL). The penalties may be civil or criminal and include fines, injunctions, contempt of court, and even a prison sentence. In addition, the unlicensed person may be unable to collect fees for services provided. Prohibitions against UPL apply not only to nonlawyers, but also to lawyers whose licenses have been suspended or who are practicing law in a jurisdiction other than the one in which they are licensed. This chapter briefly addresses UPL by nonlawyers, then focuses on the difficulty of applying traditional UPL rules to lawyers licensed in one jurisdiction who travel (either physically or virtually) across state or national boundaries in the course of their practices. This latter phenomenon is known as multijurisdictional practice (MJP).

A. UPL BY NONLAWYERS

Everyone agrees that when nonlawyers hold themselves out as lawyers, they are engaged in the unauthorized practice of law. In the absence of a false representation, however, there is considerable disagreement over what constitutes the practice of law by a nonlawyer. An ABA Task Force on the Model Definition of the Practice of Law gave up an attempt to provide a uniform definition, instead urging states to develop their own definitions and providing a state-by-state guide to how the practice of law is defined.[1]

Certain elements are standard in defining law practice. These include the application of *professional judgment*—the use of legal education, training, and experience—to address a *specific client need*. Representing clients in court and

---

1. *See* ABA, State Definitions of the Practice of Law, https://www.americanbar.org/groups/professional_responsibility/task_force_model_definition_practice_law/.

drafting certain types of legal documents are generally included, as are negotiating settlements, giving legal advice, and recording documents such as deeds. Jurisdictions differ as to when nonlawyers may prepare simple documents or fill in standardized forms, participate in real estate closings, or represent parties in administrative or quasi-judicial proceedings such as arbitration.

Even when the nature of the activity appears to come within the definition of practicing law, many jurisdictions recognize limited exceptions in certain types of proceedings, such as permitting nonlawyers to represent parties in unemployment insurance hearings,[2] or to perform activities incident to another profession, such as accountants preparing tax returns or real estate brokers preparing forms for residential real estate transactions. In Campbell v. Asbury Automotive, Inc., 381 S.W.3d 21 (Ark. 2011), a court held that the completion of standard, simple forms by a nonlawyer constitutes the practice of law but will be permitted if the forms are prepared by a lawyer and are used only in limited circumstances, including where the forms are incidental to common business dealings, such as real estate transactions or motor vehicle sales, and the nonlawyer does not charge for the service.

The stated purpose of UPL restrictions is to protect the public from unqualified persons who are not subject to professional regulation. Nevertheless, in view of the unmet need for legal services, often as a result of an inability to pay a lawyer's fees,[3] many jurisdictions have modified their definitions of the practice of law. In addition, some jurisdictions have adopted rules permitting the limited practice of law by trained and licensed nonlawyers known as "limited license legal technicians,"[4] "limited practice officers,"[5] or "legal document preparers."[6]

A recent controversy concerns the online preparation of legal documents by companies such as LegalZoom, RocketLawyer, and SmartLegalForms. Available documents include business formation and business contracts, lease agreements and other landlord-tenant documents, and personal documents such as wills, durable powers of attorney, and divorce settlements. Several lawsuits have been filed against LegalZoom, but the company has had some success in settling the disputes by agreeing to limited modifications of its business practices.[7]

---

2. *See* Unauthorized Practice of Law Comm. v. Employers Unity, Inc., 716 P.2d 460 (Colo. 1986).

3. *See, e.g.,* Rebecca L. Sandefur, Accessing Justice in the Contemporary USA: Findings from the Community Needs and Services Study 3 (Am. Bar Found. 2014) (reporting that concerns about cost were a factor in 17 percent of cases where survey recipients handled civil justice situations on their own; another reason is that the recipients did not understand the situations to be legal). Recent responses to the access to justice problem are discussed in Chapter 16: Nonlawyer Ownership, Multidisciplinary Practice, and Alternative Legal Service Providers.

4. *See* Washington State Court Rules: Admission and Practice Rules, Rule 28.

5. *Id.* at Rule 12.

6. Ariz. Code of Jud. Admin. §7-208.

7. *See, e.g.,* Caroline Shipman, Unauthorized Practice of Law Claims Against Legal Zoom—Who Do These Lawsuits Protect, and Is the Rule Outdated?, 32 Geo. J. Legal Ethics 939 (2019).

Lawyers can be disciplined for assisting a nonlawyer in the unauthorized practice of law, including working with nonlawyer-owned companies to provide legal services. *See* Model Rule 5.5(a) (lawyer may not "assist another" in the unauthorized practice of law).

Are UPL laws necessary to protect the public, or do they provide lawyers with an unjustified monopoly over the provision of legal services? The Federal Trade Commission argues that nonlawyers should be able to compete with lawyers, especially "where no specialized legal knowledge and training is demonstrably necessary to protect the interests of consumers."[8] Should we get rid of UPL entirely, prohibiting only pretending to be a lawyer? Or is there a more carefully tailored approach available? For a variety of perspectives on the value of UPL laws, *see generally* Colloquium: The Legal Profession's Monopoly on the Practice of Law, 82 Fordham L. Rev. 2563-3090 (2014). For an argument in favor of authorizing more nonlawyers to "participate in the legal marketplace [but] with some form of regulatory oversight," *see* Andrew M. Perlman, Towards the Law of Legal Services, 37 Cardozo L. Rev. 49, 53 (2015).

B. UPL BY LAWYERS

1. The MJP Problem

Model Rule 5.5(a) provides that "[a] lawyer shall not practice law in a jurisdiction in violation of the regulation of the legal profession in that jurisdiction. . . ." This rule applies in a straightforward manner to lawyers who are suspended or disbarred, including lawyers suspended for administrative reasons, such as failure to pay bar dues or to complete continuing legal education requirements. The difficulty arises, however, when the lawyer is properly licensed in one (or more) jurisdictions, but engages in activities that constitute the practice of law "in" another jurisdiction in which the lawyer is not licensed. This includes not only lawyers who physically move to the new jurisdiction and establish an office for the purpose of representing residents in the new jurisdiction, but also lawyers who temporarily travel to the new jurisdiction when necessary to properly represent clients in their home jurisdiction. It can even include lawyers whose presence in the new jurisdiction is not physical but rather "virtual," through such technologies as email and videoconferencing.

Although recognizing that they are not permitted to move to a new jurisdiction and set up an office there, lawyers were fairly complacent about *temporary* presence in another jurisdiction until 1998, when the following decision sent shock waves throughout the legal profession.

---

8. Letter from the Fed. Trade Comm'n Office of Policy Planning to the Rules Comm. of the Superior Courts 2 (May 17, 2007).

Birbrower, Montalbano, Condon & Frank, P.C. v. Superior Court
949 P.2d 1 (Cal. 1998)

CHIN, Justice

Business and Professions Code section 6125 states: "No person shall practice law in California unless the person is an active member of the State Bar." We must decide whether an out-of-state law firm, not licensed to practice law in this state, violated section 6125 when it performed legal services in California for a California-based client under a fee agreement stipulating that California law would govern all matters in the representation.

Although we are aware of the interstate nature of modern law practice and mindful of the reality that large firms often conduct activities and serve clients in several states, we do not believe these facts excuse law firms from complying with section 6125. Contrary to the Court of Appeal, however, we do not believe the Legislature intended section 6125 to apply to those services an out-of-state firm renders in its home state. We therefore conclude that, to the extent that the defendant law firm Birbrower, Montalbano, Condon & Frank, P.C. (Birbrower), practiced law in California without a license, it engaged in the unauthorized practice of law in this state. We also conclude that Birbrower's fee agreement with real party in interest, ESQ Business Services, Inc. (ESQ), is invalid to the extent it authorizes payment for the substantial legal services Birbrower performed in California. If, however, Birbrower can show it generated fees under its agreement for limited services it performed in New York, and it earned those fees under the otherwise invalid fee agreement, it may, on remand, present to the trial court evidence justifying its recovery of fees for those New York services. . . .

I. BACKGROUND

The facts with respect to the unauthorized practice of law question are essentially undisputed. Birbrower is a professional law corporation incorporated in New York, with its principal place of business in New York. During 1992 and 1993, Birbrower attorneys, defendants Kevin F. Hobbs and Thomas A Condon (Hobbs and Condon), performed substantial work in California relating to the law firm's representation of ESQ. Neither Hobbs nor Condon has ever been licensed to practice law in California. None of Birbrower's attorneys were licensed to practice law in California during Birbrower's ESQ representation.

ESQ is a California corporation with its principal place of business in Santa Clara County. In July 1992, the parties negotiated and executed the fee agreement in New York, providing that Birbrower would perform legal services for ESQ, including "All matters pertaining to the investigation of and prosecution of all claims and causes of action against TANDEM COMPUTERS INCORPORATED [Tandem]." The "claims and causes of action" against Tandem, a Delaware corporation with its principal place of business in Santa Clara County, California, related to a software development and marketing contract between

Tandem and ESQ dated March 16, 1990 (Tandem Agreement). The Tandem Agreement stated that "The internal laws of the State of California (irrespective of its choice of law principles) shall govern the validity of this Agreement, the construction of its terms, and the interpretation and enforcement of the rights and duties of the parties hereto." Birbrower asserts, and ESQ disputes, that ESQ knew Birbrower was not licensed to practice law in California. . . .

ESQ eventually settled the Tandem dispute, and the matter never went to arbitration . . .

In January 1994, ESQ sued Birbrower for legal malpractice and related claims. [The trial court granted summary adjudication in favor of ESQ.]

We granted review to determine whether Birbrower's actions and services performed while representing ESQ in California constituted the unauthorized practice of law under section 6125 and, if so, whether a section 6125 violation rendered the fee agreement wholly unenforceable.

II. DISCUSSION

A. The Unauthorized Practice of Law

The California Legislature enacted section 6125 in 1927 as part of the State Bar Act (the Act), a comprehensive scheme regulating the practice of law in the state. Since the Act's passage, the general rule has been that, although persons may represent themselves and their own interests regardless of State Bar membership, no one but an active member of the State Bar may practice law for another person in California. The prohibition against unauthorized law practice is within the state's police power and is designed to ensure that those performing legal services do so competently. . . .

Although the Act did not define the term "practice law," case law explained it as "'the doing and performing services in a court of justice in any matter depending therein throughout its various stages and in conformity with the adopted rules of procedure.'" [The California Supreme Court] included in its definition legal advice and legal instrument and contract preparation, whether or not these subjects were rendered in the course of litigation. . . .

In addition to not defining the term "practice law," the Act also did not define the meaning of "in California." In today's legal practice, questions often arise concerning whether the phrase refers to the nature of the legal services, or restricts the Act's application to those out-of-state attorneys who are physically present in the state.

Section 6125 has generated numerous opinions on the meaning of "practice law" but none on the meaning of "in California." In our view, the practice of law "in California" entails sufficient contact with the California client to render the nature of the legal service a clear legal representation. In addition to a quantitative analysis, we must consider the nature of the unlicensed lawyer's activities in the state. Mere fortuitous or attenuated contacts will not sustain a finding that the unlicensed lawyer practiced law "in California." The primary inquiry is whether the unlicensed lawyer engaged in sufficient activities in the state, or created a continuing relationship with the California client that included legal duties and obligations.

Our definition does not necessarily depend on or require the unlicensed lawyer's physical presence in the state. Physical presence here is one factor we may consider in deciding whether the unlicensed lawyer has violated section 6125, but it is by no means exclusive. For example, one may practice law in the state in violation of section 6125 although not physically present here by advising a California client on California law in connection with a California legal dispute by telephone, fax, computer, or other modern technological means. Conversely, although we decline to provide a comprehensive list of what activities constitute sufficient contact with the state, we do reject the notion that a person automatically practices law "in California" whenever that person practices California law anywhere, or "virtually" enters the state by telephone, fax, e-mail or satellite. . . .

This interpretation acknowledges the tension that exists between interjurisdictional practice and the need to have a state-regulated bar. . . .

Exceptions to 6125 do exist, but are generally limited to allowing out-of-state attorneys to make appearances before a state court or tribunal. They are narrowly drawn and strictly interpreted . . .

[W]ith the permission of the California court in which a particular cause is pending, out-of-state counsel may appear before a court as counsel pro hac vice. A court will approve a pro hac vice application only if the out-of-state attorney is a member in good standing of another state bar and is eligible to practice in any United States court or the highest court in another jurisdiction. The out-of-state attorney must also associate an active member of the California Bar as attorney of record and is subject to the Rules of Professional Conduct of the State Bar . . .

Finally, California Rules of Court, rule 988, permits the State Bar to issue registration certificates to foreign legal consultants who may advise on the law of the foreign jurisdiction where they are admitted. The consultants may not, however, appear as attorneys before a California court or judicial officer or otherwise prepare pleadings and instruments in California or give advice on the law of California or any other state or jurisdiction except those where they are admitted. . . .

B. THE PRESENT CASE

. . . [A]s the Court of Appeal observed, Birbrower engaged in unauthorized law practice *in California* on more than a limited basis, and no firm attorney engaged in that practice was an active member of the California State Bar. As noted, in 1992 and 1993, Birbrower attorneys traveled to California to discuss with ESQ and others various matters pertaining to the dispute between ESQ and Tandem. Hobbs and Condon discussed strategy for resolving the dispute and advised ESQ on this strategy. Furthermore, during California meetings with Tandem representatives in August 1992, Hobbs demanded Tandem pay $15 million, and Condon told Tandem he believed damages in the matter would exceed that amount if the parties proceeded to litigation. Also in California, Hobbs met with ESQ for the stated purpose of helping to reach a settlement agreement and to discuss the agreement that was eventually proposed. Birbrower attorneys also traveled to California to initiate arbitration proceedings before the matter was settled. As the Court of Appeal concluded, " . . . the Birbrower firm's in-state activities clearly constituted the [unauthorized] practice of law" *in California*.

Birbrower contends, however, that section 6125 is not meant to apply to *any* out-of-state *attorneys*. Instead, it argues that the statute is intended solely to prevent nonattorneys from practicing law. This contention is without merit because it contravenes the plain language of the statute. Section 6125 clearly states that *no person* shall practice law in California unless that person is a member of the State Bar. The statute does not differentiate between attorneys or nonattorneys, nor does it excuse a person who is a member of another state bar. It is well settled that, in determining the meaning of a statute, we look to its words and give them their usual and ordinary meaning. . . .

Birbrower next argues that we do not further the statute's intent and purpose — to protect California citizens from incompetent attorneys — by enforcing it against out-of-state attorneys. Birbrower argues that because out-of-state attorneys have been licensed to practice in other jurisdictions, they have already demonstrated sufficient competency to protect California clients. But Birbrower's argument overlooks the obvious fact that other states' laws may differ substantially from California law. Competence in one jurisdiction does not necessarily guarantee competence to another. By applying section 6125 to out-of-state attorneys who engage in the extensive practice of law in California without becoming licensed in our state, we serve the statute's goal of assuring the competence of all attorneys practicing law in this state.

California is not alone in regulating who practices law in its jurisdiction. . . . Whether an attorney is duly admitted in another state and is, in fact, competent to practice in California is irrelevant in the face of section 6125's language and purpose. Moreover, as the North Dakota Supreme Court pointed out . . . : "It may be that such an [out-of-state attorney] exception is warranted, but such a plea is more properly made to a legislative committee considering a bill enacting such an exception or to this court in its rule-making function than it is in a juridical decision." . . .

Assuming that section 6125 does apply to out-of-state attorneys not licensed here, Birbrower alternatively asks us to create an exception to section 6125 for work incidental to private arbitration or other alternative dispute resolution proceedings. Birbrower points to fundamental differences between private arbitration and legal proceedings, including procedural differences relating to discovery, rules of evidence, compulsory process, cross-examination of witnesses, and other areas. As Birbrower observes, at least one court has decided that an out-of-state attorney could recover fees for services rendered in an arbitration proceeding. . . .

We decline Birbrower's invitation to craft an arbitration exception to section 6125's prohibition of the unlicensed practice of law in this state. Any exception for arbitration is best left to the Legislature, which has the authority to determine qualifications for admission to the State Bar and to decide what constitutes the practice of law. . . . Section 6125 . . . articulates a strong public policy favoring the practice of law in California by licensed State Bar members. In the face of the Legislature's silence, we will not create an arbitration exception under the facts presented. . . .

C. COMPENSATION FOR LEGAL SERVICES

Because Birbrower violated section 6125 when it engaged in the unlawful practice of law in California, the Court of Appeal found its fee agreement with ESQ unenforceable in its entirety. Without crediting Birbrower for some services performed in New York, for which fees were generated under the fee agreement, the court reasoned that the agreement was void and unenforceable because it included payment for services rendered to a California client in the state by an unlicensed out-of-state lawyer. . . . The Court of Appeal let stand, however, the trial court's decision to allow Birbrower to pursue its fifth cause of action in quantum meruit. We agree with the Court of Appeal to the extent it barred Birbrower from recovering fees generated under the fee agreement for the unauthorized legal services it performed in California. We disagree with the same court to the extent it implicitly barred Birbrower from recovering fees generated under the fee agreement for the limited legal services the firm performed in New York.

It is a general rule that an attorney is barred from recovering compensation for services rendered in another state where the attorney was not admitted to the bar. The general rule, however, has some recognized exceptions.

[The court dismissed Birbrower's argument based on three possible exceptions. The first was for practice in federal court, but none of Birbrower's activities related to this exception. The second exception, recognized in several state court opinions, concerned "[s]ervices not involving courtroom appearances," which the court refused to recognize as too broad. The third exception, also recognized by some jurisdictions, was for attorneys who fully disclosed their lack of licensure in the jurisdiction. ESQ disputed that it had been so informed, but the court held that even if Birbrower had disclosed its lack of licensure in California, the court would reject this exception based on the plain language and underlying policy of section 6125.]

We agree with Birbrower that it may be able to recover fees under the fee agreement for the limited legal services it performed for ESQ in New York to the extent they did not constitute practicing law in California, even though those services were performed for a California client. Because section 6125 applies to the practice of law in California, it does not, in general, regulate law practice in other states. Thus, although the general rule against compensation to out-of-state attorneys precludes Birbrower's recovery under the fee agreement for its actions in California, the severability doctrine may allow it to receive its New York fees generated under the fee agreement, if we conclude the illegal portions of the agreement pertaining to the practice of law in California may be severed from those parts regarding services Birbrower performed in New York.

[The court remanded the case to the trial court to determine how much of the legal fees were attributable to services Birbrower performed in New York.]

NOTES AND QUESTIONS

1. A dissenting opinion described how Birbrower, a New York law firm, came to represent ESQ.[9] Birbrower had previously represented the owners of a sister corporation, which was a New York corporation, including reviewing the agreement with Tandem, to be governed under California law. The California corporation, which the dissent refers to as ESQ-CAL, consulted Birbrower concerning Tandem's performance under the agreement, and the two sister corporations jointly hired Birbrower to resolve the dispute with Tandem. The arbitration was initiated on behalf of both ESQ corporations.

2. Under *Birbrower*, the law firm could recover fees for work it performed for ESQ in New York. If the work involved interpreting and applying California law, why didn't that also constitute the unauthorized practice of law? What is the significance of the finding that the Birbrower lawyers practiced law "in" California?

3. In Estate of Condon v. McHenry,[10] an intermediate California appellate court permitted a Colorado lawyer retained by a Colorado client to obtain legal fees for legal services performed in connection with a California probate proceeding. The Colorado client had been appointed as co-executor of the California estate, and the Colorado lawyer's services included negotiating a settlement with the California co-executor and her California attorneys.[11] Although most of the Colorado lawyer's contacts with California were virtual (by telephone, letter, and email), the court stated that the result would have been the same if the lawyer had physically traveled to California. It distinguished *Birbrower* on the basis that the Colorado lawyer's client was not a California resident. Is this distinction warranted? Based on the dissenting opinion in *Birbrower*, we know that the New York law firm was representing both ESQ-CAL and its New York sister corporation in resolving the dispute with Tandem. Should the law firm be permitted to recover fees from one client (the New York corporation) but not the other (the California corporation) for providing exactly the same services? Although the

---

9. 949 P.2d at 13 (Kennard, Justice, dissenting).

10. 76 Cal.Rptr.2d 922 (Cal. Ct. App. 1998).

11. The client retained a California law firm to appear and file documents in the probate proceedings.

Birbrower firm would likely have had to sue the New York sister corporation in New York to recover its legal fees, Rule 5.5(a) provides that it is a violation for a lawyer to "practice law in a jurisdiction in violation of the regulation of the legal profession in that jurisdiction," meaning that California law (i.e., *Birbrower*) would determine whether a New York lawyer representing a New York client by providing legal services to that client "in" California engaged in the unauthorized practice of law in California.

4. In In re Estate of Waring,[12] the New Jersey Supreme Court permitted a New York law firm to recover fees in connection with an estate probated in New Jersey. The law firm represented the New Jersey executors and were retained, because of their long-time association with the decedent's family, to prepare and file the federal income tax return and federal estate tax return, and in miscellaneous other activities, including terminating a lease on a summer residence in Massachusetts. Because the firm's work was performed "largely outside the borders of New Jersey and dealt for the most part with federal tax matters," the court concluded that the firm could recover its fees, stating that "questions of unlawful practice will turn on the particular facts presented." The court further commented that "[m]ultistate relationships are a common part of today's society and are to be dealt with in a commonsense fashion" and that protection of the public has to be weighed against clients' "freedom of choice in the selection of their own counsel [unburdened by] 'technical restrictions which have no reasonable justification.'" Given that the firm's work was performed for a New Jersey client, and the work involved some physical and virtual presence in New Jersey, would *Birbrower* have prevented the New York law firm from recovering fees for the work it performed in New Jersey? Should law firms practicing federal law, such as federal tax and securities law, be permitted to represent clients from all states, including physical or virtual presence in those states, regardless of their licensure limitations? What about the *Waring* law firm's work in terminating a Massachusetts residential lease? The firm wasn't representing a Massachusetts client, but the representation probably involved physical or virtual contact with the Massachusetts landlord. Would Massachusetts likely consider that to be the unauthorized practice of law in Massachusetts?

5. Perhaps the most shocking aspect of *Birbrower* was the court's view that the lawyers' virtual presence "in" California was as significant as their physical presence. *Should* courts treat virtual and physical presence as equivalent? Some lawyers have no brick and mortar office but rather represent all their clients "virtually," through telephone, email, digital document-sharing, and videoconferencing. Should it matter where these lawyers are physically located? Attorney Richard Granat

---

12. 221 A.2d 193 (N.J. 1966).

is licensed in Maryland and has an office address and telephone number in Maryland, but he lives in Florida, where he performs the legal work. He describes himself as a virtual lawyer. He does not advertise in Florida and does not represent Florida citizens. Is he engaged in the unauthorized practice of law in Florida?[13] The Eleventh Circuit Court of Appeals upheld the right of the Florida Bar to prevent a New York-licensed lawyer living in Florida from advertising his willingness to represent clients on "New York Legal Matters Only," stating that the lawyer, "who is not admitted to the Florida Bar, does not have the authority to practice New York law in Florida."[14] Does Florida have a legitimate interest in preventing Granat from practicing Maryland law in Florida? The Florida Supreme Court recently approved a proposed State Bar advisory opinion concluding that a New Jersey-licensed lawyer could provide federal intellectual property legal services for New Jersey clients from his residence in Florida; he worked for a New Jersey law firm, his clients could not contact him except by calling him at his New Jersey office (which rerouted calls to his cellphone), and there was no indication of his presence in Florida other than the fact that he worked at his computer in his Florida home.[15] Does this opinion apply to Granat? Should it?

6. Several commentators have concluded that the primary goal of territorial limitations on law practice is to protect in-state lawyers from out-of-state competition, and that the stated goal of protection of the public is merely self-serving rhetoric. One such commentator argued that "[t]he goal of limiting the practice of law to those 'who are possessed of the requisite ability and character' is achieved when a lawyer receives his first license."[16] If so, then the possession of any valid state license would justify multijurisdictional practice, including permanently moving to another state and opening an office for the practice of law there. Do you agree that at the very least, lawyers should generally be prohibited from using their first state license to justify opening an office in another state? Why or why not?

7. A variation on a portable single license model is a driver's license model, under which valid licensure in the lawyer's home state would justify temporary practice in another jurisdiction; however, just like someone with an out-of-state driver's license, the out-of-state lawyer would be governed by the host state's rules of professional conduct

---

13. For an interesting discussion among Granat and participants in a legal ethics forum, *see* https://www.legalethicsforum.com/blog/2009/08/living-in-fl-practice-in-md-and-dc-100m-pa-for-30-minutes-per-day.html.

14. *See* Gould v. Florida Bar, 259 Fed. Appx. 208 (11th Cir. 2007).

15. Fla. Sup. Ct., The Florida Bar Re: Advisory Opinion—Out-of-State Attorney Working Remotely from Florida Home (May 20, 2021).

16. Pamela A. McManus, Have Law License; Will Travel, 15 Geo. J. Legal Ethics 527, 537 (2002).

while present in the host state. Are there significant differences between temporarily driving and temporarily practicing law in a jurisdiction in which the person is not licensed?

8. If you believe that state-by-state licensing is archaic in view of the increasingly interstate and even global needs of today's clients, what about federal legislation that would create a national license to practice law within the United States? Congress probably has the power to regulate lawyers through the interstate commerce clause, but it has not yet demonstrated any willingness to do so.[17] Are there any benefits of retaining the current state-by-state regulatory model?

2. The ABA's "Safe Harbors"[18] Solution

Following *Birbrower*, the ABA created a Commission on Multijurisdictional Practice. The Commission considered and rejected some of the proposed solutions discussed above. Instead, it recommended keeping the existing model of state licensure and regulation, but liberalizing the rules restricting the practice of law in other states. The ABA adopted the Commission's recommendations in August 2002.

The centerpiece of the Commission's recommendations consisted of amendments to Model Rules 5.5 (Unauthorized Practice of Law; Multijurisdictional Practice of Law) and 8.5 (Disciplinary Authority: Choice of Law). In addition, the Commission also recommended the adoption of additional model court rules, including a Model Rule on Pro Hac Vice Admission, a Model Rule on Admission by Motion, a Model Rule for the Licensing of Legal Consultants, and a Model Rule for Temporary Practice by Foreign Lawyers. In all, the Commission made nine final reports, all of which were adopted by the ABA House of Delegates.

Model Rule 5.5(b) states the general rule that a lawyer not admitted in the jurisdiction may not "establish an office or other systematic and continuous presence in the jurisdiction" to practice law. The comment does not define "other systematic presence," except to incorporate the *Birbrower* holding that "[p]resence may be systematic and continuous even if the lawyer is not physically present" in the jurisdiction.[19] Can you think of some clear examples of what it might take for a lawyer to have a "systematic presence" in a jurisdiction, either physically or virtually, without establishing an office there?

---

17. *See* Fred C. Zacharias, Federalizing Legal Ethics, 73 Tex. L. Rev. 335, 337 (1994).

18. The term "safe harbors" was used by the ABA Commission on Multijurisdictional Practice in a November 2001 Report. None of the Commission's recommendations used that term, but it is one that is familiar to lawyers and is viewed "as a useful metaphor for conceptualizing the categories of legal work that a lawyer admitted in one jurisdiction may do in another jurisdiction." *See* Client Representation in the 21st Century, Report of the Commission on Multijurisdictional Practice, p. 22, n.33 (2002).

19. MR 5.5, cmt [4].

Model Rule 5.5(c) establishes four "safe harbors" for out-of-state lawyers' temporary presence in a jurisdiction where they are not licensed, and Model Rule 5.5(d) establishes two "safe harbors" for establishing an office or other systematic presence.

a. Safe Harbors for Temporary Practice

Model Rule 5.5(c) creates four safe harbors for providing legal services "on a temporary basis" in the jurisdiction. Look at Comment [6] for a very brief discussion of what might distinguish "temporary" from "systematic" presence in a jurisdiction. Is this discussion sufficient? Could the comment have provided more guidance to lawyers?

The following opinion discusses several of the safe harbors created under subsection (c). We will look more closely at each of the four provisions in the notes following the opinion.

In Re Charges of Unprofessional Conduct in Panel File No. 39302
884 N.W.2d 661 (Minn. 2016)

PER CURIAM.

The Director of the Office of Lawyers Professional Conduct (the Director) issued a private admonition to appellant[20] for engaging in the unauthorized practice of law in Minnesota. . . .

Appellant is an attorney licensed to practice law in the state of Colorado, where he maintains an office and has been practicing environmental law since 1986. He has also practiced personal injury law for approximately 7 years. Part of his litigation practice includes debt collection. . . .

Appellant's mother- and father-in-law live in Minnesota. They contacted appellant in May 2014 to obtain assistance regarding a judgment entered against them in conciliation court in Minnesota for $2,368.13 in favor of their condominium association, Voyager Condominium Homeowners' Association, Inc. (VCHA). The couple told appellant that VCHA's attorney, D.R., a Minnesota-based lawyer and the complainant in this case, was harassing them with telephone calls attempting to collect on the judgment. The couple asked appellant for his assistance in negotiating with D.R. regarding payment of the outstanding judgment.

Appellant sent an e-mail to D.R. in late May 2014, informing D.R. that he was representing his in-laws and instructing D.R. to direct all future communications to him instead. Appellant and D.R. exchanged approximately two dozen e-mails between May 2014 and September 2014. In his first responsive e-mail to appellant, D.R. asked whether appellant was licensed to practice in Minnesota. Appellant replied that he was not licensed in Minnesota and that

---

20. [Because the admonition was private, the court does not name the disciplined lawyer. — ED.]

if he needed to file suit in Minnesota he would hire local counsel. The subsequent e-mails consisted of discussions regarding the in-laws' assets and ability to pay and whether the VCHA judgment would have priority in a foreclosure sale. Appellant attached financial disclosure forms to one of his e-mails and made a settlement offer.

In the penultimate e-mail exchange between the two attorneys, D.R. asserted that appellant was engaging in the unauthorized practice of law because he was not licensed in Minnesota. The final e-mail prior to D.R. filing an ethics complaint was a settlement proposal from appellant to D.R. on that same day. The Director received D.R.'s ethics complaint in October 2014. Approximately 2 months after filing the complaint, D.R. sent additional e-mails to appellant to determine whether the settlement offer was still available and whether appellant still represented his in-laws. Appellant did not respond to the subsequent e-mails and had no further involvement in the case.

Nothing in the record shows that appellant researched whether his activities constituted the unauthorized practice of law under the Minnesota Rules of Professional Conduct. When asked by the Panel at the evidentiary hearing whether he researched the rules in Minnesota, appellant said that he did not recall. Appellant admitted that he had not researched Minnesota law on foreclosure and how it would apply to his in-laws' case. Appellant also admitted that when he considered the relevant law and the rules of professional conduct, he was more familiar with the laws and rules in Colorado.

The Panel affirmed the Director's admonition, finding that clear and convincing evidence demonstrated a violation of Minn. R. Prof. Conduct 5.5(a). . . .

Appellant contends that he did not violate Rule 5.5(a) because he did not practice law in *in* Minnesota. According to appellant, a lawyer practices *in* a jurisdiction in one of three ways: (1) by being physically present in the jurisdiction; (2) by establishing an office or other systematic and continuous presence in the jurisdiction; or (3) by entering an appearance in a matter through the filing of documents with a tribunal. Appellant argues that e-mail communication directed to a jurisdiction in which the lawyer is not admitted to practice does not fall within the definition of practicing law *in* a jurisdiction, and thus the Panel erred in its determination that he violated Rule 5.5(a). . . .

Appellant concedes for the purpose of this appeal that he engaged in the practice of law, albeit in Colorado. Such a concession is consistent with our prior cases holding that negotiating the resolution of a claim on behalf of a client constitutes the practice of law. Appellant maintains, however, that an attorney does not practice law in another jurisdiction merely by engaging in e-mail communications with individuals in that jurisdiction. Whether an attorney engages in the practice of law *in* Minnesota by sending e-mails from *another* jurisdiction is a matter of first impression. . . .

Other courts have addressed the issue of whether an attorney practices law in a jurisdiction even though the attorney was not physically present in that jurisdiction. In *Birbower, Montalbano, Condon & Frank, P.C. v. Superior Court*, the

California Supreme Court analyzed what constituted the practice of law in a jurisdiction by looking at the nature of the legal representation in the jurisdiction, instead of focusing solely on physical presence. . . . The court determined that a lawyer "may practice law in the state . . . although not physically present here by advising a California client on California law in connection with a California legal dispute by telephone, fax, computer, or other modern technological means."

The reasoning in *Birbrower* is persuasive. Based on that reasoning, we conclude that the Panel did not clearly err by finding that appellant practiced law *in* Minnesota, in violation of Minn. R. Prof. Conduct 5.5(a). Appellant contacted D.R., a Minnesota lawyer, and stated that he represented Minnesota clients in a Minnesota legal dispute. This legal dispute was not interjurisdictional; instead, it involved only Minnesota residents and a debt arising from a judgment entered by a Minnesota court. . . . By multiple emails sent over several months, appellant advised Minnesota clients on Minnesota law in connection with a Minnesota legal dispute and attempted to negotiate a resolution of that dispute with a Minnesota attorney. Appellant had a clear, ongoing attorney-client relationship with his Minnesota clients, and his contacts with Minnesota were not fortuitous or attenuated. Thus, there is ample support for the Panel's finding that appellant practiced law in Minnesota. . . .

Next, we turn to appellant's claim that even if the Panel did not err in determining that he was practicing law in Minnesota in violation of Minn. R. Prof. Conduct 5.5(a), his conduct was permitted under one of the exceptions in Minn. R. Prof. Conduct 5.5(c). Appellant argues that Rule 5.5(c)(2) authorized his conduct because he reasonably believed that he would be able to associate with local counsel and be admitted pro hac vice if necessary. Appellant further claims that Rule 5.5(c)(4) authorized his conduct because his in-laws reached out to him for assistance on a matter within his expertise; thus the matter "arose out of [Appellant's] law practice."

Rule 5.5(c) permits an attorney to practice temporarily in a jurisdiction in which the attorney is not admitted. [The Minnesota version of Rule 5.5(c) is identical in all relevant respects to the Model Rule.]

Under Minnesota Rules of Professional Conduct 5.5(c)(2), a lawyer admitted in another jurisdiction may provide legal services in Minnesota on a temporary basis if the lawyer's services are reasonably related to a pending or potential proceeding before a tribunal and the lawyer reasonably expects to be authorized by law to appear in the proceeding. Comment 10 explains that a lawyer rendering services in Minnesota on a temporary basis is permitted to engage in conduct in anticipation of a proceeding or hearing in which the lawyer reasonably expects to be admitted pro hac vice. Minn. R. Prof. Conduct 5.5(c).

Appellant suggests that there was a potential proceeding that could be brought on behalf of his in-laws. Because of this belief, appellant contends Rule 5.5(c)(2) protects him. The Director persuasively argues that appellant knew further litigation was unlikely because a court had already decided the underlying case involving his in-laws, and appellant was simply negotiating a potential debt resolution. In addition, Rule 5.5(c)(2), by its plain language, requires more than an attorney's speculation that the attorney can find local counsel and be admitted to practice pro hac vice. Appellant's e-mail correspondence does not indicate that he took steps to secure local counsel or investigate the possibility of pro hac vice admission. Thus, we conclude there is no support for appellant's claim that his conduct was authorized by Rule 5.5(c)(2).

Under Minnesota Rules of Professional Conduct 5.5(c)(4), a lawyer admitted in another jurisdiction may provide legal services in Minnesota on a temporary basis if the lawyer's services are not covered by paragraphs (c)(2) and (c)(3) and "arise out of or are reasonably related to the lawyer's practice in a jurisdiction in which the lawyer is admitted to practice." Appellant contends that his services arose out of or were reasonably related to his practice in Colorado because the clients are his relatives who "reached out to him for assistance" and appellant's environmental and personal-injury practice involves debt collection.

Comment 14 of the Minnesota Rules of Professional Conduct 5.5 provides guidance on this issue. Specifically, comment 14 instructs that several factors may demonstrate that an attorney's temporary legal services in Minnesota reasonably relate to the lawyer's practice in a jurisdiction in which the lawyer is admitted to practice ("lawyer's home jurisdiction"), including: whether the client is a resident of or has substantial contacts with the lawyer's home jurisdiction; whether the client has previously been represented by the lawyer; whether a significant aspect of the matter involves the law of the lawyer's home jurisdiction; whether the client's activities or the legal issues involve multiple jurisdictions; or whether the services "draw on the lawyer's recognized expertise developed through the regular practice of law on behalf of clients in matters involving a particular body of federal, nationally-uniform, foreign, or international law."

The legal services appellant provided to his in-laws were unrelated to his environmental and personal-injury practice in Colorado. The record establishes that appellant was involved in litigation in Colorado state court, including eight trials in the past 7 years in which collection issues arose, and that appellant negotiated the resolution of a debt with an out-of-state creditor on behalf of several Colorado residents. Although Rule 5.5(c) may permit appellant to negotiate a Colorado client's out-of-state creditor because this representation is reasonably related to appellant's Colorado practice, the facts of this case are substantially different. Appellant's in-laws are not Colorado residents, and appellant had no prior attorney-client relationship with them.

Moreover, appellant's representation of his in-laws did not "arise out of" or "reasonably relate" to his practice in Colorado simply because his in-laws contacted him in Colorado or appellant has done collections work in Colorado. As the Director notes, appellant's in-laws were not longstanding clients; nor was there any connection between the in-laws' case and the state or laws of Colorado. And while appellant's Colorado practice may involve judgment collections work, nothing in the record establishes that this work was based on a body of federal or nationally uniform law.[21] To the contrary, appellant's clients were Minnesota residents with a debt that arose in Minnesota that they owed to a Minnesota resident and that was governed by Minnesota law. Accordingly, Rule 5.5(c)(4) does not apply to appellant's conduct. . . .

Affirmed.

ANDERSON, Justice (dissenting). . . .

Appellant argues that Rule 5.5(c)(4) applies because his in-law's judgment-collection matter was "reasonably related" to his practice in Colorado, which includes judgment-collection work. Appellant contends that he has experience with judgment collections and that collection work is an integral and necessary part of his litigation practice in Colorado. Upon review of the record, I agree that appellant's temporary provision of legal assistance to his parents-in-law regarding the negotiation of a small collection matter in Minnesota is "reasonably related" to appellant's practice of law in Colorado. Therefore, the exception in Rule 5.5(c)(4) applies, and respectfully, I dissent.

In concluding that appellant's work for his parents-in-law was not "reasonably related" to his practice in Colorado, the court primarily focuses on appellant's practice in the areas of environmental and personal-injury law. But, as the court notes, appellant also has experience with collection work, as reflected in the record. Appellant argues that he has engaged in and developed experience with collection work in his litigation practice. More specifically, appellant testified to the Panel that "collection work" is "an integral part of my litigation practice." He testified that in the past seven years, he has engaged in judgment-collection work and has participated in eight trials in this area of practice. In addition, he demonstrated that, in a single previous month, he had made three filings dealing with judgment collections, which he submitted to the Panel as exhibits.

Based on this record, I would conclude that appellant's assistance with a small judgment-collection negotiation for his parents-in-law, including the emails to D.R., were "reasonably related" to appellant's practice in Colorado,

---

21. [Fn. 4 in Original] The dissent's reliance on comment 14 to Rule 5.5 to support its claim that appellant's representation of his in-laws was reasonably related to his Colorado practice is misplaced. According to the dissent, the representation was reasonably related to appellant's Colorado practice because "appellant has developed experience and expertise in the area of judgment collections through his participation in eight trials and multiple filings." The dissent acknowledges, however, that the record does not establish that "appellant's collection practice is 'nationally uniform.'" In fact, the record establishes the opposite. When appellant asked D.R. whether relevant Minnesota law was the same as Colorado law, D.R. indicated that it was not.

Instead, the dissent argues, without citing any legal support for its claim, that the subject on which an attorney has expertise need not [] be nationally uniform in order for legal services provided outside the attorney's home jurisdiction to reasonably relate to the attorney's practice in his or her home jurisdiction. We disagree. Rule 5.5(c) is an exception to the general prohibition on the unauthorized practice of law. By interpreting the exception to apply to expertise in any subject matter, the dissent allows the exception to swallow the general rule.

which satisfies Rule 5.5(c)(4). The "reasonably related" exception in Rule 5.5(c)(4) is a *broad*, catch-all exception that is intended to exempt circumstances such as those presented here. Moreover, the familial connection between appellant and his in-laws, and the fact that they contacted appellant in Colorado for assistance, should be an additional consideration that supports a finding that the matter was "reasonably related" to his practice in Colorado under Rule 5.5(c)(4).

The exception established by ABA Model Rule 5.5(c)(4)—which is identical in wording to our Rule 5.5(c)(4)—is described as a *"broad catch-all"* and a "safe harbor" for out-of-state lawyers to engage in temporary practice that is "reasonably related to the lawyer's home state practice." Ronald D. Rotunda & John S. Dzienkowski, Legal Ethics: The Lawyer's Deskbook on Professional Responsibility §5.5-2, at 1112 (2016) (emphasis added).

As explained in the Restatement [(Third) of the Law Governing Lawyers], the prior, more restrictive rules governing interstate practice by nonlocal lawyers "were formed at a time when lawyers conducted very little [interstate] practice" and thus "imposed little actual inconvenience." By contrast today, "as interstate and international commerce, transportation, and communications have expanded, clients have increasingly required a truly interstate . . . practice by their lawyers." The ABA recognized that rule changes were needed as the frequency and ease of multistate practice increased, supported by electronic communication and remote services (e.g., e-mails, phone and video conferencing, electronic filings). In this modern context, lawyers routinely communicate from one jurisdiction with a client located in another jurisdiction. Thus, the ABA Model Rules "encouraged [the removal of] unnecessary restrictions on interstate practice."

The comments to Rule 5.5(c)(4) provide guidance on whether a "reasonable relationship" exists between the lawyer's temporary services in Minnesota and the lawyer's practice in another jurisdiction. Comment 14 explains that "[a] variety of factors" may evidence such a reasonable relationship. The examples and factors to consider in comment 14 are not exhaustive, nor are they mandatory. . . .

The Director argues that the guidance in comment 14 weighs against applying the Rule 5.5(c)(4) exception because the record does not establish that appellant's parents-in-laws specifically sought appellant for his "recognized expertise . . . involving a particular body of federal, nationally-uniform, foreign, or international law." I agree that the record does not meticulously detail the extent to which the law applicable to appellant's collection practice is "nationally uniform" or the extent to which his experience with collection work is "recognized." But as discussed above, the explanatory language in the comments is not mandatory or exhaustive—it merely provides examples of the types of temporary legal services that may satisfy the broad, "reasonably related" catch-all exception under Rule 5.5(c)(4). The broad, "reasonably related" requirement and the principles underlying the guidance in comment 14 surely apply here. The record reflects that appellant developed experience and "expertise" with a particular body of law — collections — in at least eight trials over seven years, including three judgement-collection filings within a single month.

In addition, the clients' relationship to appellant, including their familial connection and the clients' contacts with appellant in his home state, should be considered in the "reasonable relationship" analysis. The comments to the Restatement advise that, in determining whether an out-of-state lawyer's activities "reasonably relate" to the lawyer's practice in a state of admission, "several factors are relevant, including the following: [whether the client] is from the lawyer's home state, has extensive contacts with that state, *or contacted the lawyer there.*" Restatement (Third) of the Law Governing Lawyers §3 cmt. e (emphasis added). Here, the clients contacted their son-in-law, appellant, in his home state of Colorado.

Additional analogous support is provided in comment 14 to Rule 5.5(c)(4), which states that one factor to consider is whether the "lawyer's client may have been previously represented by the lawyer." Although the record does not indicate whether appellant ever previously represented his parents-in-law, the principle underlying this comment — a relationship of trust and familiarity with the lawyer's capabilities — is applicable here. The recognition that a sustained lawyer-client relationship would allow an attorney to perform legal work for the client in other jurisdictions, based on confidence and trust, is reflected in the ABA's recommendation for the proposed Model Rule 5.5. Regarding the exception under Rule 5.5(c)(4), the ABA stated:

> [Model Rule 5.5(c)(4)] would respect . . . client-lawyer relationships by permitting a client to retain a lawyer to work on multiple related matters, including *some having no connection to the jurisdiction* in which the lawyer is licensed. . . . [C]lients are better served by having a *sustained relationship with a lawyer or law firm in whom the client has confidence.*

[ABA Comm'n on Multijurisdictional Practice Report] (emphasis added). The ABA recommendation further explains that in such cases of reasonably related, temporary services under Rule 5.5(c)(a)(4), it is "sufficient to rely on the lawyer's home state as the jurisdiction with the primary responsibility to ensure that the lawyer has the requisite character and fitness to practice law" because the home state "has a substantial interest in ensuring that all aspects of the lawyer's provision of legal services, wherever they occur, are conducted competently and professionally."

Finally, as a policy matter, the implications of the court's decision are troubling and counterproductive. The ABA Model Rule 5.5(c), as adopted by our state, was intended as a broad catch-all that "represent[s] a bold step towards new latitude in [a] multijurisdictional practice of law," which accommodates the increasingly mobile and electronic nature of modern, national legal practice. *See* Rotunda & Dzienkowski, *supra.* Today's decision represents a step backwards. By the court's reasoning, when family members or friends — an abundant source of clients — email or call a practitioner admitted in another state, seeking assistance in areas in which the practitioner is experienced and competent, relying on a relationship of trust and confidence, they must be turned away. Those potential clients must then expend unnecessary time and resources to research and hire local counsel—even for minor, temporary services in which the out-of-state lawyer could have provided efficient, inexpensive, and competent service. Simply put, the court's decision is contrary to the principles and policy goals intended by Rule 5.5(c).

NOTES AND QUESTIONS

1. Rule 5.5(c)(1) authorizes temporary practice when the out-of-state lawyer associates with a local lawyer "who actively participates in the matter." The Colorado lawyer in *Charges of Unprofessional Conduct* said he would associate with a local lawyer if there was litigation, so why didn't he form such an association from the outset? Why isn't this the obvious solution for multijurisdictional practice in transactional matters?

2. Rule 5.5(c)(2) authorizes temporary practice for legal services "in or reasonably related to a pending or *potential* proceeding before a tribunal in this or *another* jurisdiction, if the lawyer, *or a person the lawyer is assisting*, is authorized by law or order to appear in such proceeding or reasonably expects to be so authorized." (Emphasis added.) This provision concerns pro hac vice admission, in which an out-of-state lawyer formally applies to a tribunal, typically a court, for permission to appear as an attorney of record in a particular proceeding. Pro hac vice admission long predated the 2002 ABA MJP amendments and provides a clear path for litigators to engage in multistate practice. If pro hac vice admission already existed, what purpose is served by Rule 5.5(c)(2) other than a formal acknowledgment of the status quo? Consider the italicized portions of the rule and ask yourself how these three terms expand the range of services already permitted by traditional pro hac vice admission. The Colorado lawyer in *Charges of Unprofessional Conduct* argued that this provision authorized his conduct in attempting to negotiate a resolution of the dispute between his in-laws and their creditor. Why didn't his argument succeed? What was the significance of the fact that the Colorado lawyer had not made any effort to locate a local counsel? If California had adopted the ABA MJP amendments, could the *Birbrower* lawyers have taken advantage of this safe harbor? Given the existence of a safe harbor for lawyers representing clients in an arbitration (in Rule 5.5(c)(3)), why might it have been important for the *Birbrower* lawyers to rely on Rule 5.5(c)(2) instead?

3. Rule 5.5(c)(3) authorizes temporary practice for legal services "in or reasonably related to a pending or potential arbitration, mediation, or other alternative dispute resolution pending in this or another jurisdiction." An arbitration proceeding (but not mediation or other alternative

dispute resolution) is considered to be a "tribunal" for purposes of Rule 5.5(c)(2);[22] however, arbitrators typically have no authority to grant pro hac vice admission to out-of-state lawyers; hence the need for this rule. Unlike Rule 5.5(c)(2), however, this provision contains an additional requirement—that the services "arise out of or are reasonably related to the lawyer's practice" in the lawyer's home state. If litigation services in alternative dispute resolution are similar to those provided in court proceedings, for which pro hac vice admission is available, why does the arbitration/ADR provision require that the matter have some special relationship to the lawyer's home state practice? Would the *Birbrower* lawyers have collected their entire fee if California had adopted this provision at the time they were preparing for an arbitration in that state? Keep in mind how the New York lawyers came to represent the California corporate client in the dispute with Tandem.[23]

4. Transactional lawyers have never had the ability, like litigators, to be officially admitted for temporary practice outside their home jurisdiction. Hence Rule 5.5(c)(4), or something like it, was necessary to permit them to lawfully engage in some temporary multijurisdictional practice. This provision takes the requirement from Rule 5.5(c)(3) that the legal services "arise out of or are reasonably related to the lawyer's practice" in the home jurisdiction and makes it the sole basis for temporary practice in another jurisdiction for services not otherwise authorized by 5.5(c). The dissent in *Charges of Unprofessional Conduct* describes this provision as a "broad catch-all," but the question remains exactly how broad it is. That case was decided on a 4-3 vote of the Minnesota Supreme Court, and it is unclear how other state courts will resolve the issue. Both opinions cited comment [14]. How did the majority and dissenting opinions differently interpret and apply this comment? Which opinion did you find most persuasive? Do you agree with the majority's argument in footnote 4 (footnote 21 in this text) that the dissent's interpretation "allows the exception to swallow the general rule"?

5. Think for a moment about a state court considering whether to adopt Rule 5.5(c). These changes liberalize UPL rules for *out-of-state* lawyers coming into the adopting state, but do nothing to help *in-state* lawyers who want to travel to another state to provide legal services. *See* Model Rule 5.5(a) (in-state lawyer subject to discipline for out-of-state practice in violation of that state's rules). So why would a state court agree to adopt these amendments? In addition to the many states that have substantially adopted the ABA amendments, some have gone even further. For example, Colorado permits out-of-state attorneys to practice in Colorado so long as they do not hold themselves out as practicing

---

22. *See* MR 1.0(m).

23. *See supra* Note 1 following *Birbrower.*

Colorado law, solicit or accept Colorado clients, and apply for pro hac vice admission where available.[24] As a result, Colorado is more generous to out-of-state lawyers than these lawyers' home states are to Colorado lawyers. What motivates the Colorado Supreme Court to help out-of-state lawyers?

6. Has Model Rule 5.5 solved "the MJP problem"? A 2017 article argued that it has not.[25] One of the reasons given is that the rule has not been uniformly adopted. Some jurisdictions have not provided any safe harbors, while others have adopted significantly more restrictive versions of the ABA safe harbors, particularly the "catch-all" safe harbor in MR 5.5(c)(4).[26] Other continuing problems are the failure to adequately address virtual practice (for example, by a lawyer who commutes to work and works on evenings and weekends remotely from a state where the lawyer is not licensed to practice) and the difficulty of determining when a temporary out-of-state representation arises out of or is "reasonably related" to the lawyer's in-state practice.[27] The authors proposed federal legislation that would permit lawyers licensed in any U.S. jurisdiction to practice law in every other U.S. jurisdiction with respect to certain matters, including those "affecting interstate or foreign commerce."[28]

b. Safe Harbors for Systematic Presence

Model Rule 5.5(d) provides two safe harbors for a lawyer's more permanent presence in a jurisdiction in which the lawyer is not licensed. The first is for in-house lawyers. Rule 5.5(d)(1) authorizes them to provide legal services to their employer "or its organizational affiliates," except for services requiring pro hac vice admission. The need for such an exception arises from the fact that in-house lawyers are often expected to move from state to state as the employer's needs dictate, and it is impractical to expect such lawyers to obtain a new admission to practice each time the lawyer moves. In addition, organizational clients with in-house lawyers are typically sophisticated clients who can evaluate the lawyer's qualifications; as a result, such clients are unlikely to need the protection that UPL laws afford to other clients. Many jurisdictions require out-of-state in-house lawyers to register with the host state, pay fees for client protection funds, and complete mandatory continuing legal education requirements applicable to in-state lawyers. Some states also permit such lawyers to provide pro bono services for indigent clients.[29]

---

24. *See* Colo. R. Civ. P. 205 1(1)-(2). *See also* Va. UP Op. 2001 (out-of-state lawyers may practice from a Virginia office so long as they limit their practice to the law of their home state or federal law and they include these limitations on their letterhead and in public communications).

25. James W. Jones et al., Reforming Lawyer Mobility—Protecting Turf or Serving Clients?, 30 Geo. J. Legal Ethics 125 (2017).

26. *Id.* at 131-33.

27. *Id.* at 133-35.

28. *Id.* at 189-93.

29. *See, e.g.,* Erica M. Spitzig, License to Serve: Reevaluating Multijurisdictional Pro Bono Rules for In-House Counsel, 21 Geo. J. Legal Ethics 1081 (2008).

Model Rule 5.5(d)(2) permits a lawyer to establish an office or other systematic presence if the lawyer is authorized to do so "by federal law or by other law of the jurisdiction." Authorization by federal law includes admission to practice before a federal court or agency, although lawyers sometimes get in trouble by failing to limit their practice to federal matters. An example of practice authorized by state law other than the rules of professional conduct are state court rules that permit the spouses of full-time active-duty military personnel to practice law without taking the state's bar examination.[30]

3. Regulating Out-of-State Lawyers

a. Authority to Discipline

What happens when an out-of-state lawyer engages in conduct, in the host state, that violates a rule of professional conduct? Traditionally, each state limited its disciplinary authority to lawyers who were licensed to practice in that state. The home state can itself discipline the lawyer for conduct that occurred in another, host state, but it may be unlikely to do so, in part because the complainant typically resides in the host state and does not file a complaint with disciplinary authorities in the lawyer's home state.

As part of the ABA's 2002 amendments, Rule 8.5(a) was amended to provide that "[a] lawyer not admitted in this jurisdiction is subject to the disciplinary authority of this jurisdiction if the lawyer provides or offers to provide any legal services in this jurisdiction." As a result, the host state now has the authority to discipline the out-of-state lawyer who commits professional conduct while providing legal services in that state or offering to do so through advertising or solicitations. But what sort of discipline can a non-licensing state impose? The host state cannot disbar or suspend the lawyer's license to practice, and although it can reprimand the lawyer, as in *Charges of Unprofessional Conduct*, it is unclear whether such a limited sanction is of much value. One additional sanction that host state courts can impose is to announce that the out-of-state lawyer may not seek pro hac vice or other form of admission to practice in the host state without further action on the part of the court.[31]

In addition, the host state may conclude that it would have imposed a more serious sanction, such as suspension or disbarment, and then rely on "reciprocal discipline," a concept that appears in Rule 22 of the ABA Model

---

30. *See, e.g.*, Military Spouse Authorization to Engage in the Practice of Law in Florida, ch. 21, Rules Regulating the Florida Bar (2020). These rules were prompted by federal legislation directing the Department of Defense to work with the states to relax licensure requirements that make it difficult for spouses to join military personnel who are permanently relocated to another jurisdiction.

31. *See, e.g.*, In re Jardine, 764 S.E.2d 924 (S.C. 2014) (sanctioning Utah lawyer who solicited by direct mail a South Carolina resident, without providing information required under the South Carolina Rules of Professional Conduct).

Rules for Lawyer Disciplinary Enforcement. Under this rule, whenever one state disciplines a lawyer, that discipline should be respected and enforced in any state where the lawyer is licensed. The rule had traditionally been used when a lawyer was licensed in multiple jurisdictions, but it now includes discipline that would have been imposed in a state where the lawyer was not licensed.[32] Rule 22 provides an exception when there were serious deficiencies in the process whereby the lawyer was initially disciplined or where "[t]he discipline imposed would result in grave injustice or be offensive to the public policy of the jurisdiction."

b. *Choice of Law*

Regardless whether it is the host state or a home state that is exercising its authority to discipline a lawyer, which state's rules of professional conduct will apply when the lawyer's conduct involves multiple states and the content of their rules differ? This "choice of law" problem is addressed in Model Rule 8.5(b), which has separate provisions for litigation and transactional matters.

For litigation, Rule 8.5(b)(1) provides that "for conduct in connection with a matter pending before a tribunal, the rules of the jurisdiction in which the tribunal sits [shall be applied], unless the rules of the tribunal provide otherwise." A prior version of this rule did not require that the matter be "pending" so long as it involved the lawyer engaged in "conduct in connection" with a subsequent proceeding,[33] and some states retain this prior, broader provision of (b)(1). Even when the matter is pending, the choice-of-law question may be difficult, as when the parties seek to modify a fee agreement or fee-splitting agreement initially made prior to the filing of a lawsuit.

Consider, for example, a lawyer and client who both reside in State A and who negotiate a contingent fee agreement for a lawsuit to be filed in State B. Which state's rules govern the lawyer's conduct in entering into this agreement? What if the lawyer and the client seek to modify the fee agreement after the lawsuit is filed? Does it make sense to say that a different state's rules govern the initial agreement and its subsequent modification?[34]

These difficulties are compounded when there is aggregate or other complex litigation. For example, consider a lawyer representing hundreds of individual clients with tort claims against a common defendant. Some of the claims have been filed in a lawsuit (often in multiple lawsuits pending in different state and/or federal courts), whereas other claims have not yet been filed. Which state's version of Rule 1.8(g) governs the ability of the lawyer to

---

32. *See, e.g.,* In re Harper, 785 A.2d 311 (D.C. 2001) (disbarring D.C. lawyer who had been "disbarred" by Maryland court for unlawful practice of law and other disciplinary violations in Maryland).

33. *See* MR 8.5(b)(1) (1993).

34. *See* Nancy J. Moore, Choice of Law for Professional Responsibility Issues in Aggregate Litigation, 14 Roger Williams U. L. Rev. 73, 81 (2009).

enter into an aggregate settlement offered by the defendant that is intended to settle all of the clients' claims?[35]

As for transactional matters, Rule 8.5(b)(2) provides that the rules to be applied are "the rules of the jurisdiction in which the lawyer's conduct occurred, or, if the predominant effect of the conduct is in a different jurisdiction, the rules of that jurisdiction. . . ." Where does a lawyer's conduct occur when the lawyer is engaged in multijurisdictional practice through telephone, email, or other form of digital communication? Imagine, for example, three lawyers negotiating a deal from their offices in three different states, say New Jersey, Pennsylvania, and Rhode Island. Where are their conversations occurring? And where is the predominant effect of their negotiations? One of the lawyers may have recently learned that the lawyer's client is committing a crime or fraud in connection with the transaction being negotiated. New Jersey's rules of professional conduct *require* disclosure, Pennsylvania's rules *permit* disclosure, and Rhode Island's rules *prohibit* disclosure. In determining which state's rules apply, does it matter where the lawyer is licensed? Where the lawyer's client and the other parties reside? What other factors might affect the resolution of this difficult choice-of-law problem? A New York ethics opinion includes as relevant factors where the clients live and work, where any payments will be deposited, where any contract will be performed, and where a new business will operate.[36]

The comment to Rule 8.5 was amended in 2013 to permit lawyers to enter into "a written agreement between the lawyer and client that reasonably specifies a particular jurisdiction," but only with respect to conflicts of interest and only when "the agreement was obtained with the client's informed consent confirmed in the agreement." MR 8.5, cmt [5].

Review Problems

15-1 A lawyer is a sole practitioner whose practice targets low- to middle-income clients for routine legal services, such as simple wills, no-fault divorces, home purchases, and representation in landlord-tenant disputes. In order to make a profit, the lawyer must obtain a high volume of clients. To represent large numbers of clients, the lawyer employs several paralegals, each of whom is trained to focus on a particular type of matter. After training and supervising the paralegals to the point where the lawyer is satisfied that they can operate on their own with minimal supervision, the lawyer permits the paralegals to meet with clients, identify their needs, provide them with the necessary advice, and negotiate with adversaries and other parties. They are instructed to come to the lawyer with any questions, particularly

---

35. *See id.* at 90-91. Although states generally adopt a similar version of Rule 1.8(g), there are potential differences in how courts determine such issues as what constitutes an aggregate settlement and precisely what information the lawyer must convey to the clients with respect to "the existence and nature of all the claims . . . involved and the participation of each person in the settlement."

36. *See* N.Y. State Ethics Op. 1027 (2014).

if the client's matter is at all complex. They prepare pleadings for litigation matters, although the lawyer reviews and signs any papers filed with a court. Is the lawyer's conduct proper? What are the possible consequences for any improper conduct?

15-2 A trusts and estates lawyer is licensed to practice in State A. The lawyer has an office in State A but resides in State B. Most of her clients come from referrals from existing and former clients. Many of the lawyer's clients reside in State B. Some of the State B clients meet with the lawyer in the lawyer's office in State A, where the lawyer advises them on the legal requirements for executing a will or creating a trust in State B and assists them in executing any necessary documents. With respect to State B clients who are unable or unwilling to travel to the lawyer's office in State A, the lawyer uses the telephone and videoconferencing for the initial meeting and advising sessions and then meets with them either at the clients' homes or at the lawyer's residence in order to execute the necessary documents. In the evenings and on weekends, the lawyer works at the lawyer's residence, including calling and emailing clients. A competitor filed a complaint with the State B disciplinary authority, and that authority is investigating whether the lawyer has engaged in the unauthorized practice of law in State B. How should the lawyer respond? Is the lawyer engaged in the practice of law in State B? If so, do any of the Model Rule 5.5 "safe harbors" apply?

15-3 A lawyer is employed by a company as in-house counsel. The lawyer is licensed in State A and began working for the company when it was headquartered in that state. The lawyer moved to State B, where the lawyer is not licensed, when the company moved its headquarters to that state. The lawyer provides legal services to the company and to its affiliates, many of whom are located in various states in all parts of the country. With the permission of the company's board of directors, which is fully aware of the limits of the lawyer's licensure, the lawyer also provides occasional legal services to the company's executives. When the services provided to an executive relate to the lawyer's representation of the company, such as when the government is investigating both the company and its executives, the lawyer obtains the informed consent of the board to any conflict of interest. When the services are personal and unrelated, such as assisting the executive in the purchase of a new home, no specific board approval is required. Is the lawyer engaged in the unauthorized practice of law in State B?

CHAPTER 16

NONLAWYER OWNERSHIP, MULTIDISCIPLINARY PRACTICE, AND ALTERNATIVE LEGAL SERVICE PROVIDERS

Model Rule 5.4

All but two U.S. jurisdictions currently prohibit lawyers from forming a business entity with a nonlawyer owner when any of the entity's activities constitute the practice of law.[1] These restrictions preclude nonlawyer ownership in law firms, including both nonlawyer professionals who actively assist in client representation and passive investors who could provide a firm with greater access to capital to expand or improve legal services. Also precluded are multidisciplinary practices (MDP), in which an entity provides legal services along with other goods or services. Outside the United States, countries are increasingly permitting a wide range of nontraditional structures known as alternative business structures (ABS).

This chapter addresses the current U.S. prohibitions on nonlawyer ownership in law firms and lawyer participation in multidisciplinary practices. The chapter also describes recent innovations outside the United States, noting some of the legal and practical difficulties confronting efforts to reform the U.S. legal profession along similar lines. Finally, it highlights what appears to be a growing movement by states to consider a variety of reforms, with the goal of promoting greater access to justice, as well as innovations in the private sector that deliver services that look much like legal services but which arguably do not constitute the unauthorized practice of law.

---

1. As discussed below, this prohibition is based in large part on Model Rule 5.4(d)(1). The Supreme Court of Arizona recently eliminated Rule 5.4 entirely. Arizona's decision to welcome innovation in lawyer and nonlawyer collaboration, as well as Utah's creation of a pilot program and some other states' appointment of task forces to study similar proposals, are discussed in Section E below. The District of Columbia's more limited reform of Rule 5.4, which permits a limited form of nonlawyer ownership of law firms, is discussed below in this section.

A. UPL, MODEL RULE 5.4, AND THE CURRENT STRUCTURE OF LAW PRACTICE

Unauthorized practice of law restrictions, addressed in the preceding chapter, prohibit not only nonlawyer individuals, but also for-profit entities such as corporations and partnerships from engaging in the practice of law, even when the person providing the legal services is a licensed lawyer.[2] In addition, Model Rule 5.4, which has been adopted in substance by all U.S. jurisdictions except Arizona and the District of Columbia,[3] prohibits a variety of practices that would otherwise permit or enhance a lawyer's ability to work alongside nonlawyers in law firms and to participate in multidisciplinary practices, or other forms of alternative business structures.

Model Rule 5.4(a) provides that, with certain limited exceptions, lawyers may not share legal fees with nonlawyers. Rule 5.4(b) prohibits a lawyer from "form[ing] a partnership with a nonlawyer if any of the activities of the partnership consist of the practice of law."[4] Rule 5.4(c) prohibits a lawyer from "permit[ting] a person who recommends, employs, or pays the lawyer to render legal services for another to direct or regulate the lawyer's professional judgment in rendering such legal services." And, finally, Rule 5.4(d) provides:

> A lawyer shall not practice with or in the form of a professional corporation or association authorized to practice law for a profit if:
> (1) a nonlawyer owns any interest therein . . . ;[5]
> (2) a nonlawyer is a corporate director or officer thereof or occupies the position of similar responsibility in any form of association other than a corporation; or
> (3) a nonlawyer has the right to direct or control the professional judgment of a lawyer.

The sole explanation provided for the rule is that these limitations are traditional and serve "to protect the lawyer's professional independence of judgment." MR 5.4, cmt [1]. Critics object that these rules serve the interests of established law firms, at the expense of lawyers who could benefit from increased employment opportunities in alternative business structures, and that they harm the public by limiting access to cheaper, more efficient, and otherwise beneficial law and law-related services.[6]

---

2. These prohibitions obviously do not apply to professional corporations or other entities owned solely by licensed lawyers.

3. *See supra* n. 1.

4. This provision has been construed to encompass other forms of entities with nonlawyer ownership that provide legal services. Some state versions of this rule expressly acknowledge this extension of the rule. *See, e.g.,* Mass. Rules of Prof'l Conduct, R. 5.4(b) ("A lawyer shall not form a partnership or other business entity with a nonlawyer if any of the activities of the entity consist of the practice of law.")

5. This provision contains an exception for the fiduciary representative of a deceased lawyer who holds the lawyer's stock for a reasonable time during the administration of the estate.

6. For criticism of the ABA's refusal to adopt a version of Rule 5.4 that would have permitted lawyers to work for nonlawyer entities so long as they did not permit nonlawyers to direct or regulate their independent judgment, *see* Stephen Gillers, What We Talked About When We Talked About Ethics: A Critical View of the Model Rules, 46 Ohio St.L.J. 243, 266-69 (1985).

B. PROHIBITING NONLAWYER OWNERSHIP OF LAW FIRMS

1. Nonlawyers Actively Assisting in Client Representation

The District of Columbia's version of Rule 5.4 permits lawyers to practice law in for-profit entities in which ownership or managerial authority "is exercised by an individual nonlawyer who performs professional services which assist the organization in providing legal services to clients" if the following conditions are met: the entity provides only legal services; all such nonlawyer professionals agree to abide by the rules of professional conduct; and the lawyer owners and managers agree to be responsible for the nonlawyer professionals to the same extent that they are responsible for other firm lawyers.[7] The assurances must be set forth in writing.

According to the ABA Commission on Ethics 20/20's Working Group on Alternative Business Structures, "the purpose of [reforms such as contained in the D.C. rule] regarding the possession of a financial interest or the exercise of management authority by a nonlawyer is to permit nonlawyer professionals to work with lawyers in the delivery of legal services without being relegated to the role of an employee."[8] Thus the D.C. rule "permits economists to work in a firm with antitrust or public utility practitioners, psychologists or psychiatric social workers to work with family law practitioners to assist in counseling clients, nonlawyer lobbyists to work with lawyers who perform legislative services, certified public accounts to work in conjunction with tax lawyers or others who use accountants' services in performing legal services, and professional managers to serve as office managers, executive directors, or in similar positions."[9]

In 2011, the Ethics 20/20 Commission circulated a draft proposal that mimicked the D.C. rule, but contained the additional restrictions that lawyers would have to maintain the controlling financial interest and a majority of voting rights and that the lawyer partners would have to conduct an inquiry establishing the good character of any nonlawyer owner.[10] Shortly thereafter, presumably after receiving substantial objections to the proposal, the Commission decided not to propose any changes on nonlawyer ownership of law firms.[11]

---

7. D.C. Rules of Prof'l Conduct, R. 5.4. The responsibility of partners, managers, and supervisors for the conduct of other firm lawyers is set forth in D.C. Rule 5.1, which closely tracks Model Rule 5.1.

8. *See* ABA Commission on Ethics 20/20 Working Group on Alternative Business Structures, for Comment: Issues Paper Concerning Alternative Business Structures 18-19 (Apr. 5, 2011).

9. *Id.* at 19.

10. *See* Jamie S. Gorelick & Michael Traynor, Co-Chairs, ABA Commission on Ethics 20/20, For Comment: Discussion Paper on Alternative Law Practice Structures (Dec. 2, 2011).

11. *See* ABA Commission on Ethics 20/20 Will Not Propose Changes to ABA Policy Prohibiting Nonlawyer Ownership of Law Firms (Apr. 16, 2012).

474   Chapter 16 Nonlawyer Ownership, Multidisciplinary Practice

NOTES AND QUESTIONS

1. Nonlawyers are currently permitted to assist lawyers within a law firm if they are non-managerial employees rather than owners.[12] In what way does nonlawyer ownership or management threaten a lawyer's "professional independence of judgment"? Isn't a lawyer's independent judgment also threatened by lawyer owners motivated to improve "profits per partner," which is frequently the measure of a law firm's success in the legal marketplace?[13]

2. If the salary is high enough, shouldn't law firms be able to secure the services of qualified nonlawyer professionals as employees? How does Model Rule 5.4 limit the ability of law firms to work with such nonlawyer professionals?

3. If one of the concerns underlying the current restrictions is that non-lawyer owners and managers will not act in accordance with rules of professional conduct, isn't it sufficient that, under both the D.C. rule and the proposed ABA rule, the lawyer owners are held responsible for the conduct of the nonlawyer owners? The proposed ABA rule would have also required nonlawyer owners to state, in writing, that "they have read and understand the Rules of Professional Conduct and agree in writing to undertake to conform their conduct to the Rules."

4. According to the Ethics 20/20 Commission, one of the objections to the proposed ABA rule is that nonlawyer ownership of law firms "could diminish the profession's current judicially-based system of regulation by expanding the scope of professional regulation beyond its traditional focus on lawyers, thus making external regulation more likely."[14] Given that both the D.C. rule and the proposed ABA rule depend on firm lawyers to control the conduct of nonlawyer owners and managers, is this concern valid? Later in this chapter we discuss alternative legal service providers (ALSP), that is, nonlawyer-owned entities that are currently providing services that arguably do not violate current unauthorized practice of law restrictions.[15] One of the questions raised there is how, as nonlawyers, these entities and their nonlawyer owners and participants can be adequately regulated.

---

12. Model Rule 5.3 requires lawyer supervision over such nonlawyer employees. It also requires lawyer supervision over nonlawyers outside a firm who are retained by a lawyer to assist in the representation of a client.

13. For example, the AM Law 100 ranks law firms by profits per equity partner. *See, e.g.,* https://www.law.com/americanlawyer/2020/04/21/the-2020-am-law-100-ranked-by-profits-per-equity-partner/?slreturn=20201109144614.

14. *See* Gorelick & Traynor, *supra* note 10 at 3.

15. *See infra* Section E.

2. Passive Investment in Law firms

A law firm's ability to access the capital needed to finance its future growth is currently limited to individual partner contributions, bank loans, and other forms of credit, including loan products such as anticipated attorney fee advances.[16] Outside investment in the law firm, if permitted, would provide additional capital that could be used to expand and improve the firm's delivery of legal services, including through enhanced technology that makes legal services more efficient and therefore cheaper. These potential benefits were at the heart of consumer law firm Jacoby & Meyers's constitutional challenge to New York's prohibition on outside investment in law firms, as described in the following court decision rejecting that challenge.

Jacoby & Meyers, LLP v. Presiding Justices
852 F.3d 178 (2d Cir. 2017)

SUSAN L. CARNEY, Circuit Judge;

Though a set of prohibitions of long standing in New York and similar to those widely prevalent in the fifty states and the District of Columbia, the State of New York prohibits non-attorneys from investing in law firms. The prohibition is generally seen as helping to ensure the independence and ethical conduct of lawyers. Plaintiffs-Appellants Jacoby & Meyers, LLP, a limited liability partnership (the "LLP"), and Jacoby & Meyers USA II, PLLC, a related professional limited liability company (the "PLLC"; together, "plaintiffs" or the "J&M Firms") bring a putative class action challenging New York's rules, regulations, and statutes prohibiting such investments. The infusions of additional capital that the regulations now prevent, they declare, would enable the J&M Firms to improve the quality of the legal services that they offer and at the same time to reduce their fees, expanding their ability to serve needy clients. They assert that, were they able to do so, they would act on that ability in the interests of such potential clients. Because the laws currently restrict their ability to accomplish those goals, they maintain, the state regime unlawfully interferes with their rights *as lawyers* to associate with clients and to access the courts—rights they see as grounded in the First Amendment.

The United States District Court for the Southern District of New York (Kaplan, *Judge*), dismissed the complaint for failure to allege the infringement of any cognizable constitutional right. On de novo review, we identify no error in that conclusion. Neither as a for-profit law partnership nor as a professional limited liability company do the J&M Firms have the associational or petition rights that they claim. Even were we to assume, given the evolving

---

16. In addition, plaintiffs' law firms have recently benefitted from litigation funding agreements, in which lenders provide capital to underwrite litigation, in return for a share of any recovery. For a discussion of some ethical issues that arise in connection with these agreements, *see, e.g.,* ABA Comm'n on Ethics 20/20, Informational Report to the House of Delegates (Feb. 2012).

nature of commercial speech protections, that they possess some such First Amendment interests, the regulations at issue here are adequately supported by state interests and have too little effect on the attorney-client relationship to be viewed as imposing an unlawful burden on the J&M Firms' constitutional interests. . . .

Founded in 1972, Jacoby & Meyers, LLP, is a New York-based law partnership that "maintains a network of affiliated law offices across the country, including in Southern California, New York, Alabama, Florida, and Arizona." The LLP presents as its mission the following: "[T]o ensure that people of modest or average means, who could often not afford to hire a lawyer, ha[ve] a practical alternative to obtain competent, qualified counsel at reasonable rates." . . .

The LLP alleges that it "wishes to expand its operations, hire additional attorneys and staff, acquire new technology, and improve its physical offices and infrastructure to increase its ability to serve its existing clients and to attract and retain new clients and qualified attorneys." To make these improvements, the LLP asserts, it requires capital contributions. It reports receiving "numerous offers" from "prospective non-lawyer investors . . . who are prepared to invest capital in exchange for owning an interest in the firm." These include some "high net-worth individuals" and "institutional investors." And it would accept such contributions through the vehicle of the professional limited liability company that it has formed for this purpose. But in light of New York's prohibitions, it has "been relegated to obtaining capital from (i) the personal contributions of the partners, (ii) retained earnings on fees generated and collected, and (iii) commercial bank loans, which invariably come with onerous interest rates and intrusive covenants and conditions." Moreover, these potential alternative sources of capital are either not available in practice, or too costly to be used.

In 2011, the LLP sued the Presiding Justices of New York Supreme Court's Appellate Divisions (who administer Rule 5.4) and others. . . . [A] second amended complaint . . . attempted to articulate a constitutional challenge to the entire New York regulatory regime. [The district court granted the state's motion to dismiss, holding that the amended complaint failed to state a claim for a violation of any constitutional right.]

[The Second Circuit court addressed and rejected plaintiffs' claims based on the First Amendment. It held that individual attorneys who engage in litigation "for their own commercial rewards" have no First Amendment expressive rights to associate with clients, unlike attorneys who "are part of an advocacy group like the ACLU or the NAACP." It next rejected the plaintiffs' claim that their lawyers have First Amendment rights of access to courts on behalf of their clients or that they have a right "to associate with clients *qua* clients." It then assumed that the law might evolve to recognize that the J&M Firms could be found to have some First Amendment right to associate with clients or bring lawsuits on behalf of their clients, but concluded that "the regulations are supported by substantial government interests and impose an insubstantial burden on the exercise of any such First Amendment rights."]

Because we hold that the J&M Firms' complaint does not plausibly allege the infringement of any First Amendment right, we need not stay long with the question whether New York's interests as a state justify its regulations regarding non-lawyer investments.

The J&M Firms ask us to apply strict scrutiny to the regulations. . . . Strict scrutiny applies only when a challenged regulation imposes "severe burdens" on associational rights. As discussed above, however, no First Amendment right of the J&M Firms is even implicated by the challenged regulations, much less substantially burdened by them.

Accordingly, rational basis review applies. The regulations at issue plainly survive that standard because they are rationally related to a legitimate government interest. As the District Court noted, and as we think is cognizable even on a motion to dismiss, the challenged laws serve New York State's well-established interest in regulating attorney conduct and in maintaining ethical behavior and independence among the members of the legal profession. For example, by proscribing the involvement of unrelated third parties in the attorney-client relationship, the regulations preclude the creation of incentives for attorneys to violate ethical norms, such as those requiring attorneys to put their clients' interests foremost. They therefore easily pass muster under rational basis review. . . .

We AFFIRM the judgment of the District Court.

NOTES AND QUESTIONS

1. Competitive pressures create an increasing need for law firms to find additional sources of capital to finance the acquisition of the information technology necessary to provide more efficient legal services, to open more offices (including foreign law offices), and to develop innovative legal structures.[17] Because these types of long-term developments may not be profitable in the short term, current law firm partners are reluctant to fund them through capital contributions or reduced annual profits.[18] Outside investment by nonlawyers could provide such capital. An additional argument in favor of outside investment, including the public trading of law firm shares, is that the ability of current law firm partners to purchase such shares, or receive them as stock options in lieu of cash bonuses, would incentivize these partners to make the long-term investments that will create future law firm value. Aside from the benefits accruing to the law firms themselves, proponents

---

17. *See* Milton C. Regan, Jr., Lawyers, Symbols, and Money: Outside Investment in Law Firms, 27 Penn State Int'l L. Rev. 407, 422 (2009).

18. *Id.*

of outside investment argue, as did Jacoby & Meyers, that additional funding can lower the cost of legal services and increase the public's access to legal services.

2. As with nonlawyer owners who actively assist in representation, the primary concern with passive outside investment is that nonlawyer investors will adversely affect the independent judgment of lawyers in favor of increasing the value of their investment. According to Milton Regan, the risk is even greater with outside investors because, unlike both lawyer and nonlawyer active partners, an investor's interest in the firm is typically one-dimensional, focused on either share price or an immediate return on the investment.[19] And even if outside investors are limited to a minority of firm shares or given non-voting shares, they can influence the direction of the firm by selling (or threatening to sell) their shares.[20] But is their ability to influence lawyer conduct any different than the similar ability of current law firm lenders, who may require "financial benchmarks for the firm that can effectively constrain firms' freedom of action"?[21]

3. Australia and the United Kingdom amended their laws in 2000 and 2007, respectively, to permit outside investment, among other innovations. And in the United States, the Supreme Court of Arizona, by order dated August 2020, deleted Rule 5.4 from its rules of professional conduct, effective January 1, 2021, thereby also permitting outside investment, as well as other reforms that were adopted in Australia and the United Kingdom, such as multidisciplinary practices. These reforms are discussed in Sections D and E below.

C. PROHIBITING MULTIDISCIPLINARY PRACTICES

Multidisciplinary practices (MDPs) are entities that provide legal services along with other goods or services. The legal services are provided by lawyers, but because the entity is owned by nonlawyers, or by a combination of lawyers and nonlawyers, lawyer participation in such entities is prohibited by Rule 5.4. One form of MDP provides legal services along with related professional services in order to provide clients with "one-stop shopping," rather than forcing them to retain separate service providers. Another form of MDP involves a variation on nonlawyer ownership of law firms, in which lawyers would work in a law-firm-like setting, but within a larger business entity that would play a more-or-less active role in the "law firm's" operations.

---

19. *See id.* at 426. With respect to lawyers' obligations to third persons and to the public generally, Regan notes that "[o]ur experience with publicly owned corporations suggests that concern for share price can place significant pressure on behavior." *Id.* at 430.

20. *Id.* at 425.

21. *Id.* at 427.

1. Interdisciplinary Service Providers

The following Wisconsin State Bar Ethics Opinion describes how an interdisciplinary, "one-stop shopping" MDP might work and illustrates an unsuccessful attempt to work around the current prohibition on such practices.

State Bar of Wisconsin

Lawyer Practicing in Interdisciplinary Organization
Formal Op. E-84-21 (1998)

FACTS

A lawyer is considering becoming involved in an organization "to provide the public with an interdisciplinary approach to financial planning." The organization would be composed of a lawyer, an accountant, a licensed securities broker and two life insurance agents and intends to offer itself to the public as a planning organization that works strictly on a "fee as a percentage of income basis."

This organization would collect data, talk with the individual, discuss the individual's options between and among the professionals involved and then make a series of recommendations to the individual over a broad range of financial planning possibilities. It would be contemplated that the disciplines of each of the professionals involved would be used to make the kinds of recommendations in areas traditionally dealt with by those professionals. However, it is felt that the interdisciplinary approach will allow a unified or complete plan.

QUESTION

Presuming that there is no ethical problem with a lawyer becoming a part owner in such an organization and receiving a salary and/or dividends, or in the alternative, participating with this organization on an independent basis for a fee, what is the appropriate use of referrals and the division of fees in such an organization?

OPINION

Before questions concerning referrals and the division of fees may be addressed, the propriety of a lawyer being involved in an organization as discussed above needs to be examined. The Wisconsin Code of Professional Responsibility . . . states that a lawyer may not form a partnership with a non-lawyer if any of the activities of the partnership consist of the practice of law.[22] Accordingly it would be improper for a lawyer to be a partner in the

---

22. [This same prohibition now appears in Model Rule 5.4(b). — ED.]

organization described above if any of his or her activities as a partner would consist of the practice of law.

In the alternative, it is suggested that the lawyer's participation with the organization could be on an independent basis for a fee. However, in Formal Opinion E-61-1, the Committee on Professional Ethics stated that under no circumstance may a lawyer permit his or her professional services to be controlled or exploited by any lay agency or other intermediary by intervention between himself or herself and any client. The committee continued, a lawyer "shall avoid all relationships by which the performances of his duties may be directed by, or *in the interest of* such intermediary" (emphasis added).

In addition to the above, there are several problems inherent in the proposed participation in this organization, even if it were on an "independent basis." First, [the Wisconsin Code of Professional Responsibility] states that a lawyer may not request a person or organization to recommend employment, as a private practitioner, of herself or himself.[23] Participation in the organization, however, would be tantamount to a request for recommendations. Second, [the Wisconsin Code of Professional Responsibility] states that the obligations of a lawyer to exercise professional judgment solely on behalf of a client requires that she disregard the desires of others that might impair his or her free judgment.[24] It is certainly possible that a lawyer participant in such an organization could be subject to strong economic, political or social pressures by other professionals involved in the organization. In light of the fact that a lawyer should work solely for the benefit of the client, subjecting himself or herself to such pressures is highly undesirable.

Finally, [the Wisconsin Code of Professional Responsibility] states that a lawyer should preserve the confidences and secrets of a client.[25] The purpose of the organization is to provide a "unified or complete" financial plan for clients whereby the clients' options would be discussed "between and among the professionals involved." Although clients may of course waive the attorney-client privilege, the situation presented involving discussions by a group of financial planning professionals would seem to require some form of "blanket consent" to disclosure of client confidences and secrets before effective assistance could being. However, requiring such "blanket consent" before representation may begin is not permissible conduct. Rather, [the Wisconsin Code of Professional Responsibility] requires "full disclosure" to a client of the effect of his or her consent to disclosures of confidences and secrets. In

---

23. [Model Rule 7.2 generally prohibits compensating something of value in return for such a recommendation, but it does not prohibit requesting recommendations or referrals from either lawyers or nonlawyers.—ED.]

24. [As discussed above, Model Rule 5.4(c) prohibits a lawyer from permitting a person who recommends, employs, or pays a lawyer to render legal services to direct or regulate the lawyer's professional judgment.—ED.]

25. [Model Rule 1.6 governs the confidentiality of client information. See *supra* Chapter 4: Privilege and Confidentiality.—ED.]

C. Prohibiting Multidisciplinary Practices   **481**

order to fully disclose such effects, the client's representative must take the client's individual circumstances into account. . . .

In light of the above, it appears that it would be improper for a lawyer to be a part owner or to participate independently with a financial planning organization as described. Accordingly, it is unnecessary to specifically address the referral and division of fee questions posed.

NOTES AND QUESTIONS

1. In 1998, the year the Wisconsin ethics opinion was issued, the then-ABA president created a Commission on Multidisciplinary Practice "to determine what changes, if any, should be made to the ABA Model Rules of Professional Conduct with respect to the delivery of legal services by professional services firms."[26] The Commission recommended changes to permit some forms of MDPs; however, in July 2000 the ABA House of Delegates voted overwhelmingly to reject any form of MDP and to precipitously end the work of the Commission.[27] The approved resolution expressed the sponsors' concerns that "the ownership and control of the practice of law by nonlawyers" was incompatible with the "core principles and values" of the legal profession, including "undivided loyalty to a client, competence, and confidentiality."[28] Since then, various efforts have been made within the ABA to revive the discussion, including by the ABA Commission on Ethics 20/20 and the ABA Commission on the Future of Legal Services; however, all that has been achieved is a lukewarm statement by the Commission on the Future of Legal Services that "continued exploration of [MDPs and other alternative business structures (ABS)] will be useful" and a recommendation that the ABA engage in "an organized and centralized effort to collect ABS-related information and data."[29]

2. One of the cited core values, "undivided loyalty," is reflected not only in the concern for lawyer independence that underlies Model Rule 5.4, but also in the conflict-of-interest rules embodied in Model Rules 1.7-1.10. Consider how the MDP proposed in Ethics Opinion 84-21 would implicate current conflicts of interest under Model Rules 1.7 and 1.10. For example, what if the lawyer's client wants to engage in a transaction that is adverse to one of the accountant's financial services clients?

---

26. ABA Comm'n on Multidisciplinary Practice, Report of the Commission on Multidisciplinary Practice to the ABA House of Delegates, 10 Prof. Law. 1 (Spring 1999).

27. *See* Paul D. Paton, Multidisciplinary Practice Redux: Globalization, Core Values, and Revising the MDP Debate in America, 78 Fordham L. Rev. 2193, 2209-10 (2010).

28. ABA House of Delegates Recommendation 10F (adopted July 11, 2000), *available at* http://www.americanbar.org/groups/professional_responsibility/commission_multidisciplinary _practice/mdprecom10f.html [https://perma.cc/3YFL-AN8H?type=image].

29. ABA, Comm'n on the Future of Legal Services, Report on the Future of Legal Services in the United States 42 (2016).

Will Rule 1.10(a) impute conflicts among all of the professional service providers?[30] Such conflicts might be manageable in the context of MDPs comprised of small numbers of professional service providers, but what about a lawyer working for one of the Big Four accounting firms, each of which has far more clients than any of the largest U.S. law firms?[31] One reason that the Big Four accounting firms are so much larger than the largest U.S. law firms is that accounting rules do not require imputation of conflicts to the same extent as do the rules of professional conduct for lawyers.[32] How will the lawyers and the accountants in a single MDP reconcile their different professional ethics rules? Would it be enough to impute conflicts of interests to all of the lawyers in an MDP? Should firms be permitted to use screens to avoid the imputation of conflicts within the MDP?[33]

3. Confidentiality is another "core value" cited in opposition to MDPs. Wisconsin Ethics Opinion 84-21 concluded that clients could not ethically provide "blanket consent" to the sharing of information among the different professionals. Do you agree that such consent is impermissible under Model Rule 1.6? What about the attorney-client privilege? A client's confidential communications to a lawyer will not be privileged if made in the presence of a nonlawyer professional providing related nonlegal services or if subsequently disclosed to the nonlawyer professional for similar nonlegal purposes.[34] And if the goal of the MDP is to offer holistic services, and not separate, compartmentalized services,

---

30. According to John Dzienkowski and Robert Peroni, if the lawyer imputation rules were applied to nonlawyer professionals within an MDP, the firms "would have to consider all of the present and former clients of all service providers in the MDP for purposes of determining whether a conflict exists for the legal department," and therefore "the imputation rules may need to be revised to reflect the modern realities" of large MDPs with a global presence. *See* John S. Dzienkowski & Robert J. Peroni, Multidisciplinary Practice and the American Legal Profession: A Market Approach to Regulating the Delivery of Legal Services in the Twenty-First Century, 69 Fordham L. Rev. 83, 185-86 (2000).

31. According to a 2015 news story, "[t]he largest of the Big Four firms, Deloitte, has more than 13-times the revenue of the largest global law firms, such as Baker & Mackenzie, DLA Piper, Latham, etc." and "[t]he Big Four together have more revenue ($120 billion) than all of the AmLaw 100 firms combined ($89 billion)." *See* David Curie, Why Size Matters: Big Four Accounting Firms Posed to Move In (Apr. 8, 2015), available at https://www.legalexecutiveinstitute.com/why-size-matters-big-four-accounting-firms-poised-to-move-in-by-david-curle/. The reason for this is that the accounting industry is more concentrated, allowing each to serve "many more corporate clients than any law firm ever could." *Id.*

32. *See, e.g.,* James M. McCauley, The Delivery of Legal Services Through Multidisciplinary Practices, 4 Rich. J. L. & Pub. Int. 101, 111 (2000). In addition, accountants apply a narrower test for identifying potentially impermissible conflicts. *See* Laurel S. Terry, A Primer on MDPs: Should the "No" Rule Become a New Rule, 72 Temp. L. Rev. 869, 901-02 (1999).

33. Both suggestions were made by Ernst & Young, one of the Big Four, before the ABA MDP Commission. *See* Kathryn A. Oberly, Ernst and Young General Counsel Statement to the MDP Commission, 1999 Tax Notes Today 29-22 (Feb. 12, 1999).

34. *See supra* Chapter 4: Privilege and Confidentiality. Although common law does not recognize an accountant-client privilege, a federal statute recognizes a limited privilege for federal tax preparers, and some state statutes recognize an accountant-client privilege.

then even a communication made to the lawyer alone might not be protected, because the communication might not have been made predominantly for the purpose of securing legal advice.[35] How can lawyers in an MDP protect a client's attorney-client privilege?

4. At the same time that the ABA House of Delegates slammed the door shut on MDPs, it indicated tacit approval of an argument that the benefits of an MDP could be obtained through "strategic alliances between law firms and non-law firms."[36] In 2002 the ABA agreed to modify Model Rule 7.2 to permit non-exclusive reciprocal referral agreements between a lawyer and a nonlawyer professional, as long as "the client is informed of the existence and nature of the agreement." MR 7.2(b)(4). Are reciprocal referral agreements an adequate substitute for a full MDP? Do they avoid the conflicts of interest inherent in MDPs? For an in-depth treatment of reciprocal referral agreements and an argument that the current rule is "inconsistent with fundamental rules promulgated in the ethics codes," *see* John S. Dzienkowski and Robert J. Peroni, Conflicts of Interest in Lawyer Referral Arrangements with Nonlawyer Professionals, 21 Geo. J. Legal Ethics 197 (2008).

2. Retail and Other Commercial Businesses Offering Legal Services

Sears, Roebuck & Co. is a chain of U.S. department stores. In the 1980s it was the largest retailer in the United States, with brand recognition similar to that of Walmart today. In 1982 the Kutak Commission proposed the original draft of Model Rule 5.4, which would have permitted lawyers to be employed by an entity owned by nonlawyers if "there is no interference with the lawyer's independence of professional judgment or with the client-lawyer relationship" and if the organization complied with the rule regulating the confidentiality of client information, advertising and solicitation, and legal fees.[37] This proposal was rejected by the ABA House of Delegates. Geoffrey Hazard, reporter for the Kutak Commission, recalled that "[d]uring the debate someone asked if [the] proposal would allow Sears, Roebuck to open a law office. When they found out that it would, that was the end of the debate."[38]

In addition to retail goods, Walmart offers financial services, as well as a pharmacy and an optical shop where customers can get an eye exam. It is possible that were it permitted to do so, Walmart would offer legal services, possibly even within its retail stores. What are the advantages to consumers

---

35. *See id.*

36. John S. Dzienkowski & Robert J. Peroni, Conflicts of Interest in Lawyer Referral Arrangements with Nonlawyer Professionals, 21 Geo. J. Legal Ethics 197, 206 (2008).

37. *See* ABA, A Legislative History: The Development of the ABA Model Rules of Professional Conduct, 1982-2013 610 (2013).

38. *See* David Kaplan, Ethics Change in Works: Want to Invest in a Law Firm?, 19 Nat'l L.J. 1 (Jan. 19, 1987).

of being able to purchase their legal services at a retail department store like Walmart? What are the risks to consumers of having their lawyers be salaried employees of Walmart? Are these risks different from those that exist with active and passive nonlawyer ownership of law firms providing only legal services? From the risks associated with interdisciplinary MDPs offering related professional services? As we will see in the following sections, all of these various forms of alternative business structures are currently permitted in some countries outside the United States and in one U.S. jurisdiction.

D. DEVELOPMENTS OUTSIDE THE UNITED STATES: PERMITTING ALTERNATIVE BUSINESS STRUCTURES

The United Kingdom, Australia, and several European countries have authorized the delivery of legal services by alternative business structures (ABSs), that is, entities with some form of ownership by nonlawyers. These countries now permit both nonlawyer ownership of an otherwise traditional law firm and multidisciplinary practices. Lawyers in an ABS are still bound by regulations applicable to other lawyers, and there must be at least one lawyer in each ABS who is responsible for ensuring that the professional rules are followed in the provision of legal services.

The extent of entity regulation differs from country to country. In Australia, for example, nonlawyer ABS firms are required only to register with an appropriate regulator. In the United Kingdom, however, an ABS must be licensed, and potential nonlawyer owners with more than a 10 percent interest must pass a "fit to own" test. Although the focus of regulators is on the conduct of the lawyers delivering legal services through an ABS, both the entities themselves and individual nonlawyers are subject to regulation in some form, including the imposition of sanctions such as excluding a nonlawyer owner from future involvement in an ABS.

In 2016, Judith McMorrow published an analysis of several new UK ABS firms, including: (1) some small law firms that chose ABS status to provide key nonlawyer actors with an ownership interest in the firm; (2) a cooperative that expanded from providing "food, banking, and funeral services to provide more affordable legal services to middle-income clients"; (3) LegalZoom, which can now openly practice law[39] and hopes "to provide more integrated legal services with their online resources"; (4) personal injury firms, including firms owned by insurance and private equity companies; and (5) "[s]pecialty firms [that] have created non-profit and for-profit partnerships, with any profits used to support the non-profit unit."[40] In addition, McMorrow describes an

---

39. LegalZoom is a corporation with nonlawyer ownership that offers online document preparation services. It has been accused in various lawsuits of engaging in the unauthorized practice of law, although it has to date successfully survived such challenges. *See infra* Section E.

40. Judith A. McMorrow, UK Alternative Business Structures for Legal Practice: Emerging Models and Lessons for the U.S., 47 Geo. J. Int'l Law 665, 668 (2016).

ABS called Riverview Law, which "focuses on providing systematized legal services to corporate clients through flat fee and team-based services." The following excerpt provides a detailed description of Riverview Law (since acquired by Big Four accounting firm Ernst & Young), including an analysis of how it differs from a traditional law firm.

Judith McMorrow

UK Alternative Business Structures for Legal Practice: Emerging Models and Lessons for the US
47 Geo. J. Int'l L. 665, 684-91 (2016) . . .

Riverview Law has attracted a great deal of attention, with indication that it is emerging as a success story. Riverview offers a conceptual shift from an income-driven model to a capital appreciation model. Riverview focuses on "legal advisory outsourcing," which "is focused on the 60-70% of legal work that large organizations do every day of the week, every week of the month, every month of the year that can be packaged into long-term contracts." It focuses on the more routinized work, including litigation, leaving in-house counsel to handle the policy and other high-end work, although Riverview input may affect that policy development. Riverview enters into long-term contracts with corporations with the goal of providing tailored legal services.

The law firm arose from the perspective of a customer-oriented service industry that happens to offer legal services. It is no accident that the prime mover, Karl Chapman, has a strong track record in forming and nurturing new businesses. Prior to Riverview Law he had formed AdviserPlus Business Solutions, which is an advisory outsourcing business that provides human resources and health and safety advice and services to a range of businesses. This gave Chapman insights into the infrastructure needs of businesses. It was AdviserPlus client requests wishing for legal services to be offered in a similar model that was one impetus for Riverview. . . .

At first blush it may look like Riverview Law offers the same traditional legal services in the same way, except through flat fee rates. Beneath the surface, however, are both cultural and structural changes from the typical income-driven model of a U.S. law firm. It appears that the business model is built on three key features: (1) team approach to service delivery that allows for flat fee billing and long-term contracts; (2) heavy investment in human capital; and (3) a robust IT system to support the model and provide business value-added to their clients. All three of these aspects of their business model are possible because they have access to capital to build this service.

1. CLIENT TEAM WORK & FLAT FEE

Riverview Law uses fixed fees, coupled with long-term contracts, as a central feature of its business model. Fixed fees are emerging in traditional law firms as well. But the long-term contracts, with a goal of contract renewal, create a very strong alignment of interests between the law firm and clients. This fixed-price model encourages Riverview to invest in efficiency in delivering its own legal services. It creates a structural incentive to reduce the legal problems confronting the client, which advances the business interests of the clients. This model relies heavily on both developing a very competent and effective team at Riverview to serve the needs of the client and an IT infrastructure that will allow Riverview to provide business as well as legal insights. Under this model, the best indication of providing quality services is renewal of the contracts.

2. HUMAN CAPITAL

To actively serve a client's needs, Riverview Law states that it promotes a culture of team service to clients. Most traditional firms claim to offer teamwork and efficiency, but here the structural incentives in the business model promote the goals of teamwork and client satisfaction. Riverview started with no legacy issues of jealousy in guarding billable hours or need to retain client credit, which makes it easier to build a team approach.

With hiring focused on meeting the needs of particular long-term clients, and tailoring skill sets to that client, Riverview Law has an incentive to hire carefully for fit both in terms of Riverview culture and client needs, and train and retain their employees to service the long-term contracts. As a recent Harvard Business School case study noted, Riverview founders worked to build "a culture of autonomy, personal responsibility, a focus on quality, and trust between employees and their managers." Team members have an incentive to develop strong client expertise and, unlike the billable hour model, if team members leave then Riverview, not the client, will pay for the costs of educating and training new team members. Of course it is difficult to penetrate whether there truly is autonomy, responsibility, and trust within the Riverview model, but they at least give voice to these goals. . . .

This investment in human capital also includes creating a work environment that is more attractive to talented professionals. The goal is to create "a strong corporate culture" in which "its hiring, onboarding, performance management, and compensation systems all reinforce the firm's service culture." This means that Riverview Law spends a great deal of time on "recruitment, induction, and training" to assure that employees understand "the company's overall vision and its specific strategy for a particular customer." Riverview conducts much of the day-to-day service in lower cost areas, such as their main offices in Bromborough, Wirral, and Manchester. It emphasizes the liberating effects of shedding the billable hour, and a "positive, energetic and innovative environment." They claim "competitive" salaries although their website is understandably silent on specifics.

3. TECHNOLOGY

A strong team model allows every member of the service team at Riverview Law to contribute data and information. For some business contracts they offer big data analytics by using a sophisticated IT structure to monitor legal issues and claims and pinpoint patterns to the client. With the commitment to long-term contracts, it becomes in Riverview's best interest to reduce the legal problems of the client. Building a robust IT platform that was tailored to the needs of in-house clients has allowed Riverview to launch two new endeavors. In December 2014, Riverview expanded its offerings to create a technology business, creating a unit to license software modules to in-house legal teams and even competing law firms. This does not appear in the original descriptions of Riverview's business, but it is a natural outgrowth of its IT investments. Riverview has also undertaken a partnership with University of Liverpool to bring the university's computer science expertise to the rapidly developing Riverview systems.

4. ACCESS TO CAPITAL

The business model requires heavy investment in personnel and technology in order to service the long-term contracts, and the marketing and business development necessary to acquire these contracts. The investors created an entity called LawVest and the initial business plan anticipated ten years before they would reach profitability. The firm has grown more rapidly than anticipated and it is on track to become profitable. Among Riverview Law's key early investors are DLA Piper, one of the three largest law firms in the world. . . . Having DLA Piper as a key investor means that this cohort of owners understands the professional obligations of Riverview. But even the non-lawyer owners know that they are building a business in a regulated enterprise, so that compliance is a central obligation of the business.

5. LESSONS FOR THE U.S. MARKET

The Riverview Law model might in theory be possible in the United States—flat fees, long term contracts, and heavy IT investment are occurring at some firms. But the Riverview model required an investment of approximately £10 million ($15 million) in setting up the system. There are many barriers to obtaining that kind of investment by U.S. firms. One significant challenge is whether the firms would be able to buy the business expertise needed to launch this model. Individuals with business and IT knowledge who are risk-takers and willing to invest their labors in a service industry start-up are likely to want the ability to be more than a paid employee. They will want to have an equity interest. In addition, the relentless pressure of the AmLaw 100 and emphasis on profits per partner pressures U.S. law firms to have more immediate payout of profits rather than significant investment into the firm. . . . In terms of outside investment, the traditional way to access capital in U.S. law firms is through bank loans. But what rational bank would invest that kind of money in a law firm start up?

As noted above, another advantage of the ABS structure is mind-set and attitude. The mindset issues are twofold. First, as Prof. Bill Henderson has argued, large U.S. law firms are a victim of their own success, with a locked-in business structure that is difficult to change. In an Indiana University Law School competition set up in 2009 to build a new business model for U.S. law firms, all four teams came up with the same basic attributes of customized alternative billing arrangements, new data collection, information sharing with clients, and intensive training. Under this business model associates took lower salaries in exchange for better long-term career prospects, training and more attractive firm cultures. Strikingly, these are attributes of the Riverview Law model. But Riverview did not have the "baggage" of an existing firm. Why should partners in a U.S. law firm with a large book of business invest in this model, rather than elect a short-term and less risky path of moving to another firm that would allow the partner to maintain high per partner profits, or simply taking their profits? If the most profitable partners leave, the firm goes into a death spiral. Bill Henderson concludes that the problem ailing U.S. law firms is "the settled expectations and dulled imagination produced by several decades of large profits and high prestige."

The second mindset problem is the tendency of experienced U.S. lawyers to want control. The ABS model envisions that a team of service professionals can come together as equals. The ABS model requires that the team, whether solicitors, barristers, licensed conveyancers, IT, or managers, knows it has professional obligations to maintain confidences and avoid conflicts, and is exposed to professional malpractice if it violates fiduciary duties.

An ongoing concern of any new delivery model is monitoring the quality of legal services provided. Corporate actors, Riverview Law's target clients, are generally more sophisticated and have greater ability to monitor for quality and assess value in light of the business needs. It seems likely that this Riverview structure will encourage at least as much, if not more, attention to client needs, as the client defines them, than U.S. models of service delivery.

One emerging area of concern has to do with how ABS structure can erode the more public-minded aspects of lawyering. Lawyers, in theory, have three professional obligations: "A lawyer, as a member of the legal profession, is a representative of clients, an officer of the legal system and a public citizen having special responsibility for the quality of justice." The vast majority of attention is given to client focus, and the ABS structure holds promise to improve in many cases the client service.

The second and third obligations—officer of the legal system and a public citizen with special responsibility for the quality of justice—are less clear. [I]t is not apparent that the current regulatory structure puts much emphasis on these obligations beyond limiting lying to a court and third persons. With outside investors it is not clear how much emphasis will be placed on contributing to pro bono activities and putting resources into that special

D. Developments Outside the United States: Permitting Alternative Business Structures

responsibility to improve justice. . . . [T]here appears to be a risk that profit maximization and efficiency concerns may squeeze out these public duties. [I]t is difficult to assess how this risk compares to the serious challenges of promoting public duties, such as pro bono, in the current U.S. service delivery models. Riverview Law mentions its "collective responsibility" and that it is "committed to positively impacting our colleagues, [its] business . . . customers businesses and the wider community" and has a commitment to "act with integrity and are proud of what we do, the role we play in supporting each other and our customers and in shaping the legal profession." It is unclear, however, whether the fast-growing Riverview business has actually included those more public dimensions in their work beyond excellent client service.

NOTES AND QUESTIONS

1. McMorrow had little empirical information concerning the benefits of an ABS like Riverview Law. The fact that the firm was subsequently acquired by Ernst & Young is evidence of its profitability to its owners, but is there any evidence of the benefits of Riverview Law's unique business model to its customers? (Note that Riverview Law uses the term "customers" rather than "clients.") What additional information might help assess the existence and extent of these benefits? Why did McMorrow conclude that these benefits are not otherwise available from traditional law firms?

2. McMorrow also concluded that the business structure of Riverview Law does not compromise the client protection concerns of MDP-objectors in the United States, based on the fact that Riverview Law's customers are sophisticated businesses that can decide for themselves whether they are being adequately served. But what about less sophisticated clients such as individuals seeking family law, real estate, wills and trusts, and even business-related legal advice? Can they be adequately served by an ABS? McMorrow described two UK ABS firms targeting individual clients. The first, Co-Operative Legal Services Limited, "builds on a strong cooperative model in which the firm is owned by its workers, customers and suppliers."[41] It initially offered legal services through solicitors[42] who agreed to charge set fees and meet minimum standards, but subsequently shifted to hiring and supervising solicitors to do the legal work. With the financial backing of its parent company, the legal unit was able to invest heavily in infrastructure and personnel, permitting it to incur losses while it built its client base.

---

41. *Id.* at 691.

42. In the United Kingdom, the legal profession traditionally has been divided between barristers, representing clients in higher courts, and solicitors, representing clients in other matters, including in lower courts. The distinctions between the two branches are breaking down as result of the Legal Services Act of 2007 and other recent reforms.

Unfortunately, economic and management issues plaguing the parent company adversely affected profits from the legal services unit, and it was unclear how committed the parent company was to offering legal services.[43]

3. The second ABS McMorrow described as targeting individual clients is LegalZoom, a corporation with nonlawyer ownership that provides online services such as document preparation. At the time of her study, LegalZoom was still in the planning stages to become a real law firm, with the financial backing of a European private-equity firm. Interestingly, McMorrow noted that because unauthorized practice of law restrictions are less onerous in the United Kingdom than in the United States, LegalZoom did not need to become licensed as an ABS, but nevertheless chose to do so, thereby voluntarily submitting to ABS regulation. She concluded that LegalZoom's decision to submit to regulation "is a very positive signal for the legal profession" because "[b]eing able to call itself a law firm" continues to be "powerful and valuable" as a "signal of quality and professionalism."[44]

4. McMorrow is generally optimistic about the potential benefits of the ABS structure. Her primary concern is for what she calls the "public-minded aspects of lawyering," including not only mandatory duties to courts and third parties, but an aspirational commitment to improve the legal system and to provide pro bono services to clients who cannot otherwise afford them. If the profession's commitments to improve the legal system and provide pro bono services are not currently enforceable,[45] why might lawyers who work in an ABS be less likely to fulfill those commitments than lawyers who work for a traditional law firm? Is it because of the lack of commitment and support from the entity itself? How do more traditional law firms support these aspirational commitments?

5. Nick Robinson has also studied several UK ABS firms, and he is less optimistic than McMorrow about their promise for the United States.[46] Unlike McMorrow, Robinson focused on the proponents' claim that nonlawyer ownership will make civil legal services more affordable and reliable for poor and moderate-income persons. Although given the dearth of empirical information, his conclusions are merely tentative, Robinson found no evidence of a positive impact on the accessibility of affordable legal services.[47] In addition, he pointed to evidence of the emergence of entirely new conflicts of interest, such as insurance companies purchasing personal injury firms when insurance companies

---

43. *Id.* at 694-95.

44. *Id.* at 699.

45. *See supra* Chapter 3: Competence and Diligence; Control and Communication; Fees.

46. *See* Nick Robinson, When Lawyers Don't Get All the Profits: Non-Lawyer Ownership, Access, and Professionalism, 29 Geo. J. Leg. Ethics 1 (2016).

47. *See id.* at 21-28.

have an interest in keeping recoveries low and avoiding certain types of reforms of the structure regulating these companies.[48] Robinson suggested that a similar conflict could emerge if Walmart, which has been criticized for its employment practices, were to offer employment law legal services, even if Walmart lawyers never accepted an employment law case against Walmart itself.[49] Can you explain how such a conflict would arise?

6. Robinson agrees with McMorrow that nonlawyer ownership might also undermine lawyers' public spirited ideals, for example, by catering to concerns "about the enterprise's reputation within the investor community" and by declining "to offer legal services to publicly unpopular clients out of fear of harming the larger brand of their company."[50] However, both McMorrow and Robinson have observed that the United Kingdom's Legal Ombudsman has not received more formal complaints about ABS firms than about non-ABS law firms.[51]

7. The political forces that prompted reform in the United Kingdom — vigorous antitrust regulators and powerful consumer groups with long-standing complaints concerning the existing disciplinary system — do not currently exist in the United States.[52] In addition, the UK reforms were adopted by Parliament, the national legislature, whereas in the United States, lawyers have traditionally been regulated by state courts. Congress probably has the authority to regulate the legal profession generally, but to date it has shown no inclination to do so. Why is state court regulation an obstacle to reforms such as those adopted in the United Kingdom?

E. RECENT DEVELOPMENTS IN THE UNITED STATES

There is little disagreement that poor and moderate-income persons are not currently receiving the legal help they need. Numerous studies have documented the so-called "justice gap."[53] This gap exists for two reasons: (1) many

---

48. *See id.* at 24, 46-48.

49. *See id.* at 48.

50. *Id.* at 51.

51. *See* McMorrow, *supra* n. 40, at 707; Robinson, *supra* n. 46 at 50-51.

52. *See* Ted Schneyer, Thoughts on the Compatibility of Recent U.K. and Australian Reforms with U.S. Traditions in Regulating Law Practice, 2009 J. Prof. Law. 13, 24-25 (2009).

53. *See, e.g.*, The State Bar of California, 2019 California Justice Gap Study, Executive Report; Legal Services Corporation, The Justice Gap: Measuring the Unmet Civil Legal Needs of Low-income Americans (2017); Rebecca L. Sandefur, Accessing Justice in the Contemporary USA: Findings from the Community Needs and Services Study (Am Bar Found. 2014). The ABA Commission on the Future of Legal Services has identified and provided links to many of these reports. *See* ABA Comm'n on the Future of Legal Services, Selected Reports Relating to the Delivery of Legal Services, https://www.americanbar.org/groups/bar_services/resources/resourcepages/future/.

individuals do not know either the existence of legal remedies to their problems or how to access legal help — "the knowledge gap"; and (2) the current system for delivering legal services, including limitations on the resources available to publicly sponsored legal aid for the poor, cannot meet existing legal need — "the service gap."[54]

State courts recognize this "justice gap" and have taken steps to make it easier for these individuals to meet their legal needs. Such efforts include streamlined court procedures, self-help centers, online dispute resolution, and "judicially-authorized-and-regulated legal service providers" (LSPs).[55] These nonlawyer LSPs include courthouse navigators, courthouse facilitators, limited practice officers, limited license legal technicians, and document preparers. In addition, federally authorized LSPs include bankruptcy petition preparers and nonlawyers authorized by federal agencies such as the IRS, the Patent and Trademark Office, the Social Security Administration, and the Board of Immigration Appeals, to represent individuals in proceedings before those agencies.

The private sector has also responded with innovative delivery services, including online document preparation services currently offered by companies like LegalZoom. LegalZoom has been accused of engaging in the unauthorized practice of law; however, it has managed so far to survive these challenges either by establishing that its disclaimers effectively insulate it against a UPL challenge[56] or by settling the cases in a manner permitting it to continue to offer its document preparation services.[57]

Perhaps the greatest growth in recent years, however, has been directed not at poor or moderate-income persons, but rather at business entities, including both large and mid-size companies. Led by the Big Four accounting firms, these so-called "alternative legal service providers" (ALSPs) perform many of the functions traditionally provided by law firms, including litigation and investigation support, legal research, document

---

54. The State Bar of California, California Justice Gap Study, The Service Gap — Findings and Recommendations (May 1, 2020).

55. ABA Comm'n on the Future of Legal Services, A Report on the Future of Legal Services in the United States 18-24 (2016).

56. *See* Medlock v. LegalZoom.Com., Inc. 2013 S.C. LEXIS 362, at *17-18 (S.C. 2013).

57. *See* Debra Cassens Weiss, LegalZoom Can Continue to Offer Documents in Missouri Under Proposed Settlement, ABA Journal (Aug. 23, 2011) (discussing settlement following denial of LegalZoom's motion for summary judgment in Janson v. LegalZoom, Inc., 802 F.Supp.2d 1053 (W.D. Mo. 2011)), https://www.abajournal.com/news/article/suit_claims _legalzooms_document_prep_is_unauthorized_practice; Daniel Fisher, LegalZoom Settles Fight with North Carolina Bar over Online Law, FORBES (Oct. 22, 2015), https://www.forbes. com/sites/danielfisher/2015/10/22/legalzoom-settles-fight-with-north-carolina-bar-over -online-law/?sh=1fca703eb286. An action filed in California against LegalZoom by an intellectual property lawyer is currently in arbitration. Kat Greene, LegalZoom Can Arbitrate IP Firm's Ad, Competition Claims, Law360 (Apr. 10, 2018) (discussing LegalForce RAPC Worldwide v. LegalZoom.com, 2017 WL 6505183 (N.D. Cal. Dec. 19, 2017)), https://www.law360.com/ articles/1032015/legalzoom-can-arbitrate-ip-firm-s-ad-competition-claims.

review, eDiscovery, due diligence in mergers and acquisitions, regulatory risk and compliance, and project management.[58] These nonlawyer ALSPs have many of the same advantages over law firms as do MDPs, such as greater access to capital, specialized expertise, and technology, including the use of artificial intelligence. Even large law firms are making use of ALSPs, including outsourcing work that was previously performed within the law firm and forming partnerships and other affiliations with existing ALSPs, in order to provide an interdisciplinary mix of professional services. With the growth of ASLPs offering services that are arguably outside the unauthorized practice of law, as well as their increasing affiliations with traditional law firms, perhaps the demand for full-fledged ABS firms has been lessened.

Finally, there is a growing interest among some state courts in considering permitting ABS firms. In August 2020, the Arizona Supreme Court amended its court rules—including deleting Rule 5.4—to permit nonlawyers to own entities providing legal services through lawyer owners or employees.[59] As in the United Kingdom, these new entities are called alternative business structures and must be licensed.[60] Also in August 2020, the Utah Supreme Court authorized a pilot program to test similar changes, allowing individuals and entities to explore innovative means of allowing lawyers and nonlawyers to deliver legal services.[61] Other state supreme courts are considering similar changes. The State Bar of California's board of trustees has formed a sandbox working group to examine permitting nonlawyer ownership of law firms.[62]

If only a handful of small states like Arizona and Utah permit ABS firms to operate, it is unlikely that large-scale entities such as the Big Four accounting firms or a retail store like Walmart will participate. On the other hand, if a larger state like California were to adopt these reforms, then these entities

---

58. *See* Thomson Reuters, Alternative Legal Service Providers 2019: Fast Growth, Expanding Use and Increasing Opportunity (2019), https://legal.thomsonreuters.com/content/dam/ewp-m/documents/legal/en/pdf/reports/alsp-report-final.pdf?cid=9008178&sfdccampaignid=7011B000002OF6AQAW&chl=pr.

59. Order Amending the Ariz. Rules of the Supreme Court and the Ariz. Rules of Evidence, No. R-20-0034 (2020) (order effective January 1, 2021).

60. *See* Ariz. Code Judic. Admin. §7-209 (creating court structure for licensing and regulating alternative business structures and defining an ABS as "a business entity that includes nonlawyers who have an economic interest or decision-making authority in the firm and provide legal services").

61. *See* Utah Supreme Court Standing Order No. 15 (effective Aug. 14, 2020). Initially approved for two years, the program was recently expanded to seven years: as of May 2021, the state had approved 26 of 47 regulatory sandbox applications. *See* Rhys Dipshan, Utah Adds 5 Years to Regulatory Sandbox Program Fostering Legal Services Innovation (May 4, 2021), https://www.law.com/legaltechnews/2021/05/04/utah-adds-five-years-to-regulatory-sandbox-program-fostering-legal-services-innovation/.

62. Lyle Moran, California bar gives approval to broad sandbox proposal (May 15, 2020), https://law.stanford.edu/press/california-bar-gives-approval-to-broad-sandbox-proposal/.

might well jump into the direct legal services market as full-fledged multidisciplinary practices. What difficulties do you anticipate states will encounter in attempting to regulate the delivery of legal services in MDPs with a national, indeed international, presence?

Andrew Perlman has urged the legal profession to support a broader regulatory approach to the delivery of both legal and law-related services, including the type of services now being offered by ALSPs. Here is an excerpt from one of his recent essays on this topic, written for an online symposium reviewing several recent books about the emerging frontier of law, technology, and professional regulation.[63]

Andrew M. Perlman

Reflections on the Future of Legal Services
Suffolk University Law School Research Paper No. 17-10 (May 9, 2017)[64]

Towards the Law of Legal Services: Reflections on Gillian Hadfield's "Rules for a Flat World" Sunday, February 26, 2017 . . .

THE INADEQUACY OF THE LAW OF LAWYERING

I come to this subject having written a bit about it. In an article, "Towards the Law of Legal Services," I argued that it is time for us to broaden our thinking about the regulation of legal services. Rather than focusing on the "law of lawyering" — the body of rules and law regulating lawyers — I suggested that we need to develop a broader "law of legal services" that authorizes, but appropriately regulates, the delivery of more legal and law-related assistance by people who do not have a J.D. degree and who do not work alongside lawyers. Here is one way to visualize the point. . . .

The "law of lawyering" branch of the tree includes the traditional subjects that have occupied legal profession scholars for decades, such as rules of professional conduct, the law of malpractice, and administrative regulations directed at lawyers. Of course, some of these subjects overlap with other doctrinal areas (e.g., civil procedure, SEC regulations, and IRS regulations), but the point is that there is now a fairly robust body of law governing lawyers' work.

---

63. *See* Law's New Frontiers: An On-line Symposium" (Feb. 8, 2017) at https://prawfsblawg. blogs.com/prawfsblawg/2017/02/laws-new-frontiers-an-on-line-symposium.html. The books reviewed were Richard & Daniel Susskind, The Future of the Professions: How Technology Will Transform the Work of Human Experts (2016), and Gillian K. Hadfield, Rules for a Flat World: Why Humans Invented Law and How to Reinvent It for a Complex Global Economy (2016).

64. Available at SSRN: https://ssrn.com/abstract=2965592.

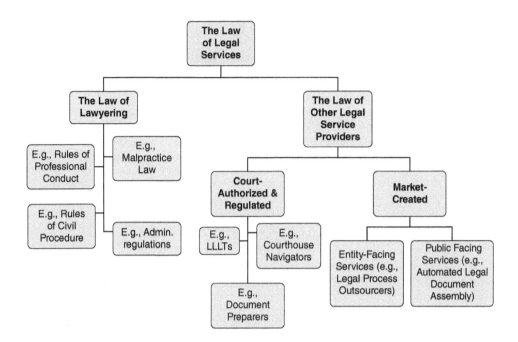

In my article, I argued that we need to spend a lot more time thinking about (and growing) the right side of the tree—the law of other legal service providers. This means devoting more attention to the increasing array of legal services professionals who are authorized and regulated by courts, such as Limited License Legal Technicians, Legal Practice Officers, courthouse navigators, and document preparers. . . . Other kinds of service providers are emerging in the marketplace and are either public-facing (e.g., Legal Zoom) or delivering services to law firms and corporate legal departments (e.g., legal process outsourcers and e-discovery companies).

For the public-facing providers who are not authorized and regulated by courts (the bottom right corner of the diagram), the regulatory framework has not been particularly robust. It has consisted primarily of restrictions on the unauthorized practice of law and consumer protection laws. Put another way, new players are either accused of engaging in the unauthorized practice of law or they are subject to the minimal regulatory constraints of ordinary consumer protection provisions.

I believe that this binary approach is inadequate. Unauthorized practice of law provisions are notoriously vague, have been used in anti-competitive ways, and are stifling competition without any clear public benefit. At the same time, a laissez faire approach is also problematic, because it provides the public with only modest protections when purchasing these services, as if they are no different from (say) purchasing a pair of shoes. A third way is possible and desirable—the development of new kinds of regulations that expressly authorize these emerging providers and subject those providers to more rigorous regulations than currently exist. . . .

Toward "Right Regulation"

Gillian's book tackles these and many other broader issues, such as how we might develop more effective legal infrastructure for a modern world. . . . Gillian develops two ideas that nicely supplement what I have sketched out above.

First, Gillian describes a concept that she refers to as "right regulation." For all intents and purposes, it is the "third way" that I think needs to exist when regulating new kinds of legal service providers. She explains:

> Challenges to the existing regulation of legal markets by bar associations are sometimes cast as proposals to deregulate legal markets. But the name of the game is not deregulation; it's what I call right regulation: putting in place intelligent regulations that ensure the markets for legal goods and services are functional and competitive. (p. 244)

Gillian cites the UK's Legal Services Act of 2007 as an example of such an approach; that is, it liberalizes, but appropriately regulates, the legal services market in the U.K.

"Right regulation" also has some applications to the left side of the tree. For example, Gillian argues that lawyers should be permitted to partner and share fees with people who are not lawyers (currently prohibited in nearly all U.S. jurisdictions under Rule 5.4 of the rules of professional conduct), but with appropriate regulatory arrangements, as is the case in the U.K.

Who Does the Regulating?

One of the greatest strengths of Gillian's book is that she provides a conceptual framework for addressing a particularly challenging question: who should be responsible for drafting the relevant "right regulations"? This is not an easy question to answer. . . .

One possible answer is that we should leave these issues to the courts, which historically have regulated legal services. Another possible answer is to have legislatures more actively involved, with appropriate delegation to administrative agencies. Both of these answers have benefits and costs, but neither offers an ideal solution.

Gillian's innovative answer, drawing on the U.K. for inspiration, is to have private market-based approaches to regulation and to use government as a so-called "super-regulator" (regulating the regulators). She describes it this way:

> Instead of civil servants or the managers of a regulated company designating the details of how to achieve politically set goals, . . . private for-profit and non-profit companies could offer this as a service in the market, for a fee. In order to participate in this market, these companies would have to be approved as private regulators by the government. Approval would be based on meeting the policy objectives established by the government for regulation — developing a system that ensures that regulated businesses meet targets [of various kinds related to the industry]. (p. 266)

I came away from the book with a much greater appreciation for the ways in which we might go about creating a more flexible legal infrastructure in the future. Although the approach won't work in every setting (as Gillian concedes), I think there are some interesting implications not just for the law of legal services, but for many other regulatory structures in a rapidly changing world.

NOTES AND QUESTIONS

1. Currently, authorized legal service providers (LSP) are subject to the training, licensing, and conduct regulations adopted by the specific authorizing court or agency. Given that courts and agencies are frequently starved for funding, is it realistic to expect that they can devote significant resources to regulating nonlawyer providers? What sort of regulatory solution might a legislature provide?

2. In the United Kingdom, ABS firms are regulated by "frontline regulators," which are typically bar association–established agencies that are independent from the bar associations' representative bodies. The frontline regulators are approved and then subject to oversight by an "external regulator," the Legal Services Board. This regulation occurs at a national level and is not too great a departure from prior practice, in which national bar associations were permitted to regulate their own members. Can this model be adapted to the U.S. tradition of regulating lawyers at the state level? Might firms interested in becoming an ABS appeal to Congress to provide authorization and regulation at the national level?[65]

3. What do you think of Hadfield's suggestion of state or federal approval of private companies as regulators? How would such companies be financed? If funded by the ABS or ALSP firms themselves (as the cost of obtaining and maintaining their licenses), wouldn't the private regulators be subject to undue influence by the firms subject to their regulation?

4. If ALSP firms are providing law-related but not legal services, is it sufficient to regulate them in the same way that other commercial businesses are regulated, that is, by general consumer protection law and legislation targeted to specific bad practices?

Review Problems

16-1 What is the ethical propriety of the following scenarios under: (1) the Model Rules; (2) the D.C. Rules; and (3) the Arizona Rules?

(a) A law firm wants to use a nonlawyer with an MBA as its business manager. It will hire her as a salaried employee with the right to participate in annual bonuses based on net law firm profits. She will have access to

---

65. *See, e.g.,* Anthony E. Davis, Regulation of the Legal Profession in the United States and the Future of Global Law, 19 Prof'l Law. 1, 8-10 (2009).

confidential information of clients as necessary in the performance of her duties.

(b) Same, except that the nonlawyer MBA will be brought in as a partner in the law firm, but will not have access to confidential information of clients.

(c) A recently admitted lawyer is starting his own law firm. His father has offered to provide the necessary capital to lease office space and purchase office furniture and computers, but only on condition that he will be given a 5 percent ownership in the law firm, with the loan to be repaid from a distribution of annual profits. The father will not have access to confidential information of clients and will not participate in or direct the provision of any legal services.

(d) A recently admitted lawyer wants to form a partnership to provide interdisciplinary services to families, including legal, accounting, and counseling services to families seeking a divorce or adoption.

(e) A recently admitted lawyer has proposed a reciprocal referral agreement among the lawyer, an accountant, and a psychologist to provide legal, accounting, and counseling services to families seeking a divorce or adoption. They have agreed that, except where there is a conflict of interest, each will refer clients in need of the others' services.

CHAPTER 17

MARKETING LEGAL SERVICES

Model Rules 7.1, 7.2, 7.3, 8.4(c)

Prior to 1977, lawyers were generally prohibited from advertising their legal services and from directly soliciting potential clients. Professional responsibility casebooks that wanted to raise the issue had to resort to hypothetical ads that a lawyer might use. In 1997, however, the U.S. Supreme Court decided Bates v. State Bar of Arizona,[1] in which it held that the general ban on attorney advertising violated the First Amendment. One year later, in Ohralik v. Ohio State Bar Assn.,[2] the Court upheld a ban on in-person solicitation of clients for pecuniary gain.

After *Bates* was decided, the ABA and the states revised their rules to permit lawyer advertising but continued to heavily regulate what lawyers could or couldn't say in their ads. Between 1982 and 1990, the Supreme Court decided three additional lawyer advertising cases, each time striking down a state rule as violating the First Amendment. In In re R.M.J.,[3] the Court struck down Missouri's limitation on the precise language or terms a lawyer could use to describe the lawyer's area of practice; for example, prohibiting lawyers from using the terms "personal injury" and "real estate" instead of the approved terms "tort law" and "property law."[4] That case was followed by Zauderer v. Office of Disciplinary Counsel,[5] in which the Court reversed Ohio's discipline of a lawyer based on a newspaper advertisement that contained an accurate illustration of an intrauterine contraceptive device (the Dalkon Shield), as well as truthful legal advice describing the lawyer's representation of women in lawsuits against the manufacturer and encouraging other users to contact

---

1. 433 U.S. 350 (1977).
2. 436 U.S. 447 (1978).
3. 455. U.S. 191 (1982).
4. The advertisement also stated that the lawyer was licensed in both Missouri and Illinois and that he was "Admitted to Practice Before THE UNITED STATES SUPREME COURT." Missouri had prohibited the use of any content that had not been explicitly approved.
5. 471 U.S. 626 (1985).

him to determine their legal rights. And in Peel v. Attorney Registration & Disciplinary Commission,[6] the Court struck down an Illinois rule prohibiting lawyers from holding themselves out as "certified" or as a "specialist," thereby permitting the lawyer to communicate that he had been certified by the National Board of Trial Advocacy as a certified civil trial specialist.[7]

The Supreme Court has also addressed several additional cases concerning solicitation of clients. In In re Primus,[8] decided on the same day as *Ohralik*, the Court upheld the associational rights of a lawyer cooperating with a branch of the American Civil Liberties Union who provided in-person legal advice to women who had been sterilized or threatened with sterilization as a condition of receiving Medicaid assistance; the lawyer also sent a follow-up letter to one of the women offering free legal assistance from the ACLU. In Shapero v. Kentucky Bar Ass'n,[9] the Court struck down a ban on truthful solicitation letters to persons known to have specific legal problems, even when the solicitation was for pecuniary gain. Finally, in Florida Bar v. Went For It, Inc.,[10] the Court upheld a Florida rule banning solicitation letters to personal injury accident victims or their families within 30 days after an accident or disaster.

The first goal of this chapter is to introduce you to the Supreme Court's approach to assessing the constitutionality of state rules regulating lawyer marketing under the First Amendment. Beginning with the adoption of the Model Rules in 1983, the ABA has taken a relatively minimalist approach to lawyer marketing efforts,[11] including adopting amendments in August 2018 designed to further simplify and streamline the lawyer marketing rules.[12] However, there is considerable variation in state regulation, and many states continue to take what one commentator has described as a "high regulatory" approach, particularly with respect to television advertising.[13] The constitutionality of these rules may be doubtful, but some states have demonstrated a willingness to litigate the validity of their provisions.

Given the disparity in state rules, the second goal of this chapter is to highlight the difficulty facing lawyers who are increasingly using cross-border, even national marketing efforts. These difficulties are compounded by the variety of new and ever-changing digital marketing tools such as websites,

---

6. 496 U.S. 91 (1990).

7. The lawyer was also disciplined for advertising his availability on a contingent fee basis without disclosing that the clients would have to pay costs even if their lawyers were unsuccessful. The Court upheld the Ohio rule requiring such disclosure.

8. 436 U.S. 412 (1978).

9. 486 U.S. 466 (1988).

10. 515 U.S 618 (1995).

11. *See generally* ABA, A Legislative History: The Development of the ABA Model Rules of Professional Conduct, 1983-2013 (Rules 7.1-7.5).

12. *See* ABA Standing Committee on Ethics and Professional Responsibility, Report to the House of Delegates (August 2018) (explaining resolution to amend Rules 7.1 through 7.5 and their comments).

13. *See* Margaret Raymond, Inside, Outside: Cross-Border Enforcement of Attorney Advertising Restrictions, 43 Akron L. Rev. 801, 803 (2010).

search engines, banners, hyperlinks, and social media. Aside from the uncertainty concerning which state rules govern, it is frequently unclear how particular rules apply to this new "arsenal of cyberspace advertising options."[14]

This chapter addresses these issues in separate sections on "advertising" and "solicitation," although the borderline between the two is sometimes uncertain. A final section briefly discusses other marketing rules, including those governing referrals from both lawyers and nonlawyers.

A. RESTRICTIONS ON LAWYER ADVERTISING

Model Rule 7.1, captioned "Communications Concerning a Lawyer's Services," provides that "[a] lawyer shall not make a false or misleading communication about the lawyer or the lawyer's services. A communication is false or misleading if it contains a material misrepresentation of fact or law, or omits a fact necessary to make the statement as a whole not materially misleading." All states have the same or a similar rule, which applies not just to advertisements but to "*all* communications about a lawyer's services."[15]

Prior to the 2018 amendments, Model Rule 7.2 contained specific rules concerning "Advertising," while Model Rule 7.3 was directed to "Solicitation of Clients." Model Rules 7.4 and 7.5 concerned "Communication of Fields of Practice and Specialization" and "Firm Names and Letterheads," respectively, and covered matters that occur in both advertising and solicitation. As a result of the 2018 amendments, Rule 7.2 is now more broadly captioned "Communications Concerning a Lawyer's Services: Specific Rules," so there is no longer a rule directed specifically to "advertisements."[16]

As a result of the 2018 amendments, the Model Rules now contain only two rules that regulate the content of a lawyer advertisement. First, under Rule 7.1, a lawyer may not make a false or misleading communication. Second, under Rule 7.2(c), the lawyer may not "state or imply that [the] lawyer is certified as a specialist" except in certain limited situations.[17]

By contrast, "high regulatory" states have numerous regulations concerning the content of lawyer advertisements, including the inclusion of endorsements, testimonials, or dramatizations and the use of actors to portray either the lawyer, a client, or a judge. In the following case, the Second Circuit

---

14. Ashley M. London, Something Wicked This Way Thumbs: Personal Contact Concerns of Text-Based Attorney Marketing, 58 Houston L. Rev. 99, 119 (2020).

15. MR 7.1, cmt [1] (emphasis added).

16. Rule 7.2 now also includes the material about fields of practice and specialization that were previously found in Rule 7.4. The material on firm names and letterhead was moved to a comment under Rule 7.1. The new rules are more streamlined, with a total of only three, as opposed to five rules on lawyer marketing.

17. The lawyer must have been certified as a specialist "by an organization that has been approved by an appropriate authority of the state or the District of Columbia or a U.S. Territory or that has been accredited by the American Bar Association"; in addition, "the name of the certifying organization [must be] clearly identified."

Chapter 17 Marketing Legal Services

invalidated all but one of the newly amended New York advertising rules, which had been challenged by a law firm because they prevented the firm from using some of its commercials.

Alexander v. Cahill
598 F.3d 79 (2d Cir. 2010)

CALEBRESI, Circuit Judge: . . .

The [Plaintiffs] are an individual (James Alexander), a law firm (Alexander & Catalano), and a not-for-profit consumer rights organization (Public Citizen). Alexander is the managing partner of Alexander & Catalano, a personal injury law firm with offices in Syracuse and Rochester. Alexander & Catalano use various broadcast and print media to advertise. Prior to the adoption of New York's new attorney advertising rules, the firm's commercials often contained jingles and special effects, including wisps of smoke and blue electrical currents surrounding the firm's name. Firm advertisements also featured dramatizations, comical scenes, and special effects—for instance, depicting Alexander and his partner as giants towering above local buildings, running to a client's house so quickly they appear as blurs, and providing legal assistance to space aliens. Another advertisement depicted a judge in the courtroom and stated that the judge is there "to make sure [the trial] is fair." The firm's ads also frequently included the firm's slogan "heavy hitters," and phrases like "think big" and "we'll give you a big helping hand." To date, no disciplinary actions have been brought against the firm or its lawyers based on firm advertising. The new rules, however, caused the firm to halt its advertisements for fear of such action. . . .

We consider below a subset of [the new New York] rules. The first group of amendments imposes a series of content-based restrictions:

N.Y. Comp. Codes R & Regs. Tit. 22, § 1200.50(c):

(c) An advertisement shall not:
    (1) include an endorsement of, or testimonial about, a lawyer or law firm from a client with respect to a matter that is still pending . . .
    (3) include the portrayal of a judge, the portrayal of a fictitious law firm, the use of a fictitious name to refer to lawyers not associated together in a law firm, or otherwise imply that lawyers are associated in a law firm if that is not the case . . .
    (5) rely on techniques to obtain attention that demonstrate a clear and intentional lack of relevance to the selection of counsel, including the portrayal of lawyers exhibiting characteristics clearly unrelated to legal competence . . .
    (7) utilize a nickname, moniker, motto or trade name that implies an ability to obtain results in a matter. . . .

This case calls on us once again to assess the scope of First Amendment protection accorded to commercial speech, and the measure of evidence a state must present in regulating such speech. Because this action was resolved on summary judgment, we review the District Court's decision *de novo*, drawing all factual inferences in favor of the non-moving party.

The Supreme Court has established a four-part inquiry for determining whether regulations of commercial speech are consistent with the First Amendment:

> [1] whether the expression is protected by the First Amendment. For commercial speech to come within that provision, it at least must concern lawful activity and not be misleading. Next, we ask [2] whether the asserted governmental interest is substantial. If both inquiries yield positive answers, we must determine [3] whether the regulation directly advances the governmental interest asserted, and [4] whether it is not more extensive than is necessary to serve that interest.

Central Hudson Gas & Elec. Corp. v. Pub. Serv. Comm'n of N.Y. . . . .

A. THE DISPUTED PROVISIONS REGULATE COMMERCIAL SPEECH PROTECTED BY THE FIRST AMENDMENT . . .

The Supreme Court first recognized attorney advertising as within the scope of protected speech in *Bates v. State of Arizona*, in which the Court invalidated a ban on price advertising for what the Court deemed "routine" legal services. In doing so, the Court reserved the question whether similar protection would extend to "advertising claims as to the quality of services [that] are not, susceptible of measurement or verification."

In the years since *Bates*, the Supreme Court has offered differing, and not always fully consistent, descriptions as to what constitutes fully protected commercial speech, particularly with respect to attorney advertising. Speaking generally, the Supreme Court has said that states may impose regulations to ensure that "the stream of commercial information flow[s] cleanly as well as freely." But this Court has nonetheless observed that there are "doctrinal uncertainties left in the wake of Supreme Court decisions from which the modern commercial speech doctrine has evolved. In particular, these decisions have created some uncertainty as to the degree of protection for commercial advertising that lacks precise informational content."

In the end, we agree with the District Court that, with one exception discussed below, the content-based restrictions in the disputed provisions of § 1200.50(c) regulate commercial speech protected by the First Amendment. . . . [T]he only categories that *Central Hudson*, and its *sequellae*, clearly excludes from protection are speech that is false, deceptive, or misleading, and speech that concerns unlawful activities. . . . The Supreme Court has also emphasized that "States may not place an absolute prohibition on certain types of potentially misleading information . . . if the information also may be presented in a way that is not deceptive." We conclude from these precedents that the *Central Hudson* analysis applies to regulations of commercial speech that is only *potentially* misleading.

The speech that Defendants' content-based restrictions seeks to regulate—that which is irrelevant, unverifiable, and non-informational—is not inherently false, deceptive, or misleading. . . .

There is one exception to this conclusion. Subsection §1200.50(c)(3) prohibits "the portrayal of a fictitious law firm, the use of a fictitious name to refer to lawyers not associated together in a law firm, or otherwise imply that lawyers are associated in a law firm if that is not the case.". . .

[T]he Attorney general, representing the Defendants [chief counsels of the N.Y. disciplinary committees] suggested a narrow[] interpretation of this regulation. He asked that we construe this language as applying only to situations in which lawyers from different firms give the misleading impression that they are from the same firm (i.e., "The Dream Team") So read, this portion of §1200.50(c)(3) addresses only advertising techniques that are actually misleading (as to the existence or membership of a firm), and such advertising is not entitled to First Amendment protection. . . .

B. *CENTRAL HUDSON* AND THE CONTENT-BASED REGULATIONS

1. SUBSTANTIAL INTEREST

Under the second prong of *Central Hudson*, the State must identify "a substantial interest in support of its regulation[s].". . . Before the District Court and again on appeal, Defendants proffered a state interest in "prohibiting attorney advertisements from containing deceptive or misleading content.". . . This state interest is substantial — indeed, states have a generally unfettered right to prohibit inherently or actually misleading commercial speech. The disputed regulations codified at §1200.50(c) therefore survive the second prong of the *Central Hudson* analysis.

Defendants also assert an interest in "protecting the legal profession's image and reputation." In Florida Bar [v. Went-For-It, Inc.], the Supreme Court recognized a substantial interest "in preventing the erosion of confidence in the [legal] profession." Defendants explain that their interest in preventing misleading attorney advertising is "inextricably linked to its overarching interest" in maintaining attorney professionalism and respect for the bar. This interest also supports the disputed regulations.

2. MATERIALLY ADVANCED

"The penultimate prong of the *Central Hudson* test requires that a regulation impinging upon commercial expression 'directly advance the state interest involved; the regulation may not be sustained if it provides only ineffective or remote support for the government's purpose.'" The state's burden with respect to this prong "is not satisfied by mere speculation or conjecture; rather, a governmental body seeking to sustain a restriction on commercial speech must demonstrate that the harms it recites are real and that its restrictions will in fact alleviate them to a material degree. Moreover, "[i]f the protections afforded commercial speech are to retain their force, we cannot allow rote invocation of the words 'potentially misleading' to supplant this burden.". . .

a. Subsection 1200.50(c)(1): Client Testimonials

This subsection prohibits advertisements that include "an endorsement of, or testimonial about, a lawyer or law firm from a client with respect to a matter that is still pending." The Task Force Report observed that testimonials can be misleading because they may suggest that past results indicate future performance. The Task Force Report, however, did not recommend outright prohibition of all testimonials on this basis. Instead, as the District Court observed, the Task Force Report "recommended a different approach." The Report suggested "strengthening the rules governing testimonials to prohibit the use of an actor or spokesperson who is not a member or employee of the advertising lawyer or law firm absent disclosure thereof." The Task Force noted, moreover, that "it would be an improper restriction on a client's free speech rights to prohibit client testimonials outright." The Task Force Report therefore does not support Defendants' assertion that prohibiting testimonials from current clients will materially advance an interest in preventing misleading advertising. . . .

Nor does consensus or common sense support the conclusion that client testimonials are inherently misleading. Testimonials may, for example, mislead if they suggest that past results indicate future performance—but not all testimonials will do so, especially if they include a disclaimer. The District Court properly concluded that Defendants failed to satisfy this prong of *Central Hudson* with respect to client testimonials.

b. Subsection 1200.50(c)(3): Portrayal of a Judge

This subsection prohibits "the portrayal of a judge." The Task Force observes that "a communication that states or implies that the lawyer has the ability to influence improperly a court" is "likely to be false, deceptive or misleading." The District Court found this comment to be persuasive evidence that a ban on portrayals of judges would materially advance the State's interest in preventing misleading advertising. We disagree. Although it seems plainly true that implying an ability to influence a court is likely to be misleading, Defendants have failed to draw the requisite connection between that common sense observation and portrayals of judges in advertisements generally. The advertisement in which Alexander & Catalano use the portrayal of a judge, for instance, depicts a judge in the courtroom and states that the judge is there "to make sure [the trial] is fair." This sort of advertisement does not imply an ability to influence a court improperly. We believe the Task Force Report fails to support Defendants' prohibition on portrayals of judges and conclude that Defendants have not met their burden with respect to the wholesale prohibition of portrayals of judges. This prohibition consequently must fail.

c. Subsection 1200.5(c)(5): Irrelevant Techniques

This subsection prohibits advertisements that "rely on techniques to obtain attention that demonstrate a clear and intentional lack of relevance to the selection of counsel, including the portrayal of lawyers exhibiting characteristics clearly unrelated to legal competence." Defendants note that the New York Code of Professional Responsibility has long declared that the purpose of attorney advertising is to "educate the public to an awareness of legal needs and to provide information relevant to the selection of the most appropriate counsel." Defendants contend that their rule excluding attention-getting techniques unrelated to attorney competence reflects this principle and so materially advances "New York's interest in factual, relevant attorney advertisements."

A rule barring irrelevant advertising components certainly advances an interest in keeping attorney advertising factual and relevant. But this interest is quite different from an interest in preventing misleading advertising. Like Defendants' claim that the First Amendment does not protect irrelevant and unverifiable components in advertising, Defendants here appear to conflate *irrelevant* components of advertising with *misleading* advertising. These are not one and the same. Questions of taste or effectiveness in advertising are generally matters of subjective judgment. Moreover, as the Task Force Report acknowledged, "limiting the information that may be advertised . . . assumes that the bar can accurately forecast the kind of information that the public would regard as relevant."

Defendants have introduced no evidence that the sorts of irrelevant advertising components proscribed by subsection 1200.5(c)(5) are, in fact, misleading and so subject to proscription. Significantly, the Task Force Report expressly recognized that "communications involving puffery and claims that cannot be measured or verified" were not specifically addressed in its proposed rules, although such communications would already be prohibited "to the extent that they are false, deceptive or misleading."

Moreover, the sorts of gimmicks that this rule appears designed to reach—such as Alexander & Catalano's wisps of smoke, blue electrical currents, and special effects—do not actually seem likely to mislead. It is true that Alexander and his partner are not giants towering above local buildings; they cannot run to a client's house so quickly that they appear as blurs; and they do not actually provide legal assistance to space aliens. But given the prevalence of these and other kinds of special effects in advertising and entertainment, we cannot seriously believe—purely as a matter of "common sense"—that ordinary individuals are likely to be misled into thinking that these advertisements depict true characteristics. Indeed, some of these gimmicks, while seemingly irrelevant, may actually serve "important communicative functions: [they] attract[] the attention of the audience to the advertiser's message, and [they] may also serve to impart information directly.". . .

d. Section 1200.50(c)(7): Nicknames, Mottos, and Trade Names

This subsection bars advertisements "utiliz[ing] a nickname, moniker, motto or trade name that implies an ability to obtain results in a matter." We conclude, once again, that the evidence on which Defendants rely fails to support this regulation.

There is a compelling, commonsense argument that, given the uncertainties of litigation, names that imply an ability to obtain results are usually misleading. The Task Force Report made precisely this observation, stating in its recommendations that "the use of dollar signs, the terms 'most cash' or 'maximum dollar,' or like terms that suggest the outcome of a legal matter" is "likely to be false, deceptive or misleading." Like its recommendations on irrelevant advertising techniques, however, the Task Force Report did not recommend outright prohibition of all such trade names or mottos — it simply acknowledged that such names are often misleading. Defendants' rule, by contrast, goes further and prohibits such descriptors — including, according to the Attorney General, Alexander & Catalano's own "Heavy Hitters" motto — even when they are not actually misleading. . . .

There is a dearth of evidence in the present record supporting the need for section 1200.50(c)(7)'s prohibition on names that imply an ability to get results when the names are akin to, and no more than, the kind of puffery that is commonly seen, and indeed expected, in commercial advertisements generally. Defendants have once against failed to provide evidence that consumers have, in fact, been misled by the sorts of names and promotional devices targeted by section 1200.50(c)(7), and so have failed to meet their burden for sustaining this prohibition under *Central Hudson*.

3. NARROWLY TAILORED

The final prong of *Central Hudson* asks whether the "fit" between the goals identified (the state's interests) and the means chosen to advance these goals is reasonable; the fit need not be perfect. . . .

On this basis, even if we were to find that all of the disputed Section 1200.50(c) restrictions survived scrutiny under *Central Hudson*'s third prong, each would fail the final inquiry because each wholly prohibits a category of advertising speech that is *potentially* misleading, but is not inherently or actually misleading in all cases. Contrary to Defendants' assertions, the fact that New York's rules do also permit substantial information in attorney advertising does not render the disputed provisions any less categorical. Significantly, *Zauderer* deemed a rule barring illustrations a "blanket ban." And New York's rules prohibiting, *inter alia*, all testimonials by current clients, all portrayals of judges, and all depictions of lawyers exhibiting characteristics unrelated to legal competence are similarly categorical. Because these advertising techniques are no more than potentially misleading, the categorical nature of New York's prohibitions would alone be enough to render the prohibitions invalid.

Moreover, "nowhere does the State cite any evidence or authority of any kind for its contention that the potential abuses associated with the [disputed provisions] cannot be combated by any means short of a blanket ban." As the District Court observed, the State could have, for example, required disclaimers similar to the one already required for fictional scenes. Nothing in the record suggests that such disclaimers would have been ineffective. . . .

508   Chapter 17 Marketing Legal Services

Defendants have failed to carry their burden with respect to *Central Hudson's* final prong. We therefore conclude, like the District Court, that the disputed portions of subsections 1200.50(c)(1), (3), (5) and (7) are unconstitutional.

NOTES AND QUESTIONS

1. Under the four-part *Central Hudson* test, some commercial speech is simply not entitled to First Amendment protection and therefore may be regulated without requiring the state to further justify its regulation. The only challenged New York rule deemed to fall outside the scope of First Amendment protection was Subsection 1200.50(c)(3), which prohibits "the portrayal of a fictitious law firm, the use of a fictitious name to refer to lawyers not associated together in a law firm, or otherwise imply that lawyers are associated in a law firm if that is not the case." Why was that provision not protected by the First Amendment?

2. With respect to the remaining challenged provisions, the first prong of the *Central Hudson* test is whether the government has asserted a "substantial interest in support of its regulation." We can all agree with the *Alexander* court's finding that New York's stated interest in preventing the transmission of false or misleading information was substantial, but what about the court's further approval of the state's asserted interest in "protecting the legal profession's image and reputation" and "maintaining attorney professionalism and respect for the bar." In *Zauderer*, the U.S. Supreme Court had questioned whether "preserving the dignity of attorneys" was sufficiently substantial to warrant abridgment of a lawyer's First Amendment rights.[18] In *Florida Bar*, however, the Supreme Court acknowledged the substantiality of the state's interest in "protect[ing] the flagging reputation of Florida lawyers by preventing them from engaging in conduct [i.e., sending solicitation letters to personal injury victims within 30 days of an accident or disaster] that 'is universally regarded as deplorable and beneath common decency.'"[19] In that case, the state had evidence that such solicitation letters had lowered public regard "for the legal profession and for the judicial process as a whole."[20] Does that explain why preserving the reputation of the profession was found to be a substantial state interest in *Florida Bar*? Is *Florida Bar* distinguishable from *Alexander*?[21]

---

18. 471 U.S. at 647-48. Shortly after that decision, then-Chief Justice Warren Burger, who had dissented in *Zauderer*, told an ABA panel that legal advertising was "sheer shysterism" and compared lawyers who advertise to those touting "automobiles, dog food, cosmetics and hair tonics." N.Y. Times News Service, Burger Rips "Shysterism" in Lawyer Ads, July 9, 1985.

19. 515 U.S. at 625.

20. *Id.* at 627.

21. In Public Citizen, Inc. v. La. Attorney Disciplinary Board, 632 F.3d 212 (5th Cir. 2011), the court cited *Zauderer* for the proposition that "an interest in preserving attorneys' dignity in their communications with the public is not substantial," but nevertheless held that the state's asserted interest in "preserving the ethical integrity of the legal profession" was substantial. *Id.* at 220. What exactly is "the ethical integrity of the legal profession," and how is it different from the "dignity" of the legal profession?

A. Restrictions on Lawyer Advertising **509**

3. Even if the state's interest is substantial, *Central Hudson*'s second prong requires that the rule "materially advance" that interest, which in turn requires that the state demonstrate that the harm is real and that the restriction will materially alleviate that harm. In *Alexander*, the court found that none of the provisions in question satisfied this prong. Why not? Do you agree with the court's decision as to each provision? Contrary to the Second Circuit opinion, a Fifth Circuit decision upheld a Louisiana rule prohibiting advertising using "a nickname, moniker, motto or trade name that stated or implied an ability to obtain results."[22] There the state relied on surveys and focus groups in which members of the public were shown specific mottos used by Louisiana lawyers; the results demonstrated that a majority of the public believed that the ads implied that the featured lawyers could manipulate courts and that the lawyer would achieve a positive result, regardless of facts or law.[23] Are the Second and Fifth Circuit decisions distinguishable? Might the Fifth Circuit have upheld the New York rule prohibiting ads that "rely on techniques to obtain attention that demonstrate a clear and intentional lack of relevance to the section of counsel"?

4. The fourth and final prong of the *Central Hudson* test is that the regulation "is not more extensive than is necessary to serve [the state's substantial] interest." In *Florida Bar*, the Supreme Court explained that the means chosen must be "reasonable," but the fit need not be perfect.[24] As applied to the Louisiana rule prohibiting nicknames and monikers that imply an ability to obtain results, the Fifth Circuit held that the rule was not unconstitutionally vague because Louisiana had provided lawyers with a handbook providing examples, such as "The Smith Law Firm: The Winning Law Firm" or "The Cash Machine Legal Clinic, L.L.C."[25] Do you agree that these types of examples provide sufficient guidance to Louisiana lawyers to enable them to comply with the rule? What about Alexander & Catalon's "Heavy Hitters" motto? South Carolina specifically identifies that motto as implying an ability to obtain results in a matter.[26]

5. New York and Louisiana are clearly "high regulatory" states, as is Florida. The Florida rules contain numerous specific prohibitions on lawyer advertising, including the use of testimonials that are "written or drafted by the lawyer" or do not contain a "disclaimer that the prospective client may not obtain the same or similar results."[27] How would you advise a lawyer whose advertisement will be

---

22. Public Citizen v. La. Attorney Disciplinary Bd., 632 F.2d 212 (5th Cir. 2011).

23. *Id.* at 224-25.

24. 515 U.S. at 632. Thus, when regulating commercial speech, the state need not use the "least restrictive means" test used for noncommercial speech. *Id.*

25. 632 F.3d at 226 & n.10.

26. *See* S.C. Rules of Prof'l Conduct, R. 7.1, cmt [4].

27. *See* Rules and Regulations of the Florida Bar, R. 4-7.13(b)(8)(C) & (F) (2020). Florida also has detailed rules concerning "potentially misleading advertisements," *id.* at R. 4-7.14, and "unduly manipulative or intrusive advertisements," *id.* at R. 4-7.15.

simultaneously displayed in high, moderate, and low regulatory states? Perhaps the lawyer would be safe by complying with the strictest rules, but that would require the lawyer to research all the applicable state rules, including ethics committee opinions interpreting and applying those rules. And with respect to various recordkeeping and disclosure provisions, one commentator has suggested that "the labeling requirements of the various jurisdictions may be so different that it is impossible to be in compliance with multiple language, print size, and color requirements of several states."[28] For a discussion of the complex choice-of-law questions raised in cross-border lawyer advertising, *see* Margaret Raymond, Inside, Outside: Cross-Border Enforcement of Attorney Advertising Restrictions, 43 Akron L. Rev. 801 (2010).

6. In advising a lawyer who seeks to use a cross-border advertisement, should you tell the lawyer that complaints about lawyer advertising are rare, that most complaints are handled informally, and that only a few states engage in active monitoring of lawyer ads?[29]

7. State regulations are difficult enough to interpret and apply to traditional print and television advertising; however, today's lawyers are increasingly using digital forms of communication, including "websites, attorney blogs, microblogs (such as Twitter), YouTube® infomercials, webinars, postings on social media such as Facebook and LinkedIn, online review sites, text messaging, the use of smart phones, 'apps,' links, video technology and tag lines."[30] In addition, "lawyers and law firms are engaged in much more sophisticated forms of marketing and advertising, including 'advertorials,' cooperative lawyer ads, retargeting, search engine optimization, online referral and lead-sharing sites, and 'pay-per-click' or 'pay-per-deal' arrangements."[31] Do lawyer advertising rules apply to a lawyer's use of this new technology? The Virginia Supreme Court held that a lawyer's blog discussing cases in which he obtained successful outcomes for his clients was commercial, not political speech, and was therefore subject to a Virginia advertising rule requiring prominent disclaimers for case-related discussions.[32] Imagine the difficulty of complying with a state rule requiring that ads include the lawyer's name and office location, while maintaining Twitter's limit of 160 characters.[33]

---

28. Daniel Backer, Choice of Law in Online Legal Ethics: Changing a Vague Standard for Attorney Advertising on the Internet, 70 Fordham L. Rev. 2409, 2427 (2002).

29. *See* Association of Professional Responsibility Lawyers, 2015 Report of the Regulation of Lawyer Advertising Committee 28 (Jun. 22, 2015) (reporting results of survey of 51 U.S. lawyer regulation offices).

30. *Id.* at 19.

31. *Id.* at 20. The report also discusses various online lawyer rating services and social networking websites for lawyers. *id.*

32. Hunter v. Virginia State Bar ex rel. Third District Comm., 744 S.E.2d 611 (Va. 2013).

33. A law school ethics professor was reported to have remarked, "Pity the lawyer trying to use Twitter in . . . Little Harbor on the Hillsboro, Fla." David L. Hudson, Jr., A Net Loss: Firm Challenges Florida Bar Over Website Ad Limits, A.B.A. Journal 22 (Mar. 2014).

8. The New York State Bar Association publishes and periodically updates Social Media Ethics Guidelines, including a discussion of when advertising rules are applicable, the prohibited use of the term "specialists" in social media, a lawyer's responsibility to monitor or remove social media content by others on a lawyer's social media page, attorney endorsements, and positional conflicts created when a lawyer communicates positions on issues that are inconsistent with those being advanced on behalf of firm clients.[34] The Guidelines focus on New York rules and ethics opinions, but also refer to ethics opinions in other states.

9. Law other than rules of professional conduct may regulate the content of some lawyer advertisements. For example, in Milavetz, Gallop & Milavetz, P.A. v. United States,[35] the U.S. Supreme Court upheld the constitutionality of a provision of the Bankruptcy Abuse Prevention and Consumer Protection Act that requires advertisements for bankruptcy lawyers to describe themselves as "debt relief agencies" and to include a statement to the effect that a debt relief agency "help[s] people file for bankruptcy relief under the Bankruptcy Code."

B. RESTRICTIONS ON LAWYER SOLICITATION

Model Rule 7.3(b) provides that, with several exceptions, "[a] lawyer shall not solicit professional employment by live person-to-person contact when a significant motive for the lawyer's doing so is the lawyer's or law firm's pecuniary gain." The exceptions permit a lawyer to solicit the following: (1) another lawyer; (2) a person who has a "family, close personal, or prior professional relationship with the lawyer or law firm"; and (3) a "person who routinely uses for business purposes the type of legal services offered by the lawyer."

The comment explains the reason for the broad ban on "live person-to-person contact":

> This form of contact subjects a person to the private importuning of the trained advocate in a direct interpersonal encounter. The person, who may already feel overwhelmed by the circumstances giving rise to the need for legal services, may find it difficult to fully evaluate all available alternatives with reasoned judgment and appropriate self-interest in the face of the lawyer's presence and insistence upon an immediate response. The situation is fraught with the possibility of undue influence, intimidation, and overreaching.[36]

As noted earlier, the U.S. Supreme Court upheld an even broader ban on in-person solicitation in *Ohralik v. Ohio State Bar Ass'n*, which is reproduced below. As you read the opinion, consider the fact that the Supreme Court upheld the state's right to adopt broad "prophylactic measures" to protect against the

---

34. NYSBA, Social Media Ethics Guidelines (Apr. 29, 2019).
35. 559 U.S. 229 (2010).
36. MR 7.3(b), cmt [2].

512   Chapter 17 Marketing Legal Services

potential evils of in-person solicitation, even though the court below made no finding that the persons targeted were harmed by the solicitation.

Ohralik v. Ohio State Bar Ass'n
436 U.S. 447 (1978)

Mr. Justice POWELL delivered the opinion of the Court.

In *Bates v. State Bar of Arizona*, this Court held that truthful advertising of "routine" legal services is protected by the First and Fourteenth Amendments against blanket prohibition by a State. The Court expressly reserved the question of the permissible scope of regulation of "in-person solicitation of clients — at the hospital room or the accident site, or in any other situation that breeds undue influence — by attorneys or their agents or 'runners.'" Today we answer part of the question so reserved, and hold that the State — or the Bar acting with state authorization — constitutionally may discipline a lawyer for soliciting clients in person, for pecuniary gain, under circumstances likely to pose dangers that the State has a right to prevent.

I

Appellant, a member of the Ohio Bar, lives in Montville Ohio. . . . On February 13, 1974, . . . appellant learned . . . about an automobile accident that had taken place on February 2 in which Carol McClintock, a young woman with whom appellant was casually acquainted, had been injured. Appellant made a telephone call to Ms. McClintock's parents, who informed him that their daughter was in the hospital. Appellant suggested that he might visit Carol in the hospital. Mrs. McClintock assented to the idea, but requested that appellant first stop by at her home.

During appellant's visit with the McClintocks, they explained that their daughter had been driving the family automobile on a local road when she was hit by an uninsured motorist. Both Carol and her passenger, Wanda Lou Holbert, were injured and hospitalized. In response to the McClintocks' expression of apprehension that they might be sued by Holbert, appellant explained that Ohio's guest statute would preclude such a suit. When appellant suggested to the McClintocks that they hire a lawyer, Mrs. McClintock retorted that such a decision would be up to Carol, who was 18 years old and would be the beneficiary of a successful claim.

Appellant proceeded to the hospital, where he found Carol lying in traction in her room. After a brief conversation about her condition, appellant told Carol he would represent her and asked her to sign an agreement. Carol said she would have to discuss the matter with her parents. She did not sign the agreement, but asked appellant to have her parents come to see her. Appellant also attempted to see Wanda Lou Holbert, but learned that she had just been released from the hospital. He then departed for another visit with the McClintocks.

On his way, appellant detoured to the scene of the accident, where he took a set of photographs. He also picked up a tape recorder, which he concealed under his raincoat before arriving at the McClintocks' residence. Once there, [a]ppellant discovered that the McClintocks' insurance policy would provide benefits of up to $12,500 each for Carol and Wanda Lou under an uninsured-motorist clause. . . . The McClintocks . . . told appellant that Carol had phoned to say that appellant could "go ahead" with her representation. Two days later appellant returned to Carol's hospital room to have her sign a contract, which provided that he would receive one-third of her recovery.

In the meantime, appellant obtained Wanda Lou's name and address from the McClintocks after telling them he wanted to ask her some questions about the accident. He then visited Wanda Lou at her home, without having been invited. He again concealed his tape recorder and recorded most of the conversation with Wanda Lou. After a brief, unproductive inquiry about the facts of the accident, appellant told Wanda Lou that he was representing Carol and that he had a "little tip" for Wanda Lou: the McClintocks' insurance policy contained an uninsured-motorist clause which might provide her with a recovery of up to $12,500. The young woman, who was 18 years of age and not a high school graduate at the time, replied to appellant's query about whether she was going to file a claim by stating that she really did not understand what was going on. Appellant offered to represent her, also, for a contingent fee of one-third of any recovery, and Wanda Lou stated "O.K."

Wanda's mother attempted to repudiate her daughter's oral assent the following day, when appellant called on the telephone to speak to Wanda. . . . Appellant insisted that Wanda had entered into a binding agreement. A month later Wanda confirmed in writing that she wanted neither to sue nor to be represented by appellant. She requested that appellant notify the insurance company that he was not her lawyer, as the company would not release a check to her until he did so. Carol also eventually discharged appellant. Although another lawyer represented her in concluding a settlement with the insurance company, she paid appellant one-third of her recovery in settlement of his lawsuit against her for breach of contract.

Both Carol McClintock and Wanda Lou Holbert filed complaints against appellant. [After a disciplinary hearing, appellant was found by an Ohio state board to have violated DR 2-103(A) and 2-104(A) of the Ohio Code of Professional Responsibility.[37] The Supreme Court of Ohio adopted the board's findings and sanctioned appellant to an indefinite suspension.]

---

37. [Fn. 9 in Original] DR 2-103(A) of the Ohio Code (1970) provides:

"A lawyer shall not recommend employment, as a private practitioner, of himself, his partner, or associate to a non-lawyer who has not sought his advice regarding employment of a lawyer."

DR 2-104(A)(1970) provides in relevant part:

"A lawyer who has given unsolicited advice to a layman that he should obtain counsel or take legal action shall not accept employment resulting from that advice, except that:

"(1) A lawyer may accept employment by a close friend, relative, former client (if the advice is germane to the former employment), or one whom the lawyer reasonably believes to be a client."

II . . .

A

Appellant contends that his solicitation of the two young women as clients is indistinguishable, for purposes of constitutional analysis, from the advertisement in *Bates*. Like that advertisement, his meetings with the prospective clients apprised them of their legal rights and of the availability of a lawyer to pursue their claims. According to appellant, such conduct is "presumptively an exercise of free speech rights" which cannot be curtailed in the absence of proof that it actually caused a specific harm that the State has a compelling interest in preventing. But in-person solicitation of professional employment by a lawyer does not stand on a par with truthful advertising about the availability and terms of routine legal services, let alone with forms of speech more traditionally within the concern of the First Amendment. . . .

As applied in this case, the Disciplinary Rules are said to have limited the communication of two kinds of information. First, appellant's solicitation imparted to Carol McClintock and Wanda Lou Holbert certain information about his availability and the terms of his proposed legal services. In this respect, in-person solicitation serves much the same function as the advertisement at issue in *Bates*. But there are significant differences as well. Unlike a public advertisement, which simply provides information and leaves the recipient free to act upon it or not, in-person solicitation may exert pressure and often demands an immediate response, without providing an opportunity for comparison or reflection. The aim and effect of in-person solicitation may be to provide a one-sided presentation and to encourage speedy and perhaps uninformed decisionmaking: there is no opportunity for intervention or counter-education by agencies of the Bar, supervisory authorities, or persons close to the solicited individual. . . . In-person solicitation is as likely as not to discourage persons needing counsel from engaging in a critical comparison of the "availability, nature and prices" of legal services; it actually may disserve the individual and societal interest, identified in *Bates*, in facilitating "informed and reliable decisionmaking."

It also is argued that in-person solicitation may provide the solicited individual with information about his or her legal rights and remedies. In this case, appellant gave Wanda Lou a "tip" about the prospect of recovery based on the uninsured-motorist clause in the McClintocks' insurance policy, and he explained that clause and Ohio's guest statute to Carol McClintock's parents. But neither of the Disciplinary Rules here at issue prohibited appellant from communicating information to these young women about their legal rights and the prospects of obtaining a monetary recovery, or from recommending that they obtain counsel. . . . The Rule does not prohibit a lawyer from giving unsolicited legal advice; it proscribes the acceptance of employment resulting from such advice. . . .

B

The state interests implicated in this case are particularly strong. In addition to its general interest in protecting consumers and regulating commercial transactions, the State bears a special responsibility for maintaining standards among members of the licensed professions. "The interest of the States in regulating lawyers is especially great since lawyers are essential to the primary governmental function of administering justice, and have historically been 'officers of the courts.'" While lawyers act in part as "self-employed businessmen," they also act "as trusted agents of their clients, and as assistants to the court in search of a just solution to disputes."...

The substantive evils of solicitation have been stated over the years in sweeping terms: stirring up litigation, assertion of fraudulent claims, debasing the legal profession, and potential harm to the solicited client in the form of overreaching, overcharging, underrepresentation, and misrepresentation. The American Bar Association, as *amicus curiae*, defends the rule against solicitation primarily on three broad grounds: It is said that the prohibitions embodied in DR 2-103(A) and 2-104(A) serve to reduce the likelihood of overreaching and the exertion of undue influence on lay persons, to protect the privacy of individuals, and to avoid situations where the lawyer's exercise of judgment on behalf of the client will be clouded by his own pecuniary interest.

We need not discuss or evaluate each of these interests in detail as appellant has conceded that the State has a legitimate and indeed "compelling" interest in preventing those aspects of solicitation that involve fraud, undue influence, intimidation, overreaching, and other forms of "vexatious conduct." We agree that protection of the public from these aspects of solicitation is a legitimate and important state interest.

III

Appellant's concession that strong state interests justify regulation to prevent the evils he enumerates would end this case but for his insistence that none of those evils was found to be present in his acts of solicitation. He challenges what he characterizes as the "indiscriminate application" of the Rules to him and thus attacks the validity of DR 2-103(A) and DR 2-104(A) not facially, but as applied to his acts of solicitation. And because no allegations or findings were made of the specific wrongs appellant concedes would justify disciplinary action, appellant terms his solicitation "pure," meaning "soliciting and obtaining agreements from Carol McClintock and Wanda Lou Holbert to represent each of them," without more. Appellant, therefore argues that we must decide whether a State may discipline him for solicitation *per se* without offending the First and Fourteenth Amendments.

We agree that the appropriate focus is on appellant's conduct. And, as appellant urges, we must undertake an independent review of the record to determine whether that conduct was constitutionally protected. But appellant errs in assuming that the constitutional validity of the judgment below depends on proof that his conduct constituted actual overreaching or inflicted some specific injury on Wanda Holbert or Carol McClintock. . . .

Appellant's argument misconceives the nature of the State's interest. The Rules prohibiting solicitation are prophylactic measures whose objective is the prevention of harm before it occurs. The Rules were applied in this case to discipline a lawyer for soliciting employment for pecuniary gain under circumstances likely to result in the adverse consequences the State seeks to avert. In such a situation, which is inherently conducive to overreaching and other forms of misconduct, the State has a strong interest in adopting and enforcing rules of professional conduct designed to protect the public from harmful solicitation by lawyers whom it has licensed.

The State's perception of the potential for harm in circumstances such as those presented in this case is well founded. The detrimental aspects of face-to-face selling even of ordinary consumer products have been recognized and addressed by the Federal Trade Commission, and it hardly need be said that the potential for overreaching is significantly greater when a lawyer, a professional trained in the art of persuasion, personally solicits an unsophisticated, injured, or distressed lay person. Such an individual may place his trust in a lawyer, regardless of the latter's qualifications or the individual's actual need for legal representation, simply in response to persuasion under circumstances conducive to uninformed acquiescence. Although it is argued that personal solicitation is valuable because it may apprise a victim of misfortune of his legal rights, the very plight of that person not only makes him more vulnerable to influence but also may make advice all the more intrusive. Thus, under these adverse conditions the overtures of an uninvited lawyer may distress the solicited individual simply because of their obtrusiveness and the invasion of the individual's privacy, even when no other harm materializes. Under such circumstances, it is not unreasonable for the State to presume that in-person solicitation by lawyers more often than not will be injurious to the person solicited.

The efficacy of the State's effort to prevent such harm to prospective clients would be substantially diminished if, having proved a solicitation in circumstances like those of this case, the State were required in addition to prove actual injury. Unlike the advertising in *Bates*, in-person solicitation is not visible or otherwise open to public scrutiny. Often there is no witness other than the lawyer and the lay person whom he has solicited, rendering it difficult or impossible to obtain reliable proof of what actually took place. This would be especially true if the lay person were so distressed at the time of the solicitation that he could not recall specific details at a later date. If appellant's view were sustained, in-person solicitation would be virtually immune to effective oversight and regulation by the State or by the legal profession, in contravention of the State's strong interest in regulating members of the Bar in an effective, objective, and self-enforcing manner. It therefore is not unreasonable, or violative of the Constitution, for a State to respond with what in effect is a prophylactic rule. . . .

B. Restrictions on Lawyer Solicitation 517

On the basis of the undisputed facts of record, we conclude that the Disciplinary Rules constitutionally could be applied to appellant. He approached two young accident victims at a time when they were especially incapable of making informed judgments or of assessing and protecting their own interest. He solicited Carol McClintock in a hospital room where she lay in traction and sought out Wanda Lou Holbert on the day she came home from the hospital, knowing from his prior inquiries that she had just been released. Appellant urged his services upon the young women and used the information he had obtained from the McClintocks, and the fact of his agreement with Carol, to induce Wanda to say "O.K." in response to his solicitation. He employed a concealed tape recorder, seemingly to insure that he would have evidence of Wanda's oral assent to the representation. He emphasized that his fee would come out of the recovery, thereby tempting the young women with what sounded like a cost-free and therefore irresistible offer. . . .

The court below did not hold that these or other facts were proof of actual harm to Wanda Holbert or Carol McClintock but rested on the conclusion that appellant had engaged in the general misconduct proscribed by the Disciplinary Rules. Under our view of the State's interest in averting harm by prohibiting solicitation in circumstances where it is likely to occur, the absence of explicit proof or findings or harm or injury is immaterial. The facts in this case present a striking example of the potential for overreaching that is inherent in a lawyer's in-person solicitation of professional employment. They also demonstrate the need for prophylactic regulation in furtherance of the State's interest in protecting the lay public. We hold that the application of DR 2-103(A) and 2-104(A) to appellant does not offend the Constitution.

Accordingly, the judgment of the Supreme Court of Ohio is
Affirmed.

NOTES AND QUESTIONS

1. Prior to the 2018 amendments, Rule 7.3 did not permit live, in-person solicitation of a "person who routinely uses for business purposes the type of legal services offered by the lawyer," and many states do not currently recognize this exception. Do lawyers have a constitutional right to solicit businesses? In 1993, the U.S. Supreme Court decided Edenfield v. Fane,[38] holding that an accountant had a constitutional right to solicit business clients and stating that "[w]hile *Ohralik* discusses the generic hazards of personal solicitation, the opinion made clear that a preventative rule was justified only in situations 'inherently conducive to overreaching and other forms of misconduct.'" The Court further noted that "[u]nlike a lawyer, a CPA is not 'a professional trained in the art of persuasion.'" Is live, in-person solicitation by *a*

---

38. 507 U.S. 761 (1993).

Chapter 17 Marketing Legal Services

lawyer always "inherently conducive to overreaching and other forms of misconduct"? What was it about the solicitation in *Ohralik* that constituted such a situation?

2. Rule 7.3(a), which was also added in 2018, defines "solicitation" as "a communication initiated by or on behalf of a lawyer or law firm that is directed to a specific person the lawyer knows or reasonably should know needs legal services in a particular matter and that offers to provide, or reasonably can be understood as offering to provide, legal services for that matter." May a lawyer cold call businesses to offer general employment law services, such as drafting employment agreements, nondisclosure and noncompetition agreements, and advising on antidiscrimination laws? What if the lawyer has no idea whether any particular business has in-house counsel or routinely uses a lawyer to perform this sort of work?

3. As with many other legal ethics issues, the increasing use of technology has complicated the application of the solicitation rules. Prior to 2018, the general antisolicitation rule applied to "in-person, live telephone or real-time electronic contact." The ABA deleted the reference to "real-time electronic contact" and defines "live person-to-person" in the comment to mean "in-person, face-to-face, live telephone and other real time visual or auditory person-to-person communications where the person is subject to a direct personal encounter without time for reflection." MR 7.3, cmt [2]. Email solicitation is clearly permitted, as are text messages. *Id.* Even prior to the rule amendment, at least one ethics opinion had concluded that using social media for solicitation purposes should be generally acceptable because they are all "characterized by an ability on the part of the prospective client to 'turn off' the soliciting lawyer and respond or not as he or she sees fit, and an ability to keep a record of its contents."[39] A recent article describes cognition studies suggesting that it is "virtually impossible for the recipient [of a text] not to open [it] immediately and most likely respond," resulting in "an incredible 98% open rate and 90% of these are read within three minutes of receipt."[40] *Should* lawyers be prohibited from soliciting persons by means of a text message?

4. Prior to the 2018 amendments, Rule 7.3(c) required that written, recorded or other nonprohibited electronic communications soliciting professional employment must "include the words 'Advertising Material' on the outside envelope, if any, and at the beginning and

---

39. Phila. Ethics Op. 2010-6. *But see, e.g.,* W. Va. Ethics Op. 2015-02 (2015) (real-time electronic contact "arguably" includes live social media chat and comments to posts); N.Y. State Ethics Op. 1049 (2015) (tweet inviting potential client to contact lawyer concerning particular issue constitutes solicitation).

40. Ashley M. London, Something Wicked This Way Thumbs: Personal Contact Concerns of Text-based Attorney Marketing, 58 Houston L. Rev. 99, 100 (2020).

ending of any recorded or electronic communication, unless the recipient of the communication is a person [exempted from live, in-person solicitation]." Many states continue to require this type of labeling. As with disclaimers and other required disclosures under the advertising rules, the labeling requirement is often difficult to satisfy when lawyers use various forms of digital media for their solicitation. In addition, the precise wording required may differ from jurisdiction to jurisdiction,[41] or the jurisdiction may make it difficult for lawyers to engage in cross-border solicitation; additionally, some jurisdictions require that a sample copy of each communication be filed with the state bar.[42]

C. PAYING FOR REFERRALS

Model Rule 7.2(b) provides that, with certain exceptions, "[a] lawyer shall not compensate, give or promise anything of value to a person for recommending the lawyer's services." The rule applies to payments to both lawyers and nonlawyers. Under Model Rule 1.5(e), lawyers in different firms may divide a legal fee, but only if "the division is in proportion to the services performed by each lawyer or each lawyer assumes joint responsibility for the representation."[43] Although the Model Rules do not permit payment of a pure referral fee to either a lawyer or a nonlawyer, some states permit pure referral fees to other lawyers[44] in order to encourage lawyers to refer cases to the lawyer most competent to perform the work.[45]

Historically, the rule against compensation for referrals arose out of a concern for lawyers who pay a "runner" to drum up business. Modern examples of the use of such "runners" include a lawyer who hired a minister as a

---

41. *See, e.g.,* Ala. Rules of Prof'l Conduct, Rule 7.3(b) ("the word 'Advertisement' shall appear prominently in red ink on each page of the written communication and on the lower left corner of the envelope in 14-point or larger type and in red ink"); Ark. Rules of Prof'l Conduct, Rule 7.3(b)(5) (written communication must "begin with the statement that 'If you have already retained a lawyer, please disregard this letter'"), 7.4(b)(6) (written communication must include the following statement in capital letters: "ANY COMPLAINTS ABOUT THIS LETTER OR THE REPRESENTATION OF ANY LAWYER MAY BE DIRECTED TO THE SUPREME COURT COMMITTEE ON PROFESSIONAL CONDUCT, C/O CLERK, ARKANSAS SUPREME COURT, 625 MARSHALL STREET, LITTLE ROCK, ARKANSAS 72201)").

42. *See, e.g.,* Ala. Rules of Prof'l Conduct, Rule 7.3(b)(2)(i) (requiring sample copy of both communication and sample envelope, along with "a list of the names and addresses of the recipients").

43. The rule further requires that "the client agree[s] to the arrangement, including the share each lawyer will receive, and the agreement is confirmed in writing" and that "the total fee is reasonable." MR 1.5(e)(2), (3).

44. These states include Alabama, California, Connecticut, Delaware, Kansas, Maine, Michigan, Nevada, New Hampshire, Pennsylvania, Oregon, and Washington. As with other fee divisions, lawyers paying these pure referral fees must inform the client that they are doing so, and may need to obtain the affirmative consent of the client to do so.

45. *See* RLGL at §47, cmt b.

"paralegal" to solicit clients from accident victims whom he met in his role as a hospital chaplain,[46] and a lawyer who paid a kickback to an in-house corporate counsel in return for counsel referring corporate business.[47]

The rule applies not only to direct payments, but also to giving "anything of value" in return for the referral. For example, an Ohio ethics opinion concluded that the rule applied to a lawyer who not only offered to pay an annual fee to a real estate brokerage for recommendations, but also agreed to provide discounted legal services to the brokerage's customers as part of the same arrangement.[48] Similarly a Maryland ethics opinion condemned an arrangement whereby lawyers would participate as panelists for seminars sponsored by a financial services company, in return for referrals from the company when consumers called them with a request for legal services.[49]

Many companies provide comparative ratings of lawyers. These ratings clearly constitute a form of "referral"; however, the companies typically receive their revenue from advertising and do not require or even permit lawyers to pay to receive the rating.[50] As a result, lawyers may advertise their selection without violating Rule 7.2(b). There are, however, a number of "online legal directories" that charge lawyers to be listed. Paying an annual fee to be listed in a directory is permissible if the company does not recommend particular lawyers. But if the listings are limited and the lawyers are deemed to be paying for that exclusivity, the service may be deemed an impermissible for-profit referral agency.[51] Some ethics committees, however, have approved such payments if the service clearly discloses that each lawyer has paid for an exclusive listing.[52] Sole practitioners or small firm lawyers sometimes pool their resources to market their services. These group marketing efforts are permissible if they provide basic directory services and don't screen cases or match lawyers with particular clients.[53]

Lawyers' marketing efforts have become highly creative in the digital age, and the possibilities are ever-changing. At one point, "daily deals" and "group coupons" were the rage. A website company markets these deals or coupons for deeply discounted products or services, including legal services. Typically, the company receives the client's payment, retains a portion, and then forwards the rest to the lawyer. A host of ethical issues are raised by these types of marketing efforts. For example, the portion of the payment retained by the company may constitute the reasonable cost

---

46. *See* Fla. Bar v. Barrett, 897 So.2d 1269 (Fla. 2005).

47. *See* Ohio State Bar Ass'n v. Kanter, 715 N.E.2d 1140 (Ohio 1999).

48. *See* Ohio Bd. of Prof. Conduct Ethics Op. 2020-09 (2020).

49. *See* Maryland Ethics Op. 2000-35 (2001).

50. *See, e.g.,* Super Lawyers, https://www.superlawyers.com; Best Lawyers, https://www.bestlawyers.com/america.

51. *See* Ill. Ethics Op. 92-23 (1992) (listings limited to four attorneys in each category).

52. *See, e.g.,* Ariz. Ethics Op. 11-02 (2011) (permissible for lawyer to pay for exclusive right to sole listing in the zip code where the client lives).

53. *See* Ky. Ethics Op. E-429 (2008).

of lawyer advertising; however, when the payment is calculated as a percentage of the client's legal fees, some ethics committees have found that the payment constitutes both an impermissible payment for a referral and impermissible fee sharing with a lay person.[54] Other concerns expressed by ethics committees include: (1) the initial payment of legal fees is deposited in the company's account, not in the lawyer's client trust account, as required by Rule 1.15(a);[55] and (2) if the consumer does not use the coupon before it expires, the lawyer will be charging an excessive legal fee unless the lawyer returns not only the lawyer's portion of the fee paid, but also an amount equal to the portion retained by the company.[56] A few ethics committees have found that lawyers may ethically participate in such programs if they follow certain guidelines, including explaining that the relationship is contingent upon a conflicts check and providing a full refund, even when the voucher has expired.[57]

An amendment to Rule 7.2(b) adopted in 2002 permits lawyers to enter into reciprocal referral agreements with other lawyers or nonlawyer professionals, but only if the referral agreement is not exclusive and the client is fully informed of the existence and nature of the agreement.[58] One purpose of the non-exclusivity agreement is to acknowledge the possibility of conflicts of interests or other circumstances where a particular referral would be inappropriate. A comment to the rule states that such arrangements may not "interfere with the lawyer's professional judgment as to making referrals." What does "independent judgment" require of a lawyer in making referrals to another lawyer or nonlawyer professional? Does it require that in each instance, the lawyer's decision as to whom to refer the client is uninfluenced by external considerations such as the lawyer's interest in receiving reciprocal referrals? If so, then what is the point of the reciprocal referral agreement? And what about referrals to other lawyers in the same law firm?

An amendment to Rule 7.2 adopted in 2018 permits lawyers to give "nominal gifts" as a token of appreciation for a referral.[59] The comment explains that "[t]he gift may not be more than a token item as might be given for holidays, or other ordinary social hospitality."[60] May a lawyer send a $100 bottle of wine to another lawyer who referred a client? Even a nominal gift will violate the rule if "intended [] or reasonably expected to be a form of compensation for recommending the lawyer's services."

---

54. *See, e.g.*, Ind. State Bar Ass'n Legal Ethics Comm., Op. No. 1, JDH-1 (2012).
55. *See, e.g., id.*
56. *See, e.g.*, N.Y. State Bar Ass'n Comm. on Prof'l Ethics, Op. 897 (2011).
57. *See, e.g.*, N.C. State Bar, Formal Op. 10 (2011).
58. MR 7.2(b)(4), discussed *supra* Chapter 16: Nonlawyer Ownership, Multidisciplinary Practice, and Alternative Legal Service Providers.
59. *See* MR 7.2(b)(5).
60. *Id.* at cmt [4].

Review Problems

17-1 A lawyer would like to use a television advertisement in which a client would appear, saying the following:

> I was ten months behind on my mortgage payments and was in real danger of losing my home. The lender didn't care. I had nowhere to turn. That's when I found attorney _____. He not only saved my house but helped me get my mortgage payments reduced. Suddenly my home was in jeopardy. I tried to work things out with the bank but it was as if I were talking to a brick wall. I would have lost everything. My life would have been ruined if I had not found attorney _____. He was truly a godsend.

A narrator would then conclude as follows:

> If you're in need of help, turn to the law offices of _____, which has helped hundreds of homeowners reduce their mortgage payments to lenders and stay in their homes. Our office will review your situation and help you decide what strategy is right for you.

The client testimonial reflects the truthful experience of an actual client. Is the ad permissible? Does it matter whether the "client" in the television ad is the real client or an actor portraying the client (with the actual client's consent)? The concluding narration is also truthful, although there were a few clients whose homes were sold at a foreclosure sale despite the lawyer's best efforts.

17-2 A litigation law firm aired a television advertisement in which it displayed the logo of a pit bull with a spiked collar, accompanied by the law firm's telephone number—"1-800-PIT-BULL." Does the ad violate the Model Rules? What about a jurisdiction that has the following provision: "Visual or verbal descriptions, depictions, or portrayals of persons, things, or events must be objectively relevant to the selection of an attorney"? Does such a provision violate the First Amendment? The stated purpose of the provision is to prevent lawyers from appealing to emotions or sentiments that are unrelated to the selection of an attorney and to avoid advertisements that demean the profession.

17-3 A real estate lawyer who recently moved her office to the suburb where she lives is considering a variety of marketing efforts to increase her client base. Consider whether the following actions would be ethical:

(a) Hosting seminars at the local community center with the following title: "Thinking about selling your home? What you need to know about the seller's contract." She will have firm brochures available on a table near the door and plans to hand out her business card to any attendee who approaches her with a question, saying, "If you have further questions, please call me at my office."

(b) Telephoning local businesses to let them know that she provides legal services with respect to lease negotiations.

(c) Telephoning, emailing, or texting homeowners with a "For Sale" sign, letting them know that she is available to represent them in any home sale.

(d) Informally partnering with a friend who is a real estate agent, letting the agent know that the lawyer plans to refer clients to the agent, and expecting that the agent will do the same, although they will have no explicit agreement to do so.

TABLE OF CASES

Principal cases are italicized.

Aboyade, In re, 434
Ackert; United States v., 299
Akzo Nobel Chems. Ltd. & Akcros Chems. Ltd. v. European Comm'n, 401
Alexander v. Cahill, 502, 508, 509
Alexander; United States v., 79
Allied Concrete Co. v. Lester, 215
Alvarez; United States v., 299
Amendment to Rule Regulating the Florida Bar 6-10.3, In re, 442
American Legacy Found. v. Lorillard Tobacco Co., 71
Amway Corp. v. Procter & Gamble Co., 404
Analytica, Inc. v. NPD Research, Inc., 152, 157-159, 160, 161, 165, 166, 168, 169, 170, 171
Application of ____. *See name of applicant*
Applied Asphalt Techs. v. Sam B. Corp., 311
Armstrong v. McAlpin, 177, 178
Arpadi v. First MSP Corp., 273
Asia Glob. Crossing, Ltd., In re, 72
Attorney Grievance Comm'n v. Bereano, 434
Attorney Grievance Comm'n v. Coppola, 220
Attorney Grievance Comm'n v. Gore, 434

Baker v. Wilmer Cutler Pickering Hale & Dorr LLP, 270
Baldesarre v. Butler, 109
Balla v. Gambro, 410
Bank Brussels Lambert v. Fiddler, Gonzalez & Rodriguez, 112
Bates v. State Bar of Ariz., 7, 499
BDO Seidman LLP; United States v., 119
Bedoya v. Aventura Limousine & Transp. Serv., 188

Belge; People v., 97
Bevill, Bresler & Schulman Asset Mgmt. Corp., In re, 329, 330
Birbrower, Montalbano, Condon & Frank, P.C. v. Superior Court, 448, 453-454, 456, 464, 465
Board of Educ. v. Nyquist, 132
Bobbitt v. Victorian House, Inc., 264, 269-270
Bourdon's Case, 136
Brennans, Inc. v. Brennan's Rests., Inc., 160
BSP Software, LLC v. Motio, Inc., 299
Burch, In re Application of, 426, 430-431, 432
Burger v. Kemp, 214
Burkhart v. Semitool, Inc., 418

Campbell v. Asbury Auto., Inc., 446
Campellone v. Cragon, 330
Cantey Hanger, LLP v. Byrd, 245
Cantrell, In re, 221
Carambio, Estate of, 199
Caremark Int'l Inc. Derivative Litig., In re, 405
Carnegie Cos., Inc. v. Summit Props., Inc., 134
Celgene Corp. v. KV Pharm. Co., 131
Central Bank of Denver v. First Interstate Bank of Denver, 374
Central Hudson Gas & Elec. Corp. v. Pub. Serv. Comm'n of N.Y., 508, 509
Charges of Unprofessional Conduct, In re, 442
Charges of Unprofessional Conduct in Panel File No. 39302, In re, 457, 464, 465, 467
Chem-Age Industries, Inc. v. Glover, 239, 242-243, 244, 271
Coleman v. State, 212

523

524 Table of Cases

Collmar, In re, 30
Commodity Futures Trading Comm'n v. Weintraub, 300
Condon, Estate of, v. McHenry, 453
Consolidated Coal Co. v. Bucyrus-Erie Co., 282, 290
Cooperman, In re, 57
Copper Market Antitrust Litigation, In re, 294, 298-299
Cord v. Gibb, 426
Crews v. Buckman Laboratories International, Inc., 412, 417-418
Cromley v. Board of Educ., 172
Cunningham v. Ky. Bar Ass'n, 433
Cuyler v. Sullivan, 143, 147, 210, 213-214

Daniels v. Alander, 194
Disciplinary Action Against Stoneburner, In re, 435
Dodge, In re, 193
Doughty, In re, 434

Edenfield v. Fane, 517
E.F. Hutton & Co. v. Brown, 259, 263, 278
Egan v. McNamara, 271
Eicher, In re, 435
Enron Corp. Sec., Derivative & ERISA Litig., 136
Enron, In re, 5
Estate of _____. *See name of decedent*

Faraone, In re, 237-238
Farris v. Fireman's Fund Ins. Co., 160
Fassihi v. Sommers, Schwartz, Silver, Schwartz & Tyler, P.C., 270
FDIC v. _____. *See name of opposing party*
Feeley, In re, 218
Fire Ins. Exch. v. Bell, 228, 238
Florida Bar v. Barrett, 520
Florida Bar v. Bartholf, 435
Florida Bar v. Joy, 224
Florida Bar v. Martocci, 437
Florida Bar v. Went For It, Inc., 500, 508, 509
Fordham, In re, 56, 57
Fox Searchlight Pictures, Inc. v. Paladino, 417
Frazier, United States ex rel., v. IASIS Healthcare Corp., 409, 418
Freescale Semiconductor, Inc. v. Maxim Integrated Prods., Inc., 409

Galderma Labs., L.P. v. Actavis Mid Atl. LLC, 131
Garner v. Wolfinbarger, 292
General Dynamics v. Superior Court, 417-418
Genesis Merchant Partners, L.P. v. Gilbride, Tusa, Last & Spellane, LLC, 23, 25, 28, 29, 30, 82
Gifford; People v., 218
Goesel v. Boley Int'l (H.K.), Ltd., 59
Goldfarb v. Va. State Bar, 7
Gould v. Fla. Bar, 455
Grand Jury Investigation, In re, 70
Great Hill Equity Partners IV, LP v. SIG Growth Equity Fund I, LLLP, 307, 312
Greater Se. Cmty. Hosp. Corp., In re, 373
Greenberg v. Haggerty, 442
Greycas, Inc. v. Proud, 246
Grutter v. Bollinger, 442
GSI Commerce Solutions, Inc. v. BabyCenter, L.L.C., 338, 344-345

Hale v. Comm. on Character & Fitness, 431
Harper, In re, 468
Haynes & Boone, LLP v. NFTD, LLC, 245
Heathcoat v. Santa Fe Int'l Corp., 35
Hechinger Inv. Co. of Del., Inc., In re, 312
Himmel, In re, 435
Holloway v. Arkansas, 147
Humphrey, State ex rel., v. Philip Morris Inc., 405
Hunter v. Va. State Bar ex rel. Third Dist. Comm., 74, 510

IBM v. Levin, 122
Iowa Supreme Court Bd. of Prof'l Ethics & Conduct v. Polson, 435
Isselmann, SEC v., 354-356, 360, 372

Jacoby & Meyers, LLP v. Presiding Justices, 475
Janson v. LegalZoom, Inc., 492
Janus Capital Grp., Inc. v. First Derivative Traders, 383, 389
Jardine, In re, 467
Johnson v. Schultz, 20, 238
JPMorgan Chase Bank ex rel. Mahonia Ltd. v. Liberty Mut. Ins. Co., 345

Table of Cases

525

Kinsey, In re, 271
Kirschner v. K&L Gates, 271
Kirschner v. KPMG LLP, 373
Kovel; United States v., 299
Kramer v. Ciba-Geigy Corp., 113, 117, 120, 142, 143
Krug; United States v., 119

Law Students Civil Rights Research Council Inc. v. Wadmond, 426
Leazure v. Apria Healthcare Inc., 402
LegalForce RAPC Worldwide v. LegalZoom.com, 492
Ligon v. Clouette, 434
Lorenzo v. SEC, 384, 389
Los Angeles, City of, v. Superior Court, 99

Manoir-ElectroAlloys Corp. v. Amalloy Corp., 31, 34-35, 102, 121, 151
Maritrans GP Inc. v. Pepper, Hamilton & Scheetz, 9
McDowell; State v., 211
McGhee v. State, 195, 199
Medlock v. LegalZoom.com, Inc., 492
Meredith; People v., 71
Meyerhofer v. Empire Fire & Marine Insurance Co., 91, 94, 96
Midgett; United States v., 211
Milavetz, Gallop & Milavetz, P.A. v. United States, 511
Mississippi Bar v. McGuire, 423
Murphy & Demory, Ltd. v. Murphy, 271
Musheno v. Gensemer, 330, 335, 336-337
Mustafa, In re, 426
Mylan, Inc. v. Kirkland & Ellis LLP, 133, 134

Nam v. Quichocho, 18, 102, 237
Nathanson v. Mass. Comm'n Against Discrimination, 35
Nguyen v. Knowles, 211-212
Nicholas; United States v., 322, 335, 336, 346
Nichols v. Keller, 29, 30
Niswander v. Cincinnati Ins. Co., 418
Nix v. Whiteside, 202, 210, 211, 213
North Shore Gas Co. v. Elgin, Joliet & E. Ry. Co., 73

Ohio State Bar Ass'n v. Kanter, 520
Ohralik v. Ohio State Bar Ass'n, 499, 500, 511, *512*, 518

Oklahoma Bar Ass'n, State ex rel., v. Wilcox, 434
Olfe v. Gordon, *48*, 50, 51
O'Melveny & Myers; FDIC v., 373
Opinion 668 of Advisory Comm. on Prof'l Ethics, In re, 8
Oppenheimer-Palmieri Fund, L.P. v. Peat Marwick Main & Co., 373
Orbit One Commc'ns, Inc. v. Numerex Corp., 312
Orr; State v., 42

Pacific Investment Management Co. LLC v. Mayer Brown LLP, 374, 382, 383, 389
Pacific Pictures Corp., In re, 81
Passante v. McWilliam, *138*, 139-141
Pasyanos, In re, 430
Patsy's Brand, Inc. v. I.O.B. Realty, Inc., 201
Pearlstein v. Blackberry Ltd., 71, 293, 298, 299
Peel v. Attorney Registration & Disciplinary Comm'n, 500
People v. ____. *See name of opposing party*
Peterson v. Katten Muchin Rosenman LLP, 369, 372
Peterson v. Winston & Strawn LLP, 367, 372, 373
Picker Int'l, Inc. v. Varian Assocs., Inc., 132
Price v. Price, 160
Primus, In re, 500
Public Citizen, Inc. v. La. Attorney Disciplinary Bd., 508, 509
Purcell v. District Attorney for the Suffolk District, 68, 73, *75*, 78-79, 84, 87, 93

Quinlan v. Curtiss-Wright Corp., 418

Regents of Univ. of Cal. v. Bakke, 442-443
Republican Party of Minn. v. White, 56
Reynolds v. Schrock, 244-245
Rice v. Strunk, 271, 278
Richter v. Van Amberg, 274
Rishel; People v., 434
Rite Aid Corp. Sec. Litig., In re, 351
R.M.J., In re, 499
Roots, In re, 432
Rosman v. Shapiro, 267, 270, 272
Ruehle; United States v., 328-329
Ruffalo, In re, 432

SCB Diversified Municipal Portfolio v. Crews & Associates, 26, 28-29, 30
Schiessle v. Stephens, 166, 169, 170
Scholastic Corp. Sec. Litig., In re, 382
Schware v. N.M. Bd. of Bar Exam'rs, 426
Schwartz; United States v., 148
SEC v. ___. *See name of opposing party*
Shapero v. Ky. Bar Ass'n, 500
Sheppard, Mullin, Richter & Hampton, LLP v. J-M Manufacturing Co., 123, 131, 132, 135, 352
Siegel, In re, 218
Silver Chrysler Plymouth, Inc. v. Chrysler Motors Corp., 161, 165, 166
Simpson v. James, 104, 109, 111, 112, 132
Smith v. Scripto-Tokai Corp., 199, 200
State ex rel. ___. *See name of related party*
State v. ___. *See name of opposing party*
Steele, In re, 201
Stone v. Ritter, 405
Stoneridge Inv. Partners, LLC v. Sci.-Atlanta, Inc., 380
Strickland v. Washington, 147, 210, 211, 214
Stropnicky v. Nathanson, 441
Sullivan v. Cuyler, 147
Supreme Court Disciplinary Bd. v. Kress, 434
Swanson, State ex rel., v. 3M Co., 132
Swihart, In re, 136

Tekni-Plex, Inc. v. Meyner & Landis, 300, 311, 312
Tesini v. Zawistowski, 52
Thomas H. Lee Equity Fund V, L.P. v. Mayer Brown, Rowe & Maw LLP, 382-383, 389

3M Co.; State v., 159
Togstad v. Vesely, Otto, Miller & Keefe, 20
Tyler v. State, 194, 196, 199

Unauthorized Practice of Law Comm. v. Emp'rs Unity, Inc., 446
(Under Seal); United States v., 79
United States ex rel. ___. *See name of related party*
United States v. ___. *See name of opposing party*
Upjohn Co. v. United States, 282, *285,* 290, 291, 318
USI Ins. Servs., LLC v. Ryan, 311

Van Asdale v. International Game Tech., 418
Vega v. Jones, Day, Reavis & Pogue, 238
Vioxx Prods. Liab. Litig., In re, 404
Visa U.S.A. Inc. v. First Data Corp., 130

Warhaftig, In re, 433
Waring, In re Estate of, 454
Watkins, In re, 201
Watkins v. TransUnion, LLC, 160
Wayland v. Shore Lobster & Shrimp Corp., 270
Westinghouse Elec. Corp. v. Kerr-McGee Corp., 160
Wieder v. Skala, 436
William F. Shea, LLC v. Bonutti Research, Inc., 73
Witherspoon v. United States, 211

Zador Corp., N.V. v. Kwan, 130, 352
Zauderer v. Office of Disciplinary Counsel, 499, 508

INDEX

ABA/Bloomberg Law Lawyers' Manual on Professional Conduct, 8
ABS. *See* Alternative business structures (ABS)
ACC. *See* Association of Corporate Counsel (ACC)
ACCA. *See* American Corporate Counsel Association (ACCA)
Access to justice
  gap, 61, 491-497
  knowledge gap, 492
  service gap, 492
  unbundled legal services, 31
"Accidental" clients, 22
Accommodation clients, 118, 346-352
Accountant-client privilege, 482
Accreditation, 1, 423, 424
Actual authority, 52
Actual knowledge, 243
Admission to practice, 423-432
  bar examinations, 423, 424-425
  candor on law school applications, 425-430
  character and fitness, 423, 425-432
  court-adopted rules, 423
  educational requirements, 423, 424
  foreign-trained lawyers, 424
  out-of-state lawyers, 423-424
  professional responsibility bar examination, 423, 424
  requirements for, 423-432
Advance waivers
  conflicts of interest, 123-131, 352
Adversary system, 181, 182-188
  adversary zeal, limits on, 188-215
  failure to disclose adverse law or facts, 193, 194-200
  fairness to opposing party and counsel, 214-215
  misrepresentation by lawyer to court or other tribunal, 191-194
  perjury by client or witness, 201-214

pleadings in civil and criminal cases, 188-191
  zealous representation, limits of, 181-188
Advertising by lawyers, 7. *See also* Solicitation
  cross-border, 500-501, 510
  cyberspace options, 500-501
  disclaimers, 519
  restrictions on, 501-511
  technological developments, 510
Advocacy, ethics of, 182-183
Affiliate, corporate
  defined, 337
  representation of, 337-346
Agency, law of
  actual authority, 52
  apparent authority, 52
  imputation, 366
  vicarious liability, 366
Aiding and abetting, 5, 238-245, 250, 374
Alabama
  referral fees, 519
  solicitation labeling requirement, 519
Alaska
  adverse legal authority, disclosure of, 194-199
ALSP. *See* Alternative legal service providers (ALSP)
Alternative business structures (ABS), 471, 484-491
Alternative legal service providers (ALSP), 474, 492-493, 494-497
American Bar Association (ABA)
  accreditation by, 1, 423, 424
  Annotated Model Rules of Professional Conduct, 8, 9
  Canons of Professional Ethics, 7
  Center for Professional Responsibility, 6
  Commission on Ethics 20/20, 45, 473, 474, 481

528   Index

Commission on Multidisciplinary
Practice, 481
Commission on Multijurisdictional
Practice, 456
Commission on the Future of Legal
Services, 481
Committee on Lawyer Business
Ethics, 54-55
Criminal Justice Standards for the
Defense Function, 193
diverse faculty on CLE programs, 443
Ethics 2000 Commission, 158
Formal Ethics Op. 00-418, 141
Formal Ethics Op. 01-424, 417
Formal Ethics Op. 06-439, 227
Formal Ethics Op. 10-456, 95
Formal Ethics Op. 11-461, 236
Formal Ethics Op. 18-480, 74
Formal Ethics Op. 18-481, 22, 34
Formal Ethics Op. 18-483, 83
Formal Ethics Op. 18-491, 151
Formal Ethics Op. 20-491, 219, 220
Formal Ethics Op. 21-496, 96
Formal Ethics Op. 91-361, 272, 273
Formal Ethics Op. 92-366, 222
Formal Ethics Op. 95-390, 345
Formal Ethics Op. 95-397, 193
Formal Ethics Op. 98-410, 137
Formal Ethics Op. 98-411, 83
House of Delegates, 258, 456, 481, 483
Informal Ethics Op. 86-1518, 228, 229
Legal Technology Resource Center,
45, 98
Model Code of Professional
Responsibility, 7
Model Codes, 6-7
Model Rules for Lawyer Disciplinary
Enforcement, 432
Model Rules of Professional Conduct.
See Model Rules of Professional
Conduct
Standing Committee on Ethics and
Professional Responsibility, 31
Task Force on the Model Definition of
the Practice of Law, 445
Unbundling Resource Center, 31
Working Group on Alternative
Business Structures, 473
American Civil Liberties Union, 500
American Corporate Counsel Association
(ACCA), 392, 400
American Law Institute (ALI), 7. *See also*
specific Restatements

Antidiscrimination rules, 7, 436-443
Apparent authority, 52
Arizona
legal document preparers, 446
legal fees, 57
nonlawyer and lawyer collaboration,
471, 472, 493
outside investment, 478
Arkansas
solicitation labeling requirement, 519
Association of Corporate Counsel (ACC),
392, 400
Association of Professional
Responsibility Lawyers (APRL),
10
Attorney-client privilege, 67, 70-74,
281-312
basic doctrinal approaches, 281-292
changes in entity control, 300-312
communications, 71, 281
"in confidence" requirement, 72, 281
confidentiality duty vs., 67-70, 79
consultants, 292-299
"control group" test, 282-291, 318-319
crime-fraud exception, 75-80
email communications, 72
entities, representation of, 281-312
exceptions, 75-82
express consent, 75, 81-82
fiduciary-lawyer exception, 292
"functional equivalents" test, 294-298,
298-299
identity of client, 72
implied waiver, 75, 81-82
inadvertent waiver, 81-82
in-house counsel, 292, 402-405
joint clients in action between them,
75, 80-81
joint representation, 82-83
limited waiver, 81
organizational fiduciary exception,
292
personal privilege, 329
privileged persons, between, 71-72,
281
for purpose of obtaining or providing
legal assistance, 73-74, 281
selective waiver, 81
"subject matter" test, 282-291, 318
third-party agents, 71, 292-299
Attorney-client relationship
decision-making authority, allocation
of, 47-51

determining whether to represent client, 35-38

duties owed, 17

formation of. *See* Formation of attorney-client relationship

morally repugnant client or cause, 36-38

scope of representation. *See* Scope of representation

termination of. *See* Termination of attorney-client relationship

unpopular clients, representation of, 36-38

withdrawal from representation, 36, 52

Attorney fees. *See* Legal fees

"Attribution" test, 383

At-will employment, 435
  public policy exception, 410
  wrongful discharge suits, 411, 412-417

Audit committee
  importance of, 354
  members of, 354

Auditors, 365

Australia
  alternative business structures, 484
  multidisciplinary practices, 478
  outside investment, 478

Autonomy, 51-52

Bankruptcy Abuse Prevention and Consumer Protection Act, 511

Bankruptcy petition preparers, 492

Bar examinations
  admission to practice, 424-425
  criticisms of, 425

Bias or prejudice, 436-443, 440

Big Four accounting firms, 482, 485, 492

"Blind eye" doctrine, 219

Bloomberg Law, 8

Board of Immigration Appeals
  nonlawyers representing individuals, 492

Bond counsel, 26

Bond, defined, 26

Boswell, James, 190-191

Business judgment rule, 334, 336

Business lawyers, defined, 2

Business transactions with client, 137-142

California
  advance waivers, 123-131
  attorney-client relationship, 21-22

business or financial transactions between lawyer and client, 138-141

conflicts of interest, 138-141

consent of president on behalf of organization, 330

disclosures to prevent or rectify economic harm, 364

indemnification of employee, 372

informed consent, 112

justice gap, 492

legal education through law office study, 424

non-accredited law schools, graduates of, 424

nonlawyer ownership of law firms, sandbox working group on, 493

partnership, representation of, 276

pro bono service, 63

referral fees, 519

represented person, communication with, 230-236

retaliatory discharge, 417-418

rules of professional conduct, 6, 12

state-accredited law schools, 424

temporary presence and UPL, 447-453

work product doctrine, 99

Candor
  to third persons, 433
  to tribunal, 433

Central Hudson test, 508-509

Character and fitness
  admission to practice, 425-432
  criticism of requirement, 432

Choice of law, 468-469, 510

Civility codes, 188

Client trust accounts. *See* Trust accounts

Closely held corporations, 264-272, 274-276
  corporate shareholder, action against, 274-276
  defined, 264
  fiduciary duties to shareholders, 270-271

Closing attorney, responsibilities of, 20

Colorado
  out-of-state attorneys, practice by, 465-466

Commercial businesses offering legal services, 483-484

Commercial speech, 502-508

Commingling funds, 433

Common interest privilege, 119

Communication, 53-54
  entity client, 277-278
  fee agreement, 54, 60
  triggering events, 53
  type of explanation to be provided, 54
Competence, 41-46
  confidentiality, protection of, 98
  cultural, 45-46
  franchising case, 42-44
  global environment, 45-46
  gross incompetence, 42-44
  specialists, 44-45
  technology, 45
Compliance officers, 405-411
Confidences, defined, 74
Confidentiality, duty of, 67, 68, 74
  attorney-client privilege vs., 67-70
  claims against client, assertion of, 90-96
  competence in protection of, 98
  compliance with other law, 96-97
  conflicts of interest, detection of, 97
  economic harm, prevention of, 84-89
  entities, representation of, 312-313
  exceptions whereby lawyer is
    permitted to disclose, 83-97
  former clients, 31
  implied authority to disclose, 83
  informed consent, 82-83
  joint representation, 82-83
  legal advice about compliance with
    rules, 89-90
  past crimes or frauds, 89
  physical harm, prevention of, 84
  self-defense, 90-96
  waiver, 53
Conflicts of interest
  advance waivers, 123-131, 352
  confidentiality duty, exceptions to, 97
  criminal cases, 143-148
  current clients. *See* Current-client
    conflicts
  directly adverse. *See* Directly adverse
    conflicts
  entity representation, 321-352
  former arbitrators, 101
  former clients. *See* Former-client
    conflicts
  former government lawyers, 101,
    176-178
  former judges, 101
  imputation. *See* Imputation
  material limitation. *See* Material
    limitation conflicts

prospective clients. *See* Prospective-
    client conflicts
  remedies, 101
  screening. *See* Screening
  sexual or romantic interest in client,
    136, 142
  transient lawyer, 97
  waiver, 53, 123-131
Connecticut
  referral fees, 519
"Conscious avoidance of facts" doctrine,
    220
Consentability, 103, 109, 110, 118, 121,
    122, 134, 328. *See also* Conflicts of
    interest; Informed consent
Constituent, defined, 257
Constitutional standards
  commercial speech, 502-508
  conflicts of interest, 143-148
  effective assistance of counsel. *See*
    Effective assistance of counsel
Constructive fraud, 218
Constructive knowledge, 233, 240, 243
Contacting a represented entity
  in-house counsel, 319
Contingent fees, 54, 58-59
Contract, breach of, 18, 223, 244
Control
  allocation of decision-making
    authority, 47-53
  implied authorization, 48
"Control group" test, 282-291, 318-319
Corporate governance requirements, 395.
    See also Sarbanes-Oxley Act (SOX)
Corporate wrongdoing, 353-390
  lawyer liability, 366-389
  liability to client entity, 366-373
  reporting out, 5, 10, 361-366
  reporting up, 3-5, 10, 353-361, 365
  SEC regulations, 358-360, 362-364
  securities laws, liability for violation
    of, 374-389
Corporations
  affiliates, representation of, 337-346
  business judgment rule, 334, 336
  care, duty of, 336
  closely held. *See* Closely held
    corporations
  conflicts of interest, 321, 337-346
  "corporate family" conflicts, 321,
    337-346
  fiduciary duties of officers and
    directors, 336

independent directors, 336
loyalty, duty of, 336
make or buy decision, 394
publicly held. *See* Publicly held corporations
sister corporations, 337
subsidiaries, 337
wrongdoing. *See* Corporate wrongdoing
Counsel, right to, 143-148. *See also* Effective assistance of counsel
Crime or fraud of client
 aiding and abetting, lawyers' liability for, 238-245, 250, 374
 attorney-client privilege, crime-fraud exception to, 75-80
 counseling or assisting, 218-221
Criminal conduct, discipline for, 434-435
Cultural challenges for in-house counsel, 391-393
Current-client conflicts, 31-35, 101-150
 business transactions with client, 137-142
 client identification, 102
 conflict identification, 102
 consentability, 103
 constitutional standards, 143-148
 "corporate family" conflicts, 321, 337-346
 criminal cases, 143-148
 directly adverse conflicts. *See* Directly adverse conflicts
 entity and constituent, simultaneous representation of, 321-337
 financial transactions with clients, 18-19, 137-142
 identification of client and conflict, 102
 imputation among associated lawyers, 135
 informed consent. *See* Informed consent
 material limitation conflicts. *See* Material limitation conflicts
 other specific conflicts rules, 142-143
 personal interest conflicts, 136-137
 potentially impermissible conflicts, 102

Debt relief agencies, 511
Delaware
 attorney-client privilege, 307-310, 310-312

changes in entity control, 307-310, 310-312
compliance officers, 405
disclosure of client information because of moral compulsion, 12-13
referral fees, 519
Derivative actions, 330-337
Digital forms of communication, 469, 510
Diligence, 46-47, 181. *See also* Zealous representation
Directly adverse conflicts, 120-135. *See also* Conflicts of interest
 advance waivers, 123-131, 352
 defined, 103, 321
 disqualification cases, 132
 entity representation, 321, 345
 hostile takeover attempt, 133
 in litigation, 120-133
 "punch-pulling" conflicts, 122, 338
 "thrust upon" conflicts, 132
 in transactions, 133-135
Discipline, 218-238, 432-443
 active counseling or assisting crime or fraud of client, 218-221
 bias, 436-443
 common grounds for, 433-436
 criminal conduct, 434-435
 discrimination, 436-443
 dishonesty, forms of, 433-434
 failure to disclose, 221-223
 failure to report misconduct, 435-436
 formal charges, 432, 433
 harassment, 436-443
 informal complaints, 432
 interactions with persons other than clients, 224
 knowingly counseling or assisting wrongful client acts, 223-224
 mishandling client funds, 433
 out-of-state lawyers
  authority to discipline, 467-468
  regulation of, 467-469
 prejudice, 436-443
 represented person, communication with, 229-236
 sanctions, 432
 serious misconduct of another lawyer, failure to report, 435-436
 unrepresented person, communication with, 236-238
 violent crimes, 435

Disclaimers, 22, 81, 175-176, 345, 492, 509, 510, 519
Disclosure committee, 355
Discovery reforms, 187
Discretion in lawyering, 11
Discrimination, discipline for, 436-443
Dishonesty, 433-434
Disqualification, 5, 40, 95, 96, 122, 131-132, 158-161, 165, 166, 171
  common law test, 169
  former government lawyers, 176-178
  imputed, 135, 152
  reasonable belief in prior representation, 264-270
  remedy for impermissible conflict, 101
  remedy for violation of law governing lawyers, 8
District of Columbia
  closely held corporation, representation of, in action against shareholder, 274-276
  nonlawyer assistance in client representation, 473
  nonlawyer ownership of law firm, 471, 472, 473
  outside counsel guidelines, 394-395
  perjured testimony, 211, 212, 213
  personal interest conflict, 136
  "thrust upon" conflict of interest, 132
Diversity, racial and gender, 395
Dodd-Frank Wall Street Reform and Consumer Protection Act, 419
Domestic abuse, 435
Domestic violence, 435
Dual representation. *See* Joint representation
Duty of communication. *See* Communication
Duty of confidentiality. *See* Confidentiality, duty of

Earnings call, defined, 293
Educational requirements admission to practice, 424
Effective assistance of counsel, 143-148, 202
Efficient breach, 223
Email
  exchanges, 235
  solicitation, 518
Employee Retirement Income Security Act of 1974 (ERISA), 252

Enforcement actions, 381-382
England. *See also* United Kingdom
  barristers, 38, 489
  "cab rank" rule, 38
  "public access" cases, 38
  solicitors, 38, 489
Enron scandal, 3, 5, 357
Entities, representation of, 255, 257-280
  affiliates, 337-346
  attorney-client privilege, 281, 300-312
  changes in control, 300-312
  client identification, 258-274
  closely held corporations. *See* Closely held corporations
  communication, 277-278
  confidentiality, duty of, 281, 312-313
  conflicts of interest, 321-352
  constituents, 257
  contacting represented entity, 279, 313-319
  control, 274-276
  corporate wrongdoing. *See* Corporate wrongdoing
  corporations. *See* Closely held corporations; Corporations; Publicly held corporations
  current and former constituents of represented organization, contact with, 313-318
  deposition of employee, defending, 264
  entity theory, 258
  formal associations, 273-274
  general partnerships, 272
  group theory, 258
  informal associations, 273-274
  joint representation in shareholder derivative lawsuit, 330-337
  joint representation of entity and constituent, 329-330
  large, publicly held corporations. *See* Publicly held corporations
  limited liability companies, 273
  limited liability limited partnership, 273
  limited liability partnership, 273
  limited partnerships, 272-273
  "reasonable expectations" test, 273
  shareholder derivative lawsuit, 330-337
  subsidiaries, 337-346
Entity theory, 258
Episodic client, 22, 31-35

ERISA. *See* Employee Retirement Income Security Act of 1974 (ERISA)
Ernst & Young, 485, 489
Ethics of lawyering, 10-13
Ex parte communications, transactional practice, 230-236
Ex parte proceedings, 194, 200

Failure to disclose
adverse law or facts, 193, 194-200
material fact to avoid assisting in crime or fraud by client, 221-223
Failure to report misconduct, 435-436
Fairness to opposing party and counsel, 214-215
False Claims Act, 418-419
Federal Judicial Center
Mandatory Initial Discovery Pilot Project, 200
Federal Rules of Civil Procedure, 188
Federal Rules of Criminal Procedure, 190-191
Federal Rules of Evidence, 69
Federal tax preparers, privilege for, 482
Fees. *See* Legal fees
Fiduciary duties
breach of, 10, 18-19, 223, 239-244, 251, 374
care, 245, 246-250, 333, 336
confidentiality. *See* Confidentiality, duty of
loyalty. *See* Loyalty, duty of
Fiduciary relationship, defined, 242
Financial transactions with clients, 18-19, 137-142
Firm, defined, 135
First Amendment
commercial speech, 502-508
lawyer marketing, 500
Florida
advertising, 509
course approval for CLE requirements, 442-443
diverse faculty on CLE programs, 442-443
harassment or discrimination by lawyer, 437-439
multijurisdictional practice, 455
truthfulness in statements to others, 224-226
Form 10-K, 92
Formal associations, representation of, 263-274

Formation of attorney-client relationship, 17-22
"accidental" clients, 22
disclaimers, 22
episodic client, 22, 31-35
oral agreement, 17
unintended clients, 22
written retention agreements, 17
Former clients
confidentiality, duty of, 31
conflicts of interest. *See* Former-client conflicts
Former-client conflicts, 31-35, 151, 152-172
accommodation clients, 346-352
disqualification, 152-158
entities, representation of, 346-352
former government client, 151
imputation. *See* Imputation
migrating to another firm, 152, 161-165, 166-172
new firm of individual migrating lawyer, 166-172
rebuttable vs. irrebuttable presumption, 164, 165, 166-172
screening. *See* Screening
stable firm, individual private lawyer in, 152-161
"substantial relationship" test, 156-160, 164
Franchise Disclosure Document (FDD), 43
Fraud
crime or fraud of client. *See* Crime or fraud of client
defined, 218
reporting of, 3-4
Future of legal services, reflections on, 494-497

Gatekeeper, defined, 365
Gender diversity, 395
General partnerships, representation of, 272
Georgia
conduct prejudicial to administration of justice, 440
harassment or discrimination by lawyer, 440
Group theory, 258

Harassment
discipline for, 436-443
rules, 7
"Hot potato" rule, 132

Illinois
advertising, 500
character and fitness for admission to practice, 431
disclosure of another lawyer's serious misconduct, 435
limited scope representation, 30
nonclients, liability to, for negligence, 246-250
Impropriety, appearance of, 93, 158
Imputation, 120-121, 135, 137, 152, 161, 166, 169, 170, 171, 177, 178, 482. *See also* Screening
In pari delicto, doctrine of, 366, 372-373
Independence of judgment, professional, 472, 474
Independent counsel, defined, 131, 337
Independent directors, 336
Ineffective assistance of counsel, 143-148, 202-210, 214
Informal associations, representation of, 273-274
Informed consent, 53, 54
confidentiality duty, 82-83
confirmed in writing, 112
conflicts of interest, 82, 103, 111
current-client conflicts, 103, 111
defined, 82
limited scope representation, 23-25, 28-29, 82
writing, defined, 112
In-house counsel, 391-420
attorney-client privilege, 402-405
compliance officers, lawyers as, 405-411
contacting a represented entity, 319
cultural challenges, 391-393
European model of corporate counsel, 401
evolving role, 391-396
globalization of business, 391-393, 395-396
government regulation, scope of, 395
"independence" of, questions concerning, 396-402
license to practice in jurisdiction where located, 405
make or buy decision, 394
malpractice lawsuits against, scarcity of, 372
modern, 391-396
obstruction of justice, 319
outside counsel guidelines, 394

reform proposals, 401
regulation of lawyers in compliance, 406-409
retaliatory discharge, 365
roles of, 396
significant internal investigations, outside counsel for, 401, 404-405
wrongful discharge, 410, 411-419
Inquisitorial system, 181, 182, 185, 186, 187. *See also* Adversary system
Interdisciplinary service providers, 479-483
Internal Revenue Service
nonlawyers representing individuals, 492
Iowa
confidential information, disclosure of, 84

Joint defense agreement, 118-119
Joint defense privilege, 75, 80-81
Joint representation
confidentiality duty, 82-83
Judicially-authorized-and-regulated legal service providers, 492
Jury trial, right to, 185
Justice gap. *See* Access to justice

Kansas
referral fees, 519
Kentucky
reporting serious violations of rules by other lawyers, 436
Knowingly, defined, 191-192, 218
Knowledge
actual, 243
constructive. *See* Constructive knowledge
proof of, 219-221
Kutak Commission, 188, 200, 222, 258, 483

Lawyer discipline. *See* Discipline
Legal document preparers, 446
Legal fees, 54-65
alternative fee billing, 59-60
basis of, advising client up front, 23
bill padding, 56
blended rates, 59
budgets, 59
caps, 59
client trust accounts, 57
contingent, 54, 58-59
cost-plus arrangements, 59

Index **535**

discounted hourly rates, 59
division by lawyers not in same firm, 54
firm estimates, 59
fixed, 23, 57-58
forfeiture, 132
general retainer, 57
hourly, 23, 56
incentive billing, 59
loaned lawyer, 59, 60
midstream termination, effect of, 35
minimum billing increments, 56
minimum fee schedules, 7
modification of fee agreement, 41, 60
nonrefundable, 57-58
partner-based rule structures, 59
phased billings, 59
pro bono public service, 41, 60-63
reasonableness standard, 54-55
result-based billing, 59
reverse contingency fees, 58
sharing with nonlawyers, rule
      against, 11
success fees, 56
task-based flat fees, 59
types of arrangements, 56-60
unbundled fees, 59
value billing, 59
volume rates, 59
written agreements, 54, 58
Legal malpractice. *See* Malpractice
Legal service providers (LSP), 492, 497
LegalZoom, 31, 446, 484, 490, 492
Leveraged buyout, 382
Lexis Advance, 8
Limited liability company (LLC),
      representation of, 273
Limited liability limited partnership
      (LLLP), representation of, 273
Limited liability partnership (LLP),
      representation of, 273
Limited license legal technicians, 446
Limited partnerships, representation of,
      272-273
Limited practice officers, 446
Limited scope representation, 23-25, 28-
      29, 30, 53, 82, 108
Litigation funding agreements, 475
Litigation, adversary system. *See*
      Adversary system
LLC. *See* Limited liability company
      (LLC)
LLLP. *See* Limited liability limited
      partnership (LLLP)

LLP. *See* Limited liability partnership
      (LLP)
Louisiana
    advertising, 509
Loyalty, duty of, 31, 67, 101, 122, 275,
      322-328, 333, 336, 338-344
    former clients, 31
    undivided loyalty, 481-482
LSP. *See* Legal service providers (LSP)

Maine
    harassment or discrimination by
        lawyer, 436
    legal education through law office
        study, 424
    limiting practice to particular clients,
        441
    referral fees, 519
Malpractice, 5, 8, 10, 23-25, 104-107, 271,
      366, 372
Marketing legal services, 499-522
    advertising. *See* Advertising by
        lawyers
    false or misleading communication, 501
    referrals. *See* Referrals, paying for
    social media, use of, 511
    solicitation. *See* Solicitation of clients
    specialist certification, rules against
        use of term, 501, 511
    websites as tool, 173-176, 500-501
Maryland
    personal interest conflict, 136
    privity requirement in wills cases, 250
    referral, anything of value in return
        for, 520
Massachusetts
    attorney-client privilege, 68-69, 75-78
    disclosure of confidential information,
        85, 87
    gender discrimination in public
        accommodation, 35
    nonlawyer, formation of business
        entity with, 472
    perjured testimony, 212, 213
    scope of representation and basis
        or rate of fee and expenses in
        writing, 17
    work-life balance, 47
Material limitation conflicts, 103-120, 121
    defined, 103, 321
    entity representation, 321-329
    in litigation, 112-120
    in transactions, 103-112

MBE. *See* Multistate Bar Exam (MBE)
MDP. *See* Multidisciplinary practices (MDP)
MEE. *See* Multistate Essay Exam (MEE)
Mens rea, 218, 440
Michigan
    counseling or assisting wrongful client acts, 223
    disclosure of confidential information, 84
    limited scope representation, 30
    referral fees, 519
Migratory lawyers, 152, 161-165
Minnesota
    temporary practice, safe harbors for, 457-464
    truthfulness in statements to others, 224
Mishandling client funds, 433
Misleading statements, 224
Misrepresentation
    to court or other tribunal, 191-194
    negligent, 434
Mississippi
    court's regulation of lawyers, 423
Missouri
    advertising, 499
MJP. *See* Multijurisdictional practice (MJP)
Model Code of Professional Responsibility, 7
Model Rule for Temporary Practice by Foreign Lawyers, 456
Model Rule for the Licensing of Legal Consultants, 456
Model Rule on Admission by Motion, 456
Model Rule on Pro Hac Vice Admission, 456
Model Rules for Lawyer Disciplinary Enforcement, 432, 467-468
Model Rules of Professional Conduct. *See also subject matter of rules*
    adoption of, 7
    preamble, 1
Money laundering, 219
Moral compulsion, 12-13
MPRE. *See* Multistate Professional Responsibility Exam (MPRE)
MPT. *See* Multistate Performance Test (MPT)
Multidisciplinary practice (MDP)
    defined, 471
    one-stop shopping, 478, 479-481

    opposition to, 481-483
    outside United States, 484-491. *See also* Alternative business structures (ABS)
    prohibition on, 478-484
    recent developments in United States, 491-497
    reciprocal referral agreements, 483
Multijurisdictional practice (MJP)
    choice of law, 468-469
    discipline, authority to, 467-468
    in-house counsel, 405
    regulation of out-of-state lawyers, 467-469
    "safe harbors," 456-467
    systematic presence, safe harbors for, 456, 466-467
    temporary practice, safe harbors for, 457-466
    temporary presence, 447-453, 454
    UPL and, 447-467. *See also* Unauthorized practice of law (UPL)
    "virtual" presence, 447-453, 454, 466
Multistate Bar Exam (MBE), 424, 425
Multistate Essay Exam (MEE), 424, 425
Multistate Performance Test (MPT), 424, 425
Multistate Professional Responsibility Exam (MPRE), 424

National Association of Bond Lawyers Committee on Professional Responsibility, 29
National Board of Trial Advocacy, 500
National Conference of Bar Examiners (NCBE), 423
Nebraska
    competence, 42-44, 46
    privity requirement in wills cases, 250
Negligence
    misrepresentation, 434
    nonclients, liability to, 245-251
Negotiation, ethics in, 227-228
Nevada
    personal interest conflict, 136
    referral fees, 519
New Hampshire
    bar examination exemption for honors program students, 424
    referral fees, 519
New Jersey
    conflicts of interest, 109, 113-117

counseling or assisting wrongful
client acts, 223
disclosure of confidential information,
85
emails, copying clients on, 235
employment discrimination, 441
material limitation conflicts in
litigation, 113-117
multijurisdictional practice, 455
represented person, communication
with, 235
rules of professional conduct, 8
New Mexico
harassment or discrimination by
lawyer, 436
New York
advertising rules, 502-508
attorney-client privilege, 300-307,
310-312
changes in entity control, 300-307,
310-312
choice of law, 469
confidential information, 74
court rules, 17
differing interests, 134
directly adverse conflict, 134
disclosure of confidential information,
85-87, 88, 89
embarrassment or harm to third
person by lawyer, 439
ex parte proceeding, 200
fee agreements in writing, 5
informed consent, 82
legal education through law office
study, 424
limited scope representation, 82
migratory lawyers, 170-171
multijurisdictional practice, 453, 454,
455
noisy withdrawal, 222
nonrefundable legal fees, 57
outside investment in law firms,
475-478
partnerships, 272
privity requirement in wills cases, 250
pro bono service, 62-63
reporting serious violations of rules
by other lawyers, 436
rules of professional conduct, 5, 8,
23-25
screening, 170-171
Social Media Ethics Guidelines, 511
solicitation via tweet, 518

technological competence, 45
"thrust upon" conflict of interest, 132
truthfulness in statements to others,
224
NextGen Bar Exam, 425
Noisy withdrawal, 88-89, 222, 362, 363-
364, 365
Nolo contendere, plea of, 190
Nominal gifts for referrals, 521
Nonaccountability principle, 37
Nonclients
negligence, lawyers' liability for,
245-251
Nonlawyer ownership of law firms,
473-478
nonlawyers actively assisting in client
representation, 473-474
passive investment in law firms,
475-478
prohibition of, 473-478
Nonlawyer representation of individuals
before certain federal agencies,
492
North Carolina
disclosure vs. SOX regulations, 364
implied authority to disclose
confidential information, 83
North Dakota
truthfulness in statements to others,
224
Northern Mariana Islands
attorney-client relationship, formation
of, 18-19

Obstruction of justice, 319
Ohio
advertising, 500
character and fitness for admission to
practice, 426-431
counseling or assisting wrongful
client acts, 223
illegal client conduct, 223
privity requirement in wills cases,
250
referral, anything of value in return
for, 520
Omissions in statements, 224-226
One-sided partisan zeal, 199, 201
Online dispute resolution, 492
Online document preparation services,
31
Online legal directories, 520
Oral retention agreement, 17

Oregon
  referral fees, 519
  substantial assistance to client's
    breach of fiduciary duty, 243
Organizational clients. *See* Entities,
    representation of
Out-of-state lawyers, regulation of,
    467-469
Ownership of law firms
  by nonlawyers. *See* Nonlawyer
    ownership of law firms

Partisan justice, 183-185
Partnerships, representation of,
    272-273
Pennsylvania
  harassment or discrimination by
    lawyer, 442
  referral fees, 519
Perjury by client or witness, 201-214
Personal interest conflicts, 136-137
Philadelphia
  solicitation using social media, 518
Philosophical approach to legal ethics, 2
"Playbook" information, 159
Pleadings in civil and criminal cases,
    188-191
Practice of law, defined, 445-446
Private placement, 232
Private Securities Litigation Reform Act
    of 1995, 381-382
Privity, 250-251
Pro bono public service, 41, 60-63, 490
  mandatory, 61-62
Pro hac vice admission, 456, 464-465, 466,
    467
Promissory estoppel, 20
Prospective-client conflicts, 172-176
  websites, obligations triggered by,
    173-176
Protection of client information
  attorney-client privilege. *See*
    Attorney-client privilege
  confidentiality. *See* Confidentiality,
    duty of
Publicly held corporations, 258-264
Puffing, 227
"Punch-pulling" conflicts, 122, 338

Qualified immunity, 244, 245
Qui tam actions, 123-132, 135

Racial diversity, 395
Ratings of lawyers, 520
Reaffirmation agreement, 30
"Reasonable expectations" test, 20
Reasons for professional responsibility,
    13-14
Reciprocal referral agreements, 483
Referral agreements, 483
Referrals, paying for, 501, 519-521
Registered agent, 241
Regulation of profession. *See* Admission
    to practice; Discipline
"Reporting out," 5, 10, 353, 361-366, 411
"Reporting up," 3-5, 10, 353-361, 411
Represented person, communication
    with, 229-236, 313-319
Researching law of lawyering, 8-9
Resources for interpreting rules, 8-9
Restatement (Second) of Contracts, 9
Restatement (Second) of Torts, 9
Restatement (Third) of Agency, 9
Restatement (Third) of the Law
    Governing Lawyers (RLGL), 2
  actual authority, 52
  adoption of, 7-8
  attorney-client privilege, 70, 72, 73, 78,
    81, 292
  client instructions to lawyer, 50, 51
  confidentiality, 79-80
  conflicts of interest, 110
  contingent fee, reasonableness of, 59
  counseling or assisting wrongful
    client acts, 223
  crime-fraud exception, 78
  decisions reserved to lawyer, 52
  description of, 7-8
  forfeiture of fee, 132
  general law, lawyers are subject to, 238
  identity of client, 72
  inadvertent waiver of attorney-client
    privilege, 81
  informal associations, 273
  insured, representation of, 120
  invitation to rely, 250
  legal fees, information about, 55
  misrepresentation by lawyer, 194
  modification of fee agreement, 60
  nonclients, duty of care to, 245
  nonconsentability, 110
  organizational fiduciary exception to
    attorney-client privilege, 292

privity exceptions, 250-251
referral fees, 519
third-party beneficiary exception to
privity requirement, 250
work product, 99
Restatement (Third) of Torts, 9
Restatement (Third) of Torts: Liability for
Economic Harm, 242-243, 244
Retail businesses offering legal services,
483-484
Retaliatory discharge, 365, 410, 412-418
Retention agreement, 271
oral, 17
written, 17
Reverse contingency fees, 58
Revolving door, 178
Rhode Island
character and fitness for admission to
practice, 432
confidential information, disclosure
of, 84, 88, 89
Riverview Law, 485-489
RLGL. *See* Restatement (Third) of the
Law Governing Lawyers
(RLGL)
RocketLawyer, 446
Rule 10b-5, 374-381, 382-383, 384-389
"Runners," 519-520. *See also* Solicitation
of clients

Sarbanes-Oxley Act (SOX), 3-5, 6, 10, 11,
353-361, 362-366, 395, 407, 411,
418
Scope of representation, 17, 23-31
discrete-task representation, 31
informed consent, 23-25, 28-29
limited scope representation. *See*
Limited scope representation
unbundled representation, 31
Screening, 152, 161, 166-172, 178. *See also*
Imputation
Scrivener, 108, 229
Sears, Roebuck & Co., 483
SEC. *See* Securities and Exchange
Commission (SEC)
Secondary actor, 374
Secrets, defined, 74
Securities and Exchange Commission
(SEC), 3-5
corporate wrongdoing, regulations on,
358-360, 362-364

enforcement actions, 381-382
liability of lawyer for violating
securities laws, 374-389
"reporting out" regulations, 362-364
"reporting up" regulations, 358-360
Rule 10b-5, 374-381, 382-383, 384-389
Standards of Conduct for Attorneys, 3
Securities Exchange Act of 1934, 374
Self-defense
confidentiality duty and, 90-96
Self-help centers, 492
Sentencing guidelines, 395
Serious attorney error, 210
Serious misconduct of another lawyer,
failure to report, 435-436
Service of process, 241
Sexual relations with client, 136, 142
Shareholder derivative lawsuits, 330-337
Sherman Act, 7
Singer, Hutner law firm, 85-87, 88, 89, 90,
91, 217-219, 221-222, 242
Sixth Amendment, 143-148, 202-210
SmartLegalForms, 446
Social media
access to evidence on accounts,
214-215
ethics guidelines, 511
Social responsibility, 395
Social Security Administration
nonlawyers representing individuals,
492
Solicitation of clients, 500, 511-519
cross-border, 519
defined, 518
electronic communications, 518-519
email, 518
labeling requirement, 519
technology, increasing use of, 518
text messages, 518
South Carolina
limited scope representation, 30
South Dakota
aiding and abetting breach of
fiduciary duty, 239-242, 243
SOX. *See* Sarbanes-Oxley Act (SOX)
Stable firm, defined, 152
State rules of professional conduct, 5-6, 7.
See also specific states
Streamlined court procedures, 492
"Subject matter" test, 282-291, 318. *See
also* Attorney-client privilege

540   Index

Subsidiaries
    representation of, 337-346
    subsidiary, defined, 337
Substantial assistance, defined, 242-244
Systematic presence safe harbors,
          456, 466-467. *See also*
          Multijurisdictional practice
          (MJP)

Temporary practice safe harbors, 457-
          466. *See also* Multijurisdictional
          practice (MJP)
Tennessee
    perjured testimony, 212
    wrongful discharge, 412-417
Termination of attorney-client
          relationship, 31-35
    client discharge of attorney, 35
    lawyer withdrawal, good cause
          for, 35
    wrongful termination, 35
Terrorism, 219
Texas
    immunity doctrine, 245
    malpractice, 5
    privity requirement in wills
          cases, 250
Third-party beneficiaries, 250
"Thrust upon" conflicts, 132. *See also*
          Conflicts of interest
Timeliness, 46-47. *See also* Diligence
Tortious conduct of client
    aiding and abetting, lawyers' liability
          for, 238-245, 250
    substantial assistance in, 242-244
Transient lawyer
    conflicts of interest, 97
Tribunal, defined, 192
Trust accounts, 20, 57, 58, 218, 226, 433,
          521
Trustworthiness, 89, 228, 434, 435
Truthfulness in statements to others,
          224-229
    misleading statements, 224
    omissions, 224-226

UBE. *See* Uniform Bar Exam (UBE)
Unauthorized practice of law (UPL),
          445-470
    authority to discipline out-of-state
          lawyers, 467-468
    current structure of law practice, 472

    by lawyers, 447-469
    MJP problem, 447-456. *See also*
          Multijurisdictional practice
          (MJP)
    by nonlawyers, 445-447
    out-of-state lawyers, regulation of,
          467-469
    practice of law, defined, 445-446
    value of laws on, 447
Unbundled fees, 59
Unbundled legal services, 31
Unbundled representation, 31
Unconscionability, 55
Underdeveloped state of law of
          lawyering, 9-10
Uniform Bar Exam (UBE), 424-425
Uniform Franchising Offering Circular
          (UFOC), 43
Unintended clients, 22
United Kingdom
    alternative business structures, 484,
          485-490, 493, 497
    barristers, 38, 489
    frontline regulators, 497
    Legal Ombudsman, 491
    Legal Services Act of 2007, 489
    Legal Services Board, 497
    multidisciplinary practices, 478
    outside investment, 478
    solicitors, 38, 489
Unrepresented person, communication
          with, 236-238
UPL. *See* Unauthorized practice of law
          (UPL)
Utah
    legal services innovation, 493
    pilot program on nonlawyer and
          lawyer services, 471, 493

Vermont
    harassment or discrimination by
          lawyer, 436
    legal education through law office
          study, 424
    nonrefundable legal fees, 58
Violent crimes, discipline for, 435
Virginia
    confidential information, 74
    legal education through law office
          study, 424
    truthfulness in statements to others, 224
Virtual practice, 447-453, 454, 466

Waiver
confidentiality duty, 53
conflicts of interest, 53, 123-131
directly adverse conflicts, 123-131
future conflicts, 123-131
Washington
disclosure vs. SOX regulations, 364
legal education through law office
study, 424
limited license legal technicians, 446
limited practice officers, 446
referral fees, 519
Websites
as marketing tools, 500-501
obligations triggered by, 173-176
West Virginia
legal education through law office
study, 424
real-time electronic contact, 518
Westinghouse doctrine, 160-161
Whistleblower programs, 136, 365, 395,
409, 411
bounties, 418-419
financial rewards, 12, 418-419
retaliation statutes, 418
"Willful blindness" doctrine, 219
Wisconsin
bar examination exemption for state
law school graduates, 424
client's instructions, failure to follow,
48-50

control, 48-50
interdisciplinary service providers,
479-481, 482
lawyer practicing in
interdisciplinary organization,
479-481, 482
MPRE not adopted, 424
perjured testimony, 211
represented entity, contact with
constituents of, 313-318
Withdrawal, noisy. *See* Noisy
withdrawal
Witnesses, credibility of, 201
Work product immunity, 67-68,
98-99, 281, 293-298, 394, 408
opinion work product, 99
ordinary work product, 99
Written retention agreements, 17
Wrongful client acts
counseling or assisting, 223-224
crime or fraud. *See* Crime or fraud of
client
Wrongful discharge, 35, 90, 173, 403, 410,
411-419
Wrongful termination. *See* Wrongful
discharge

Zealous representation, 36, 37, 47
limits of, 181-188
litigation, limits in, 181-216
transactions, limits in, 217-253